2008 DOCUMENTS SUPPLEMENT
TO
INTERNATIONAL LAW AND LITIGATION IN THE U.S.

By

Jordan J. Paust
Mike and Teresa Baker Professor
Law Center, University of Houston

Jon M. Van Dyke
Professor of Law
William S. Richardson School of Law, University of Hawaii at Manoa

Linda A. Malone
Marshall-Wythe Foundation Professor of Law
College of William and Mary, Marshall-Wythe School of Law

AMERICAN CASEBOOK SERIES®

THOMSON
WEST™

Mat #40769101

Thomson/West have created this publication to provide you with accurate and authoritative information concerning the subject matter covered. However, this publication was not necessarily prepared by persons licensed to practice law in a particular jurisdiction. Thomson/West are not engaged in rendering legal or other professional advice, and this publication is not a substitute for the advice of an attorney. If you require legal or other expert advice, you should seek the services of a competent attorney or other professional.

610 Opperman Drive
St. Paul, MN 55123
1–800–313–9378

Printed in the United States of America

ISBN: 978–0–314–19890–7

TEXT IS PRINTED ON 10% POST CONSUMER RECYCLED PAPER

Table of Contents

*

Alphabetical List of Documents

*

Table of Abbreviations

Eur. T.S.	European Treaty Series
G.A.	General Assembly
GAOR	General Assembly Official Records
L.N.T.S.	League of Nations Treaty Series
O.A.S.	Organization of American States
O.A.U.	Organization of African Unity
Stat.	U.S. Statutes at Large
T.I.A.S.	Treaties and Other International Acts Series
T.S.	Treaty Series
U.N.T.S.	United Nations Treaty Series
U.S.T.	United States Treaties and Other International Agreements
Y.B.U.N.	Yearbook of the United Nations

*

2008 DOCUMENTS SUPPLEMENT
TO
INTERNATIONAL LAW AND LITIGATION IN THE U.S.

*

Document 1
UNITED STATES CONSTITUTION

(Extracts)

Article I.

Section 1. All legislative Powers herein granted shall be vested in a Congress of the United States, which shall consist of a Senate and House of Representatives.

Section 7. [1] All Bills for raising Revenue shall originate in the House of Representatives....

Section 8. [1] The Congress shall have Power To lay and collect Taxes, Duties, Imposts and Excises, to pay the Debts and provide for the common Defence and general Welfare of the United States; but all Duties, Imposts and Excises shall be uniform throughout the United States;

[2] To borrow money on the credit of the United States;

[3] To regulate Commerce with foreign Nations, and among the several States, and with the Indian Tribes;

[4] To establish an uniform Rule of Naturalization, and uniform Laws on the subject of Bankruptcies throughout the United States;

[5] To coin Money, regulate the Value thereof, and of foreign Coin, and fix the Standard of Weights and Measures;

[6] To provide for the Punishment of counterfeiting the Securities and current Coin of the United States;

[7] To Establish Post Offices and Post Roads;

[8] To promote the Progress of Science and useful Arts, by securing for limited Times to Authors and Inventors the exclusive Right to their respective Writings and Discoveries;

[9] To constitute Tribunals inferior to the supreme Court;

[10] To define and punish Piracies and Felonies committed on the high Seas, and Offences against the Law of Nations;

[11] To declare War, grant Letters of Marque and Reprisal, and make Rules concerning Captures on Land and Water;

[12] To raise and support Armies, but no Appropriation of Money to that Use shall be for a longer Term than two Years;

[13] To provide and maintain a Navy;

[14] To make Rules for the Government and Regulation of the land and naval Forces;

[15] To provide for calling forth the Militia to execute the Laws of the Union, suppress Insurrections and repel Invasions;

[16] To provide for organizing, arming, and disciplining, the Militia, and for governing such Part of them as may be employed in the

Service of the United States, reserving to the States respectively, the Appointment of the Officers, and the Authority of training the Militia according to the discipline prescribed by Congress; . . .

[18] To make all Laws which shall be necessary and proper for carrying into Execution the foregoing Powers, and all other Powers vested by this Constitution in the Government of the United States, or in any Department or Officer thereof.

Section 9.

[2] The privilege of the Writ of Habeas Corpus shall not be suspended, unless when in Case of Rebellion or Invasion the public Safety may require it.

[3] No Bill of Attainder or ex post facto Law shall be passed.

[7] No money shall be drawn from the Treasury, but in Consequence of Appropriations made by law. . . .

Section 10.

[1] No State shall enter into any Treaty, Alliance, or Confederation; grant Letters of Marque and Reprisal. . . .

[3] No State shall, without the Consent of Congress, . . . enter into any Agreement or Compact with another State, or with a foreign Power or engage in War, unless actually invaded, or in such imminent Danger as will not admit of delay.

Article II.

Section 1. [1] The executive Power shall be vested in a President of the United States of America.

[8] Before he enter on the Execution of his Office, he shall take the following Oath or Affirmation:—"I do solemnly swear (or affirm) that I will faithfully execute the Office of President of the United States, and will to the best of my Ability, preserve, protect and defend the Constitution of the United States."

Section 2. [1] The President shall be Commander in Chief of the Army and Navy of the United States, and of the militia of the several States, when called into the actual Service of the United States; he may require the Opinion, in writing, of the principal Officer in each of the Executive Departments, upon any Subject relating to the Duties of their respective Offices, and he shall have Power to grant Reprieves and Pardons for Offenses against the United States, except in Cases of Impeachment.

[2] He shall have Power, by and with the Advice and Consent of the Senate to make Treaties, provided two thirds of the Senators present concur; and he shall nominate, and by and with the Advice and Consent of the Senate, shall appoint Ambassadors, other public Ministers and Consuls, Judges of the supreme Court, and all other Officers of the United States, whose Appointments are not herein otherwise provided for, and which shall be established by Law; but the Congress may by Law vest the Appointment of such inferior Officers, as they think proper, in the President alone, in the Courts of Law, or in the Heads of Departments. . . .

Section 3. . . . [H]e shall receive Ambassadors and other public Ministers; he shall take Care that the Laws be faithfully executed, and shall Commission all the Officers of the United States.

Article III.

Section 1. The judicial Power of the United States, shall be vested in one supreme Court, and in such inferior Courts as the Congress may from time to time ordain and establish. . . .

Section 2. [1] The judicial Power shall extend to all Cases, in Law and Equity, arising under this Constitution, the Laws of the United States, and Treaties made, or which shall be made, under their Authority;—to all Cases affecting Ambassadors, other public Ministers and Consuls;—to all Cases of admiralty and maritime Jurisdiction;—to Controversies to which the United States shall be a Party;—to Controversies between two or more States;—between a State and Citizens of another State;—between Citizens of different States;—between Citizens of the same State claiming Lands under the Grants of different States, and between a State, or the Citizens thereof, and foreign States, Citizens or Subjects.

[2] In all Cases affecting Ambassadors, other public Ministers and Consuls, and those in which a State shall be a Party, the supreme Court shall have original Jurisdiction. In all the other Cases before mentioned, the supreme Court shall have appellate Jurisdiction, both as to Law and Fact, with such Exceptions, and under such Regulations as the Congress shall make. . . .

Article VI.

[2] This Constitution, and the Laws of the United States which shall be made in Pursuance thereof; and all Treaties made, or which shall be made, under the Authority of the United States, shall be the supreme Law of the Land; and the Judges in every State shall be bound thereby, any Thing in the Constitution or Laws of any State to the Contrary notwithstanding. . . .

Amendment I.

Congress shall make no law respecting an establishment of religion, or prohibiting the free exercise thereof; or abridging the freedom of speech, or of the press; or the right of the people peaceably to assemble, and to petition the Government for a redress of grievances. . . .

Amendment IV.

The right of the people to be secure in their persons, houses, papers, and effects, against unreasonable searches and seizures, shall not be violated, and no Warrants shall issue, but upon probable cause, supported by Oath or affirmation, and particularly describing the place to be searched, and the persons or things to be seized.

Amendment V.

No person shall be held to answer for a capital, or otherwise infamous crime, unless on a presentment of a Grand Jury, except in cases arising in the land or naval forces, or in the Militia, when in actual service in time of War or public danger; nor shall any person be subject for the same offence to be twice put in jeopardy of life and limb; nor be deprived of life, liberty, or property, without due process of law; nor shall private property be taken for public use, without just compensation.

Amendment VI.

In all criminal prosecutions, the accused shall enjoy the right to a speedy and public trial, by an impartial jury of the State and district wherein the crime shall have been committed, which district shall have been previously ascertained by law, and to be informed of the nature and cause of the accusation; to be confronted with the witnesses against him; to have compulsory process for obtaining witnesses in his favor, and to have the Assistance of Counsel for his defence....

Amendment VIII.

Excessive bail shall not be required, nor excessive fines imposed, nor cruel and unusual punishments inflicted.

Amendment IX.

The enumeration in the Constitution, of certain rights, shall not be construed to deny or disparage others retained by the people.

Amendment X.

The powers not delegated to the United States by the Constitution, nor prohibited by it to the States, are reserved to the States respectively, or to the people.

Amendment XI.

The judicial power of the United States shall not be construed to extend to any suit in law or equity, commenced or prosecuted against one of the United States by Citizens of another State, or by Citizens or Subjects of any Foreign State....

Amendment XIII.

Section 1. Neither slavery nor involuntary servitude, except as a punishment for crimes whereof the party shall have been duly convicted, shall exist within the United States, or any place subject to its jurisdiction.

Section 2. Congress shall have power to enforce this article by appropriate legislation.

Amendment XIV.

Section 1. All persons born or naturalized in the United States, and subject to the jurisdiction thereof, are citizens of the United States and of the State wherein they reside. No State shall make or enforce any law which shall abridge the privileges or immunities of citizens of the United States; nor shall any State deprive any person of life, liberty, or property without due process of law; nor deny to any person within its jurisdiction the equal protection of the laws....

Document 2
CHARTER OF THE UNITED NATIONS

T.S. 993, 59 Stat. 1031, 1976 Y.B.U.N. 1043 (June 26, 1945)

WE THE PEOPLES OF THE UNITED NATIONS DETERMINED to save succeeding generations from the scourge of war, which twice in our lifetime has brought untold sorrow to mankind, and to reaffirm faith in fundamental human rights, in the dignity and worth of the human person, in the equal rights of men and women and of nations large and small, and to establish conditions under which justice and respect for the obligations arising from treaties and other sources of international law can be maintained, and to promote social progress and better standards of life in larger freedom,

AND FOR THESE ENDS to practice tolerance and live together in peace with one another as good neighbours, and to unite our strength to maintain international peace and security, and to ensure by the acceptance of principles and the institution of methods, that armed force shall not be used, save in the common interest, and to employ international machinery for the promotion of the economic and social advancement of all peoples,

HAVE RESOLVED TO COMBINE OUR EFFORTS TO ACCOMPLISH THESE AIMS Accordingly, our respective Governments, through representatives assembled in the city of San Francisco, who have exhibited their full powers found to be in good and due form, have agreed to the present Charter of the United Nations and do hereby establish an international organization to be known as the United Nations.

CHAPTER I. PURPOSES AND PRINCIPLES

Article 1

The Purposes of the United Nations are:

1. To maintain international peace and security, and to that end: to take effective collective measures for the prevention and removal of threats to the peace, and for the suppression of acts of aggression or other breaches of the peace, and to bring about by peaceful means, and in conformity with the principles of justice and international law, adjustment or settlement of international disputes or situations which might lead to a breach of the peace;

2. To develop friendly relations among nations based on respect for the principle of equal rights and self-determination of peoples, and to take other appropriate measures to strengthen universal peace;

3. To achieve international co-operation in solving international problems of an economic, social, cultural, or humanitarian character, and in promoting and encouraging respect for human rights and for fundamental freedoms for all without distinction as to race, sex, language, or religion; and

4. To be a centre for harmonizing the actions of nations in the attainment of these common ends.

Article 2

The Organization and its Members, in pursuit of the Purposes stated in Article 1, shall act in accordance with the following Principles.

1. The Organization is based on the principle of the sovereign equality of all its Members.

2. All Members, in order to ensure to all of them the rights and benefits resulting from membership, shall fulfil in good faith the obligations assumed by them in accordance with the present Charter.

3. All Members shall settle their international disputes by peaceful means in such a manner that international peace and security, and justice, are not endangered.

4. All Members shall refrain in their international relations from the threat or use of force against the territorial integrity or political independence of any state, or in any other manner inconsistent with the Purposes of the United Nations.

5. All Members shall give the United Nations every assistance in any action it takes in accordance with the present Charter, and shall refrain from giving assistance to any state against which the United Nations is taking preventive or enforcement action.

6. The Organization shall ensure that states which are not Members of the United Nations act in accordance with these Principles so far as may be necessary for the maintenance of international peace and security.

7. Nothing contained in the present Charter shall authorize the United Nations to intervene in matters which are essentially within the domestic jurisdiction of any state or shall require the Members to submit such matters to settlement under the present Charter; but this principle shall not prejudice the application of enforcement measures under Chapter VII.

CHAPTER II. MEMBERSHIP

Article 3

The original Members of the United Nations shall be the states which, having participated in the United Nations Conference on International Organization at San Francisco, or having previously signed the Declaration by United Nations of 1 January 1942, sign the present Charter and ratify it in accordance with Article 110.

Article 4

1. Membership in the United Nations is open to a other peace-loving states which accept the obligations contained in the present Charter and, in the judgment of the Organization, are able and willing to carry out these obligations.

2. The admission of any such state to membership in the Nations will be effected by a decision of the General Assembly upon the recommendation of the Security Council.

Article 5

A Member of the United Nations against which preventive or enforcement action has been taken by the Security Council may be suspended from the exercise of the rights and privileges of membership by the General Assembly upon the recommendation of the Security Council. The exercise of these rights and privileges may be restored by the Security Council.

Article 6

A Member of the United Nations which has persistently violated the Principles contained in the present Charter may be' expelled from the Organization by the General Assembly upon the recommendation of the Security Council.

CHAPTER III. ORGANS

Article 7

1. There are established as the principal organs of the United Nations: a General Assembly, a Security Council, an Economic and Social Council, a Trusteeship Council, an International Court of Justice, and a Secretariat.

2. Such subsidiary organs as may be found necessary may be established in accordance with the present Charter.

Article 8

The United Nations shall place no restrictions on the eligibility of men and women to participate in any capacity and under conditions of equality in its principal and subsidiary organs.

CHAPTER IV. THE GENERAL ASSEMBLY

Composition

Article 9

1. The General Assembly shall consist of all the Members of the United Nations.

2. Each Member shall have not more than five representatives in the General Assembly.

Functions and Powers

Article 10

The General Assembly may discuss any questions or any matters within the scope of the present Charter or relating to the powers and functions of any organs provided for in the present Charter, and, except as provided in Article 12, may make recommendations to the Members of the United Nations or to the Security Council or to both on any such questions or matters.

Article 11

1. The General Assembly may consider the general principles of co-operation in the maintenance of international peace and security, including the principles governing disarmament and the regulation of armaments, and may make recommendations with regard to such principles to the Members or to the Security Council or to both.

2. The General Assembly may discuss any questions relating to the maintenance of international peace and security brought before it by any Member of the United Nations, or by the Security Council, or by a state which is not a Member of the United Nations in accordance with Article 35, paragraph 2, and, except as provided in Article 12, may make recommendations with regard to any such questions to the state or states concerned or to the Security Council or to both. Any such question on which action is necessary shall be referred to the Security Council by the General Assembly either before or after discussion.

3. The General Assembly may call the attention of the Security Council to situations which are likely to endanger international peace and security.

4. The powers of the General Assembly set forth in this Article shall not limit the general scope of Article 10.

Article 12

1. While the Security Council is exercising in respect of any dispute or situation the functions assigned to it in the present Charter, the General Assembly shall not make any recommendations with regard to that dispute or situation unless the Security Council so requests.

2. The Secretary–General, with the consent of the Security Council, shall notify the General Assembly at each session of any matters relative to the maintenance of international peace and security which are being dealt with by the Security Council and similarly notify the General Assembly, or the Members of the United Nations if the General Assembly is not in session, immediately the Security Council ceases to deal with such matters.

Article 13

1. The General Assembly shall initiate studies and make recommendations for the purpose of:

a. promoting international cooperation in the political field and encouraging the progressive development of international law and its codification;

b. promoting international cooperation in the economic, social, cultural, educational, and health fields, and assisting in the realization of human rights and fundamental freedoms for all without distinction as to race, sex, language, or religion.

2. The further responsibilities, functions, and powers of the General Assembly with respect to matters mentioned in paragraph 1 (b) above are set forth in Chapters IX and X.

Article 14

Subject to the provisions of Article 12, the General Assembly may recommend measures for the peaceful adjustment of any situation, regardless of origin, which it deems likely to impair the general welfare or friendly relations among nations, including situations resulting from a violation of the provisions of the present Charter setting forth the Purposes and Principles of the United Nations.

Article 15

1. The General Assembly shall receive and consider annual and special reports from the Security Council; these reports shall include an account of the measures that the Security Council has decided upon or taken to maintain international peace and security.

2. The General Assembly shall receive and consider reports from the other organs of the United Nations.

Article 16

The General Assembly shall perform such functions with respect to the international trusteeship system as are assigned to it under Chapters XII and XIII, including the approval of the trusteeship agreements for areas not designated as strategic.

Article 17

1. The General Assembly shall consider and approve the budget of the Organization.

2. The expenses of the Organization shall be borne by the Members as apportioned by the General Assembly.

3. The Assembly shall consider and approve any financial and budgetary arrangements with specialize agencies referred to in Article 57 and shall examine the administrative budgets of such specialized agencies with a view to making recommendations to the agencies concerned.

Voting

Article 18

1. Each member of the General Assembly shall have one vote.

2. Decisions of the General Assembly on important questions shall be made by a two-thirds majority of the members present and voting. These questions shall include: recommendations with respect to the maintenance of international peace and security, the election of the non-permanent members of the Security Council, the election of the mem-

bers of the Economic and Social Council, the election of members of the Trusteeship Council in accordance with paragraph 1 of Article 86, the admission of new Members to the United Nations, the suspension of the rights and privileges of membership, the expulsion of Members, questions relating to the operation of the trusteeship system, and budgetary questions.

3. Decisions on other questions, including the determination of additional categories of questions to be decided by a two-thirds majority, shall be made by a majority of the members present and voting.

Article 19

A Member of the United Nations which is in arrears in the payment of its financial contributions to the Organization shall have no vote in the General Assembly if the amount of its arrears equals or exceeds the amount of the contributions due from it for the preceding two full years. The General Assembly may, nevertheless, permit such a Member to vote if it is satisfied that the failure to pay is due to conditions beyond the of the Member.

Procedure

Article 20

The General Assembly shall meet in regular annual sessions and in such special sessions as occasion may require. Special sessions shall be convoked by the Secretary–General at the request of the Security Council or of a majority of the Members of the United Nations.

Article 21

The General Assembly shall adopt its own rules of procedure. It shall elect its President for each session.

Article 22

The General Assembly may establish such subsidiary organs as it deems necessary for the performance of its functions.

CHAPTER V. THE SECURITY COUNCIL COMPOSITION

Article 23

1. The Security Council shall consist of fifteen Members of the United Nations. The Republic of China, France, the Union of Soviet Socialist Republics, the United Kingdom of Great Britain and Northern Ireland, and the United States of America shall be permanent members of the Security Council. The General Assembly shall elect ten other Members of the United Nations to be non-permanent members of the Security Council, due regard being specially paid, in the first instance to the contribution of Members of the United Nations to the maintenance of international peace and security and to the other purposes of the Organization, and also to equitable geographical distribution.

2. The non-permanent members of the Security Council shall be elected for a term of two years. In the first election of the non-

permanent members after the increase of the membership of the Security Council from eleven to fifteen, two of the four additional members shall be chosen for a term of one year. A retiring member shall not be eligible for immediate re-election.

3. Each member of the Security Council shall have one representative.

Functions and Powers

Article 24

1. In order to ensure prompt and effective action by the United Nations, its Members confer on the Security Council primary responsibility for the maintenance of international peace and security, and agree that in carrying out its duties under this responsibility the Security Council acts on their behalf.

2. In discharging these duties the Security Council shall act in accordance with the Purposes and Principles of the United Nations. The specific powers granted to the Security Council for the discharge of these duties are laid down in Chapters VI, VII, VIII, and XII.

3. The Security Council shall submit annual and, when necessary, special reports to the General Assembly for its consideration.

Article 25

The Members of the United Nations agree to accept and carry out the decisions of the Security Council in accordance with the present Charter.

Article 26

1. In order to promote the establishment and maintenance of international peace and security with the least diversion for armaments of the world's human and economic resources, the Security Council shall be responsible for formulating, with the assistance of the Military Staff Committee referred to in Article 47, plans to be submitted to the Members of the United–Nations for the establishment of a system for the regulation of armaments.

Voting

Article 27

1. Each member of the Security Council shall have one vote.

2. Decisions of the Security Council on procedural matters shall be made by an affirmative vote of nine members.

3. Decisions of the Security Council on all other matters shall be made by an affirmative vote of nine members including the concurring votes of the permanent members; provided that, in decisions under Chapter VI, and under paragraph 3 of Article 52, a party to a dispute shall abstain from voting.

Procedure

Article 28

1. The Security Council shall be so organized as to be able to function continuously. Each member of the Security Council shall for this purpose be represented at times at the seat of the Organization.

2. The Security Council shall hold meetings at which each of its members may, if it so desires, be represented by a member of the government or by some other specially designated representative.

3. The Security Council may hold meetings at such places other than the seat of the Organization as in its judgment will best facilitate its work.

Article 29

The Security Council may establish such subsidiary organs as it deems necessary for the performance of its functions.

Article 30

The Security Council shall adopt its own rules of procedure, including the method of selecting its President.

Article 31

Any Member of the United Nations which is not a member of the Security Council may participate, without vote, in the discussion of any question brought before the Security Council whenever the latter considers that the interests of that Member are specially affected.

Article 32

1. Any Member of the United Nations which is not a member of the Security Council or any state which is not a Member of the United Nations, if it is a party to a dispute under consideration by the Security Council, shall be invited to participate, without vote, in the discussion relating to the dispute. The Security Council shall any down such conditions as it deems just for the participation of a state which is not a Member of the United Nations.

CHAPTER VI. PACIFIC SETTLEMENT OF DISPUTES

Article 33

1. The parties to any dispute, the continuance of which is likely to endanger the maintenance of international peace and security, shall, first of all, seek a solution by negotiation, enquiry, mediation, conciliation, arbitration, judicial settlement, resort to regional agencies or arrangements, or other peaceful means of their own choice.

2. The Security Council shall, when it deems necessary, call upon the parties to settle their dispute by such means.

Article 34

The Security Council may investigate any dispute, or any situation which might lead to international friction or give rise to a dispute, in order to determine whether the continuance of the dispute or situation is likely to endanger the maintenance of international peace and security.

Article 35

1. Any Member of the United Nations may bring any dispute, or any situation of the nature referred to in Article 34, to the attention of the Security Council or of the General Assembly.

2. A state which is not a Member of the United Nations may bring to the attention of the Security Council or of the General Assembly any dispute to which it is a party if it accepts in advance, for the purposes of the dispute, the obligations of pacific settlement provided in the present Charter.

3. The proceedings of the General Assembly in respect of matters brought to its attention under this Article will be subject to the provisions of Articles 11 and 12.

Article 36

1. The Security Council may, at any stage of a dispute of the nature referred to in Article 33 or of a situation of like nature, recommend appropriate procedures or methods of adjustment.

2. The Security Council should take into consideration any procedures for the settlement of the dispute which have already been adopted by the parties.

3. In making recommendations under this Article the Security Council should also take into consideration that legal disputes should as a general rule be referred by the parties to the International Court of Justice in accordance with the provisions of the Statute of the Court.

Article 37

1. Should the parties to a dispute of the nature referred to in Article 33 fail to settle it by the means indicated in that Article, they shall refer it to the Security Council.

2. If the Security Council deems that the continuance of the dispute is in fact likely to endanger the maintenance of international peace and security, it shall decide whether to take action under Article 36 or to recommend such terms of settlement as it may consider appropriate.

Article 38

Without prejudice to the provisions of Articles 33 to 37, the Security Council may, if all the parties to any dispute so request, make recommendations to the parties with a view to a pacific settlement of the dispute.

CHAPTER VII. ACTION WITH RESPECT TO THREATS TO THE PEACE, BREACHES OF THE PEACE, OR ACTS OF AGGRESSION

Article 39

The Security Council shall determine the existence of any threat to the peace, breach of the peace, or act of aggression and shall make recommendations, or decide what measures shall be taken in accordance with Articles 41 and 42, to maintain or restore international peace and security.

Article 40

In order to prevent an aggravation of the situation, the Security Council may, before making the recommendations or deciding upon the measures provided for in Article 39, call upon the parties concerned to comply with such provisional measures as it deems necessary or desirable. Such provisional measures shall be without prejudice to the rights, claims, or position of the parties concerned. The Security Council shall duly take account of failure to comply with such provisional measures.

Article 41

The Security Council may decide what measures not involving the use of armed force are to be employed to give effect to its decisions, and it may call upon the Members of the United Nations to apply such measures. These may include complete or partial interruption of economic relations and of rail, sea, air, postal, telegraphic, radio, and other means of communication, and the severance of diplomatic relations.

Article 42

Should the Security Council consider that measures provided for in Article 41 would be inadequate or have proved inadequate, it may take such action by air, sea, or land forces as may be necessary to maintain or restore international peace and security. Such action may include demonstrations, blockade, and other operations by air, sea, or land forces of Members of the United Nations.

Article 43

1. All Members of the United Nations, in order to contribute to the maintenance of international peace and security, undertake to make available to the Security Council, on its call and in accordance with a special agreement or agreements, armed forces, assistance, and facilities, including rights of passage, necessary for the purpose of maintaining international peace and security.

2. Such agreement or agreements shall govern the numbers and types of forces, their degree of readiness and general location, and the nature of the facilities and assistance to be provided.

3. The agreement or agreements shall be negotiated as soon as possible on the initiative of the Security Council. They shall be concluded between the Security Council and Members or between the Security Council and groups of Members and shall be subject to ratification by the signatory states in accordance with their respective constitutional processes.

Article 44

1. When Security Council has decided to use force it shall, before calling upon a Member not represented on it to provide armed forces in

fulfilment of the obligations assumed under Article 43, invite that Member, if the Member so desires, to participate in the decisions of the Security Council concerning the employment of contingents of that Member's armed forces.

Article 45

In order to enable the United Nations to take urgent military measures, Members shall hold immediately available national air-force contingents for combined international enforcement action. The strength and degree of readiness of these contingents and plans for their combined action shall be determined, within the limits laid down in the special agreement or agreements referred to in Article 43, by the Security Council with the assistance of the Military Staff Committee.

Article 46

1. Plans for the application of armed force shall be made by the Security Council with the assistance of the Military Staff Committee.

Article 47

1. There shall be established a Military Staff Committee to advise and assist the Security Council on questions relating to the Security Council's military requirements for the maintenance of international peace and security, the employment and command of forces placed at its disposal, the regulation of armaments, and possible disarmament.

2. The Military Staff Committee consist of the Chiefs of Staff of the permanent members of the Security Council or their representatives. Any Member of the United Nations not permanently represented on the Committee shall be invited by the Committee to be associated with it when the efficient discharge of the Committee's responsibilities requires the participation of that Member its work.

3. The Military Staff Committee be responsible under the Security Council for the strategic direction of any armed forces paced at the disposal of the Security Council. Questions relating to the command of such forces shall be worked out subsequently.

4. The Military Staff Committee, with the authorization of the security Council and after consultation with appropriate regional agencies, may establish sub-committees.

Article 48

1. The action required to carry out the decisions of the Security Council for the maintenance of international peace and security shall be taken by all the Members of the United Nations or by some of them, as the Security Council may determine.

2. Such decisions shall be carried out by the members of the United Nations directly and through their action in the appropriate international agencies of which they are members.

Article 49

The Members of the United Nations shall join in affording mutual assistance in carrying out the measures decided upon by the Security Council.

Article 50

If preventive or enforcement measures against any state are taken by the Security Council, any other state, whether a Member of the United Nations or not, which finds itself confronted with special economic problems arising from the carrying out of those measures shall have the right to consult with the Security Council with regard to a solution of those problems.

Article 51

Nothing in the present Charter shall impair the inherent right of individual or collective self-defence if an armed attack occurs against a Member of the United Nations, until the Security Council has taken measures necessary to maintain international peace and security. Measures taken by Members in the exercise of this right of self-defence shall be immediately reported to the Security Council and shall not in any way affect the authority and responsibility of the Security Council under the present Charter to take at any time such action as it deems necessary in order to maintain or restore international peace and security.

CHAPTER VIII. REGIONAL ARRANGEMENTS

Article 52

1. Nothing in the present Charter precludes the existence of regional arrangements or agencies for dealing with such matters relating to the maintenance of international peace and security as are appropriate for regional action, provided that such arrangements or agencies and their activities are consistent with the Purposes and Principles of the United Nations.

2. The Members of the United Nations entering into such arrangements or constituting such agencies shall make every effort to achieve pacific settlement of local disputes through such regional arrangements or by such regional agencies before referring them to the Security Council.

3. The Security Council shall encourage the development of pacific settlement of local disputes through such regional arrangements or by such regional agencies either on the initiative of the states concerned or by reference from the Security Council.

4. This Article in no way impairs the application of Articles 34 and 35.

Article 53

1. The Security Council shall, where appropriate, utilize such regional arrangements or agencies for enforcement action under its authority. But no enforcement action shall be taken under regional ar-

rangements or by regional agencies without the authorization of the Security Council, with the exception of measures against any enemy state, as defined in paragraph 2 of this Article, provided for pursuant to Article 107 or in regional arrangements directed against renewal of aggressive policy on the part of any such state, until such time as the Organization may, on request of the Governments concerned, be charged with the responsibility for preventing further aggression by such a state.

2. The term enemy state as used in paragraph 1 of this Article applies to any state which during the Second World War has been an enemy of any signatory of the present Charter.

Article 54

The Security Council shall at all times be kept fully informed of activities undertaken or in contemplation under regional arrangements or by regional agencies for the maintenance of international peace and security.

CHAPTER IX. INTERNATIONAL ECONOMIC AND SOCIAL COOPERATION

Article 55

With a view to the creation of conditions of stability and well-being which are necessary for peaceful and friendly relations among nations based on respect for the principle of equal rights and self-determination of peoples, the United Nations shall promote:

a. higher standards of living, full employment, and conditions of economic and social progress and development;

b. solutions of international economic, social, health, and related problems; and international cultural and educational cooperation; and

c. universal respect for, and observance of, human rights and fundamental freedoms for all without distinction as to race, sex, language, or religion.

Article 56

All Members pledge themselves to take joint and separate action in cooperation with the Organization for the achievement of the purposes set forth in Article 55.

Article 57

1. The various specialized agencies, established by intergovernmental agreement and having wide international responsibilities, as defined in their basic instruments, in economic, social, cultural, educational, health, and related fields, shall be brought into relationship with the United Nations in accordance with the provisions of Article 63.

2. Such agencies thus brought into relationship with the United Nations are hereinafter referred to as specialized agencies.

Article 58

The Organization shall make recommendations for the coordination of the policies and activities of the specialized agencies.

Article 59

The Organization shall, where appropriate, initiate negotiations among the states concerned for the creation of any new specialized agencies required for the accomplishment of the purposes set forth in Article 55.

Article 60

Responsibility for the discharge of the functions of the Organization set forth in this Chapter shall be vested in the General Assembly and, under the authority of the General Assembly, in the Economic and Social Council, which shall have for this purpose the powers set forth in Chapter X.

CHAPTER X. THE ECONOMIC AND SOCIAL COUNCIL

Composition

Article 61

1. The Economic and Social Council shall consist of fifty-four Members of the United Nations elected by the General Assembly.

2. Subject to the provisions of paragraph 3, eighteen members of the Economic and Social Council shall be elected each year for a term of three years. A retiring member shall be eligible for immediate re-election.

3. At the first election after the increase in the membership of the Economic and Social Council from twenty-seven to fifty-four members, in addition to the members elected in place of the nine members whose term of office expires at the end of that year, twenty-seven additional members shall be elected. Of these twenty-seven additional members, the term of office of nine members so elected shall expire at the end of one year, and of nine other members at the end of two years, in accordance with arrangements made by the General Assembly.

4. Each member of the Economic and Social Council shall have one representative.

Functions and Powers

Article 62

1. The Economic and Social Council may make or initiate studies and reports with respect to international economic, social, cultural, educational, health, and related matters and may make recommendations with respect to any such matters to the General Assembly, to the Members of the United Nations, and to the specialized agencies concerned.

2. It may make recommendations for the purpose of promoting respect for and observance of, human rights and fundamental freedoms for all.

3. It may prepare draft conventions for submission to the General Assembly, with respect to matters falling within its competence.

4. It may call, in accordance with the rules prescribed by the United Nations, international conferences on matters falling within its competence.

Article 63

1. The Economic and Social Council may enter into agreements with any of the agencies referred to in Article 57, defining the terms on which the agency concerned shall be brought into relationship with the United Nations. Such agreements shall be subject to approval by the General Assembly.

2. It may coordinate the activities of the specialized agencies through consultation with and recommendations to such agencies and through recommendations to the General Assembly and to the Members of the United Nations.

Article 64

1. The Economic and Social Council may take appropriate steps to obtain regular reports from the specialized agencies. It may make arrangements with the Members of the United Nations and with the specialized agencies to obtain reports on the steps taken to give effect to its own recommendations and to recommendations on matters falling within its competence made by the General Assembly.

2. It may communicate its observations on these reports to the General Assembly.

Article 65

The Economic and Social Council may furnish information to the Security Council and shall assist the Security Council upon its request.

Article 66

1. The Economic and Social Council shall perform such functions as fall within its competence in connection with the carrying out of the recommendations of the General Assembly.

2. It may, with the approval of the General Assembly, perform services at the request of Members of the United Nations and at the request of specialized agencies.

3. It shall perform such other functions as are specified elsewhere in the present Charter or as may be assigned to it by the General Assembly.

Voting

Article 67

1. Each member of the Economic and Social Council shall have one vote.

2. Decisions of the Economic and Social Council shall be made by a majority of the members present and voting.

Article 68

The Economic and Social Council shall set up commissions in economic and social fields and for the promotion of human rights, and such other commissions as may be required for the performance of its functions.

Article 69

The Economic and Social Council shall invite any Member of the United Nations to participate, without vote, in its deliberations on any matter of particular concern to that Member.

Article 70

The Economic and Social Council may make arrangements for representatives of the specialized agencies to participate, without vote, in its deliberations and in those of the commissions established by it, and for its representatives to participate in the deliberations of the specialized agencies.

Article 71

The Economic and Social Council may make suitable arrangements for consultation with nongovernmental organizations which are concerned with matters within its competence. Such arrangements may be made with international organizations and, where appropriate, with national organizations after consultation with the Member of the United Nations concerned.

Article 72

1. The Economic and Social Council shall adopt its own rules of procedure, including the method of selecting its President.

2. The Economic and Social Council shall meet as required in accordance with its rules, which shall include provision for the convening of meetings on the request of a majority of its members.

CHAPTER XI. DECLARATION REGARDING NON-SELF-GOVERNING TERRITORIES

Article 73

Members of the United Nations which have or assume responsibilities for the administration of territories whose peoples have not yet attained a full measure of self-government recognize the principle that the interests of the inhabitants of these territories are paramount, and accept as a sacred trust the obligation to promote to the utmost, within the system of international peace and security established by the present

Charter, the well-being of the inhabitants of these territories, and, to this end:

a. to ensure, with due respect for the culture of the peoples concerned, their political, economic, social, and educational advancement, their just treatment, and their protection against abuses;

b. to develop self-government, to take due account of the political aspirations of the peoples, and to assist them in the progressive development of their free political institutions, according to the particular circumstances of each territory and its peoples and their varying stages of advancement;

c. to further international peace and security;

d. to promote constructive measures of development, to encourage research, and to co-operate with one another and, when and where appropriate, with specialized international bodies with a view to the practical achievement of the social, economic, and scientific purposes set forth in this Article; and

e. to transmit regularly to the Secretary–General for information purposes, subject to such limitation as security and constitutional considerations may require, statistical and other information of a technical nature relating to economic, social, and educational conditions in the territories for which they are respectively responsible other than those territories to which Chapters XII and XIII apply.

Article 74

Members of the United Nations also agree that their policy in respect of the territories to which this Chapter applies, no less than in respect of their metropolitan areas, must be based on the general principle of good-neighbourliness, due account being taken of the interests and well-being of the rest of the world, in social, economic, and commercial matters.

CHAPTER XII. INTERNATIONAL TRUSTEESHIP SYSTEM

Article 75

The United Nations shall establish under its authority an international trusteeship system for the administration and supervision of such territories as may be placed thereunder by subsequent individual agreements. These territories are hereinafter referred to as trust territories.

Article 76

The basic objectives of the trusteeship system, in accordance with the Purposes of the United Nations laid down in Article 1 of the present Charter, shall be:

a. to further international peace and security;

b. to promote the political, economic, social, and educational advancement of the inhabitants of the trust territories, and their progressive development towards self-government or independence as may be appropriate to the particular circumstances of each territory and its peoples and the freely expressed wishes of the peoples concerned, and as may be provided by the terms of each trusteeship agreement;

c. to encourage respect for human rights and for fundamental freedoms for all without distinction as to race, sex, language, or religion, and to encourage recognition of the interdependence of the peoples of the world; and

d. to ensure equal treatment in social, economic, and commercial matters for all Members of the United Nations and their nationals, and also equal treatment for the latter in the administration of justice, without prejudice to the attainment of the foregoing objectives and subject to the provisions of Article 80.

Article 77

1. The trusteeship system shall apply to such territories in the following categories as may be placed thereunder by means of trusteeship agreements:

a. territories now held under mandate;

b. territories which may be detached from enemy states as a result of the Second World War; and

c. territories voluntarily placed under the system by states responsible for their administration.

2. It will be a matter for subsequent agreement as to which territories in the foregoing categories will be brought under the trusteeship system and upon what terms.

Article 78

The trusteeship system shall not apply to territories which have become Members of the United Nations, relationship among which shall be based on respect for the principle of sovereign equality.

Article 79

The terms of trusteeship for each territory to be placed under the trusteeship system, including any alteration or amendment, shall be agreed upon by the states directly concerned, including the mandatory power in the case of territories held under mandate by a Member of the United Nations, and shall be approved as provided for in Articles 83 and 85.

Article 80

1. Except as may be agreed upon in individual trusteeship agreements, made under Articles 77, 79, and 81, placing each territory under the trusteeship system, and until such agreements have been concluded, nothing in this Chapter shall be construed in or of itself to alter in any manner the rights whatsoever of any states or any peoples or the terms of existing international instruments to which Members of the United Nations may respectively be parties.

2. Paragraph 1 of this Article shall not be interpreted as giving grounds for delay or postponement of the negotiation and conclusion of

agreements for placing mandated and other territories under the trusteeship system as provided for in Article 77.

Article 81

The trusteeship agreement shall in each case include the terms under which the trust territory will be administered and designate the authority which will exercise the administration of the trust territory. Such authority, hereinafter called the administering authority, may be one or more states or the Organization itself.

Article 82

There may be designated, in any trusteeship agreement, a strategic area or areas which may include part or all of the trust territory to which the agreement applies, without prejudice to any special agreement or agreements made under Article 43.

Article 83

1. All functions of the United Nations relating to strategic areas, including the approval of the terms of the trusteeship agreements and of their alteration or amendment, shall be exercised by the Security Council.

2. he basic objectives set forth in Article 76 shall be applicable to the people of each strategic area.

3. The Security Council shall, subject to the provisions of the trusteeship agreements and without prejudice to security considerations, avail itself of the assistance of the Trusteeship Council to perform those functions of the United Nations under the trusteeship system relating to political, economic, social, and educational matters in the strategic areas.

Article 84

It shall be the duty of the administering authority to ensure that the trust territory shall play its part in the maintenance of international peace and security. To this end the administering authority may make use of volunteer forces, facilities, and assistance from the trust territory in carrying out the obligations towards the Security Council undertaken in this regard by the administering authority, as well as for local defence and the maintenance of law and order within the trust territory.

Article 85

1. The functions of the United Nations with regard to trusteeship agreements for all areas not designated as strategic, including the approval of the terms of the trusteeship agreements and of their alteration or amendment, shall be exercised by the General Assembly.

2. The Trusteeship Council, operating under the authority of the General Assembly, shall assist the General Assembly in carrying out these functions.

CHAPTER XIII. THE TRUSTEESHIP COUNCIL

Composition

Article 86

1. The Trusteeship Council shall consist of the following Members of the United Nations:

a. those Members administering trust territories;

b. such of those Members mentioned by name in Article 23 as are not administering trust territories; and

c. as many other Members elected for three-year terms by the General Assembly as may be necessary to ensure that the total number of members of the Trusteeship Council is equally divided between those Members of the United Nations which administer trust territories and those which do not.

2. Each member of the Trusteeship Council shall designate one specially qualified person to represent it therein.

Functions and Powers

Article 87

The General Assembly and, under its authority, the Trusteeship Council, in carrying out their functions, may:

a. consider reports submitted by the administering authority;

b. accept petitions and examine them in consultation with the administering authority;

c. provide for periodic visits to the respective trust territories at times agreed upon with the administering authority; and

d. take these and other actions in conformity with the terms of the trusteeship agreements.

Article 88

The Trusteeship Council shall formulate a questionnaire on the political, economic, social, and educational advancement of the inhabitants of each trust territory, and the administering authority for each trust territory within the competence of the General Assembly shall make an annual report to the General Assembly upon the basis of such questionnaire.

Voting

Article 89

1. Each member of the Trusteeship Council shall have one vote.

2. Decisions of the Trusteeship Council shall be made by a majority of the members present and voting.

Procedure

Article 90

1. The Trusteeship Council shall adopt its own rules of procedure, including the method of selecting its President.

2. The Trusteeship Council shall meet as required in accordance with its rules, which shall include provision for the convening of meetings on the request of a majority of its members.

Article 91

The Trusteeship Council shall, when appropriate, avail itself of the assistance of the Economic and Social Council and of the specialized agencies in regard to matters with which they are respectively concerned.

CHAPTER XIV. THE INTERNATIONAL COURT OF JUSTICE

Article 92

The International Court of Justice shall be the principal judicial organ of the United Nations. It shall function in accordance with the annexed Statute, which is based upon the Statute of the Permanent Court of International Justice and forms an integral part of the present Charter.

Article 93

1. All Members of the United Nations are *ipso facto* parties to the Statute of the International Court of Justice.

2. A state which is not a Member of the United Nations may become a party to the Statute of the International Court of Justice on conditions to be determined in each case by the General Assembly upon the recommendation of the Security Council.

Article 94

1. Each Member of the United Nations undertakes to comply with the decision of the International Court of Justice in any case to which it is a party.

2. If any party to a case fails to perform the obligations incumbent upon it under a judgment rendered by the Court, the other party may have recourse to the Security Council, which may, if it deems necessary, make recommendations or decide upon measures to be taken to give effect to the judgment.

Article 95

Nothing in the present Charter shall prevent Members of the United Nations from entrusting the solution of their differences to other tribunals by virtue of agreements already in existence or which may be concluded in the future.

Article 96

1. The General Assembly or the Security Council may request the International Court of Justice to give an advisory opinion on any legal question.

2. Other organs of the United Nations and specialized agencies, which may at any time be so authorized by the General Assembly, may

also request advisory opinions of the Court on legal questions arising within the scope of their activities.

CHAPTER XV. THE SECRETARIAT

Article 97

The Secretariat shall comprise a Secretary–General and such staff as the Organization may require. The Secretary–General shall be appointed by the General Assembly upon the recommendation of the Security Council. He shall be the chief administrative officer of the Organization.

Article 98

The Secretary–General shall act in that capacity in all meetings of the General Assembly, of the Security Council, of the Economic and Social Council, and of the Trusteeship Council, and shall perform such other functions as are entrusted to him by these organs. The Secretary–General shall make an annual report to the General Assembly on the work of the Organization.

Article 99

The Secretary–General may bring to the attention of the Security Council any matter which in his opinion may threaten the maintenance of international peace and security.

Article 100

1. In the performance of their duties the Secretary–General and the staff shall not seek or receive instructions from any government or from any other authority external to the Organization. They shall refrain from any action which might reflect on their position as international officials responsible only to the Organization.

2. Each Member of the United Nations undertakes to respect the exclusively international character of the responsibilities of the Secretary–General and the staff and not to seek to influence them in the discharge of their responsibilities.

Article 101

1. The staff shall be appointed by the Secretary–General under regulations established by the General Assembly.

2. Appropriate staffs shall be permanently assigned to the Economic and Social Council, the Trusteeship Council, and, as required, to other organs of the United Nations. These staffs shall form a part of the Secretariat.

3. The paramount consideration in the employment of the staff and in the determination of the conditions of service shall be the necessity of securing the highest standards of efficiency, competence, and integrity. Due regard shall be paid to the importance of recruiting the staff on as wide a geographical basis as possible.

CHAPTER XVI. MISCELLANEOUS PROVISIONS

Article 102

1. Every treaty and every international agreement entered into by any Member of the United Nations after the present Charter comes into force shall as soon as possible be registered with the Secretariat and published by it.

2. No party to any such treaty or international agreement which has not been registered in accordance with the provisions of paragraph 1 of this Article may invoke that treaty or agreement before any organ of the United Nations.

Article 103

In the event of a conflict between the obligations of the Members of the United Nations under the present Charter and their obligations under any other international agreement, their obligations under the present Charter shall prevail.

Article 104

The Organization shall enjoy in the territory of each of its Members such legal capacity as may be necessary for the exercise of its functions and the fulfillment of its purposes.

Article 105

1. The Organization shall enjoy in the territory of each of its Members such privileges and immunities as are necessary for the fulfillment of its purposes.

2. Representatives of the Members of the United Nations and officials of the Organization shall similarly enjoy such privileges and immunities as are necessary for the independent exercise of their functions in connection with the Organization.

3. The General Assembly may make recommendations with a view to determining the details of the application of paragraphs 1 and 2 of this Article or may propose conventions to the Members of the United Nations for this purpose.

Article 106

Pending the coming into force of such special agreements referred to in Article 43 as in the opinion of the Security Council enable it to begin the exercise of its responsibilities under Article 42, the parties to the Four–Nation Declaration, signed at Moscow, 30 October 1943, and France, shall, in accordance with the provisions of paragraph 5 of that Declaration, consult with one another and as occasion requires with other Members of the United Nations with a view to such joint action on behalf of the Organization as may be necessary for the purpose of maintaining international peace and security.

Article 107

Nothing in the present Charter shall invalidate or preclude action, in relation to any state which during the Second World War has been an enemy of any signatory to the present Charter, taken or authorized as a result of that war by the Governments having responsibility for such action.

CHAPTER XVIII. AMENDMENTS

Article 108

Amendments to the present Charter shall come into force for all Members of the United Nations when they have been adopted by a vote of two thirds of the members of the General Assembly and ratified in accordance with their respective constitutional processes by two thirds of the Members of the United Nations, including all the permanent members of the Security Council.

Article 109

1. A General Conference of the Members of the United Nations for the purpose of reviewing the present Charter may be held at a date and place to be fixed by a two-thirds vote of the members of the General Assembly and by a vote of any nine members of the Security Council. Each Member of the United Nations shall have one vote in the conference.

2. Any alteration of the present Charter recommended by a two-thirds vote of the conference shall take effect when ratified in accordance with their respective constitutional processes by two thirds of the Members of the United Nations including the permanent members of the Security Council.

3. If such a conference has not been held before the tenth annual session of the General Assembly following the coming into force of the present Charter, the proposal to call such a conference shall be placed on the agenda of that session of the General Assembly, and the conference shall be held if so decided by a majority vote of the members of the General Assembly and by a vote of any seven members of the Security Council.

CHAPTER XIX. RATIFICATION AND SIGNATURE

Article 110

1. The present Charter shall be ratified by the signatory states in accordance with their respective constitutional processes.

2. The shall be deposited with the Government of the United States of America, which shall notify a the signatory states of each deposit as well as the Secretary–General of the Organization when he has been appointed.

3. The present Charter shall come into force upon the deposit of by the Republic of China, France, the Union of Soviet Socialist, the United Kingdom of Great Britain and Northern Ireland, and the United States of America, and by a majority of the other signatory states. A protocol of

the deposited shall thereupon be drawn up by the Government of the United States of America which shall communicate copies thereof to all the signatory states.

4. The states signatory to the present Charter which ratify it after it has come into force will become original Members of the United Nations on the date of the deposit of their respective ratifications.

Article 111

The present Charter, of which the Chinese, French, Russian, English, and Spanish texts are equally authentic, shall remain deposited in the archives of the Government of -the United States of America. Duly certified copies thereof shall be transmitted by that Government to the Governments of the other signatory states.

IN FAITH WHEREOF the representatives of the Governments of the United Nations have signed the present Charter.

DONE at the city of San Francisco the twenty-sixth day of June, one thousand nine hundred and forty-five.

Document 3
STATUTE OF THE INTERNATIONAL COURT OF JUSTICE

T.S. No. 993, 59 Stat. 1055 (June 26, 1945)

Article 34

1. Only states may be parties in cases before the Court.

2. The Court, subject to and in conformity with its Rules, may request of public international organizations information relevant to cases before it, and shall receive such information presented by such organizations on their own initiative.

3. Whenever the construction of the constituent instrument of a public international organization or of an international convention adopted thereunder is in question in a case before the Court, the Registrar shall so notify the public international organization concerned and shall communicate to it copies of all the written proceedings.

Article 35

1. The Court shall be open to the states parties to the present Statute.

2. The conditions under which the Court shall be open to other states shall, subject to the special provisions contained in treaties in force, be laid down by the Security Council, but in no case shall such conditions place the parties in a position of inequality before the Court.

3. When a state which is not a Member of the United Nations is a party to a case, the Court shall fix the amount which that party is to contribute towards the expenses of the Court. This provision shall not apply if such state is bearing a share of the expenses of the Court.

Article 36

1. The jurisdiction of the Court comprises all cases which the parties refer to it and all matters specially provided for in the Charter of the United Nations or in treaties and conventions in force.

2. The states parties to the present Statute may at any time declare that they recognize as compulsory *ipso facto* and without special agreement, in relation to any other state accepting the same obligation, the jurisdiction of the Court in all legal disputes concerning:

a. the interpretation of a treaty;

b. any question of international law;

c. the existence of any fact which, if established, would constitute a breach of an international obligation;

d. the nature or extent of the reparation to be made for the breach of an international obligation.

3. The declarations referred to above may be made unconditionally or on condition of reciprocity on the part of several or certain states or for a certain time.

4. Such declarations shall be deposited with the Secretary–General of the United Nations, who shall transmit copies thereof to the parties to the Statute and to the Registrar of the Court.

5. Declarations made under Article 36 of the Statute of the Permanent Court of International Justice and which are still in force shall be deemed, as between the parties to the present Statute, to be acceptances of the compulsory jurisdiction of the International Court of Justice for the period which they still have to run and in accordance with their terms.

6. In the event of a dispute as to whether the Court has jurisdiction the matter shall be settled by the decision of the Court.

Article 37

Whenever a treaty or convention in force provides for reference of a matter to a tribunal to have been instituted by the League of Nations, or to the Permanent Court of International Justice, the matter shall, as between the parties to the present Statute, be referred to the International Court of Justice.

Article 38

1. The Court, whose function is to decide in accordance with international law such disputes as are submitted to it, shall apply:

a. international conventions, whether general or particular, establishing rules expressly recognized by the contesting states;

b. international custom, as evidence of a general practice accepted as law;

c. the general principles of law recognized by civilized nations;

d. subject to the provisions of Article 59, judicial decisions and the teachings of the most highly qualified publicists of the various nations, as subsidiary means for the determination of rules of law.

2. This provision shall not prejudice the power of the Court to decide a case *ex aequo et bono,* if the parties agree thereto.

Article 53

1. Whenever one of the parties does not appear before the Court, or fails to defend its case, the other party may call upon the Court to decide in favor of its claim.

2. The Court must, before doing so, satisfy itself, not only that it has jurisdiction in accordance with Articles 36 and 37, but also that the claim is well founded in fact and law.

Article 55

1. All questions shall be decided by a majority of the judges present.

2. In the event of an equality of votes, the President or the judge who acts in his place shall have a casting vote.

Article 59

The decision of the Court has no binding force except between the parties in respect of that particular case.

Article 60

The judgment is final and without appeal. In the event of dispute as to the meaning or scope of the judgment, the Court shall construe it upon the request of any party.

Article 62

1. Should a state consider that it has an interest of a legal nature which may be affected by the decision in the case, it may submit a request to the Court to be permitted to intervene.

2. It shall be for the Court to decide upon this request.

Article 65

1. The Court may give an advisory opinion on any legal question at the request of whatever body may be authorized by or in accordance with the Charter of the United Nations to make a request.

2. Questions upon which the advisory opinion of the Court is asked shall be laid before the Court by means of a written request containing an exact statement of the question upon which an opinion is required, and accompanied by all documents likely to throw light upon the question.

Document 4
VIENNA CONVENTION ON THE LAW OF TREATIES

1155 U.N.T.S. 331 (May 23, 1969)

PART I

INTRODUCTION

Article 1. Scope of the Present Convention

The present Convention applies to treaties between States.

Article 2. Use of Terms

1. For the purposes of the present Convention:

(a) "treaty" means an international agreement concluded between States in written form and governed by international law, whether embodied in a single instrument or in two or more related instruments and whatever its particular designation;

(b) "ratification", "acceptance", "approval" and "accession" mean in each case the international act so named whereby a State establishes on the international plane its consent to be bound by a treaty;

(c) "full powers" means a document emanating from the competent authority of a State designating a person or persons to represent the State for negotiating, adopting or authenticating the text of a treaty, for expressing the consent of the State to be bound by a treaty, or for accomplishing any other act with respect to a treaty;

(d) "reservation" means a unilateral statement, however phrased or named, made by a State, when signing, ratifying, accepting, approving or acceding to a treaty, whereby it purports to exclude or to modify the legal effect of certain provisions of the treaty in their application to that State;

(e) "negotiating State" means a State which took part in the drawing up and adoption of the text of the treaty;

(f) "contracting State" means a State which has consented to be bound by the treaty, whether or not the treaty has entered into force;

(g) "party" means a State which has consented to be bound by the treaty and for which the treaty is in force;

(h) "third State" means a State not a party to the treaty;

(i) "international organization" means an intergovernmental organization.

2. The provisions of paragraph 1 regarding the use of terms in the present Convention are without prejudice to the use of those terms or to the meanings which may be given to them in the internal law of any State.

Article 3. International Agreements Not Within the Scope of the Present Convention

The fact that the present Convention does not apply to international agreements concluded between States and other subjects of international law or between such other subjects of international law, or to international agreements not in written form, shall not affect:

(a) the legal force of such agreements;

(b) the application to them of any of the rules set forth in the present Convention to which they would be subject under international law independently of the Convention;

(c) the application of the Convention to the relations of States as between themselves under international agreements to which other subjects of international law are also parties.

Article 4. Non–Retroactivity of the Present Convention

Without prejudice to the application of any rules set forth in the present Convention to which treaties would be subject under international law independently of the Convention, the Convention applies only to treaties which are concluded by States after the entry into force of the present Convention with regard to such States.

Article 5. Treaties Constituting International Organizations and Treaties Adopted Within an International Organization

The present Convention applies to any treaty which is the constituent instrument of an international organization and to any treaty adopted within an international organization without prejudice to any relevant rules of the organization.

PART II

CONCLUSION AND ENTRY INTO FORCE OF TREATIES

SECTION 1. CONCLUSION OF TREATIES

Article 6. Capacity of States to Conclude Treaties

Every State possesses capacity to conclude treaties.

Article 7. Full Powers

1. A person is considered as representing a State for the purpose of adopting or authenticating the text of a treaty or for the purpose of expressing the consent of the State to be bound by a treaty if:

(a) he produces appropriate full powers; or

(b) it appears from the practice of the States concerned or from other circumstances that their intention was to consider that person as representing the State for such purposes and to dispense with full powers.

2. In virtue of their functions and without having to produce full powers, the following are considered as representing their State:

(a) Heads of State, Heads of Government and Ministers for Foreign Affairs, for the purpose of performing all acts relating to the conclusion of a treaty;

(b) heads of diplomatic missions, for the purpose of adopting the text of a treaty between the accrediting State and the State to which they are accredited;

(c) representatives accredited by States to an international conference or to an international organization or one of its organs, for the purpose of adopting the text of a treaty in that conference, organization or organ.

Article 8. Subsequent Confirmation of an Act Performed Without Authorization

An act relating to the conclusion of a treaty performed by a person who cannot be considered under article 7 as authorized to represent a State for that purpose is without legal effect unless afterwards confirmed by that State.

Article 9. Adoption of the Text

1. The adoption of the text of a treaty takes place by the consent of all the States participating in its drawing up except as provided in paragraph 2.

2. The adoption of the text of a treaty at an international conference takes place by the vote of two-thirds of the States present and voting, unless by the same majority they shall decide to apply a different rule.

Article 10. Authentication of the Text

The text of a treaty is established as authentic and definitive:

(a) by such procedure as may be provided for in the text or agreed upon by the States participating in its drawing up; or

(b) failing such procedure, by the signature, signature ad referendum or initialing by the representatives of those States of the text of the treaty or of the Final Act of a conference incorporating the text.

Article 11. Means of Expressing Consent to Be Bound by a Treaty

The consent of a State to be bound by a treaty may be expressed by signature, exchange of instruments constituting a treaty, ratification, acceptance, approval or accession, or by any other means if so agreed.

Article 12. Consent to Be Bound by a Treaty Expressed by Signature

1. The consent of a State to be bound by a treaty is expressed by the signature of its representative when:

(a) the treaty provides that signature shall have that effect;

(b) it is otherwise established that the negotiating States were agreed that signature should have that effect; or

(c) the intention of the State to give that effect to the signature appears from the full powers of its representative or was expressed during the negotiation.

2. For the purposes of paragraph 1:

(a) the initialing of a text constitutes a signature of the treaty when it is established that the negotiating States so agreed;

(b) the signature ad referendum of a treaty by a representative, if confirmed by his State, constitutes a full signature of the treaty.

Article 13. Consent to Be Bound by a Treaty Expressed by an Exchange of Instruments Constituting a Treaty

The consent of States to be bound by a treaty constituted by instruments exchanged between them is expressed by that exchange when:

(a) the instruments provide that their exchange shall have that effect; or

(b) it is otherwise established that those States were agreed that the exchange of instruments should have that effect

Article 14. Consent to Be Bound by a Treaty Expressed by Ratification, Acceptance or Approval

1. The consent of a State to be bound by a treaty is expressed by ratification when:

(a) the treaty provides for such consent to be expressed by means of ratification;

(b) it is otherwise established that the negotiating States were agreed that ratification should be required;

(c) the representative of the State has signed the treaty subject to ratification; or

(d) the intention of the State to sign the treaty subject to ratification appears from the full powers of its representative or was expressed during the negotiation.

2. The consent of a State to be bound by a treaty is expressed by acceptance or approval under conditions similar to those which apply to ratification.

Article 15. Consent to Be Bound by a Treaty Expressed by Accession

The consent of a State to be bound by a treaty is expressed by accession when:

(a) the treaty provides that such consent may be expressed by that State by means of accession;

(b) it is otherwise established that the negotiating States were agreed that such consent may be expressed by that State by means of accession; or

(c) all the parties have subsequently agreed that such consent may be expressed by that State by means of accession.

Article 16. Exchange or Deposit of Instruments of Ratification, Acceptance, Approval or Accession

Unless the treaty otherwise provides, instruments of ratification, acceptance, approval or accession establish the consent of a State to be bound by a treaty upon:

(a) their exchange between the contracting States;

(b) their deposit with the depositary; or

(c) their notification to the contracting States or to the depositary, if so agreed.

Article 17. Consent to Be Bound by Part of a Treaty and Choice of Differing Provisions

1. Without prejudice to articles 19 to 23, the consent of a State to be bound by part of a treaty is effective only if the treaty so permits or the other contracting States so agree.

2. The consent of a State to be bound by a treaty which permits a choice between differing provisions is effective only if it is made clear to which of the provisions the consent relates.

Article 18. Obligation not to Defeat the Object and Purpose of a Treaty Prior to its Entry into Force

A State is obligated to refrain from acts which would defeat the object and purpose of a treaty when:

(a) it has signed the treaty or has exchanged instruments constituting the treaty subject to ratification, acceptance or approval, until it shall have made its intention clear not to become a party to the treaty; or

(b) it has expressed its consent to be bound by the treaty, pending the entry into force of the treaty and provided that such entry into force is not unduly delayed.

Article 19. Formulation of Reservations

A State may, when signing, ratifying, accepting, approving or acceding to a treaty, formulate a reservation unless:

(a) the reservation is prohibited by the treaty;

(b) the treaty provides that only specified reservations, which do not include the reservation in question, may be made; or

(c) in cases not falling under sub-paragraphs (a) and (b), the reservation is incompatible with the object and purpose of the treaty.

Article 20. Acceptance of an Objection to Reservations

1. A reservation expressly authorized by a treaty does not require any subsequent acceptance by the other contracting States unless the treaty so provides.

2. When it appears from the limited number of the negotiating States and the object and purpose of a treaty that the application of the treaty in its entirety between all the parties is an essential condition of the consent of each one to be bound by the treaty, a reservation requires acceptance by all the parties.

3. When a treaty is a constituent instrument of an international organization and unless it otherwise provides, a reservation requires the acceptance of the competent organ of that organization.

4. In cases not falling under the preceding paragraphs and unless the treaty otherwise provides:

(a) acceptance by another contracting State of a reservation constitutes the reserving State a party to the treaty in relation to that other State if or when the treaty is in force for those States;

(b) an objection by another contracting State to a reservation does not preclude the entry into force of the treaty as between the objecting and reserving States unless a contrary intention is definitely expressed by the objecting State;

(c) an act expressing a State's consent to be bound by the treaty and containing a reservation is effective as soon as at least one other contracting State has accepted the reservation.

5. For the purposes of paragraphs 2 and 4 and unless the treaty otherwise provides, a reservation is considered to have been accepted by a State if it shall have raised no objection to the reservation by the end of a period of twelve months after it was notified of the reservation or by the date on which it expressed its consent to be bound by the treaty, whichever is later.

Article 21. Legal Effects of Reservations and of Objections to Reservations

1. A reservation established with respect to another party in accordance with Articles 19, 20 and 23:

(a) modifies for the reserving State in its relations with that other party the provisions of the treaty to which the reservation relates to the extent of the reservation; and

(b) modifies those provisions to the same extent for that other party in its relations with the reserving State.

2. The reservation does not modify the provisions of the treaty for the other parties to the treaty *inter se*.

3. When a State objecting to a reservation has not opposed the entry into force of the treaty between itself and the reserving State, the provisions to which the reservation relates do not apply as between the two States to the extent of the reservation.

Article 22. Withdrawal of Reservations and of Objections to Reservations

1. Unless the treaty otherwise provides, a reservation may be withdrawn at any time and the consent of a State which has accepted the reservation is not required for its withdrawal.

2. Unless the treaty otherwise provides, an objection to a reservation may be withdrawn at any time.

3. Unless the treaty otherwise provides, or it is otherwise agreed:

(a) the withdrawal of a reservation becomes operative in relation to another contracting State only when notice of it has been received by that State;

(b) the withdrawal of an objection to a reservation becomes operative only when notice of it has been received by the State which formulated the reservation.

Article 23. Procedure Regarding Reservations

1. A reservation, an express acceptance of a reservation and an objection to a reservation must be formulated in writing and communicated to the contracting States and other States entitled to become parties to the treaty.

2. If formulated when signing the treaty subject to ratification, acceptance or approval, a reservation must be formally confirmed by the reserving State when expressing its consent to be bound by the treaty. In such a case the reservation shall be considered as having been made on the date of its confirmation.

3. An express acceptance of, or an objection to, a reservation made previously to confirmation of the reservation does not itself require confirmation.

4. The withdrawal of a reservation or of an objection to a reservation must be formulated in writing.

SECTION 3. ENTRY INTO FORCE AND PROVISIONAL APPLICATION OF TREATIES

Article 24. Entry into Force

1. A treaty enters into force in such manner and upon such date as it may provide or as the negotiating States may agree.

2. Failing any such provision or agreement, a treaty enters into force as soon as consent to be bound by the treaty has been established for all the negotiating States.

3. When the consent of a State to be bound by a treaty is established on a date after the treaty has come into force, the treaty enters into force for that State on that date, unless the treaty otherwise provides.

4. The provisions of a treaty regulating the authentication of its text, the establishment of the consent of States to be bound by the treaty, the manner or date of its entry into force, reservations, the

functions of the depositary and other matters arising necessarily before the entry into force of the treaty apply from the time of the adoption of its text.

Article 25. Provisional Application

1. A treaty or a part of a treaty is applied provisionally pending its entry into force if:

(a) the treaty itself so provides; or

(b) the negotiating States have in some other manner so agreed.

2. Unless the treaty otherwise provides or the negotiating States have otherwise agreed, the provisional application of a treaty or a part of a treaty with respect to a State shall be terminated if that State notifies the other States between which the treaty is being applied provisionally of its intention not to become a party to the treaty.

PART III

OBSERVANCE, APPLICATION AND INTERPRETATION OF TREATIES

SECTION 1. OBSERVANCE OF TREATIES

Article 26. *Pacta Sunt Servanda*

Every treaty in force is binding upon the parties to it and must be performed by them in good faith.

Article 27. Internal Law and Observance of Treaties

A party may not invoke the provisions of its internal law as justification for its failure to perform a treaty. This rule is without prejudice to article 46.

SECTION 2. APPLICATION OF TREATIES

Article 28. Non–Retroactivity of Treaties

Unless a different intention appears from the treaty or is otherwise established, its provisions do not bind a party in relation to any act or fact which took place or any situation which ceased to exist before the date of the entry into force of the treaty with respect to that party.

Article 29. Territorial Scope of Treaties

Unless a different intention appears from the treaty or is otherwise established, a treaty is binding upon each party in respect of its entire territory.

Article 30. Application of Successive Treaties Relating to the Same Subject–Matter

1. Subject to Article 103 of the Charter of the United Nations, the rights and obligations of States parties to successive treaties relating to the same subject-matter shall be determined in accordance with the following paragraphs.

2. When a treaty specifies that it is subject to, or that it is not to be considered as incompatible with, an earlier or later treaty, the provisions of that other treaty prevail.

3. When all the parties to the earlier treaty are parties also to the later treaty but the earlier treaty is not terminated or suspended in operation under article 59, the earlier treaty applies only to the extent that its provisions are compatible with those of the latter treaty.

4. When the parties to the later treaty do not include all the parties to the earlier one:

(a) as between States parties to both treaties the same rule applies as in paragraph 3;

(b) as between a State party to both treaties and a State party to only one of the treaties, the treaty to which both States are parties governs their mutual rights and obligations.

5. Paragraph 4 is without prejudice to article 41, or to any question of the termination or suspension of the operation of a treaty under article 60 or to any question of responsibility which may arise for a State from the conclusion or application of a treaty, the provisions of which are incompatible with its obligations towards another State under another treaty.

SECTION 3. INTERPRETATION OF TREATIES

Article 31. General Rule of Interpretation

1. A treaty shall be interpreted in good faith in accordance with the ordinary meaning to be given to the terms of the treaty in their context and in light of its object and purpose.

2. The context for the purpose of the interpretation of a treaty shall comprise, in addition to the text, including its preamble and annexes:

(a) any agreement relating to the treaty which was made between all the parties in connection with the conclusion of the treaty;

(b) any instrument which was made by one or more parties in connection with the conclusion of the treaty and accepted by the other parties as an instrument related to the treaty.

3. There shall be taken into account, together with the context:

(a) any subsequent agreement made between the parties regarding the interpretation of the treaty or the application of its provisions;

(b) any subsequent practice in the application of the treaty which establishes the agreement of the parties regarding its interpretation;

(c) any relevant rules of international law applicable in the relations between the parties.

4. A special meaning shall be given to a term if it is established that the parties so intended.

Article 32. Supplementary Means of Interpretation

Recourse may be had to supplementary means of interpretation, including the preparatory work of the treaty and the circumstances of its conclusion, in order to confirm the meaning resulting from the application of Article 31, or to determine the meaning when the interpretation according to Article 31:

(a) leaves the meaning ambiguous or obscure; or

(b) leads to a result which is manifestly absurd or unreasonable.

Article 33. Interpretation of Treaties Authenticated in Two or More Languages

1. When a treaty has been authenticated in two or more languages, the text is equally authoritative in each language, unless the treaty provides or the parties agree that, in case of divergence, a particular text shall prevail.

2. A version of the treaty in a language other than one of those in which the text was authenticated shall be considered an authentic text only if the treaty so provides or the parties so agree.

3. The terms of the treaty are presumed to have the same meaning in each authentic text.

4. Except where a particular text prevails in accordance with paragraph 1, when a comparison of the authentic texts discloses a difference of meaning which the application of articles 31 and 32 does not remove, the meaning which best reconciles the texts, having regard to the object and purpose of the treaty, shall be adopted.

SECTION 4. TREATIES AND THIRD STATES

Article 34. General Rule Regarding Third States

A treaty does not create either obligations or rights for a third State without its consent.

Article 35. Treaties Providing for Obligations for Third States

An obligation arises for a third State from a provision of a treaty if the parties to the treaty intend the provision to be the means of establishing the obligation and the third State expressly accepts that obligation in writing.

Article 36. Treaties Providing for Rights for Third States

1. A right arises for a third State from a provision of a treaty if the parties to the treaty intend the provision to accord that right either to the third State, or to a group of States to which it belongs, or to all States, and the third State assents thereto. Its assent shall be presumed so long as the contrary is not indicated, unless the treaty otherwise provides.

2. A State exercising a right in accordance with paragraph 1 shall comply with the conditions for its exercise provided for in the treaty or established in conformity with the treaty.

Article 37. Revocation or Modification of Obligations or Rights of Third States

1. When an obligation has arisen for a third State in conformity with article 35, the obligation may be revoked or modified only with the consent of the parties to the treaty and of the third State, unless it is established that they had otherwise agreed.

2. When a right has arisen for a third State in conformity with article 36, the right may not be revoked or modified by the parties if it is established that the right was intended not to be revocable or subject to modification without the consent of the third State.

Article 38. Rules in a Treaty Becoming Binding on Third States through International Custom

Nothing in articles 34 to 37 precludes a rule set forth in a treaty from becoming binding upon a third State as a customary rule of international law, recognized as such.

PART IV

AMENDMENT AND MODIFICATION OF TREATIES

Article 39. General Rule Regarding the Amendment of Treaties

A treaty may be amended by agreement between the parties. The rules laid down in Part II apply to such an agreement except in so far as the treaty may otherwise provide.

Article 40. Amendment of Multilateral Treaties

1. Unless the treaty otherwise provides, the amendment of multilateral treaties shall be governed by the following paragraphs.

2. Any proposal to amend a multilateral treaty as between all the parties must be notified to all the contracting States, each one of which shall have the right to take part in:

(a) the decision as to the action to be taken in regard to such proposal;

(b) the negotiation and conclusion of any agreement for the amendment of the treaty.

3. Every State entitled to become a party to the treaty shall also be entitled to become a party to the treaty as amended.

4. The amending agreement does not bind any State already a party to the treaty which does not become a party to the amending agreement; article 30, paragraph 4(b), applies in relation to such State.

5. Any State which becomes a party to the treaty after the entry into force of the amending agreement shall, failing an expression of a different intention by that State:

(a) be considered as a party to the treaty as amended; and

(b) be considered as a party to the unamended treaty in relation to any party to the treaty not bound by the amending agreement.

Article 41. Agreements to Modify Multilateral Treaties Between Certain of the Parties Only

1. Two or more of the parties to a multilateral treaty may conclude an agreement to modify the treaty as between themselves alone if:

(a) the possibility of such a modification is provided for by the treaty; or

(b) the modification in question is not prohibited by the treaty and:

(i) does not affect the enjoyment by the other parties of their rights under the treaty or the performance of their obligations;

(ii) does not relate to a provision, derogation from which is incompatible with the effective execution of the object and purpose of the treaty as a whole.

2. Unless in a case falling under paragraph 1(a) the treaty otherwise provides, the parties in question shall notify the other parties of their intention to conclude the agreement and of the modification to the treaty for which it provides.

PART V

INVALIDITY, TERMINATION AND SUSPENSION OF THE OPERATION OF TREATIES

SECTION 1. GENERAL PROVISIONS

Article 42. Validity and Continuance in Force of Treaties

1. The validity of a treaty or of the consent of a State to be bound by a treaty may be impeached only through the application of the present Convention.

2. The termination of a treaty, its denunciation or the withdrawal of a party, may take place only as a result of the application of the provisions of the treaty or of the present Convention. The same rule applies to suspension of the operation of a treaty.

Article 43. Obligations Imposed by International Law Independently of a Treaty

The invalidity, termination or denunciation of a treaty, the withdrawal of a party from it, or the suspension of its operation, as a result of the application of the present Convention or of the provisions of the treaty, shall not in any way impair the duty of any State to fulfil any obligation embodied in the treaty to which it would be subject under international law independently of the treaty.

Article 44. Separability of Treaty Provisions

1. A right of a party, provided for in a treaty or arising under article 56, to denounce, withdraw from or suspend the operation of the treaty may be exercised only with respect to the whole treaty unless the treaty otherwise provides or the parties otherwise agree.

2. A ground for invalidating, terminating, withdrawing from or suspending the operation of a treaty recognized in the present Convention may be invoked only with respect to the whole treaty except as provided in the following paragraphs or in article 60.

3. If the ground relates solely to particular clauses, it may be invoked only with respect to those clauses where:

(a) the said clauses are separable from the remainder of the treaty with regard to their application;

(b) it appears from the treaty or is otherwise established that acceptance of those clauses was not an essential basis of the consent of the other party or parties to be bound by the treaty as a whole; and

(c) continued performance of the remainder of the treaty would not be unjust.

4. In cases falling under articles 49 and 50 the State entitled to invoke the fraud or corruption may do so with respect either to the whole treaty or, subject to paragraph 3, to the particular clauses alone.

5. In cases falling under articles 51, 52 and 53, no separation of the provisions of the treaty is permitted

Article 45. Loss of a Right to Invoke a Ground for Invalidating, Terminating, Withdrawing from or Suspending the Operation of a Treaty

A State may no longer invoke a ground for invalidating, terminating, withdrawing form or suspending the operation of a treaty under Articles 46 to 50 or Articles 60 and 62 if, after becoming aware of the facts:

(a) it shall have expressly agreed that the treaty is valid or remains in force or continues in operation, as the case may be; or

(b) it must by reason of its conduct be considered as having acquiesced in the validity of the treaty or in its maintenance in force or in operation, as the case may be.

SECTION 2. INVALIDITY OF TREATIES

Article 46. Provisions of Internal Law Regarding Competence to Conclude Treaties

1. A State may not invoke the fact that its consent to be bound by a treaty has been expressed in violation of a provision of its internal law regarding competence to conclude treaties as invalidating its consent unless that violation was manifest and concerned a rule of its internal law of fundamental importance.

2. A violation is manifest if it would be objectively evident to any State conducting itself in the matter in accordance with normal practice and in good faith.

Article 47. Specific Restrictions on Authority to Express the Consent of a State

If the authority of a representative to express the consent of a State to be bound by a particular treaty has been made subject to a specific restriction, his omission to observe that restriction may not be invoked as invalidating the consent expressed by him unless the restriction was notified to the other negotiating States prior to his expressing such consent.

Article 48. Error

1. A State may invoke an error in a treaty as invalidating its consent to be bound by the treaty if the error relates to a fact or situation which was assumed by that State to exist at the time when the treaty was concluded and formed an essential basis of its consent to be bound by the treaty.

2. Paragraph 1 shall not apply if the State in question contributed by its own conduct to the error or if the circumstances were such as to put that State on notice of a possible error.

3. An error relating only to the wording of the text of a treaty does not affect its validity; article 79 then applies.

Article 49. Fraud

If a State has been induced to conclude a treaty by the fraudulent conduct of another negotiating State, the State may invoke the fraud as invalidating its consent to be bound by the treaty.

Article 50. Corruption of a Representative of a State

If the expression of a State's consent to be bound by a treaty has been procured through the corruption of its representative directly or indirectly by another negotiating State, the State may invoke such corruption as invalidating its consent to be bound by the treaty.

Article 51. Coercion of a Representative of a State

The expression of a State's consent to be bound by a treaty which has been procured by the coercion of its representative through acts or threats directed against him shall be without any legal effect.

Article 52. Coercion of a State by the Threat or Use of Force

A treaty is void if its conclusion has been procured by the threat or use of force in violation of the principles of international law embodied in the Charter of the United Nations.

Article 53. Treaties Conflicting with a Peremptory Norm of General International Law (*Jus Cogens*)

A treaty is void if, at the time of its conclusion, it conflicts with a peremptory norm of general international law. For the purposes of the present Convention, a peremptory norm of general international law is a norm accepted and recognized by the international community of States as a whole as a norm from which no derogation is permitted and which can be modified only by a subsequent norm of general international law having the same character.

SECTION 3. TERMINATION AND SUSPENSION OF THE OPERATION OF TREATIES

Article 54. Termination of or Withdrawal from a Treaty Under Its Provisions or by Consent of the Parties

The termination of a treaty or the withdrawal of a party may take place:

(a) in conformity with the provisions of the treaty; or

(b) at any time by consent of all the parties after consultation with the other contracting States.

Article 55. Reduction of the Parties to a Multilateral Treaty Below the Number Necessary for Its Entry into Force

Unless the treaty otherwise provides, a multilateral treaty does not terminate by reason only of the fact that the number of the parties falls below the number necessary for its entry into force.

Article 56. Denunciation of or Withdrawal from a Treaty Containing No Provision Regarding Termination, Denunciation or Withdrawal

1. A treaty which contains no provision regarding its termination and which does not provide for denunciation or withdrawal is not subject to denunciation or withdrawal unless:

(a) it is established that the parties intended to admit the possibility of denunciation or withdrawal; or

(b) a right of denunciation or withdrawal may be implied by the nature of the treaty.

2. A party shall give not less than twelve months' notice of its intention to denounce or withdraw from a treaty under paragraph 1.

Article 57. Suspension of the Operation of a Treaty Under Its Provisions or by Consent of the Parties

The operation of a treaty in regard to all the parties or to a particular party may be suspended:

(a) in conformity with the provisions of the treaty; or

(b) at any time by consent of all the parties after consultation with the other contracting States.

Article 58. Suspension of the Operation of a Multilateral Treaty by Agreement Between Certain of the Parties Only

1. Two or more parties to a multilateral treaty may conclude an agreement to suspend the operation of provisions of the treaty, temporarily and as between themselves alone, if:

(a) the possibility of such a suspension is provided for by the treaty; or

(b) the suspension in question is not prohibited by the treaty and:

(i) does not affect the enjoyment by the other parties of their rights under the treaty or the performance of their obligations;

(ii) is not incompatible with the object and purpose of the treaty.

2. Unless in a case falling under paragraph 1(a) the treaty otherwise provides, the parties in question shall notify the other parties of their intention to conclude the agreement and of those provisions of the treaty the operation of which they intend to suspend.

Article 59. Termination or Suspension of the Operation of a Treaty Implied by Conclusion of a Later Treaty

1. A treaty shall be considered as terminated if all the parties to it conclude a later treaty relating to the same subject-matter and:

(a) it appears from the later treaty or is otherwise established that the parties intended that the matter should be governed by that treaty; or

(b) the provisions of the later treaty are so far incompatible with those of the earlier one that the two treaties are not capable of being applied at the same time.

2. The earlier treaty shall be considered as only suspended in operation if it appears from the later treaty or is otherwise established that such was the intention of the parties.

Article 60. Termination or Suspension of the Operation of a Treaty as a Consequence of its Breach

1. A material breach of a bilateral treaty by one of the parties entitles the other to invoke the breach as a ground for terminating the treaty or suspending its operation in whole or in part.

2. A material breach of a multilateral treaty by one of the parties entitles:

(a) the other parties by unanimous agreement to suspend the operation of the treaty in whole or in part or to terminate it either:

(i) in the relations between themselves and the defaulting State, or

(ii) as between all the parties;

(b) a party specially affected by the breach to invoke it as a ground for suspending the operation of the treaty in whole or in part in the relations between itself and the defaulting State;

(c) any party other than the defaulting State to invoke the breach as a ground for suspending the operation of the treaty in whole or in part with respect to itself if the treaty is of such a character that a material breach of its provisions by one party radically changes the position of every party with respect to the further performance of its obligations under the treaty.

3. A material breach of a treaty, for the purposes of this article, consists in:

(a) a repudiation of the treaty not sanctioned by the present Convention; or

(b) the violation of a provision essential to the accomplishment of the object or purpose of the treaty.

4. The foregoing paragraphs are without prejudice to any provision in the treaty applicable in the event of a breach.

5. Paragraphs 1 to 3 do not apply to provisions relating to the protection of the human person contained in treaties of a humanitarian character, in particular to provisions prohibiting any form of reprisals against persons protected by such treaties.

Article 61. Supervening Impossibility of Performance

1. A party may invoke the impossibility of performing a treaty as a ground for terminating or withdrawing from it if the impossibility results from the permanent disappearance or destruction of an object indispensable for the execution of the treaty. If the impossibility is temporary, it may be invoked only as a ground for suspending the operation of the treaty.

2. Impossibility of performance may not be invoked by a party as a ground for terminating, withdrawing from or suspending the operation of a treaty if the impossibility is the result of a breach by that party either of an obligation under the treaty or of any other international obligation owed to any other party to the treaty.

Article 62. Fundamental Change of Circumstances

1. A fundamental change of circumstances which has occurred with regard to those existing at the time of the conclusion of a treaty, and which was not foreseen by the parties, may not be invoked as a ground for terminating or withdrawing from the treaty unless:

(a) the existence of those circumstances constituted an essential basis of the consent of the parties to be bound by the treaty; and

(b) the effect of the change is radically to transform the extent of obligations still to be performed under the treaty.

2. A fundamental change of circumstances may not be invoked as a ground for terminating or withdrawing from a treaty:

(a) if the treaty establishes a boundary; or

(b) if the fundamental change is the result of a breach by the party invoking it either of an obligation under the treaty or of any other international obligation owed to any other party to the treaty.

3. If, under the foregoing . . . [one could terminate or withdraw] it may also invoke the change as a ground for suspending the operation of the treaty.

Article 63. Severance of Diplomatic or Consular Relations

The severance of diplomatic or consular relations between parties to a treaty does not affect the legal relations established between them by the treaty except in so far as the existence of diplomatic or consular relations is indispensable for the application of the treaty.

Article 64. Emergence of a New Peremptory Norm of General International Law (*Jus Cogens*)

If a new peremptory norm of general international law emerges, any existing treaty which is in conflict with that norm becomes void and terminates.

SECTION 4. PROCEDURE

Article 65. Procedure to Be Followed with Respect to Invalidity, Termination, Withdrawal from or Suspension of the Operation of a Treaty

1. A party which, under the provisions of the present Convention, invokes either a defect in its consent to be bound by a treaty or a ground for impeaching the validity of a treaty, terminating it, withdrawing from it or suspending its operation, must notify the other parties of its claim. The notification shall indicate the measure proposed to be taken with respect to the treaty and the reasons therefor.

2. If, after the expiry of a period which, except in cases of special urgency, shall not be less than three months after the receipt of the notification, no party has raised any objection, the party making the notification may carry out in the manner provided in article 67 the measure which it has proposed.

3. If, however, objection has been raised by any other party, the parties shall seek a solution through the means indicated in article 33 of the Charter of the United Nations.

4. Nothing in the foregoing paragraphs shall affect the rights or obligations of the parties under any provisions in force binding the parties with regard to the settlement of disputes.

5. Without prejudice to article 45, the fact that a State has not previously made the notification prescribed in paragraph 1 shall not prevent it from making such notification in answer to another party claiming performance of the treaty or alleging its violation.

Article 66. Procedures for Judicial Settlement, Arbitration and Conciliation

If, under paragraph 3 of article 65, no solution has been reached within a period of 12 months following the date on which the objection was raised, the following procedures shall be followed:

(a) any one of the parties to a dispute concerning the application or the interpretation of articles 53 or 64 may, by a written application, submit it to the International Court of Justice for a decision unless the parties by common consent agree to submit the dispute to arbitration;

(b) any one of the parties to a dispute concerning the application or the interpretation of any of the other articles in Part V of the present Convention may set in motion the procedure specified in the Annexe to the Convention by submitting a request to that effect to the Secretary–General of the United Nations.

Article 67. Instruments for Declaring Invalid, Terminating, Withdrawing from or Suspending the Operation of a Treaty

1. The notification provided for under article 65 paragraph 1 must be made in writing.

2. Any act declaring invalid, terminating, withdrawing from or suspending the operation of a treaty pursuant to the provisions of the treaty or of paragraphs 2 or 3 of article 65 shall be carried out through an instrument communicated to the other parties. If the instrument is not signed by the Head of State, Head of Government or Minister for Foreign Affairs, the representative of the State communicating it may be called upon to produce full powers.

Article 68. Revocation of Notifications and Instruments Provided for in Articles 65 and 67

A notification or instrument provided for in articles 65 or 67 may be revoked at any time before it takes effect.

SECTION 5. CONSEQUENCES OF THE INVALIDITY, TERMINATION OR SUSPENSION OF THE OPERATION OF A TREATY

Article 69. Consequences of the Invalidity of a Treaty

1. A treaty the invalidity of which is established under the present Convention is void. The provisions of a void treaty have no legal force.

2. If acts have nevertheless been performed in reliance on such a treaty:

(a) each party may require any other party to establish as far as possible in their mutual relations the position that would have existed if the acts had not been performed;

(b) acts performed in good faith before the invalidity was invoked are not rendered unlawful by reason only of the invalidity of the treaty.

3. In cases falling under articles 49, 50, 51 or 52, paragraph 2 does not apply with respect to the party to which the fraud, the act of corruption or the coercion is imputable.

4. In the case of the invalidity of a particular State's consent to be bound by a multilateral treaty, the foregoing rules apply in the relations between that State and the parties to the treaty.

Article 70. Consequences of the Termination of a Treaty

1. Unless the treaty otherwise provides or the parties otherwise agree, the termination of a treaty under its provisions or in accordance with the present Convention:

(a) releases the parties from any obligation further to perform the treaty;

(b) does not affect any right, obligation or legal situation of the parties created through the execution of the treaty prior to its termination.

2. If a State denounces or withdraws from a multilateral treaty, paragraph 1 applies in the relations between that State and each of the other parties to the treaty from the date when such denunciation or withdrawal takes effect.

Article 71. Consequences of the Invalidity of a Treaty which Conflicts with a Peremptory Norm of General International Law

1. In the case of a treaty which is void under article 53 the parties shall:

(a) eliminate as far as possible the consequences of any act performed in reliance on any provision which conflicts with the peremptory norm of general international law; and

(b) bring their mutual relations into conformity with the peremptory norm of general international law.

2. In the case of a treaty which becomes void and terminates under article 64, the termination of the treaty:

(a) releases the parties from any obligation further to perform the treaty;

(b) does not affect any right, obligation or legal situation of the parties created through the execution of the treaty prior to its termination; provided that those rights, obligations or situations may thereafter be maintained only to the extent that their maintenance is not in itself in conflict with the new peremptory norm of general international law.

Article 72. Consequences of the Suspension of the Operation of a Treaty

1. Unless the treaty otherwise provides or the parties otherwise agree, the suspension of the operation of a treaty under its provisions or in accordance with the present Convention:

(a) releases the parties between which the operation of the treaty is suspended from the obligation to perform the treaty in their mutual relations during the period of the suspension;

(b) does not otherwise affect the legal relations between the parties established by the treaty.

2. During the period of the suspension the parties shall refrain from acts tending to obstruct the resumption of the operation of the treaty.

PART VI

MISCELLANEOUS PROVISIONS

Article 73. Cases of State Succession, State Responsibility and Outbreak of Hostilities

The provisions of the present Convention shall not prejudge any question that may arise in regard to a treaty from a succession of States or from the international responsibility of a State or from the outbreak of hostilities between States.

Article 74. Diplomatic and Consular Relations and the Conclusion of Treaties

The severance or absence of diplomatic or consular relations between two or more States does not prevent the conclusion of treaties between those States. The conclusion of a treaty does not in itself affect the situation in regard to diplomatic or consular relations.

Article 75. Case of an Aggressor State

The provisions of the present Convention are without prejudice to any obligation in relation to a treaty which may arise for an aggressor State in consequence of measures taken in conformity with the Charter of the United Nations with reference to that State's aggression.

PART VII

DEPOSITORIES, NOTIFICATIONS, CORRECTIONS AND REGISTRATION

Article 76. Depositories of Treaties

1. The designation of the depositary of a treaty may be made by the negotiating States, either in the treaty itself or in some other manner. The depositary may be one or more States, an international organization or the chief administrative officer of the organization.

2. The functions of the depositary of a treaty are international in character and the depositary is under an obligation to act impartially in their performance. In particular, the fact that a treaty has not entered into force between certain of the parties or that a difference has appeared between a State and a depositary with regard to the performance of the latter's functions shall not affect that obligation.

Article 77. Functions of Depositories

1. The functions of a depositary, unless otherwise provided in the treaty or agreed by the contracting States, comprise in particular:

(a) keeping custody of the original text of the treaty and of any full powers delivered to the depositary;

(b) preparing certified copies of the original text and preparing any further text of the treaty in such additional languages as may be required by the treaty and transmitting them to the parties and to the States entitled to become parties to the treaty;

(c) receiving any signatures to the treaty and receiving and keeping custody of any instruments, notifications and communications relating to it;

(d) examining whether the signature or any instrument, notification or communication relating to the treaty is in due and proper form and, if need be, bringing the matter to the attention of the State in question;

(e) informing the parties and the States entitled to become parties to the treaty of acts, notifications and communications relating to the treaty;

(f) informing the States entitled to become parties to the treaty when the number of signatures or of instruments of ratification, acceptance, approval or accession required for the entry into force of the treaty has been received or deposited;

(g) registering the treaty with the Secretariat of the United Nations;

(h) performing the functions specified in other provisions of the present Convention.

2. In the event of any difference appearing between a State and the depositary as to the performance of the latter's functions, the depositary shall bring the question to the attention of the signatory States and the contracting States or, where appropriate, of the competent organ of the international organization concerned.

Article 78. Notifications and Communications

Except as the treaty or the present Convention otherwise provide, any notification or communication to be made by any State under the present Convention shall:

(a) if there is no depositary, be transmitted direct to the States for which it is intended, or if there is a depositary, to the latter;

(b) be considered as having been made by the State in question only upon its receipt by the State to which it was transmitted or, as the case may be, upon its receipt by the depositary;

(c) if transmitted to a depositary, be considered as received by the State for which it was intended only when the latter State has been informed by the depositary in accordance with article 77, paragraph 1(e).

Article 79. Correction of Errors in Texts or in Certified Copies of Treaties

1. Where, after the authentication of the text of a treaty, the signatory States and the contracting States are agreed that it contains an error, the error shall, unless they decide upon some other means of correction, be corrected:

(a) by having the appropriate correction made in he text and causing the correction to be initialed by duly authorized representatives;

(b) by executing or exchanging an instrument or instruments setting out the correction which it has been agreed to make; or

(c) by executing a corrected text of the whole treaty by the same procedure as in the case of the original text.

2. Where the treaty is one for which there is a depositary, the latter shall notify the signatory States and the contracting States of the error and of the proposal to correct it and shall specify an appropriate

time-limit within which objection to the proposed correction may be raised.

If, on the expiry of the time-limit:

(a) no objection has been raised, the depositary shall make and initial the correction in the text and shall execute a procès-verbal of the rectification of the text and communicate a copy of it to the parties and to the States entitled to become parties to the treaty;

(b) an objection has been raised, the depositary shall communicate the objection to the signatory States and to the contracting States.

3. The rules in paragraphs 1 and 2 apply also where the text has been authenticated in two or more languages and it appears that there is a lack of concordance which the signatory States and the contracting States agree should be corrected.

4. The corrected text replaces the defective text ab initio, unless the signatory States and the contracting States otherwise decide.

5. The correction of the text of a treaty that has been registered shall be notified to the Secretariat of the United Nations.

6. Where an error is discovered in a certified copy of a treaty, the depositary shall execute a procès-verbal specifying the rectification and communicate a copy of it to the signatory States and to the contracting States.

Article 80. Registration and Publication of Treaties

1. Treaties shall, after their entry into force, be transmitted to the Secretariat of the United Nations for registration or filing and recording, as the case may be, and for publication.

2. The designation of a depositary shall constitute authorization for it to perform the acts specified in the preceding paragraph.

PART VIII

FINAL PROVISIONS

Article 81. Signature

The present Convention shall be open for signature by all States Members of the United Nations or of any of the specialized agencies or of the International Atomic Energy Agency or parties to the Statute of the International Court of Justice, and by any other State invited by the General Assembly of the United Nations to become a party to the Convention, as follows: until 30 November 1969, at the Federal Ministry for Foreign Affairs of the Republic of Austria, and subsequently, until 30 April 1970, at United Nations Headquarters, New York.

Article 82. Ratification

The present Convention is subject to ratification. The instruments of ratification shall be deposited with the Secretary–General of the United Nations.

Article 83. Accession

The present Convention shall remain open for accession by any State belonging to any of the categories mentioned in article 81. The instruments of accession shall be deposited with the Secretary–General of the United Nations.

Article 84. Entry into Force

1. The present Convention shall enter into force on the thirtieth day following the date of deposit of the thirty-fifth instrument of ratification or accession.

2. For each State ratifying or acceding to the Convention after the deposit of the thirty-fifth instrument of ratification or accession, the Convention shall enter into force on the thirtieth day after deposit by such State of its instrument of ratification or accession.

Article 85. Authentic Texts

The original of the present Convention, of which the Chinese, English, French, Russian and Spanish texts are equally authentic, shall be deposited with the Secretary–General of the United Nations.

Document 5
DECLARATION ON PRINCIPLES OF INTERNATIONAL LAW CONCERNING FRIENDLY RELATIONS AND CO-OPERATION AMONG STATES IN ACCORDANCE WITH THE CHARTER OF THE UNITED NATIONS

October 24, 1970, U.N. G.A. Res. 2625, 25 U.N. GAOR, Supp. No. 28, at 121, U.N. Doc. A/8028 (1971)

Preamble

The General Assembly,

Reaffirming in the terms of the Charter of the United Nations that the maintenance of international peace and security and the development of friendly relations and co-operation between nations are among the fundamental purposes of the United Nations,

Recalling that the peoples of the United Nations are determined to practice tolerance and live together in peace with one another as good neighbours,

Bearing in mind the importance of maintaining and strengthening international peace founded upon freedom, equality, justice and respect for fundamental human rights and of developing friendly relations among nations irrespective of their political, economic and social systems or the levels of their development,

Bearing in mind also the paramount importance of the Charter of the United Nations in the promotion of the rule of law among nations,

Considering that the faithful observance of the principles of international law concerning friendly relations and co-operation among States and the fulfillment in good faith of the obligations assumed by States, in accordance with the Charter, is of the greatest importance for the maintenance of international peace and security and for the implementation of the other purposes of the United Nations,

Convinced that the strict observance by States of the obligation not to intervene in the affairs of any other State is an essential condition to ensure that nations live together in peace with one another, since the practice of any form of intervention not only violates the spirit and letter of the Charter, but also leads to the creation of situations which threaten international peace and security,

Recalling the duty of States to refrain in their international relations from military, political, economic or any other form of coercion aimed against the political independence or territorial integrity of any State,

Considering it essential that all States shall refrain in their international relations from the threat or use of force against the territorial integrity or political independence of any State, or in any other manner inconsistent with the purposes of the United Nations,

Considering it equally essential that all States shall settle their international disputes by peaceful means in accordance with the Charter,

Reaffirming, in accordance with the Charter, the basic importance of sovereign equality and stressing that the purposes of the United Nations can be implemented only if States enjoy sovereign equality and comply fully with the requirements of this principle in their international relations,

Convinced that the subjection of peoples to alien subjugation, domination and exploitation constitutes a major obstacle to the promotion of international peace and security,

Convinced that the principle of equal rights and self-determination of peoples constitutes a significant contribution to contemporary international law, and that its effective application is of paramount importance for the promotion of friendly relations among States, based on respect for the principle of sovereign equality,

Convinced in consequence that any attempt aimed at the partial or total disruption of the national unity and territorial integrity of a State or country or at its political independence is incompatible with the purposes and principles of the Charter,

Considering the provisions of the Charter as a whole and taking into account the role of relevant resolutions adopted by the competent organs of the United Nations relating to the content of the principles,

Considering the progressive development and codification of the following principles:

(a) The principle that States shall refrain in their international relations from the threat or use of force against the territorial integrity or political independence of any State, or in any other manner inconsistent with the purposes of the United Nations,

(b) The principle that States shall settle their international disputes by peaceful means in such a manner that international peace and security and justice are not endangered,

(c) The duty not to intervene in matters within the domestic jurisdiction of any state, in accordance with the Charter,

(d) The duty of States to co-operate with one another in accordance with the Charter,

(e) The principle of equal rights and self-determination of peoples,

(f) The principle of sovereign equality of States,

(g) The principle that States shall fulfill in good faith the obligations assumed by them in accordance with the Charter, so as to secure their more effective application within the international community, would promote the realization of the purposes of the United Nations.

Having considered the principles of international law relating to friendly relations and co-operation among States,

1. *Solemnly proclaims* the following principles:

The principle that States shall refrain in their international relations from the threat or use of force against the territorial integrity or political independence of any State, or in any other manner inconsistent with the purposes of the United Nations

Every State has the duty to refrain in its international relations from the threat or use of force against the territorial integrity or political independence of any State, or in any other manner inconsistent with the purposes of the United Nations. Such a threat or use of force constitutes a violation of international law and the Charter of the United Nations and shall never be employed as a means of settling international issues.

A war of aggression constitutes a crime against the peace for which there is responsibility under international law.

In accordance with the purposes and principles of the United Nations, States have the duty to refrain from propaganda for wars of aggression.

Every State has the duty to refrain from the threat or use of force to violate international boundaries of another State or as a means of solving international disputes, including territorial disputes and problems concerning frontiers of States.

Every State likewise has the duty to refrain from the threat or use of force to violate international lines of demarcation, such as armistice lines, established by or pursuant to an international agreement to which it is a party or which it is otherwise bound to respect. Nothing in the foregoing shall be construed as prejudicing the positions of the parties concerned with regard to the status and effects of such lines under their special regimes or as affecting their temporary character.

States have a duty to refrain from acts of reprisal involving the use of force.

Every State has the duty to refrain from any forcible action which deprives peoples referred to in the elaboration of the principle of equal rights and self-determination of their right to self-determination and freedom and independence.

Every State has the duty to refrain from organizing or encouraging the organization of irregular forces or armed bands, including mercenaries, for incursion into the territory of another State.

Every State has the duty to refrain from organizing, instigating, assisting or participating in acts of civil strife or terrorist acts in another State or acquiescing in organized activities within its territory directed towards the commission of such acts, when the acts referred to in the present paragraph involve a threat or use of force.

The territory of a State shall not be the object of military occupation resulting from the use of force in contravention of the provisions of the Charter. The territory of a State shall not be the object of acquisition by another State resulting from the threat or use of force. No territorial acquisition resulting from the threat or use of force shall be recognized as legal. Nothing in the foregoing shall be construed as affecting:

(a) Provisions of the Charter or any international agreement prior to the Charter regime and valid under international law; or

(b) The powers of the Security Council under the Charter. . . .

Nothing in the foregoing paragraphs shall be construed as enlarging or diminishing in any way the scope of the provisions of the Charter concerning cases in which the use of force is lawful. . . .

The duty of States to co-operate with one another in accordance with the Charter

States have the duty to co-operate with one another, irrespective of the differences of their political, economic and social systems, in the various spheres of international relations, in order to maintain international peace and security and to promote international economic stability and progress, the general welfare of nations and international cooperation free from discrimination based on such differences.

To this end:

(a) States shall co-operate with other States in the maintenance of international peace and security;

(b) States shall co-operate in the promotion of universal respect for, and observance of, human rights and fundamental freedoms for all, and in the elimination of all forms of racial discrimination and all forms of religious intolerance;

(c) States shall conduct their international relations in the economic, social, cultural technical and trade fields in accordance with the principles of sovereign equality and non-intervention,

(d) States Members of the United Nations have the duty to take joint and separate action in co-operation with the United Nations in accordance with the relevant provisions of the Charter.

States should co-operate in the economic, social and cultural fields as well as in the field of science and technology and for the promotion of international cultural and educational progress. States should cooperate in the promotion of economic growth throughout the world, especially that of the developing countries.

The principle of equal rights and self-determination of peoples

By virtue of the principle of equal rights and self-determination of peoples enshrined in the Charter of the United Nations, all peoples have the right freely to determine, without external interference their political status and to pursue their economic, social and cultural development, and every State has the duty to respect this right in accordance with the provisions of the Charter.

Every State has the duty to promote, through joint and separate action, realization of the principle of equal rights and self-determination of peoples, in accordance with the provisions of the Charter, and to render assistance to the United Nations in carrying out the responsibilities entrusted to it by the Charter regarding the implementation of the principle, in order:

(a) To promote friendly relations and co-operation among States, and

(b) To bring a speedy end of colonialism, having due regard to the freely expressed will of the peoples concerned;

and bearing in mind that subjection of peoples to alien subjugation, domination and exploitation constitutes a violation of the principle, as well as a denial of fundamental human rights, and is contrary to the Charter.

Every State has the duty to promote through joint and separate action universal respect for and observance of human rights and fundamental freedoms in accordance with the Charter.

The establishment of a sovereign and independent State, the free association or integration with an independent State or the emergence into any other political status freely determined by a people constitute modes of implementing the right of self-determination by that people.

Every State has the duty to refrain from any forcible action which deprives peoples referred to above in the elaboration of the present principle of their right to self-determination and freedom and independence. In their actions against, and resistance to, such forcible action in pursuit of the exercise of their right to self-determination, such peoples are entitled to seek and to receive support in accordance with the purposes and principles of the Charter.

The territory of a colony of other Non–Self–Governing Territory has, under the Charter, a status separate and distinct from the territory of the State administering it; and such separate and distinct status under the Charter shall exist until the people of the colony or Non–Self–Governing Territory have exercised their right of self-determination in accordance with the Charter, and particularly its purposes and principles.

Nothing in the foregoing paragraphs shall be construed as authorizing or encouraging any action which would dismember or impair, totally or in part, the territorial integrity or political unity of sovereign and independent States conducting themselves in compliance with the principle of equal rights and self-determination of peoples as described above and thus possessed of a government representing the whole people belonging to the territory without distinction as to race, creed or colour.

Every State shall refrain from any action aimed at the partial or total disruption of the national unity and territorial integrity of any other State or country.

The principle of sovereign equality of States

All States enjoy sovereign quality. They have equal rights and duties and are equal members of the international community, notwithstanding differences of an economic, social, political or other nature.

In particular, sovereign equality includes the following elements:

(a) States are judicially equal;

(b) Each State enjoys the rights inherent in full sovereignty;

(c) Each State has the duty to respect the personality of other States;

(d) The territorial integrity and political independence of the State are inviolable;

(e) Each State has the right freely to choose and develop its political, social, economic and cultural systems;

(f) Each State has the duty to comply fully and in good faith with its international obligations and to live in peace with other states.

The principle that States shall fulfill in good faith the obligations assumed by them in accordance with the Charter

Every State has the duty to fulfil in good faith the obligations assumed by it in accordance with the Charter of the United Nations. . . .

General Part

2. *Declares* that:

In their interpretation and application the above principles are interrelated and each principle should be construed in the context of the other principles.

Nothing in this Declaration shall be construed as prejudicing in any manner the provisions of the Charter or the rights and duties of Member States under the Charter or the rights of peoples under the Charter, taking into account the elaboration of these rights in this Declaration.

3. *Declares further* that:

The principles of the Charter which are embodied in this Declaration constitute basic principles of international law, and consequently appeals to all States to be guided by these principles in their international conduct and to develop their mutual relations on the basis of the strict observance of these principles.

Document 6
RESOLUTION ON THE DEFINITION OF AGGRESSION

December 14, 1974, U.N. G.A. Res. 3314, 29 U.N. GAOR, Supp. (No. 31) 142, U.N. Doc. A/9631, Annex (1975)

The General Assembly,

Basing itself on the fact that one of the fundamental purposes of the United Nations is to maintain international peace and security and to take effective collective measures for the prevention and removal of threats to the peace, and for the suppression of acts of aggression or other breaches of the peace,

Recalling that the Security Council, in accordance with Article 39 of the Charter of the United Nations, shall determine the existence of any threat to the peace, breach of the peace or act of aggression and shall make recommendations, or decide what measures shall be taken in accordance with Articles 41 and 42, to maintain or restore international peace and security.

Recalling also the duty of States under the Charter to settle their international disputes by peaceful means in order not to endanger international peace, security and justice,

Bearing in mind, that nothing in this Definition shall be interpreted as in any way affecting the scope of the provisions of the Charter with respect to the functions and powers of the organs of the United Nations.

Considering also that, since aggression is the most serious and dangerous form of the illegal use of force, being fraught, in the conditions created by the existence of all types of weapons of mass destruction, with the possible threat of a world conflict and all its catastrophic consequences, aggression should be defined at the present stage,

Reaffirming the duty of States not to use armed force to deprive peoples of their right to self-determination, freedom and independence, or to disrupt territorial integrity,

Reaffirming also that the territory of a State shall not be violated by being the object, even temporarily, of military occupation or of other measures of force taken by another State in contravention of the Charter, and that it shall not be the object of acquisition by another State resulting from such measures or the threat thereof,

Reaffirming also the provisions of the Declaration on Principles of International Law concerning Friendly Relations and Co-operation among States in accordance with the Charter of the United Nations,

Convinced that the adoption of a definition of aggression ought to have the effect of deterring a potential aggressor, would simplify the determination of acts of aggression and the implementation of measures to suppress them and would also facilitate the protection of the rights and lawful interests of, and the rendering of assistance to, the victim,

Believing that, although the question whether an act of aggression has been committed must be considered in the light of all the circumstances of each particular case, it is nevertheless desirable to formulate basic principles as guidance for such determination,

Adopts the following Definition of Aggression.

Article 1

Aggression is the use of armed force by a State against the sovereignty, territorial integrity or political independence of another State, or in any other manner inconsistent with the Charter of the United Nations, as set out in this Definition. . . .

Article 2

The first use of armed force by a State in contravention of the Charter shall constitute *prima facie* evidence of an act of aggression although the Security Council may, in conformity with the Charter, conclude that a determination that an act of aggression has been committed would not be justified in the light of other relevant circumstances, including the fact that the acts concerned or their consequences are not a sufficient gravity.

Article 3

Any of the following acts, regardless of a declaration of war, shall, subject to and in accordance with the provisions of article 2, qualify as an act of aggression:

(a) The invasion or attack by the armed forces of a State of the territory of another State, or any military occupation, however temporary, resulting from such invasion or attack, or any annexation by the use of force of the territory of another State or part thereof;

(b) Bombardment by the armed forces of a State against the territory of another State or the use of any weapons by a State against the territory of another State;

(c) The blockade of the ports or coasts of a State by the armed forces of another State;

(d) An attack by the armed forces of a State on the land, sea or air forces, or marine and air fleets of another State;

(e) The use of armed forces of one State which are within the territory of another State with the agreement of the receiving State, in contravention of the conditions provided for in the agreement or any extension of their presence in such territory beyond the termination of the agreement;

(f) The action of a State in allowing its territory, which it has placed at the disposal of another State, to be used by that other State for perpetrating an act of aggression against a third State;

(g) The sending by or on behalf of a State of armed bands, groups, irregulars or mercenaries, which carry out acts of armed force against another State of such gravity as to amount to the acts listed above, or its substantial involvement therein.

Article 4

The acts enumerated above are not exhaustive and the Security Council may determine that other acts constitute aggression under the provisions of the Charter.

Article 5

1. No consideration of whatever nature, whether political, economic, military or otherwise, may serve as a justification for aggression.

2. A war of aggression is a crime against international peace. Aggression gives rise to international responsibility.

3. No territorial acquisition or special advantage resulting from aggression is or shall be recognized as lawful.

Article 6

Nothing is this Definition shall be construed as in any way enlarging or diminishing the scope of the Charter, including its provisions concerning cases in which the use of force is lawful.

Article 7

Nothing in this definition, and in particular Article 3, could in any way prejudice the right to self-determination, freedom and independence, as derived from the Charter, of peoples forcibly deprived of that right and referred to in the Declaration on Principles of International Law concerning Friendly Relations and Cooperation among States in accordance with the Charter of the United Nations, particularly peoples under colonial and racist regimes or other forms of alien domination; nor the right of these peoples to struggle to that end and to seek and receive support, in accordance with the principles of the Charter and in conformity with the above-mentioned Declaration.

Article 8

In their interpretation and application the above provisions are interrelated and each provision should be construed in the context of the other provisions.

Document 7
NORTH ATLANTIC TREATY

34 U.N.T.S. 243, T.I.A.S. No. 1964, 63 Stat. 2241 (1949)

The Parties to this Treaty reaffirm their faith in the purposes and principles of the Charter of the United Nations and their desire to live in peace with all peoples and all governments.

They are determined to safeguard the freedom, common heritage and civilization of their peoples, founded on the principles of democracy, individual liberty and the rule of law.

They seek to promote stability and well-being in the North Atlantic area.

They are resolved to unite their efforts for collective defense and for the preservation of peace and security.

They therefore agree to this North Atlantic Treaty:

Article 1

The Parties undertake, as set forth in the Charter of the United Nations, to settle any international disputes in which they may be involved by peaceful means in such a manner that international peace and security, and justice, are not endangered, and to refrain in their international relations from the threat or use of force in any manner inconsistent with the purposes of the United Nations.

Article 2

The Parties will contribute toward the further development of peaceful and friendly international relations by strengthening their free institutions, by bringing about a better understanding of he principles upon which these institutions are founded, and by promoting conditions of stability and well-being. They will seek to eliminate conflict in their international economic policies and will encourage economic collaboration between any or all of them.

Article 3

In order more effectively to achieve the objectives of this Treaty, the Parties, separately and jointly, by means of continuous and effective self-help and mutual aid, will maintain and develop their individual and collective capacity to resist armed attack.

Article 4

The Parties will consult together whenever, in the opinion of any of them, the territorial integrity, political independence or security of any of the Parties is threatened.

Article 5

The Parties agree that an armed attack against one or more of them in Europe or North America shall be considered an attack against them all; and consequently they agree that, if such an armed attack occurs, each of them, in exercise of the right of individual or collective self-defense recognized by Article 51 of the Charter of the United Nations, will assist the Party or Parties so attacked by taking forthwith, individually and in concert with the other Parties, such action as it deems necessary, including the use of armed force, to restore and maintain the security of the North Atlantic area.

Any such armed attack and all measures taken as a result thereof shall immediately be reported to the Security Council. Such measures shall be terminated when the Security Council has taken the measures necessary to restore and maintain international peace and security.

Article 6

For the purpose of Article 5 an armed attack on any one or more of the Parties is deemed to include an armed attack on the territory of any of the Parties in Europe or North America . . ., on the islands under the jurisdiction of any Party in the North Atlantic area north of the Tropic of Cancer or on the vessels or aircraft in this area of any of the Parties.

Article 7

This Treaty does not affect, and shall not be interpreted as affecting, in any way the rights and obligations under the Charter of the Parties which are members of the United Nations, or the primary responsibility of the Security Council for the maintenance of international peace and security.

Article 9

The Parties hereby establish a council, on which each of them shall be represented, to consider matters concerning the implementation of this Treaty. The council shall be so organized as to be able to meet promptly at any time. The council shall set up such subsidiary bodies as may be necessary; in particular it shall establish immediately a defense committee which shall recommend measures for the implementation of Articles 3 and 5.

Article 11

This Treaty shall be ratified and its provisions carried out by the Parties in accordance with their respective constitutional processes. . . .

Document 8

TREATY ON EXTRADITION BETWEEN THE GOVERNMENT OF CANADA AND THE GOVERNMENT OF THE UNITED STATES OF AMERICA

Washington, December 3, 1971; Instruments of Ratification exchanged March 22, 1976; in force March 22, 1976, 1976 Can. T.S. No. 3 (amended by an Exchange of Notes)

Canada and the United States of America, desiring to make more effective the co-operation of the two countries in the repression of crime by making provision for the reciprocal extradition of offenders, agree as follows:

Article 1

Each contracting Party agrees to extradite to the other, in the circumstances and subject to the conditions described in this Treaty, persons found in its territory who have been charged with, or convicted of, any of the offenses covered by Article 2 of this Treaty committed within the territory of the other, or outside thereof under the conditions specified in Article 3(3) of this Treaty.

Article 2

(1) Persons shall be delivered up according to the provisions of this Treaty for any of the offenses listed in the Schedule annexed to this Treaty, which is an integral part of this Treaty, provided these offenses are punishable by the laws of both contracting Parties by a term of imprisonment exceeding one year.

(2) Extradition shall also be granted for attempts to commit, or conspiracy to commit or being party to any of the offenses listed in the annexed Schedule.

(3) Extradition shall also be granted for any offense against a federal law of the United States in which one of the offenses listed in the annexed Schedule, or made extraditable by paragraph (2) of this article, is a substantial element, even if transporting, transportation, the use of the mails or interstate facilities are also elements of the specific offense.

Article 3

(1) For the purpose of this Treaty the territory of a Contracting Party shall include all territory under the jurisdiction of that Contract-

ing Party, including air space and territorial waters and vessels and aircraft registered in that principal place of business, or, if the lessee has no such place of business, his permanent residence in, that contracting Party if any such aircraft is in flight, or if any such vessel is on the high seas when the offense is committed. For the purposes of this treaty an aircraft shall be considered in flight from the moment when power is applied for the purpose of the take-of until the moment when the landing run ends.

(2) In a case when offense 23 of the annexed Schedule is committed on board an aircraft at any time form the moment when all its external doors are closed following embarkation until the moment when any such door is opened for disembarkation, such offense and any other offense covered by Article 2 committed against passengers or crew of that aircraft in connection with such offense shall be considered to have been committed within the territory of a Contracting Party if the aircraft was registered in that Contracting Party, if the aircraft landed in the territory of that contracting party with the alleged offender still on board, or if the aircraft was leased without crew to a lessee who has his principal place of business, or if the lessee has no such place of business, his permanent residence in that Contracting Party.

(3) When the offense of which extradition has been requested has been committed outside the territory of the requesting State, the executive or other appropriate authority of the requested State shall have the power to grant the extradition if the laws of the requested State provide for jurisdiction over such an offense committed in similar circumstances.

Article 4

(1) Extradition shall not be granted in any of the following circumstances:

(i) When the person whose surrender is sought is being proceeded against, or has been tried and discharged or punished in the territory of the requested State of the offense for which his extradition is requested.

(ii) When the prosecution for the offenses has become barred by lapse of time according to the laws of the requesting State.

(iii) When the offense in respect of which extradition is requested is of a political character, or the person whose extradition is requested proves that the extradition request has been made for the purpose of trying or punishing him for an offense of the above-mentioned character. If any question arises as to whether a case comes within the provisions of this subparagraph, the authorities of the Government on which the requisition is made shall decide.

(2) The provisions of subparagraph (iii) of paragraph (1) of this article shall not be applicable to the following:

(i) A kidnaping, murder or other assault against the life or physical integrity of a person to whom a Contracting Party has the duty according to international law to give special protection, or any attempt to commit such an offense with respect to any such person.

(ii) When offense 23 of the annexed Schedule, or an attempt to commit, or a conspiracy to commit, or being a party to the commission of that offense, has been committed on board an aircraft engaged in commercial services carrying passengers.

Article 5

If a request for extradition is made under this Treaty for a person who at the time of such request, or at the time of the commission of the offense for which extradition is sought, is under the age of eighteen years and is considered by the requested State to be one of its residents, the requested State, upon a determination that extradition would disrupt the social readjustment and rehabilitation of that person, may recommend to the requesting State that the request for extradition be withdrawn, specifying the reasons therefor.

Article 6

When the offense for which extradition is requested is punishable by death under the laws of the requesting State and the laws of the requested State do not permit such punishment for that offense, extradition may be refused unless the requesting State Provides such assurances as the requested State considers sufficient that the death penalty shall not be imposed, or, if imposed, shall not be executed.

Article 7

When the person whose extradition is requested is being proceeded against or is serving a sentence in the territory of the requested State for an offense other than for which extradition has been requested, his surrender may be deferred until the conclusion of the proceedings and the full execution of any punishment he may be or may have been awarded.

Article 8

The determination that extradition should or should not be granted shall be made in accordance with the law of the requested State and the person whose extradition is sought shall have the right to use all remedies and recourses provided by such law.

Article 9

(1) The request for extradition shall be made through the diplomatic channel.

(2) The request shall be accompanied by a description of the person sought, a statement of the facts of the case, the text of the laws of the requesting State describing the offense and prescribing the punishment for the offense, and a statement of the law relating to the limitation of the legal proceedings.

(3) When the request relates to a person who has not yet been convicted, it must also be accompanied by a warrant of arrest issued by a judge or other judicial office of the requesting State and by such evidence as, according to the laws of the requested State, would justify his arrest

and committal for trial if the offense had been committed there, including evidence proving the person requested is the person to whom the warrant of arrest refers.

(4) When the request relates to a person already convicted, it must be accompanied by the judgement of conviction and sentence passed against him in the territory of the requesting State, by a statement showing how much of the sentence has not been served, and by evidence proving that the person requested is the person to whom the sentence refers.

Article 10

(1) Extradition shall be granted only if the evidence be found sufficient, according to the laws of the place where the person sought shall be found, either to justify his committal for trial if the offense of which he is accused had been committed in its territory or to prove that he is the identical person convicted by the courts of the requesting State.

(2) The documentary evidence in support of a request for extradition or copies of these documents shall be admitted in evidence in the examination of the request for extradition when, in the case of a request emanating from Canada, they are authenticated by an officer of the Department of Justice of Canada and are certified by the principal diplomatic or consular officer of the United States in Canada, or when, in the case of a request emanating from the United States, they are authenticated by an officer of the Department of State of the United States and are certified by the principal diplomatic or consular officer of Canada in the United States.

Article 11

(1) In case of urgency a Contracting Party may apply for the provisional arrest of the person sought pending the presentation of the request for extradition through the diplomatic channel. Such application shall contain a description of the person sought, and indication of intention to request the extradition of the person sought and a statement of the existence of a warrant of arrest had the offense been committed, or the person sought been convicted, in the territory of the requested State.

(2) On receipt of such application the requested State shall take the necessary steps to secure the arrest of the person claimed.

(3) A person arrested shall be set at liberty upon the expiration of forty-five days from the date of his arrest pursuant to such application if a request for his extradition accompanied by the documents specified in Article 9 shall not have been received. This stipulation shall not prevent the institution of proceedings with a view to extraditing the person sought if the request is subsequently received.

Article 12

(1) A person extradited under the present treaty shall not be detained, tried or punished in the territory of the requesting State for an

offense other than that for which extradition has been granted nor be extradited by that State to a third State unless:

(i) He has left the territory of the requesting State after his extradition and has voluntarily returned to it;

(ii) He has not left the territory of the requesting State within thirty days after being free to do so.

(iii) The requested State has consented to his detention, trial, punishment for an offense other than that for which extradition was granted or to his extradition to a third State, provided such other offense is covered by Article 2.

(2) The foregoing shall not apply to offenses committed after the extradition.

Article 13

(1) A requested State upon receiving two or more requests for the extradition of the same person either for the same offense, or for different offenses, shall determine to which of the requesting States it will extradite the person sought.

(2) Among the matters which the requested State may take into consideration are the possibility of a later extradition between the requesting States, the seriousness of each offense, the place where the offense was committed, the dates upon which the requests were received and the provisions of any extradition agreements between the requested State and the other requesting State or States.

Article 14

(1) The requested State shall promptly communicate to the requesting State through the diplomatic channel the decision on the request for extradition.

(2) If a warrant or order for the extradition of a person sought has been issued by the competent authority and he is not removed from the territory of the requested State within such time as may be prescribed by the laws of that State, he may be set at liberty and the requested State may subsequently refuse to extradite that person for the same offense.

Article 15

(1) To the extent permitted under the law of the requested State and subject to the rights of third parties, which shall be duly respected, all articles acquired as a result of the offense or which may be required as evidence shall, if found, be surrendered to the requesting State if extradition is granted.

(2) Subject to the qualifications of paragraph (1) of this article, the above-mentioned articles shall be returned to the requesting State even if the extradition, having been agreed to, cannot be carried out owing to the death or escape of the person sought.

Article 16

(1) The right to transport through the territory of one of the Contracting Parties a person surrendered to the other Contracting Party by a third State shall be granted on request made through the diplomatic channel, provided that conditions are present which would warrant extradition of such person by the State of transit and reasons of public order are not opposed to the transit.

(2) The party to which the person has been extradited shall reimburse the Party through whose territory such person is transported for any expenses incurred by the latter in connection with such transportation.

Article 17

(1) Expenses related to the transportation of the person sought to the requesting State shall be paid by the requesting State. The appropriate legal officers of the State in which the extradition proceedings take place shall, by all legal means within their power, assist the requesting State before the respective judges and magistrates.

(2) No pecuniary claim, arising out of the arrest, detention, examination and surrender of persons sought under the terms of this Treaty, shall be made by the requested State against the requesting State.

Article 18

(1) This Treaty shall be ratified and the instruments of ratification shall be exchanged at Ottawa as soon as possible.

(2) This Treaty shall terminate and replace any extradition agreements and provisions on extradition in any other agreement in force between Canada and the United States; except that the crimes listed in such agreements and committed prior to entry into force of this Treaty shall be subject to extradition pursuant to the provisions of such agreements.

(3) This Treaty shall enter into force upon the exchange of ratifications. It may be terminated by either Contracting Party giving notice of termination to the other Contracting Party at any time and the termination shall be effective six months after the date of receipt of such notice.

Schedule

1. Murder; assault with intent to commit murder.

2. Manslaughter.

3. Wounding; maiming; or assault occasioning bodily harm.

4. Unlawful throwing or application of any corrosive substances at or upon the person of another.

5. Rape; indecent assault.

6. Unlawful sexual acts with or upon children under the age specified by the laws of both the requesting and requested States.

7. Willful nonsupport or willful abandonment of a minor when such minor is or is likely to be injured or his life is or is likely to be endangered.

8. Kidnapping; child stealing; abduction; false imprisonment.

9. Robbery; assault with intent to steal.

10. Burglary; housebreaking.

11. Larceny, theft or embezzlement.

12. Obtaining property, money or valuable securities by false pretenses or by threat of force or by defrauding the public or any person by deceit or falsehood or other fraudulent means, whether such deceit or falsehood or any fraudulent means would or would not amount to a false pretense.

13. Bribery, including soliciting, offering and accepting.

14. Extortion.

15. Receiving any money, valuable securities or other property knowing the same to have been unlawfully obtained.

16. Fraud by a banker, agent, or by a director of officer of any company.

17. Offenses against the laws relating to counterfeiting or forgery.

18. Perjury in any proceeding whatsoever.

19. Making a false affidavit or statutory declaration of any extrajudicial purpose.

20. Arson.

21. Any act done with intent to endanger the safety of any person traveling upon a railway, or in any aircraft or vessel or other means of transportation.

22. Piracy, by statute or by law of nations; mutiny or revolt on board a vessel against the authority of the captain or commander of such vessel.

23. Any unlawful seizure or exercise of control of an aircraft, by force or violence or threat of force or violence, or by any other form of intimidation, on board such aircraft.

24. Willful injury to property.

25. Offenses against the bankruptcy laws.

26. Offenses against the laws relating to the traffic in, production, manufacture, or importation of narcotic drugs, Cannabis sativa L., hallucinogenic drugs, amphetamines, barbiturates, cocaine and its derivatives.

27. Use of the mails or other means of communication in connection with schemes devised or intended to deceive or defraud the public or for the purpose of obtaining money or property by false pretenses.

28. Offenses against federal laws relating to the sale or purchase of securities.

29. Making or having in possession any explosive substance with intent to endanger life, or to cause severe damage to property.

30. Obstructing the course of justice in a judicial proceeding, existing or proposed, by:

a) dissuading or attempting to dissuade a person by threats, bribes, or other corrupt means from giving evidence;

b) influencing or attempting to influence by threat, bribes, or other corrupt means a person in his conduct as a juror; or

c) accepting a bribe or other corrupt consideration to abstain from giving evidence or to do or to refrain from doing anything as a juror.

Document 9
PROTOCOL AMENDING THE TREATY ON EXTRADITION

1991 Can. T.S. No. 37

The Government of the United States of America and the Government of Canada;

Desiring to make more effective the Extradition Treaty between the Contracting Parties, signed at Washington on December 3, 1971, as amended by the agreement effected by an Exchange of Notes on June 28 and July 9, 1974 (hereinafter referred to as "the Extradition Treaty");

Have agreed as follows:

Article I

Article 2 of the extradition Treaty is deleted and replaced by the following:

Article 2

"(1) Extradition shall be granted for conduct which constitutes an offense punishable by the laws of both Contracting Parties by imprisonment or other form of detention for a term exceeding one year or any greater punishment.

"(2) An offense is extraditable notwithstanding

"(i) that conduct such as interstate transportation or use of the mails or of other facilities affecting interstate or foreign commerce, required for the purpose of establishing jurisdiction, forms part of the offense in the United States, or,

"(ii) that it relates to taxation or revenue or is one of a purely fiscal character."

Article II

The Schedule to the Extradition Treaty, as amended, is deleted.

Article III

Paragraph (2) of Article 3 of the Extradition Treaty is deleted. Paragraph (3) of Article 3 of the Extradition Treaty is amended to read as follows:

"(2) When the offense for which extradition is requested was committed outside the territory of the requesting State, the executive or other appropriate authority of the requested State shall grant extradition if the laws of the requested State provide for jurisdiction over such an offense committed in similar circumstances. If the laws in the requested State do not so provide, the executive authority in the requested State may, in its discretion, grant extradition.''

Article IV

Paragraph (2) of Article 4 of the Extradition Treaty, as amended, is deleted and replaced by the following:

''(2) For the purpose of this Treaty, the following offenses shall be deemed not to be offenses within subparagraph (iii) of paragraph 1 of this article:

''(i) An offense for which each Contracting Party has the obligation pursuant to a multilateral international agreement to extradite the person sought or to submit the case to its competent authorities for the purpose of prosecution;

''(ii) Murder, manslaughter or other culpable homicide, malicious wounding or inflicting grievous bodily harm;

''(iii) an offense involving kidnapping, abduction, or any form of unlawful detention, including taking a hostage;

''(iv) An offense involving the placing or use of explosives, incendiaries or destructive devices or substances capable of endangering life or of causing grievous bodily harm or substantial property damage; and

''(v) An attempt or conspiracy to commit, or counselling the commission of, any of the foregoing offenses, or aiding or abetting a person who commits or attempts to commit such offenses.''

Article V

Article 7 of the Extradition Treaty is deleted and replaced by the following:

Article 7

''When the person sought is being proceeded against or is serving a sentence in the requested State for an offense other than that for which extradition is requested, the requested State may surrender the person sought or postpone surrender until the conclusion of the proceedings or the service of the whole or any part of the sentence imposed.''

Article VI

Paragraph (3) of Article 11 of the Extradition treaty is deleted and replaced by the following:

''(3) A person arrested shall be set at liberty upon the expiration of sixty days from the date of arrest pursuant to such application if a request for extradition and the documents specified in Article 9 have not been received. This stipulation shall not prevent the institution of proceedings with a view to extraditing the person sought if the request and documents are subsequently received.''

Article VII

The Extradition Treaty is amended by adding the following after Article 17:

"Article 17 BIS

"If both contracting Parties have jurisdiction to prosecute the person for the offense for which extradition is sought, the executive authority of the requested State, after consulting with the executive authority of the requesting State, shall decide whether to extradite the person or to submit the case to its competent authorities for the purpose of prosecution. In making its decision, the requested State shall consider all relevant factors, including but not limited to:

"(i) the place where the act was committed or intended to be committed or the injury occurred or was intended to occur;

"(ii) the respective interests of the Contracting Parties;

"(iii) the nationality of the victim or the intended victim; and

"(iv) the availability and location of the evidence."

Article VIII

Notwithstanding paragraph (2) of Article 18 of the Extradition Treaty, this Protocol shall apply in all cases where the request for extradition is made after its entry into force regardless of whether the offense was committed before or after that date.

Article IX

(1) This Protocol shall be subject to ratification in accordance with the applicable procedures of the Government of the United States and the Government of Canada and instruments of ratification shall be exchanged as soon as possible.

(2) The Protocol shall enter into force upon the exchange of instruments of ratification.

In Witness Whereof, the undersigned, being duly authorized thereto by their respective Governments, have signed this Protocol.

Done in duplicate at Ottawa, this 11th day of January 1988, in the English and French languages, the two texts being equally authentic.

Document 10
UNIVERSAL DECLARATION OF HUMAN RIGHTS

U.N. G.A. Res. 217A, 3 U.N. GAOR, U.N. Doc. A/810, at 71 (1948)

Preamble

Whereas recognition of the inherent dignity and of the equal and inalienable rights of all members of the human family is the foundation of freedom, justice and peace in the world,

Whereas disregard and contempt for human rights have resulted in barbarous acts which have outraged the conscience of mankind, and the advent of a world in which human beings shall enjoy freedom of speech and belief and freedom from fear and want has been proclaimed as the highest aspiration of the common people,

Whereas it is essential, if man is not to be compelled to have recourse, as a last resort, to rebellion against tyranny and oppression, that human rights should be protected by the rule of law,

Whereas it is essential to promote the development of friendly relations between nations,

Whereas the peoples of the United Nations have in the Charter reaffirmed their faith in fundamental human rights, in the dignity and worth of the human person and in the equal rights of men and women and have determined to promote social progress and better standards of life in larger freedom,

Whereas Member States have pledged themselves to achieve, in cooperation with the United Nations, the promotion of universal respect for and observance of human rights and fundamental freedoms,

Whereas a common understanding of these rights and freedoms is of the greatest importance for the full realization of this pledge. *Now Therefore*, The General Assembly *proclaims this universal declaration of human rights* as a common standard of achievement for all peoples and all nations, to the end that every individual and every organ of society, keeping this Declaration constantly in mind, shall strive by teaching and education to promote respect for these rights and freedoms and by progressive measures, national and international, to secure their universal and effective recognition and observance, both among the peoples of Member States themselves and among the peoples of territories under their jurisdiction.

Article 1

All human beings are born free and equal in dignity and rights. They are endowed with reason and conscience and should act towards one another in a spirit of brotherhood.

Article 2

Everyone is entitled to all the rights and freedoms set forth in this declaration, without discrimination of any kind, such as race, colour, sex, language, religion, political or other opinion, national or social origin, property, birth or other status.

Furthermore, no distinction shall be made on the basis of the political, jurisdictional or international status of the country or territory to which a person belongs, whether it be independent, trust, non-self-governing or under any other limitation of sovereignty.

Article 3

Everyone has the right to life, liberty and the security of person.

Article 4

No one shall be held in slavery or servitude; slavery and the slave trade shall be prohibited in all their forms.

Article 5

No one shall be subjected to torture or to cruel, inhuman or degrading treatment or punishment.

Article 6

Everyone has the right to recognition everywhere as a person before the law.

Article 7

All are equal before the law and are entitled without any discrimination to equal protection of the law. All are entitled to equal protection against any discrimination in violation of this Declaration and against any incitement to such discrimination.

Article 8

Everyone has the right to an effective remedy by the competent national tribunals for acts violating the fundamental rights granted him by the constitution or by law.

Article 9

No one shall be subjected to arbitrary arrest, detention or exile.

Article 10

Everyone is entitled in full equality to a fair and public hearing by an independent and impartial tribunal, in the determination of his rights and obligations and of any criminal charge against him.

Article 11

1. Everyone charged with a penal offence has the right to be presumed innocent until proved guilty according to law in a public trial at which he has had all the guarantees necessary for his defense.

2. No one shall be held guilty of any penal offence on account of any act or omission which did not constitute a penal offence, under

national or international law, at the time when it was committed. Nor shall a heavier penalty be imposed than the one that was applicable at the time the penal offence was committed.

Article 12

No one shall be subjected to arbitrary interference with his privacy, family, home or correspondence, nor to attacks upon his honour and reputation. Everyone has the right to the protection of the law against such interference or attacks.

Article 13

1. Everyone has the right to freedom of movement and residence within the borders of each State.

2. Everyone has the right to leave any country, including his own, and to return to his country.

Article 14

1. Everyone has the right to seek and to enjoy in other countries asylum from persecution.

2. This right may not be invoked in the case of prosecutions genuinely arising from non-political crimes or from acts contrary to the purposes and principles of the United Nations.

Article 15

1. Everyone has the right to a nationality.

2. No one shall be arbitrarily deprived of his nationality nor denied the right to change his nationality.

Article 16

1. Men and women of full age, without any limitation due to race, nationality or religion, have the right to marry and to found a family. They are entitled to equal rights as to marriage, during marriage and at its dissolution.

2. Marriage shall be entered into only with the free and full consent of the intending spouses.

3. The family is the natural and fundamental group unit of society and is entitled to protection by society and the State.

Article 17

1. Everyone has the right to own property alone as well as in association with others.

2. No one shall be arbitrarily deprived of his property.

Article 18

Everyone has the right to freedom of thought, conscience and religion; this right includes freedom to change his religion or belief, and freedom, either alone or in community with others and in public or private, to manifest his religion or belief in teaching, practice, worship and observance.

Article 19

Everyone has the right to freedom of opinion and expression; this right includes freedom to hold opinions without interference and to seek, receive and impart information and ideas through any media and regardless of frontiers.

Article 20

1. Everyone has the right to freedom of peaceful assembly and association.

2. No one may be compelled to belong to an association.

Article 21

1. Everyone has the right to take part in the government of his country, directly or through freely chosen representatives.

2. Everyone has the right official access to public service in his country.

3. The will of the people shall be the basis of the authority of government; this will shall be expressed in periodic and genuine elections which shall be by universal and equal suffrage and shall be held by secret vote or by equivalent free voting procedures.

Article 22

Everyone, as a member of society, has the right to social security and is entitled to realization, through national effort and international cooperation and in accordance with the organization and resources of each State, of the economic, social and cultural rights indispensable for his dignity and the free development of his personality.

Article 23

1. Everyone has the right to work, to free choice of employment, to just and favorable conditions of work and to protection against unemployment.

2. Everyone, without any discrimination, has the right to equal pay for equal work.

3. Everyone who works has the right to just and favourable remuneration ensuring for himself and his family and existence worthy of human dignity, and supplemented, if necessary, by other means of social protection.

4. Everyone has the right to form and to join trade unions for the protection of his interests.

Article 24

Everyone has the right to rest and leisure, including reasonable limitation of working hours and periodic holidays with pay.

Article 25

1. Everyone has the right to a standard of living adequate for the health and well-being of himself and of his family, including food,

clothing, housing and medical care and necessary social services, and the right to security in the event of unemployment, sickness, disability, widowhood, old age or other lack of livelihood in circumstances beyond his control.

2. Motherhood and childhood are entitled to special care and assistance. All children, whether born in or out of wedlock, shall enjoy the same social protection.

Article 26

1. Everyone has the right to education. Education shall be free, at least in the elementary and fundamental stages. Elementary education shall be compulsory. Technical and professional education shall be made generally available and higher education shall be equally accessible to all on the basis of merit.

2. Education shall be directed to the full development of the human personality and to the strengthening of respect for human rights and fundamental freedoms. It shall promote understanding, tolerance and friendship among all nations, racial or religious groups, and shall further the activities of the United Nations for the maintenance of peace.

3. Parents have a right to choose the kind of education that shall be given to their children.

Article 27

1. Everyone has the right freely to participate in the cultural life of the community, to enjoy the arts and to share in scientific advancement and its benefits.

2. Everyone has the right to the protection of the moral and material interests resulting from any scientific, literary or artistic production of which he is the author.

Article 28

Everyone is entitled to a social and international order in which the rights and freedoms set forth in this Declaration can be fully realized.

Article 29

1. Everyone has duties to the community in which alone the free and full development of his personality is possible.

2. In the exercise of his rights and freedoms, everyone shall be subject only to such limitations as are determined by law solely for the purpose of securing due recognition and respect for the rights and freedoms of others and of meeting the just requirements of morality, public order and the general welfare in a democratic society.

3. These rights and freedoms may in no case be exercised contrary to the purposes and principles of the United Nations.

Article 30

Nothing in this Declaration may be interpreted as implying for any State, group or person any right to engage in any activity or to perform any act aimed at the destruction of any of the rights and freedoms set forth herein.

Document 11
INTERNATIONAL COVENANT ON CIVIL AND POLITICAL RIGHTS

999 U.N.T.S. 171 (Dec. 9, 1966)

Preamble

The States Parties to the present Covenant,

Considering that, in accordance with the principles proclaimed in the Charter of the United Nations, recognition of the inherent dignity and of the equal and inalienable rights of all members of the human family is the foundation of freedom, justice and peace in the world,

Recognizing that these rights derive from the inherent dignity of the human person,

Recognizing that, in accordance with the Universal Declaration of Human Rights, the ideal of free human beings enjoying civil and political freedom and freedom from fear and want can only be achieved if conditions are created whereby everyone may enjoy his civil and political rights, as well as his economic, social and cultural rights,

Considering the obligation of States under the Charter of the United Nations to promote universal respect for, and observance of, human rights and freedoms,

Realizing that the individual, having duties to other individuals and to the community to which he belongs, is under a responsibility to strive for the promotion and observance of the rights recognized in the present Covenant,

Agree upon the following articles:

PART I

Article 1

1. All peoples have the right of self-determination. By virtue of that right they freely determine their political status and freely pursue their economic, social and cultural development.

2. All peoples may, for their own ends, freely dispose of their natural wealth and resources without prejudice to any obligations arising out of international economic co-operation, based upon the principle of mutual benefit, and international law. In no case may a people be deprived of its own means of subsistence.

3. The States Parties to the present Covenant, including those having responsibility for the administration of Non–Self–Governing and Trust Territories, shall promote the realization of the right of self-

determination, and shall respect that right, in conformity with the provisions of the Charter of the United Nations.

PART II

Article 2

1. Each State Party to the present Covenant undertakes to respect and to ensure to all individuals within its territory and subject to its jurisdiction the rights recognized in the present Covenant, without distinction of any kind, such as race, colour, sex, language, religion, political or other opinion, national or social origin, property, birth or other status.

2. Where not already provided for by existing legislative or other measures, each State Party to the present Covenant undertakes to take the necessary steps, in accordance with its constitutional processes and with the provisions of the present Covenant, to adopt such legislative or other measures as may be necessary to give effect to the rights recognized in the present Covenant.

3. Each State Party to the present Covenant undertakes:

(a) To ensure that any person whose rights or freedoms as herein recognized are violated shall have an effective remedy, notwithstanding that the violation has been committed by persons acting in an official capacity;

(b) To ensure that any person claiming such a remedy shall have his right thereto determined by competent judicial, administrative or legislative authorities, or by any other competent authority provided for by the legal system of the State, and to develop the possibilities of judicial remedy;

(c) To ensure that the competent authorities shall enforce such remedies when granted.

Article 3

The States Parties to the present Covenant undertake to ensure the equal right of men and women to the enjoyment of all civil and political rights set forth in the present Covenant.

Article 4

1. In time of public emergency which threatens the life of the nation and the existence of which is officially proclaimed, the States Parties to the present Covenant may take measures derogating from their obligations under the present Covenant to the extent strictly required by the exigencies of the situation, provided that such measures are not inconsistent with their other obligations under international law and do not involve discrimination solely on the ground of race, colour, sex, language, religion or social origin.

2. No derogation from Articles 6, 7, 8 (paragraphs 1 and 2), 11, 15, 16 and 18 may be made under this provision.

3. Any State Party to the present Covenant availing itself of the right of derogation shall immediately inform the other States Parties to the present Covenant, through the intermediary of the Secretary–General of the United Nations, of the provisions from which it has derogated and of the reasons by which it was actuated. A further communication shall be made, through the same intermediary, on the date on which it terminates such derogation.

Article 5

1. Nothing in the present Covenant may be interpreted as implying for any State, group or person any right to engage in any activity or perform any act aimed at the destruction of any of the rights and freedoms recognized herein or at their limitation to a greater extent than is provided for in the present Covenant.

2. There shall be no restriction upon or derogation from any of the fundamental human rights recognized or existing in any State Party to the present Covenant pursuant to law, conventions, regulations or custom on the pretext that the present Covenant does not recognize such rights or that it recognizes them to a lesser extent.

PART III

Article 6

1. Every human being has the inherent right to life. This right shall be protected by law. No one shall be arbitrarily deprived of his life.

2. In countries which have not abolished the death penalty, sentence of death may be imposed only for the most serious crimes in accordance with the law in force at the time of the commission of the crime and not contrary to the provisions of the present Covenant and to the Convention on the Prevention and Punishment of the Crime of Genocide. This penalty can only be carried out pursuant to a final judgment rendered by a competent court.

3. When deprivation of life constitutes the crime of genocide, it is understood that nothing in this article shall authorize any State Party to the present Covenant to derogate in any way from any obligation assumed under the provisions of the Convention on the Prevention and Punishment of the Crime of Genocide.

4. Anyone sentenced to death shall have the right to seek pardon or commutation of the sentence. Amnesty, pardon or commutation of the sentence of death may be granted in all cases.

5. Sentence of death shall not be imposed for crimes committed by persons below eighteen years of age and shall not be carried out on pregnant women.

6. Nothing in this article shall be invoked to delay or to prevent the abolition of capital punishment by any State Party to the present Covenant.

Article 7

No one shall be subjected to torture or to cruel, inhuman or degrading treatment or punishment. In particular, no one shall be subjected without his free consent to medical or scientific experimentation.

Article 8

1. No one shall be held in slavery; slavery and the slave trade in all their forms shall be prohibited.

2. No one shall be held in servitude.

3. (a) No one shall be required to perform forced or compulsory labour;

(b) Paragraph 3(a) shall not be held to preclude, in countries where imprisonment with hard labour may be imposed as a punishment for a crime, the performance of hard labour in pursuance of a sentence to such punishment by a competent court;

(c) For the purpose of this paragraph the term "forced or compulsory labour" shall not include:

(i) Any work or service, not referred to in sub-paragraph (b), normally required of a person who is under detention in consequence of a lawful order of a court, or of a person during conditional release from such detention;

(ii) Any service of a military character and, in countries where conscientious objection is recognized, any national service required by law of conscientious objectors;

(iii) Any service exacted in cases of emergency or calamity threatening the life or well-being of the community;

(iv) Any work or service which forms part of normal civil obligations.

Article 9

1. Everyone has the right to liberty and security of person. No one shall be subjected to arbitrary arrest or detention. No one shall be deprived of his liberty except on such grounds and in accordance with such procedure as are established by law.

2. Anyone who is arrested shall be informed, at the time of arrest, of the reasons for his arrest and shall be promptly informed of any charges against him.

3. Anyone arrested or detained on a criminal charge shall be brought promptly before a judge or other officer authorized by law to exercise judicial power and shall be entitled to trial within a reasonable time or to release. It shall not be the general rule that persons awaiting trial shall be detained in custody, but release may be subject to guarantees to appear for trial, at any other stage of the judicial proceedings, and, should occasion arise, for execution of the judgment.

4. Anyone who is deprived of his liberty by arrest or detention shall be entitled to take proceedings before a court, in order that that court may decide without delay on the lawfulness of his detention and order his release if the detention is not lawful.

5. Anyone who has been the victim of unlawful arrest or detention shall have an enforceable right to compensation.

Article 10

1. All persons deprived of their liberty shall be treated with humanity and with respect for the inherent dignity of the human person.

2. (a) Accused persons shall, save in exceptional circumstances, be segregated from convicted persons and shall be subject to separate treatment appropriate to their status as unconvicted persons;

(b) Accused juvenile persons shall be separated from adults and brought as speedily as possible for adjudication.

3. The penitentiary system shall comprise treatment of prisoners the essential aim of which shall be their reformation and social rehabilitation. Juvenile offenders shall be segregated from adults and be accorded treatment appropriate to their age and legal status.

Article 11

No one shall be imprisoned merely on the ground of inability to fulfil a contractual obligation.

Article 12

1. Everyone lawfully within the territory of a State shall, within that territory, have the right to liberty of movement and freedom to choose his residence.

2. Everyone shall be free to leave any country, including his own.

3. The above-mentioned rights shall not be subject to any restrictions except those which are provided by law, are necessary to protect national security, public order (*ordre public*), public health or morals or the rights and freedoms of others, and are consistent with the other rights recognized in the present Covenant.

4. No one shall be arbitrarily deprived of the right to enter his own country.

Article 13

An alien lawfully in the territory of a State Party to the present Covenant may be expelled therefrom only in pursuance of a decision reached in accordance with law and shall, except where compelling reasons of national security otherwise require, be allowed to submit the reasons against his expulsion and to have his case reviewed by, and be represented for the purpose before, the competent authority or a person or persons especially designated by the competent authority.

Article 14

1. All persons shall be equal before the courts and tribunals. In the determination of any criminal charge against him, or of his rights and obligations in a suit at law, everyone shall be entitled to a fair and public hearing by a competent, independent and impartial tribunal established by law. The Press and the public may be excluded from all or part of a trial for reasons of morals, public order (*ordre public*) or national security in a democratic society, or when the interest of the private lives of the parties so requires, or to the extent strictly necessary in the opinion of the court in special circumstances where publicity would prejudice the interests of justice; but any judgment rendered in a criminal case or in a suit at law shall be made public except where the interest of juvenile persons otherwise requires or the proceedings concern matrimonial disputes or the guardianship of children.

2. Everyone charged with a criminal offence shall have the right to be presumed innocent until proved guilty according to law.

3. In the determination of any criminal charge against him, everyone shall be entitled to the following minimum guarantees, in full equality:

(a) To be informed promptly and in detail in a language which he understands of the nature and cause of the charge against him;

(b) To have adequate time and facilities for the preparation of his defence and to communicate with counsel of his own choosing;

(c) To be tried without undue delay;

(d) To be tried in his presence, and to defend himself in person or through legal assistance of his own choosing; to be informed, if he does not have legal assistance, of this right; and to have legal assistance assigned to him, in any case where the interests of justice so require, and without payment by him in any such case if he does not have sufficient means to pay for it;

(e) To examine, or have examined, the witnesses against him and to obtain the attendance and examination of witnesses on his behalf under the same conditions as witnesses against him;

(f) To have the free assistance of an interpreter if he cannot understand or speak the language used in court;

(g) Not to be compelled to testify against himself or to confess guilt.

4. In the case of juvenile persons, the procedure shall be such as will take account of their age and the desirability of promoting their rehabilitation.

5. Everyone convicted of a crime shall have the right to his conviction and sentence being reviewed by a higher tribunal according to law.

6. When a person has by a final decision been convicted of a criminal offence and when subsequently his conviction has been reversed or he has been pardoned on the ground that a new or newly discovered

fact shows conclusively that there has been a miscarriage of justice, the person who has suffered punishment as a result of such conviction shall be compensated according to law, unless it is proved that the non-disclosure of the unknown fact in time is wholly or partly attributable to him.

7. No one shall be liable to be tried or punished again for an offence for which he has already been finally convicted or acquitted in accordance with the law and penal procedure of each country.

Article 15

1. No one shall be held guilty of any criminal offence on account of any act or omission which did not constitute a criminal offence, under national or international law, at the time when it was committed. Nor shall a heavier penalty be imposed than the one that was applicable at the time when the criminal offence was committed. If, subsequent to the commission of the offence, provision is made by law for the imposition of a lighter penalty, the offender shall benefit thereby.

2. Nothing in this article shall prejudice the trial and punishment of any person for any act or omission which, at the time when it was committed, was criminal according to the general principles of law recognized by the community of nations.

Article 16

Everyone shall have the right to recognition everywhere as a person before the law.

Article 17

1. No one shall be subjected to arbitrary or unlawful interference with his privacy, family, home or correspondence, nor to unlawful attacks on his honour and reputation.

2. Everyone has the right to the protection of the law against such interference or attacks.

Article 18

1. Everyone shall have the right to freedom of thought, conscience and religion. This right shall include freedom to have or to adopt a religion or belief of his choice, and freedom, either individually or in community with others and in public or private, to manifest his religion or belief in worship, observance, practice and teaching.

2. No one shall be subject to coercion which would impair his freedom to have or to adopt a religion or belief of his choice.

3. Freedom to manifest one's religion or beliefs may be subject only to such limitations as are prescribed by law and are necessary to protect public safety, order, health, or morals or the fundamental rights and freedoms of others.

4. The States Parties to the present Covenant undertake to have respect for the liberty of parents and, when applicable, legal guardians to

ensure the religious and moral education of their children in conformity with their own convictions.

Article 19

1. Everyone shall have the right to hold opinions without interference.

2. Everyone shall have the right to freedom of expression; this right shall include freedom to seek, receive and impart information and ideas of all kinds, regardless of frontiers, either orally, in writing or in print, in the form of art, or through any other media of his choice.

3. The exercise of the rights provided for in paragraph 2 of this article carries with it special duties and responsibilities. It may therefore be subject to certain restrictions, but these shall only be such as are provided by law and are necessary:

(a) For respect of the rights or reputations of others;

(b) For the protection of national security or of public order (*ordre public*), or of public health or morals.

Article 20

1. Any propaganda for war shall be prohibited by law.

2. Any advocacy of national, racial or religious hatred that constitutes incitement to discrimination, hostility or violence shall be prohibited by law.

Article 21

The right of peaceful assembly shall be recognized. No restrictions may be placed on the exercise of this right other than those imposed in conformity with the law and which are necessary in a democratic society in the interests of national security or public safety, public order (*ordre public*), the protection of public health or morals or the protection of the rights and freedoms of others.

Article 22

1. Everyone shall have the right to freedom of association with others, including the right to form and join trade unions for the protection of his interests.

2. No restrictions may be placed on the exercise of this right other than those which are prescribed by law and which are necessary in a democratic society in the interests of national security or public safety, public order (*ordre public*), the protection of public health or morals or the protection of the rights and freedoms of others. This article shall not prevent the imposition of lawful restrictions on members of the armed forces and of the police in their exercise of this right.

3. Nothing in this article shall authorize States Parties to the International Labour Organization Convention of 1948 concerning Freedom of Association and Protection of the Right to Organize to take legislative measures which would prejudice, or to apply the law in such a manner as to prejudice, the guarantees provided for in that Convention.

Article 23

1. The family is the natural and fundamental group unit of society and is entitled to protection by society and the State.

2. The right of men and women of marriageable age to marry and to found a family shall be recognized.

3. No marriage shall be entered into without the free and full consent of the intending spouses.

4. States Parties to the present Covenant shall take appropriate steps to ensure equality of rights and responsibilities of spouses as to marriage, during marriage and at its dissolution. In the case of dissolution, provision shall be made for the necessary protection of any children.

Article 24

1. Every child shall have, without any discrimination as to race, colour, sex, language, religion, national or social origin, property or birth, the right to such measures of protection as are required by his status as a minor, on the part of his family, society and the State.

2. Every child shall be registered immediately after birth and shall have a name.

3. Every child has the right to acquire a nationality.

Article 25

Every citizen shall have the right and the opportunity, without any of the distinctions mentioned in Article 2 and without unreasonable restrictions:

(a) To take part in the conduct of public affairs, directly or through freely chosen representatives;

(b) To vote and to be elected at genuine periodic elections which shall be by universal and equal suffrage and shall be held by secret ballot, guaranteeing the free expression of the will of the electors;

(c) To have access, on general terms of equality, to public service in his country.

Article 26

All persons are equal before the law and are entitled without any discrimination to the equal protection of the law. In this respect, the law shall prohibit any discrimination and guarantee to all persons equal and effective protection against discrimination on any ground such as race, colour, sex, language, religion, political or other opinion, national or social origin, property, birth or other status.

Article 27

In those States in which ethnic, religious or linguistic minorities exist, persons belonging to such minorities shall not be denied the right, in community with the other members of their group, to enjoy their own culture, to profess and practice their own religion, or to use their own language.

PART IV

Article 28

1. There shall be established a Human Rights Committee (hereafter referred to in the present Covenant as the Committee). It shall consist of eighteen members and shall carry out the functions hereinafter provided.

2. The Committee shall be composed of nationals of the States Parties to the present Covenant who shall be persons of high moral character and recognized competence in the field of human rights, consideration being given to the usefulness of the participation of some persons having legal experience.

3. The members of the Committee shall be elected and shall serve in their personal capacity.

Article 29

1. The members of the Committee shall be elected by secret ballot from a list of persons possessing the qualifications prescribed in Article 28 and nominated for the purpose by the State Parties to the present Covenant.

2. Each State Party to the present Covenant may nominate not more than two persons. These persons shall be nationals of the nominating State.

3. A person shall be eligible for renomination.

Article 30

1. The initial election shall be held no later than six months after the date of the entry into force of the present Covenant.

2. At least four months before the date of each election to the Committee, other than an election to fill a vacancy declared in accordance with Article 34, the Secretary–General of the United Nations shall address a written invitation to the States Parties to the present Covenant to submit their nominations for membership of the Committee within three months.

3. The Secretary–General of the United Nations shall prepare a list in alphabetical order of all the persons thus nominated, with an indication of the States Parties which have nominated them, and shall submit it to the States Parties to the present Covenant no later than one month before the date of each election.

4. Elections of the members of the Committee shall be held at a meeting of the States Parties to the present Covenant convened by the Secretary–General of the United Nations at the Headquarters of the United Nations. At that meeting, for which two thirds of the States Parties to the present Covenant shall constitute a quorum, the persons elected to the Committee shall be those nominees who obtain the largest

number of votes and an absolute majority of the votes of the representatives of States Parties present and voting.

Article 31

1. The Committee may not include more than one national of the same State.

2. In the election of the Committee, consideration shall be given to equitable geographical distribution of membership and to the representation of the different forms of civilization and of the principal legal systems.

Article 32

1. The members of the Committee shall be elected for a term of four years. They shall be eligible for re-election if renominated. However, the terms of nine of the members elected at the first election shall expire at the end of two years; immediately after the first election, the names of these nine members shall be chosen by lot by the Chairman of the meeting referred to in Article 30, paragraph 4.

2. Elections at the expiry of office shall be held in accordance with the preceding articles of this part of the present Covenant.

Article 33

1. If, in the unanimous opinion of the other members, a member of the Committee has ceased to carry out his functions for any cause other than absence of a temporary character, the Chairman of the Committee shall notify the Secretary–General of the United Nations, who shall then declare the seat of that member to be vacant.

2. In the event of the death or the resignation of a member of the Committee, the Chairman shall immediately notify the Secretary–General of the United Nations, who shall declare the seat vacant from the date of death or the date on which the resignation takes effect.

Article 34

1. When a vacancy is declared in accordance with Article 33 and if the term of office of the member to be replaced does not expire within six months of the declaration of the vacancy, the Secretary–General of the United Nations shall notify each of the States Parties to the present Covenant, which may within two months submit nominations m accordance with Article 29 for the purpose of filling the vacancy.

2. The Secretary–General of the United Nations shall prepare a list in alphabetical order of the persons thus nominated and shall submit it to the States Parties to the present Covenant. The election to fill the vacancy shall then take place in accordance with the relevant provisions of this part of the present Covenant.

3. A member of the Committee elected to fill a vacancy declared in accordance with Article 33 shall hold office for the remainder of the term of the member who vacated the seat on the Committee under the provisions of that article.

Article 35

The members of the Committee shall, with the approval of the General Assembly of the United Nations, receive emoluments from United Nations resources on such terms and conditions as the General Assembly may decide, having regard to the importance of the Committee's responsibilities.

Article 36

The Secretary–General of the United Nations shall provide the necessary staff and facilities for the effective performance of the functions of the Committee under the present Covenant.

Article 37

1. The Secretary–General of the United Nations shall convene the initial meeting of the Committee at the Headquarters of the United Nations.

2. After its initial meeting, the Committee shall meet at such times as shall be provided in its rules of procedure.

3. The Committee shall normally meet at the Headquarters of the United Nations or at the United Nations Office at Geneva.

Article 38

Every member of the Committee shall, before taking up his duties, make a solemn declaration in open committee that he will perform his functions impartially and conscientiously.

Article 39

1. The Committee shall elect its officers for a term of two years. They may be re-elected.

2. The Committee shall establish its own rules of procedure, but these rules shall provide, *inter alia*, that:

(a) Twelve members shall constitute a quorum;

(b) Decisions of the Committee shall be made by a majority vote of the members present.

Article 40

1. The States Parties to the present Covenant undertake to submit reports on the measures they have adopted which give effect to the rights recognized herein and on the progress made in the enjoyment of those rights:

(a) Within one year of the entry into force of the present Covenant for the States Parties concerned;

(b) Thereafter whenever the Committee so requests.

2. All reports shall be submitted to the Secretary–General of the United Nations, who shall transmit them to the Committee for consideration. Reports shall indicate the factors and difficulties, if any, affecting the implementation of the present Covenant.

3. The Secretary–General of the United Nations may, after consultation with the Committee, transmit to the specialized agencies concerned copies of such parts of the reports as may fall within their field of competence.

4. The Committee shall study the reports submitted by the States Parties to the present Covenant. It shall transmit its reports, and such general comments as it may consider appropriate, to the States Parties. The Committee may also transmit to the Economic and Social Council these comments along with the copies of the reports it has received from States Parties to the present Covenant.

5. The States Parties to the present Covenant may submit to the Committee observations on any comments that may be made in accordance with paragraph 4 of this article.

Article 41

1. A State Party to the present Covenant may at any time declare under this article that it recognizes the competence of the Committee to receive and consider communications to the effect that a State Party claims that another State Party is not fulfilling its obligations under the present Covenant. Communications under this article may be received and considered only if submitted by a State Party which has made a declaration recognizing in regard to itself the competence of the Committee. No communication shall be received by the Committee if it concerns a State Party which has not made such a declaration. Communications received under this article shall be dealt with in accordance with the following procedure:

(a) If a State Party to the present Covenant considers that another State Party is not giving effect to the provisions of the present Covenant, it may, by written communication, bring the matter to the attention of that State Party. Within three months after the receipt of the communication, the receiving State shall afford the State which sent the communication an explanation or any other statement in writing clarifying the matter, which should include, to the extent possible and pertinent, reference to domestic procedures and remedies taken, pending, or available in the matter.

(b) If the matter is not adjusted to the satisfaction of both States Parties concerned within six months after the receipt by the receiving State of the initial communication, either State shall have the right to refer the matter to the Committee, by notice given to the Committee and to the other State.

(c) The Committee shall deal with a matter referred to it only after it has ascertained that all available domestic remedies have been invoked and exhausted in the matter, in conformity with the generally recognized principles of international law. This shall not be the rule where the application of the remedies is unreasonably prolonged.

(d) The Committee shall hold closed meetings when examining communications under this article.

(e) Subject to the provisions of sub-paragraph (c), the Committee shall make available its good offices to the States Parties concerned with a view to a friendly solution of the matter on the basis of respect for human rights and fundamental freedoms as recognized in the present Covenant.

(f) In any matter referred to it, the Committee may call upon the States Parties concerned, referred to in sub-paragraph (b), to supply any relevant information.

(g) The States Parties concerned, referred to in sub-paragraph (b), shall have the right to be represented when the matter is being considered in the Committee and to make submissions orally and/or in writing.

(h) The Committee shall, within twelve months after the date of receipt of notice under sub-paragraph (b), submit a report:

(i) If a solution within the terms of sub-paragraph (e) is reached, the Committee shall confine its report to a brief statement of the facts and of the solution reached;

(ii) If a solution within the terms of sub-paragraph (e) is not reached, the Committee shall confine its report to a brief statement of the facts; the written submissions and record of the oral submissions made by the States Parties concerned shall be attached to the report. In every matter, the report shall be communicated to the States Parties concerned.

2. The provisions of this article shall come into force when ten States Parties to the present Covenant have made declarations under paragraph 1 of this article. Such declarations shall be deposited by the States Parties with the Secretary–General of the United Nations, who shall transmit copies thereof to the other States Parties. A declaration may be withdrawn at any time by notification to the Secretary–General. Such a withdrawal shall not prejudice the consideration of any matter which is the subject of a communication already transmitted under this article; no further communication by any State Party shall be received after the notification of withdrawal of the declaration has been received by the Secretary–General, unless the State Party concerned has made a new declaration.

Article 42

1. (a) If a matter referred to the Committee in accordance with Article 41 is not resolved to the satisfaction of the States Parties concerned, the Committee may, with the prior consent of the States Parties concerned, appoint an ad hoc Conciliation Commission (hereinafter referred to as the Commission). The good offices of the Commission shall be made available to the States Parties concerned with a view to an amicable solution of the matter on the basis of respect for the present Covenant;

(b) The Commission shall consist of five persons acceptable to the States Parties concerned. If the States Parties concerned fail to reach agreement within three months on all or part of the composition of the Commission, the members of the Commission concerning whom no agreement has been reached shall be elected by secret ballot by a two-thirds majority vote of the Committee from among its members.

2. The members of the Commission shall serve in their personal capacity. They shall not be nationals of the States Parties concerned, or of a State not party to the present Covenant, or of a State Party which has not made a declaration under Article 41.

3. The Commission shall elect its own Chairman and adopt its own rules of procedure.

4. The meetings of the Commission shall normally be held at the Headquarters of the United Nations or at the United Nations Office at Geneva. However, they may be held at such other convenient places as the Commission may determine in consultation with the Secretary–General of the United Nations and the States Parties concerned.

5. The secretariat provided in accordance with Article 36 shall also service the commissions appointed under this article.

6. The information received and collated by the Committee shall be made available to the Commission and the Commission may call upon the States Parties concerned to supply any other relevant information.

7. When the Commission has fully considered the matter, but in any event not later than twelve months after having been seized of the matter, it shall submit to the Chairman of the Committee a report for communication to the States Parties concerned:

(a) if the Commission is unable to complete its consideration of the matter within twelve months, it shall confine its report to a brief statement or the status of its consideration of the matter;

(b) if an amicable solution to the matter on the basis of respect for human rights as recognized in the present Covenant is reached, the Commission shall confine its report to a brief statement of the facts and of the solution reached;

(c) if a solution within the terms of sub-paragraph (b) is not reached, the Commission's report shall embody its findings on all questions of fact relevant to the issues between the States Parties concerned, and its views on the possibilities of an amicable solution of the matter. This report shall also contain the written submissions and a record of the oral submissions made by the States Parties concerned;

(d) if the Commission's report is submitted under subparagraph (c), the States Parties concerned shall, within three months of the receipt of the report, notify the Chairman of the Committee whether or not they accept the contents of the report of the Commission.

8. The provisions of this article are without prejudice to the responsibilities of the Committee under Article 41

9. The States Parties concerned shall share equally all the expenses of the members of the Commission in accordance with estimates to be provided by the Secretary–General of the United Nations.

10. The Secretary–General of the United Nations shall be empowered to pay the expenses of the members of the Commission, if necessary, before reimbursement by the States Parties concerned, in accordance with paragraph 9 of this article.

Article 43

The members of the Committee, and of the ad hoc conciliation commissions which may be appointed under Article 42, shall be entitled to the facilities, privileges and immunities of experts on mission for the United Nations as laid down in the relevant sections of the Convention on the Privileges and Immunities of the United Nations.

Article 44

The provisions for the implementation of the present Covenant shall apply without prejudice to the procedures prescribed in the field of human rights by or under the constituent instruments and the conventions of the United Nations and of the specialized agencies and shall not prevent the States Parties to the present Covenant from having recourse to other procedures for settling a dispute in accordance with general or special international agreements in force between them.

Article 45

The Committee shall submit to the General Assembly of the United Nations, through the Economic and Social Council, an annual report on its activities.

PART V

Article 46

Nothing in the present Covenant shall be interpreted as impairing the provisions of the Charter of the United Nations and of the constitutions of the specialized agencies which define the respective responsibilities of the various organs of the United Nations and of the specialized agencies in regard to the matters dealt with in the present Covenant.

Article 47

Nothing in the present Covenant shall be interpreted as impairing the inherent right of all peoples to enjoy and utilize fully and freely their natural wealth and resources.

Part VI

Article 48

1. The present Covenant is open for signature by any State Member of the United Nations or member of any of its specialized agencies, by any State Party to the Statute of the International Court of Justice, and by any other State which has been invited by the General Assembly of the United Nations to become a party to the present Covenant.

2. The present Covenant is subject to ratification. Instruments of ratification shall be deposited with the Secretary–General of the United Nations.

3. The present Covenant shall be open to accession by any State referred to in paragraph 1 of this article.

4. Accession shall be effected by the deposit of an instrument of accession with the Secretary–General of the United Nations.

5. The Secretary–General of the United Nations shall inform all States which have signed this Covenant or acceded to it of the deposit of each instrument of ratification or accession.

Article 49

1. The present Covenant shall enter into force three months after the date of the deposit with the Secretary–General of the United Nations of the thirty-fifth instrument of ratification or instrument of accession.

2. For each State ratifying the present Covenant or acceding to it after the deposit of the thirty-fifth instrument of ratification or instrument of accession, the present Covenant shall enter into force three months after the date of the deposit of its own instrument of ratification or instrument of accession.

Article 50

The provisions of the present Covenant shall extend to all parts of federal States without any limitations or exceptions.

Article 51

1. Any State Party to the present Covenant may propose an amendment and file it with the Secretary–General of the United Nations. The Secretary–General of the United Nations shall thereupon communicate any proposed amendments to the States Parties to the present Covenant with a request that they notify him whether they favour a conference of States Parties for the purpose of considering and voting upon the proposals. In the event that at least one third of the States Parties favours such a conference, the Secretary–General shall convene the conference under the auspices of the United Nations. Any amendment adopted by a majority of the States Parties present and voting at the conference shall be submitted to the General Assembly of the United Nations for approval.

2. Amendments shall come into force when they have been approved by the General Assembly of the United Nations and accepted by a two-thirds majority of the States Parties to the present Covenant in accordance with their respective constitutional processes.

3. When amendments come into force, they shall be binding on those States Parties which have accepted them, other States Parties still being bound by the provisions of the present Covenant and any earlier amendment which they have accepted.

Article 52

Irrespective of the notifications made under Article 48, paragraph 5, the Secretary–General of the United Nations shall inform all States referred to in paragraph 1 of the following particulars:

(a) Signatures, ratifications and accessions under Article 48;

(b) The date of the entry into force of the present Covenant under Article 49 and the date of the entry into force of any amendments under Article 51.

Article 53

1. The present Covenant, of which the Chinese, English, French, Russian and Spanish texts are equally authentic, shall be deposited in the archives of the United Nations.

Document 12
OPTIONAL PROTOCOL TO THE INTERNATIONAL COVENANT ON CIVIL AND POLITICAL RIGHTS

999 U.N.T.S. 171 (1966)

The States Parties to the present Protocol,

Considering that in order further to achieve the purposes of the Covenant on Civil and Political Rights (hereinafter referred to as the Covenant) and the implementation of its provisions it would be appropriate to enable the Human Rights Committee set up in Part IV of the Covenant (hereafter referred to as the Committee) to receive and consider, as provided in the present Protocol, communications from individuals claiming to be victims of violations of any of the rights set forth in the Covenant,

Have agreed as follows:

Article 1

A State Party to the Covenant that becomes a party to the present Protocol recognizes the competence of the Committee to receive and consider communications from individuals subject to its jurisdiction who claim to be victims of a violation by that State Party of any of the rights set forth in the Covenant. No communication shall be received by the Committee if it concerns a State Party to the Covenant which is not a party to the present Protocol.

Article 2

Subject to the provisions of Article 1, individuals who claim that any of their rights enumerated in the Covenant have been violated and who have exhausted all available domestic remedies may submit a written communication to the Committee for consideration.

Article 3

The Committee shall consider inadmissible any communication under the present Protocol which is anonymous, or which it considers to be an abuse of the right of submission of such communications or to be incompatible with the provisions of the Covenant.

Article 4

1. Subject to the provisions of Article 3, the Committee shall bring any communications submitted to it under the present Protocol to the

attention of the State Party to the present Protocol alleged to be violating any provision of the Covenant.

2. Within six months, the receiving State shall submit to the Committee written explanations or statements clarifying the matter and the remedy, if any, that may have been taken by that State.

Article 5

1. The Committee shall consider communications received under the present Protocol in the light of all written information made available to it by the individual and by the State Party concerned.

2. The Committee shall not consider any communication from an individual unless it has ascertained that:

(a) The same matter is not being examined under another procedure of international investigation or settlement;

(b) The individual has exhausted all available domestic remedies. This shall not be the rule where the application of the remedies is unreasonably prolonged.

3. The Committee shall hold closed meetings when examining communications under the present Protocol.

4. The Committee shall forward its views to the State Party concerned and to the individual.

Article 6

The Committee shall include in its annual report under Article 45 of the Covenant a summary of its activities under the present Protocol.

Article 7

Pending the achievement of the objectives of resolution 1514(XV) adopted by the General Assembly of the United Nations on 14 December 1960 concerning the Declaration on the Granting of Independence to Colonial Countries and Peoples, the provisions of the present Protocol shall in no way limit the right of petition granted to these peoples by the Charter of the United Nations and other international conventions and instruments under the United Nations and its specialized agencies.

Article 8

1. The present Protocol is open for signature by any State which has signed the Covenant.

2. The present Protocol is subject to ratification by any State which has ratified or acceded to the Covenant. Instruments of ratification shall be deposited with the Secretary–General of the United Nations.

3. The present Protocol shall be open to accession by any State which has ratified or acceded to the Covenant.

4. Accession shall be effected by the deposit of an instrument of accession with the Secretary–General of the United Nations.

5. The Secretary–General of the United Nations shall inform all States which have signed the present Protocol or acceded to it of the deposit of each instrument of ratification or accession.

Article 9

1. Subject to the entry into force of the Covenant, the present Protocol shall enter into force three months after the date of the deposit with the Secretary–General of the United Nations of the tenth instrument of ratification or instrument of accession.

2. For each State ratifying the present Protocol or acceding to it after the deposit of the tenth instrument of accession, the present Protocol shall enter into force three months after the date of the deposit of its own instrument of ratification or instrument of accession.

Article 10

The provisions of the present Protocol shall extend to all parts of federal States without any limitations or exceptions.

Article 11

1. Any State Party to the present Protocol may propose an amendment and file it with the Secretary–General of the United Nations. The Secretary–General shall thereupon communicate any proposed amendments to the States Parties to the present Protocol with a request that they notify him whether they favour a conference of States Parties for the purpose of considering and voting upon the proposal. In the event that at least one third of the States Parties favours such a conference, the Secretary–General shall convene the conference under the auspices of the United Nations. Any amendment adopted by a majority of the States Parties present and voting at the conference shall be submitted to the General Assembly of the United Nations for approval.

2. Amendments shall come into force when they have been approved by the General Assembly of the United Nations and accepted by a two-thirds majority of the States Parties to the present Protocol in accordance with their respective constitutional processes.

3. When amendments come into force, they shall be binding on those States Parties which have accepted them, other States Parties still being bound by the provisions of the present Protocol and any earlier amendment which they have accepted.

Article 12

1. Any State Party may denounce the present Protocol at any time by written notification addressed to the Secretary–General of the United Nations. Denunciation shall take effect three months after the date of receipt of the notification by the Secretary–General.

2. Denunciation shall be without prejudice to the continued application of the provisions of the present Protocol to any communication submitted under Article 2 before the effective date of denunciation.

Article 13

Irrespective of the notifications made under Article 8, paragraph 5, of the present Protocol, the Secretary–General of the United Nations shall inform all States referred to in Article 48, paragraph 1, of the Covenant of the following particulars:

(a) Signatures, ratifications and accessions under Article 8;

(b) The date of the entry into force of the present Protocol under Article 9 and the date of the entry into force of any amendments under Article 11;

(c) Denunciations under Article 12.

Article 14

1. The present Protocol, of which the Chinese, English, French, Russian and Spanish texts are equally authentic, shall be deposited in the archives of the United Nations.

2. The Secretary–General of the United Nations shall transmit certified copies of the present Protocol to all States referred to in Article 48 of the Covenant.

Document 13
SECOND OPTIONAL PROTOCOL, AIMING AT THE ABOLITION OF THE DEATH PENALTY

U.N. G.A. Res. 44/128, 44 U.N. GAOR, Supp. No. 49, at 206, U.N. Doc. A/44/49 (1989)

The States Parties to the present Protocol,

Believing that abolition of the death penalty contributes to enhancement of human dignity and progressive development of human rights,

Recalling Article 3 of the Universal Declaration of Human Rights, adopted on 10 December 1948, and Article 6 of the International Covenant on Civil and Political Rights, adopted on 16 December 1966,

Noting that Article 6 of the International Covenant on Civil and Political Rights refers to abolition of the death penalty in terms that strongly suggest that abolition is desirable,

Convinced that all measures of abolition of the death penalty should be considered as progress in the enjoyment of life,

Desirous to undertake hereby an international commitment to abolish the death penalty,

Have agreed as follows:

Article 1

1. No one within the jurisdiction of a State Party to the present Protocol shall be executed.

2. Each State party shall take all necessary measures to abolish the death penalty within its jurisdiction.

Article 2

1. No reservation is admissible to the present Protocol, except for a reservation made at the time of ratification or accession that provides for the application of the death penalty in time of war pursuant to a conviction for a most serious crime of a military nature committed during wartime.

2. The State Party making such a reservation shall at the time of ratification or accession communicate to the Secretary–General of the United Nations the relevant provisions of its national legislation applicable during wartime.

3. The State Party having made such a reservation shall notify the Secretary–General of the United Nations of any beginning or ending of a state of war applicable to its territory.

Article 3

The States Parties to the present Protocol shall include in the reports they submit to the Human Rights Committee, in accordance with Article 40 of the Covenant, information on the measures that they have adopted to give effect to the present Protocol.

Article 4

With respect to the States Parties to the Covenant that have made a declaration under Article 41, the competence of the Human Rights Committee to receive and consider communications when a State Party claims that another State Party is not fulfilling its obligations shall extend to the provisions of the present Protocol, unless the State Party concerned has made a statement to the contrary at the moment of ratification or accession.

Article 5

With respect to the States Parties to the first Optional Protocol to the International Covenant on Civil and Political Rights adopted on 16 December 1966, the competence of the Human Rights Committee to receive and consider communications from individuals subject to its jurisdiction shall extend to the provisions of the present Protocol, unless the State Party concerned has made a statement to the contrary at the moment of ratification or accession.

Article 6

1. The provisions of the present Protocol shall apply as additional provisions to the Covenant.

2. Without prejudice to the possibility of a reservation under Article 2 of the present Protocol, the right guaranteed in Article 1, paragraph 1, of the present Protocol shall not be subject to any derogation under Article 4 of the Covenant. . . .

Article 9

The provisions of the present Protocol shall extend to all parts of federal States without any limitations or exceptions. . . .

Document 14
INTERNATIONAL COVENANT ON ECONOMIC, SOCIAL, AND CULTURAL RIGHTS

993 U.N.T.S. 3 (1966)

Preamble

The States Parties to the present Covenant,

Considering that, in accordance with the principles proclaimed in the Charter of the United Nations, recognition of the inherent dignity and of the equal and inalienable rights of all members of the human family is the foundation of freedom, justice and peace in the world,

Recognizing that these rights derive from the inherent dignity of the human person,

Recognizing that, in accordance with the Universal Declaration of Human Rights, the ideal of free human beings enjoying freedom from fear and want can only be achieved if conditions are created whereby everyone may enjoy his economic, social and cultural rights, as well as his civil and political rights,

Considering the obligation of States under the Charter of the United Nations to promote universal respect for, and observance of, human rights and freedoms,

Realizing that the individual, having duties to other individuals and to the community to which he belongs, is under a responsibility to strive for the promotion and observance of the rights recognized in the present Covenant,

Agree upon the following articles:

PART I

Article 1

1. All peoples have the right of self-determination. By virtue of that right they freely determine their political status and freely pursue their economic, social and cultural development.

2. All peoples may, for their own ends, freely dispose of their natural wealth and resources without prejudice to any obligations arising out of international economic co-operation, based upon the principle of mutual benefit, and international law. In no case may a people be deprived of its own means of subsistence.

3. The States Parties to the present Covenant, including those having responsibility for the administration of Non–Self–Governing and Trust Territories, shall promote the realization of the right of self-

determination, and shall respect that right, in conformity with the provisions of the Chatter of the United Nations.

PART II

Article 2

1. Each State Party to the present Covenant undertakes to take steps, individually and through international assistance and co-operation, especially economic and technical, to the maximum of its available resources, with a view to achieving progressively the full realization of the rights recognized in the present Covenant by all appropriate means, including particularly the adoption of legislative measures.

2. The States Parties to the present Covenant undertake to guarantee that the rights enunciated in the present Covenant will be exercised without discrimination of any kind as to race, colour, sex, language, religion, political or other opinion, national or social origin, property, birth or other status.

3. Developing countries, with due regard to human rights and their national economy, may determine to what extent they would guarantee the economic rights recognized in the present Covenant to non-nationals.

Article 3

The States Parties to the present Covenant undertake to ensure the equal right of men and women to the enjoyment of all economic, social and cultural rights set forth in the present Covenant.

Article 4

The States Parties to the present Covenant recognize that, in the enjoyment of those rights provided by the State in conformity with the present Covenant, the State may subject such rights only to such limitations as are determined by law only in so far as this may be compatible with the nature of these rights and solely for the purpose of promoting the general welfare in a democratic society.

Article 5

1. Nothing in the present Covenant may be interpreted as implying for any State, group or person any right to engage in any activity or to perform any act aimed at the destruction of any of the rights or freedoms recognized herein, or at their limitation to a greater extent than is provided for in the present Covenant.

2. No restriction upon or derogation from any of the fundamental human rights recognized or existing in any country in virtue of law, conventions, regulations or custom shall be admitted on the pretext that the present Covenant does not recognize such rights or that it recognizes them to a lesser extent.

PART III

Article 6

1. The States Parties to the present Covenant recognize the right to work, which includes the right of everyone to the opportunity to gain

his living by work which he freely chooses or accepts, and will take appropriate steps to safeguard this right.

2. The steps to be taken by a State Party to the present Covenant to achieve the full realization of this right shall include technical and vocational guidance and training programmes, policies and techniques to achieve steady economic, social and cultural development and full and productive employment under conditions safeguarding fundamental political and economic freedoms to the individual.

Article 7

The States Parties to the present Covenant recognize the right of everyone to the enjoyment and favourable conditions of work which ensure, in particular:

(a) Remuneration which provides all workers, as a minimum, with:

(i) Fair wages and equal remuneration for work of equal value without distinction of any kind, in particular women being guaranteed conditions of work inferior to those enjoyed by men, with equal pay for equal work;

(ii) A decent living for themselves and their families in accordance with the provisions of the present Covenant;

(b) Safe and healthy working conditions;

(c) Equal opportunity for everyone to be promoted in his employment to an appropriate higher level, subject to no considerations other than those of seniority and competence;

(d) Rest, leisure and reasonable limitation of working hours and periodic holidays with pay, as well as remuneration for public holidays.

Article 8

1. The States Parties to the present Covenant undertake to ensure:

(a) The right of everyone to form trade unions and join the trade union of his choice, subject only to the rules of the organization concerned, for the promotion and protection of his economic and social interests. No restrictions may be placed on the exercise of this right other than those prescribed by law and which are necessary in a democratic society in the interests of national security or public order or for the protection of the rights and freedoms of others;

(b) The right of trade unions to establish national federations or confederations and the right of the latter to form or join international trade-union organizations;

(c) The right of trade unions to function freely subject to no limitations other than those prescribed by law and which are necessary in a democratic society in the interests of national security or public order or for the protection of the rights and freedoms of others;

(d) The right to strike, provided that it is exercised in conformity with the laws of the particular country.

2. This article shall not prevent the imposition of lawful restrictions on the exercise of these rights by members of the armed forces or of the police or of the administration of the State.

3. Nothing in this article shall authorize States Parties to the International Labour Organisation Convention of 1948 concerning Freedom of Association and Protection of the Right to Organize to take legislative measures which would prejudice, or apply the law in such a manner as would prejudice, the guarantees provided for in that Convention.

Article 9

The States Parties to the present Covenant recognize the right of everyone to social security, including social insurance.

Article 10

The States Parties to the present Covenant recognize that:

1. The widest possible protection and assistance should be accorded to the family, which is the natural and fundamental group unit of society, particularly for its establishment and while it is responsible for the care and education of dependent children. Marriage must be entered into with the free consent of the intending spouses.

2. Special protection should be accorded to mothers during a reasonable period before and after childbirth. During such period working mothers should be accorded paid leave or leave with adequate social security benefits.

3. Special measures of protection and assistance should be taken on behalf of all children and young persons without any discrimination for reasons of parentage or other conditions. Children and young persons should be protected from economic and social exploitation. Their employment in work harmful to their morals or health or dangerous to life or likely to hamper their normal development should be punishable by law. States should also set age limits below which the paid employment of child labour should be prohibited and punishable by law.

Article 11

1. The States Parties to the present Covenant recognize the right of everyone to an adequate standard of living for himself and his family, including adequate food, clothing and housing, and to the continuous improvement of living conditions. The States Parties will take appropriate steps to ensure the realization of this right, recognizing to this effect the essential importance of international co-operation based on free consent.

2. The States Parties to the present Covenant, recognizing the fundamental right of everyone to be free from hunger, shall take, individually and through international co-operation, the measures, including specific programmes, which are needed:

(a) To improve methods of production, conservation and distribution of food by making full use of technical and scientific knowledge, by disseminating knowledge of the principles of nutrition and by developing or reforming agrarian systems in such a way as to achieve the most efficient development and utilization of natural resources;

(b) Taking into account the problems of both food-importing and food-exporting countries, to ensure an equitable distribution of world food supplies in relation to need.

Article 12

1. The States Parties to the present Covenant recognize the right of everyone to the enjoyment of the highest attainable standard of physical and mental health.

2. The steps to be taken by the States Parties to the present Covenant to achieve the full realization of this right shall include those necessary for:

(a) The provision for the reduction of the stillbirth-rate and of infant mortality and for the healthy development of the child;

(b) The improvement of all aspects of environmental and industrial hygiene;

(c) The prevention, treatment and control of epidemic, endemic, occupational and other diseases;

(d) The creation of conditions which would assure to all medical service and medical attention in the event of sickness.

Article 13

1. The States Parties to the present Covenant recognize the right of everyone to education. They agree that education shall be directed to the full development of the human personality and the sense of its dignity, and shall strengthen the respect for human rights and fundamental freedoms. They further agree that education shall enable all persons to participate effectively in a free society, promote understanding, tolerance and friendship among all nations and all racial, ethnic or religious groups, and further the activities of the United Nations for the maintenance of peace.

2. The States Parties to the present Covenant recognize that, with a view to achieving the full realization of this right:

(a) Primary education shall be compulsory and available free to all;

(b) Secondary education in its different forms, including technical and vocational secondary education, shall be made generally available and accessible to all by every appropriate means, and in particular by the progressive introduction of free education;

(c) Higher education shall be made equally accessible to all, on the basis of capacity, by every appropriate means, and in particular by the progressive introduction of free education;

(d) Fundamental education shall be encouraged or intensified as far as possible for those persons who have not received or completed the whole period of their primary education;

(e) The development of a system of schools at all levels shall be actively pursued, an adequate fellowship system shall be established, and the material conditions of teaching staff shall be continuously improved.

3. The States Parties to the present Covenant undertake to have respect for the liberty of parents and, when applicable, legal guardians to choose for their children schools, other than those established by the public authorities, which conform to such minimum educational standards as may be laid down or approved by the State and to ensure the religious and moral education of their children in conformity with their own convictions.

4. No part of this article shall be construed so as to interfere with the liberty of individuals and bodies to establish and direct educational institutions, subject always to the observance of the principles set forth in paragraph 1 of this article and to the requirement that the education given in such institutions shall conform to such minimum standards as may be laid down by the State.

Article 14

Each State Party to the present Covenant which, at the time of becoming a Party, has not been able to secure in its metropolitan territory or other territories under its jurisdiction compulsory primary education, free of charge, undertakes, within two years, to work out and adopt a detailed plan of action for the progressive implementation, within a reasonable number of years, to be fixed in the plan, of the principle of compulsory education free of charge for all.

Article 15

1. The States Parties to the present Covenant recognize the right of everyone:

(a) To take part in cultural life;

(b) To enjoy the benefits of scientific progress and its applications;

(c) To benefit from the protection of the moral and material interests resulting from any scientific, literary or artistic production of which he is the author.

2. The steps to be taken by the States Parties to the present Covenant to achieve the full realization of this right shall include those necessary for the conservation, the development and the diffusion of science and culture.

3. The States Parties to the present Covenant undertake to respect the freedom indispensable for scientific research and creative activity.

4. The States Parties to the present Covenant recognize the benefits to be derived from the encouragement and development of international contacts and co-operation in the scientific and cultural fields.

PART IV

Article 16

1. The States Parties to the present Covenant undertake to submit in conformity with this part of the Covenant reports on the measures which they have adopted and the progress made in achieving the observance of the rights recognized herein.

2. (a) All reports shall be submitted to the Secretary–General of the United Nations, who shall transmit copies to the Economic and Social Council for consideration in accordance with the provisions of the present Covenant;

(b) The Secretary–General of the United Nations shall also transmit to the specialized agencies copies of the reports, or any relevant parts therefrom, from States Parties to the present Covenant which are also members of these specialized agencies in so far as these reports, or parts therefrom, relate to any matters which fall within the responsibilities of the said agencies in accordance with their constitutional instruments.

Article 17

1. The States Parties to the present Covenant shall furnish their reports in stages, in accordance with a programme to be established by the Economic and Social Council within one year of the entry into force of the present Covenant after consultation with the States Parties and the specialized agencies concerned.

2. Reports may indicate factors and difficulties affecting the degree of fulfilment of obligations under the present Covenant.

3. Where relevant information has previously been furnished to the United Nations or to any specialized agency by any State Party to the present Covenant, it will not be necessary to reproduce that information, but a precise reference to the information so furnished will suffice.

Article 18

Pursuant to its responsibilities under the Charter of the United Nations in the field of human rights and fundamental freedoms, the Economic and Social Council may make arrangements with the specialized agencies in respect of their reporting to it on the progress made in achieving the observance of the provisions of the present Covenant falling within the scope of their activities. These reports may include particulars of decisions and recommendations on such implementation adopted by their competent organs.

Article 19

The Economic and Social Council may transmit to the Commission on Human Rights for study and general recommendation or, as appropriate, for information the reports concerning human rights submitted by States in accordance with Articles 16 and 17, and those concerning human rights submitted by the specialized agencies in accordance with Article 18.

Article 20

The States Parties to the present Covenant and the specialized agencies concerned may submit comments to the Economic and Social Council on any general recommendation under Article 19 or reference to such general recommendation in any report of the Commission on Human Rights or any documentation referred to therein.

Article 21

The Economic and Social Council may submit from time to time to the General Assembly reports with recommendations of a general nature and a summary of the information received from the States Parties to the present Covenant and the specialized agencies on the measures taken and the progress made in achieving general observance of the rights recognized in the present Covenant.

Article 22

The Economic and Social Council may bring to the attention of other organs of the United Nations, their subsidiary organs and specialized agencies concerned with furnishing technical assistance any matters arising out of the reports referred to in this part of the present Covenant which may assist such bodies in deciding, each within its field of competence, on the advisability of international measures likely to contribute to the effective progressive implementation of the present Covenant.

Article 23

The States Parties to the present Covenant agree that international action for the achievement of the rights recognized in the present Covenant includes such methods as the conclusion of conventions, the adoption of recommendations, the furnishing of technical assistance and the holding of regional meetings and technical meetings for the purpose of consultation and study organized in conjunction with the Governments concerned.

Article 24

Nothing in the present Covenant shall be interpreted as impairing the provisions of the Charter of the United Nations and of the constitutions of the specialized agencies which define the respective responsibilities of the various organs of the United Nations and of the specialized agencies in regard to the matters dealt with in the present Covenant.

Article 25

Nothing in the present Covenant shall be interpreted as impairing the inherent right of all peoples to enjoy and utilize fully and freely their natural wealth and resources.

PART V

Article 26

1. The present Covenant is open for signature by any State Member of the United Nations or member of any of its specialized agencies, by any State Party to the Statute of the International Court of Justice, and by any other State which has been invited by the General Assembly of the United Nations to become a party to the present Covenant.

2. The present Covenant is subject to ratification. Instruments of ratification shall be deposited with the Secretary–General of the United Nations.

3. The present Covenant shall be open to accession by any State referred to in paragraph 1 of this article.

4. Accession shall be effected by the deposit of an instrument of accession with the Secretary–General of the United Nations.

5. The Secretary–General of the United Nations shall inform all States which have signed the present Covenant or acceded to it of the deposit of each instrument of ratification or accession.

Article 27

1. The present Covenant shall enter into force three months after the date of the deposit with the Secretary–General of the United Nations of the thirty-fifth instrument of ratification or instrument of accession.

2. For each State ratifying the present Covenant or acceding to it after the deposit of the thirty-fifth instrument of ratification or instrument of accession, the present Covenant shall enter into force three months after the date of the deposit of its own instrument of ratification or instrument of accession.

Article 28

The provisions of the present Covenant shall extend to all parts of federal States without any limitations or exceptions.

Article 29

1. Any State Party to the present Covenant may propose an amendment and file it with the Secretary–General of the United Nations. The Secretary–General shall thereupon communicate any proposed amendments to the States Parties to the present Covenant with a request that they notify him whether they favour a conference of States Parties for the purpose of considering and voting upon the proposals. In the event that at least one third of the States Parties favours such a conference, the Secretary–General shall convene the conference under the auspices of the United Nations. Any amendment adopted by a majority of the States Parties present and voting at the conference shall be submitted to the General Assembly of the United Nations for approval.

2. Amendments shall come into force when they have been approved by the General Assembly of the United Nations and accepted by a

two-thirds majority of the States Parties to the present Covenant in accordance with their respective constitutional processes.

3. When amendments come into force they shall be binding on those States Parties which have accepted them, other States Parties still being bound by the provisions of the present Covenant and any earlier amendment which they have accepted.

Article 30

Irrespective of the notifications made under Article 26, paragraph 5, the of the United Nations shall inform all States referred to in paragraph 1 of the following particulars:

(a) Signatures, ratifications and accessions under Article 26;

(b) The date of the entry into force of the present Covenant under Article 27 and the date of the entry into force of any amendments under Article 29.

Article 31

1. The present Covenant, of which the Chinese, English, French, Russian and Spanish texts are equally authentic, shall be deposited in the archives of the United Nations.

2. The Secretary–General of the United Nations shall transmit certified copies of the present Covenant to all States referred to in Article 26.

Document 15
PROCEDURE FOR DEALING WITH COMMUNICATIONS RELATING TO VIOLATIONS OF HUMAN RIGHTS AND FUNDAMENTAL FREEDOMS

E.S.C. Res. 1503, 48 U.N. ESCOR Supp. No. 1A, at 8, U.N. Doc. E/4832/Add.1 (1970)

The Economic and Social Council,

Noting resolutions 7 (XXVI) and 17 (XXV) of the Commission on Human Rights and resolution 2 (XXI) of the Sub–Commission on Prevention of Discrimination and Protection of Minorities,

1. *Authorizes* the Sub–Commission on Prevention of Discrimination and Protection of Minorities to appoint a working group consisting of not more than five of its members, with due regard to geographical distribution, to meet once a year in private meetings for a period not exceeding ten days immediately before the sessions of the Sub–Commission to consider all communications, including replies of Governments thereon, received by the Secretary–General under Council resolution 728 F (XXVIII) of 30 July 1959 with a view to bringing to the attention of the Sub–Commission those communications, together with replies of Governments, if any, which appear to reveal a consistent pattern of gross and reliably attested violations of human rights and fundamental freedoms within the terms of reference of the Sub–Commission;

2. *Decides* that the Sub–Commission on Prevention of Discrimination and Protection of Minorities should, as the first stage in the implementation of the present resolution, devise at its twenty-third session appropriate procedures for dealing with the question of admissibility of communications received by the Secretary–General under Council resolution 728 F (XXVIII) and in accordance with Council resolution 1235 (XLII) of 6 June 1967;

3. *Requests* the Secretary–General to prepare a document on the question of admissibility of communications for the Sub–Commission's consideration at its twenty-third session;

4. *Further requests* the Secretary–General:

(a) To furnish to the members of the Sub–Commission every month a list of communications prepared by him in accordance with Council resolution 728 F (XXVIII) and a brief description of them, together with the text of any replies received from Governments;

(b) To make available to the members of the working group at their meetings the originals of such communications listed as they may request, having due regard to the provisions of paragraph 2(b) of Council resolution 728 F (XXVIII) concerning the divulging of the identity of the authors of communications;

(c) To circulate to the members of the Sub–Commission, in the working languages, the originals of such communications as are referred to the Sub–Commission by the working group;

5. *Requests* the Sub–Commission on Prevention of Discrimination and Protection of Minorities to consider in private meetings, in accordance with paragraph 1 above, the communications brought before it in accordance with the decision of a majority of the members of the working group and any replies of Governments relating thereto and other relevant information, with a view to determining whether to refer to the Commission on Human Rights particular situations which appear to reveal a consistent pattern of gross and reliably attested violations of human rights requiring consideration by the Commission;

6. *Requests* the Commission on Human Rights after it has examined any situation referred to it by the Sub–Commission to determine:

(a) Whether it requires a thorough study by the Commission and a report and recommendations thereon to the Council in accordance with paragraph 3 of Council resolution 1235 (XLII);

(b) Whether it may be a subject of an investigation by an ad hoc committee to be appointed by the Commission which shall be undertaken only with the express consent of the State concerned and shall be conducted in constant co-operation with that State and under conditions determined by agreement with it. In any event, the investigation may be undertaken only if:

(i) All available means at the national level have been resorted to and exhausted;

(ii) The situation does not relate to a matter which is being dealt with under other procedures prescribed in the constituent instruments of, or conventions adopted by, the United Nations and the specialized agencies, or in regional conventions, or which the State concerned wishes to submit to other procedures in accordance with general or special international agreements to which it is a party.

7. *Decides* that if the Commission on Human Rights appoints an ad hoc committee to carry on an investigation with the consent of the State concerned:

(a) The composition of the committee shall be determined by the Commission. The members of the committee shall be independent persons whose competence and impartiality is beyond question. Their appointment shall be subject to the consent of the Government concerned;

(b) The committee shall establish its own rules of procedure. It shall be subject to the quorum rule. It shall have authority to receive communications and hear witnesses, as necessary. The investigation shall be conducted in co-operation with the Government concerned;

(c) The committee's procedure shall be confidential, its proceedings shall be conducted in private meetings and its communications shall not he publicized in any way;

(d) The committee shall strive for friendly solutions before, during and even after the investigation;

(e) The committee shall report to the Commission on Human Rights with such observations and suggestions as it may deem appropriate;

8. *Decides* that all actions envisaged in the implementation of the present resolution by the Sub–Commission on Prevention of Discrimination and Protection of Minorities or the Commission on Human Rights shall remain confidential until such time as the Commission may decide to make recommendations to the Economic and Social Council;

9. *Decides* to authorize the Secretary–General to provide all facilities which may be required to carry out the present resolution, making use of the existing staff of the Division of Human Rights of the United Nations Secretariat;

10. *Decides* that the procedure set out in the present resolution for dealing with communications relating to violations of human rights and fundamental freedoms should be reviewed if any new organ entitled to deal with such communications should be established within the United Nations or by international agreement.

Document 16
AMERICAN DECLARATION OF THE RIGHTS AND DUTIES OF MAN

O.A.S. Res. XXX (1948), O.A.S. Off. Rec. OEA/Ser. L/V/I.4 Rev. (1965)

Preamble

All men are born free and equal, in dignity and in rights, and, being endowed by nature with reason and conscience, they should conduct themselves as brothers one to another.

The fulfillment of duty by each individual is a prerequisite to the rights of all. Rights and duties are interrelated in every social and political activity of man. While rights exalt individual liberty, duties express the dignity of that liberty.

Duties of a juridical nature presuppose others of a moral nature which support them in principle and constitute their basis.

Inasmuch as spiritual development is the supreme end of human existence and the highest expression thereof, it is the duty of man to serve that end with all his strength and resources.

Since culture is the highest social and historical expression of that spiritual development, it is the duty of man to preserve, practice and foster culture by every means within his power.

And, since moral conduct constitutes the noblest flowering of culture, it is the duty of every man always to hold it in high respect.

CHAPTER ONE. RIGHTS

Article I. Every human being has the right to life, liberty and the security of his person.

Article II. All persons are equal before the law and have the rights and duties established in this Declaration, without distinction as to race, sex, language, creed or any other factor.

Article III. Every person has the right freely to profess a religious faith, and to manifest and practice it both in public and in private.

Article IV. Every person has the right to freedom of investigation, of opinion, and of the expression and dissemination of ideas, by any medium whatsoever.

Article V. Every person has the right to the protection of the law against abusive attacks upon his honor, his reputation, and his private and family life.

Article VI. Every person has the right to establish a family, the basic element of society, and to receive protection therefor.

Article VII. All women, during pregnancy and the nursing period, and all children have the right to special protection, care and aid.

Article VIII. Every person has the right to fix his residence within the territory of the state of which he is a national, to move about freely within such territory, and not to leave it except by his own will.

Article IX. Every person has the right to the inviolability of his home.

Article X. Every person has the right to the inviolability and transmission of his correspondence.

Article XI. Every person has the right to the preservation of his health through sanitary and social measures relating to food, clothing, housing and medical care, to the extent permitted by public and community resources.

Article XII. Every person has the right to an education, which should be based on the principles of liberty, morality and human solidarity.

Likewise every person has the right to an education that will prepare him to attain a decent life, to raise his standard of living, and to be a useful member of society.

The right to an education includes the right to equality of opportunity in every case in accordance with natural talents, merit and the desire to utilize the resources that the state or the community is in a position to provide.

Every person has the right to receive, free, at least a primary education.

Article XIII. Every person has the right to take part in the cultural life of the community, to enjoy the arts, and to participate in the benefits that result from intellectual progress, especially scientific discoveries.

He likewise has the right to the protection of his moral and material interests as regards his inventions or any literary, scientific or artistic works of which he is the author.

Article XIV. Every person has the right to work, under proper conditions, and to follow his vocation freely, in so far as existing conditions of employment permit.

Every person who works has the right to receive such remuneration as will, in proportion to his capacity and skill, assure him a standard of living suitable for himself and for his family.

Article XV. Every person has the right to leisure time, to wholesome recreation, and to the opportunity for advantageous use of his free time to his spiritual, cultural and physical benefit.

Article XVI. Every person has the right to social security which will protect him from the consequences of unemployment, old age, and any disability arising from causes beyond his control that make it physically or mentally impossible for him to earn a living.

Article XVII. Every person has the right to be recognized everywhere as a person having rights and obligations, and to enjoy the basic civil rights.

Article XVIII. Every person may resort to the courts to ensure respect for his legal rights. There should likewise be available to him a simple, brief procedure whereby the courts will protect him from acts of authority that, to his prejudice, violate any fundamental constitutional rights.

Article XIX. Every person has the right to the nationality to which he is entitled by law and to change it, if he so wishes, for the nationality of any other country that is willing to grant it to him.

Article XX. Every person having legal capacity is entitled to participate in the government of his country, directly or through his representatives, and to take part in popular elections, which shall be by secret ballot, and shall be honest, periodic and free.

Article XXI. Every person has the right to assemble peaceably with others in a formal public meeting or an informal gathering, in connection with matters of common interest of any nature.

Article XXII. Every person has the right to associate with others to promote, exercise and protect his legitimate interests of a political, economic, religious, social, cultural, professional, labor union or other nature.

Article XXIII. Every person has a right to own such private property as meets the essential needs of decent living and helps to maintain the dignity of the individual and of the home.

Article XXIV. Every person has the right to submit respectful petitions to any competent authority, for reasons of either general or private interest, and the right to obtain a prompt decision thereon.

Article XXV. No person may be deprived of his liberty except in the cases and according to the procedures established by pre-existing law.

No person may be deprived of liberty for nonfulfillment of obligations of a purely civil character.

Every individual who has been deprived of his liberty has the right to have the legality of his detention ascertained without delay by a court, and the right to be tried without undue delay, or otherwise, to be released. He also has the right to humane treatment during the time he is in custody.

Article XXVI. Every accused person is presumed to be innocent until proved guilty.

Every person accused of an offense has the right to be given an impartial and public hearing, and to be tried by courts previously established in accordance with pre-existing laws, and not to receive cruel, infamous or unusual punishment.

Article XXVII. Every person has the right, in case of pursuit not resulting from ordinary crimes, to seek and receive asylum in foreign territory, in accordance with the laws of each country and with international agreements.

Article XXVIII. The rights of man are limited by the rights of others, by the security of all, and by the just demands of the general welfare and the advancement of democracy.

CHAPTER TWO. DUTIES

Article XXIX. It is the duty of the individual so to conduct himself in relation to others that each and every one may fully form and develop his personality.

Article XXX. It is the duty of every person to aid, support, educate and protect his minor children, and it is the duty of children to honor their parents always and to aid, support and protect them when they need it.

Article XXXI. It is the duty of every person to acquire at least an elementary education.

Article XXXII. It is the duty of every person to vote in the popular elections of the country of which he is a national, when he is legally capable of doing so.

Article XXXIII. It is the duty of every person to obey the law and other legitimate commands of the authorities of his country and those of the country in which he may be.

Article XXXIV. It is the duty of every able-bodied person to render whatever civil and military service his country may require for its defense and preservation, and, in case of public disaster, to render such services as may be in his power.

It is likewise his duty to hold any public office to which he may be elected by popular vote in the state of which he is a national.

Article XXXV. It is the duty of every person to cooperate with the state with respect to social security and welfare, in accordance with existing circumstances.

Article XXXVI. It is the duty of every person to pay the taxes established by law for the support of public services.

Article XXXVII. It is the duty of every person to work, as far as his capacity and possibilities permit, in order to obtain the means of livelihood or to benefit his community.

Article XXXVIII. It is the duty of every person to refrain from taking part in political activities that, according to law, are reserved exclusively to the citizens of the state in which he is an alien.

Document 17
AMERICAN CONVENTION ON HUMAN RIGHTS

O.A.S. Treaty Ser. No. 36 (1969), 144 U.N.T.S. 123

Preamble

The American states signatory to this present Convention,

Reaffirming their intention to consolidate in this hemisphere, within the framework of democratic institutions, a system of personal liberty and social justice based on respect for the essential rights of man;

Recognizing that the essential rights of man are not derived from one's being a national of a certain state, but are based upon attributes of the human personality, and that they therefore justify international protection in the form of a convention reinforcing or complementing the protection provided by the domestic law of the American states;

Considering that these principles have been set forth in the Charter of the Organization of American States, in the American Declaration of the Rights and Duties of Man, and in the Universal Declaration of Human Rights, and that they have been reaffirmed and refined in other international instruments, worldwide as well as regional in scope;

Reiterating that, in accordance with the Universal Declaration of Human Rights, the ideal of free men enjoying freedom from fear and want can be achieved only if conditions are created whereby everyone may enjoy his economic, social, and cultural rights, as well as his civil and political rights; and

Considering that the Third Special Inter–American Conference (Buenos Aires, 1967) approved the incorporation into the Charter of the Organization itself of broader standards with respect to economic, social, and educational rights and resolved that an inter-American convention on human rights should determine the structure, competence, and procedure of the organs responsible for these matters,

Have agreed upon the following:

PART I. STATE OBLIGATIONS AND RIGHTS PROTECTED

CHAPTER I. GENERAL OBLIGATIONS

Article 1. Obligation to Respect Rights

1. The States Parties to this Convention undertake to respect the rights and freedoms recognized herein and to ensure to all persons subject to their jurisdiction the free and full exercise of those rights and freedoms, without any discrimination for reasons of race, color, sex, language, religion, political or other opinion, national or social origin, economic status, birth, or any other social condition.

2. For the purposes of this Convention, "person" means every human being.

Article 2. Domestic Legal Effects

Where the exercise of any of the rights or freedoms referred to in Article 1 is not already ensured by legislative or other provisions, the States Parties undertake to adopt, in accordance with their constitutional processes and the provisions of this Convention, such legislative or other measures as may be necessary to give effect to those rights or freedoms.

CHAPTER II. CIVIL AND POLITICAL RIGHTS

Article 3. Right to Juridical Personality

Every person has the right to recognition as a person before the law.

Article 4. Right to Life

1. Every person has the right to have his life respected. This right shall be protected by law, and, in general, from the moment of conception. No one shall be arbitrarily deprived of his life.

2. In countries that have not abolished the death penalty, it may be imposed only for the most serious crimes and pursuant to a final judgment rendered by a competent court and in accordance with a law establishing such punishment, enacted prior to the commission of the crime. The application of such punishment shall not be extended to crimes to which it does not presently apply.

3. The death penalty shall not be reestablished in states that have abolished it.

4. In no case shall capital punishment be inflicted for political offences or related common crimes.

5. Capital punishment shall not be imposed upon persons who, at the time the crime was committed, were under 18 years of age or over 70 years of age; nor shall it be applied to pregnant women.

6. Every person condemned to death shall have the right to apply for amnesty, pardon, or commutation of sentence, which may be granted in all cases. Capital punishment shall not be imposed while such a petition is pending decision by the competent authority.

Article 5. Right to Humane Treatment

1. Every person has the right to have his physical, mental, and moral integrity respected.

2. No one shall be subjected to torture or to cruel, inhuman, or degrading punishment or treatment. All persons deprived of their liberty shall be treated with respect for the inherent dignity of the human person.

3. Punishment shall not be extended to any person other than the criminal.

4. Accused persons shall, save in exceptional circumstances, be segregated from convicted persons, and shall be subject to separate treatment appropriate to their status as unconvicted persons.

5. Minors while subject to criminal proceedings shall be separated from adults and brought before specialized tribunals, as speedily as possible, so that they may be treated in accordance with their status as minors.

6. Punishments consisting of deprivation of liberty shall have as an essential aim the reform and social readaptation of the prisoners.

Article 6. Freedom from Slavery

1. No one shall be subject to slavery or to involuntary servitude, which are prohibited in all their forms, as are the slave trade and traffic in women.

2. No one shall be required to perform forced or compulsory labor. This provision shall not be interpreted to mean that, in those countries in which the penalty established for certain crimes is deprivation of liberty at forced labor, the carrying out of such a sentence imposed by a competent court is prohibited. Forced labor shall not adversely affect the dignity or the physical or intellectual capacity of the prisoner.

3. For the purposes of this article the following do not constitute forced or compulsory labor:

(a) work or service normally required of a person imprisoned in execution of a sentence or formal decision passed by the competent judicial authority. Such work or service shall be carried out under the supervision and control of public authorities, and any persons performing such work or service shall not be placed at the disposal of any private party, company, or juridical person;

(b) military service and, in countries in which conscientious objectors are recognized, national service that the law may provide for in lieu of military service;

(c) service exacted in time of danger or calamity that threatens the existence or the well-being of the community; or

(d) work or service that forms part of normal civil obligations.

Article 7. Right to Personal Liberty

1. Every person has the right to personal liberty and security.

2. No one shall be deprived of his physical liberty except for the reasons and under the conditions established beforehand by the constitution of the State Party concerned or by a law established pursuant thereto.

3. No one shall be subject to arbitrary arrest or imprisonment.

4. Anyone who is detained shall be informed of the reasons for his detention and shall be promptly notified of the charge or charges against him.

5. Any person detained shall be brought promptly before a judge or other officer authorized by law to exercise judicial power and shall be entitled to trial within a reasonable time or to be released without prejudice to the continuation of the proceedings. His release may be subject to guarantees to assure his appearance for trial.

6. Anyone who is deprived of his liberty shall be entitled to recourse to a competent court, in order that the court may decide without delay on the lawfulness of his arrest or detention and order his release if the arrest or detention is unlawful. In States Parties whose laws provide that anyone who believes himself to be threatened with deprivation of his liberty is entitled to recourse to a competent court in order that it may decide on the lawfulness of such threat, this remedy may not be restricted or abolished. The interested party or another person in his behalf is entitled to seek these remedies.

7. No one shall be detained for debt. This principle shall not limit the orders of a competent judicial authority issued for nonfulfillment of duties of support.

Article 8. Right to a Fair Trial

1. Every person has the right to a hearing, with due guarantees and within a reasonable time, by a competent, independent, and impartial tribunal, previously established by law, in the substantiation of any accusation of a criminal nature made against him or for the determination of his rights and obligations of a civil, labor, fiscal, or any other nature.

2. Every person accused of a criminal offense has the right to be presumed innocent so long as his guilt has not been proven according to law. During the proceedings, every person is entitled, with full equality, to the following minimum guarantees:

(a) the right of the accused to be assisted without charge by a translator or interpreter, if he does not understand or does not speak the language of the tribunal or court;

(b) prior notification in detail to the accused of the charges against him;

(c) adequate time and means for the preparation of his defense;

(d) the right of the accused to defend himself personally or to be assisted by legal counsel of his own choosing, and to communicate freely and privately with his counsel;

(e) the inalienable right to be assisted by counsel provided by the state, paid or not as the domestic law provides, if the accused does not defend himself personally or engage his own counsel within the time period established by law;

(f) the right of the defense to examine witnesses present in the court and to obtain the appearance, as witnesses, of experts or other persons who may throw light on the facts;

(g) the right not to be compelled to be a witness against himself or to plead guilty; and

(h) the right to appeal the judgment to a higher court.

3. A confession of guilt by the accused shall be valid only if it is made without coercion of any kind.

4. An accused person acquitted by a nonappealable judgment shall not be subjected to a new trial for the same cause.

5. Criminal proceedings shall be public, except insofar as may be necessary to protect the interests of justice.

Article 9. Freedom from Ex Post Facto Laws

No one shall be convicted of any act or omission that did not constitute a criminal offense, under the applicable law, at the time it was committed. A heavier penalty shall not be imposed than the one that was applicable at the time the criminal offense was committed. If subsequent to the commission of the offense the law provides for the imposition of a lighter punishment, the guilty person shall benefit therefrom.

Article 10. Right to Compensation

Every person has the right to be compensated in accordance with the law in the event he has been sentenced by a final judgment through a miscarriage of justice.

Article 11. Right to Privacy

1. Everyone has the right to have his honor respected and his dignity recognized.

2. No one may be the object of arbitrary or abusive interference with his private life, his family, his home, or his correspondence, or of unlawful attacks on his honor or reputation.

3. Everyone has the right to the protection of the law against such interference or attacks.

Article 12. Freedom of Conscience and Religion

1. Everyone has the right to freedom of conscience and religion. this right includes freedom to maintain or to change one's religion or beliefs, and freedom to profess or disseminate one's religion or beliefs either individually or together with others, in public or in private.

2. No one shall be subject to restrictions that might impair his freedom to maintain or to change his religion or beliefs.

3. Freedom to manifest one's religion and beliefs may be subject only to the limitations prescribed by law that are necessary to protect public safety, order, health, or morals, or the rights or freedoms of others.

4. Parents or guardians, as the case may be, have the right to provide for the religious and moral education of their children or wards that is in accord with their own convictions.

Article 13. Freedom of Thought and Expression

1. Everyone shall have the right to freedom of thought and expression. This right shall include freedom to seek, receive, and impart information and ideas of all kinds, regardless of frontiers, either orally, in writing, in print, in the form of art, or through any other medium of his choice.

2. The exercise of the right provided for in the foregoing paragraph shall not be subject to prior censorship but shall be subject to subsequent imposition of liability, which shall be expressly established by law to the extent necessary in order to ensure:

(a) respect for the rights or reputations of others; or

(b) the protection of national security, public order, or public health or morals.

3. The right of expression may not be restricted by indirect methods or means, such as the abuse of government or private controls over newsprint, radio broadcasting frequencies, or equipment used in the dissemination of information, or by any other means tending to impede the communication and circulation of ideas and opinions.

4. Notwithstanding the provisions of paragraph 2 above, public entertainments may be subject by law to prior censorship for the sole purpose of regulating access to them for the moral protection of childhood and adolescence.

5. Any propaganda for war and any advocacy of national, racial, or religious hatred that constitute incitements to lawless violence or to any other similar illegal action against any person or group of persons on any grounds including those of race, color, religion, language, or national origin shall be considered as offenses punishable by law.

Article 14. Right of Reply

1. Anyone injured by inaccurate or offensive statements or ideas disseminated to the public in general by a legally regulated medium of communication has the right to reply or make a correction using the same communications outlet, under such conditions as the law may establish.

2. The correction or reply shall not in any case remit other legal liabilities that may have been incurred.

3. For the effective protection of honor and reputation, every publisher, and every newspaper, motion picture, radio, and television company, shall have a person responsible, who is not protected by immunities or special privileges.

Article 15. Right of Assembly

The right of peaceful assembly, without arms, is recognized. No restrictions may be placed on the exercise of this right other than those imposed in conformity with the law and necessary in a democratic society in the interest of national security, public safety, or public order, or to protect public health, or morals or the rights or freedoms of others.

Article 16. Freedom of Association

1. Everyone has the right to associate freely for ideological, religious, political, economic, labor, social, cultural, sports, or other purposes.

2. The exercise of this right shall be subject only to such restrictions established by law as may be necessary in a democratic society, in the interest of national security, public safety, or public order, or to protect public health or morals or the rights and freedoms of others.

3. The provisions of this article do not bar the imposition of legal restrictions, including even deprivation of the exercise of the right of association, on members of the armed forces and the police.

Article 17. Rights of the Family

1. The family is the natural and fundamental group unit of society and is entitled to protection by society and the state.

2. The right of men and women of marriageable age to marry and to raise a family shall be recognized, if they meet the conditions required by domestic laws, insofar as such conditions do not affect the principle of nondiscrimination established in this Convention.

3. No marriage shall be entered into without the free and full consent of the intending spouses.

4. The States Parties shall take appropriate steps to ensure the equality of rights and the adequate balancing of responsibilities of the spouses as to marriage, during marriage, and in the event of its dissolution. In case of dissolution, provision shall be made for the necessary protection of any children solely on the basis of their own best interests.

5. The law shall recognize equal rights for children born out of wedlock and those born in wedlock.

Article 18. Right to a Name

Every person has the right to a given name and to the surnames of his parents or that of one of them. The law shall regulate the manner in which this right shall be ensured for all, by the use of assumed names if necessary.

Article 19. Rights of the Child

Every minor child has the right to the measures of protection required by his condition as a minor on the part of his family, society, and the state.

Article 20. Right to Nationality

1. Every person has the right to a nationality.

2. Every person has the right to the nationality of the state in whose territory he was born if he does not have the right to any other nationality.

3. No one shall be arbitrarily deprived of his nationality or of the right to change it.

Article 21. Right to Property

1. Everyone has the right to the use and enjoyment of his property. The law may subordinate such use and enjoyment to the interest of society.

2. No one shall be deprived of his property except upon payment of just compensation, for reasons of public utility or social interest, and in the cases and according to the forms established by law.

3. Usury and any other form of exploitation of man by man shall be prohibited by law.

Article 22. Freedom of Movement and Residence

1. Every person lawfully in the territory of a State Party has the right to move about in it and to reside in it subject to the provisions of the law.

2. Every person has the right to leave any country freely, including his own.

3. The exercise of the foregoing rights may be restricted only pursuant to a law to the extent necessary in a democratic society to prevent crime or to protect national security, public safety, public order, public morals, public health, or the rights or freedoms of others.

4. The exercise of the rights recognized in paragraph 1 may also be restricted by law in designated zones for reasons of public interest.

5. No one can be expelled from the territory of the state of which he is a national or be deprived of the right to enter it.

6. An alien lawfully in the territory of a State Party to this Convention may be expelled from it only pursuant to a decision reached in accordance with law.

7. Every person has the right to seek and be granted asylum in a foreign territory, in accordance with the legislation of the state and international conventions, in the event he is being pursued for political offenses or related common crimes.

8. In no case may an alien be deported or returned to a country, regardless of whether or not it is his country of origin, if in that country his right to life or personal freedom is in danger of being violated because of his race, nationality, religion, social status, or political opinions.

9. The collective expulsion of aliens is prohibited.

Article 23. Right to Participate in Government

1. Every citizen shall enjoy the following rights and opportunities:

(a) to take part in the conduct of public affairs, directly or through freely chosen representatives;

(b) to vote and to be elected in genuine periodic elections, which shall be by universal and equal suffrage and by secret ballot that guarantees the free expression of the will of the voters; and

(c) to have access, under general conditions of equality, to the public services of his country.

2. The law may regulate the exercise of the rights and opportunities referred to in the preceding paragraph only on the basis of age, nationality, residence, language, education, civil and mental capacity, or sentencing by a competent court in criminal proceedings.

Article 24. Right to Equal Protection

All persons are equal before the law. Consequently, they are entitled, without discrimination, to equal protection of the law.

Article 25. Right to Judicial Protection

1. Everyone has the right to simple and prompt recourse, or any other effective recourse, to a competent court or tribunal for protection against acts that violate his fundamental rights recognized by the constitution or laws of the state concerned or by this Convention, even though such violation may have been committed by persons acting in the course of their official duties.

2. The States Parties undertake:

(a) to ensure that any person claiming such remedy shall have his rights determined by the competent authority provided for by the legal system of the state;

(b) to develop the possibilities of judicial remedy; and

(c) to ensure that the competent authorities shall enforce such remedies when granted.

CHAPTER III. ECONOMIC, SOCIAL, AND CULTURAL RIGHTS

Article 26. Progressive Development

The States Parties undertake to adopt measures, both internally and through international cooperation, especially those of an economic and technical nature, with a view to achieving progressively, by legislation or other appropriate means, the full realization of the rights implicit in the economic, social, educational, scientific, and cultural standards set forth in the Charter of the Organization of American States as amended by the Protocol of Buenos Aires.

CHAPTER IV. SUSPENSION OF GUARANTEES, INTERPRETATION, AND APPLICATION

Article 27. Suspension of Guarantees

1. In time of war, public danger, or other emergency that threatens the independence or security of a State Party, it may take measures derogating from its obligations under the present Convention to the extent and for the period of time strictly required by the exigencies of the situation, provided that such measures are not inconsistent with its other obligations under international law and do not involve discrimination on the ground of race, color, sex, language, religion, or social origin.

2. The foregoing provision does not authorize any suspension of the following articles: Article 3 (Right to Juridical Personality), Article 4 (Right to Life), Article 5 (Right to Humane Treatment), Article 6 (Freedom from Slavery), Article 9 (Freedom from Ex Post Facto Laws), Article 12 (Freedom of Conscience and Religion), Article 17 (Rights of the Family), Article 18 (Right to a Name), Article 19 (Rights of the Child), Article 20 (Right to Nationality), and Article 23 (Right to Participate in Government), or of the judicial guarantees essential for the protection of such rights.

3. Any State Party availing itself of the right of suspension shall immediately inform the other States Parties, through the Secretary General of the Organization of American States, of the provisions the application of which it has suspended, the reasons that gave rise to the suspension, and the date set for the termination of such suspension.

Article 28. Federal Clause

1. Where a State Party is constituted as a federal state, the national government of such State Party shall implement all the provisions of the Convention over whose subject matter it exercises legislative and judicial jurisdiction.

2. With respect to the provisions over whose subject matter the constituent units of the federal state have jurisdiction, the national government shall immediately take suitable measures, in accordance with its constitution and its laws, to the end that the competent authorities of the constituent units may adopt appropriate provisions for the fulfillment of this Convention.

3. Whenever two or more States Parties agree to form a federation or other type of association, they shall take care that the resulting federal or other compact contains the provisions necessary for continuing and rendering effective the standards of this Convention in the new state that is organized.

Article 29. Restrictions Regarding Interpretation

No provision of this Convention shall be interpreted as:

(a) permitting any State Party, group, or person to suppress the enjoyment or exercise of the rights and freedoms recognized in this Convention or to restrict them to a greater extent than is provided for herein;

(b) restricting the enjoyment or exercise of any right or freedom recognized by virtue of the laws of any State Party or by virtue of another convention to which one of the said states is a party;

(c) precluding other rights or guarantees that are inherent in the human personality or derived from representative democracy as a form of government; or

(d) excluding or limiting the effect that the American Declaration of the Rights and Duties of Man and other international acts of the same nature may have.

Article 30. Scope of Restrictions

The restrictions that, pursuant to this Convention, may be placed on the enjoyment or exercise of the rights or freedoms recognized herein may not be applied except in accordance with laws enacted for reasons of general interest and in accordance with the purpose for which such restrictions have been established.

Article 31. Recognition of Other Rights

Other rights and freedoms recognized in accordance with the procedures established in Articles 76 and 77 may be included in the system of protection of this Convention.

CHAPTER V. PERSONAL RESPONSIBILITIES

Article 32. Relationship Between Duties and Rights

1. Every person has responsibilities to his family, his community, and mankind.

2. The rights of each person are limited by the rights of others, by the security of all, and by the just demands of the general welfare, in a democratic society.

PART III. MEANS OF PROTECTION

CHAPTER VI. COMPETENT ORGANS

Article 33

The following organs shall have competence with respect to matters relating to the fulfillment of the commitments made by the States Parties to this Convention:

(a) the Inter–American Commission on Human Rights, referred to as "The Commission"; and

(b) the Inter–American Court of Human Rights, referred to as "The Court."

CHAPTER VII. INTER–AMERICAN COMMISSION ON HUMAN RIGHTS

Section 1. Organization

Article 34

The Inter–American Commission on Human Rights shall be composed of seven members, who shall be persons of high moral character and recognized competence in the field of human rights.

Article 35

The Commission shall represent all the member countries of the Organization of American States.

Article 36

1. The Members of the Commission shall be elected in a personal capacity by the General Assembly of the Organization from a list of candidates proposed by the governments of the member states. . . .

Section 2. Functions

Article 41

The main functions of the Commission shall be to promote respect for and defense of human rights. In the exercise of its mandate it shall have the following functions and powers:

(a) to develop an awareness of human rights among the peoples of America;

(b) to make recommendations to the governments of the member states, when it considers such action advisable, for the adoption of progressive measures in favor of human rights within the framework of their domestic law and constitutional provisions as well as appropriate measures to further the observance of those rights;

(c) to prepare such studies or reports as it considers advisable in the performance of its duties;

(d) to request the governments of the member states to supply it with information on the measures adopted by them in matters of human rights;

(e) to respond, through the General Secretariat of the Organization of American States, to inquiries made by the member states on matters related to human rights and, within the limits of its possibilities, to provide those states with the advisory services they request;

(f) to take action on petitions and other communications pursuant to its authority, under the provisions of Article 44 through 51 of this Convention; and

(g) to submit an annual report to the General Assembly of the Organization of American States.

Article 42

The States Parties shall transmit to the Commission a copy of each of the reports and studies that they submit annually to the Executive Committees of the Inter–American Economic and Social Council and the Inter–American Council for Education, Science, and Culture, in their respective fields, so that the Commission may watch over the promotion of the rights implicit in the economic, social, educational, scientific, and cultural standards set forth in the Charter of the Organization of American States as amended by the Protocol of Buenos Aires.

Article 43

The States Parties undertake to provide the Commission with such information as it may request of them as to the manner in which their domestic law ensures the effective application of any provisions of this Convention.

Section 3. Competence

Article 44

Any person or group of persons, or any nongovernmental entity legally recognized in one or more member states of the Organization, may lodge petitions with the Commission containing denunciations or complaints of violation of this Convention by a State Party.

Article 45

1. Any State Party may, when it deposits its instrument of ratification of or adherence to this Convention, or at any later time, declare that it recognizes the competence of the Commission to receive and examine communications in which a State Party alleges that another State Party has committed a violation of a human right set forth in this Convention.

2. Communications presented by virtue of this article may be admitted and examined only if they are presented by a State Party that has made a declaration recognizing the aforementioned competence of the Commission. The Commission shall not admit any communication against a State Party that has not made such a declaration.

3. A declaration concerning recognition of competence may be made to be valid for an indefinite time, for a specified period, or for a specific case.

4. Declarations shall be deposited with the General Secretariat of the Organization of American States, which shall transmit copies thereof to the member states of that Organization.

Article 46

1. Admission by the Commission of a petition or communication lodged in accordance with Articles 44 or 45 shall be subject to the following requirements:

(a) that the remedies under domestic law have been pursued and exhausted, in accordance with generally recognized principles of international law;

(b) that the petition or communication is lodged within a period of six months from the date on which the party alleging violation of his rights was notified of the final judgment;

(c) that the subject of the petition or communication is not pending before another international procedure for settlement; and

(d) that, in the case of Article 44, the petition contains the name, nationality, profession, domicile, and signature of the person or persons or of the legal representative of the entity lodging the petition.

2. The provisions of paragraphs 1 (a) and 1 (b) of this article shall not be applicable when:

(a) the domestic legislation of the state concerned does not afford due process of law for the protection of the right or rights that have allegedly been violated;

(b) the party alleging violation of his rights has been denied access to the remedies under domestic law or has been prevented from exhausting them; or

(c) there has been unwarranted delay in rendering a final judgment under the aforementioned remedies.

Article 47

The Commission shall consider inadmissible any petition or communication submitted under Articles 44 or 45 if:

(a) any of the requirements indicated in Article 46 has not been met;

(b) the petition or communication does not state facts that tend to establish a violation of the rights guaranteed by this Convention;

(c) the statements of the petitioner or of the state indicate that the petition or communication is manifestly groundless or obviously out of order; or

(d) the petition or communication is substantially the same as one previously studied by the Commission or by another international organization.

Section 4. Procedure

Article 48

1. When the Commission receives a petition or communication alleging violation of any of the rights protected by this Convention, it shall proceed as follows:

(a) If it considers the petition or communication admissible, it shall request information from the government of the state indicated as being responsible for the alleged violations and shall furnish that government a transcript of the pertinent portions of the petition or communication. This information shall be submitted within a reasonable period to be determined by the Commission in accordance with the circumstances of each case.

(b) After the information has been received, or after the period established has elapsed and the information has not been received, the Commission shall ascertain whether the grounds for the petition or communication still exist. If they do not, the Commission shall order the record to be closed.

(c) The Commission may also declare the petition or communication inadmissible or out of order on the basis of information or evidence subsequently received.

(d) If the record has not been closed, the Commission shall, with the knowledge of the parties, examine the matter set forth in the petition or communication in order to verify the facts. If necessary and advisable, the Commission shall carry out an investigation, for the effective conduct of which it shall request, and the state concerned shall furnish to it, all necessary facilities.

(e) The Commission may request the states concerned to furnish any pertinent information and, if so requested, shall hear oral statements or receive written statements from the parties concerned.

(f) The Commission shall place itself at the disposal of the parties concerned with a view to reaching a friendly settlement of the matter on the basis of respect for the human rights recognized in this Convention.

2. However, in serious and urgent cases, only the presentation of a petition or communication that fulfills all the formal requirements of admissibility shall be necessary in order for the Commission to conduct an investigation with the prior consent of the state in whose territory a violation has allegedly been committed.

Article 49

If a friendly settlement has been reached in accordance with paragraph 1 (f) of Article 48, the Commission shall draw up a report, which shall be transmitted to the petitioner and to the States Parties to this Convention, and shall then be communicated to the Secretary General of the Organization of American States for publication. This report shall contain a brief statement of the facts and of the solution reached. If any party in the case so requests, the fullest possible information shall be provided to it.

Article 50

1. If a settlement is not reached, the Commission shall, within the time limit established by its Statute, draw up a report setting forth the facts and stating its conclusions. If the report, in whole or in part, does not represent the unanimous agreement of the members of the Commission, any member may attach to it a separate opinion. The written and oral statements made by the parties in accordance with paragraph 1 (e) of Article 48 shall also be attached to the report.

2. The report shall be transmitted to the states concerned, which shall not be at liberty to publish it.

3. In transmitting the report, the Committee may make such proposals and recommendations as it sees fit.

Article 51

1. If, within a period of three months from the date of the transmittal of the report of the Commission to the states concerned, the matter has not either been settled or submitted by the Commission or by the state concerned to the Court and its jurisdiction accepted, the Commission may, by the vote of an absolute majority of its members, set forth its opinion and conclusions concerning the question submitted for its consideration.

2. Where appropriate, the Commission shall make pertinent recommendations and shall prescribe a period within which the state is to take the measures that are incumbent upon it to remedy the situation examined.

3. When the prescribed period has expired, the Commission shall decide by the vote of an absolute majority of its members whether the state has taken adequate measures and whether to publish its report.

CHAPTER VIII. INTER–AMERICAN COURT OF HUMAN RIGHTS

Section 1. Organization

Article 52

1. The Court shall consist of seven judges, nationals of the member states of the Organization, elected in an individual capacity from among jurists of the highest moral authority and of recognized competence in the field of human rights, who possess the qualifications required for the exercise of the highest judicial functions in conformity with the law of the state of which they are nationals or of the state that proposes them as candidates.

2. No two judges may be nationals of the same state. . . .

Article 55

1. If a judge is a national of any of the States Parties to a case submitted to the Court, he shall retain his right to hear the case.

2. If one of the judges called upon to hear a case should be a national of one of the States Parties to the case, any other State Party in the case may appoint a person of its choice to serve on the Court as an *ad hoc* judge.

3. If among the judges called upon to hear a case none is a national of any of the States Parties to the case, each of the latter may appoint an *ad hoc* judge.

4. An *ad hoc* judge shall possess the qualifications indicated in Article 52.

5. If several States Parties should have the same interest in a case, they shall be considered as a single party for purposes of the above provisions. In case of doubt, the Court shall decide.

Article 56

Five judges shall constitute a quorum for the transaction of business by the Court.

Article 57

The Commission shall appear in all cases before the Court. . . .

Article 60

The Court shall draw up its Statute which it shall submit to the General Assembly for approval. It shall adopt its own Rules of Procedure.

Section 2. Jurisdiction and Functions

Article 61

1. Only the States Parties and the Commission shall have the right to submit a case to the Court.

2. In order for the Court to hear a case, it is necessary that the procedures set forth in Articles 48 to 50 shall have been completed.

Article 62

1. A State Party may, upon depositing its instrument of ratification or adherence to this Convention, or at any subsequent time, declare that it recognizes as binding, *ipso facto,* and not requiring special agreement, the jurisdiction of the Court on all matters relating to the interpretation or application of this Convention.

2. Such declaration may be made unconditionally, on the condition of reciprocity, for a specified period, or for specific cases. It shall be presented to the Secretary General of the Organization, who shall transmit copies thereof to the other member states of the Organization and to the Secretary of the Court.

3. The jurisdiction of the Court shall comprise all cases concerning the interpretation and application of the provisions of this Convention that are submitted to it, provided that the States Parties to the case recognize or have recognized such jurisdiction, whether by special declaration pursuant to the preceding paragraphs, or by a special agreement.

Article 63

1. If the Court finds that there has been a violation of a right or freedom protected by this Convention, the Court shall rule that the injured party be ensured the enjoyment of his right or freedom that was violated. It shall also rule, if appropriate, that the consequences of the measure or situation that constituted the breach of such right or freedom be remedied and that fair compensation be paid to the injured party.

2. In cases of extreme gravity and urgency, and when necessary to avoid irreparable damage to persons, the Court shall adopt such provisional measures as it deems pertinent in matters it has under consideration. With respect to a case not yet submitted to the Court, it may act at the request of the Commission.

Article 64

1. The member states of the Organization may consult the Court regarding the interpretation of this Convention or of other treaties concerning the protection of human rights in the American States. Within their spheres of competence, the organs listed in Chapter X of the Charter of the Organization of American States, as amended by the Protocol of Buenos Aires, may in like manner consult the Court.

2. The Court, at the request of a member state of the Organization, may provide that state with opinions regarding the compatibility of any of its domestic laws with the aforesaid international instruments.

Article 65

To each regular session of the General Assembly of the Organization of American States the Court shall submit, for the Assembly's consideration, a report on its work during the previous year. It shall specify, in particular, the cases in which a state has not complied with its judgments, making any pertinent recommendations.

Section 3. Procedure

Article 66

1. Reasons shall be given for the judgment of the Court.

2. If the judgment does not represent in whole or in part the unanimous opinion of the judges, any judge shall be entitled to have his dissenting or separate opinion attached to the judgment.

Article 67

The judgment of the Court shall be final and not subject to appeal. In case of disagreement as to the meaning or scope of the judgment, the Court shall interpret it at the request of any of the parties, provided the request is made within ninety days from the date of notification of the judgment.

Article 68

1. The States Parties to the Convention undertake to comply with the judgment of the Court in any case to which they are parties.

2. That part of a judgment that stipulates compensatory damages may be executed in the country concerned in accordance with domestic procedure governing the execution of judgments against the state.

Article 69

The parties to the case shall be notified of the judgment of the Court and it shall be transmitted to the States Parties to the Convention....

Document 18
PROTOCOL TO THE AMERICAN CONVENTION ON HUMAN RIGHTS TO ABOLISH THE DEATH PENALTY

O.A.S. T.S. No. 73, O.A.S. G.A. Res. 1042, 20th Sess. (8 June 1990)

Article 1

The States Parties to this Protocol shall not apply the death penalty in their territory to any person subject to their jurisdiction.

Article 2

1. No reservations may be made to this Protocol. However, at the time of ratification or accession, the States Parties to this instrument may declare that they reserve the right to apply the death penalty in wartime in accordance with international law, for extremely serious crimes of a military nature.

2. The State Party making this reservation shall, upon ratification or accession, inform the Secretary General of the Organization of American States of the pertinent provisions of its national legislation applicable in wartime, as referred to in the preceding paragraph.

3. Said State Party shall notify the Secretary General of the Organization of American States of the beginning or end of any state of war in effect in its territory.

Document 19
STATUTE OF THE INTER-AMERICAN COMMISSION ON HUMAN RIGHTS

Reprinted in Basic Documents pertaining to Human Rights in the Inter-American System, O.A.S. Doc. OEA/Ser. L.V/II.82, doc. 6, rev. 1, at 93 (1992)

I. Nature and Purposes

Article 1

1. The Inter-American Commission on Human Rights is an organ of the Organization of the American States, created to promote the observance and defense of human rights and to serve as consultative organ of the Organization in this matter.

2. For the purposes of the present Statute, human rights are understood to be:

a. The rights set forth in the American Convention on Human Rights, in relation to the States Parties thereto;

b. The rights set forth in the American Declaration of the Rights and Duties of Man, in relation to the other member states.

II. Membership and Structure

Article 2

1. The Inter-American Commission on Human Rights shall be composed of seven members, who shall be persons of high moral character and recognized competence in the field of human rights.

2. The Commission shall represent all the member states of the Organization.

Article 3

1. The members of the Commission shall be elected in a personal capacity by the General Assembly of the Organization from a list of candidates proposed by the governments of the member states....

Article 6

The members of the Commission shall be elected for a term of four years and may be reelected only once. Their terms of office shall begin on January 1 of the year following the year in which they are elected.

Article 7

No two nationals of the same state may be members of the Commission.

Article 8

1. Membership on the Inter-American Commission on Human Rights is incompatible with engaging in other functions that might affect the independence or impartiality of the member or the dignity or prestige of his post on the Commission.

2. The Commission shall consider any case that may arise regarding incompatibility in accordance with the provisions of the first paragraph of this Article, and in accordance with the procedures provided by its Regulations. If the Commission decides, by an affirmative vote of at least five of its members, that a case of incompatibility exists, it will submit the case, with its background, to the General Assembly for decision.

3. A declaration of incompatibility by the General Assembly shall be adopted by a majority of two thirds of the member states of the Organization and shall occasion the immediate removal of the member of the Commission from his post, but it shall not invalidate any action in which he may have participated.

Article 9

The duties of the members of the Commission are:

1. Except when justifiably prevented, to attend the regular and special meetings the Commission holds at its permanent headquarters or in any other place to which it may have decided to move temporarily.

2. To serve, except when justifiably prevented, on the special committees which the Commission may form to conduct on-site observations, or to perform any other duties within their ambit.

3. To maintain absolute secrecy about all matters which the Commission deems confidential.

4. To conduct themselves in their public and private life as befits the high moral authority of the office and the importance of the mission entrusted to the Commission....

Article 12

1. In those member states of the Organization that are Parties to the American Convention on Human Rights, the members of the Commission shall enjoy, from the time of their election and throughout their term of office, such immunities as are granted to diplomatic agents under international law. While in office, they shall also enjoy the diplomatic privileges required for the performance of their duties.

2. In those member states of the Organization that are not Parties to the American Convention on Human Rights, the members of the Commission shall enjoy the privileges and immunities pertaining to their posts that are required for them to perform their duties with independence.

3. The system of privileges and immunities of the members of the Commission may be regulated or supplemented by multilateral or bilateral agreements between the Organization and the member states....

III. Headquarters and Meetings

Article 16

1. The headquarters of the Commission shall be in Washington, D.C.

2. The Commission may move to and meet in the territory of any American State when it so decides by an absolute majority of votes, and with the consent, or at the invitation of the government concerned.

3. The Commission shall meet in regular and special sessions, in conformity with the provisions of the Regulations.

Article 17

1. An absolute majority of the members of the Commission shall constitute a quorum.

2. In regard to those States that are Parties to the Convention, decisions shall be taken by an absolute majority vote of the members of the Commission in those cases established by the American Convention on Human Rights and the present Statute. In other cases, an absolute majority of the members present shall be required.

3. In regard to those States that are not Parties to the Convention, decisions shall be taken by an absolute majority vote of the members of the Commission, except in matters of procedure, in which case, the decisions shall be taken by simple majority.

IV. Functions and Powers

Article 18

The Commission shall have the following powers with respect to the member states of the Organization of American States:

a. to develop an awareness of human rights among the peoples of the Americas;

b. to make recommendations to the governments of the states on the adoption of progressive measures in favor of human rights in the framework of their legislation, constitutional provisions and international commitments, as well as appropriate measures to further observance of those rights;

c. to prepare such studies or reports as it considers advisable for the performance of its duties;

d. to request that the governments of the states provide it with reports on measures they adopt in matters of human rights;

e. to respond to inquiries made by any member state through the General Secretariat of the Organization on matters related to human rights in the state and, within its possibilities, to provide those states with the advisory services they request;

f. to submit an annual report to the General Assembly of the Organization, in which due account shall be taken of the legal regime applicable to those States Parties to the American Convention on Human Rights and of that system applicable to those that are not Parties;

g. to conduct on-site observations in a state, with the consent or at the invitation of the government in question; and

h. to submit the program-budget of the Commission to the Secretary General, so that he may present it to the General Assembly.

Article 19

With respect to the States Parties to the American Convention on Human Rights, the Commission shall discharge its duties in conformity with the powers granted under the Convention and in the present Statute, and shall have the following powers in addition to those designated in Article 18:

a. to act on petitions and other communications, pursuant to the provisions of Articles 44 to 51 of the Convention;

b. to appear before the Inter-American Court of Human Rights in cases provided for in the Convention;

c. to request the Inter-American Court of Human Rights to take such provisional measures as it considers appropriate in serious and urgent cases which have not yet been submitted before it for consideration, whenever this becomes necessary to prevent irreparable injury to persons;

d. to consult the Court on the interpretation of the American Convention on Human Rights or of other treaties concerning the protection of human rights in the American states;

e. to submit additional draft protocols to the American Convention on Human Rights to the General Assembly, in order to progressively include other rights and freedoms under the system of protection of the Convention; and

f. to submit to the General Assembly, through the Secretary General, proposed amendments to the American Convention on Human Rights, for such action as the General Assembly deems appropriate.

Article 20

In relation to those member states of the Organization that are not parties to the American Convention on Human Rights, the Commission shall have the following powers, in addition to those designated in Article 18:

a. to pay particular attention to the observance of the human rights referred to in Articles I, II, III, IV, XVIII, XXV, and XXVI of the American Declaration of the Rights and Duties of Man;

b. to examinc communications submitted to it and any other available information, to address the government of any member state not a Party to the Convention for information deemed pertinent by this Commission, and to make recommendations to it, when it finds this appropriate, in order to bring about more effective observance of fundamental human rights; and

c. to verify, as a prior condition to the exercise of the powers granted under subparagraph b above, whether the domestic legal procedures and remedies of each member state not a Party to the Convention have been duly applied and exhausted.

V. Secretariat

Article 21

1. The Secretariat services of the Commission shall be provided by a specialized administrative unit under the direction of an Executive Secretary. This unit shall be provided with the resources and staff required to accomplish the tasks the Commission may assign to it.

2. The Executive Secretary, who shall be a person of high moral character and recognized competence in the field of human rights, shall be responsible for the work of the Secretariat and shall assist the Commission in the performance of its duties in accordance with the Regulations.

3. The Executive Secretary shall be appointed by the Secretary General of the Organization, in consultation with the Commission. Furthermore, for the Secretary General to be able to remove the Executive Secretary, he shall consult with the Commission and inform its members of the reasons for his decision.

VI. Statute and Regulations

Article 22

1. The present Statute may be amended by the General Assembly.

2. The Commission shall prepare and adopt its own Regulations, in accordance with the present Statute.

Article 23

1. In accordance with the provisions of Articles 44 to 51 of the American Convention on Human Rights, the Regulations of the Commission shall determine the procedure to be followed in cases of petitions or communications alleging violation of any of the rights guaranteed by the Convention, and imputing such violation to any State Party to the Convention.

2. If the friendly settlement referred to in Articles 44 to 51 of the Convention is not reached, the Commission shall draft, within 180 days, the report required by Article 50 of the Convention.

Article 24

1. The Regulations shall establish the procedure to be followed in cases of communications containing accusations or complaints of violations of human rights imputable to States that are not Parties to the American Convention on Human Rights. . . .

Document 20
AFRICAN [BANJUL] CHARTER ON HUMAN AND PEOPLES' RIGHTS

O.A.U. Doc. CAB/LEG/67/3 Rev. 5 (1981)

Preamble

The African States members of the Organization of African Unity, parties to the present convention entitled "Banjul Charter on Human and Peoples' Rights,"

Recalling Decision 115 (XVI) of the Assembly of Heads of State and Government at its Sixteenth Ordinary Session held in Monrovia, Liberia, from 17 to 20 July 1979 on the preparation of "a preliminary draft on an African Charter on Human and Peoples' Rights providing *inter alia* for the establishment of bodies to promote and protect human and peoples' rights";

Considering the Charter of the Organization of African Unity, which stipulates that "freedom, equality, justice and dignity are essential objectives for the achievement of the legitimate aspirations of the African peoples";

Reaffirming the pledge they solemnly made in Article 2 of the said Charter to eradicate all forms of colonialism from Africa, to coordinate and intensify their cooperation and efforts to achieve a better life for the peoples of Africa and to promote international cooperation having due regard to the Charter of the United Nations and the Universal Declaration of Human Rights;

Taking into consideration the virtues of their historical tradition and the values of African civilization which should inspire and characterize their reflection on the concept of human and peoples' rights;

Recognizing on the one hand, that fundamental human rights stem from the attributes of human beings, which justifies their international protection and on the other hand that the reality and respect of peoples' rights should necessarily guarantee human rights;

Considering that the enjoyment of rights and freedom also implies the performance of duties on the part of everyone;

Convinced that it is henceforth essential to pay particular attention to the right to development and that civil and political rights cannot be dissociated from economic, social and cultural rights in their conception as well as universality and that the satisfaction of economic, social and cultural rights is a guarantee for the enjoyment of civil and political rights;

Conscious of their duty to achieve the total liberation of Africa, the peoples of which are still struggling for their dignity and genuine independence, and undertaking to eliminate colonialism, neo-colonialism, apartheid, zionism and to dismantle aggressive foreign military bases and all forms of discrimination, particularly those based on race, ethnic group, colour, sex, language, religion or political opinion;

Reaffirming their adherence to the principles of human and peoples' rights and freedoms contained in the declarations, conventions and other instruments adopted by the Organization of African Unity, the Movement of Non–Aligned Countries and the United Nations;

Firmly convinced of the duty to promote and protect human and peoples' rights and freedoms taking into account the importance traditionally attached to these rights and freedoms in Africa;

Have agreed as follows:

PART I. RIGHTS AND DUTIES

CHAPTER I. HUMAN AND PEOPLES' RIGHTS

Article 1

The Member States of the Organization of African Unity parties to the present Charter shall recognize the rights, duties and freedoms enshrined in this Charter and shall undertake to adopt legislative or other measures to give effect to them.

Article 2

Every individual shall be entitled to the enjoyment of the rights and freedoms recognized in the present Charter without distinction of any kind such as race, ethnic group, colour, sex, language, religion, political or any other opinion, national and social origin, fortune, birth or other status.

Article 3

1. Every individual shall be equal before the law.
2. Every individual shall be entitled to equal protection of the law.

Article 4

Human beings are inviolable. Every human being shall be entitled to respect for his life and the integrity of his person. No one may be arbitrarily deprived of this right.

Article 5

Every individual shall have the right to the respect of the dignity inherent in a human being and to the recognition of his legal status. All forms of exploitation and degradation of man, particularly slavery, slave trade, torture, cruel, inhuman or degrading punishment or treatment shall be prohibited.

Article 6

Every individual shall have the right to liberty and to the security of his person. No one may be deprived of his freedom except for reasons and conditions previously laid down by law. In particular, no one may be arbitrarily arrested or detained.

Article 7

1. Every individual shall have the right to have his cause heard. This comprises:

a. The right to an appeal to competent national organs against acts violating his fundamental rights as recognized and guaranteed by conventions, laws, regulations and customs in force;

b. The right to be presumed innocent until proved guilty by a competent court or tribunal;

c. The right to defence, including the right to be defended by counsel of his choice;

d. The right to be tried within a reasonable time by an impartial court or tribunal.

2. No one may be condemned for an act or omission which did not constitute a legally punishable offence at the time it was committed. No penalty may be inflicted for an offence for which no provision was made at the time it was committed. Punishment is personal and can be imposed only on the offender.

Article 8

Freedom of conscience, the profession and free practice of religion shall be guaranteed. No one may, subject to law and order, be submitted to measures restricting the exercise of these freedoms.

Article 9

1. Every individual shall have the right to receive information.

2. Every individual shall have the right to express and disseminate his opinions within the law.

Article 10

1. Every individual shall have the right to free association provided that he abides by the law.

2. Subject to the obligation of solidarity provided for in Article 29 no one may be compelled to join an association.

Article 11

Every individual shall have the right to assemble freely with others. The exercise of this right shall be subject only to necessary restrictions provided for by law in particular those enacted in the interest of national security, the safety, health, ethics and rights and freedoms of others.

Article 12

1. Every individual shall have the right to freedom of movement and residence within the borders of a State provided he abides by the law.

2. Every individual shall have the right to leave any country including his own, and to return to his country. This right may only be subject to restrictions provided for by law for the protection of national security, law and order, public health or morality.

3. Every individual shall have the right, when persecuted, to seek and obtain asylum in other countries in accordance with the laws of those countries and international conventions.

4. A non-national legally admitted in a territory of a State Party to the present Charter may only be expelled from it by virtue of a decision taken in accordance with the law.

5. The mass expulsion of non-nationals shall be prohibited. Mass expulsion shall be that which is aimed at national, racial, ethnic or religious groups.

Article 13

1. Every citizen shall have the right to participate freely in the government of his country, either directly or through freely chosen representatives in accordance with the provisions of the law.

2. Every citizen shall have the right of equal access to the public service of his country.

3. Every individual shall have the right of access to public property and services in strict equality of all persons before the law.

Article 14

The right to property shall be guaranteed. It may only be encroached upon in the interest of public need or in the general interest of the community and in accordance with the provisions of appropriate laws.

Article 15

Every individual shall have the right to work under equitable and satisfactory conditions and shall receive equal pay for equal work.

Article 16

1. Every individual shall have the right to enjoy the best attainable state of physical and mental health.

2. States Parties to the present Charter shall take the necessary measures to protect the health of their people and to ensure that they receive medical attention when they are sick.

Article 17

1. Every individual shall have the right to education.

2. Every individual may freely take part in the cultural life of his community.

3. The promotion and protection of morals and traditional values recognized by the community shall be the duty of the State.

Article 18

1. The family shall be the natural unit and basis of society. It shall be protected by the State which shall take care of its physical health and morals.

2. The State shall have the duty to assist the family which is the custodian of morals and traditional values recognized by the community.

3. The State shall ensure the elimination of every discrimination against women and also ensure the protection of the rights of the women and the child as stipulated in international declarations and conventions.

4. The aged and the disabled shall also have the right to special measures of protection in keeping with their physical and moral needs.

Article 19

All peoples shall be equal; they shall enjoy the same respect and shall have the same rights. Nothing shall justify the domination of a people by another.

Article 20

1. All peoples shall have the right to existence. They shall have the unquestionable and inalienable right to self-determination. They shall freely determine their political status and shall pursue their economic and social development according to the policy they have freely chosen.

2. Colonized or oppressed peoples shall have the right to free themselves from the bonds of domination by resorting to any means recognized by the international community.

3. All peoples shall have the right to the assistance of the States Parties to the present Charter in their liberation struggle against foreign domination, be it political, economic or cultural.

Article 21

1. All peoples shall freely dispose of their wealth and natural resources. This right shall be exercised in the exclusive interest of the people. In no case shall a people be deprived of it.

2. In case of spoliation the dispossessed people shall have the right to the lawful recovery of its property as well as to an adequate compensation.

3. The free disposal of wealth and natural resources shall be exercised without prejudice to the obligation of promoting international economic cooperation based on mutual respect, equitable exchange and the principles of international law.

4. States Parties to the present Charter shall individually and collectively exercise the right to free disposal of their natural wealth and

natural resources with a view to strengthening African unity and solidarity.

5. States Parties to the present Charter shall undertake to eliminate all forms of foreign economic exploitation particularly that practiced by international monopolies so as to enable their peoples to fully benefit from the advantages derived from their natural resources.

Article 22

1. All peoples shall have the right to their economic, social and cultural development with due regard to their freedom and identity and in the equal enjoyment of the common heritage of mankind.

2. States shall have the duty, individually or collectively, to ensure the exercise of the right to development.

Article 23

1. All peoples shall have the right to national and international peace and security. The principles of solidarity and friendly relations implicitly affirmed by the Charter of the United Nations and reaffirmed by that of the Organization of African Unity shall govern relations between States.

2. For the purpose of strengthening peace, solidarity and friendly relations, States Parties to the present Charter shall ensure that:

a. any individual enjoying the right of asylum under Article 12 of the present Charter shall not engage in subversive activities against his country of origin or any other State Party to the present Charter;

b. their territories shall not be used as bases for subversive or terrorist activities against the people of any other State Party to the present Charter.

Article 24

All peoples have the right to a general satisfactory environment favourable to their development.

Article 25

States Parties to the present Charter shall have the duty to promote and ensure through teaching, education and publication, the respect of the rights and freedoms contained in the present Charter and to see to it that these freedoms and rights as well as corresponding obligations and duties are understood.

Article 26

States Parties to the present Charter shall have the duty to guarantee the independence of the Courts and shall allow the establishment and improvement of appropriate national institutions entrusted with the promotion and protection of the rights and freedoms guaranteed by the present Charter.

CHAPTER II. DUTIES

Article 27

1. Every individual shall have duties towards his family and society, the State and other legally recognized communities and the international community.

2. The rights and freedoms of each individual shall be exercised with due regard to the rights of others, collective security, morality and common interest.

Article 28

Every individual shall have the duty to respect and consider his fellow beings without discrimination, and to maintain relations aimed at promoting, safeguarding and reinforcing mutual respect and tolerance.

Article 29

The individual shall also have the duty:

1. To preserve the harmonious development of the family and to work for the cohesion and respect of the family, to respect his parents at all times, to maintain them in case of need;

2. To serve the national community by placing his physical and intellectual abilities at its service;

3. Not to compromise the security of the State whose national or resident he is;

4. To preserve and strengthen social and national solidarity, particularly when the latter is threatened;

5. To preserve and strengthen the national independence and the territorial integrity of his country and to contribute to its defence in accordance with the law;

6. To work to the best of his abilities and competence, and to pay taxes imposed by law in the interest of the society;

7. To preserve and strengthen positive African cultural values in his relations with other members of the society, in the spirit of tolerance, dialogue and consultation and, in general, to contribute to the promotion of the moral well being of society;

8. To contribute to the best of his abilities, at all times and at all levels, to the promotion and achievement of African unity.

PART II. MEASURES OF SAFEGUARD

CHAPTER I. ESTABLISHMENT AND ORGANIZATION OF THE AFRICAN COMMISSION ON HUMAN AND PEOPLES' RIGHTS

Article 30

An African Commission on Human and Pcoplcs' Rights, hereinafter called "the Commission," shall be established within the Organization of African Unity to promote human and peoples' rights and ensure their protection in Africa.

CHAPTER II. MANDATE OF THE COMMISSION

Article 45

The functions of the Commission shall be:

1. To promote Human and Peoples' Rights and in particular:

a. To collect documents, undertake studies and researches on African problems in the field of human and peoples' rights, organize seminars, symposia and conferences, disseminate information, encourage national and local institutions concerned with human and peoples' rights, and should the case arise, give its views or make recommendations to Governments.

b. To formulate and lay down principles and rules aimed at solving legal problems relating to human and peoples' rights and fundamental freedoms upon which African Governments may base their legislations.

c. Co-operate with other African and international institutions concerned with the promotion and protection of human and peoples' rights.

2. Ensure the protection of human and peoples' rights under conditions laid down by the present Charter.

3. Interpret all the provisions of the present Charter at the request of a State Party, an institution of the OAU or an African organization recognized by the OAU.

4. Perform any other tasks which may be entrusted to it by the Assembly of Heads of State and Government.

CHAPTER III. PROCEDURE OF THE COMMISSION

Article 46

The Commission may resort to any appropriate method of investigation; it may hear from the Secretary–General of the Organization of African Unity or any other person capable of enlightening it.

Communication from States

Article 47

If a State Party to the present Charter has good reasons to believe that another State Party to this Charter has violated the provisions of the Charter, it may draw, by written communication, the attention of that State to the matter. This communication shall also be addressed to the Secretary–General of the OAU and to the Chairman of the Commission. Within three months of the receipt of the communication, the State to which the communication is addressed shall give the enquiring State written explanation or statement elucidating the matter. This should include as much as possible relevant information relating to the laws and rules of procedure applied and applicable and the redress already given or course of action available.

Article 48

If within three months from the date on which the original communication is received by the State to which it is addressed, the issue is not settled to the satisfaction of the two States involved through bilateral negotiation or by any other peaceful procedure, either State shall have the right to submit the matter to the Commission through the Chairman and shall notify the other States involved.

Article 49

Notwithstanding the provisions of Article 47, if a State Party to the present Charter considers that another State Party has violated the provisions of the Charter, it may refer the matter directly to the Commission by addressing a communication to the Chairman, to the Secretary–General of the Organization of African Unity and the State concerned.

Article 50

The Commission can only deal with a matter submitted to it after making sure that all local remedies, if they exist, have been exhausted, unless it is obvious to the Commission that the procedure of achieving these remedies would be unduly prolonged.

Article 51

1. The Commission may ask the States concerned to provide it with all relevant information.

2. When the Commission is considering the matter, States concerned may be represented before it and submit written or oral representation.

Article 52

After having obtained from the States concerned and other sources all the information it deems necessary and after having tried all appropriate means to reach an amicable solution based on the respect of Human and Peoples' Rights, the Commission shall prepare, within a reasonable period of time from the notification referred to in Article 48, a report stating the facts and its findings. This report shall be sent to the States concerned and communicated to the Assembly of Heads of State and Government.

Article 53

While transmitting its report, the Commission may make to the Assembly of Heads of State and Government such recommendations as it deems useful.

Article 54

The Commission shall submit to each Ordinary Session of the Assembly of Heads of State and Government a report on its activities.

Other Communications

Article 55

1. Before each Session, the Secretary of the Commission shall make a list of the communications other than those of States Parties to the present Charter and transmit them to the Members of the Commission, who shall indicate which communications should be considered by the Commission.

2. A communication shall be considered by the Commission if a simple majority of its members so decide.

Article 56

Communications relating to human and peoples' rights referred to in Article 55 received by the Commission, shall be considered if they:

1. indicate their authors even if the latter request anonymity,

2. are compatible with the Charter of the Organization of African Unity or with the present Charter,

3. are not written in disparaging or insulting language directed against the State concerned and its institutions or to the Organization of African Unity,

4. are not based exclusively on news disseminated through the mass media,

5. are sent after exhausting local remedies, if any, unless it is obvious that this procedure is unduly prolonged,

6. are submitted within a reasonable period from the time local remedies are exhausted or from the date the Commission is seized of the matter, and

7. do not deal with cases which have been settled by these States involved in accordance with the principles of the Charter of the United Nations, or the Charter of the Organization of African Unity or the provisions of the present Charter.

Article 57

Prior to any substantive consideration, all communications shall be brought to the knowledge of the State concerned by the Chairman of the Commission.

Article 58

1. When it appears after deliberation of the Commission that one or more communications apparently relate to special cases which reveal the existence of a series or serious or massive violations of human and peoples' rights, the Commission shall draw the attention of the Assembly of Heads of State and Government to these special cases.

2. The Assembly of Heads of State and Government may then request the Commission to undertake an in-depth study of these situations and make a factual report, accompanied by its findings and recommendations.

3. A case of emergency duly noticed by the Commission shall be submitted by the latter to the Chairman of the Assembly of Heads of State and Government who may request an in-depth study.

Article 59

1. All measures taken within the provisions of the present Chapter shall remain confidential until such a time as the Assembly of Heads of State and Government shall otherwise decide.

2. However, the report shall be published by the Chairman of the Commission upon the decision of the Assembly of Heads of State and Government.

3. The report on the activities of the Commission shall be published by its Chairman after it has been considered by the Assembly of Heads of State and Government.

CHAPTER IV. APPLICABLE PRINCIPLES

Article 60

The Commission shall draw inspiration from international law on human and peoples' rights, particularly from the provisions of various African instruments on human and peoples' rights, the Charter of the United Nations, the Charter of the Organization of African Unity, the Universal Declaration of Human Rights, other instruments adopted by the United Nations and by African countries in the field of human and peoples' rights as well as from the provisions of various instruments adopted within the Specialized Agencies of the United Nations of which the parties to the present Charter are members.

Article 61

The Commission shall also take into consideration, as subsidiary measures to determine the principles of law, other general or special international conventions, laying down rules expressly recognized by member states of the Organization of African Unity, African practices consistent with international norms on human and peoples' rights, customs generally accepted as law, general principles of law recognized by African states as well as legal precedents and doctrine.

Article 62

Each State Party shall undertake to submit every two years, from the date the present Charter comes into force, a report on the legislative and other measures taken with a view to giving effect to the rights and freedoms recognized and guaranteed by the present Charter. . . .

Document 21
PROTOCOL TO THE AFRICAN CHARTER ON HUMAN AND PEOPLES' RIGHTS ON THE ESTABLISHMENT OF AN AFRICAN COURT ON HUMAN AND PEOPLES' RIGHTS

(Adopted by the 34th Ordinary Session of the Assembly of Heads of State and Government meeting in Ouagadougou, Burkina Faso from 8–10 June 1998. In a signing ceremony held thereafter, at the same venue, thirty Member States signed the Protocol)

The Member States of the Organization of African Unity hereinafter referred to as the OAU, States Parties to the African Charter on Human and Peoples' Rights:

Considering that the Charter of the Organization of African Unity recognizes that freedom, equality, justice, peace and dignity are essential objectives for the achievement of the legitimate aspirations of the African peoples;

Noting that the African Charter on Human and Peoples' Rights reaffirms adherence to the principles of human and peoples' rights, freedoms and duties contained in the declarations, conventions and other instruments adopted by the Organization of African Unity, and other international organizations;

Recognizing that the twofold objective of the African Charter on Human and Peoples' Rights is to ensure on the one hand promotion and on the other protection of human and peoples' rights, freedoms and duties;

Recognizing further, the efforts of the African Commission on Human and Peoples' Rights in the promotion and protection of human and peoples' rights since its inception in 1987;

Recalling resolution AHGIRe5.230 (XXX) adopted by the Assembly of Heads of State and Government in June 1994 in Tunis, Tunisia, requesting the Secretary–General to convene a Government experts' meeting to ponder, in conjunction with the African Commission, over the means to enhance the efficiency of the African Commission and to consider in particular the establishment of an African Court on Human and Peoples' Rights;

Noting the first and second Government legal experts' meetings held respectively in Cape Town, South Africa (September, 1995) and Nouakchott, Mauritania (April, 1997), and the third Government Legal Experts meeting held in Addis Ababa, Ethiopia (December, 1997), which was enlarged to include Diplomats;

Firmly convinced that the attainment of the objectives of the African Charter on Human and Peoples' Rights requires the establishment of an African Court on Human and Peoples' Rights to complement and reinforce the functions of the African Commission on Human and Peoples' Rights.

Have agreed as follows:

Article 1. Establishment of the Court

There shall be established within the Organization of African Unity an African Court on Human and Peoples' Rights (hereinafter referred to as "the Court"), the organization, jurisdiction and functioning of which shall be governed by the present Protocol.

Article 2. Relationship between the Court and the Commission

The Court shall, bearing in mind the provisions of this Protocol, complement the protective mandate of the African Commission on Human and Peoples' Rights (hereinafter referred to as "the Commission") conferred upon it by the African Charter on Human and Peoples' Rights (hereinafter referred to as "the Charter").

Article 3. Jurisdiction

1. The jurisdiction of the Court shall extend to all cases and disputes submitted to it concerning the interpretation and application of the Charter, this Protocol and any other relevant Human Rights instrument ratified by the States concerned.

2. In the event of a dispute as to whether the Court has jurisdiction, the Court shall decide.

Article 4. Advisory Opinions

1. At the request of a Member State of the OAU, the OAU, any of its organs, or any African organization recognized by the OAU, the Court may provide an opinion on any legal matter relating to the Charter or any other relevant human rights instruments, provided that the subject matter of the opinion is not related to a matter being examined by the Commission.

2. The Court shall give reasons for its advisory opinions provided that every judge shall be entitled to deliver a separate or dissenting decision.

Article 5. Access to the Court

1. The following are entitled to submit cases to the Court:

   a. The Commission;

b. The State Party which has lodged a complaint to the Commission.

c. The State Party against which the complaint has been lodged at the Commission;

d. The State Party whose citizen is a victim of human rights violation;

e. African Intergovernmental Organizations.

2. When a State Party has an interest in a case, it may submit a request to the Court to be permitted to join.

3. The Court may entitle relevant Non Governmental Organizations (NGOs) with observer status before the Commission and individuals to institute cases directly before it, in accordance with article 34 (6) of this Protocol.

Article 6. Admissibility of Cases

1. The Court, when deciding on the admissibility of a case instituted under article 5 (3) of this Protocol, may request the opinion of the Commission which shall give t as soon as possible.

2. The Court shall rule on the admissibility of cases taking into account the provisions of article 56 of the Charter.

3. The Court may consider cases or transfer them to the Commission.

Article 7. Sources of Law

The Court shall apply the provisions of the Charter and any other relevant human rights instruments ratified by the States concerned.

Article 8. Consideration of Cases

The Rules of Procedure of the Court shall lay down the detailed conditions under which the Court shall consider cases brought before it, bearing in mind the complementarity between the Commission and the Court.

Article 9. Amicable Settlement

The Court may try to reach an amicable settlement in a case pending before it in accordance with the provisions of the Charter.

Article 10. Hearings and Representation

1. The Court shall conduct its proceedings in public. The Court may, however, conduct proceedings in camera as may be provided for in the Rules of Procedure.

2. Any party to a case shall be entitled to be represented by a legal representative of the party's choice. Free legal representation may be provided where the interests of justice so require.

3. Any person, witness or representative of the parties, who appears before the Court, shall enjoy protection and all facilities, in

accordance with international law, necessary for the discharging of their functions, tasks and duties in relation to the Court.

Article 11. Composition

1. The Court shall consist of eleven judges, nationals of Member States of the OAU, elected in an individual capacity from among jurists of high moral character and of recognized practical, judicial or academic competence and experience in the field of human and peoples' rights.

2. No two judges shall be nationals of the same State.

Article 12. Nominations

1. States Parties to the Protocol may each propose up to three candidates, at least two of whom shall be nationals of that State.

2. Due consideration shall be given to adequate gender representation in the nomination process.

Article 13. List of Candidates

1. Upon entry into force of this Protocol, the Secretary–General of the OAU shall request each State Party to the Protocol to present, within ninety (90) days of such a request, its nominees for the office of judge of the Court.

2. The Secretary–General of the OAU shall prepare a list in alphabetical order of the candidates nominated and transmit it to the Member States of the OAU at least thirty days prior to the next session of the Assembly of Heads of State and Government of the OAU hereinafter referred to as "the Assembly".

Article 14. Elections

1. The judges of the Court shall be elected by secret ballot by the Assembly from the list referred to in Article 13 (2) of the present Protocol.

2. The Assembly shall ensure that in the Court as a whole there is representation of the main regions of Africa and of theft principal legal traditions.

3. In the election of the judges, the Assembly shall ensure that there is adequate gender representation.

Article 15. Term of Office

1. The judges of the Court shall be elected for a period of six years and may be re-elected only once. The terms of four judges elected at the first election shall expire at the end of two years, and the terms of four more judges shall expire at the end of four years.

2. The judges whose terms are to expire at the end of the initial periods of two and four years shall be chosen by lot to be drawn by the Secretary–General of the OAU immediately after the first election has been completed.

3. A judge elected to replace a judge whose term of office has not expired shall hold office for the remainder of the predecessor's term.

4. All judges except the President shall perform their functions on a part-time basis. However, the Assembly may change this arrangement as it deems appropriate.

Article 16. Oath of Office

After their election, the judges of the Court shall make a solemn declaration to discharge their duties impartially and faithfully.

Article 17. Independence

1. The independence of the judges shall be fully ensured in accordance with international law.

2. No judge may hear any case in which the same judge has previously taken part as agent, counsel or advocate for one of the parties or as a member of a national or international court or a commission of enquiry or in any other capacity. Any doubt on this point shall be settled by decision of the Court.

3. The judges of the Court shall enjoy, from the moment of theft election and throughout their term of office, the immunities extended to diplomatic agents in accordance with international law.

4. At no time shall the judges of the Court be held liable for any decision or opinion issued in the exercise of theft functions.

Article 18. Incompatibility

The position of judge of the Court is incompatible with any activity that might interfere with the independence or impartiality of such a judge or the demands of the office, as determined in the Rules of Procedure of the Court.

Article 19. Cessation of Office

1. A judge shall not be suspended or removed from office unless, by the unanimous decision of the other judges of the Court, the judge concerned has been found to be no longer fulfilling the required conditions to be a judge of the Court.

2. Such a decision of the Court shall become final unless it is set aside by the Assembly at its next session.

Article 20. Vacancies

1. In case of death or resignation of a judge of the Court, the President of the Court shall immediately inform the Secretary General of the Organization of African Unity, who shall declare the seat vacant from the date of death or from the date on which the resignation takes effect.

2. The Assembly shall replace the judge whose office became vacant unless the remaining period of the term is less than one hundred and eighty (180) days.

3. The same procedure and considerations as set out in Articles 12, 13 and 14 shall be followed for the filling of vacancies.

Article 21. Presidency of the Court

1. The Court shall elect its President and one Vice–President for a period of two years. They may be re-elected only once.

2. The President shall perform judicial functions on a full-time basis and shall reside at the seat of the Court.

3. The functions of the President and the Vice–President shall be set out in the Rules of Procedure of the Court.

Article 22. Exclusion

If a judge is a national of any State which is a party to a case submitted to the Court, the judge shall not hear the case.

Article 23. Quorum

The Court shall examine cases brought before it, if it has a quorum of at least seven judges.

Article 24. Registry of the Court

1. The Court shall appoint its own Registrar and other staff of the registry from among nationals of Member States of the OAU according to the Rules of Procedure.

2. The office and residence of the Registrar shall be at the place where the Court has its seat.

Article 25. Seat of the Court

1. The Court shall have its seat at the place determined by the Assembly from among States parties to this Protocol. However, it may convene in the territory of any Member State of the OAU when the majority of the Court considers it desirable, and with the prior consent of the State concerned.

2. The seat of the Court may be changed by the Assembly after due consultation with the Court.

Article 26. Evidence

1. The Court shall hear submissions by all parties and if deemed necessary, hold an enquiry. The States concerned shall assist by providing relevant facilities for the efficient handling of the case.

2. The Court may receive written and oral evidence including expert testimony and shall make its decision on the basis of such evidence.

Article 27. Findings

1. If the Court finds that there has been violation of a human or peoples' right, it shall make appropriate orders to remedy the violation, including the payment of fair compensation or reparation.

2. In cases of extreme gravity and urgency, and when necessary to avoid irreparable harm to persons, the Court shall adopt such provisional measures as it deems necessary.

Article 28. Judgment

1. The Court shall render its judgment within ninety (90) days of having completed its deliberation.

2. The judgment of the Court decided by majority shall be final and not subject to appeal.

3. Without prejudice to sub-article 2 above, the Court may review its decision in the light of new evidence under conditions to be set out in the Rules of Procedure.

4. The Court may interpret its own decision.

5. The judgement of the Court shall be read in open court, due notice having been given to the parties.

6. Reasons shall be given for the judgement of the Court.

7. If the judgment of the Court does not represent, in whole or in part, the unanimous decision of the judges, any judge shall be entitled to deliver a separate or dissenting opinion.

Article 29. Notification of Judgment

1. The parties to the case shall be notified of the judgment of the Court and it shall he transmitted to the Member States of the OAU and the Commission.

2. The Council of Ministers shall also be notified of the judgment and shall monitor its execution on behalf of the Assembly.

Article 30. Execution of Judgment

The States parties to the present Protocol undertake to comply with the judgment in any case to which they are parties within the time stipulated by the Court and to guarantee its execution.

Article 31. Report

The Court shall submit to each regular session of the Assembly, a report on its work during the previous year. The report shall specify, in particular, the cases in which a State has not complied with the Court's judgment.

Article 32. Budget

Expenses Of the Court, emoluments and allowances for judges and the budget of its registry, shall be determined and borne by the OAU, in accordance with criteria laid down by the OAU in consultation with the Court.

Article 33. Rules of Procedure

The Court shall draw up its Rules and determine its own procedures. The Court shall consult the Commission as appropriate.

Article 34. Ratification

1. This Protocol shall be open for signature and ratification or accession by any State Party to the Charter.

2. The instrument of ratification or accession to the present Protocol shall be deposited with the Secretary–General of the OAU.

3. The Protocol shall come into force thirty days after fifteen instruments of ratification or accession have been deposited.

4. For any State Party ratifying or acceding subsequently, the present Protocol shall come into force in respect of that State on the date of the deposit of its instrument of ratification or accession.

5. The Secretary–General of the OAU shall inform all Member States of the entry into force of the present Protocol.

6. At the time of the ratification of this Protocol or any time thereafter, the State shall make a declaration accepting the competence of the Court to receive cases under article 5 (3) of this Protocol. The Court shall not receive any petition under article 5 (3) involving a State Party which has not made such a declaration.

7. Declarations made under sub-article (6) above shall be deposited with the Secretary General, who shall transmit copies thereof to the State parties.

Article 35. Amendments

1. The present Protocol may be amended if a State Party to the Protocol makes a written request to that effect to the Secretary–General of the OAU. The Assembly may adopt, by simple majority, the draft amendment after all the States Parties to the present Protocol have been duly informed of it and the Court has given its opinion on the amendment.

2. The Court shall also be entitled to propose such amendments to the present Protocol as it may deem necessary, through the Secretary–General of the OAU.

3. The amendment shall come into force for each State Party which has accepted it thirty days after the Secretary–General of the OAU has received notice of the acceptance.

Document 22
EUROPEAN CONVENTION FOR THE PROTECTION OF HUMAN RIGHTS AND FUNDAMENTAL FREEDOMS

213 U.N.T.S. 221, Eur. T.S. No. 5 (1950), revised by Protocol 11, Eur. T.S. No. 155

The Governments signatory hereto, being Members of the Council of Europe,

Considering the Universal Declaration of Human Rights proclaimed by the General Assembly of the United Nations on 10 December 1948;

Considering that this Declaration aims at securing the universal and effective recognition and observance of the Rights therein declared;

Considering that the aim of the Council of Europe is the achievement of greater unity between its Members and that one of the methods by which that aim is to be pursued is the maintenance and further realisation of Human Rights and Fundamental Freedoms;

Reaffirming their profound belief in those Fundamental Freedoms which are the foundation of justice and peace in the world and are best maintained on the one hand by an effective political democracy and on the other by a common understanding and observance of the Human Rights upon which they depend;

Being resolved, as the Governments of European countries which are like-minded and have a common heritage of political traditions, ideals, freedom and the rule of law, to take the first steps for the collective enforcement of certain of the Rights stated in the Universal Declaration,

Have agreed as follows:

Article 1. Obligation to respect human rights

The High Contracting Parties shall secure to everyone within their jurisdiction the rights and freedoms defined in Section 1 of this Convention.

Section I. Rights and Freedom

Article 2. Right to life

1. Everyone's right to life shall be protected by law. No one shall be deprived of his life intentionally save in the execution of a sentence of

a court following his conviction of a crime for which this penalty is provided by law.

2. Deprivation of life shall not be regarded as inflicted in contravention of this article when it results from the use of force which is no more than absolutely necessary:

a. in defence of any person from unlawful violence;

b. in order to effect a lawful arrest or to prevent the escape of a person lawfully detained;

c. in action lawfully taken for the purpose of quelling a riot or insurrection.

Article 3. Prohibition of torture

No one shall be subjected to torture or to inhuman or degrading treatment or punishment.

Article 4. Prohibition of slavery and forced labour

1. No one shall be held in slavery or servitude.

2. No one shall be required to perform forced or compulsory labour.

3. For the purpose of this article the term "forced or compulsory labour" shall not include:

a. any work required to be done in the ordinary course of detention imposed according to the provisions of Article 5 of this Convention or during conditional release from such detention;

b. any service of a military character or, in case of conscientious objectors in countries where they are recognized, service exacted instead of compulsory military service;

c. any service exacted in case of an emergency or calamity threatening the life or well-being of the community;

d. any work or service which forms part of normal civic obligations.

Article 5. Right to liberty and security

1. Everyone has the right to liberty and security of person. No one shall be deprived of his liberty save in the following cases and in accordance with a procedure described by law;

a. the lawful detention of a person after conviction by a competent court;

b. the lawful arrest or detention of a person for non-compliance with the lawful order of a court or in order to secure the fulfilment of any obligation prescribed by law;

c. the lawful arrest or detention of a person effected for the purpose of bringing him before the competent legal authority on reasonable suspicion of having committed an offence or when it is reasonably considered necessary to prevent his committing an offence or fleeing after having done so;

d. the detention of a minor by lawful order for the purpose of educational supervision or his lawful detention for the purpose of bringing him before the competent legal authority;

e. the lawful detention of persons for the prevention of the spreading of infectious diseases, of persons of unsound mind, alcoholics or drug addicts or vagrants;

f. the lawful arrest or detention of a person to prevent his effecting an unauthorized entry into the country or of a person against whom action is being taken with a view to deportation or extradition.

2. Everyone who is arrested shall be informed promptly, in a language which he understands, of the reasons for his arrest and of any charge against him.

3. Everyone arrested or detained in accordance with the provisions of paragraph 1(c) of this article shall be brought promptly before a judge or other officer authorised by law to exercise judicial power and shall be entitled to trial within a reasonable time or to release pending trial. Release may be conditioned by guarantees to appear for trial.

4. Everyone who is deprived of his liberty by arrest or detention shall be entitled to take proceedings by which the lawfulness of his detention shall be decided speedily by a court and his release ordered if the detention is not lawful.

5. Everyone who has been the victim of arrest or detention in contravention of the provisions of this article shall have an enforceable right to compensation.

Article 6. Right to a fair trial

1. In the determination of his civil rights and obligations or of any criminal charge against him, everyone is entitled to a fair and public hearing within a reasonable time by an independent and impartial tribunal established by law. Judgment shall be pronounced publicly but the press and public may be excluded from all or part of the trial in the interest of morals, public order or national security in a democratic society, where the interests of juveniles or the protection of the private life of the parties so require, or to the extent strictly necessary in the opinion of the court in special circumstances where publicity would prejudice the interests of justice.

2. Everyone charged with a criminal offence shall be presumed innocent until proved guilty according to law.

3. Everyone charged with a criminal offence has the following minimum rights:

a. to be informed promptly, in a language which he understands and in detail, of the nature and cause of the accusation against him;

b. to have adequate time and facilities for the preparation of his defence;

c. to defend himself in person or through legal assistance of his own choosing or, if he has not sufficient means to pay for legal assistance, to be given it free when the interests of justice so require;

d. to examine or have examined witness against him and to obtain the attendance and examination of witnesses on his behalf under the same conditions as witnesses against him;

e. to have the free assistance of an interpreter if he cannot understand or speak the language used in court.

Article 7. No punishment without law

1. No one shall be held guilty of any criminal offence on account of any act or omission which did not constitute a criminal offence under national or international law at the time it was committed.

2. This Article shall not prejudice the trial and punishment of a person for any act or omission which at the time when it was committed, was criminal according to the general principles of law recognized by civilized nations.

Article 8. Right to respect for private and family life

1. Everyone has the right to respect for private and family life, his home and his correspondence.

2. There shall be no interference by a public authority with the exercise of this right except such as is in accordance with the law and is necessary in a democratic society in the interests of national security, public safety or the economic well-being of the country, for the prevention of disorder or crime, for the protection of health or morals, or for the protection of the rights and freedoms of others.

Article 9. Freedom of thought, conscience and religion

1. Everyone has the right to freedom of thought, conscience and religion; this right includes freedom to change his religion or belief and freedom, either alone or in community with others and in public or private, to manifest his religion or belief, in worship, teaching, practice and observance.

2. Freedom to manifest one's religion or belief shall be subject only to such limitations as are prescribed by law and are necessary in a democratic society in the interests of public order, health or morals, or for the protection of the rights and freedoms of others.

Article 10. Freedom of expression

1. Everyone has the right to freedom of expression. This right shall include freedom to hold opinions and to receive and impart information and ideas without interference by public authority and regardless of frontiers. This article shall not prevent States from requiring the licensing of broadcasting, television or cinema enterprises.

2. The exercise of these freedoms, since it carries with it duties and responsibilities, may be subject to such formalities, conditions, restric-

tions or penalties as are prescribed by law and are necessary in a democratic society, in the interests of national security, territorial integrity or public safety, for the prevention of disorder or crime, for the protection of the reputation or rights of others, for preventing the disclosure of information received in confidence, or for maintaining the authority and impartiality of the judiciary.

Article 11. Freedom of assembly and association

1. Everyone has the right to freedom of peaceful assembly and to freedom of association with others, including the right to form and to join trade unions for the protection of his interests.

2. No restrictions shall be placed on the exercise of these rights other than such as are prescribed by law and are necessary in a democratic society in the interests of national security or public safety, for the prevention of disorder or crime, for the protection of health or morals or for the protection of the rights and freedoms of others. This article shall not prevent the imposition of lawful restrictions on the exercise of these rights by members of the armed forces, of the police or the administration of the State.

Article 12. Right to marry

Men and women of marriageable age have the right to marry and to found a family, according to the national laws governing the exercise of this right.

Article 13. Right to an effective remedy

Everyone whose rights and freedoms as set forth in this Convention are violated shall have an effective remedy before a national authority notwithstanding that the violation has been committed by persons acting in an official capacity.

Article 14. Prohibition of discrimination

The enjoyment of the rights and freedoms as set forth in this Convention shall be secured without discrimination on any ground such as sex, race, colour, language, religion, political or other opinion, national or social origin, association with a national minority, property, birth or other status.

Article 15. Derogation in time of emergency

1. In time of war or other public emergency threatening the life of the nation any High Contracting Party may take measures derogating from its obligations under this Convention to the extent strictly required by the exigencies of the situation, provided that such measures are not inconsistent with its other obligations under international law.

2. No derogation from Article 2, except in respect of deaths resulting from lawful acts of war, or from Articles 3, 4 (paragraph 1) and 7 shall be made under this provision.

3. Any High Contracting Party availing itself of this right of derogation shall keep the Secretary General of the Council of Europe

fully informed of the measures which it has taken and the reasons therefor. It shall also inform the Secretary General of the Council of Europe when such measures have ceased to operate and the provisions of the Convention are again being fully executed.

Article 16. Restrictions on political activity of aliens

Nothing in Articles 10, 11, and 14 shall be regarded as preventing the High Contracting Parties from imposing restrictions on the political activity of aliens.

Article 17. Prohibition of abuse of rights

Nothing in this Convention may be interpreted as implying for any State, group or person any right to engage in any activity or perform any act aimed at the destruction of any of the rights and freedoms set forth herein or at their limitation to a greater extent than is provided for in the Convention.

Article 18. Limitation on use of restrictions or rights

The restrictions permitted under this Convention to the said rights and freedoms shall not be applied for any purpose other than those for which they have been prescribed.

Section II. European Court of Human Rights

Article 19. Establishment of the Court

To ensure the observance of the engagements undertaken by the High Contracting Parties in the Convention and the Protocols thereto, there shall be set up a European Court of Human Rights, hereinafter referred to as "the Court". It shall function on a permanent basis.

Article 20. Number of judges

The Court shall consist of a number of judges equal to that of the High Contracting Parties.

Article 21. Criteria for office

1. The judges shall be of high moral character and must either possess the qualifications required to high judicial office or be jurisconsults of recognised competence.

2. The judges shall sit on the Court in their individual capacity.

3. During their term of office the judges shall not engage in any activity which is incompatible with their independence, impartiality or with the demands of a full-time office; all questions arising from the application of this paragraph shall be decided by the Court.

Article 22. Election of judges

1. The judges shall be elected by the Parliamentary Assembly with respect to each High Contracting Party by a majority of votes cast from a list of three candidates nominated by the High Contracting Party.

2. The same procedure shall be followed to complete the Court in the event of the accession of new High Contracting Parties and in filling casual vacancies.

Article 23. Terms of office

1. The judges shall be elected for a period of six years. They may be re-elected. However, the terms of office of one-half of the judges elected at the first election shall expire at the end of three years.

2. The judges whose terms of office are to expire at the end of the initial period of three years shall be chosen by lot by the Secretary General of the Council of Europe immediately after their election.

3. In order to ensure that, as far as possible, the terms of office of one-half of the judges are renewed every three years, the Parliamentary Assembly may decide, before proceeding to any subsequent election, that the term or terms of office of one or more judges to be elected shall be for a period other than six years but not more than nine and not less than three years.

4. In cases where more than one term of office is involved and where the Parliamentary Assembly applies the preceding paragraph, the allocation of the terms of office shall be effected by a drawing of lots by the Secretary General of the Council of Europe immediately after the election.

5. A judge elected to replace a judge whose term of office has not expired shall hold office for the remainder of his predecessor's term.

6. The terms of office of judges shall expire when they reach the age of 70.

7. The judges shall hold office until replaced. They shall, however, continue to deal with such cases as they already have under consideration.

Article 24. Dismissal

No judge may be dismissed from his office unless the other judges decide by a majority of two-thirds that he has ceased to fulfil the required conditions.

Article 25. Registry and legal secretaries

The Court shall have a registry, the functions and organisation of which shall be laid down in the rules of the Court. The Court shall be assisted by legal secretaries.

Article 26. Plenary Court

The plenary Court shall

a. elect its President and one or two Vice–Presidents for a period of three years; they may be re-elected;

b. set up Chambers, constituted for a fixed period of time;

c. elect the Presidents of the Chambers of the Court; they may be re-elected;

d. adopt the rules of the Court; and

e. elect the Registrar and one or more Deputy Registrars.

Article 27. Committees, Chambers and Grand Chamber

1. To consider cases brought before it, the Court shall sit in committees of three judges, in Chambers of seven judges and in a Grand Chamber of seventeen judges. The Court's Chambers shall set up committees for a fixed period of time.

2. There shall sit as an ex officio member of the Chamber and the Grand Chamber the judge elected in respect of the State Party concerned or, if there is none or if he is unable to sit, a person of its choice who shall sit in the capacity of judge.

3. The Grand Chamber shall also include the President of the Court, the Vice–Presidents, the Presidents of the Chambers and other judges chosen in accordance with the rules of the Court. When a case is referred to the Grand Chamber under Article 43, no judge from the Chamber which rendered the judgment shall sit in the Grand Chamber, with the exception of the President of the Chamber and the judge who sat in respect of the State Party concerned.

Article 28. Declarations of inadmissibility by committees

A committee may, by a unanimous vote, declare inadmissible or strike out of its list of cases an individual application submitted under Article 34 where such a decision can be taken without further examination. The decision shall be final.

Article 29. Decisions by Chambers on admissibility and merits

1. If no decision is taken under Article 28, a Chamber shall decide on the admissibility and merits of individual applications submitted under Article 34.

2. A Chamber shall decide on the admissibility and merits of inter-State applications submitted under Article 33.

3. The decision on admissibility shall be taken separately unless the Court, in exceptional cases, decides otherwise.

Article 30. Relinquishment of jurisdiction to the Grand Chamber

Where a case pending before a Chamber raises a serious question affecting the interpretation of the Convention or the protocols thereto, or where the resolution of a question before the Chamber might have a result inconsistent with a judgment previously delivered by the Court, the Chamber may, at any time before it has rendered its judgment, relinquish jurisdiction in favour of the Grand Chamber, unless one of the parties to the case objects.

Article 31. Powers of the Grand Chamber

The Grand Chamber shall

a. determine applications submitted either under Article 33 or Article 34 when a Chamber has relinquished jurisdiction under

Article 30 or when the case has been referred to it under Article 43; and

b. consider requests for advisory opinions submitted under Article 47.

Article 32. Jurisdiction of the Court

1. The jurisdiction of the Court shall extend to all matters concerning the interpretation and application of the Convention and the protocols thereto which are referred to it as provided in Articles 33, 34 and 47.

2. In the event of dispute as to whether the Court has jurisdiction, the Court shall decide.

Article 33. Inter–State cases

Any High Contracting Party may refer to the Court any alleged breach of the provisions of the Convention and the protocols thereto by Another High Contracting Party.

Article 34. Individual applications

The Court may receive applications from any person, non-governmental organisation or group of individuals claiming to be the victim of a violation by one of the High Contracting Parties of the rights set forth in the Convention or the protocols thereto. The High Contracting Parties undertake not to hinder in any way the effective exercise of this right.

Article 35. Admissibility criteria

1. The Court may only deal with the matter after all domestic remedies have been exhausted, according to the generally recognised rules of international law, and within a period of six months from the date on which the final decision was taken.

2. The Court shall not deal with any individual application submitted under Article 34 that

a. is anonymous; or

b. is substantially the same as a matter that has already been examined by the Court or has already been submitted to another procedure of international investigation or settlement and contains no relevant new information.

3. The Court shall declare inadmissible any individual application submitted under Article 34 which it considers incompatible with the provisions of the Convention or the protocols thereto, manifestly ill-founded, or an abuse of the right of application.

4. The Court shall reject any application which it considers inadmissible under this Article. It may do so at any stage of the proceedings.

Article 36. Third-party intervention

1. In all cases before a Chamber or the Grand Chamber, a High Contracting Party one of whose nationals is an applicant shall have the right to submit written comments and to take part in hearings.

2. The President of the Court may, in the interest of the proper administration of justice, invite any High Contracting Party which is not a party to the proceedings or any person concerned who is not the applicant to submit written comments or take part in hearings.

Article 37. Striking out applications

1. The Court may at any stage of the proceedings decide to strike an application out of its list of cases where the circumstances lead to the conclusion that

a. the applicant does not intend to pursue his application; or

b. the matter has been resolved; or

c. for any other reason established by the Court, it is no longer justified to continue the examination of the application.

However, the Court shall continue the examination of the application if respect for human rights as defined in the Convention and the protocols thereto so requires.

2. The Court may decide to restore an application to its list of cases if it considers that the circumstances justify such a course.

Article 38. Examination of the case and friendly settlement proceedings

1. If the Court declares the application admissible, it shall

a. pursue the examination of the case, together with the representatives of the parties, and if need be, undertake an investigation, for the effective conduct of which the States concerned shall furnish all necessary facilities;

b. place itself at the disposal of the parties concerned with a view to securing a friendly settlement of the matter on the basis of respect for human rights as defined in the Convention and the protocols thereto.

2. Proceedings conducted under paragraph 1 b shall be confidential.

Article 39. Finding of a friendly settlement

If a friendly settlement is effected, the Court shall strike the case out of its list by means of a decision which shall be confined to a brief statement of the facts and of the solution reached.

Article 40. Public hearings and access to documents

1. Hearings shall be public unless the Court in exceptional circumstances decides otherwise.

2. Documents deposited with the Registrar shall be accessible to the public unless the President of the Court decides otherwise.

Article 41. Just satisfaction

If the Court finds that there has been a violation of the Convention or the protocols thereto, and if the internal law of the High Contracting

Party concerned allows only partial reparation to be made, the Court shall, if necessary, afford just satisfaction to the injured party.

Article 42. Judgments of Chambers

Judgments of Chambers shall become final in accordance with the provisions of Article 44, paragraph 2.

Article 43. Referral to the Grand Chamber

1. Within a period of three months from the date of the judgment of the Chamber, any party to the case may, in exceptional cases, request that the case be referred to the Grand Chamber.

2. A panel of five judges of the Grand Chamber shall accept the request if the case raises a serious question affecting the interpretation or application of the Convention or the protocols thereto, or a serious issue of general importance.

3. If the panel accepts the request, the Grand Chamber shall decide the case by means of a judgment.

Article 44. Final judgements

1. The judgment of the Grand Chamber shall be final.

2. The judgment of a Chamber shall become final

a. when the parties declare that they will not request that the case be referred to the Grand Chamber; or

b. three months after the date of the judgment, if reference of the case to the Grand Chamber has not been requested; or

c. when the panel of the Grand Chamber rejects the request to refer under Article 43.

3. The final judgment shall be published.

Article 45. Reasons for judgments and decisions

1. Reasons shall be given for judgments as well as for decisions declaring applications admissible or inadmissible.

2. If a judgment does not represent, in whole or in part, the unanimous opinion of the judges, any judge shall be entitled to deliver a separate opinion.

Article 46. Binding force and execution of judgments

1. The High Contracting Parties undertake to abide by the final judgment of the Court in any case to which they are parties.

2. The final judgment of the Court shall be transmitted to the Committee of Ministers, which shall supervise its execution.

Article 47. Advisory opinions

1. The Court may, at the request of the Committee of Ministers, give advisory opinions on legal questions concerning the interpretation of the Convention and the protocols thereto.

2. Such opinions shall not deal with any question relating to the content or scope of the rights or freedoms defined in Section I of the Convention and the protocols thereto, or with any other question which the Court or the Committee of Ministers might have to consider in consequence of any such proceedings as could be instituted in accordance with the Convention.

3. Decisions of the Committee of Ministers to request an advisory opinion of the Court shall require a majority vote of the representatives entitled to sit on the Committee.

Article 48. Advisory jurisdiction of the Court

The Court shall decide whether a request for an advisory opinion submitted by the Committee of Ministers is within its competence as defined in Article 47.

Article 49. Reasons for advisory opinions

1. Reasons shall be given for advisory opinions of the Court.

2. In the advisory opinion does not represent, in whole or in part, the unanimous opinion of the judges, any judge shall be entitled to deliver a separate opinion.

3. Advisory opinions of the Court shall be communicated to the Committee of Ministers.

Article 50. Expenditure of Court

The expenditure of the Court shall be borne by the Council of Europe.

Article 51. Privileges and immunities of judges

The judges hall be entitled, during the exercise of their functions, to the privileges and immunities provided for in Article 40 or the Statute of the Council of Europe and in the agreements made thereunder.

Section III. Miscellaneous Provisions

Article 52. Inquires by the Secretary General

On receipt of a request from the Secretary General of the Council of Europe and High Contracting Party shall furnish an explanation of the manner in which its internal law ensures the effective implementation of any of the provisions of the Convention.

Article 53. Safeguard for existing human rights

Nothing in this Convention shall be construed as limiting or derogating from any of the human rights and fundamental freedoms which may be ensured under the laws of any High Contracting Party or under any other agreement to which it is a Party.

Article 54. Powers of the Committee of Ministers

Nothing in this Convention shall prejudice the powers conferred on the Committee of Ministers by the Statute of the Council of Europe.

Document 23
PROTOCOL NO. 1 TO THE EUROPEAN CONVENTION

Eur. T.S. 9 (excerpt)

Article 1

Every natural or legal person is entitled to the peaceful enjoyment of his possessions.

No one shall be deprived of his possessions except in the public interest and subject to the conditions provided for by law and by the general principles of international law.

The preceding provisions shall not, however, in any way impair the right of a State to enforce such laws as it deems necessary to control the use of property in accordance with the general interest or to secure the payment of taxes or other contributions or penalties.

Article 2

No person shall be denied the right to education. In the exercise of any functions which it assumes in relation to education and to teaching, the State shall respect the right of parents to ensure such education and teaching in conformity with their own religious and philosophical convictions.

Article 3

The High Contracting Parties undertake to hold free elections at reasonable intervals by secret ballot, under conditions which will ensure the free expression of the opinion of the people in the choice of the legislature.

Document 24
PROTOCOL NO. 2 TO THE EUROPEAN CONVENTION

Eur. T.S. 44 (excerpt)

Article 1

1. The Court may, at the request of the Committee of Ministers, give advisory opinions on legal questions concerning the interpretation of the Convention and the Protocols thereto.

2. Such opinions shall not deal with any question relating to the content or scope of the rights or freedoms defined in Section I of the Convention and in the Protocols thereto, or with any other question which the Commission, the Court or the Committee of Ministers might have to consider in consequence of any such proceedings as could be instituted in accordance with the Convention.

3. Decisions of the Committee of Ministers to request an advisory opinion of the Court shall require a two-thirds majority vote of the representatives entitled to sit on the Committee.

Document 25
PROTOCOL NO. 4 TO THE EUROPEAN CONVENTION

Eur. T.S. 46 (excerpt)

Article 1

No one shall be deprived of his liberty merely on the ground of inability to fulfil a contractual obligation.

Article 2

1. Everyone lawfully within the territory of a State shall, within that territory, have the right to liberty of movement and freedom to choose his residence.

2. Everyone shall be free to leave any country, including his own.

3. No restrictions shall be placed on the exercise of these rights other than such as are in accordance with law and are necessary in a democratic society in the interests of national security or public safety, for the maintenance of *ordre public*, for the prevention of crime, for the protection of health or morals, or for the protection of the rights and freedoms of others.

4. The rights set forth in paragraph 1 may also be subject, in particular areas, to restrictions imposed in accordance with law and justified by the public interest in a democratic society.

Article 3

1. No one shall be expelled, by means either of an individual or of a collective measure, from the territory of the State of which he is a national.

2. No one shall be deprived of the right to enter the territory of the State of which he is a national.

Article 4

Collective expulsion of aliens is prohibited.

Document 26
PROTOCOL NO. 6 TO THE EUROPEAN CONVENTION

Eur. T.S. 114 (1985) (excerpt)

Article 1

The death penalty shall be abolished. No one shall be condemned to such penalty or executed.

Article 2

A State may make provisions in its law for the death penalty in respect of acts committed in time of war or of imminent threat of war; such penalty shall be applied only in the instances laid down in the law and in accordance with its provisions. The State shall communicate to the Secretary General of the Council of Europe the relevant provisions of that law.

Article 3

No derogation from the provisions of this Protocol shall be made under Article 15 of the Convention.

Article 4

No reservation may be made under Article 64 of the Convention in respect of the provisions of this Protocol.

Document 27
PROTOCOL NO. 7 TO THE EUROPEAN CONVENTION

Eur. T.S. 117 (1988) (excerpt)

Article 1

1. An alien lawfully resident in the territory of a State shall not be expelled therefrom except in pursuance of a decision reached in accordance with law and shall be allowed:

a. to submit reasons against his expulsion,

b. to have his case reviewed, and

c. to be represented for these purposes before the competent authority or a person or persons designated by that authority.

2. An alien may be expelled before the exercise of his rights under paragraph 1.a, b and c of this article, when such expulsion is necessary in the interests of public order or is grounded on reasons of national security.

Article 2

1. Everyone convicted of a criminal offence by a tribunal shall have the right to have his conviction or sentence reviewed by a higher tribunal. The exercise of this right, including the grounds on which it may be exercised, shall be governed by law.

2. The right may be subject to exceptions in regard to offences of a minor character, as prescribed by law, or in cases in which the person concerned was tried in the first instance by the highest tribunal or was convicted following an appeal against acquittal.

Article 3

When a person has by a final decision been convicted of a criminal offence and when subsequently his conviction has been reversed, or he has been pardoned, on the ground that a new or newly discovered fact shows conclusively that there has been a miscarriage of justice, the person who has suffered punishment as a result of such conviction shall be compensated according to the law or the practice of the State concerned, unless it is proved that the nondisclosure of the unknown fact in time is wholly or partly attributable to him.

Article 4

1. No one shall be liable to be tried or punished again in criminal proceedings under the jurisdiction of the same State for an offence for

which he has already been finally acquitted or convicted in accordance with the law and penal procedure of that State.

2. The provisions of the preceding paragraph shall not prevent the reopening of the case in accordance with the law and penal procedure of the State concerned, if there is evidence of new or newly discovered facts, or if there has been a fundamental defect in the previous proceedings, which could affect the outcome of the case.

3. No derogation from this article shall be made under Article 15 of the Convention.

Article 5

Spouses shall enjoy equality of rights and responsibilities of a private law character between them, and in their relations with their children, as to marriage, during marriage and in the event of its dissolution. This article shall not prevent States from taking such measures as are necessary in the interests of the children.

Document 28
BASIC PRINCIPLES AND GUIDELINES ON THE RIGHT TO A REMEDY AND REPARATION FOR VICTIMS OF GROSS VIOLATIONS OF INTERNATIONAL HUMAN RIGHTS AND SERIOUS VIOLATIONS OF INTERNATIONAL HUMANITARIAN LAW

U.N. G.A. Res. 60/147 (16 Dec. 2005)

The General Assembly,

Guided by the Charter of the United Nations, the Universal Declaration of Human Rights, the International Covenants on Human Rights, other relevant human rights instruments and the Vienna Declaration and Programme of Action,

Affirming the importance of addressing the question of remedies and reparation for victims of gross violations of international human rights law and serious violations of international humanitarian law in a systematic and thorough way at the national and international levels,

Recognizing that, in honouring the victims' right to benefit from remedies and reparation, the international community keeps faith with the plight of victims, survivors and future human generations and reaffirms international law in the field,

Recalling the adoption of the Basic Principles and Guidelines on the Right to a Remedy and Reparation for Victims of Gross Violations of International Human Rights Law and Serious Violations of International Humanitarian Law by the Commission on Human Rights in its resolution 2005/35 of 19 April 2005 and by the Economic and Social Council in its resolution 2005/30 of 25 July 2005, in which the Council recommended to the General Assembly that it adopt the Basic Principles and Guidelines,

1. *Adopts* the Basic Principles and Guidelines on the Right to a Remedy and Reparation for Victims of Gross Violations of International Human Rights Law and Serious Violations of International Humanitarian Law annexed to the present resolution;

2. *Recommends* that States take the Basic Principles and Guidelines into account, promote respect thereof and bring them to the attention of members of the executive bodies of government, in particular law enforcement officials and military and security forces, legislative

bodies, the judiciary, victims and their representatives, human rights defenders and lawyers, the media and the public in general;

3. *Requests* the Secretary–General to take steps to ensure the widest possible dissemination of the Basic Principles and Guidelines in all the official languages of the United Nations, including by transmitting them to Governments and intergovernmental and non-governmental organizations and by including the Basic Principles and Guidelines in the United Nations publication entitled *Human Rights: A Compilation of International Instruments.*

Annex

Basic Principles and Guidelines on the Right to a Remedy and Reparation for Victims of Gross Violations of International Human Rights Law and Serious Violations of International Humanitarian Law

Preamble

The General Assembly,

Recalling the provisions providing a right to a remedy for victims of violations of international human rights law found in numerous international instruments, in particular article 8 of the Universal Declaration of Human Rights, article 2 of the International Covenant on Civil and Political Rights, article 6 of the International Convention on the Elimination of All Forms of Racial Discrimination, article 14 of the Convention against Torture and Other Cruel, Inhuman or Degrading Treatment or Punishment, and article 39 of the Convention on the Rights of the Child, and of international humanitarian law as found in article 3 of the Hague Convention respecting the Laws and Customs of War on Land of 18 October 1907 (Convention IV), article 91 of the Protocol Additional to the Geneva Conventions of 12 August 1949, and relating to the Protection of Victims of International Armed Conflicts (Protocol I) of 8 June 1977, and articles 68 and 75 of the Rome Statute of the International Criminal Court,

Recalling the provisions providing a right to a remedy for victims of violations of international human rights found in regional conventions, in particular article 7 of the African Charter on Human and Peoples' Rights, article 25 of the American Convention on Human Rights, and article 13 of the Convention for the Protection of Human Rights and Fundamental Freedoms,

Recalling the Declaration of Basic Principles of Justice for Victims of Crime and Abuse of Power emanating from the deliberations of the Seventh United Nations Congress on the Prevention of Crime and the Treatment of Offenders and General Assembly resolution 40/34 of 29 November 1985 by which the Assembly adopted the text recommended by the Congress,

Reaffirming the principles enunciated in the Declaration of Basic Principles of Justice for Victims of Crime and Abuse of Power, including that victims should be treated with compassion and respect for their dignity, have their right to access to justice and redress mechanisms fully respected, and that the establishment, strengthening and expansion of national funds for compensation to victims should be encouraged, together with the expeditious development of appropriate rights and remedies for victims,

Noting that the Rome Statute of the International Criminal Court requires the establishment of "principles relating to reparations to, or in respect of, victims, including restitution, compensation and rehabilitation", requires the Assembly of States Parties to establish a trust fund for the benefit of victims of crimes within the jurisdiction of the Court, and of the families of such victims, and mandates the Court "to protect the safety, physical and psychological well-being, dignity and privacy of victims" and to permit the participation of victims at all "stages of the proceedings determined to be appropriate by the Court",

Affirming that the Basic Principles and Guidelines contained herein are directed at gross violations of international human rights law and serious violations of international humanitarian law which, by their very grave nature, constitute an affront to human dignity,

Emphasizing that the Basic Principles and Guidelines contained herein do not entail new international or domestic legal obligations but identity mechanisms, modalities, procedures and methods for the implementation of existing legal obligations under international human rights law and international humanitarian law which arc complementary though different as to their norms,

Recalling that international law contains the obligation to prosecute perpetrators of certain international crimes in accordance with international obligations of States and the requirements of national law or as provided for in the applicable statutes of international judicial organs, and that the duty to prosecute reinforces the international legal obligations to be carried out in accordance with national legal requirements and procedures and supports the concept of complementarity,

Noting that contemporary forms of victimization, while essentially directed against persons, may nevertheless also be directed against groups of persons who are targeted collectively,

Recognizing that, in honouring the victims' right to benefit from remedies and reparation, the international community keeps faith with the plight of victims, survivors and future human generations and reaffirms the international legal principles of accountability, justice and the rule of law,

Convinced that, in adopting a victim-oriented perspective, the international community affirms its human solidarity with victims of violations of international law, including violations of international human rights law and international humanitarian law, as well as with humanity at large, in accordance with the following Basic Principles and Guidelines,

Adopts the following Basic Principles and Guidelines:

I. Obligation to respect, ensure respect for and implement international human rights law and international humanitarian law

1. The obligation to respect, ensure respect for and implement international human rights law and international humanitarian law as provided for under the respective bodies of law emanates from:

(a) Treaties to which a State is a party;

(b) Customary international law;

(c) The domestic law of each State.

2. If they have not already done so, States shall, as required under international law, ensure that their domestic law is consistent with their international legal obligations by:

(a) Incorporating norms of international human rights law and international humanitarian law into their domestic law, or otherwise implementing them in their domestic legal system;

(b) Adopting appropriate and effective legislative and administrative procedures and other appropriate measures that provide fair, effective and prompt access to justice;

(c) Making available adequate, effective, prompt and appropriate remedies, including reparation, as defined below;

(d) Ensuring that their domestic law provides at least the same level of protection for victims as that required by their international obligations.

II. Scope of the obligation

3. The obligation to respect, ensure respect for and implement international human rights law and international humanitarian law as provided for under the respective bodies of law, includes, inter alia, the duty to:

(a) Take appropriate legislative and administrative and other appropriate measures to prevent violations;

(b) Investigate violations effectively, promptly, thoroughly and impartially and, where appropriate, take action against those allegedly responsible in accordance with domestic and international law;

(c) Provide those who claim to be victims of a human rights or humanitarian law violation with equal and effective access to justice, as described below, irrespective of who may ultimately be the bearer of responsibility for the violation; and

(d) Provide effective remedies to victims, including reparation, as described below.

III. Gross violations of international human rights law and serious violations of international humanitarian law that constitute crimes under international law

4. In cases of gross violations of international human rights law and serious violations of international humanitarian law constituting crimes under international law, States have the duty to investigate and, if there is sufficient evidence, the duty to submit to prosecution the person allegedly responsible for the violations and, if found guilty, the duty to punish her or him. Moreover, in these cases, States should, in accordance with international law, cooperate with one another and assist international judicial organs competent in the investigation and prosecution of these violations.

5. To that end, where so provided in an applicable treaty or under other international law obligations, States shall incorporate or otherwise implement within their domestic law appropriate provisions for universal jurisdiction. Moreover, where it is so provided for in an applicable treaty or other international legal obligations, States should facilitate extradition or surrender offenders to other States and to appropriate international judicial bodies and provide judicial assistance and other forms of cooperation in the pursuit of international justice, including assistance to, and protection of, victims and witnesses, consistent with international human rights legal standards and subject to international legal requirements such as those relating to the prohibition of torture and other forms of cruel, inhuman or degrading treatment or punishment.

IV. Statutes of limitations

6. Where so provided for in an applicable treaty or contained in other international legal obligations, statutes of limitations shall not apply to gross violations of international human rights law and serious violations of international humanitarian law which constitute crimes under international law.

7. Domestic statutes of limitations for other types of violations that do not constitute crimes under international law, including those time limitations applicable to civil claims and other procedures, should not be unduly restrictive.

V. Victims of gross violations of international human rights law and serious violations of international humanitarian law

8. For purposes of the present document, victims are persons who individually or collectively suffered harm, including physical or mental injury, emotional suffering, economic loss or substantial impairment of their fundamental rights, through acts or omissions that constitute gross violations of international human rights law, or serious violations of international humanitarian law. Where appropriate, and in accordance with domestic law, the term "victim" also includes the immediate family or dependants of the direct victim and persons who have suffered harm in intervening to assist victims in distress or to prevent victimization.

9. A person shall be considered a victim regardless of whether the perpetrator of the violation is identified, apprehended, prosecuted, or convicted and regardless of the familial relationship between the perpetrator and the victim.

VI. Treatment of victims

10. Victims should be treated with humanity and respect for their dignity and human rights, and appropriate measures should be taken to ensure their safety, physical and psychological well-being and privacy, as well as those of their families. The State should ensure that its domestic laws, to the extent possible, provide that a victim who has suffered violence or trauma should benefit from special consideration and care to avoid his or her re-traumatization in the course of legal and administrative procedures designed to provide justice and reparation.

VII. Victims' right to remedies

11. Remedies for gross violations of international human rights law and serious violations of international humanitarian law include the victim's right to the following as provided for under international law:

(a) Equal and effective access to justice;

(b) Adequate, effective and prompt reparation for harm suffered;

(c) Access to relevant information concerning violations and reparation mechanisms.

VIII. Access to justice

12. A victim of a gross violation of international human rights law or of a serious violation of international humanitarian law shall have equal access to an effective judicial remedy as provided for under international law. Other remedies available to the victim include access to administrative and other bodies, as well as mechanisms, modalities and proceedings conducted in accordance with domestic law. Obligations arising under international law to secure the right to access justice and fair and impartial proceedings shall be reflected in domestic laws. To that end, States should:

(a) Disseminate, through public and private mechanisms, information about all available remedies for gross violations of international human rights law and serious violations of international humanitarian law;

(b) Take measures to minimize the inconvenience to victims and their representatives, protect against unlawful interference with their privacy as appropriate and ensure their safety from intimidation and retaliation, as well as that of their families and witnesses, before, during and after judicial, administrative, or other proceedings that affect the interests of victims;

(c) Provide proper assistance to victims seeking access to justice;

(d) Make available all appropriate legal, diplomatic and consular means to ensure that victims can exercise their rights to remedy for gross violations of international human rights law or serious violations of international humanitarian law.

13. In addition to individual access to justice, States should endeavour to develop procedures to allow groups of victims to present claims for reparation and to receive reparation, as appropriate.

14. An adequate, effective and prompt remedy for gross violations of international human rights law or serious violations of international humanitarian law should include all available and appropriate international processes in which a person may have legal standing and should be without prejudice to any other domestic remedies.

IX. Reparation for harm suffered

15. Adequate, effective and prompt reparation is intended to promote justice by redressing gross violations of international human rights

law or serious violations of international humanitarian law. Reparation should be proportional to the gravity of the violations and the harm suffered. In accordance with its domestic laws and international legal obligations, a State shall provide reparation to victims for acts or omissions which can be attributed to the State and constitute gross violations of international human rights law or serious violations of international humanitarian law. In cases where a person, a legal person, or other entity is found liable for reparation to a victim, such party should provide reparation to the victim or compensate the State if the State has already provided reparation to the victim.

16. States should endeavour to establish national programmes for reparation and other assistance to victims in the event that the parties liable for the harm suffered are unable or unwilling to meet their obligations.

17. States shall, with respect to claims by victims, enforce domestic judgements for reparation against individuals or entities liable for the harm suffered and endeavour to enforce valid foreign legal judgements for reparation in accordance with domestic law and international legal obligations. To that end, States should provide under their domestic laws effective mechanisms for the enforcement of reparation judgements.

18. In accordance with domestic law and international law, and taking account of individual circumstances, victims of gross violations of international human rights law and serious violations of international humanitarian law should, as appropriate and proportional to the gravity of the violation and the circumstances of each case, be provided with full and effective reparation, as laid out in principles 19 to 23, which include the following forms: restitution, compensation, rehabilitation, satisfaction and guarantees of non-repetition.

19. *Restitution* should, whenever possible, restore the victim to the original situation before the gross violations of international human rights law or serious violations of international humanitarian law occurred. Restitution includes, as appropriate: restoration of liberty, enjoyment of human rights, identity, family life and citizenship, return to one's place of residence, restoration of employment and return of property.

20. *Compensation* should be provided for any economically assessable damage, as appropriate and proportional to the gravity of the violation and the circumstances of each case, resulting from gross violations of international human rights law and serious violations of international humanitarian law, such as:

(a) Physical or mental harm;

(b) Lost opportunities, including employment, education and social benefits;

(c) Material damages and loss of earnings, including loss of earning potential;

(d) Moral damage;

(e) Costs required for legal or expert assistance, medicine and medical services, and psychological and social services.

21. *Rehabilitation* should include medical and psychological care as well as legal and social services.

22. *Satisfaction* should include, where applicable, any or all of the following:

(a) Effective measures aimed at the cessation of continuing violations;

(b) Verification of the facts and full and public disclosure of the truth to the extent that such disclosure does not cause further harm or threaten the safety and interests of the victim, the victim's relatives, witnesses, or persons who have intervened to assist the victim or prevent the occurrence of further violations;

(c) The search for the whereabouts of the disappeared, for the identities of the children abducted, and for the bodies of those killed, and assistance in the recovery, identification and reburial of the bodies in accordance with the expressed or presumed wish of the victims, or the cultural practices of the families and communities;

(d) An official declaration or a judicial decision restoring the dignity, the reputation and the rights of the victim and of persons closely connected with the victim;

(e) Public apology, including acknowledgement of the facts and acceptance of responsibility;

(f) Judicial and administrative sanctions against persons liable for the violations;

(g) Commemorations and tributes to the victims;

(h) Inclusion of an accurate account of the violations that occurred in international human rights law and international humanitarian law training and in educational material at all levels.

23. *Guarantees of non-repetition* should include, where applicable, any or all of the following measures, which will also contribute to prevention:

(a) Ensuring effective civilian control of military and security forces;

(b) Ensuring that all civilian and military proceedings abide by international standards of due process, fairness and impartiality;

(c) Strengthening the independence of the judiciary;

(d) Protecting persons in the legal, medical and health-care professions, the media and other related professions, and human rights defenders;

(e) Providing, on a priority and continued basis, human rights and international humanitarian law education to all sectors of society and training for law enforcement officials as well as military and security forces;

(f) Promoting the observance of codes of conduct and ethical norms, in particular international standards, by public servants, including law enforcement, correctional, media, medical, psychological, social service and military personnel, as well as by economic enterprises;

(g) Promoting mechanisms for preventing and monitoring social conflicts and their resolution;

(h) Reviewing and reforming laws contributing to or allowing gross violations of international human rights law and serious violations of international humanitarian law.

X. Access to relevant information concerning violations and reparation mechanisms

24. States should develop means of informing the general public and, in particular, victims of gross violations of international human rights law and serious violations of international humanitarian law of the rights and remedies addressed by these Basic Principles and Guidelines and of all available legal, medical, psychological, social, administrative and all other services to which victims may have a right of access. Moreover, victims and their representatives should be entitled to seek and obtain information on the causes leading to their victimization and on the causes and conditions pertaining to the gross violations of international human rights law and serious violations of international humanitarian law and to learn the truth in regard to these violations.

XI. Non-discrimination

25. The application and interpretation of these Basic Principles and Guidelines must be consistent with international human rights law and international humanitarian law and be without any discrimination of any kind or on any ground, without exception.

XII. Non-derogation

26. Nothing in these Basic Principles and Guidelines shall be construed as restricting or derogating from any rights or obligations arising under domestic and international law. In particular, it is understood that the present Basic Principles and Guidelines are without prejudice to the right to a remedy and reparation for victims of all violations of international human rights law and international humanitarian law. It is further understood that these Basic Principles and Guidelines are without prejudice to special rules of international law.

XIII. Rights of others

27. Nothing in this document is to be construed as derogating from internationally or nationally protected rights of others, in particular the right of an accused person to benefit from applicable standards of due process.

Document 29
2005 WORLD SUMMIT OUTCOME

U.N. G.A. Res. 60/1 (24 Oct. 2005)

The General Assembly

Adopts the following 2005 World Summit Outcome:

I. Values and Principles

1. We, Heads of State and Government, have gathered at United Nations Headquarters in New York from 14 to 16 September 2005....

4. We reaffirm our common fundamental values, including freedom, equality, solidarity, tolerance, respect fo all human rights, respect for nature and shared responsibility, are essential to international relations.

5. We are determined to establish a just and lasting peace all over the world in accordance with the purposes and principles of the Charter. We rededicate ourselves to support all efforts to uphold the sovereign equality of all States, respect their territorial integrity and political independence, to refrain in our international relations from the threat or use of force in any manner inconsistent with the purposes and principles of the United Nations, to uphold resolution of disputes by peaceful means and in conformity with the principles of justice and international law, the right to self-determination of peoples which remain under colonial domination and foreign occupation, non-interference in the internal affairs of States, respect for human rights and fundamental freedoms, respect for the equal rights of all without distinction as to race, sex, language or religion, international cooperation in solving international problems of an economic, social, cultural or humanitarian character and the fulfilment in good faith of the obligations assumed in accordance with the Charter....

9. We acknowledge that peace and security, development and human rights are the pillars of the United Nations system and the foundations for collective security and well-being. We recognize that development, peace and security and human rights are interlinked and mutually reinforcing.

10. We reaffirm that development is a central goal in itself and that sustainable development in its economic, social and environmental aspects constitutes a key element of the overarching framework of United Nations activities.

11. We acknowledge that good governance and the rule of law at the national and international levels are essential for sustained economic growth, sustainable development and the eradication of poverty and hunger.

12. We reaffirm that gender equality and the promotion and protection of the full enjoyment of all human rights and fundamental freedoms for all are essential to advance development and peace and security. We are committed to creating a world fit for future generations, which takes into account the best interests of the child.

13. We reaffirm the universality, indivisibility, interdependence and interrelatedness of all human rights.

14. Acknowledging the diversity of the world, we recognize that all cultures and civilizations contribute to the enrichment of humankind. We acknowledge the importance of respect and understanding for religious and cultural diversity throughout the world. In order to promote international peace and security, we commit ourselves to advancing human welfare, freedom and progress everywhere, as well as to encouraging tolerance, respect, dialogue and cooperation among different cultures, civilizations and peoples.

15. We pledge to enhance the relevance, effectiveness, efficiency, accountability and credibility of the United Nations system. This is our shared responsibility and interest.

16. We therefore resolve to create a more peaceful, prosperous and democratic world and to undertake concrete measures to continue finding ways to implement the outcome of the Millennium Summit and the other major United Nations conferences and summits so as to provide multilateral solutions to problems in the four following areas: development, peace and collective security, human rights and the rule of law, strengthening of the United Nations. . . .

Gender equality and empowerment of women

58. We remain convinced that progress for women is progress for all. We reaffirm that the full and effective implementation of the goals and objectives of the Beijing Declaration and Platform for Action and the outcome of the twenty-third special session of the General Assembly is an essential contribution to achieving the internationally agreed development goals, including those contained in the Millennium Declaration, and we resolve to promote gender equality and eliminate pervasive gender discrimination by:

(a) Eliminating gender inequalities to primary and secondary education by the earliest possible date and at all educational levels by 2015;

(b) Guaranteeing the free and equal right of women to own and inherit property and ensuring tenure of property and housing by women;

(c) Ensuring equal access to reproductive health;

(d) Promoting women's equal access to labour markets, sustainable employment and adequate labour protection;

(e) Ensuring equal access of women to productive assets and resources, including land, credit and technology;

(f) Eliminating all forms of discrimination and violence against women and the girl child, including by ending impunity and by ensuring the protection of civilians, in particular women and the girl child, during and after armed conflicts in accordance with the obligations of States under international humanitarian law and international human rights law;

(g) Promoting increased representation of women in Government decision-making bodies, including through ensuring their equal opportunity to participate fully in the political process.

59. We recognize the importance of gender mainstreaming as a tool for achieving gender equality. To that end, we undertake to actively promote the mainstreaming of a gender perspective in the design, implementation, monitoring and evaluation of policies and programmes in all political, economic and social spheres, and further undertake to strengthen the capabilities of the United Nations system in the area of gender....

III. Peace and Collective Security

69. We recognize that we are facing a whole range of threats that require our urgent, collective and more determined response.

70. We also recognize that, in accordance with the Charter, addressing such threats requires cooperation among all the principal organs of the United Nations within their respective mandates.

71. We acknowledge that we are living in an interdependent and global world and that many of today's threats recognize no national boundaries, are interlinked and must be tackled at the global, regional and national levels in accordance with the Charter and international law.

72. We therefore reaffirm our commitment to work towards a security consensus based on the recognition that many threats are interlinked, that development, peace, security and human rights are mutually reinforcing, that no State can best protect itself by acting entirely alone and that all States need an effective and efficient collective security system pursuant to the purposes and principles of the Charter....

79. We reaffirm that the relevant provisions of the Charter are sufficient to address the full range of threats to international peace and security. We further reaffirm the authority of the Security Council to mandate coercive action to maintain and restore international peace and security. We stress the importance of acting in accordance with the purposes and principles of the Charter.

80. We also reaffirm that the Security Council has primary responsibility in the maintenance of international peace and security. We also note the role of the General Assembly relating to the maintenance of peace and security in accordance with the relevant provisions of the Charter.

Terrorism

81. We strongly condemn terrorism in all its forms and manifestations, committed by whomever, wherever and for whatever purposes, as

it constitutes one of the most serious threats to international peace and security....

85. We recognize that international cooperation to fight terrorism must be conducted in conformity with international law, including the Charter and relevant international conventions and protocols. States must ensure that any measures taken to combat terrorism comply with their obligations under international law, in particular human rights law, refugee law and international humanitarian law.

86. We reiterate our call upon States to refrain from organizing, financing, encouraging, providing training for or otherwise supporting terrorist activities and to take appropriate measures to ensure that their territories are not used for such activities....

Peacekeeping

93. Recognizing the important contribution to peace and security by regional organizations as provided for under Chapter VII of the Charter and the importance of forging predictable partnerships and arrangements between the United Nations and regional organizations, and noting in particular, given the special needs of Africa, the importance of a strong African Union:

(a) We support the efforts of the European Union and other regional entities to develop capacities such as for rapid deployment, standby and bridging arrangements;

(b) We support the development and implementation of a ten-year plan for capacity-building with the African Union....

Protecting children in situations of armed conflict

117. We reaffirm our commitment to promote and protect the rights and welfare of children in armed conflicts.... We also call upon States to take effective measures, as appropriate, to prevent the recruitment and use of children in armed conflict, contrary to international law, by armed forces and groups, and to prohibit and criminalize such practices.

118. We therefore call upon all States concerned to take concrete measures to ensure accountability and compliance by those responsible for grave abuses against children. We also reaffirm our commitment to ensure that children in armed conflicts receive timely and effective humanitarian assistance, including education, for their rehabilitation and reintegration into society.

IV. Human Rights and the Rule of Law

119. We recommit ourselves to actively protecting and promoting all human rights, the rule of law and democracy and recognize that they are interlinked and mutually reinforcing and that they belong to the universal and indivisible core values and principles of the United Nations, and call upon all parts of the United Nations to promote human rights and fundamental freedoms in accordance with their mandates....

Human Rights

121. We reaffirm that all human rights are universal, indivisible, interrelated, interdependent and mutually reinforcing and that all human rights must be treated in a fair and equal manner, on the same footing and with the same emphasis. While the significance of national and regional particularities and various historical, cultural and religious backgrounds must be borne in mind, all States, regardless of their political, economic and cultural systems, have the duty to promote and protect all human rights and fundamental freedoms.

122. We emphasize the responsibilities of all States, in conformity with the Charter, to respect human rights and fundamental freedoms for all, without distinction of any kind as to race, colour, sex, language or religion, political or other opinion, national or social origin, property, birth or other status. . . .

Democracy

135. We reaffirm that democracy is a universal value based on the freely expressed will of people to determine their own political, economic, social and cultural systems and their full participation in all aspects of their lives. We also reaffirm that while democracies share common features, there is no single model of democracy, that it does not belong to any country or region, and reaffirm the necessity of due respect for sovereignty and the right of self-determination. We stress that democracy, development and respect for all human rights and fundamental freedoms are interdependent and mutually reinforcing. . . .

Responsibility to Protect Populations from Genocide, War Crimes, Ethnic Cleansing and Crimes Against Humanity

138. Each individual State has the responsibility to protect its populations from genocide, war crimes, ethnic cleansing and crimes against humanity. This responsibility entails the prevention of such crimes, including their incitement, through appropriate and necessary means. We accept that responsibility and will act in accordance with it. The international community should, as appropriate, encourage and help States to exercise this responsibility and support the United Nations in establishing an early warning capability.

139. The international community, through the United Nations, also has the responsibility to use appropriate diplomatic, humanitarian and other peaceful means, in accordance with Chapters VI and VII of the Charter, to help to protect populations from genocide, war crimes, ethnic cleansing and crimes against humanity. In this context, we are prepared to take collective action, in a timely and decisive manner, through the Security Council, in accordance with the Charter, including Chapter VII, on a case-by-case basis and in cooperation with relevant regional organizations as appropriate, should peaceful means be inadequate and national authorities are manifestly failing to protect their populations from genocide, war crimes, ethnic cleansing and crimes against humanity. We stress the need for the General Assembly to continue consideration of the responsibility to protect populations from genocide, war crimes, ethnic cleansing and crimes against humanity and its implications,

bearing in mind the principles of the Charter and international law. We also intend to commit ourselves, as necessary and appropriate, to helping States build capacity to protect their populations from genocide, war crimes, ethnic cleansing and crimes against humanity and to assisting those which are under stress before crises and conflicts break out....

Children's rights

141. We express dismay at the increasing number of children involved in and affected by armed conflict, as well as all other forms of violence, including domestic violence, sexual abuse and exploitation and trafficking. We support cooperation policies aimed at strengthening national capacities to improve the situation of those children and to assist in their rehabilitation and reintegration into society....

Human security

143. We stress the right of people to live in freedom and dignity, free from poverty and despair. We recognize that all individuals, in particular vulnerable people, are entitled to freedom from fear and freedom from want, with an equal opportunity to enjoy all their rights and full develop their human potential. To this end, we commit ourselves to discussing and defining the notion of human security in the General Assembly....

V. Strengthening the United Nations

Human Rights Council

157. Pursuant to our commitment to further strengthen the United Nations human rights machinery, we resolve to create a Human Rights Council.

158. The Council will be responsible for promoting universal respect for the protection of all human rights and fundamental freedoms for all, without distinction of any kind and in a fair and equal manner.

159. The Council should address situations of violations of human rights, including gross and systematic violations, and make recommendations thereon. It should also promote effective coordination and the mainstreaming of human rights within the United Nations system....

Document 30
UNITED NATIONS DECLARATION ON THE RIGHTS OF INDIGENOUS PEOPLES

U.N. G.A. Res. 61/295 (13 Sept. 2007)

The General Assembly,

Taking note of the recommendation of the Human Rights Council contained in its resolution 1/2 of 29 June 2006, by which the Council adopted the text of the United Nations Declaration on the Rights of Indigenous Peoples,

Recalling its resolution 61/178 of 20 December 2006, by which it decided to defer consideration of and action on the Declaration to allow time for further consultations thereon, and also decided to conclude its consideration before the end of the sixty-first session of the General Assembly,

Adopts the United Nations Declaration on the Rights of Indigenous Peoples as contained in the annex to the present resolution.

Annex

United Nations Declaration on the Rights of Indigenous Peoples

The General Assembly,

Guided by the purposes and principles of the Charter of the United Nations, and good faith in the fulfilment of the obligations assumed by States in accordance with the Charter,

Affirming that indigenous peoples are equal to all other peoples, while recognizing the right of all peoples to be different, to consider themselves different, and to be respected as such,

Affirming also that all peoples contribute to the diversity and richness of civilizations and cultures, which constitute the common heritage of humankind,

Affirming further that all doctrines, policies and practices based on or advocating superiority of peoples or individuals on the basis of national origin or racial, religious, ethnic or cultural differences are racist, scientifically false, legally invalid, morally condemnable and socially unjust,

Reaffirming that indigenous peoples, in the exercise of their rights, should be free from discrimination of any kind,

Concerned that indigenous peoples have suffered from historic injustices as a result of, inter alia, their colonization and dispossession of their lands, territories and resources, thus preventing them from exercising, in particular, their right to development in accordance with their own needs and interests,

Recognizing the urgent need to respect and promote the inherent rights of indigenous peoples which derive from their political, economic and social structures and from their cultures, spiritual traditions, histories and philosophies, especially their rights to their lands, territories and resources,

Recognizing also the urgent need to respect and promote the rights of indigenous peoples affirmed in treaties, agreements and other constructive arrangements with States,

Welcoming the fact that indigenous peoples are organizing themselves for political, economic, social and cultural enhancement and in order to bring to an end all forms of discrimination and oppression wherever they occur,

Convinced that control by indigenous peoples over developments affecting them and their lands, territories and resources will enable them to maintain and strengthen their institutions, cultures and traditions, and to promote their development in accordance with their aspirations and needs,

Recognizing that respect for indigenous knowledge, cultures and traditional practices contributes to sustainable and equitable development and proper management of the environment,

Emphasizing the contribution of the demilitarization of the lands and territories of indigenous peoples to peace, economic and social progress and development, understanding and friendly relations among nations and peoples of the world,

Recognizing in particular the right of indigenous families and communities to retain shared responsibility for the upbringing, training, education and well-being of their children, consistent with the rights of the child,

Considering that the rights affirmed in treaties, agreements and other constructive arrangements between States and indigenous peoples are, in some situations, matters of international concern, interest, responsibility and character,

Considering also that treaties, agreements and other constructive arrangements, and the relationship they represent, are the basis for a strengthened partnership between indigenous peoples and States,

Acknowledging that the Charter of the United Nations, the International Covenant on Economic, Social and Cultural Rights and the International Covenant on Civil and Political Rights, as well as the Vienna Declaration and Programme of Action, affirm the fundamental importance of the right to self-determination of all peoples, by virtue of which they freely determine their political status and freely pursue their economic, social and cultural development,

Bearing in mind that nothing in this Declaration may be used to deny any peoples their right to self-determination, exercised in conformity with international law,

Convinced that the recognition of the rights of indigenous peoples in this Declaration will enhance harmonious and cooperative relations between the State and indigenous peoples, based on principles of justice, democracy, respect for human rights, non-discrimination and good faith,

Encouraging States to comply with and effectively implement all their obligations as they apply to indigenous peoples under international instruments, in particular those related to human rights, in consultation and cooperation with the peoples concerned,

Emphasizing that the United Nations has an important and continuing role to play in promoting and protecting the rights of indigenous peoples,

Believing that this Declaration is a further important step forward for the recognition, promotion and protection of the rights and freedoms of indigenous peoples and in the development of relevant activities of the United Nations system in this field,

Recognizing and reaffirming that indigenous individuals are entitled without discrimination to all human rights recognized in international law, and that indigenous peoples possess collective rights which are indispensable for their existence, well-being and integral development as peoples,

Recognizing that the situation of indigenous peoples varies from region to region and from country to country and that the significance of national and regional particularities and various historical and cultural backgrounds should be taken into consideration,

Solemnly proclaims the following United Nations Declaration on the Rights of Indigenous Peoples as a standard of achievement to be pursued in a spirit of partnership and mutual respect:

Article 1

Indigenous peoples have the right to the full enjoyment, as a collective or as individuals, of all human rights and fundamental freedoms as recognized in the Charter of the United Nations, the Universal Declaration of Human Rights and international human rights law.

Article 2

Indigenous peoples and individuals are free and equal to all other peoples and individuals and have the right to be free from any kind of discrimination, in the exercise of their rights, in particular that based on their indigenous origin or identity.

Article 3

Indigenous peoples have the right to self-determination. By virtue of that right they freely determine their political status and freely pursue their economic, social and cultural development.

Article 4

Indigenous peoples, in exercising their right to self-determination, have the right to autonomy or self-government in matters relating to their internal and local affairs, as well as ways and means for financing their autonomous functions.

Article 5

Indigenous peoples have the right to maintain and strengthen their distinct political, legal, economic, social and cultural institutions, while retaining their right to participate fully, if they so choose, in the political, economic, social and cultural life of the State.

Article 6

Every indigenous individual has the right to a nationality.

Article 7

1. Indigenous individuals have the rights to life, physical and mental integrity, liberty and security of person.

2. Indigenous peoples have the collective right to live in freedom, peace and security as distinct peoples and shall not be subjected to any act of genocide or any other act of violence, including forcibly removing children of the group to another group.

Article 8

1. Indigenous peoples and individuals have the right not to be subjected to forced assimilation or destruction of their culture.

2. States shall provide effective mechanisms for prevention of, and redress for:

(a) Any action which has the aim or effect of depriving them of their integrity as distinct peoples, or of their cultural values or ethnic identities;

(b) Any action which has the aim or effect of dispossessing them of their lands, territories or resources;

(c) Any form of forced population transfer which has the aim or effect of violating or undermining any of their rights;

(d) Any form of forced assimilation or integration;

(e) Any form of propaganda designed to promote or incite racial or ethnic discrimination directed against them.

Article 9

Indigenous peoples and individuals have the right to belong to an indigenous community or nation, in accordance with the traditions and customs of the community or nation concerned. No discrimination of any kind may arise from the exercise of such a right.

Article 10

Indigenous peoples shall not be forcibly removed from their lands or territories. No relocation shall take place without the free, prior and informed consent of the indigenous peoples concerned and after agreement on just and fair compensation and, where possible, with the option of return.

Article 11

1. Indigenous peoples have the right to practice and revitalize their cultural traditions and customs. This includes the right to maintain, protect and develop the past, present and future manifestations of their cultures, such as archaeological and historical sites, artefacts, designs, ceremonies, technologies and visual and performing arts and literature.

2. States shall provide redress through effective mechanisms, which may include restitution, developed in conjunction with indigenous peoples, with respect to their cultural, intellectual, religious and spiritual property taken without their free, prior and informed consent or in violation of their laws, traditions and customs.

Article 12

1. Indigenous peoples have the right to manifest, practice, develop and teach their spiritual and religious traditions, customs and ceremonies; the right to maintain, protect, and have access in privacy to their religious and cultural sites; the right to the use and control of their ceremonial objects; and the right to the repatriation of their human remains.

2. States shall seek to enable the access and/or repatriation of ceremonial objects and human remains in their possession through fair, transparent and effective mechanisms developed in conjunction with indigenous peoples concerned.

Article 13

1. Indigenous peoples have the right to revitalize, use, develop and transmit to future generations their histories, languages, oral traditions, philosophies, writing systems and literatures, and to designate and retain their own names for communities, places and persons.

2. States shall take effective measures to ensure that this right is protected and also to ensure that indigenous peoples can understand and be understood in political, legal and administrative proceedings, where necessary through the provision of interpretation or by other appropriate means.

Article 14

1. Indigenous peoples have the right to establish and control their educational systems and institutions providing education in their own languages, in a manner appropriate to their cultural methods of teaching and learning.

2. Indigenous individuals, particularly children, have the right to all levels and forms of education of the State without discrimination.

3. States shall, in conjunction with indigenous peoples, take effective measures, in order for indigenous individuals, particularly children, including those living outside their communities, to have access, when

possible, to an education in their own culture and provided in their own language.

Article 15

1. Indigenous peoples have the right to the dignity and diversity of their cultures, traditions, histories and aspirations which shall be appropriately reflected in education and public information.

2. States shall take effective measures. in consultation and cooperation with the indigenous peoples concerned, to combat prejudice and eliminate discrimination and to promote tolerance, understanding and good relations among indigenous peoples and all other segments of society.

Article 16

1. Indigenous peoples have the right to establish their own media in their own languages and to have access to all forms of non-indigenous media without discrimination.

2. States shall take effective measures to ensure that State-owned media duly reflect indigenous cultural diversity. States, without prejudice to ensuring full freedom of expression, should encourage privately owned media to adequately reflect indigenous cultural diversity.

Article 17

1. Indigenous individuals and peoples have the right to enjoy fully all rights established under applicable international and domestic labour law.

2. States shall in consultation and cooperation with indigenous peoples take specific measures to protect indigenous children from economic exploitation and from performing any work that is likely to be hazardous or to interfere with the child's education, or to be harmful to the child's health or physical, mental, spiritual, moral or social development, taking into account their special vulnerability and the importance of education for their empowerment.

3. Indigenous individuals have the right not to be subjected to any discriminatory conditions of labour and, inter alia, employment or salary.

Article 18

Indigenous peoples have the right to participate in decision-making in matters which would affect their rights, through representatives chosen by themselves in accordance with their own procedures, as well as to maintain and develop their own indigenous decision-making institutions.

Article 19

States shall consult and cooperate in good faith with the indigenous peoples concerned through their own representative institutions in order to obtain their free, prior and informed consent before adopting and implementing legislative or administrative measures that may affect them.

Article 20

1. Indigenous peoples have the right to maintain and develop their political, economic and social systems or institutions, to be secure in the enjoyment of their own means of subsistence and development, and to engage freely in all their traditional and other economic activities.

2. Indigenous peoples deprived of their means of subsistence and development are entitled to just and fair redress.

Article 21

1. Indigenous peoples have the right, without discrimination, to the improvement of their economic and social conditions, including, inter alia, in the areas of education, employment, vocational training and retraining, housing, sanitation, health and social security.

2. States shall take effective measures and, where appropriate, special measures to ensure continuing improvement of their economic and social conditions. Particular attention shall be paid to the rights and special needs of indigenous elders, women, youth, children and persons with disabilities.

Article 22

1. Particular attention shall be paid to the rights and special needs of indigenous elders, women, youth, children and persons with disabilities in the implementation of this Declaration.

2. States shall take measures, in conjunction with indigenous peoples, to ensure that indigenous women and children enjoy the full protection and guarantees against all forms of violence and discrimination.

Article 23

Indigenous peoples have the right to determine and develop priorities and strategies for exercising their right to development. In particular, indigenous peoples have the right to be actively involved in developing and determining health, housing and other economic and social programmes affecting them and, as far as possible, to administer such programmes through their own institutions.

Article 24

1. Indigenous peoples have the right to their traditional medicines and to maintain their health practices, including the conservation of their vital medicinal plants, animals and minerals. Indigenous individuals also have the right to access, without any discrimination, to all social and health services.

2. Indigenous individuals have an equal right to the enjoyment of the highest attainable standard of physical and mental health. States

shall take the necessary steps with a view to achieving progressively the full realization of this right.

Article 25

Indigenous peoples have the right to maintain and strengthen their distinctive spiritual relationship with their traditionally owned or otherwise occupied and used lands, territories, waters and coastal seas and other resources and to uphold their responsibilities to future generations in this regard.

Article 26

1. Indigenous peoples have the right to the lands, territories and resources which they have traditionally owned, occupied or otherwise used or acquired.

2. Indigenous peoples have the right to own, use, develop and control the lands, territories and resources that they possess by reason of traditional ownership or other traditional occupation or use, as well as those which they have otherwise acquired.

3. States shall give legal recognition and protection to these lands, territories and resources. Such recognition shall be conducted with due respect to the customs, traditions and land tenure systems of the indigenous peoples concerned.

Article 27

States shall establish and implement, in conjunction with indigenous peoples concerned, a fair, independent, impartial, open and transparent process, giving due recognition to indigenous peoples' laws, traditions, customs and land tenure systems, to recognize and adjudicate the rights of indigenous peoples pertaining to their lands, territories and resources, including those which were traditionally owned or otherwise occupied or used. Indigenous peoples shall have the right to participate in this process.

Article 28

1. Indigenous peoples have the right to redress, by means that can include restitution or, when this is not possible, just, fair and equitable compensation, for the lands, territories and resources which they have traditionally owned or otherwise occupied or used, and which have been confiscated, taken, occupied, used or damaged without their free, prior and informed consent.

2. Unless otherwise freely agreed upon by the peoples concerned, compensation shall take the form of lands, territories and resources equal in quality, size and legal status or of monetary compensation or other appropriate redress.

Article 29

1. Indigenous peoples have the right to the conservation and protection of the environment and the productive capacity of their lands or territories and resources. States shall establish and implement assistance

programmes for indigenous peoples for such conservation and protection, without discrimination.

2. States shall take effective measures to ensure that no storage or disposal of hazardous materials shall take place in the lands or territories of indigenous peoples without their free, prior and informed consent.

3. States shall also take effective measures to ensure, as needed, that programmes for monitoring, maintaining and restoring the health of indigenous peoples, as developed and implemented by the peoples affected by such materials, are duly implemented.

Article 30

1. Military activities shall not take place in the lands or territories of indigenous peoples, unless justified by a relevant public interest or otherwise freely agreed with or requested by the indigenous peoples concerned.

2. States shall undertake effective consultations with the indigenous peoples concerned, through appropriate procedures and in particular through their representative institutions, prior to using their lands or territories for military activities.

Article 31

1. Indigenous peoples have the right to maintain, control, protect and develop their cultural heritage, traditional knowledge and traditional cultural expressions, as well as the manifestations of their sciences, technologies and cultures, including human and genetic resources, seeds, medicines, knowledge of the properties of fauna and flora, oral traditions, literatures, designs, sports and traditional games and visual and performing arts. They also have the right to maintain, control, protect and develop their intellectual property over such cultural heritage, traditional knowledge, and traditional cultural expressions.

2. In conjunction with indigenous peoples, States shall take effective measures to recognize and protect the exercise of these rights.

Article 32

1. Indigenous peoples have the right to determine and develop priorities and strategies for the development or use of their lands or territories and other resources.

2. States shall consult and cooperate in good faith with the indigenous peoples concerned through their own representative institutions in order to obtain their free and informed consent prior to the approval of any project affecting their lands or territories and other resources, particularly in connection with the development, utilization or exploitation of mineral, water or other resources.

3. States shall provide effective mechanisms for just and fair redress for any such activities, and appropriate measures shall be taken to mitigate adverse environmental, economic, social, cultural or spiritual impact.

Article 33

1. Indigenous peoples have the right to determine their own identity or membership in accordance with their customs and traditions. This does not impair the right of indigenous individuals to obtain citizenship of the States in which they live.

2. Indigenous peoples have the right to determine the structures and to select the membership of their institutions in accordance with their own procedures.

Article 34

Indigenous peoples have the right to promote, develop and maintain their institutional structures and their distinctive customs, spirituality, traditions, procedures, practices and, in the cases where they exist, juridical systems or customs, in accordance with international human rights standards.

Article 35

Indigenous peoples have the right to determine the responsibilities of individuals to their communities.

Article 36

1. Indigenous peoples, in particular those divided by international borders, have the right to maintain and develop contacts, relations and cooperation, including activities for spiritual, cultural, political, economic and social purposes, with their own members as well as other peoples across borders.

2. States, in consultation and cooperation with indigenous peoples, shall take effective measures to facilitate the exercise and ensure the implementation of this right.

Article 37

1. Indigenous peoples have the right to the recognition, observance and enforcement of treaties, agreements and other constructive arrangements concluded with States or their successors and to have States honour and respect such treaties, agreements and other constructive arrangements.

2. Nothing in this Declaration may be interpreted as diminishing or eliminating the rights of indigenous peoples contained in treaties, agreements and other constructive arrangements.

Article 38

States in consultation and cooperation with indigenous peoples, shall take the appropriate measures, including legislative measures, to achieve the ends of this Declaration.

Article 39

Indigenous peoples have the right to have access to financial and technical assistance from States and through international cooperation, for the enjoyment of the rights contained in this Declaration.

Article 40

Indigenous peoples have the right to access to and prompt decision through just and fair procedures for the resolution of conflicts and disputes with States or other parties, as well as to effective remedies for all infringements of their individual and collective rights. Such a decision shall give due consideration to the customs, traditions, rules and legal systems of the indigenous peoples concerned and international human rights.

Article 41

The organs and specialized agencies of the United Nations system and other intergovernmental organizations shall contribute to the full realization of the provisions of this Declaration through the mobilization, inter alia, of financial cooperation and technical assistance. Ways and means of ensuring participation of indigenous peoples on issues affecting them shall be established.

Article 42

The United Nations, its bodies, including the Permanent Forum on Indigenous Issues, and specialized agencies, including at the country level, and States shall promote respect for and full application of the provisions of this Declaration and follow up the effectiveness of this Declaration.

Article 43

The rights recognized herein constitute the minimum standards for the survival, dignity and well-being of the indigenous peoples of the world.

Article 44

All the rights and freedoms recognized herein are equally guaranteed to male and female indigenous individuals.

Article 45

Nothing in this Declaration may be construed as diminishing or extinguishing the rights indigenous peoples have now or may acquire in the future.

Article 46

1. Nothing in this Declaration may be interpreted as implying for any State, people, group or person any right to engage in any activity or to perform any act contrary to the Charter of the United Nations or construed as authorizing or encouraging any action which would dismember or impair, totally or in part, the territorial integrity or political unity of sovereign and independent States.

2. In the exercise of the rights enunciated in the present Declaration, human rights and fundamental freedoms of all shall be respected. The exercise of the rights set forth in this Declaration shall be subject only to such limitations as are determined by law and in accordance with

international human rights obligations. Any such limitations shall be non-discriminatory and strictly necessary solely for the purpose of securing due recognition and respect for the rights and freedoms of others and for meeting the just and most compelling requirements of a democratic society.

3. The provisions set forth in this Declaration shall be interpreted in accordance with the principles of justice, democracy, respect for human rights, equality, non-discrimination, good governance and good faith.

Document 31

LIST OF WAR CRIMES PREPARED BY THE COMMISSION ON THE RESPONSIBILITY OF THE AUTHORS OF THE WAR AND ON ENFORCEMENT OF PENALTIES, PRESENTED TO THE PRELIMINARY PEACE CONFERENCE

Paris, 29 March 1919 (members: Belgium, British Empire, France, Greece, Italy, Japan, Poland, Roumania, Serbia, United States)

1. Murder and massacres—systematic terrorism.
2. Putting hostages to death.
3. Torture of civilians.
4. Deliberate starvation of civilians.
5. Rape.
6. Abduction of girls and women for the purpose of enforced prostitution.
7. Deportation of civilians.
8. Internment of civilians under inhuman conditions.
9. Forced labour of civilians in connection with the military operations of the enemy.
10. Usurpation of sovereignty during military occupation.
11. Compulsory enlistment of soldiers among the inhabitants of occupied territory.
12. Attempts to denationalize the inhabitants of occupied territory.
13. Pillage.
14. Confiscation of property.
15. Exaction of illegitimate or of exorbitant contributions and requisitions.
16. Debasement of the currency and issue of spurious currency.
17. Imposition of collective penalties.
18. Wanton devastation and destruction of property.

19. Deliberate bombardment of undefended places.
20. Wanton destruction of religious, charitable, educational and historic buildings and monuments.
21. Destruction of merchant ships and passenger vessels without warning and without provision for the safety of passengers and crew.
22. Destruction of fishing boats and relief ships.
23. Deliberate bombardment of hospitals.
24. Attack and destruction of hospital ships.
25. Breach of other rules relating to the Red Cross.
26. Use of deleterious and asphyxiating gases.
27. Use of explosive or expanding bullets and other inhuman appliances.
28. Directions to give no quarter.
29. Ill-treatment of wounded and prisoners of war.
30. Employment of prisoners of war on unauthorized works.
31. Misuse of flags of truce.
32. Poisoning of wells.

[Item added by the War Crimes Commission]

33. Indiscriminate mass arrests.

Document 32
GENEVA CONVENTION RELATIVE TO THE PROTECTION OF CIVILIAN PERSONS IN TIME OF WAR OF AUGUST 12, 1949

75 U.N.T.S. 287, 6 U.S.T. 3516, T.I.A.S. No. 3365

Article 1

The High Contracting Parties undertake to respect and to ensure respect for the present Convention in all circumstances.

Article 2

In addition to the provisions which shall be implemented in peacetime, the present Convention shall apply to all cases of declared war or of any other armed conflict which may arise between two or more of the High Contracting Parties, even if the state of war is not recognized by one of them.

The Convention shall also apply to all cases of partial or total occupation of the territory of a High Contracting Party, even if the said occupation meets with no armed resistance.

Although one of the Powers in conflict may not be a party to the present Convention, the Powers who are parties thereto shall remain bound by it in their mutual relations. They shall furthermore be bound by the Convention in relation to the said Power, if the latter accepts and applies the provisions thereof.

Article 3

In the case of armed conflict not of an international character occurring in the territory of one of the High Contracting Parties, each party to the conflict shall be bound to apply, as a minimum, the following provisions:

(1) Persons taking no active part in the hostilities, including members of armed forces who have laid down their arms and those placed *hors de combat* by sickness, wounds, detention, or any other cause, shall in all circumstances be treated humanely, without any adverse distinction founded on race, colour, religion or faith, sex, birth or wealth, or any other similar criteria.

To this end, the following acts are and shall remain prohibited at any time and in any place whatsoever with respect to the abovementioned persons:

(a) violence to life and person, in particular murder of all kinds, mutilation, cruel treatment and torture;

(b) taking of hostages;

(c) outrages upon personal dignity, in particular, humiliating and degrading treatment;

(d) the passing of sentences and the carrying out of executions without previous judgment pronounced by a regularly constituted court, affording all the judicial guarantees which are recognized as indispensable by civilized peoples.

(2) The wounded and sick shall be collected and cared for.

An impartial humanitarian body, such as the International Committee of the Red Cross, may offer its services to the Parties to the conflict.

The Parties to the conflict should further endeavor to bring into force, by means of special agreements, all or part of the other provisions of the present Convention.

The application of the preceding provisions shall not affect the legal status of the Parties to the conflict.

Article 4

Persons protected by the Convention are those who, at a given moment and in any manner whatsoever, find themselves, in case of a conflict or occupation, in the hands of a Party to the conflict or Occupying Power of which they are not nationals.

Nationals of a State which is not bound by the Convention are not protected by it. Nationals of a neutral State who find themselves in the territory of a belligerent State, and nationals of a co-belligerent State, shall not be regarded as protected persons while the State of which they are nationals has normal diplomatic representation in the State in whose hands they are.

The provisions of Part II are, however, wider in application, as defined in Article 13.

Persons protected by the Geneva Convention for the Amelioration of the Condition of the Wounded and Sick in Armed Forces in the Field of August 12, 1949, or by the Geneva Convention for the Amelioration of the Condition of Wounded, Sick and Shipwrecked Members of Armed Forces at Sea of August 12, 1949, or by the Geneva Convention Relative to the Treatment of Prisoners of War of August 12, 1949, shall not be considered as protected persons within the meaning of the present Convention.

Article 5

Where, in the territory of a Party to the conflict, the latter is satisfied that an individual protected person is definitely suspected of or engaged in activities hostile to the security of the State, such individual person shall not be entitled to claim such rights and privileges under the present Convention as would, if exercised in the favour of such individual person, be prejudicial to the security of such State.

Where in occupied territory an individual protected person is detained as a spy or saboteur, or as a person under definite suspicion of activity hostile to the security of the Occupying Power, such person shall, in those cases where absolute military security so requires, be regarded as having forfeited rights of communication under the present Convention.

In each case, such persons shall nevertheless be treated with humanity, and in case of trial, shall not be deprived of the rights of fair and regular trial prescribed by the present Convention. They shall also be granted the full rights and privileges of a protected person under the present Convention at the earliest date consistent with the security of the State or Occupying Power, as the case may be.

Article 6

The present Convention shall apply from the outset of any conflict or occupation mentioned in Article 2.

In the territory of Parties to the conflict, the application of the present Convention shall cease on the general close of military operations.

In the case of occupied territory, the application of the present Convention shall cease one year after the general close of military operations; however, the Occupying Power shall be bound, for the duration of the occupation, to the extent that such Power exercises the functions of government in such territory, by the provisions of the following articles of the present Convention: 1 to 12, 27, 29 to 34, 47, 49, 51, 52, 53, 59, 61 to 77, 143.

Protected persons whose release, repatriation or re-establishment may take place after such dates shall meanwhile continue to benefit by the present Convention.

Article 7

In addition to the agreements expressly provided for in Articles 11, 14, 15, 17, 36, 108, 109, 132, 133 and 149, the High Contracting Parties may conclude other special agreements for all matters concerning which they may deem it suitable to make separate provision. No special agreement shall adversely affect the situation of protected persons, as defined by the present Convention, nor restrict the rights which it confers upon them.

Protected persons shall continue to have the benefit of such agreements as long as the Convention is applicable to them, except where express provisions to the contrary are contained in the aforesaid or in subsequent agreements, or where more favourable measures have been taken with regard to them by one or other of the Parties to the conflict.

Article 8

Protected persons may in no circumstances renounce in part or in entirety the rights secured to them by the present Convention, and by the special agreements referred to in the foregoing article, if such there be. . . .

PART II. GENERAL PROTECTION OF POPULATIONS AGAINST CERTAIN CONSEQUENCES OF WAR

Article 13

The provisions of Part II cover the whole of the populations of the countries in conflict, without any adverse distinction based, in particular, on race, nationality, religion or political opinion, and are intended to alleviate the sufferings caused by war. . . .

Article 16

The wounded and sick, as well as the infirm, and expectant mothers, shall be the object of particular protection and respect.

As far as military considerations allow, each Party to the conflict shall facilitate the steps taken to search for the killed and wounded, to assist the shipwrecked and other persons exposed to grave danger, and to protect them against pillage and ill-treatment.

Article 17

The Parties to the conflict shall endeavour to conclude local agreements for the removal from besieged or encircled areas, of wounded, sick, infirm, and aged persons, children and maternity cases, and for the passage of ministers of all religions, medical personnel and medical equipment on their way to such areas.

Article 18

Civilian hospitals organized to give care to the wounded and sick, the infirm and maternity cases, may in no circumstances be the object of attack, but shall at all times be respected and protected by the Parties to the conflict. . . .

Article 23

Each High Contracting Party shall allow the free passage of all consignments of medical and hospital stores and objects necessary for religious worship intended only for civilians of another High Contracting Party, even if the latter is its adversary. It shall likewise permit the free passage of all consignments of essential foodstuffs, clothing and tonics intended for children under fifteen, expectant mothers and maternity cases.

The obligation of a High Contracting Party to allow the free passage of consignments indicated in the preceding paragraph is subject to the condition that this Party is satisfied that there are no serious reasons for fearing:

a. that the consignments may be diverted from their destination,

b. that the control may not be effective, or

c. that a definite advantage may accrue to the military efforts or economy of the enemy through the substitution of the above-mentioned consignments for goods which would otherwise be provided or produced by the enemy or through the release of such material, services or facilities as would otherwise be required for the production of such goods. . . .

Article 24

The Parties to the conflict shall take the necessary measures to ensure that children under fifteen, who are orphaned or are separated from their families as a result of the war, are not left to their own resources, and that their maintenance ... [is] facilitated in all circumstances. . . .

Article 25

All persons in the territory of a Party to the conflict, or in a territory occupied by it, shall be enabled to give news of a strictly personal nature to members of their families, wherever they may be, and to receive news from them. This correspondence shall be forwarded speedily and without undue delay. . . .

Article 26

Each Party to the conflict shall facilitate enquiries made by members of families dispersed owing to the war, with the object of renewing contact with one another and of meeting, if possible. It shall encourage, in particular, the work of organizations engaged on this task provided they are acceptable to it and conform to its security regulations.

PART III. STATUS AND TREATMENT OF PROTECTED PERSONS

Section I. Provisions Common to the Territories of the Parties to the Conflict and to Occupied Territories

Article 27

Protected persons are entitled, in all circumstances, to respect for their persons, their honour, their family rights, their religious convictions and practices, and their manners and customs. They shall at all times be humanely treated, and shall be protected especially against all acts of violence or threats thereof and against insults and public curiosity.

Women shall be especially protected against any attack on their honour, in particular against rape, enforced prostitution, or any form of indecent assault.

Without prejudice to the provisions relating to their state of health, age and sex, all protected persons shall be treated with the same consideration by the Party to the conflict in whose power they are, without any adverse distinction based, in particular, on race, religion or political opinion.

However, the Parties to the conflict may take such measures of control and security in regard to protected persons as may be necessary as a result of the war.

Article 28

The presence of a protected person may not be used to render certain points or areas immune from military operations.

Article 29

The Party to the conflict in whose hands protected persons may be, is responsible for the treatment accorded to them by its agents, irrespective of any individual responsibility which may be incurred.

Article 30

Protected persons shall have every facility for making application to the Protecting Powers, the International Committee of the Red Cross, the National Red Cross (Red Crescent, Red Lion and Sun) Society of the country where they may be, as well as to any organization that might assist them.

These several organizations shall be granted all facilities for that purpose by the authorities, within the bounds set by military or security considerations.

Apart from the visits of the delegates of the Protecting Powers and of the International Committee of the Red Cross, provided for by Article 143, the Detaining or Occupying Powers shall facilitate as much as possible visits to protected persons by the representatives of other organizations whose object is to give spiritual aid or material relief to such persons.

Article 31

No physical or moral coercion shall be exercised against protected persons, in particular to obtain information from them or from third parties.

Article 32

The High Contracting Parties specifically agree that each of them is prohibited from taking any measure of such a character as to cause the physical suffering or extermination of protected persons in their hands. This prohibition applies not only to murder, torture, corporal punishment, mutilation and medical or scientific experiments not necessitated by the medical treatment of a protected person, but also to any other measures of brutality whether applied by civilian or military agents.

Article 33

No protected person may be punished for an offence he or she has not personally committed. Collective penalties and likewise all measures of intimidation or of terrorism are prohibited.

Pillage is prohibited.

Reprisals against protected persons and their property are prohibited.

Article 34

The taking of hostages is prohibited.

Section II. Aliens in the Territory of a Party to the Conflict

Article 35

All protected persons who may desire to leave the territory at the outset of, or during a conflict, shall be entitled to do so, unless their departure is contrary to the national interests of the State....

Article 42

The internment or placing in assigned residence of protected persons may be ordered only if the security of the Detaining Power makes it absolutely necessary....

Article 43

Any protected person who has been interned or placed in assigned residence shall be entitled to have such action reconsidered as soon as possible by an appropriate court or administrative board designated by the Detaining Power for that purpose. If the internment or placing in assigned residence is maintained, the court or administrative board shall periodically, at least twice yearly, give consideration to his or her case with a view to the favourable amendment of the initial decision, if circumstances permit.

Unless the persons concerned object, the Detaining Power shall, as rapidly as possible, give the Protecting Power the names of any protected persons who have been interned or subjected to assigned residence, or who have been released from internment or assigned residence. The decisions of the courts or boards mentioned in the first paragraph of the present Article shall also, subject to the same conditions, be notified as rapidly as possible to the Protecting Power.

Article 44

In applying the measures of control mentioned in the present Convention, the Detaining Power shall not treat as enemy aliens exclusively on the basis of their nationality *de jure* of an enemy State, refugees who do not, in fact, enjoy the protection of any government.

Article 45

Protected persons shall not be transferred to a Power which is not a party to the Convention.

This provision shall in no way constitute an obstacle to the repatriation of protected persons, or to their return to their country of residence after the cessation of hostilities.

Protected persons may be transferred by the Detaining Power only to a Power which is a party to the present Convention and after the

Detaining Power has satisfied itself of the willingness and ability of such transferee Power to apply the present Convention. If protected persons are transferred under such circumstances, responsibility for the application of the present Convention rests on the Power accepting them, while they are in its custody. Nevertheless, if that Power fails to carry out the provisions of the present Convention in any important respect, the Power by which the protected persons were transferred shall, upon being so notified by the Protecting Power, take effective measures to correct the situation or shall request the return of the protected persons. Such request must be complied with.

In no circumstances shall a protected person be transferred to a country where he or she may have reason to fear persecution for his or her political opinions or religious beliefs.

The provisions of this Article do not constitute an obstacle to the extradition, in pursuance of extradition treaties concluded before the outbreak of hostilities, of protected persons accused of offences against ordinary criminal law.

Section III. Occupied Territories

Article 47

Protected persons who are in occupied territory shall not be deprived, in any case or in any manner whatsoever, of the benefits of the present Convention by any change introduced, as the result of the occupation of a territory, into the institutions or government of the said territory, nor by any agreement concluded between the authorities of the occupied territories and the Occupying Power, nor by any annexation by the latter of the whole or part of the occupied territory.

Article 48

Protected persons who are not nationals of the Power whose territory is occupied may avail themselves of the right to leave the territory subject to the provisions of Article 35, and decisions thereon shall be taken according to the procedure which the Occupying Power shall establish in accordance with the said article.

Article 49

Individual or mass forcible transfers, as well as deportations of protected persons from occupied territory to the territory of the Occupying Power or to that of any other country, occupied or not, are prohibited, regardless of their motive.

Nevertheless, the Occupying Power may undertake total or partial evacuation of a given area if the security of the population or imperative military reasons so demand. Such evacuations may not involve the displacement of protected persons outside the bounds of the occupied territory except when for material reasons it is impossible to avoid such displacement. Persons thus evacuated shall be transferred back to their homes as soon as hostilities in the area in question have ceased.

The Occupying Power undertaking such transfers of evacuations shall ensure, to the greatest practicable extent, that proper accommodation is provided to receive the protected persons, that the removals are effected in satisfactory conditions of hygiene, health, safety and nutrition, and that members of the same family are not separated.

The Protecting Power shall be informed of any transfers and evacuations as soon as they have taken place.

The Occupying Power shall not detain protected persons in an area particularly exposed to the dangers of war unless the security of the population or imperative military reasons so demand.

The Occupying Power shall not deport or transfer parts of its own civilian population into the territory it occupies.

Article 50

The Occupying Power shall, with the cooperation of the national and local authorities, facilitate the proper working of all institutions devoted to the care and education of children.

The Occupying Power shall take all necessary steps to facilitate the identification of children and the registration of their parentage. It may not, in any case, change their personal status, nor enlist them in formations or organizations subordinate to it....

Section III. Occupied Territories

Article 53

Any destruction by the Occupying Power of real or personal property ... is prohibited, except where such destruction is rendered absolutely necessary by military operations.

Article 55

To the fullest extent of the means available to it, the Occupying Power has the duty of ensuring the food and medical supplies of the population; it should, in particular, bring in the necessary foodstuffs, medical stores and other articles if the resources of the occupied territory are inadequate ... [and may] requisition ... [such for its forces and administrative personnel] only if the requirements of the civilian population have been taken into account.

Article 56

To the fullest extent of the means available to it, the Occupying Power has the duty of ensuring and maintaining, with the cooperation of national and local authorities, the medical and hospital establishments and services, public health and hygiene in the occupied territory, with particular reference to the adoption and application of the prophylactic and preventive measures necessary to combat the spread of contagious diseases and epidemics. Medical personnel of all categories shall be allowed to carry out their duties....

Article 59

If the whole or part of the population of an occupied territory is inadequately supplied, the Occupying Power shall agree to relief schemes on behalf of the said population, and shall facilitate them by all the means at its disposal ... [especially re:] consignments of foodstuffs, medical supplies and clothing.

All Contracting Parties shall permit the free passage of these consignments and shall guarantee their protection.

A Power granting free passage ... shall, however, have the right to search the consignments, to regulate their passage according to prescribed times and routes, and to be reasonably satisfied ... that these consignments are to be used for the relief of the needy population and are not to be used for the benefit of the Occupying Power.

Article 60

... The Occupying Power shall in no way whatsoever divert relief consignments from the purpose for which they are intended, except in cases of urgent necessity, in the interests of the population....

Article 64

The penal laws of the occupied territory shall remain in force, with the exception that they may be repealed or suspended by the Occupying Power in cases where they constitute a threat to its security or an obstacle to the application of the present Convention. Subject to the latter consideration and to the necessity for ensuring the effective administration of justice, the tribunals of the occupied territory shall continue to function in respect of all offences covered by the said laws.

The Occupying Power may, however, subject the population of the occupied territory to provisions which are essential to enable the Occupying power to fulfil its obligations under the present Convention, to maintain the orderly government of the territory, and to ensure the security of the Occupying Power, of the members and property of the occupying forces or administration, and likewise of the establishments and lines of communication used by them.

Article 65

The penal provisions enacted by the Occupying Power shall not come into force before they have been published and brought to the knowledge of the inhabitants in their own language. The effect of these penal provisions shall not be retroactive.

Article 66

In case of a breach of the penal provisions promulgated by it by virtue of the second paragraph of Article 64, the Occupying Power may hand over the accused to its properly constituted, non-political military courts, on condition that the said courts sit in the occupied country. Courts of appeal shall preferably sit in the occupied country.

Article 67

The courts shall apply only those provisions of law which were applicable prior to the offence, and which are in accordance with general principles of law, in particular the principle that the penalty shall be proportionate to the offence. They shall take into consideration the fact that the accused is not a national of the Occupying Power.

Article 68

Protected persons who commit an offence which is solely intended to harm the Occupying Power, but which does not constitute an attempt on the life or limb of members of the occupying forces or administration, nor a grave collective danger, nor seriously damage the property of the occupying forces or administration or the installations used by them, shall be liable to internment or simple imprisonment, provided the duration of such internment or imprisonment is proportionate to the offence committed. Furthermore, internment or imprisonment shall, for such offences, be the only measure adopted for depriving protected persons of liberty. The courts provided for under Article 66 of the present Convention may at their discretion convert a sentence of imprisonment to one of internment for the same period.

The penal provisions promulgated by the Occupying Power in accordance with Articles 64 and 65 may impose the death penalty on a protected person only in cases where the person is guilty of espionage, of serious acts of sabotage against the military installations of the Occupying Power or of intentional offences which have caused the death of one or more persons, provided that such offences were punishable by death under the law of the occupied territory in force before the occupation began.

The death penalty may not be pronounced against a protected person unless the attention of the court has been particularly called to the fact that since the accused is not a national of the Occupying Power, he is not bound to it by any duty of allegiance.

In any case, the death penalty may not be pronounced against a protected person who was under eighteen years of age at the time of the offence.

Article 69

In all cases, the duration of the period during which a protected person accused of an offence is under arrest awaiting trial or punishment shall be deducted from any period of imprisonment awarded.

Article 70

Protected persons shall not be arrested, prosecuted or convicted by the Occupying Power for acts committed or for opinions expressed before the occupation, or during a temporary interruption thereof, with the exception of breaches of the laws and customs of war.

Nationals of the Occupying Power who, before the outbreak of hostilities, have sought refuge in the territory of the occupied State, shall not be arrested, prosecuted, convicted or deported from the occupied territory, except for offences committed after the outbreak of hostilities, or for offence under common law committed before the outbreak of hostilities which, according to the law of the occupied State, would have justified extradition in time of peace.

Article 71

No sentence shall be pronounced by the competent courts of the Occupying Power except after a regular trial.

Accused persons who are prosecuted by the Occupying Power shall be promptly informed, in writing, in a language which they understand, of the particulars of the charges preferred against them, and shall be brought to trial as rapidly as possible. The Protecting Power shall be informed of all proceedings instituted by the Occupying Power against protected persons in respect of charges involving the death penalty or imprisonment for two years or more; it shall be enabled, at any time, to obtain information regarding the state of such proceedings. Furthermore, the Protecting Power shall be entitled, on request, to be furnished with all particulars of these and of any other proceedings instituted by the Occupying Power against protected persons.

The notification to the Protecting Power, as provided for in the second paragraph above, shall be sent immediately, and shall in any case reach the Protecting Power three weeks before the date of the first hearing. Unless, at the opening of the trial, evidence is submitted that the provisions of the article are fully complied with, the trial shall not proceed. The notification shall include the following particulars:

(a) description of the accused;

(b) place of residence or detention;

(c) specification of the charge or charges (with mention of the penal provisions under which it is brought);

(d) designation of the court which will hear the case;

(e) place and date of the first hearing.

Article 72

Accused persons shall have the right to present evidence necessary to their defence and may, in particular, call witnesses. They shall have the right to be assisted by a qualified advocate or counsel of their own choice, who shall be able to visit them freely and shall enjoy the necessary facilities for preparing the defence.

Failing a choice by the accused, the Protecting Power may provide him with an advocate or counsel. When an accused person has to meet a serious charge and the Protecting Power is not functioning, the Occupying Power, subject to the consent of the accused, shall provide an advocate or counsel.

Accused persons shall, unless they freely waive such assistance, be aided by an interpreter, both during preliminary investigation and during the hearing in court. They shall have the right at any time to object to the interpreter and to ask for his replacement.

Article 73

A convicted person shall have the right of appeal provided for by the laws applied by the court. He shall be fully informed of his right to appeal or petition and of the time limit within which he may do so.

The penal procedure provided in the present Section shall apply, as far as it is applicable, to appeals. Where the laws applied by the Court make no provision for appeals, the convicted person shall have the right to petition against the finding and sentence to the competent authority of the Occupying Power.

Article 74

Representatives of the Protecting Power shall have the right to attend the trial of any protected person, unless the hearing has, as an exceptional measure, to be held *in camera* in the interests of the security of the Occupying Power, which shall then notify the Protecting Power. A notification in respect of the date and place of trial shall be sent to the Protecting Power.

Any judgment involving a sentence of death, or imprisonment for two years or more, shall be communicated, with the relevant grounds, as rapidly as possible to the Protecting Power. The notification shall contain a reference to the notification made under Article 71, and, in the case of sentences of imprisonment, the name of the place where the sentence is to be served. A record of judgments other than those referred to above shall be kept by the court and shall be open to inspection by representatives of Protecting Power. Any period allowed for appeal in the case of sentences involving the death penalty, or imprisonment of two years or more, shall not run until notification of judgment has been received by the Protecting Power.

Article 75

In no case shall persons condemned to death be deprived of the right of petition for pardon or reprieve.

No death sentence shall be carried out before the expiration of a period of at least six months from the date of receipt by the Protecting Power of the notification of the final judgment confirming such death sentence, or of an order denying pardon or reprieve.

The six months period of suspension of the death sentence herein prescribed may be reduced in individual cases in circumstances of grave emergency involving an organized threat to the security of the Occupying Power or its forces, provided always that the Protecting Power is notified of such reduction and is given reasonable time and opportunity to make representations to the competent occupying authorities in respect of such death sentences.

Article 76

Protected persons accused of offences shall be detained in the occupied country, and if convicted they shall serve their sentences therein. They shall, if possible, be separated from other detainees and shall enjoy conditions of food and hygiene which will be sufficient to keep them in good health, and which will be at least equal to those obtaining in prisons in the occupied country.

They shall receive the medical attention required by their state of health.

They shall also have the right to receive any spiritual assistance which they may require.

Women shall be confined in separate quarters and shall be under the direct supervision of women.

Proper regard shall be paid to the special treatment due to minors.

Protected persons who are detained shall have the right to be visited by delegates of the Protecting Power and of the International Committee of the Red Cross, in accordance with the provisions of Article 143.

Such persons shall have the right to receive at least one relief parcel monthly.

Article 77

Protected persons who have been accused of offences or convicted by the courts in occupied territory, shall be handed over at the close of occupation, with the relevant records, to the authorities of the liberated territory.

Article 78

If the Occupying Power considers it necessary, for imperative reasons of security, to take safety measures concerning protected persons, it may, at the most, subject them to assigned residence or to internment.

Decisions regarding such assigned residence or internment shall be made according to a regular procedure to be prescribed by the Occupying Power in accordance with the provisions of the present Convention. This procedure shall include the right of appeal for the parties concerned. Appeals shall be decided with the least possible delay. . . .

Chapter VIII. Relations with the Exterior

Article 105

Immediately upon interning protected persons, the Detaining Powers shall inform them, the Power to which they owe allegiance and their Protecting Power of the measures taken for executing the provisions of the present Chapter. The Detaining Powers shall likewise inform the Parties concerned of any subsequent modifications of such measures.

Article 106

As soon as he is interned, or at the latest not more than one week after his arrival in a place of internment, and likewise in cases of sickness or transfer to another place of internment or to a hospital, every internee shall be enabled to send direct to his family, on the one hand, and to the Central Agency, provided for by Article 140, on the other, an internment card similar, if possible, to the model annexed to the present Convention, informing his relatives of his detention, address and state of health. The said cards shall be forwarded as rapidly as possible and may not be delayed in any way.

Article 107

Internees shall be allowed to send and receive letters and cards....

Part IV. Execution of the Convention

Section I. General Provisions.

Article 143

Representatives or delegates of the Protecting Powers shall have permission to go to all places where protected persons are, particularly to places of internment, detention and work.

They shall have access to all premises occupied by protected persons and shall be able to interview the latter without witnesses, personally or through an interpreter.

Such visits may not be prohibited except for reasons of imperative military necessity, and then only as an exceptional and temporary measure. Their duration and frequency shall not be restricted....

The delegates of the International Committee of the Red Cross shall also enjoy the above prerogatives....

Article 144

The High Contracting Parties undertake, in time of peace as in time or war, to disseminate the text of the present Convention as widely as possible in their respective countries, and in particular, to include the study thereof in their programmes of military and, if possible, civil instruction, so that the principles thereof may become known to the entire population.

Any civilian, military, police or other authorities, who in time of war assume responsibilities in respect of protected persons, must possess the text of the Conventions and be specially instructed as to its provisions.

Article 145

The High Contracting Parties shall communicate to one another through the Swiss Federal Council and, during hostilities, through the Protecting Powers, the official translations of the present Convention, as well as the laws and regulations which they may adopt to ensure the application thereof.

Article 146

The High Contracting Parties undertake to enact any legislation necessary to provide effective penal sanctions for persons committing, or ordering to be committed, any of the grave breaches of the present Convention defined in the following article.

Each High Contracting Party shall be under the obligation to search for persons alleged to have committed, or to have ordered to be committed, such grave breaches, and shall bring such persons, regardless of their nationality, before its own courts. It may also, if it prefers, and in accordance with the provisions of its own legislation, hand such persons over for trial to another High Contracting Party concerned, provided such High Contracting Party has made out a *prima facie* case.

Each High Contracting Party shall take measures necessary for the suppression of all acts contrary to the provisions of the present Convention other than grave breaches defined in the following article.

In all circumstances, the accused persons shall benefit by safeguards of proper trial and defence, which shall not be less favourable than those provided by Article 105 and those following of the Geneva Convention relative to the Treatment of Prisoners of War of August 12, 1949.

Article 147

Grave breaches to which the preceding article relates shall be those involving any of the following acts, if committed against persons or property protected by the present Convention: wilful killing, torture or inhuman treatment, including biological experiments, wilfully causing great suffering or serious injury to body or health, unlawful deportation or transfer or unlawful confinement of a protected person, compelling a protected person to serve in the forces of a hostile Power or wilfully depriving a protected person of the rights of fair and regular trial prescribed in the present Convention, taking of hostages and extensive destruction and appropriation of property, not justified by military necessity and carried out unlawfully and wantonly.

Article 148

No High Contracting Party shall be allowed to absolve itself or any other High Contracting Part of any liability incurred by itself or by another High Contracting Party in respect of breaches referred to in the preceding article.

Article 149

At the request of a Party to the conflict, an enquiry shall be instituted, in a manner to be decided between the interested Parties, concerning any alleged violation of the Convention.

If agreement has not been reached concerning the procedure for the enquiry, the Parties should agree on the choice of an umpire who will decide upon the procedure to be followed.

Once the violation has been established, the Parties to the conflict shall put an end to it and shall repress it with the least possible delay....

Document 33
GENEVA CONVENTION RELATIVE TO THE TREATMENT OF PRISONERS OF WAR OF 12 AUGUST 1949

75 U.N.T.S. 135, 6 U.S.T. 3316, T.I.A.S. No. 3364

Part I. General Provisions

Article 1

The High Contracting Parties undertake to respect and to ensure respect for the present Convention in all circumstances.

Article 2

In addition to the provisions which shall be implemented in peacetime, the present Convention shall apply to all cases of declared war or of any other armed conflict which may arise between two or more of the High Contracting Parties, even if the state of war is not recognized by one of them.

The Convention shall also apply to all cases of partial or total occupation of the territory of a High Contracting Party, even if the said occupation meets with no armed resistance.

Although one of the Powers in conflict may not be a party to the present Convention, the Powers who are parties thereto shall remain bound by it in their mutual relations. They shall furthermore be bound by the Convention in relation to the said Power, if the latter accepts and applies the provisions thereof.

Article 3

In the case of armed conflict not of an international character occurring in the territory of one of the High Contracting Parties, each party to the conflict shall be bound to apply, as a minimum, the following provisions:

(1) Persons taking no active part in the hostilities, including members of armed forces who have laid down their arms and those placed *hors de combat* by sickness, wounds, detention, or any other cause, shall in all circumstances be treated humanely, without any adverse distinction founded on race, colour, religion or faith, sex, birth or wealth, or any other similar criteria.

To this end, the following acts are and shall remain prohibited at any time and in any place whatsoever with respect to the above-mentioned persons:

(a) violence to life and person, in particular murder of all kinds, mutilation, cruel treatment and torture;

(b) taking of hostages;

(c) outrages upon personal dignity, in particular, humiliating and degrading treatment;

(d) the passing of sentences and the carrying out of executions without previous judgment pronounced by a regularly constituted court, affording all the judicial guarantees which are recognized as indispensable by civilized peoples.

(2) The wounded and sick shall be collected and cared for.

An impartial humanitarian body, such as the International Committee of the Red Cross, may offer its services to the Parties to the conflict.

The Parties to the conflict should further endeavor to bring into force, by means of special agreements, all or part of the other provisions of the present Convention.

The application of the preceding provisions shall not affect the legal status of the Parties to the conflict.

Article 4

A. Prisoners of war, in the sense of the present Convention, are persons belonging to one of the following categories, who have fallen into the power of the enemy:

1. Members of the armed forces of a Party to the conflict, as well as members of militias or volunteer corps forming part of such forces.

2. Members of other militias and members of other volunteer corps, including those of organized resistance movements, belonging to a Party to the conflict and operating in or outside their own territory, even if this territory is occupied, provided that such militias or volunteer corps, including such organized resistance movements, fulfil the following conditions:

a. that of being commanded by a person responsible for his subordinates;

b. that of having a fixed distinctive sign recognizable at a distance;

c. that of carrying arms openly;

d. that of conducting their operations in accordance with the laws and customs of war.

3. Members of regular armed forces who profess allegiance to a government or an authority not recognized by the Detaining Power. . . .

6. Inhabitants of a non-occupied territory, who on the approach of the enemy spontaneously take up arms to resist the invading forces, without having had time to form themselves into regular armed units provided they carry arms openly and respect the laws and customs of war. . . .

C. This article shall in no way affect the status of medical personnel and chaplains as provided for in Article 33 of the present Convention.

Article 5

The present Convention shall apply to the persons referred to in Article 4 from the time they fall into the power of the enemy and until their final release and repatriation.

Should any doubt arise as to whether persons, having committed a belligerent act and having fallen into the hands of the enemy, belong to any of the categories enumerated in Article 4, such persons shall enjoy the protection of the present Convention until such time as their status has been determined by a competent tribunal.

Article 6

In addition to the agreements expressly provided for in Articles 10, 23, 28, 33, 60, 65, 66, 67, 72, 73, 109, 110, 118, 119, 122 and 132, the High Contracting Parties may conclude other special agreements for all matters concerning which they may deem it suitable to make separate provision. No special agreement shall adversely affect the situation of prisoners of war, as defined by the present Convention, nor restrict the rights which it confers upon them. . . .

Article 7

Prisoners of war may in no circumstances renounce in part or in entirety the rights secured to them by the present Convention, and by the special agreements referred to in the foregoing article, if such there be. . . .

Part II. General Protection of Prisoners of War

Article 12

Prisoners of war are in the hands of the enemy Power, but not of the individuals or military units who have captured them. Irrespective of the individual responsibilities that may exist, the Detaining Power is responsible for the treatment given them.

Prisoners of war may only be transferred by the Detaining Power to a Power which is a party to the Convention and after the Detaining Power has satisfied itself of the willingness and ability of such transferee Power to apply the Convention. When prisoners of war are transferred under such circumstances, responsibility for the application of the Convention rests on the Power accepting them while they are in its custody.

Nevertheless, if that Power fails to carry out the provisions of the Convention in any important respect, the Power by whom the prisoners of war were transferred shall, upon being notified by the Protecting Power, take effective measures to correct the situation or shall request the return of the prisoners of war. Such requests must be complied with.

Article 13

Prisoners of war must at all times be humanely treated. Any unlawful act or omission by the Detaining Power causing death or seriously endangering the health of a prisoner of war in its custody is prohibited, and will be regarded as a serious breach of the present Convention. In particular, no prisoner of war may be subjected to physical mutilation or to medical or scientific experiments of any kind which are not justified by the medical, dental or hospital treatment of the prisoner concerned and carried out in his interest.

Likewise, prisoners of war must at all times be protected, particularly against acts of violence or intimidation and against insults and public curiosity.

Measures of reprisal against prisoners of war are prohibited.

Article 14

Prisoners of war are entitled in all circumstances to respect for their persons and their honour.

Women shall be treated with all the regard due to their sex and shall in all cases benefit by treatment as favourable as that granted to men.

Prisoners of war shall retain the full civil capacity which they enjoyed at the time of their capture. The Detaining Power may not restrict the exercise, either within or without its own territory, of the rights such capacity confers except in so far as the capacity requires.

Article 15

The Power detaining prisoners of war shall be bound to provide free of charge for their maintenance and for the medical attention required by their state of health.

Article 16

Taking into consideration the provisions of the present Convention relating to rank and sex, and subject to any privileged treatment which may be accorded to them by reason of their state of health, age or professional qualifications, all prisoners of war shall be treated alike by the Detaining Power, without any adverse distinction based on race, nationality, religious belief or political opinions, or any other distinction founded on similar criteria. . . .

Part III. Captivity

Section I. Beginning of Captivity

Article 18

All effects and articles of personal use, except arms, horses, military equipment and military documents, shall remain in the possession of prisoners of war, likewise their metal helmets and gas masks and like articles issued for personal protection. Effects and articles used for their clothing or feeding shall likewise remain in their possession, even if such effects and articles belong to their regulation military equipment.

At no time should prisoners of war be without identity documents. The Detaining Power shall supply such documents to prisoners of war who possess none.

Badges of rank and nationality, decorations and articles having above all a personal or sentimental value may not be taken from prisoners of war.

Sums of money carried by prisoners of war may not be taken away from them except by order of an officer, and after the amount and particulars of the owner have been recorded in a special register and an itemized receipt has been given, legibly inscribed with the name, rank and unit of the person issuing the said receipt. Sums in the currency of the Detaining Power, or which are changed into such currency at the prisoner's request, shall be placed to the credit of the prisoner's account as provided in Article 64.

The Detaining Power may withdraw articles of value from prisoners of war only for reasons of security; when such articles are withdrawn, the procedure laid down for sums of money impounded shall apply.

Such objects, likewise sums taken away in any currency other than that of the Detaining Power and the conversion of which has not been asked for by the owners, shall be kept in the custody of the Detaining Power and shall be returned in their initial shape to prisoners of war at the end of their captivity.

Article 19

Prisoners of war shall be evacuated, as soon as possible after their capture, to camps situated in an area far enough from the combat zone for them to be out of danger.

Only those prisoners of war who, owing to wounds or sickness, would run greater risks by being evacuated than by remaining where they are, may be temporarily kept back in a danger zone.

Prisoners of war shall not be unnecessarily exposed to danger while awaiting evacuation from a fighting zone.

Article 20

The evacuation of prisoners of war shall always be effected humanely and in conditions similar to those for the forces of the Detaining Power in their changes of station.

The Detaining Power shall supply prisoners of war who are being evacuated with sufficient food and potable water, and with the necessary clothing and medical attention. The Detaining Power shall take all suitable precautions to ensure their safety during evacuation, and shall establish as soon as possible a list of the prisoners of war who are evacuated.

If prisoners of war must, during evacuation, pass through transit camps, their stay in such camps shall be as brief as possible....

Section II. Internment of Prisoners of War

Chapter I. General Observations.

Article 22

Prisoners of war may be interned only in premises located on land and affording every guarantee of hygiene and healthfulness. Except in particular cases which are justified by the interest of the prisoners themselves, they shall not be interned in penitentiaries.

Prisoners of war interned in unhealthy areas, or where the climate is injurious for them, shall be removed as soon as possible to a more favourable climate.

The Detaining Power shall assemble prisoners of war in camps or camp compounds according to their nationality, language and customs, provided that such prisoners shall not be separated from prisoners of war belonging to the armed forces with which they were serving at the time of their capture, except with their consent.

Article 23

No prisoner of war may at any time be sent to, or detained in areas where he may be exposed to the fire of the combat zone, nor may his presence be used to render certain points or areas immune from military operations.

Prisoners of war shall have shelters against air bombardment and other hazards of war, to the same extent as the local civilian population. With the exception of those engaged in the protection of their quarters against the aforesaid hazards, they may enter such shelters as soon as possible after the giving of the alarm. Any other protective measure taken in favour of the population shall also apply to them.

Detaining Powers shall give the Powers concerned, through the intermediary of the Protecting Powers, all useful information regarding the geographical location of prisoner of war camps.

Whenever military considerations permit, prisoner of war camps shall be indicated in the day-time by the letters PW or PG, placed so as to be clearly visible from the air. The Powers concerned may, however, agree upon any other system or marking. Only prisoner of war camps shall be marked as such.

Article 24

Transit or screening camps of a permanent kind shall be fitted out under conditions similar to those described in the present Section, and the prisoners therein shall have the same treatment as in other camps....

Chapter II. Quarters, Food and Clothing of Prisoners of War.

Chapter III. Hygiene and Medical Attention.

Chapter IV. Medical Personnel and Chaplains
Retained to Assist Prisoners of War.

Article 33

Members of the medical personnel and chaplains while retained by the Detaining Power with a view to assisting prisoners of war, shall not be considered as prisoners of war. They shall, however, receive as a minimum the benefits and protection of the present Convention, and shall be granted all facilities necessary to provide for the medical care of, and religious ministration to prisoners of war....

I. General Provisions

Article 82

A prisoner of war shall be subject to the laws, regulations and orders in force in the armed forces of the Detaining Power; the Detaining Power shall be justified in taking judicial or disciplinary measures in respect of any offence committed by a prisoner of war against such laws, regulations or orders. However, no proceedings or punishments contrary to the provisions of this Chapter shall be allowed.

Article 83

In deciding whether proceedings in respect of an offence alleged to have been committed by a prisoner of war shall be judicial or disciplinary, the Detaining Power shall ensure that the competent authorities exercise the greatest leniency and adopt, wherever possible, disciplinary rather than judicial measures.

Article 84

A prisoner of war shall be tried only by a military court, unless the existing laws of the Detaining Power expressly permit the civil courts to try a member of the armed forces of the Detaining Power in respect of the particular offence alleged to have been committed by the prisoner of war.

In no circumstances whatever shall a prisoner of war be tried by a court of any kind which does not offer the essential guarantees of independence and impartiality as generally recognized, and, in particular, the procedure of which does not afford the accused the rights and means of defence provided for in Article 105.

Article 85

Prisoners of war prosecuted under the laws of the Detaining Power for acts committed prior to capture shall retain, even if convicted, the benefits of the present Convention.

Article 86

No prisoner of war may be punished more than once for the same act or on the same charge.

Article 87

Prisoners of war may not be sentenced by the military authorities and courts of the Detaining Power to any penalties except those provided for in respect of members of the armed forces of said Power who have committed the same acts. . . .

Collective punishment for individual acts, corporal punishment, imprisonment in premises without daylight and, in general, any form of torture or cruelty, are forbidden.

No prisoner of war may be deprived of his rank by the Detaining Power, or prevented from wearing his badges. . . .

II. Disciplinary Sanctions

III. Judicial Proceedings

Article 99

No prisoner shall be tried or sentenced for an act which is not forbidden by the law of the Detaining Power or by international law, in force at the time the said act was committed.

No moral or physical coercion may be exerted on a prisoner of war in order to induce him to admit himself guilty of the act which he is accused.

No prisoner of war may be convicted without having had an opportunity to present his defence and the assistance of a qualified advocate or counsel. . . .

Article 102

A prisoner of war can be validly sentenced only if the sentence has been pronounced by the same courts according to the same procedure as in the case of members of the armed forces of the Detaining Power, and if, furthermore, the provisions of the present Chapter have been observed. . . .

Article 104

In any case in which the Detaining Power has decided to institute judicial proceedings against a prisoner of war, it shall notify the Protecting Power as soon as possible and at least three weeks before the opening of the trial. . . .

Article 105

The prisoner of war shall be entitled to assistance by one of his prisoner comrades, to defence by a qualified advocate or counsel of his own choice, to the calling of witnesses and, if he deems it necessary, to the services of a competent interpreter. He shall be advised of these rights by the Detaining Power in due time before the trial.

Failing a choice by the prisoner of war, the Protecting Power shall find him an advocate or counsel, and shall have at least one week at its disposal for the purposes....

The advocate or counsel conducting the defence on behalf of the prisoner of war shall have at his disposal a period of two weeks at least before the opening of the trial, as well as the necessary facilities to prepare the defence of the accused. He may, in particular, freely visit the accused and interview him in private. He may also confer with any witnesses for the defence, including prisoners of war. He shall have the benefit of these facilities until the term of appeal or petition has expired.

Particulars of the charge or charges on which the prisoner of war is to be arraigned, as well as the documents which are generally communicated to the accused by virtue of the laws in force in the armed forces of the Detaining Power, shall be communicated to the accused prisoner of war in a language which he understands, and in good time before the opening of the trial. The same communication in the same circumstances shall be made to the advocate or counsel conducting the defence on behalf of the prisoner of war.

The representatives of the Protecting Power shall be entitled to attend the trial of the case, unless, exceptionally, this is held *in camera* in the interest of State security. In such a case the Detaining Power shall advise the Protecting Power accordingly.

Article 106

Every prisoner of war shall have, in the same manner as the members of the armed forces of the Detaining Power, the right of appeal or petition from any sentence pronounced upon him, with a view to the quashing or revising of the sentence or the reopening of the trial. He shall be fully informed of his right to appeal or petition and of the time limit within which he may do so....

Article 108

Sentences pronounced on prisoners of war after a conviction has become duly enforceable, shall be served in the same establishments and under the same conditions as in the case of members of the armed forces of the Detaining Power. These conditions shall in all cases conform to the requirements of health and humanity.

A woman prisoner of war on whom such a sentence has been pronounced shall be confined in separate quarters and shall be under the supervision of women....

Part IV. Termination of Captivity

Section I. Direct Repatriation and Accommodation in Neutral Countries

Section II. Release and Repatriation of Prisoners of War at the Close of Hostilities

Article 118

Prisoners of war shall be released and repatriated without delay after the cessation of active hostilities....

Article 119

Prisoners of war against whom criminal proceedings for an indictable offence are pending may be detained until the end of such proceedings, and, if necessary, until completion of the punishment. The same shall apply to prisoners of war already convicted for an indictable offence....

Part VI. Execution of the Convention

Section I. General Provisions

Article 126

Representatives or delegates of the Protecting Powers shall have permission to go to all places where prisoners of war may be, particularly to places of interment, imprisonment and labour, and shall have access to all premises occupied by prisoners of war; they shall also be allowed to go to the places of departure, passage and arrival of prisoners of war who are being transferred. They shall be able to interview the prisoners, and in particular the prisoners' representatives, without witnesses, either personally or through an interpreter.

Representatives and delegates of the Protecting Powers shall have full liberty to select the places they wish to visit. The duration and frequency of those visits shall not be restricted. Visits may not be prohibited except for reason of imperative military necessity, and then only as an exceptional and temporary measure.

The Detaining Power and the Power on which the said prisoners of war depend may agree, if necessary, that compatriots of these prisoners of war be permitted to participate in the visits.

The delegates of the International Committee of the Red Cross shall enjoy the same prerogatives. The appointment of such delegates shall be submitted to the approval of the Power detaining the prisoners of war to be visited.

Article 127

The High Contracting Parties undertake, in time of peace as in time of war, to disseminate the text of the present Convention as widely as possible in their respective countries, and, in particular, to include the study thereof in their programmes of military and, if possible, civil instruction, so that the principles thereof may become known to all their armed forces and to the entire population.

Any military or other authorities, who in time of war assume responsibilities in respect of prisoners of war, must possess the text of the Convention and be specially instructed as to its provisions.

Article 128

The High Contracting Parties shall communicate to one another through the Swiss Federal Council and, during hostilities, through the Protecting Powers, the official translations of the present Convention, as well as the laws and regulations which they may adopt to ensure the application thereof.

Article 129

The High Contracting Parties undertake to enact any legislation necessary to provide effective penal sanctions for persons committing, or ordering to be committed, any of the grave breaches of the present Convention defined in the following article.

Each High Contracting Party shall be under an obligation to search for persons alleged to have committed, or to have ordered to be committed, such grave breaches, and shall bring such persons, regardless of their nationality, before its own courts. It may also, if it prefers, and in accordance with the provisions of its own legislation, hand such persons over for trial to another High Contracting Party concerned, provided such High Contacting Party has made out a *prima facie* case.

Each High Contracting Party shall take measures necessary for the suppression of all acts contrary to the provisions of the present Convention other than grave breaches defined in the following article.

In all circumstances, the accused persons shall benefit by safeguards of proper trial and defence, which shall not be less favourable than those provided by Article 105 and those following of the present Convention.

Article 130

Grave breaches to which the preceding article relates shall be those involving any of the following acts, if committed against persons or property protected by the Convention: wilful killing, torture or inhuman treatment, including biological experiments, wilfully causing great suffering or serious injury to body or health, compelling a prisoner of war to serve in the forces of the hostile Power, or wilfully depriving a prisoner of war of the rights to fair and regular trial prescribed in this Convention.

Article 131

No High Contracting Part shall be allowed to absolve itself or any other High Contracting Party of any liability incurred by itself or by another High Contracting Party in respect of breaches referred to in the preceding article.

Article 132

At the request of a Party to the conflict, an enquiry shall be instituted, in a manner to be decided between the interested Parties, concerning any alleged violation of the Convention.

If agreement has not been reached concerning the procedure for the enquiry, the Parties should agree on the choice of an umpire who will decide upon the procedure to be followed.

Once the violation has been established, the Parties to the conflict shall put an end to it and shall repress it with the least possible delay. . . .

Document 34
PROTOCOL ADDITIONAL TO THE GENEVA CONVENTIONS OF 12 AUGUST 1949, AND RELATING TO THE PROTECTION OF VICTIMS OF INTERNATIONAL ARMED CONFLICTS (PROTOCOL I) 8 JUNE 1977

1125 U.N.T.S. 3

PREAMBLE

The High Contracting Parties, Proclaiming their earnest wish to see peace prevail among peoples,

Recalling that every State has the duty, in conformity with the Charter of the United Nations, to refrain in its international relations from the threat or use of force against the sovereignty, territorial integrity or political independence of any State, or in any other manner inconsistent with the purposes of the United Nations,

Believing it necessary nevertheless to reaffirm and develop the provisions protecting the victims of armed conflicts and to supplement measures intended to reinforce their application,

Expressing their conviction that nothing in this Protocol or in the Geneva Conventions of 12 August 1949 can be construed as legitimizing or authorizing any act of aggression or any other use of force inconsistent with the Charter of the United Nations,

Reaffirming further that the provisions of the Geneva Conventions of 12 August 1949 and of this Protocol must be fully applied in all circumstances to all persons who are protected by those instruments, without any adverse distinction based on the nature or origin of the armed conflict or on the causes espoused by or attributed to the Parties to the conflict,

Have agreed on the following:

PART I. GENERAL PROVISIONS

Article 1

General principles and scope of application

1. The High Contracting Parties undertake to respect and to ensure respect for this Protocol in all circumstances.

2. In cases not covered by this Protocol or by other international agreements, civilians and combatants remain under the protection and authority of the principles of international law derived from established custom, from the principles of humanity and from the dictates of public conscience.

3. This Protocol, which supplements the Geneva Conventions of 12 August 1949 for the protection of war victims, shall apply in the situations referred to in Article 2 common to those Conventions.

4. The situations referred to in the preceding paragraph include armed conflicts in which peoples are fighting against colonial domination and alien occupation and against racist regimes in the exercise of their right of self-determination, as enshrined in the Charter of the United Nations and the Declaration on Principles of International Law concerning Friendly Relations and Co-operation among States in accordance with the Charter of the United Nations. . . .

Article 3

Beginning and end of application

Without prejudice to the provisions which are applicable at all times:

(a) the Conventions and this Protocol shall apply from the beginning of any situation referred to in Article 1 of this Protocol;

(b) the application of the Conventions and of this Protocol shall cease, in the territory of Parties to the conflict, on the general close of military operations and, in the case of occupied territories, on the termination of the occupation, except, in either circumstance, for those persons whose final release, repatriation or re-establishment takes place thereafter. These persons shall continue to benefit from the relevant provisions of the Conventions and of this Protocol until their final release, repatriation or re-establishment.

Article 4

Legal status of the Parties to the conflict

The application of the Conventions and of this Protocol, as well as the conclusion of the agreements provided for therein, shall not affect the legal status of the Parties to the conflict. Neither the occupation of a territory nor the application of the Conventions and this Protocol shall affect the legal status of the territory in question. . . .

PART II. WOUNDED, SICK AND SHIPWRECKED

Section I. General Protection

Article 10

Protection and care

1. All the wounded, sick and shipwrecked, to whichever Party they belong, shall be respected and protected.

2. In all circumstances they shall be treated humanely and shall receive, to the fullest extent practicable and with the least possible delay,

the medical care and attention required by their condition. There shall be no distinction among them founded on any grounds other than medical ones.

Article 11

Protection of persons

1. The physical or mental health and integrity of persons who are in the power of the adverse Party or who are interned, detained or otherwise deprived of liberty as a result of a situation referred to in Article 1 shall not be endangered by any unjustified act or omission. Accordingly, it is prohibited to subject the persons described in this article to any medical procedure which is not indicated by the state of health of the person concerned and which is not consistent with generally accepted medical standards which would be applied under similar medical circumstances to persons who are nationals of the Party conducting the procedure and who are in no way deprived of their liberty.

2. It is, in particular, prohibited to carry out on such persons, even with their consent:

(a) physical mutilations;

(b) medical or scientific experiments;

(c) removal of tissue or organs for transplantation, except where these acts are justified in conformity with the conditions provided for in paragraph 1. . . .

4. Any wilful act or omission which seriously endangers the physical or mental health or integrity of any person who is in the power of a Party other than the one on which he depends and which either violates any of the prohibitions in paragraphs 1 and 2 or fails to comply with the requirements of paragraph 3 shall be a grave breach of this Protocol. . . .

PART III. METHODS AND MEANS OF WARFARE, COMBATANT AND PRISONER-OF-WAR STATUS

Section I. Methods and Means of Warfare

Article 35

Basic rules

1. In any armed conflict, the right of the Parties to the conflict to choose methods and means of warfare is not unlimited.

2. It is prohibited to employ weapons, projectiles and material and methods or warfare of a nature to cause superfluous injury or unnecessary suffering.

3. It is prohibited to employ methods or means of warfare which are intended, or may be expected, to cause widespread, long-term and severe damage to the natural environment.

Article 36

New weapons

In the study, development, acquisition or adoption of a new weapon, means or method of warfare, a High Contracting Party is under an obligation to determine whether its employment would, in some or all circumstances, be prohibited by this Protocol or by any other rule of international law applicable to the High Contracting Party.

Article 37

Prohibition of perfidy

1. It is prohibited to kill, injure or capture an adversary by resort to perfidy. Acts inviting the confidence of an adversary to lead him to believe that he is entitled to, or is obligated to accord, protection under the rules of international law applicable in armed conflict, with intent to betray that confidence, shall constitute perfidy. The following acts are examples of perfidy:

(a) the feigning of an intent to negotiate under a flag of truce or of a surrender;

(b) the feigning of an incapacitation by wounds or sickness;

(c) the feigning of civilian, non-combatant status; and

(d) the feigning of protected status by the use of signs, emblems or uniforms of the United Nations or of neutral or other States not Parties to the conflict.

2. Ruses of war are not prohibited. Such ruses are acts which are intended to mislead an adversary or to induce him to act recklessly but which infringe no rule of international law applicable in armed conflict and which are not perfidious because they do not invite the confidence of an adversary with respect to protection under that law. The following are examples of such ruses: the use of camouflage, decoys, mock operations and misinformation. . . .

Article 40

Quarter

It is prohibited to order that there shall be no survivors, to threaten an adversary therewith or to conduct hostilities on this bases. . . .

PART IV. CIVILIAN POPULATION

Section I. General Protection Against Effects of Hostilities

Chapter I. Basic Rule and Field of Application

Article 48

Basic rule

In order to ensure respect for an protection of the civilian population and civilian objects, the Parties to the conflict shall at all times distinguish between the civilian population and combatants and between civilian objects and military objectives and accordingly shall direct their operations only against military objectives. . . .

Chapter II. Civilians and Civilian Population

Article 50

Definition of civilians and civilian population

1. A civilian is any person who does not belong to one of the categories of persons referred to in Article 4(A)(1), (2), (3) and (6) of the

Third Convention [GPW] and in Article 43 of this Protocol. In case of doubt whether a person is a civilian, that person shall be considered to be a civilian.

2. The civilian population comprises all persons who are civilians.

3. The presence within the civilian population of individuals who do not come within the definition of civilians does not deprive the population of its civilian character.

Article 51

Protection of the civilian population

1. The civilian population and individual civilians shall enjoy general protection against dangers arising from military operations. To give effect to this protection, the following rules, which are additional to other applicable rules of international law, shall be observed in all circumstances.

2. The civilian population as such, as well as individual civilians, shall not be the object of attack. Acts or threats of violence the primary purpose of which is to spread terror among the civilian population are prohibited.

3. Civilians shall enjoy the protection afforded by this section, unless and for such time as they take a direct part in hostilities.

4. Indiscriminate attacks are prohibited. Indiscriminate attacks are:

(a) those which are not directed at a specific military objective;

(b) those which employ a method or means of combat which cannot be directed at a specific military objective; or

(c) those which employ a method or means of combat the effects of which cannot be limited as required by this Protocol;

and consequently, in each such case, are of a nature to strike military objectives and civilians or civilian objects without distinction.

5. Among others, the following types of attacks are to be considered as indiscriminate:

(a) an attack by bombardment by any methods or means which treats as a single military objective a number of clearly separated and distinct military objectives located in a city, town, village or other area containing a similar concentration of civilians or civilian objects; and

(b) an attack which may be expected to cause incidental loss of civilian life, injury to civilians, damage to civilian objects, or a combination thereof, which would be excessive in relation to the concrete and direct military advantage anticipated.

6. Attacks against the civilian population or civilians by way of reprisals are prohibited.

7. The presence or movements of the civilian population or individual civilians shall not be used to render certain points or areas immune from military operations, in particular in attempts to shield military

objectives from attacks or to shield, favour or impede military operations. The Parties to the conflict shall not direct the movement of the civilian population or individual civilians in order to attempt to shield military objectives from attacks or to shield military operations....

Article 52

General protection of civilian objects

1. Civilian objects shall not be the object of attack or of reprisal. Civilian objects are all objects which are not military objects as defined in paragraph 2.

2. Attacks shall be limited strictly to military objectives. In so far as objects are concerned, military objectives are limited to those objects which by their nature, location, purpose or use make an effective contribution to military action and whose total or partial destruction, capture or neutralization, in the circumstances ruling at the time, offers a definite military advantage.

3. In case of doubt whether an object which is normally dedicated to civilian purposes, such as a place of worship, a house or other dwelling or a school, is being used to make an effective contribution to military action, it shall be presumed not to be so used.

Article 53

Protection of cultural objects and places of worship

Without prejudice to the provisions of the Hague Convention for the Protection of Cultural Property in the Event of Armed Conflict of 14 May 1954, and of other relevant international instruments, it is prohibited:

(a) to commit any acts of hostility directed against the historic monuments, works of art or places of worship which constitute the cultural or spiritual heritage of peoples;

(b) to use such objects in support of the military effort;

(c) to make such objects the object of reprisals.

Article 54

Protection of objects indispensable to the survival of the civilian population

1. Starvation of civilians as a method of warfare is prohibited.

2. It is prohibited to attack, destroy, remove or render useless objects indispensable to the survival of the civilian population, such as food-stuffs, agricultural areas for the production of food-stuffs, crops, livestock, drinking water installations and supplies and irrigation works, for the specific purpose of denying them for their sustenance value to the civilian population or to the adverse Party, whatever the motive, whether in order to starve out civilians, to cause them to move away, or for any other motive.

3. The prohibitions in paragraph 2 shall not apply to such of the objects covered by it as are used by an adverse Party:

(a) as sustenance solely for the members of its armed forces; or

(b) if not as sustenance, then in direct support of military action, provided, however, that in no event shall actions against these objects be taken which may be expected to leave the civilian population with such inadequate food or water as to cause its starvation or force its movement.

4. These objects shall not be made the object of reprisals.

5. In recognition of the vital requirements of any Party to the conflict in the defence of its national territory against invasion, derogation from the prohibitions contained in paragraph 2 may be made by a Party to the conflict within such territory under its own control where required by imperative military necessity.

Article 55

Protection of the natural environment

1. Care shall be taken in warfare to protect the natural environment against widespread, long-term and severe damage. This prohibition includes a prohibition of the use of methods or means of warfare which are intended or may be expected to cause such damage to the natural environment and thereby prejudice the health or survival of the population.

2. Attacks against the natural environment by way of reprisals are prohibited.

Article 56

Protection of works and installations containing dangerous forces

1. Works or installations containing dangerous forces, namely dams, dykes and nuclear electrical generating stations, shall not be made the object of attack, even where these objects are military objectives, if such attack may cause the release of dangerous forces and consequent severe losses among the civilian population. Other military objectives located at or in the vicinity of these works or installations shall not be made the object of attack if such attack may cause the release of dangerous forces from the works or installations and consequent severe losses among the civilian population.

2. The special protection against attack provided in paragraph 1 shall cease:

(a) for a dam or a dyke if it is used for other than its normal function and in regular, significant and direct support of military operations and if such attack is the only feasible way to terminate such support;

(b) for a nuclear electrical generating station only if it provides electric power in regular, significant and direct support of military operations and if such attack is the only feasible way to terminate such support;

(c) for other military objectives located at or in the vicinity of these works or installations only if they are used in regular, significant and direct support of military operations and if such attack is the only feasible way to terminate such support. . . .

Chapter IV. Precautionary Measures

Article 57

Precautions in attack

1. In the conduct of military operations, constant care shall be taken to spare the civilian population, civilians and civilian objects.

2. With respect to attacks, the following shall be taken:

(a) those who plan or decide upon an attack shall:

(i) do everything feasible to verify that the objectives to be attacked are neither civilians nor civilian objects and are not subject to special protection but are military objectives within the meaning of paragraph 2 of Article 52 and that it is not prohibited by the provisions of this Protocol to attack them;

(ii) take all feasible precautions in the choice of means and methods of attack with a view to avoiding, and in any event to minimizing, incidental loss of civilian life, injury to civilians and damage to civilian objects;

(iii) refrain from deciding to launch an attack which may be expected to cause incidental loss of civilian life, injury to civilians, damage to civilian objects, or a combination thereof, which would be excessive in relation to the concrete and direct military advantage anticipated;

(b) an attack shall be cancelled or suspended if it becomes apparent that the objective is not a military one or is subject to special protection or that the attack may be expected to cause incidental loss of civilian life, injury to civilians, damage to civilian objects, or a combination thereof, which would be excessive n relation to the concrete and direct military advantage anticipated;

(c) effective advance warning shall be given of attacks which may affect the civilian population, unless circumstances do not permit.

3. When a choice is possible between several military objectives for obtaining a similar military advantage, the objective to be selected shall be that the attack on which may be expected to cause the least danger to civilian lives and to civilian objects.

4. In the conduct of military operations at sea or in the air, each Party to the conflict shall, in conformity with its rights and duties under the rules of international law applicable in armed conflict, take all reasonable precautions to avoid losses of civilian lives and damage to civilian objects.

5. No provision of this article may be construed as authorizing any attacks against the civilian population, civilians or civilian objects.

Article 58

Precautions against the effects of attacks

The Parties to the conflict shall, to the maximum extent feasible:

(a) without prejudice to Article 49 of the Fourth Convention, endeavour to remove the civilian population, individual civilians and civilian objects under their control from the vicinity of military objectives;

(b) avoid locating military objective within or near densely populated areas;

(c) take the other necessary precautions to protect the civilian population, individual civilians and civilian objects under their control against the dangers resulting from military operations....

Section III. Treatment of Persons in the Power of a Party to the Conflict

Chapter I. Field of Application and Protection of Persons and Objects

Article 72

Field of application

The provisions of this Section are additional to the rules concerning humanitarian protection of civilians and civilian objects in the power of a Party to the conflict contained in the Fourth Convention [GC], particularly Parts I and III thereof, as well as to other applicable rules of international law relating to protection of fundamental human rights during international armed conflict....

Article 75

Fundamental guarantees

1. In so far as they are affected by a situation referred to in Article 1 of this Protocol, persons who are in the power of a Party to the conflict and who do not benefit from more favourable treatment under the Conventions or under this Protocol shall be treated humanely in all circumstances and shall enjoy, as a minimum, the protection provided by this article without any adverse distinction based upon race, colour, sex, language, religion or belief, political or other opinion, national or social origin, wealth, birth or other status, or on any other similar criteria. Each Party shall respect the person, honour, convictions and religious practices of all such persons.

2. The following acts are and shall remain prohibited at any time and in any place whatsoever, whether committed by civilian or by military agents:

(a) violence to the life, health, or physical or mental well-being of persons, in particular:

(i) murder;

(ii) torture of all kinds, whether physical or mental;

(iii) corporal punishment; and

(iv) mutilation;

(b) outrages upon personal dignity, in particular humiliating and degrading treatment, enforced prostitution and any form of indecent assault;

(c) the taking of hostages;

(d) collective punishments; and

(e) threats to commit any of the foregoing acts.

3. Any person arrested, detained or interned for actions related to the armed conflict shall be informed promptly, in a language he understands, of the reasons why these measures have been taken. Except in cases of arrest or detention for penal offences, such persons shall be released with the minimum delay possible and in any event as soon as the circumstances justifying the arrest, detention or internment have ceased to exist.

4. No sentence may be passed and no penalty may be executed on a person found guilty of a penal offence related to the armed conflict except pursuant to a conviction pronounced by an impartial and regularly constituted court respecting the generally recognized principles of regular judicial procedure, which include the following:

(a) the procedure shall provide for an accused to be informed without delay of the particulars of the offence alleged against him and shall afford the accused before and during the trial all necessary rights and means of defence;

(b) no one shall be convicted of an offence except on the basis of individual penal responsibility;

(c) no one shall be accused or convicted of a criminal offence on account of any act or omission which did not constitute a criminal offence under the national or international law to which he was subject at the time when it was committed; nor shall any heavier penalty be imposed than that which was applicable at the time when the criminal offence was committed; if, after the commission of the offence, provision is made by law for the imposition of a lighter penalty, the offender shall benefit thereby;

(d) anyone charged with an offence is presumed innocent until proved guilty according to law;

(e) anyone charged with an offence shall have the right to be tried in his presence;

(f) no one shall be compelled to testify against himself or to confess guilt;

(g) anyone charged with an offence shall have the right to examine, or have examined, the witnesses against him and to obtain the attendance and examination of witnesses on his behalf under the same conditions as witnesses against him;

(h) no onc shall bc prosecuted or punished by the same Party for an offence in respect of which a final judgment acquitting or convicting that person has been previously pronounced under the same law and judicial procedure;

(i) anyone prosecuted for an offence shall have the right to have the judgment pronounced publicly;

(j) a convicted person shall be advised on conviction of his judicial and other remedies and of the time-limits within which they may be exercised.

5. Women whose liberty has been restricted for reasons related to the armed conflict shall be held in quarters separated from men's quarters. They shall be under the immediate supervision of women. Nevertheless, in cases where families are detained or interned, they shall, wherever possible, be held in the same place and accommodated as family units.

6. Persons arrested, detained or interned for reasons related to the armed conflict shall enjoy the protection provided by this article until their final release, repatriation or re-establishment, even after the end of the armed conflict.

7. In order to avoid any doubt concerning the prosecution and trial of persons accused of war crimes or crimes against humanity, the following principles shall apply:

(a) persons who are accused of such crimes should be submitted for the purpose of prosecution and trial in accordance with the applicable rules of international law; and

(b) any such persons who do not benefit from more favourable treatment under the Conventions or this Protocol shall be accorded the treatment provided by this article, whether or not the crimes of which they are accused constitute grave breaches of the Conventions or of this Protocol.

8. No provision of this article may be construed as limiting or infringing any other more favourable provision granting greater protection, under any applicable rules of international law, to persons covered by paragraph 1. . . .

Article 91

Responsibility

A Party to the conflict which violates the provisions of the Conventions or this Protocol shall, if the case demands, be liable to pay compensation. It shall be responsible for all acts committed by persons forming part of its armed forces.

Document 35
CONVENTION (NO. IV) RESPECTING THE LAWS AND CUSTOMS OF WAR ON LAND, ANNEX

Done at The Hague, Oct. 18, 1907
36 Stat. 2277, T.S. No. 539, 1 Bevans 631

Preamble

... Considering that, while seeking means to preserve peace and prevent armed conflicts between nations, it is likewise necessary to bear in mind the case where an appeal to arms may be brought about by events which their solicitude could not avert;

Animated by the desire to serve, even in this extreme case, the interests of humanity and the ever progressive needs of civilization;

Thinking it important, with this object, to revise the general laws and customs of war, either with a view to defining them with greater precision or to confining them within such limits as would mitigate their severity as far as possible;

Have deemed in necessary to complete and render more precise in certain particulars the work of the First Peace Conference, which, following on the Brussels Conference of 1874, and inspired by the ideas dictated by a wise and generous forethought, adopted provisions intended to define and govern the usages of war on land. According to the views of the High Contacting Parties, these provisions, the wording of which has been inspired by the desire to diminish the evils of war, so far as military requirements permit, are intended to serve as a general rule of conduct for the belligerents in their mutual relations and in their relations with the inhabitants.

It has not, however, been found possible at present to concert Regulations covering all the circumstances which arise in practice; On the other hand, the High Contracting Parties clearly do not intend that unforeseen cases should, in the absence of a written undertaking, be let to the arbitrary judgment of military commanders.

Until a more complete code of the laws of war has been issued, the High Contracting Parties deem it expedient to declare that, in cases not included in the Regulations adopted by them, the inhabitants and the belligerents remain under the protection and the rule of the principles of the law of nations, as they result from the usages established among civilized peoples, from the laws of humanity, and from the dictates of the public conscience.

They declare that it is in this sense especially that Articles 1 and 2 of the Regulations adopted must be understood....

Who, after having deposited their full powers, found in good and due form, have agreed upon the following:

Article 1

The Contracting Parties shall issue instructions to their armed land forces which shall be in conformity with the Regulations respecting the Laws and Customs of War on Land, annexed to the present Convention.

Article 2

The provisions contained in the Regulations referred to in Article 1, as well as in the present Convention, do not apply except between Contracting Powers, and then only if all the belligerents are parties to the Convention.

Article 3

A belligerent party which violates the provisions of the said Regulations shall, if the case demands, be liable to pay compensation. It shall be responsible for all acts committed by persons forming part of its armed forces. . . .

Annex to the Convention.

Regulations Respecting the Laws and Customs of War on Land

Section I. On Belligerents.

Chapter I. The Qualifications of Belligerents.

Article 1

The laws, rights, and duties of war apply not only to armies, but also to militia and volunteer corps fulfilling the following conditions:

1. To be commanded by a person responsible for his subordinates;

2. To have a fixed distinctive emblem recognizable at a distance;

3. To carry arms openly; and

4. To conduct their operations in accordance with the laws and customs of war.

In countries where militia or volunteer corps constitute the army, or form part of it, they are included under the denomination "army."

Article 2

The inhabitants of a territory which has not been occupied, who, on the approach of the enemy, spontaneously take up arms to resist the invading troops without having had time to organize themselves in accordance with Article 1, shall be regarded as belligerents if they carry arms openly and if they respect the laws and customs of war.

Article 3

The armed forces of the belligerent parties may consist of combatants and noncombatants. In the case of capture by the enemy, both have a right to be treated as prisoners of war.

Chapter II. Prisoners of War.

Article 4

Prisoners of war are in the power of the hostile Government, but not of the individuals or crops who capture them.

They must be humanely treated.

All their personal belongings, except arms, horses, and military papers, remain their property.

Article 5

Prisoners of war may be interned in a town, fortress, camp, or other place, under obligation not to go beyond certain fixed limits; but they can only be placed in confinement as an indispensable measure of safety and only while the circumstances which necessitate the measure continue to exist. . . .

Article 20

After the conclusion of peace, the repatriation of prisoners of war shall be carried out as quickly as possible.

Chapter III. The Sick and Wounded.

Article 21

The obligations of belligerents with regard to the sick and wounded are governed by the Geneva Convention [of 1906].

Section II. Hostilities

CHAPTER I. MEANS OF INJURING THE ENEMY, SIEGES, AND BOMBARDMENTS

Article 22

The right of belligerents to adopt means of injuring the enemy is not unlimited.

Article 23

In addition to the prohibitions provided by special Conventions, it is especially forbidden:

(a) To employ poison or poisoned weapons;

(b) To kill or wound treacherously individuals belonging to the hostile nation or army;

(c) To kill or wound an enemy who, having laid down his arms, or having no longer means of defence, has surrendered at discretion;

(d) To declare that no quarter will be given;

(e) To employ arms, projectiles, or material of such as nature as to cause unnecessary suffering;

(f) To make improper use of a flag of truce, of the national flag, or of the military insignia and uniform of the enemy, as well as the distinctive badges of the Geneva Convention;

(g) To destroy or seize the enemy's property, unless such destruction or seizure be imperatively demanded by the necessities of war;

(h) To declare abolished, suspended, or inadmissible in a court of law the rights and actions of the nationals of the hostile party.

A belligerent is likewise forbidden to compel the nationals of the hostile party to take part in the operations of war directed against their own country, even if they were in the belligerent's service before the commencement of the war.

Article 24

Ruses of war and the employment of measures necessary for obtaining information about the enemy and the country are considered permissible.

Article 25

The attack or bombardment, by whatever means, of towns, villages, dwellings, or buildings which are undefended is prohibited.

Article 26

The officer in command of an attacking force must, before commencing bombardment, except in cases of assault, do all in his power to warn the authorities.

Article 27

In sieges and bombardments all necessary steps must be taken to spare, as far as possible, buildings dedicated to religion, art, science, or charitable purposes, historic monuments, hospitals, and places where the sick and wounded are collected, provided they are not being used at the time for military purposes.

It is the duty of the besieged to indicate the presence of such buildings or places by distinctive and visible signs, which shall be notified to the enemy beforehand.

Article 28

The pillage of a town or place, even when taken by assault, is prohibited....

Section III. Military Authority Over the Territory of the Hostile State

Article 42

Territory is considered occupied when it is actually placed under the authority of the hostile army.

The occupation extends only to the territory where such authority has been established and can be exercised.

Article 43

The authority of the legitimate power having in fact passed into the hands of the occupant, the latter shall take all the measures in his power to restore, and ensure, as far as possible, public order and safety, while respecting, unless absolutely prevented, the laws in force in the country.

Article 44

A belligerent is forbidden to force the inhabitants of occupied territory to furnish information about the army of the other belligerent, or about its means of defence.

Article 45

It is forbidden to compel the inhabitants of occupied territory to swear allegiance to the hostile Power.

Article 46

Family honour and rights, the lives of persons, and private property, as well as religious convictions and practice, must be respected.

Private property cannot be confiscated.

Article 47

Pillage is formally forbidden.

Article 48

If, in the territory occupied, the occupant collects the taxes, dues, and tolls imposed for the benefit of the State, he shall do so, as far as is possible in accordance with the rules of assessment and incidence in force, and shall in consequence be bound to defray the expenses of the administration of the occupied territory to the same extent as the legitimate Government was so bound.

Article 49

If, in addition to the taxes mentioned in the above article, the occupant levies other money contributions in the occupied territory, this shall only be for the needs of the army or of the administration of the territory in question.

Article 50

No general penalty, pecuniary or otherwise, shall be inflicted upon the population on account of the acts of individuals for which they cannot be regarded as jointly and severally responsible.

Article 51

No contribution shall be collected except under a written order, and on the responsibility of a Commander-in-chief.

The collection of the said contribution shall only be effected as far as possible in accordance with the rules of assessment and incidence of the taxes in force.

For every contribution a receipt shall be given to the contributors....

Article 53

An army of occupation can only take possession of cash, funds, and realizable securities which are strictly the property of the State, depots of arms, means of transport, stores and supplies, and, generally, all movable property belonging to the State, which may be used for operations of the war.

All appliances, whether on land, at sea, or in the air, adapted for the transmission of news, or for the transport of persons or things, exclusive of cases governed by naval law, depots of arms, and, generally, all kinds of ammunition of war, may be seized, even if they belong to private individuals, but must be restored and compensation fixed when peace is made.

Article 54

Submarine cables connecting an occupied territory with a neutral territory shall not be seized or destroyed except in the case of absolute necessity. They must likewise be restored and compensation fixed when peace is made.

Article 55

The occupying State shall be regarded only as administrator and usufructuary of public buildings, real estate, forests, and agricultural estates belonging to the hostile State, and situated in the occupied country. It must safeguard the capital of these properties, and administer them in accordance with the rules of usufruct.

Article 56

The property of municipalities, that of institutions dedicated to religion, charity and education, the arts and sciences, even when State property, shall be treated as private property.

All seizure of, destruction or wilful damage done to institutions of this character, historic monuments, works of art and science, is forbidden, and should be made the subject of legal proceedings.

Document 36
CHARTER OF THE INTERNATIONAL MILITARY TRIBUNAL AT NUREMBERG (1945)

Article 6

The Tribunal established by the Agreement referred to in Article 1 hereof for the trial and punishment of the major war criminals of the European Axis countries shall have the power to try and punish persons who, acting in the interests of the European Axis countries, whether as individuals or as members of organizations, committed any of the following crimes.

The following acts, or any of them, are crimes coming within the jurisdiction of the Tribunal for which there shall be individual responsibility:

(a) *Crimes against peace*: namely, planning, preparation, initiation or waging of a war of aggression, or a war in violation of international treaties, agreements or assurances, or participation in a common plan or conspiracy for the accomplishment of any of the foregoing;

(b) *War crimes*: namely, violations of the laws or customs of war. Such violations shall include, but not be limited to, murder, ill-treatment or deportation to slave labour or for any other purpose of civilian population of or in occupied territory, murder or ill-treatment of prisoners of war or persons on the seas, killing of hostages, plunder of public or private property, wanton destruction of cities, towns or villages, or devastation not justified by military necessity;

(c) *Crimes against humanity*: namely, murder, extermination, enslavement, deportation, and other inhumane acts committed against any civilian population, before or during the war; or persecutions on political, racial or religious grounds in execution of or in connection with any crime within the jurisdiction of the Tribunal, whether or not in violation of the domestic law of the country where perpetrated.

Leaders, organizers, instigators and accomplices participating in the formulation or execution of a common plan or conspiracy to commit any of the foregoing crimes are responsible for all acts performed by any persons in execution of such plan.

Article 7

The official position of defendants, whether as Heads of State or responsible officials in Government Departments, shall not be considered as freeing them from responsibility or mitigating punishment.

Article 8

The fact that the Defendant acted pursuant to order of his Government or of a superior shall not free him from responsibility, but may be considered in mitigation of punishment if the Tribunal determines that justice so requires.

Document 37
TOKYO CHARTER FOR THE INTERNATIONAL MILITARY TRIBUNAL FOR THE FAR EAST (1946)

As amended by General Orders No. 20 (26 April 1946), T.I.A.S. No. 1589

Article 5

Jurisdiction Over Persons and Offenses. The Tribunal shall have the power to try and punish Far Eastern war criminals who as individuals or as members of organizations are charged with offenses which include Crimes against Peace. The following acts, or any of them, are crimes coming within the jurisdiction of the Tribunal for which there shall be individual responsibility:

a. *Crimes against Peace*: Namely, the planning, preparation, initiation or waging of a declared or undeclared war of aggression, or a war in violation of international law, treaties, agreements or assurances, or participation in a common plan or conspiracy for the accomplishment of any of the foregoing;

b. *Conventional War Crimes*: Namely, violations of the laws or customs of war;

c. *Crimes against Humanity*: Namely, murder, extermination, enslavement, deportation, and other inhumane acts committed before or during the war, or persecutions on political or racial grounds in execution of or in connection with any crime within the jurisdiction of the Tribunal, whether or not in violation of the domestic law of the country where perpetrated.

Leaders, organizers, instigators and accomplices participating in the formulation or execution of a common plan or conspiracy to commit any of the foregoing crimes are responsible for all acts performed by any person in execution of such plan.

Article 6

Responsibility of Accused. Neither the official position, at any time, of an accused, nor the fact that an accused acted pursuant to order of his government or of a superior shall, of itself, be sufficient to free such accused from responsibility for any crime with which he is charged, but such circumstances may be considered in mitigation of punishment if the Tribunal determines that justice so requires.

Document 38
ALLIED CONTROL COUNCIL LAW NO. 10 (1945)

Article II

1. Each of the following acts is recognized as a crime:

(a) *Crimes against Peace*. Initiation of invasions of other countries and wars of aggression in violation of international laws and treaties, including but not limited to planning, preparation, initiation or waging a war of aggression, or a war [in] violation of international treaties, agreements or assurances, or participation in a common plan or conspiracy for the accomplishment of any of the foregoing.

(b) *War Crimes*. Atrocities or offences against persons or property constituting violations of the laws or customs of war, including, but not limited to, murder, ill treatment or deportation to slave labour or for any other purpose, of civilian population from occupied territory, murder or ill treatment of prisoners of war or persons on the seas, killing of hostages, plunder of public or private property, wanton destruction of cities, towns or villages, or devastation not justified by military necessity.

(c) *Crimes against Humanity*. Atrocities and offenses, including but not limited to murder, extermination, enslavement, deportation, imprisonment, torture, rape, or other inhumane acts committed against any civilian population, or persecutions on political, racial or religious grounds whether or not in violation of the domestic laws of the country where perpetrated....

2. Any person without regard to nationality or the capacity in which he acted, is deemed to have committed a crime as defined in paragraph 1 of this article, if he was (a) a principal or (b) was an accessory to the commission of any such crime or ordered or abetted the same or (c) took a consenting part therein or (d) was connected with plans or enterprises involving its commission or (e) was a member of any organization or group connected with the commission of any such crime or (f) with reference to paragraph 1 (a), if he held a high political, civil or military (including General Staff) position in Germany or in one of its Allies, co-belligerents or satellites or held high position in financial, industrial or economic life of any such country....

4. (a) The official position of any person, whether as Head of State or as a responsible official in a Government Department, does not free him from responsibility for a crime or entitle him to mitigation of punishment.

(b) The fact that any person acted pursuant to the order of his Government or of a superior does not relieve him from responsibility for a crime, but may be considered in mitigation.

Document 39
PRINCIPLES OF THE NUREMBERG CHARTER AND JUDGMENT

Formulated by the International Law Commission, 5 U.N. GAOR, Supp. No. 12, at 11–14, para. 99, U.N. Doc. A/1316 (1950)

I. Any person who commits an act which constitutes a crime under international law is responsible therefor and liable to punishment.

II. The fact that internal law does not impose a penalty for an act which constitutes a crime under international law does not relieve the person who committed the act from responsibility under international law.

III. The fact that a person who committed an act which constitutes a crime under international law acted as Head of State or responsible Government official does not relieve him from responsibility under international law.

IV. The fact that a person acted pursuant to order of his Government or of a superior does not relieve him from responsibility under international law, provided a moral choice was in fact possible to him.

V. Any person charge with a crime under international law has the right to a fair trial on the facts and law.

VI. The crimes hereinafter set out are punishable as crimes under international law:

a. Crimes against peace:

(i) Planning, preparation, initiation or waging of a war of aggression, or a war in violation of international treaties, agreements or assurances;

(ii) Participation in a common plan or conspiracy for the accomplishment of any of the acts mentioned under (i).

b. War crimes: Violation of the laws and customs of war which include, but are not limited to, murder, ill-treatment of prisoners of war or of persons on the seas, killing of hostages, plunder of public or private property, wanton destruction of cities, towns, or villages, or devastation not justified by military necessity.

c. Crimes against humanity: Murder, extermination, enslavement, deportation and other inhuman acts done against any civilian population, or persecution on political, racial or religious grounds, when such acts are done or such persecutions are carried on in execution of or in connection with any crime against peace or any war crime.

VII. Complicity in the commission of a crime against peace, a war crime, or a crime against humanity as set forth in Principle VI is a crime under international law.

Document 40
ROME STATUTE OF THE INTERNATIONAL CRIMINAL COURT

Adopted by the U.N. Diplomatic Conference, July 17, 1998

Preamble

Conscious that all peoples are united by common bonds, their cultures pieced together in a shared heritage, and concerned that this delicate mosaic may be shattered at any time,

Mindful that during this century millions of children, women and men have been victims of unimaginable atrocities that deeply shock the conscience of humanity,

Recognizing that such grave crimes threaten the peace, security and well-being of the world,

Affirming that the most serious crimes of concern to the international community as a whole must not go unpunished and that their effective prosecution must be ensured by taking measures at the national level and by enhancing international cooperation,

Determined to put an end to impunity for the perpetrators of these crimes and thus to contribute to the prevention of such crimes,

Recalling that it is the duty of every State to exercise its criminal jurisdiction over those responsible for international crimes,

Reaffirming the Purposes and Principles of the Charter of the United Nations, and in particular that all States shall refrain from the threat or use of force against the territorial integrity or political independence of any State, or in any other manner inconsistent with the Purposes of the United Nations,

Emphasizing in this connection that nothing in this Statute shall be taken as authorizing any State Party to intervene in an armed conflict in the internal affairs of any State,

Determined to these ends and for the sake of present and future generations, to establish an independent permanent International Criminal Court in relationship with the United Nations system, with jurisdiction over the most serious crimes of concern to the international community as a whole,

Emphasizing that the International Criminal Court established under this Statute shall be complementary to national criminal jurisdictions,

Resolved to guarantee lasting respect for the enforcement of international justice,

Have agreed as follows:

Part 1. Establishment of the Court

Article 1. The Court

An International Criminal Court ("the Court") is hereby established. It shall be a permanent institution and shall have the power to exercise its jurisdiction over persons for the most serious crimes of international concern, as referred to in this Statute, and shall be complementary to national criminal jurisdictions. The jurisdiction and functioning of the Court shall be governed by the provisions of this Statute.

Article 2. Relationship of the Court with the United Nations

The Court shall be brought into relationship with the United Nations through an agreement to be approved by the Assembly of States Parties to this Statute and thereafter concluded by the President of the Court on its behalf.

Article 3. Seat of the Court

1. The seat of the Court shall be established at The Hague in the Netherlands ("the host State").

2. The Court shall enter into a headquarters agreement with the host State, to be approved by the Assembly of States Parties and thereafter concluded by the President of the Court on its behalf.

3. The Court may sit elsewhere, whenever it considers it desirable, as provided in this Statute.

Article 4. Legal status and powers of the Court

1. The Court shall have international legal personality. It shall also have such legal capacity as may be necessary for the exercise of its functions and the fulfilment of its purposes.

2. The Court may exercise its functions and powers, as provided in this Statute, on the territory of any State Party and, by special agreement, on the territory of any other State.

Part 2. Jurisdiction, Admissibility and Applicable Law

Article 5. Crimes within the jurisdiction of the Court

1. The jurisdiction of the Court shall be limited to the most serious crimes of concern to the international community as a whole. The Court has jurisdiction in accordance with this Statute with respect to the following crimes:

(a) The crime of genocide;

(b) Crimes against humanity;

(c) War crimes;

(d) The crime of aggression.

2. The Court shall exercise jurisdiction over the crime of aggression once a provision is adopted in accordance with Articles 121 and 123 defining the crime and setting out the conditions under which the Court shall exercise jurisdiction with respect to this crime. Such a provision shall be consistent with the relevant provisions of the Charter of the United Nations.

Article 6. Genocide

[The article provides the same customary definition found in Article II of the Genocide Convention.]

Article 7. Crimes against humanity

1. For the purpose of this Statute, "crime against humanity" means any of the following acts when committed as part of a widespread or systematic attack directed against any civilian population, with knowledge of the attack:

(a) Murder;

(b) Extermination;

(c) Enslavement;

(d) Deportation or forcible transfer of population;

(e) Imprisonment or other severe deprivation of physical liberty in violation of fundamental rules of international law;

(f) Torture;

(g) Rape, sexual slavery, enforced prostitution, forced pregnancy, enforced sterilization, or any other form of sexual violence of comparable gravity;

(h) Persecution against any identifiable group or collectivity on political, racial, national, ethnic, cultural, religious, gender as defined in paragraph 3, or other grounds that are universally recognised as impermissible under international law, in connection with any act referred to in this paragraph or any crime within the jurisdiction of the Court;

(i) Enforced disappearance of persons;

(j) The crime of apartheid;

(k) Other inhumane acts of a similar character intentionally causing great suffering, or serious injury to body or to mental or physical health.

2. For the purpose of paragraph 1:

(a) "Attack directed against any civilian population" means a course of conduct involving the multiple commission of acts referred to in paragraph 1 against any civilian population, pursuant to or in furtherance of a State or organizational policy to commit such attack;

(b) "Extermination" includes the intentional infliction of conditions of life, *inter alia* the deprivation of access to food and medicine, calculated to bring about the destruction of part of a population;

(c) "Enslavement" means the exercise of any or all of the powers attaching to the right of ownership over a person and includes the exercise of such power in the course of trafficking in persons, in particular women and children;

(d) "Deportation or forcible transfer of population" means forced displacement of the persons concerned by expulsion or other coercive acts from the area in which they are lawfully present, without grounds permitted under international law;

(e) "Torture" means the intentional infliction of severe pain or suffering, whether physical or mental, upon a person in the custody or under the control of the accused; except that torture shall not include pain or suffering arising only from, inherent in or incidental to, lawful sanctions;

(f) "Forced pregnancy" means the unlawful confinement, of a woman forcibly made pregnant, with the intent of affecting the ethnic composition of any population or carrying out other grave violations of international law. This definition shall not in any way be interpreted as affecting national laws relating to pregnancy;

(g) "Persecution" means the intentional and severe deprivation of fundamental rights contrary to international law by reason of the identity of the group or collectivity;

(h) "The crime of apartheid" means inhumane acts of a character similar to those referred to in paragraph 1, committed in the context of an institutionalized regime of systematic oppression and domination by one racial group over any other racial group or groups and committed with the intention of maintaining that regime;

(i) "Enforced disappearance of persons" means the arrest, detention or abduction of persons by, or with the authorization, support or acquiescence of, a State or a political organization, followed by a refusal to acknowledge that deprivation of freedom or to give information on the fate or whereabouts of those persons, with the intention of removing them from the protection of the law for a prolonged period of time.

3. For the purpose of this Statute, it is understood that the term "gender" refers to the two sexes, male and female, within the context of society. The term "gender" does not indicate any meaning different from the above....

Article 8

1. The Court shall have jurisdiction in respect of war crimes in particular when committed as a part of a plan or policy or as part of a large-scale commission of such crimes.

2. For the purpose of this Statute, "war crimes" means:

(a) Grave breaches of the Geneva Conventions of 12 August 1949, namely, any of the following acts against persons or property protected under the provisions of the relevant Geneva Convention:

(i) Wilful killing;

(ii) Torture or inhuman treatment, including biological experiments;

(iii) Wilfully causing great suffering, or serious injury to body or health;

(iv) Extensive destruction and appropriation of property, not justified by military necessity and carried out unlawfully and wantonly;

(v) Compelling a prisoner of war or other protected person to serve in the forces of a hostile Power;

(vi) Wilfully depriving a prisoner of war or other protected person of the rights of fair and regular trial;

(vii) Unlawful deportation or transfer or unlawful confinement;

(viii) Taking of hostages.

(b) Other serious violations of the laws and customs applicable in international armed conflict, within the established framework of international law, namely, any of the following acts:

(i) Intentionally directing attacks against the civilian population as such or against individual civilians not taking direct part in hostilities;

(ii) Intentionally directing attacks against civilian objects, that is, objects which are not military objectives;

(iii) Intentionally directing attacks against personnel, installations, material, units or vehicles involved in a humanitarian assistance or peacekeeping mission in accordance with the Charter of the United Nations, as long as they are entitled to the protection given to civilians or civilian objects under the international law of armed conflict;

(iv) Intentionally launching an attack in the knowledge that such attack will cause incidental loss of life or injury to civilians or damage to civilian objects or widespread, long-term and severe damage to the natural environment which would be clearly excessive in relation to the concrete and direct overall military advantage anticipated;

(v) Attacking or bombarding, by whatever means, towns, villages, dwellings or buildings which are undefended and which are not military objectives;

(vi) Killing or wounding a combatant who, having laid down his arms or having no longer means of defence, has surrendered at discretion;

(vii) Making improper use of a flag of truce, of the flag or of the military insignia and uniform of the enemy or of the United Nations, as well as of the distinctive emblems of the Geneva Conventions, resulting in death or serious personal injury;

(viii) The transfer, directly or indirectly, by the Occupying Power of parts of its own civilian population into the territory it occupies, or the deportation or transfer of all or parts of the population of the occupied territory within or outside this territory;

(ix) Intentionally directing attacks against buildings dedicated to religion, education, art, science or charitable purposes, historic monuments, hospitals and places where the sick and wounded are collected, provided they are not military objectives;

(x) Subjecting persons who are in the power of an adverse party to physical mutilation or to medical or scientific experiments of any kind which are neither justified by the medical, dental or hospital treatment of the person concerned nor carried out in his or her interest, and which cause death to or seriously endanger the health of such person or persons;

(xi) Killing or wounding treacherously individuals belonging to the hostile nation or army;

(xii) Declaring that no quarter will be given;

(xiii) Destroying or seizing the enemy's property unless such destruction or seizure be imperatively demanded by the necessities of war;

(xiv) Declaring abolished, suspended or inadmissible in a court of law the rights and actions of the nationals of the hostile party;

(xv) Compelling the nationals of the hostile party to take part in the operations of war directed against their own country, even if they were in the belligerent's service before the commencement of the war;

(xvi) Pillaging a town or place, even when taken by assault;

(xvii) Employing poison or poisoned weapons;

(xviii) Employing asphyxiating, poisonous or other gases, and all analogous liquids, materials or devices;

(xix) Employing bullets which expand or flatten easily in the human body, such as bullets with a hard envelope which does not entirely cover the core or is pierced with incisions;

(xx) Employing weapons, projectiles and material and methods of warfare which are of a nature to cause superfluous injury or unnecessary suffering or which are inherently indiscriminate in violation of the international law of armed conflict, provided that such weapons, projectiles and material and methods of warfare are the subject of a comprehensive prohibition and are included in an annex to this Statute, by an amendment in accordance with the relevant provisions set forth in Articles 121 and 123;

(xxi) Committing outrages upon personal dignity, in particular humiliating and degrading treatment;

(xxii) Committing rape, sexual slavery, enforced prostitution, forced pregnancy, as defined in Article 7, paragraph 2 (f), enforced sterilization, or any other form of sexual violence also constituting a grave breach of the Geneva Conventions;

(xxiii) Utilizing the presence of a civilian or other protected person to render certain points, areas or military forces immune from military operations;

(xxiv) Intentionally directing attacks against buildings, material, medical units and transport, and personnel using the distinctive emblems of the Geneva Conventions in conformity with international law;

(xxv) Intentionally using starvation of civilians as a method of warfare by depriving them of objects indispensable to their survival, including wilfully impeding relief supplies as provided for under the Geneva Conventions;

(xxvi) Conscripting or enlisting children under the age of fifteen years into the national armed forces or using them to participate actively in hostilities.

(c) In the case of an armed conflict not of an international character, serious violations of Article 3 common to the four Geneva Conventions of 12 August 1949, namely, any of the following acts committed against persons taking no active part in the hostilities, including members of armed forces who have laid down their arms and those placed *hors de combat* by sickness, wounds, detention or any other cause:

(i) Violence to life and person, in particular murder of all kinds, mutilation, cruel treatment and torture;

(ii) Committing outrages upon personal dignity, in particular humiliating and degrading treatment;

(iii) Taking of hostages;

(iv) The passing of sentences and the carrying out of executions without previous judgement pronounced by a regularly constituted court, affording all judicial guarantees which are generally recognized as indispensable.

(d) Paragraph 2 (c) applies to armed conflicts not of an international character and thus does not apply to situations of internal disturbances and tensions, such as riots, isolated and sporadic acts of violence or other acts of a similar nature.

(e) Other serious violations of the laws and customs applicable in armed conflicts not of an international character, within the established framework of international law, namely, any of the following acts:

(i) Intentionally directing attacks against the civilian population as such or against individual civilians not taking direct part in hostilities;

(ii) Intentionally directing attacks against buildings, material, medical units and transport, and personnel using the distinctive emblems of the Geneva Conventions in conformity with international law;

(iii) Intentionally directing attacks against personnel, installations, material, units or vehicles involved in a humanitarian assistance or peacekeeping mission in accordance with the Charter of the United Nations, as long as they are entitled to the protection given to civilians or civilian objects under the law of armed conflict;

(iv) Intentionally directing attacks against buildings dedicated to religion, education, art, science or charitable purposes, historic monuments, hospitals and places where the sick and wounded are collected, provided they are not military objectives;

(v) Pillaging a town or place, even when taken by assault;

(vi) Committing rape, sexual slavery, enforced prostitution, forced pregnancy, as defined in Article 7, paragraph 2 (f), enforced sterilization, and any other form of sexual violence also constituting a serious violation of Article 3 common to the four Geneva Conventions;

(vii) Conscripting or enlisting children under the age of fifteen years into armed forces or groups or using them to participate actively in hostilities;

(viii) Ordering the displacement of the civilian population for reasons related to the conflict, unless the security of the civilians involved or imperative military reasons so demand;

(ix) Killing or wounding treacherously a combatant adversary;

(x) Declaring that no quarter will be given;

(xi) Subjecting persons who are in the power of another party to the conflict to physical mutilation or to medical or scientific experiments of any kind which are neither justified by the medical, dental or hospital treatment of the person concerned nor carried out in his or her interest, and which cause death to or seriously endanger the health of such person or persons;

(xii) Destroying or seizing the property of an adversary unless such destruction or seizure be imperatively demanded by the necessities of the conflict;

(f) Paragraph 2 (e) applies to armed conflicts not of an international character and thus does not apply to situations of internal disturbances and tensions, such as riots, isolated and sporadic acts of violence or other acts of a similar nature. It applies to armed conflicts that take place in the territory of a State when there is protracted armed conflict between governmental authorities and organized armed groups or between such groups.

3. Nothing in paragraphs 2 (c) and (d) shall affect the responsibility of a Government to maintain or reestablish law and order in the State or to defend the unity and territorial integrity of the State, by all legitimate means.

Article 9

1. Elements of Crimes shall assist the Court in the interpretation and application of Articles 6, 7 and 8. They shall be adopted by a two-thirds majority of the members of the Assembly of States Parties.

2. Amendments to the Elements of Crimes may be proposed by:

(a) Any State Party;

(b) The judges acting by an absolute majority;

(c) The Prosecutor.

Such amendments shall be adopted by a two-thirds majority of the members of the Assembly of States Parties.

3. The Elements of Crimes and amendments thereto shall be consistent with this Statute.

Article 10

Nothing in this Part shall be interpreted as limiting or prejudicing in any way existing or developing rules of international law for purposes other than this Statute.

Article 11

1. The Court has jurisdiction only with respect to crimes committed after the entry into force of this Statute.

2. If a State becomes a Party to this Statute after its entry into force, the Court may exercise its jurisdiction only with respect to crimes committed after the entry into force of this Statute for that State, unless that State has made a declaration under Article 12, paragraph 3.

Article 12. Preconditions to the exercise of jurisdiction

1. A State which becomes a Party to this Statute thereby accepts the jurisdiction of the Court with respect to the crimes referred to in Article 5.

2. In the case of Article 13, paragraph (a) or (c), the Court may exercise its jurisdiction if one or more of the following States are Parties to this Statute or have accepted the jurisdiction of the Court in accordance with paragraph 3:

(a) The State on the territory of which the conduct in question occurred or, if the crime was committed on board a vessel or aircraft, the State of registration of that vessel or aircraft;

(b) The State of which the person accused of the crime is a national.

3. If the acceptance of a State which is not a Party to this Statute is required under paragraph 2, that State may, by declaration lodged with the Registrar, accept the exercise of jurisdiction by the Court with respect to the crime in question. The accepting State shall cooperate with the Court without any delay or exception in accordance with Part 9.

Article 13. Exercise of jurisdiction

The Court may exercise its jurisdiction with respect to a crime referred to in Article 5 in accordance with the provisions of this Statute if:

(a) A situation in which one or more of such crimes appears to have been committed is referred to the Prosecutor by a State Party in accordance with Article 14;

(b) A situation in which one or more of such crimes appears to have been committed is referred to the Prosecutor by the Security Council acting under Chapter VII of the United Nations; or

(c) The Prosecutor has initiated an investigation in respect of such a crime in accordance with Article 15.

Article 14. Referral of a situation by a State Party

1. A State Party may refer to the Prosecutor a situation in which one or more crimes within the jurisdiction of the Court appear to have been committed requesting the Prosecutor to investigate the situation for the purpose of determining whether one or more specific persons should be charged with the commission of such crimes.

2. As far as possible, a referral shall specify the relevant circumstances and be accompanied by such supporting documentation as is available to the State referring the situation.

Article 15. Prosecutor

1. The Prosecutor may initiate investigations *proprio motu* on the basis of information on crimes within the jurisdiction of the Court.

2. The Prosecutor shall analyze the seriousness of the information received. For this purpose, he or she may seek additional information from States, organs of the United Nations, intergovernmental or non-governmental organizations, or other reliable sources that he or she deems appropriate, and may receive written or oral testimony at the seat of the Court.

3. If the Prosecutor concludes that there is a reasonable basis to proceed with an investigation, he or she shall submit to the Pre–Trial Chamber a request for authorization of an investigation, together with any supporting material collected. Victims may make representations to the Pre–Trial Chamber, in accordance with the Rules of Procedure and Evidence.

4. If the Pre–Trial Chamber, upon examination of the request and the supporting material, considers that there is a reasonable basis to proceed with an investigation, and that the case appears to fall within the jurisdiction of the Court, it shall authorize the commencement of the investigation, without prejudice to subsequent determinations by the Court with regard to the jurisdiction and admissibility of a case.

5. The refusal of the Pre–Trial Chamber to authorize the investigation shall not preclude the presentation of a subsequent request by the Prosecutor based on new facts or evidence regarding the same situation.

6. If, after the preliminary examination referred to in paragraphs 1 and 2, the Prosecutor concludes that the information provided does not constitute a reasonable basis for an investigation, he or she shall inform those who provided the information. This shall not preclude the Prosecutor from considering further information submitted to him or her regarding the same situation in the light of new facts or evidence.

Article 16. Deferral of investigation or prosecution

No investigation or prosecution may be commenced or proceeded with under this Statute for a period of 12 months after the Security Council, in a resolution adopted under Chapter VII of the Charter of the United Nations, has requested the Court to that effect; that request may be renewed by the Council under the same conditions.

Article 17. Issues of admissibility

1. Having regard to paragraph 10 of the Preamble and Article 1, the Court shall determine that a case is inadmissible where:

(a) The case is being investigated or prosecuted by a State which has jurisdiction over it, unless the State is unwilling or unable genuinely to carry out the investigation or prosecution;

(b) The case has been investigated by a State which has jurisdiction over it and the State has decided not to prosecute the person concerned, unless the decision resulted from the unwillingness or inability of the State genuinely to prosecute;

(c) The person concerned has already been tried for conduct which is the subject of the complaint, and a trial by the Court is not permitted under Article 20, paragraph 3;

(d) The case is not of sufficient gravity to justify further action by the Court.

2. In order to determine unwillingness in a particular case, the Court shall consider, having regard to the principles of due process recognized by international law, whether one or more of the following exist, as applicable:

(a) The proceedings were or are being undertaken or the national decision was made for the purpose of shielding the person concerned from criminal responsibility for crimes within the jurisdiction of the Court referred to in Article 5;

(b) There has been an unjustified delay in the proceedings which in the circumstances is inconsistent with an intent to bring the person concerned to justice;

(c) The proceedings were not or are not being conducted independently or impartially, and they were or are being conducted in a manner which, in the circumstances, is inconsistent with an intent to bring the person concerned to justice.

3. In order to determine inability in a particular case, the Court shall consider whether, due to a total or substantial collapse or unavailability of its national judicial system, the State is unable to obtain the accused or the necessary evidence and testimony or otherwise unable to carry out its proceedings.

Article 18. Preliminary rulings regarding admissibility

1. When a situation has been referred to the Court pursuant to Article 13 (a) and the Prosecutor has determined that there would be a reasonable basis to commence an investigation, or the Prosecutor initiates an investigation pursuant to Articles 13 (c) and 15, the Prosecutor shall notify all States Parties and those States which, taking into account the information available, would normally exercise jurisdiction over the crimes concerned. The Prosecutor may notify such States on a confidential basis and, where the Prosecutor believes it necessary to protect persons, prevent destruction of evidence or prevent the absconding of persons, may limit the scope of the information provided to States.

2. Within one month of receipt of that notice, a State may inform the Court that it is investigating or has investigated its nationals or others within its jurisdiction with respect to criminal acts which may constitute crimes referred to in Article 5 and which relate to the information provided in the notification to States. At the request of that State, the Prosecutor shall defer to the State's investigation of those persons unless the Pre–Trial Chamber, on the application of the Prosecutor, decides to authorize the investigation.

3. The Prosecutor's deferral to a State's investigation shall be open to review by the Prosecutor six months after the date of deferral or at any time when there has been a significant change of circumstances based on the State's unwillingness or inability genuinely to carry out the investigation.

4. The State concerned or the Prosecutor may appeal to the Appeals Chamber against a ruling of the Pre–Trial Chamber, in accordance with Article 82, paragraph 2. The appeal may be heard on an expedited basis.

5. When the Prosecutor has deferred an investigation in accordance with paragraph 2, the Prosecutor may request that the State concerned periodically inform the Prosecutor of the progress of its investigations and any subsequent prosecutions. States Parties shall respond to such requests without undue delay.

6. Pending a ruling by the Pre–Trial Chamber, or at any time when the Prosecutor has deferred an investigation under this article, the

Prosecutor may, on an exceptional basis, seek authority from the Pre–Trial Chamber to pursue necessary investigative steps for the purpose of preserving evidence where there is a unique opportunity to obtain important evidence or there is a significant risk that such evidence may not be subsequently available.

7. A State which has challenged a ruling of the Pre–Trial Chamber under this article may challenge the admissibility of a case under Article 19 on the grounds of additional significant facts or significant change of circumstances.

Article 19. Challenges to the jurisdiction of the Court or the admissibility of a case

1. The Court shall satisfy itself that it has jurisdiction in any case brought before it. The Court may, on its own motion, determine the admissibility of a case in accordance with Article 17.

2. Challenges to the admissibility of a case on the grounds referred to in Article 17 or challenges to the jurisdiction of the Court may be made by:

(a) An accused or a person for whom a warrant of arrest or a summons to appear has been issued under Article 58;

(b) A State which has jurisdiction over a case, on the ground that it is investigating or prosecuting the case or has investigated or prosecuted; or

(c) A State from which acceptance of jurisdiction is required under Article 12.

3. The Prosecutor may seek a ruling from the Court regarding a question of jurisdiction or admissibility. In proceedings with respect to jurisdiction or admissibility, those who have referred the situation under Article 13, as well as victims, may also submit observations to the Court.

4. The admissibility of a case or the jurisdiction of the Court may be challenged only once by any person or State referred to in paragraph 2. The challenge shall take place prior to or at the commencement of the trial. In exceptional circumstances, the Court may grant leave for a challenge to be brought more than once or at a time later than the commencement of the trial. Challenges to the admissibility of a case, at the commencement of a trial, or subsequently with the leave of the Court, may be based only on Article 17, paragraph 1 (c).

5. A State referred to in paragraph 2 (b) and (c) shall make a challenge at the earliest opportunity.

6. Prior to the confirmation of the charges, challenges to the admissibility of a case or challenges to the jurisdiction of the Court shall be referred to the Pre–Trial Chamber. After confirmation of the charges, they shall be referred to the Trial Chamber. Decisions with respect to jurisdiction or admissibility may be appealed to the Appeals Chamber in accordance with Article 82.

7. If a challenge is made by a State referred to in paragraph 2 (b) or (c), the Prosecutor shall suspend the investigation until such time as the Court makes a determination in accordance with Article 17.

8. Pending a ruling by the Court, the Prosecutor may seek authority from the Court:

(a) To pursue necessary investigative steps of the kind referred to in Article 18, paragraph 6;

(b) To take a statement or testimony from a witness or complete the collection and examination of evidence which had begun prior to the making of the challenge; and

(c) In cooperation with the relevant States, to prevent the absconding of persons in respect of whom the Prosecutor has already requested a warrant of arrest under Article 58.

9. The making of challenge shall not affect the validity of any act performed by the Prosecutor or any order or warrant issued by the Court prior to the making of the challenge.

10. If the Court has decided that a case is inadmissible under Article 17, the Prosecutor may submit a request for a review of the decision when he or she is fully satisfied that new facts have arisen which negate the basis on which the case had previously been found inadmissible under Article 17.

11. If the Prosecutor, having regard to the matters referred to in Article 17, defers an investigation, the Prosecutor may request that the relevant State make available to the Prosecutor information on the proceedings. That information shall, at the request of the State concerned, be confidential. If the Prosecutor thereafter decides to proceed with an investigation, he or she shall notify the State in respect of the proceedings of which deferral has taken place.

Article 20. *Ne bis in idem*

1. Except as provided in this Statute, no person shall be tried before the Court with respect to conduct which formed the basis of crimes for which the person has been convicted or acquitted by the Court.

2. No person shall be tried before another court for a crime referred to in Article 5 for which that person has already been convicted or acquitted by the Court.

3. No person who has been tried by another court for conduct also proscribed under Articles 6, 7 or 8 shall be tried by the Court with respect to the same conduct unless the proceedings in the other court:

(a) Were for the purpose of shielding the person concerned from criminal responsibility for crimes within the jurisdiction of the Court; or

(b) Otherwise were not conducted independently or impartially in accordance with the norms of due process recognized by international law and were conducted in a manner which, in the circumstances, was inconsistent with an intent to bring the person concerned to justice.

Article 21. Applicable law

1. The Court shall apply:

(a) In the first place, this Statute, Elements of Crimes and its Rules of Procedure and Evidence;

(b) In the second place, where appropriate, applicable treaties and the principles and rules of international law, including the established principles of the international law of armed conflict;

(c) Failing that, general principles of law derived by the Court from national laws and legal systems of the world....

2. The Court may apply principles and rules of law as interpreted in its previous decisions.

3. The application and interpretation of law pursuant to this article must be consistent with internationally recognized human rights, and be without any adverse distinction founded on grounds such as gender, as defined in Article 7, paragraph 3, age, race, colour, language, religion or belief, political or other opinion, national, ethnic or social origin, wealth, birth or other status.

Part 3. General Principles of Criminal Law

Article 22. *Nullum crimen sine lege*

1. A person shall not be criminally responsible under this Statute unless the conduct in question constitutes, at the time it takes place, a crime within the jurisdiction of this Court.

2. The definition of a crime shall be strictly construed and shall not be extended by analogy. In case of ambiguity, the definition shall be interpreted in favour of the person being investigated, prosecuted or convicted.

3. This article shall not affect the characterization of any conduct as criminal under international law independently of this Statute.

Article 23. *Nulla poena sine lege*

A person convicted by the Court may be punished only in accordance with this Statute.

Article 24. Non-retroactivity *ratione personae*

1. No person shall be criminally responsible under this Statute for conduct prior to entry into force of the Statute.

2. In the event of a change in the law applicable to a given case prior to a final judgment, the law more favourable to the person being investigated, prosecuted or convicted shall apply.

Article 25. Individual criminal responsibility

1. The Court shall have jurisdiction over natural persons pursuant to this Statute.

2. A person who commits a crime within the jurisdiction of the Court shall be individually responsible and liable for punishment in accordance with this Statute.

3. In accordance with this Statute, a person shall be criminally responsible and liable for punishment for a crime within the jurisdiction of the Court if that person:

(a) Commits such a crime, whether as an individual, jointly with another or through another person, regardless of whether that other person is criminally responsible;

(b) Orders, solicits or induces the commission of such a crime which in fact occurs or is attempted;

(c) For the purpose of facilitating the commission of such a crime, aids, abets or otherwise assists in its commission or its attempted commission, including providing the means for its commission;

(d) In any other way contributes to the commission or attempted commission of such a crime by a group of persons acting with a common purpose. Such contribution shall be intentional and shall either:

(i) Be made with the aim of furthering the criminal activity or criminal purpose of the group, where such activity or purpose involves the commission of a crime within the jurisdiction of the Court; or

(ii) Be made in the knowledge of the intention of the group to commit the crime;

(e) In respect of the crime of genocide, directly and publicly incites others to commit genocide;

(f) Attempts to commit such a crime by taking action that commences its execution by means of a substantial step, but the crime does not occur because of circumstances independent of the person's intentions. However, a person who abandons the effort to commit the crime or otherwise prevents the completion of the crime shall not be liable for punishment under this Statute for the attempt to commit that crime if that person completely and voluntarily gave up the criminal purpose.

4. No provision in this Statute relating to individual criminal responsibility shall affect the responsibility of States under international law.

Article 26. Exclusion of jurisdiction over persons under eighteen

The Court shall have no jurisdiction over any person who was under the age of 18 at the time of the alleged commission of a crime.

Article 27. Irrelevance of official capacity

1. This Statute shall apply equally to all persons without any distinction based on official capacity. In particular, official capacity as a Head of State or Government, a member of a Government or parliament,

an elected representative or a government official shall in no case exempt a person from criminal responsibility under this Statute, nor shall it, in and of itself, constitute a ground for reduction of sentence.

2. Immunities or special procedural rules which may attach to the official capacity of a person, whether under national or international law, shall not bar the Court from exercising its jurisdiction over such a person.

Article 28. Responsibility of commanders and other superiors

In addition to other grounds of criminal responsibility under this Statute for crimes within the jurisdiction of the Court:

1. A military commander or person effectively acting as a military commander shall be criminally responsible for crimes within the jurisdiction of the Court committed by forces under his or her effective command and control, or effective authority and control as the case may be, as a result of his or her failure to exercise control properly over such forces, where:

(a) That military commander or person either knew or, owing to the circumstances at the time, should have known that the forces were committing or about to commit such crimes; and

(b) That military commander or person failed to take all necessary and reasonable measures within his or her power to prevent or repress their commission or to submit the matter to the competent authorities for investigation and prosecution.

2. With respect to superior and subordinate relationships not described in paragraph 1, a superior shall be criminally responsible for crimes within the jurisdiction of the Court committed by subordinates under his or her effective authority and control, as a result of his or her failure to exercise control properly over such subordinates, where:

(a) The superior either knew, or consciously disregarded information which clearly indicated, that the subordinates were committing or about to commit such crimes;

(b) The crimes concerned activities that were within the effective responsibility and control of the superior; and

(c) The superior failed to take all necessary and reasonable measures within his or her power to prevent or repress their commission or to submit the matter to the competent authorities for investigation and prosecution.

Article 29. Non-applicability of statute of limitations

The crimes within the jurisdiction of the Court shall not be subject to any statute of limitations.

Article 30. Mental Element

1. Unless otherwise provided, a person shall be criminally responsible and liable for punishment for a crime within the jurisdiction of the

Court only if the material elements are committed with intent and knowledge.

2. For the purposes of this article, a person has intent where:

(a) In relation to conduct, that person means to engage in the conduct;

(b) In relation to a consequence, that person means to cause that consequence or is aware that it will occur in the ordinary course of events.

3. For the purposes of this article, "knowledge" means awareness that a circumstance exists or a consequence will occur in the ordinary course of events. "Know" and "knowingly" shall be construed accordingly.

Article 31. Grounds for excluding criminal responsibility

1. In addition to other grounds for excluding criminal responsibility provided for in this Section, a person shall not be criminally responsible if, at the time of that person's conduct:

(a) The person suffers from a mental disease or defect that destroys that person's capacity to appreciate the unlawfulness or nature of his or her conduct, or capacity to control his or her conduct to conform to the requirements of law;

(b) The person is in a state of intoxication that destroys that person's capacity to appreciate the unlawfulness or nature of his or her conduct, or capacity to control his or her conduct to conform to the requirements of law, unless the person has become voluntarily intoxicated under such circumstances that the person knew, or disregarded the risk, that, as a result of the intoxication, he or she was likely to engage in conduct constituting a crime within the jurisdiction of the Court;

(c) The person acts reasonably to defend himself or herself or another person or, in the case of war crimes, property which is essential for the survival of the person or another person or property which is essential for accomplishing a military mission, against an imminent and unlawful use of force in a manner proportionate to the degree of danger to the person or the other person or property protected. The fact that the person was involved in a defensive operation conducted by forces shall not in itself constitute a ground for excluding criminal responsibility under this subparagraph;

(d) The conduct which is alleged to constitute a crime within the jurisdiction of the Court has been caused by duress resulting from a threat of imminent death or of continuing or imminent serious bodily harm against that person or another person, and the person acts necessarily and reasonably to avoid this threat, provided that the person does not intend to cause a greater harm than the one sought to be avoided. Such a threat may either be:

(i) Made by other persons; or

(ii) Constituted by other circumstances beyond that person's control.

2. The Court shall determine the applicability of the grounds for excluding criminal responsibility provided for in this Statute to the case before it.

3. At trial, the Court may consider a ground for excluding criminal responsibility other than those referred to in paragraph 1 where such a ground is derived from applicable law as set forth in Article 21. The procedure relating to the consideration of such a ground shall be provided for in the Rules of Procedure and Evidence.

Article 32. Mistake of fact or mistake of law

1. A mistake of fact shall be a ground for excluding criminal responsibility only if it negates the mental element required by the crime.

2. A mistake of law as to whether a particular type of conduct is a crime within the jurisdiction of the Court shall not be a ground for excluding criminal responsibility. A mistake of law may, however, be a ground for excluding criminal responsibility if it negates the mental element required by such a crime, or as provided for in Article 33.

Article 33. Superior orders and prescription of law

1. The fact that a crime within the jurisdiction of the Court has been committed by a person pursuant to an order of a Government or of a superior, whether military or civilian, shall not relieve that person of criminal responsibility unless:

(a) The person was under a legal obligation to obey orders of the Government or the superior in question;

(b) The person did not know that the order was unlawful; and

(c) The order was not manifestly unlawful.

2. For the purposes of this article, orders to commit genocide or crimes against humanity are manifestly unlawful.

Part 4. Composition and Administration of the Court

Article 34. Organs of the Court

The Court shall be composed of the following organs:

(a) The Presidency;

(b) An Appeals Division, a Trial Division and a Pre-Trial Division;

(c) The Office of the Prosecutor;

(d) The Registry.

Article 35. Service of judges

1. All judges shall be elected as full-time members of the Court and shall be available to serve on that basis from the commencement of their terms of office.

2. The judges composing the Presidency shall serve on a full-time basis as soon as they are elected.

3. The Presidency may, on the basis of the workload of the Court and in consultation with its members, decide from time to time to what extent the remaining judges shall be required to serve on a full-time basis. Any such arrangement shall be without prejudice to the provisions of Article 40.

4. The financial arrangements for judges not required to serve on a full-time basis shall be made in accordance with Article 49.

Article 36. Qualifications, nomination and election of judges

1. Subject to the provisions of paragraph 2, there shall be 18 judges of the Court.

2. (a) The Presidency, acting on behalf of the Court, may propose an increase in the number of judges specified in paragraph 1, indicating the reasons why this is considered necessary and appropriate. The Registrar shall promptly circulate any such proposal to all States Parties.

(b) Any such proposal shall then be considered at a meeting of the Assembly of States Parties to be convened in accordance with Article 112. The proposal shall be considered adopted if approved at the meeting by a vote of two-thirds of the members of the Assembly of States Parties and shall enter into force at such time as decided by the Assembly of States Parties.

(c) (i) Once a proposal for an increase in the number of judges has been adopted under subparagraph (b), the election of the additional judges shall take place at the next session of the Assembly of States Parties in accordance with paragraphs 3 to 8 inclusive, and Article 37, paragraph 2;

(ii) Once a proposal for an increase in the number of judges has been adopted and brought into effect under subparagraphs (b) and (c) (i), it shall be open to the Presidency at any time thereafter, if the workload of the Court justifies it, to propose a reduction in the number of judges, provided that the number of judges shall not be reduced below that specified in paragraph 1. The proposal shall be dealt with in accordance with the procedure laid down in subparagraphs (a) and (b). In the event that the proposal is adopted, the number of judges shall be progressively decreased as the terms of office of serving judges expire, until the necessary number has been reached.

3. (a) The judges shall be chosen from among persons of high moral character, impartiality and integrity who possess the qualifications required in their respective States for appointment to the highest judicial offices.

(b) Every candidate for election to the Court shall:

(i) Have established competence in criminal law and procedure, and the necessary relevant experience, whether as judge, prosecutor, advocate or in other similar capacity, in criminal proceedings; or

(ii) Have established competence in relevant areas of international law such as international humanitarian law and the law of human rights, and extensive experience in a professional legal capacity which is of relevance to the judicial work of the Court;

(c) Every candidate for election to the Court shall have an excellent knowledge of and be fluent in at least one of the working languages of the Court.

4. (a) Nominations of candidates for election to the Court may be made by any State Party to this Statute, and shall be made either:

(i) By the procedure for the nomination of candidates for appointment to the highest judicial offices in the State in question; or

(ii) By the procedure provided for the nomination of candidates for the International Court of Justice in the Statute of that Court. Nominations shall be accompanied by a statement in the necessary detail specifying how the candidate fulfils the requirements of paragraph 3.

(b) Each State Party may put forward one candidate for any given election who need not necessarily be a national of that State Party but shall in any case be a national of a State Party.

(c) The Assembly of States Parties may decide to establish, if appropriate, an Advisory Committee on nominations. In that event, the Committee's composition and mandate shall be established by the Assembly of States Parties.

5. For the purposes of the election, there shall be two lists of candidates:

List A containing the names of candidates with the qualifications specified in paragraph 3 (b) (i); and

List B containing the names of candidates with the qualifications specified in paragraph 3 (b) (ii).

A candidate with sufficient qualifications for both lists may choose on which list to appear. At the first election to the Court, at least nine judges shall be elected from list A and at least five judges from list B. Subsequent elections shall be so organized as to maintain the equivalent proportion on the Court of judges qualified on the two lists.

6. (a) The judges shall be elected by secret ballot at a meeting of the Assembly of States Parties convened for that purpose under Article 112. Subject to paragraph 7, the persons elected to the Court shall be the 18 candidates who obtain the highest number of votes and a two-thirds majority of the States Parties present and voting.

(b) In the event that a sufficient number of judges is not elected on the first ballot, successive ballots shall be held in accordance with the procedures laid down in subparagraph (a) until the remaining places have been filled.

7. No two judges may be nationals of the same State. A person who, for the purposes of membership in the Court, could be regarded as a national of more than one State shall be deemed to be a national of the State in which that person ordinarily exercises civil and political rights.

8. (a) The States Parties shall, in the selection of judges, take into account the need, within the membership of the Court, for:

(i) The representation of the principal legal systems of the world;

(ii) Equitable geographical representation; and

(iii) A fair representation of female and male judges.

(b) States Parties shall also take into account the need to include judges with legal expertise on specific issues, including, but not limited to, violence against women or children.

9. (a) Subject to subparagraph (b), judges shall hold office for a term of nine years and, subject to subparagraph (c) and to Article 37, paragraph 2, shall not be eligible for re-election.

(b) At the first election, one third of the judges elected shall be selected by lot to serve for a term of three years; one third of the judges elected shall be selected by lot to serve for a term of six years; and the remainder shall serve for a term of nine years.

(c) A judge who is selected to serve for a term of three years under subparagraph (b) shall be eligible for re-election for a full term.

10. Notwithstanding paragraph 9, a judge assigned to a Trial or Appeals Chamber in accordance with Article 39 shall continue in office to complete any trial or appeal the hearing of which has already commenced before that Chamber.

Article 37. Judicial Vacancies

1. In the event of a vacancy, an election shall be held in accordance with Article 36 to fill the vacancy.

2. A judge elected to fill a vacancy shall serve for the remainder of the predecessor's term and, if that period is three years or less, shall be eligible for re-election for a full term under Article 36.

Article 38. The Presidency

1. The President and the First and Second Vice–Presidents shall be elected by an absolute majority of the judges. They shall each serve for a term of three years or until the end of their respective terms of office as judges, whichever expires earlier. They shall be eligible for re-election once.

2. The First Vice–President shall act in place of the President in the event that the President is unavailable or disqualified. The Second Vice–President shall act in place of the President in the event that both

the President and the First Vice–President are unavailable or disqualified.

3. The President, together with the First and Second Vice–Presidents, shall constitute the Presidency, which shall be responsible for:

(a) The proper administration of the Court, with the exception of the Office of the Prosecutor; and

(b) The other functions conferred upon it in accordance with this Statute.

4. In discharging its responsibility under paragraph 3 (a), the Presidency shall coordinate with and seek the concurrence of the Prosecutor on all matters of mutual concern.

Article 39. Chambers

1. As soon as possible after the election of the judges, the Court shall organize itself into the divisions specified in Article 34, paragraph (b). The Appeals Division shall be composed of the President and four other judges, the Trial Division of not less than six judges and the Pre–Trial Division of not less than six judges. The assignment of judges to divisions shall be based on the nature of the functions to be performed by each division and the qualifications and experience of the judges elected to the Court, in such a way that each division shall contain an appropriate combination of expertise in criminal law and procedure and in international law. The Trial and Pre–Trial Divisions shall be composed predominantly of judges with criminal trial experience.

2. (a) The judicial functions of the Court shall be carried out in each division by Chambers.

(b) (i) The Appeals Chamber shall be composed of all the judges of the Appeals Division;

(ii) The functions of the Trial Chamber shall be carried out by three judges of the Trial Division;

(iii) The functions of the Pre–Trial Chamber shall be carried out either by three judges of the Pre–Trial Division or by a single judge of that division in accordance with this Statute and the Rules of Procedure and Evidence;

(c) Nothing in this paragraph shall preclude the simultaneous constitution of more than one Trial Chamber or Pre–Trial Chamber when the efficient management of the Court's workload so requires.

3. (a) Judges assigned to the Trial and Pre–Trial Divisions shall serve in those divisions for a period of three years, and thereafter until the completion of any case the hearing of which has already commenced in the division concerned.

(b) Judges assigned to the Appeals Division shall serve in that division for their entire term of office.

4. Judges assigned to the Appeals Division shall serve only in that division. Nothing in this article shall, however, preclude the temporary attachment of judges from the Trial Division to the Pre–Trial Division or

vice versa, if the Presidency considers that the efficient management of the Court's workload so requires, provided that under no circumstances shall a judge who has participated in the pre-trial phase of a case be eligible to sit on the Trial Chamber hearing that case.

Article 40. Independence of the judges

1. The judges shall be independent in the performance of their functions.

2. Judges shall not engage in any activity which is likely to interfere with their judicial functions or to affect confidence in their independence.

3. Judges required to serve on a full-time basis at the seat of the Court shall not engage in any other occupation of a professional nature.

4. Any question regarding the application of paragraphs 2 and 3 shall be decided by an absolute majority of the judges. Where any such question concerns an individual judge, that judge shall not take part in the decision.

Article 41. Excusing and disqualification of judges

1. The Presidency may, at the request of a judge, excuse that judge from the exercise of a function under this Statute, in accordance with the Rules of Procedure and Evidence.

2. (a) A judge shall not participate in any case in which his or her impartiality might reasonably be doubted on any ground. A judge shall be disqualified from a case in accordance with this paragraph if, *inter alia*, that judge has previously been involved in any capacity in that case before the Court or in a related criminal case at the national level involving the person being investigated or prosecuted. A judge shall also be disqualified on such other grounds as may be provided for in the Rules of Procedure and Evidence.

(b) The Prosecutor or the person being investigated or prosecuted may request the disqualification of a judge under this paragraph.

(c) Any question as to the disqualification of a judge shall be decided by an absolute majority of the judges. The challenged judge shall be entitled to present his or her comments on the matter, but shall not take part in the decision.

Article 42. The Office of the Prosecutor

1. The Office of the Prosecutor shall act independently as a separate organ of the Court. It shall be responsible for receiving referrals and any substantiated information on crimes within the jurisdiction of the Court, for examining them and for conducting investigations and prosecutions before the Court. A member of the Office shall not seek or act on instructions from any external source.

2. The Office shall be headed by the Prosecutor. The Prosecutor shall have full authority over the management and administration of the Office, including the staff, facilities and other resources thereof. The

Prosecutor shall be assisted by one or more Deputy Prosecutors, who shall be entitled to carry out any of the acts required of the Prosecutor under this Statute. The Prosecutor and the Deputy Prosecutors shall be of different nationalities. They shall serve on a full-time basis.

3. The Prosecutor and the Deputy Prosecutors shall be persons of high moral character, be highly competent in and have extensive practical experience in the prosecution or trial of criminal cases. They shall have an excellent knowledge of and be fluent in at least one of the working languages of the Court.

4. The Prosecutor shall be elected by secret ballot by an absolute majority of the members of the Assembly of States Parties. The Deputy Prosecutors shall be elected in the same way from a list of candidates provided by the Prosecutor. The Prosecutor shall nominate three candidates for each position of Deputy Prosecutor to be filled. Unless a shorter term is decided upon at the time of their election, the Prosecutor and the Deputy Prosecutors shall hold office for a term of nine years and shall not be eligible for re-election.

5. Neither the Prosecutor nor a Deputy Prosecutor shall engage in any activity which is likely to interfere with his or her prosecutorial functions or to affect confidence in his or her independence. They shall not engage in any other occupation of a professional nature.

6. The Presidency may excuse the Prosecutor or a Deputy Prosecutor, at his or her request, from acting in a particular case.

7. Neither the Prosecutor nor a Deputy Prosecutor shall participate in any matter in which their impartiality might reasonably be doubted on any ground. They shall be disqualified from a case in accordance with this paragraph if, *inter alia*, they have previously been involved in any capacity in that case before the Court or in a related criminal case at the national level involving the person being investigated or prosecuted.

8. Any question as to the disqualification of the Prosecutor or a Deputy Prosecutor shall be decided by the Appeals Chamber.

(a) The person being investigated or prosecuted may at any time request the disqualification of the Prosecutor or a Deputy Prosecutor on the grounds set out in this article.

(b) The Prosecutor or the Deputy Prosecutor, as appropriate, shall be entitled to present his or her comments on the matter.

9. The Prosecutor shall appoint advisers with legal expertise on specific issues, including, but not limited to, sexual and gender violence and violence against children.

Article 43. The Registry

1. The Registry shall be responsible for the non-judicial aspects of the administration and servicing of the Court, without prejudice to the functions and powers of the Prosecutor in accordance with Article 42.

2. The Registry shall be headed by the Registrar, who shall be the principal administrative officer of the Court. The Registrar shall exercise his or her functions under the authority of the President of the Court.

3. The Registrar and the Deputy Registrar shall be persons of high moral character, be highly competent and have an excellent knowledge of and be fluent in at least one of the working languages of the Court.

4. The judges shall elect the Registrar by an absolute majority by secret ballot, taking into account any recommendation by the Assembly of States Parties. If the need arises and upon the recommendation of the Registrar, the judges shall elect, in the same manner, a Deputy Registrar.

5. The Registrar shall hold office for a term of five years, shall be eligible for re-election once and shall serve on a full-time basis. The Deputy Registrar shall hold office for a term of five years or such shorter term as may be decided upon by an absolute majority of the judges, and may be elected on the basis that the Deputy Registrar shall be called upon to serve as required.

6. The Registrar shall set up a Victims and Witnesses Unit within the Registry. This Unit shall provide, in consultation with the Office of the Prosecutor, protective measures and security arrangements, counselling and other appropriate assistance for witnesses, victims who appear before the Court and others who are at risk on account of testimony given by such witnesses. The Unit shall include staff with expertise in trauma, including trauma related to crimes of sexual violence.

Article 44. Staff

1. The Prosecutor and the Registrar shall appoint such qualified staff as may be required to their respective offices. In the case of the Prosecutor, this shall include the appointment of investigators.

2. In the employment of staff, the Prosecutor and the Registrar shall ensure the highest standards of efficiency, competency and integrity, and shall have regard, mutatis mutandis, to the criteria set forth in Article 36, paragraph 8.

3. The Registrar, with the agreement of the Presidency and the Prosecutor, shall propose Staff Regulations which include the terms and conditions upon which the staff of the Court shall be appointed, remunerated and dismissed. The Staff Regulations shall be approved by the Assembly of States Parties.

4. The Court may, in exceptional circumstances, employ the expertise of gratis personnel offered by States Parties, intergovernmental organizations or non-governmental organizations to assist with the work of any of the organs of the Court. The Prosecutor may accept any such offer on behalf of the Office of the Prosecutor. Such gratis personnel shall be employed in accordance with guidelines to be established by the Assembly of States Parties.

Article 45. Solemn undertaking

Before taking up their respective duties under this Statute, the judges, the Prosecutor, the Deputy Prosecutors, the Registrar and the

Deputy Registrar shall each make a solemn undertaking in open court to exercise his or her respective functions impartially and conscientiously.

Article 46. Removal from office

1. A judge, the Prosecutor, a Deputy Prosecutor, the Registrar or the Deputy Registrar shall be removed from office if a decision to this effect is made in accordance with paragraph 2, in cases where that person:

(a) Is found to have committed serious misconduct or a serious breach of his or her duties under this Statute, as provided for in the Rules of Procedure and Evidence; or

(b) Is unable to exercise the functions required by this Statute.

2. A decision as to the removal from office of a judge, the Prosecutor or a Deputy Prosecutor under paragraph 1 shall be made by the Assembly of States Parties, by secret ballot:

(a) In the case of a judge, by a two-thirds majority of the States Parties upon a recommendation adopted by a two-thirds majority of the other judges;

(b) In the case of the Prosecutor, by an absolute majority of the States Parties;

(c) In the case of a Deputy Prosecutor, by an absolute majority of the States Parties upon the recommendation of the Prosecutor.

3. A decision as to the removal from office of the Registrar or Deputy Registrar shall be made by an absolute majority of the judges.

4. A judge, Prosecutor, Deputy Prosecutor, Registrar or Deputy Registrar whose conduct or ability to exercise the functions of the office as required by this Statute is challenged under this article shall have full opportunity to present and receive evidence and to make submissions in accordance with the Rules of Procedure and Evidence. The person in question shall not otherwise participate in the consideration of the matter.

Article 47. Disciplinary measures

A judge, Prosecutor, Deputy Prosecutor, Registrar or Deputy Registrar who has committed misconduct of a less serious nature than that set out in Article 46, paragraph 1, shall be subject to disciplinary measures, in accordance with the Rules of Procedure and Evidence.

Article 48. Privileges and immunities

1. The Court shall enjoy in the territory of each State Party such privileges and immunities as are necessary for the fulfilment of its purposes.

2. The judges, the Prosecutor, the Deputy Prosecutors and the Registrar shall, when engaged on or with respect to the business of the Court, enjoy the same privileges and immunities as are accorded to heads of diplomatic missions and shall, after the expiry of their terms of office, continue to be accorded immunity from legal process of every kind

in respect of words spoken or written and acts performed by them in their official capacity.

3. The Deputy Registrar, the staff of the Office of the Prosecutor and the staff of the Registry shall enjoy the privileges and immunities and facilities necessary for the performance of their functions, in accordance with the agreement on the privileges and immunities of the Court.

4. Counsel, experts, witnesses or any other person required to be present at the seat of the Court shall be accorded such treatment as is necessary for the proper functioning of the Court, in accordance with the agreement on the privileges and immunities of the Court.

5. The privileges and immunities of:

(a) A judge or the Prosecutor may be waived by an absolute majority of the judges;

(b) The Registrar may be waived by the Presidency;

(c) The Deputy Prosecutors and staff of the Office of the Prosecutor may be waived by the Prosecutor;

(d) The Deputy Registrar and staff of the Registry may be waived by the Registrar.

Article 49. Salaries, allowances and expenses

The judges, the Prosecutor, the Deputy Prosecutors, the Registrar and the Deputy Registrar shall receive such salaries, allowances and expenses as may be decided upon by the Assembly of States Parties. These salaries and allowances shall not be reduced during their terms of office.

Article 50. Official and working languages

1. The official languages of the Court shall be Arabic, Chinese, English, French, Russian and Spanish. The judgements of the Court, as well as other decisions resolving fundamental issues before the Court, shall be published in the official languages. The Presidency shall, in accordance with the criteria established by the Rules of Procedure and Evidence, determine which decisions may be considered as resolving fundamental issues for the purposes of this paragraph.

2. The working languages of the Court shall be English and French. The Rules of Procedure and Evidence shall determine the cases in which other official languages may be used as working languages.

3. At the request of any party to a proceeding or a State allowed to intervene in a proceeding, the Court shall authorize a language other than English or French to be used by such a party or State, provided that the Court considers such authorization to be adequately justified.

Article 51. Rules of Procedure and Evidence

1. The Rules of Procedure and Evidence shall enter into force upon adoption by a two-thirds majority of the members of the Assembly of States Parties.

2. Amendments to the Rules of Procedure and Evidence may be proposed by:

(a) Any State Party;

(b) The judges acting by an absolute majority; or

(c) The Prosecutor.

Such amendments shall enter into force upon adoption by a two-thirds majority of the members of the Assembly of States Parties.

3. After the adoption of the Rules of Procedure and Evidence, in urgent cases where the Rules do not provide for a specific situation before the Court, the judges may, by a two-thirds majority, draw up provisional Rules to be applied until adopted, amended or rejected at the next ordinary or special session of the Assembly of States Parties.

4. The Rules of Procedure and Evidence, amendments thereto and any provisional Rule shall be consistent with this Statute. Amendments to the Rules of Procedure and Evidence as well as provisional Rules shall not be applied retroactively to the detriment of the person who is being investigated or prosecuted or who has been convicted.

5. In the event of conflict between the Statute and the Rules of Procedure and Evidence, the Statute shall prevail.

Article 52. Regulations of the Court

1. The judges shall, in accordance with this Statute and the Rules of Procedure and Evidence, adopt, by an absolute majority, the Regulations of the Court necessary for its routine functioning.

2. The Prosecutor and the Registrar shall be consulted in the elaboration of the Regulations and any amendments thereto.

3. The Regulations and any amendments thereto shall take effect upon adoption unless otherwise decided by the judges. Immediately upon adoption, they shall be circulated to States Parties for comments. If within six months there are no objections from a majority of States Parties, they shall remain in force.

Part 5. Investigation and Prosecution

Article 53. Initiation of an investigation

1. The Prosecutor shall, having evaluated the information made available to him or her, initiate an investigation unless he or she determines that there is no reasonable basis to proceed under this Statute. In deciding whether to initiate an investigation, the Prosecutor shall consider whether:

(a) The information available to the Prosecutor provides a reasonable basis to believe that a crime within the jurisdiction of the Court has been or is being committed;

(b) The case is or would be admissible under Article 17; and

(c) Taking into account the gravity of the crime and the interests of victims, there are nonetheless substantial reasons to believe that an investigation would not serve the interests of justice.

If the Prosecutor determines that there is no reasonable basis to proceed and his or her determination is based solely on subparagraph (c) above, he or she shall inform the Pre–Trial Chamber.

2. If, upon investigation, the Prosecutor concludes that there is not a sufficient basis for a prosecution because:

(a) There is not a sufficient legal or factual basis to seek a warrant or summons under Article 58;

(b) The case is inadmissible under Article 17; or

(c) A prosecution is not in the interests of justice, taking into account all the circumstances, including the gravity of the crime, the interests of victims and the age or infirmity of the alleged perpetrator, and his or her role in the alleged crime;

The Prosecutor shall inform the Pre–Trial Chamber and the State making a referral under Article 14 or the Security Council in a case under Article 13, paragraph (b), of his or her conclusion and the reasons for the conclusion.

3. (a) At the request of the State making a referral under Article 14 or the Security Council under Article 13, paragraph (b), the Pre–Trial Chamber may review a decision of the Prosecutor under paragraph 1 or 2 not to proceed and may request the Prosecutor to reconsider that decision.

(b) In addition, the Pre–Trial Chamber may, on its own initiative, review a decision of the Prosecutor not to proceed if it is based solely on paragraph 1(c) or 2(c). In such a case, the decision of the Prosecutor shall be effective only if confirmed by the Pre–Trial Chamber.

4. The Prosecutor may, at any time, reconsider a decision whether to initiate an investigation prosecution based on new facts or information.

Article 54. Duties and powers of the Prosecutor with respect to investigations

1. The Prosecutor shall:

(a) In order to establish the truth, extend the investigation to cover all facts and evidence relevant to an assessment of whether there is criminal responsibility under this Statute, and, in doing so, investigate incriminating and exonerating circumstances equally;

(b) Take appropriate measures to ensure the effective investigation and prosecution of crimes within the jurisdiction of the Court, and in doing so, respect the interests and personal circumstances of victims and witnesses, including age, gender as defined in Article 7, paragraph 3, and health, and take into account the nature of the crime, in particular where it involves sexual violence, gender violence or violence against children; and

(c) Fully respect the rights of persons arising under this Statute.

2. The Prosecutor may conduct investigations on the territory of a State:

(a) In accordance with the provisions of Part 9; or

(b) As authorized by the Pre–Trial Chamber under Article 57, paragraph 3 (d).

3. The Prosecutor may:

(a) Collect and examine evidence;

(b) Request the presence of and question persons being investigated, victims and witnesses;

(c) Seek the cooperation of any State or intergovernmental organization or arrangement in accordance with its respective competence and/or mandate;

(d) Enter into such arrangements or agreements, not inconsistent with this Statute, as may be necessary to facilitate the cooperation of a State, intergovernmental organization or person;

(e) Agree not to disclose, at any stage of the proceedings, documents or information that the Prosecutor obtains on the condition of confidentiality and solely for the purpose of generating new evidence, unless the provider of the information consents; and

(f) Take necessary measures, or request that necessary measures be taken, to ensure the confidentiality of information, the protection of any person or the preservation of evidence.

Article 55. Rights of persons during an investigation

1. In respect of an investigation under this Statute, a person:

(a) Shall not be compelled to incriminate himself or herself or to confess guilt;

(b) Shall not be subjected to any form of coercion, duress or threat, to torture or to any other form of cruel, inhuman or degrading treatment or punishment; and

(c) Shall, if questioned in a language other than a language the person fully understands and speaks, have, free of any cost, the assistance of a competent interpreter and such translations as are necessary to meet the requirements of fairness;

(d) Shall not be subjected to arbitrary arrest or detention; and shall not be deprived of his or her liberty except on such grounds and in accordance with such procedures as are established in the Statute.

2. Where there are grounds to believe that a person has committed a crime within the jurisdiction of the Court and that person is about to be questioned either by the Prosecutor, or by national authorities pursuant to a request made under Part 9 of this Statute, that person shall also have the following rights of which he or she shall be informed prior to being questioned:

(a) To be informed, prior to being questioned, that there are grounds to believe that he or she has committed a crime within the jurisdiction of the Court;

(b) To remain silent, without such silence being a consideration in the determination of guilt or innocence;

(c) To have legal assistance of the person's choosing, or, if the person does not have legal assistance, to have legal assistance assigned to him or her, in any case where the interests of justice so require, and without payment by the person in any such case if the person does not have sufficient means to pay for it;

(d) To be questioned in the presence of counsel unless the person has voluntarily waived his or her right to counsel.

Article 56. Role of the Pre–Trial Chamber in relation to a unique investigative opportunity

1. (a) Where the Prosecutor considers an investigation to present a unique opportunity to take testimony or a statement from a witness or to examine, collect or test evidence, which may not be available subsequently for the purposes of a trial, the Prosecutor shall so inform the Pre–Trial Chamber.

(b) In that case, the Pre–Trial Chamber may, upon request of the Prosecutor, take such measures as may be necessary to ensure the efficiency and integrity of the proceedings and, in particular, to protect the rights of the defence.

(c) Unless the Pre–Trial Chamber orders otherwise, the Prosecutor shall provide the relevant information to the person who has been arrested or appeared in response to a summons in connection with the investigation referred to in subparagraph (a), in order that he or she may be heard on the matter.

2. The measures referred to in paragraph 1(b) may include:

(a) Making recommendations or orders regarding procedures to be followed;

(b) Directing that a record be made of the proceedings;

(c) Appointing an expert to assist;

(d) Authorizing counsel for a person who has been arrested, or appeared before the Court in response to a summons, to participate, or where there has not yet been such an arrest or appearance or counsel has not been designated, appointing another counsel to attend and represent the interests of the defence;

(e) Naming one of its members or, if necessary, another available judge of the Pre–Trial or Trial Division to observe and make recommendations or orders regarding the collection and preservation of evidence and the questioning of persons;

(f) Taking such other action as may be necessary to collect or preserve evidence.

3. (a) Where the Prosecutor has not sought measures pursuant to this article but the Pre–Trial Chamber considers that such measures are required to preserve evidence that it deems would be essential for the defence at trial, it shall consult with the Prosecutor as to whether there is good reason for the Prosecutor's failure to request the measures. If upon consultation, the Pre–Trial Chamber concludes that the Prosecutor's failure to request such measures is unjustified, the Pre–Trial Chamber may take such measures on its own initiative.

(b) A decision of the Pre–Trial Chamber to act on its own initiative under this paragraph may be appealed by the Prosecutor. The appeal shall be heard on an expedited basis.

4. The admissibility of evidence preserved or collected for trial pursuant to this article, or the record thereof, shall be governed at trial by Article 69, and given such weight as determined by the Trial Chamber.

Article 57. Functions and powers of the Pre–Trial Chamber

1. Unless otherwise provided for in this Statute, the Pre–Trial Chamber shall exercise its functions in accordance with the provisions of this article.

2. (a) Orders or rulings of the Pre–Trial Chamber issued under Articles 15, 18, 19, 54, paragraph 2, 61, paragraph 7, and 72 must be concurred in by a majority of its judges.

(b) In all other cases, a single judge of the Pre–Trial Chamber may exercise the functions provided for in this Statute, unless otherwise provided for in the Rules of Procedure and Evidence or by a majority of the Pre–Trial Chamber.

3. In addition to its other functions under this Statute, the Pre–Trial Chamber may:

(a) At the request of the Prosecutor, issue such orders and warrants as may be required for the purposes of an investigation;

(b) Upon the request of a person who has been arrested or has appeared pursuant to a summons under Article 58, issue such orders, including measures such as those described in Article 56, or seek such cooperation pursuant to Part 9 as may be necessary to assist the person in the preparation of his or her defence;

(c) Where necessary, provide for the protection and privacy of victims and witnesses, the preservation of evidence, the protection of persons who have been arrested or appeared in response to a summons, and the protection of national security information;

(d) Authorize the Prosecutor to take specific investigative steps within the territory of a State Party without having secured the cooperation of that State under Part 9 if, whenever possible having regard to the views of the State concerned, the Pre–Trial Chamber has determined in that case that the State is clearly unable to execute a request for cooperation due to the unavailability of any authority or any component of its judicial system competent to execute the request for cooperation under Part 9.

(e) Where a warrant of arrest or a summons has been issued under Article 58, and having due regard to the strength of the evidence and the rights of the parties concerned, as provided for in this Statute and the Rules of Procedure and Evidence, seek the cooperation of States pursuant to Article 93, paragraph 1(j), to take protective measures for the purpose of forfeiture in particular for the ultimate benefit of victims.

Article 58. Issuance by the Pre–Trial Chamber of a warrant of arrest or a summons to appear

1. At any time after the initiation of an investigation, the Pre–Trial Chamber shall, on the application of the Prosecutor, issue a warrant of arrest of a person if, having examined the application and the evidence or other information submitted by the Prosecutor, it is satisfied that:

(a) There are reasonable grounds to believe that the person has committed a crime within the jurisdiction of the Court; and

(b) The arrest of the person appears necessary:

(i) To ensure the person's appearance at trial.

(ii) To ensure that the person does not obstruct or endanger the investigation or the court proceedings, or

(iii) Where applicable, to prevent the person from continuing with the commission of that crime or a related crime which is within the jurisdiction of the Court and which arises out of the same circumstances.

2. The application of the Prosecutor shall contain:

(a) The name of the person and any other relevant identifying information;

(b) A specific reference to the crimes within the jurisdiction of the Court which the person is alleged to have committed;

(c) A concise statement of the facts which are alleged to constitute those crimes;

(d) A summary of the evidence and any other information which establish reasonable grounds to believe that the person committed those crimes; and

(e) The reason why the Prosecutor believes that the arrest of the person is necessary.

3. The warrant of arrest shall contain:

(a) The name of the person and any other relevant identifying information;

(b) A specific reference to the crimes within the jurisdiction of the Court for which the person's arrest is sought; and

(c) A concise statement of the facts which are alleged to constitute those crimes.

4. The warrant of arrest shall remain in effect until otherwise ordered by the Court.

5. On the basis of the warrant of arrest, the Court may request the provisional arrest or the arrest and surrender of the person under Part 9.

6. The Prosecutor may request the Pre–Trial Chamber to amend the warrant of arrest by modifying or adding to the crimes specified therein. The Pre–Trial Chamber shall so amend the warrant if it is satisfied that there are reasonable grounds to believe that the person committed the modified or additional crimes.

7. As an alternative to seeking a warrant of arrest, the Prosecutor may submit an application requesting that the Pre–Trial Chamber issue a summons for the person to appear. If the Pre–Trial Chamber is satisfied that there are reasonable grounds to believe that the person committed the crime alleged and that a summons is sufficient to ensure the person's appearance, it shall issue the summons, with or without conditions restricting liberty (other than detention) if provided for by national law, for the person to appear. The summons shall contain:

(a) The name of the person and any other relevant identifying information;

(b) The specified date on which the person is to appear;

(c) A specific reference to the crimes within the jurisdiction of the Court which the person is alleged to have committed; and

(d) A concise statement of the facts which are alleged to constitute the crime.

The summons shall be served on the person.

Article 59. Arrest proceedings in the custodial State

1. A State Party which has received a request for provisional arrest or for arrest and surrender shall immediately take steps to arrest the person in question in accordance with its laws and the provisions of Part 9.

2. A person arrested shall be brought promptly before the competent judicial authority in the custodial State which shall determine, in accordance with the law of that State, that:

(a) The warrant applies to that person;

(b) The person has been arrested in accordance with the proper process; and

(c) The person's rights have been respected.

3. The person arrested shall have the right to apply to the competent authority in the custodial State for interim release pending surrender.

4. In reaching a decision on any such application, the competent authority in the custodial State shall consider whether, given the gravity of the alleged crimes, there are urgent and exceptional circumstances to justify interim release and whether necessary safeguards exist to ensure

that the custodial State can fulfil its duty to surrender the person to the Court. It shall not be open to the competent authority of the custodial State to consider whether the warrant of arrest was properly issued in accordance with Article 58, paragraph 1(a) and (b).

5. The Pre–Trial Chamber shall be notified of any request for interim release and shall make recommendations to the competent authority in the custodial State. The competent authority in the custodial State shall give full consideration to such recommendations, including any recommendations on measures to prevent the escape of the person, before rendering its decision.

6. If the person is granted interim release, the Pre–Trial Chamber may request periodic reports on the status of the interim release.

7. Once ordered to be surrendered by the custodial State, the person shall be delivered to the Court as soon as possible.

Article 60. Initial proceedings before the Court

1. Upon the surrender of the person to the Court, or the person's appearance before the Court voluntarily or pursuant to a summons, the Pre–Trial Chamber shall satisfy itself that the person has been informed of the crimes which he or she is alleged to have committed, and of his or her rights under this Statute, including the right to apply for interim release pending trial.

2. A person subject to a warrant of arrest may apply for interim release pending trial. If the Pre–Trial Chamber is satisfied that the conditions set forth in Article 58, paragraph 1, are met, the person shall continue to be detained. If it is not so satisfied, the Pre–Trial Chamber shall release the person, with or without conditions.

3. The Pre–Trial Chamber shall periodically review its ruling on the release or detention of the person, and may do so at any time on the request of the Prosecutor or the person. Upon such review, it may modify its ruling as to detention, release or conditions of release, if it is satisfied that changed circumstances so require.

4. The Pre–Trial Chamber shall ensure that a person is not detained for an unreasonable period prior to trial due to inexcusable delay by the Prosecutor. If such delay occurs, the Court shall consider releasing the person, with or without conditions.

5. If necessary, the Pre–Trial Chamber may issue a warrant of arrest to secure the presence of a person who has been released.

Article 61. Confirmation of the charges before trial

1. Subject to the provisions of paragraph 2, within a reasonable time after the person's surrender or voluntary appearance before the Court, the Pre–Trial Chamber shall hold a hearing to confirm the charges on which the Prosecutor intends to seek trial. The hearing shall be held in the presence of the Prosecutor and the person charged, as well as his or her counsel.

2. The Pre–Trial Chamber may, upon request of the Prosecutor or on its own motion, hold a hearing in the absence of the person charged

to confirm the charges on which the Prosecutor intends to seek trial when the person has:

(a) Waived his or her right to be present; or

(b) Fled or cannot be found and all reasonable steps have been taken to secure his or her appearance before the Court and to inform the person of the charges and that a hearing to confirm those charges will be held.

In that case, the person shall be represented by counsel where the Pre–Trial Chamber determines that it is in the interests of justice.

3. Within a reasonable time before the hearing, the person shall:

(a) Be provided with a copy of the document containing the charges on which the Prosecutor intends to bring the person to trial; and

(b) Be informed of the evidence on which the Prosecutor intends to rely at the hearing.

The Pre–Trial Chamber may issue orders regarding the disclosure of information for the purposes of the hearing.

4. Before the hearing, the Prosecutor may continue the investigation and may amend or withdraw any charges. The person shall be given reasonable notice before the hearing of any amendment to or withdrawal of charges. In case of a withdrawal of charges, the Prosecutor shall notify the Pre–Trial Chamber of the reasons for the withdrawal.

5. At the hearing, the Prosecutor shall support each charge with sufficient evidence to establish substantial grounds to believe that the person committed the crime charged. The Prosecutor may rely on documentary or summary evidence and need not call the witnesses expected to testify at the trial.

6. At the hearing, the person may:

(a) Object to the charges;

(b) Challenge the evidence presented by the Prosecutor; and

(c) Present evidence.

7. The Pre–Trial Chamber shall, on the basis of the hearing, determine whether there is sufficient evidence to establish substantial grounds to believe that the person committed each of the crimes charged. Based on its determination, the Pre–Trial Chamber shall:

(a) Confirm those charges in relation to which it has determined that there is sufficient evidence; and commit the person to a Trial Chamber for trial on the charges as confirmed;

(b) Decline to confirm those charges in relation to which it has determined that there is insufficient evidence;

(c) Adjourn the hearing and request the Prosecutor to consider;

(i) Providing further evidence or conducting further investigation with respect to a particular charge; or

(ii) Amending a charge because the evidence submitted appears to establish a different crime within the jurisdiction of the Court.

8. Where the Pre–Trial Chamber declines to confirm a charge, the Prosecutor shall not be precluded from subsequently requesting its confirmation if the request is supported by additional evidence.

9. After the charges are confirmed and before the trial has begun, the Prosecutor may, with the permission of the Pre–Trial Chamber and after notice to the accused, amend the charges. If the Prosecutor seeks to add additional charges or to substitute more serious charges, a hearing under this article to confirm those charges must be held. After commencement of the trial, the Prosecutor may, with the permission of the Trial Chamber, withdraw the charges.

10. Any warrant previously issued shall cease to have effect with respect to any charges which have not been confirmed by the Pre–Trial Chamber or which have been withdrawn by the Prosecutor.

11. Once the charges have been confirmed in accordance with this article, the Presidency shall constitute a Trial Chamber which, subject to paragraph 8 and to Article 64, paragraph 4, shall be responsible for the conduct of subsequent proceedings and may exercise any function of the Pre–Trial Chamber that is relevant and capable of application in those proceedings

Part 6. The Trial

Article 62. Place of trial

Unless otherwise decided, the place of the trial shall be the seat of the Court.

Article 63. Trial in the presence of the accused

1. The accused shall be present during the trial.

2. If the accused, being present before the Court, continues to disrupt the trial, the Trial Chamber may remove the accused and shall make provision for him or her to observe the trial and instruct counsel from outside the courtroom, through the use of communications technology, if required. Such measures shall be taken only in exceptional circumstances after other reasonable alternatives have proved inadequate, and only for such duration as is strictly required.

Article 64. Functions and powers of the Trial Chamber

1. The functions and powers of the Trial Chamber set out in this article shall be exercised in accordance with this Statute and the Rules of Procedure and Evidence.

2. The Trial Chamber shall ensure that a trial is fair and expeditious and is conducted with full respect for the rights of the accused and due regard for the protection of victims and witnesses.

3. Upon assignment of a case for trial in accordance with this Statute, the Trial Chamber assigned to deal with the case shall:

(a) Confer with the parties and adopt such procedures as are necessary to facilitate the fair and expeditious conduct of the proceedings;

(b) Determine the language or languages to be used at trial; and

(c) Subject to any other relevant provisions of this Statute, provide for disclosure of documents or information not previously disclosed, sufficiently in advance of the commencement of the trial to enable adequate preparation for trial.

4. The Trial Chamber may, if necessary for its effective and fair functioning, refer preliminary issues to the Pre–Trial Chamber or, if necessary, to another available judge of the Pre–Trial Division.

5. Upon notice to the parties, the Trial Chamber may, as appropriate, direct that there be joinder or severance in respect of charges against more than one accused.

6. In performing its functions prior to trial or during the course of a trial, the Trial Chamber may, as necessary:

(a) Exercise any functions of the Pre–Trial Chamber referred to in Article 61, paragraph 11;

(b) Require the attendance and testimony of witnesses and production of documents and other evidence by obtaining, if necessary, the assistance of States as provided in this Statute;

(c) Provide for the protection of confidential information;

(d) Order the production of evidence in addition to that already collected prior to the trial or presented during the trial by the parties;

(e) Provide for the protection of the accused, witnesses and victims; and

(f) Rule on any other relevant matters.

7. The trial shall be held in public. The Trial Chamber may, however, determine that special circumstances require that certain proceedings be in closed session for the purposes set forth in Article 68, or to protect confidential or sensitive information to be given in evidence.

8. (a) At the commencement of the trial, the Trial Chamber shall have read to the accused the charges previously confirmed by the Pre–Trial Chamber. The Trial Chamber shall satisfy itself that the accused understands the nature of the charges. It shall afford him or her the opportunity to make an admission of guilt in accordance with Article 65 or to plead not guilty.

(b) At the trial, the presiding judge may give directions for the conduct of proceedings, including to ensure that they are conducted in a fair and impartial manner. Subject to any directions of the presiding judge, the parties may submit evidence in accordance with the provisions of this Statute.

9. The Trial Chamber shall have, *inter alia*, the power on application of a party or on its own motion to:

(a) Rule on the admissibility or relevance of evidence; and

(b) Take all necessary steps to maintain order in the course of a hearing.

10. The Trial Chamber shall ensure that a complete record of the trial, which accurately reflects the proceedings, is made and that it is maintained and preserved by the Registrar.

Article 65. Proceedings on an admission of guilt

1. Where the accused makes an admission of guilt pursuant to Article 64, paragraph 8 (a), the Trial Chamber shall determine whether:

(a) The accused understands the nature and consequences of the admission of guilt;

(b) The admission is voluntarily made by the accused after sufficient consultation with defence counsel; and

(c) The admission of guilt is supported by the facts of the case that are contained in:

(i) The charges brought by the Prosecutor and admitted by the accused;

(ii) Any materials presented by the Prosecutor which supplement the charges and which the accused accepts; and

(iii) Any other evidence, such as the testimony of witnesses, presented by the Prosecutor or the accused.

2. Where the Trial Chamber is satisfied that the matters referred to in paragraph 1 are established, it shall consider the admission of guilt, together with any additional evidence presented, as establishing all the essential facts that are required to prove the crime to which the admission of guilt relates, and may convict the accused of that crime.

3. Where the Trial Chamber is not satisfied that the matters referred to in paragraph 1 are established, it shall consider the admission of guilt as not having been made, in which case it shall order that the trial be continued under the ordinary trial procedures provided by this Statute and may remit the case to another Trial Chamber.

4. Where the Trial Chamber is of the opinion that a more complete presentation of the facts of the case is required in the interests of justice, in particular the interests of the victims, the Trial Chamber may:

(a) Request the Prosecutor to present additional evidence, including the testimony of witnesses; or

(b) Order that the trial be continued under the ordinary trial procedures provided by this Statute, in which case it shall consider the admission of guilt as not having been made and may remit the case to another Trial Chamber.

5. Any discussions between the Prosecutor and the defence regarding modification of the charges, the admission of guilt or the penalty to be imposed shall not be binding on the Court.

Article 66. Presumption of innocence

1. Everyone shall be presumed innocent until proved guilty before the Court in accordance with the applicable law.

2. The onus is on the Prosecutor to prove the guilt of the accused.

3. In order to convict the accused, the Court must be convinced of the guilt of the accused beyond reasonable doubt.

Article 67. Rights of the accused

1. In the determination of any charge, the accused shall be entitled to a public hearing, having regard to the provisions of this Statute, to a fair hearing conducted impartially, and to the following minimum guarantees, in full equality:

(a) To be informed promptly and in detail of the nature, cause and content of the charge, in a language which the accused fully understands and speaks;

(b) To have adequate time and facilities for the preparation of the defence and to communicate freely with counsel of the accused's choosing in confidence;

(c) To be tried without undue delay;

(d) Subject to Article 63, paragraph 2, to be present at the trial, to conduct the defence in person or through legal assistance of the accused's choosing, to be informed, if the accused does not have legal assistance, of this right and to have legal assistance assigned by the Court in any case where the interests of justice so require, and without payment if the accused lacks sufficient means to pay for it;

(e) To examine, or have examined, the witnesses against him or her and to obtain the attendance and examination of witnesses on his or her behalf under the same conditions as witnesses against him or her. The accused shall also be entitled to raise defences and to present other evidence admissible under this Statute;

(f) To have, free of any cost, the assistance of a competent interpreter and such translations as are necessary to meet the requirements of fairness, if any of the proceedings of or documents presented to the Court are not in a language which the accused fully understands and speaks;

(g) Not to be compelled to testify or to confess guilt and to remain silent, without such silence being a consideration in the determination of guilt or innocence;

(h) To make an unsworn oral or written statement in his or her defence; and

(i) Not to have imposed on him or her any reversal of the burden of proof or any onus of rebuttal.

2. In addition to any other disclosure provided for in this Statute, the Prosecutor shall, as soon as practicable, disclose to the defence evidence in the Prosecutor's possession or control which he or she believes shows or tends to show the innocence of the accused, or to

mitigate the guilt of the accused, or which may affect the credibility of prosecution evidence. In case of doubt as to the application of this paragraph, the Court shall decide.

Article 68. Protection of the victims and witnesses and their participation in the proceedings

1. The Court shall take appropriate measures to protect the safety, physical and psychological well-being, dignity and privacy of victims and witnesses. In so doing, the Court shall have regard to all relevant factors, including age, gender as defined in Article 2, paragraph 3, and health, and the nature of the crime, in particular, but not limited to, where the crime involves sexual or gender violence or violence against children. The Prosecutor shall take such measures particularly during the investigation and prosecution of such crimes. These measures shall not be prejudicial to or inconsistent with the rights of the accused and a fair and impartial trial.

2. As an exception to the principle of public hearings provided for in Article 67, the Chambers of the Court may, to protect victims and witnesses or an accused, conduct any part of the proceedings in camera or allow the presentation of evidence by electronic or other special means. In particular, such measures shall be implemented in the case of a victim of sexual violence or a child who is a victim or a witness, unless otherwise ordered by the Court, having regard to all the circumstances, particularly the views of the victim or witness.

3. Where the personal interests of the victims are affected, the Court shall permit their views and concerns to be presented and considered at stages of the proceedings determined to be appropriate by the Court and in a manner which is not prejudicial to or inconsistent with the rights of the accused and a fair and impartial trial. Such views and concerns may be presented by the legal representatives of the victims where the Court considers it appropriate, in accordance with the Rules of Procedure and Evidence.

4. The Victims and Witnesses Unit may advise the Prosecutor and the Court on appropriate protective measures, security arrangements, counselling and assistance as referred to in Article 43, paragraph 6.

5. Where the disclosure of evidence or information pursuant to this Statute may lead to the grave endangerment of the security of a witness or his or her family, the Prosecutor may, for the purposes of any proceedings conducted prior to the commencement of the trial, withhold such evidence or information and instead submit a summary thereof. Such measures shall be exercised in a manner which is not prejudicial to or inconsistent with the rights of the accused and a fair and impartial trial.

6. A State may make an application for necessary measures to be taken in respect of the protection of its servants or agents and the protection of confidential or sensitive information.

Article 69. Evidence

1. Before testifying, each witness shall, in accordance with the Rules of Procedure and Evidence, give an undertaking as to the truthfulness of the evidence to be given by that witness.

2. The testimony of a witness at trial shall be given in person, except to the extent provided by the measures set forth in Article 68 or in the Rules of Procedure and Evidence. The Court may also permit the giving of *viva voce* (oral) or recorded testimony of a witness by means of video or audio technology, as well as the introduction of documents or written transcripts, subject to this Statute and in accordance with the Rules of Procedure and Evidence. These measures shall not be prejudicial to or inconsistent with the rights of the accused.

3. The parties may submit evidence relevant to the case, in accordance with Article 64. The Court shall have the authority to request the submission of all evidence that it considers necessary for the determination of the truth.

4. The Court may rule on the relevance or admissibility of any evidence, taking into account, *inter alia*, the probative value of the evidence and any prejudice that such evidence may cause to a fair trial or to a fair evaluation of the testimony of a witness, in accordance with the Rules of Procedure and Evidence.

5. The Court shall respect and observe privileges on confidentiality as provided for in the Rules of Procedure and Evidence.

6. The Court shall not require proof of facts of common knowledge but may take judicial notice of them.

7. Evidence obtained by means of a violation of this Statute or internationally recognized human rights shall not be admissible if:

(a) The violation casts substantial doubt on the reliability of the evidence; or

(b) The admission of the evidence would be antithetical to and would seriously damage the integrity of the proceedings.

8. When deciding on the relevance or admissibility of evidence collected by a State, the Court shall not rule on the application of the State's national law.

Article 70. Offences against the administration of justice

1. The Court shall have jurisdiction over the following offences against its administration of justice when committed intentionally:

(a) Giving false testimony when under an obligation pursuant to Article 69, paragraph 1, to tell the truth;

(b) Presenting evidence that the party knows is false or forged;

(c) Corruptly influencing a witness, obstructing or interfering with the attendance or testimony of a witness, retaliating against a witness for giving testimony or destroying, tampering with or interfering with the collection of evidence;

(d) Impeding, intimidating or corruptly influencing an official of the Court for the purpose of forging or persuading the official not to perform, or to perform improperly, his or her duties;

(e) Retaliating against an official of the Court on account of duties performed by that or another official;

(f) Soliciting or accepting a bribe as an official of the Court in conjunction with his or her official duties.

2. The principles and procedures governing the Court's exercise of jurisdiction over offences under this articles shall be those provided for in the Rules of Procedure and Evidence. The conditions for providing international cooperation to the Court with respect to its proceedings under this article shall be governed by the domestic laws of the requested State.

3. In the event of conviction, the Court may impose a term of imprisonment not exceeding five years, or a fine in accordance with the Rules of Procedure and Evidence, or both.

4. (a) Each State Party shall extend its criminal laws penalizing offences against the integrity of its own investigative or judicial process to offences against the administration of justice referred to in this article, committed on its territory, or by one of its nationals;

(b) Upon request by the Court, whenever it deems it proper, the State Party shall submit the case to its competent authorities for the purpose of prosecution. Those authorities shall treat such cases with diligence and devote sufficient resources to enable them to be conducted effectively.

Article 71. Sanctions for misconduct before the Court

1. The Court may sanction persons present before it who commit misconduct, including disruption of its proceedings or deliberate refusal to comply with its directions, by administrative measures other than imprisonment, such as temporary or permanent removal from the courtroom, a fine or other similar measures provided for in the Rules of Procedure and Evidence.

2. The procedures governing the imposition of the measures set forth in paragraph 1 shall be those provided for in the Rules of Procedure and Evidence.

Article 72. Protection of national security information

1. This article applies in any case where the disclosure of the information or documents of a State would, in the opinion of that State, prejudice its national security interests. Such cases include those falling within the scope of Article 56, paragraphs 2 and 3, Article 61, paragraph 3, Article 64, paragraph 3, Article 67, paragraph 2, Article 68, paragraph 6, Article 87, paragraph 6 and Article 93, as well as cases arising at any other stage of the proceedings where such disclosure may be at issue.

2. This article shall also apply when a person who has been requested to give information or evidence has refused to do so or has referred the matter to the State on the ground that disclosure would

prejudice the national security interests of a State and the State concerned confirms that it is of the opinion that disclosure would prejudice its national security interests.

3. Nothing in this article shall prejudice the requirements of confidentiality applicable under Article 54, paragraph 3(e) and (f), or the application of Article 73.

4. If a State learns that information or documents of the State are being, or are likely to be, disclosed at any stage of the proceedings, and it is of the opinion that disclosure would prejudice its national security interests, that State shall have the right to intervene in order to obtain resolution of the issue in accordance with this article.

5. If, in the opinion of a State, disclosure of information would prejudice its national security interests, all reasonable steps will be taken by the State, acting in conjunction with the Prosecutor, the Defence or the Pre–Trial Chamber or Trial Chamber, as the case may be, to seek to resolve the matter by cooperative means. Such steps may include:

(a) Modification or clarification of the request;

(b) A determination by the Court regarding the relevance of the information or evidence sought, or a determination as to whether the evidence, though relevant, could be or has been obtained from a source other than the requested State;

(c) Obtaining the information or evidence from a different source or in a different form; or

(d) Agreement on conditions under which the assistance could be provided including, among other things, providing summaries or redactions, limitations on disclosure, use of in camera or *ex parte* proceedings, or other protective measures permissible under the Statute and the Rules.

6. Once all reasonable steps have been taken to resolve the matter through cooperative means, and if the State considers that there are no means or conditions under which the information or documents could be provided or disclosed without prejudice to its national security interests, it shall so notify the Prosecutor or the Court of the specific reasons for its decision, unless a specific description of the reasons would itself necessarily result in such prejudice to the State's national security interests.

7. Thereafter, if the Court determines that the evidence is relevant and necessary for the establishment of the guilt or innocence of the accused, the Court may undertake the following actions:

(a) Where disclosure of the information or document is sought pursuant to a request for cooperation under Part 9 or the circumstances described in paragraph 2, and the State has invoked the ground for refusal referred to in Article 93, paragraph 4:

(i) The Court may, before making any conclusion referred to in subparagraph 7 (a)(ii), request further consultations for the purpose of considering the State's representations, which may include, as appropriate, hearings in camera and *ex parte*;

(ii) If the Court concludes that, by invoking the ground for refusal under Article 93, paragraph 4, in the circumstances of the case, the requested State is not acting in accordance with its obligations under the Statute, the Court may refer the matter in accordance with Article 87, paragraph 7, specifying the reasons for its conclusion; and

(iii) The Court may make such inference in the trial of the accused as to the existence or non-existence of a fact, as may be appropriate in the circumstances; or

(b) In all other circumstances:

(i) Order disclosure; or

(ii) To the extent it does not order disclosure, make such inference in the trial of the accused as to the existence or non-existence of a fact, as may be appropriate in the circumstances.

Article 73. Third-party information or documents

If a State Party is requested by the Court to provide a document or information in its custody, possession or control, which was disclosed to it in confidence by a State, intergovernmental organization or international organization, it shall seek the consent of the originator to disclose that document or information. If the originator is a State Party, it shall either consent to disclosure of the information or document or undertake to resolve the issue of disclosure with the Court, subject to the provisions of Article 72. If the originator is not a State Party and refuses consent to disclosure, the requested State shall inform the Court that it is unable to provide the document or information because of a pre-existing obligation of confidentiality to the originator.

Article 74. Requirements for the decision

1. All the judges of the Trial Chamber shall be present at each stage of the trial and throughout their deliberations. The Presidency may, on a case-by-case basis, designate, as available, one or more alternate judges to be present at each stage of the trial and to replace a member of the Trial Chamber if that member is unable to continue attending.

2. The Trial Chamber's decision shall be based on its evaluation of the evidence and the entire proceedings. The decision shall not exceed the facts and circumstances described in the charges and any amendments to the charges. The Court may base its decision only on evidence submitted and discussed before it at the trial.

3. The judges shall attempt to achieve unanimity in their decision, failing which the decision shall be taken by a majority of the judges.

4. The deliberations of the Trial Chamber shall remain secret.

5. The decision shall be in writing and shall contain a full and reasoned statement of the Trial Chamber's findings on the evidence and

conclusions. The Trial Chamber shall issue one decision. When there is no unanimity, the Trial Chamber's decision shall contain the views of the majority and the minority. The decision or a summary thereof shall be delivered in open court.

Article 75. Reparations to victims

1. The Court shall establish principles relating to reparations to, or in respect of, victims, including restitution, compensation and rehabilitation. On this basis, in its decision the Court may, either upon request or on its own motion in exceptional circumstances, determine the scope and extent of any damage, loss and injury to, or in respect of, victims and will state the principles on which it is acting.

2. The Court may make an order directly against a convicted person specifying appropriate reparations to, or in respect of, victims, including restitution, compensation and rehabilitation. Where appropriate, the Court may order that the award for reparations be made through the Trust Fund provided for in Article 79.

3. Before making an order under this article, the Court may invite and shall take account of representations from or on behalf of the convicted person, victims, other interested persons or interested States.

4. In exercising its power under this article, the Court may, after a person is convicted of a crime within the jurisdiction of the Court, determine whether, in order to give effect to an order which it may make under this article, it is necessary to seek measures under Article 93, paragraph 1.

5. A State Party shall give effect to a decision under this article as if the provisions of Article 109 were applicable to this article.

6. Nothing in this article shall be interpreted as prejudicing the rights of victims under national or international law.

Article 76. Sentencing

1. In the event of a conviction, the Trial Chamber shall consider the appropriate sentence to be imposed and shall take into account the evidence presented and submissions made during the trial that are relevant to the sentence.

2. Except where Article 65 applies and before the completion of the trial, the Trial Chamber may on its own motion and shall, at the request of the Prosecutor or the accused, hold a further hearing to hear any additional evidence or submissions relevant to the sentence, in accordance with the Rules of Procedure and Evidence.

3. Where paragraph 2 applies, any representations under Article 75 shall be heard during the further hearing referred to in paragraph 2 and, if necessary, during any additional hearing.

4. The sentence shall be pronounced in public and, wherever possible, in the presence of the accused.

Part 7. Penalties

Article 77. Applicable penalties

1. Subject to Article 110, the Court may impose one of the following penalties on a person convicted of a crime under Article 5 of this Statute:

(a) Imprisonment for a specified number of years, which may not exceed a maximum of 30 years; or

(b) A term of life imprisonment when justified by the extreme gravity of the crime and the individual circumstances of the convicted person.

2. In addition to imprisonment, the Court may order:

(a) A fine under the criteria provided for in the Rules of Procedure and Evidence;

(b) A forfeiture of proceeds, property and assets derived directly or indirectly from that crime, without prejudice to the rights of bona fide third parties.

Article 78. Determination of the sentence

1. In determining the sentence, the Court shall, in accordance with the Rules of Procedure and Evidence, take into account such factors as the gravity of the crime and the individual circumstances of the convicted person.

2. In imposing a sentence of imprisonment, the Court shall deduct the time, if any, previously spent in detention in accordance with an order of the Court. The Court may deduct any time otherwise spent in detention in connection with conduct underlying the crime.

3. When a person has been convicted of more than one crime, the Court shall pronounce a sentence for each crime and a joint sentence specifying the total period of imprisonment. This period shall be no less than the highest individual sentence pronounced and shall not exceed 30 years imprisonment or a sentence of life imprisonment in conformity with Article 77, paragraph 1(b).

Article 79. Trust Fund

1. A Trust Fund shall be established by decision of the Assembly of States Parties for the benefit of victims of crimes within the jurisdiction of the Court, and of the families of such victims.

2. The Court may order money and other property collected through fines or forfeiture to be transferred, by order of the Court, to the Trust Fund.

3. The Trust Fund shall be managed according to criteria to be determined by the Assembly of States Parties.

Article 80. Non-prejudice to national application of penalties and national laws

Nothing in this Part of the Statute affects the application by States of penalties prescribed by their national law, nor the law of States which do not provide for penalties prescribed in this Part.

Part 8. Appeal and Revision

Article 81. Appeal against decision of acquittal or conviction or against sentence

1. A decision under Article 74 may be appealed in accordance with the Rules of Procedure and Evidence as follows:

(a) The Prosecutor may make an appeal on any of the following grounds:

(i) Procedural error,

(ii) Error of fact, or

(iii) Error of law;

(b) The convicted person or the Prosecutor on that person's behalf may make an appeal on any of the following grounds:

(i) Procedural error,

(ii) Error of fact,

(iii) Error of law, or

(iv) Any other ground that affects the fairness or reliability of the proceedings or decision.

2. (a) A sentence may be appealed, in accordance with the Rules of Procedure and Evidence, by the Prosecutor or the convicted person on the ground of disproportion between the crime and the sentence;

(b) If on an appeal against sentence the Court considers that there are grounds on which the conviction might be set aside, wholly or in part, it may invite the Prosecutor and the convicted person to submit grounds under Article 81, paragraph 1(a) or (b), and may render a decision on conviction in accordance with Article 83;

(c) The same procedure applies when the Court, on an appeal against conviction only, considers that there are grounds to reduce the sentence under paragraph 2 (a).

3. (a) Unless the Trial Chamber orders otherwise, a convicted person shall remain in custody pending an appeal;

(b) When a convicted person's time in custody exceeds the sentence of imprisonment imposed, that person shall be released, except that if the Prosecutor is also appealing, the release may be subject to the conditions under subparagraph (c) below;

(c) In case of an acquittal, the accused shall be released immediately, subject to the following:

(i) Under exceptional circumstances, and having regard, *inter alia*, to the concrete risk of flight, the seriousness of the offence charged and the probability of success on appeal, the Trial Chamber, at the request of the Prosecutor, may maintain the detention of the person pending appeal;

(ii) A decision by the Trial Chamber under subparagraph (c)(i) may be appealed in accordance with the Rules of Procedure and Evidence.

4. Subject to the provisions of paragraph 3(a) and (b), execution of the decision or sentence shall be suspended during the period allowed for appeal and for the duration of the appeal proceedings.

Article 82. Appeal against other decisions

1. Either party may appeal any of the following decisions in accordance with the Rules of Procedure and Evidence:

(a) A decision with respect to jurisdiction or admissibility;

(b) A decision granting or denying release of the person being investigated or prosecuted;

(c) A decision of the Pre–Trial Chamber to act on its own initiative under Article 56, paragraph 3;

(d) A decision that involves an issue that would significantly affect the fair and expeditious conduct of the proceedings or the outcome of the trial, and for which, in the opinion of the Pre–Trial or Trial Chamber, an immediate resolution by the Appeals Chamber may materially advance the proceedings.

2. A decision of the Pre–Trial Chamber under Article 57, paragraph 3(d), may be appealed against by the State concerned or by the Prosecutor, with the leave of the Pre–Trial Chamber. The appeal shall be heard on an expedited basis.

3. An appeal shall not of itself have suspensive effect unless the Appeals Chamber so orders, upon request, in accordance with the Rules of Procedure and Evidence.

4. A legal representative of the victims, the convicted person or a bona fide owner of property adversely affected by an order under Article 73 may appeal against the order for reparations, as provided in the Rules of Procedure and Evidence.

Article 83. Proceedings on appeal

1. For the purposes of proceedings under Article 81 and this article, the Appeals Chamber shall have all the powers of the Trial Chamber.

2. If the Appeals Chamber finds that the proceedings appealed from were unfair in a way that affected the reliability of the decision or sentence, or that the decision or sentence appealed from was materially affected by error of fact or law or procedural error, it may:

(a) Reverse or amend the decision or sentence; or

(b) Order a new trial before a different Trial Chamber.

For these purposes, the Appeals Chamber may remand a factual issue to the original Trial Chamber for it to determine the issue and to report back accordingly, or may itself call evidence to determine the issue. When the decision or sentence has been appealed only by the person convicted, or the Prosecutor on that person's behalf, it cannot be amended to his or her detriment.

3. If in an appeal against sentence the Appeals Chamber finds that the sentence is disproportionate to the crime, it may vary the sentence in accordance with Part 7.

4. The judgement of the Appeals Chamber shall be taken by a majority of the judges and shall be delivered in open court. The judgement shall state the reasons on which it is based. When there is no unanimity, the judgement of the Appeals Chamber shall contain the views of the majority and the minority, but a judge may deliver a separate or dissenting opinion on a question of law.

5. The Appeals Chamber may deliver its judgement in the absence of the person acquitted or convicted.

Article 84. Revision of conviction or sentence

1. The convicted person or, after death, spouses, children, parents or one person alive at the time of the accused's death who has been given express written instructions from the accused to bring such a claim, or the Prosecutor on the person's behalf, may apply to the Appeals Chamber to revise the final judgement of conviction or sentence on the grounds that:

(a) New evidence has been discovered that:

(i) Was not available at the time of trial, and such unavailability was not wholly or partially attributable to the party making application; and

(ii) Is sufficiently important that had it been proved at trial it would have been likely to have resulted in a different verdict;

(b) It has been newly discovered that decisive evidence, taken into account at trial and upon which the conviction depends, was false, forged or falsified;

(c) One or more of the judges who participated in conviction or confirmation of the charges has committed, in that case, an act of serious misconduct or serious breach of duty of sufficient gravity to justify the removal of that judge or those judges from office under Article 46.

2. The Appeals Chamber shall reject the application if it considers it to be unfounded. If it determines that the application is meritorious, it may, as appropriate:

(a) Reconvene the original Trial Chamber;

(b) Constitute a new Trial Chamber; or

(c) Retain jurisdiction over the matter, with a view to, after hearing the parties in the manner set forth in the Rules of Procedure and Evidence, arriving at a determination on whether the judgement should be revised.

Article 85. Compensation to an arrested or convicted person

1. Anyone who has been the victim of unlawful arrest or detention shall have an enforceable right to compensation.

2. When a person has by a final decision been convicted of a criminal offence, and when subsequently his or her conviction has been reversed on the ground that a new or newly discovered fact shows conclusively that there has been a miscarriage of justice, the person who has suffered punishment as a result of such conviction shall be compensated according to law, unless it is proved that the non-disclosure of the unknown fact in time is wholly or partly attributable to him or her.

3. In exceptional circumstances, where the Court finds conclusive facts showing that there has been a grave and manifest miscarriage of justice, it may in its discretion award compensation, according to the criteria provided in the Rules of Procedure and Evidence, to a person who has been released from detention following a final decision of acquittal or a termination of the proceedings for that reason.

Part 9. International Cooperation and Judicial Assistance

Article 86. General obligation to cooperate

States Parties shall, in accordance with the provisions of this Statute, cooperate fully with the Court in its investigation and prosecution of crimes within the jurisdiction of the Court.

Article 87. Requests for cooperation: general provisions

1. (a) The Court shall have the authority to make requests to States Parties for cooperation. The requests shall be transmitted through the diplomatic channel or any other appropriate channel as may be designated by each State Party upon ratification, acceptance, approval or accession. Subsequent changes to the designation shall be made by each State Party in accordance with the Rules of Procedure and Evidence.

(b) When appropriate, without prejudice to the provisions of subparagraph (a), requests may also be transmitted through the International Criminal Police Organization or any appropriate regional organization.

2. Requests for cooperation and any documents supporting the request shall either be in or be accompanied by a translation into an official language of the requested State or in one of the working languages of the Court, in accordance with the choice made by that State upon ratification, acceptance, approval or accession.

Subsequent changes to this choice shall be made in accordance with the Rules of Procedure and Evidence.

3. The requested State shall keep confidential a request for cooperation and any documents supporting the request, except to the extent that the disclosure is necessary for execution of the request.

4. In relation to any request for assistance presented under Part 9, the Court may take such measures, including measures related to the protection of information, as may be necessary to ensure the safety or physical or psychological well-being of any victims, potential witnesses and their families. The Court may request that any information that is made available under Part 9 shall be provided and handled in a manner

that protects the safety and physical or psychological well-being of any victims, potential witnesses and their families.

5. The Court may invite any State not party to this Statute to provide assistance under this Part on the basis of an ad hoc arrangement, an agreement with such State or any other appropriate basis. Where a State not party to this Statute, which has entered into an ad hoc arrangement or an agreement with the Court, fails to cooperate with requests pursuant to any such arrangement or agreement, the Court may so inform the Assembly of States Parties or, where the Security Council referred the matter to the Court, the Security Council.

6. The Court may ask any intergovernmental organization to provide information or documents. The Court may also ask for other forms of cooperation and assistance which may be agreed upon with such an organization and which are in accordance with its competence or mandate.

7. Where a State Party fails to comply with a request to cooperate by the Court contrary to the provisions of this Statute, thereby preventing the Court from exercising its functions and powers under this Statute, the Court may make a finding to that effect and refer the matter to the Assembly of States Parties or, where the Security Council referred the matter to the Court, to the Security Council.

Article 88. Availability of procedures under national law

States Parties shall ensure that there are procedures available under their national law for all of the forms of cooperation which are specified under this Part.

Article 89. Surrender of persons to the Court

1. The Court may transmit a request for the arrest and surrender of a person, together with the material supporting the request outlined in Article 91, to any State on the territory of which that person may be found and shall request the cooperation of that State in the arrest and surrender of such a person. States Parties shall, in accordance with the provisions of this Part and the procedure under their national law, comply with requests for arrest and surrender.

2. Where the person sought for surrender brings a challenge before a national court on the basis of the principle of *ne bis in idem* as provided in Article 20, the requested State shall immediately consult with the Court to determine if there has been a relevant ruling on admissibility. If the case is admissible, the requested State shall proceed with the execution of the request. If an admissibility ruling is pending, the requested State may postpone the execution of the request for surrender of the person until the Court makes a determination on admissibility.

3. (a) A State Party shall authorize, in accordance with its national procedural law, transportation through its territory of a person being surrendered to the Court by another State, except where transit through that State would impede or delay the surrender.

(b) A request by the Court for transit shall be transmitted in accordance with Article 87. The request for transit shall contain:

(i) A description of the person being transported;

(ii) A brief statement of the facts of the case and their legal characterization; and

(iii) The warrant for arrest and surrender;

(c) A person being transported shall be detained in custody during the period of transit;

(d) No authorization is required if the person is transported by air and no landing is scheduled on the territory of the transit State;

(e) If an unscheduled landing occurs on the territory of the transit State, that State may require a request for transit from the Court as provided for in subparagraph (b). The transit State shall detain the person being transported until the request for transit is received and the transit is effected; provided that detention for purposes of this subparagraph may not be extended beyond 96 hours from the unscheduled landing unless the request is received within that time.

4. If the person sought is being proceeded against or is serving a sentence in the requested State for a crime different from that for which surrender to the Court is sought, the requested State, after making its decision to grant the request, shall consult with the Court.

Article 90. Competing requests

1. A State Party which receives a request from the Court for the surrender of a person under Article 89 shall, if it also receives a request from any other State for the extradition of the same person for the same conduct which forms the basis of the crime for which the Court seeks the person's surrender, notify the Court and the requesting State of that fact.

2. Where the requesting State is a State Party, the requested State shall give priority to the request from the Court if:

(a) The Court has, pursuant to Articles 18 and 19, made a determination that the case in respect of which surrender is sought is admissible and that determination takes into account the investigation or prosecution conducted by the requesting State in respect of its request for extradition; or

(b) The Court makes the determination described in subparagraph (a) pursuant to the requested State's notification under paragraph 1.

3. Where a determination under paragraph 2 (a) has not been made, the requested State may, at its discretion, pending the determination of the Court under paragraph 2 (b), proceed to deal with the request for extradition from the requesting State but shall not extradite the person until the Court has determined that the case is inadmissible. The Court's determination shall be made on an expedited basis.

4. If the requesting State is a State not Party to this Statute the requested State, if it is not under an international obligation to extradite the person to the requesting State, shall give priority to the request for surrender from the Court, if the Court has determined that the case is admissible.

5. Where a case under paragraph 4 has not been determined to be admissible by the Court, the requested State may, at its discretion, proceed to deal with the request for extradition from the requesting State.

6. In cases where paragraph 4 applies except that the requested State is under an existing international obligation to extradite the person to the requesting State not Party to this Statute, the requested State shall determine whether to surrender the person to the Court or extradite the person to the requesting State. In making its decision, the requested State shall consider all the relevant factors, including but not limited to:

(a) The respective dates of the requests;

(b) The interests of the requesting State including, where relevant, whether the crime was committed in its territory and the nationality of the victims and of the person sought; and

(c) The possibility of subsequent surrender between the Court and the requesting State.

7. Where a State Party which receives a request from the Court for the surrender of a person also receives a request from any State for the extradition of the same person for conduct other than that which constitutes the crime for which the Court seeks the person's surrender:

(a) The requested State shall, if it is not under an existing international obligation to extradite the person to the requesting State, give priority to the request from the Court;

(b) The requested State shall, if it is under an existing international obligation to extradite the person to the requesting State, determine whether to surrender the person to the Court or extradite the person to the requesting State. In making its decision, the requested State shall consider all the relevant factors, including but not limited to those set out in paragraph 6, but shall give special consideration to the relative nature and gravity of the conduct in question.

8. Where pursuant to a notification under this article, the Court has determined a case to be inadmissible, and subsequently extradition to the requesting State is refused, the requested State shall notify the Court of this decision.

Article 91. Contents of request for arrest and surrender

1. A request for arrest and surrender shall be made in writing. In urgent cases, a request may be made by any medium capable of delivering a written record, provided that the request shall be confirmed through the channel provided for in Article 87, paragraph 1 (a).

2. In the case of a request for the arrest and surrender of a person for whom a warrant of arrest has been issued by the Pre–Trial Chamber under Article 58, the request shall contain or be supported by:

(a) Information describing the person sought, sufficient to identify the person, and information as to that person's probable location;

(b) A copy of the warrant of arrest; and

(c) Such documents, statements or information as may be necessary to meet the requirements for the surrender process in the requested State, except that those requirements should not be more burdensome than those applicable to requests for extradition pursuant to treaties or arrangements between the requested State and other States and should, if possible, be less burdensome, taking into account the distinct nature of the Court.

3. In the case of a request for the arrest and surrender of a person already convicted, the request shall contain or be supported by:

(a) A copy of any warrant of arrest for that person;

(b) A copy of the judgement of conviction;

(c) Information to demonstrate that the person sought is the one referred to in the judgement of conviction; and

(d) If the person sought has been sentenced, a copy of the sentence imposed and, in the case of a sentence for imprisonment, a statement of any time already served and the time remaining to be served.

4. Upon the request of the Court, a State Party shall consult with the Court, either generally or with respect to a specific matter, regarding any requirements under its national law that may apply under paragraph 2 (c). During the consultations, the State Party shall advise the Court of the specific requirements of its national law.

Article 92. Provisional arrest

1. In urgent cases, the Court may request the provisional arrest of the person sought, pending presentation of the request for surrender and the documents supporting the request as specified in Article 91.

2. The request for provisional arrest shall be made by any medium capable of delivering a written record and shall contain:

(a) Information describing the person sought, sufficient to identify the person, and information as to that person's probable location;

(b) A concise statement of the crimes for which the person's arrest is sought and of the facts which are alleged to constitute those crimes, including, where possible, the date and location of the crime;

(c) A statement of the existence of a warrant of arrest or a judgement of conviction against the person sought; and

(d) A statement that a request for surrender of the person sought will follow.

3. A person who is provisionally arrested may be released from custody if the requested State has not received the request for surrender and the documents supporting the request as specified in Article 91 within the time limits specified in the Rules of Procedure and Evidence. However, the person may consent to surrender before the expiration of this period if permitted by the law of the requested State. In such a case, the requested State shall proceed to surrender the person to the Court as soon as possible.

4. The fact that the person sought has been released from custody pursuant to paragraph 3 shall not prejudice the subsequent arrest and surrender of that person if the request for surrender and the documents supporting the request are delivered at a later date.

Article 93. Other forms of cooperation

1. States Parties shall, in accordance with the provisions of this Part and under procedures of national law, comply with requests by the Court to provide the following assistance in relation to investigations or prosecutions:

(a) The identification and whereabouts of persons or the location of items;

(b) The taking of evidence, including testimony under oath, and the production of evidence, including expert opinions and reports necessary to the Court;

(c) The questioning of any person being investigated or prosecuted;

(d) The service of documents, including judicial documents;

(e) Facilitating the voluntary appearance of persons as witnesses or experts before the Court;

(f) The temporary transfer of persons as provided in paragraph 7;

(g) The examination of places or sites, including the exhumation and examination of grave sites;

(h) The execution of searches and seizures;

(i) The provision of records and documents, including official records and documents;

(j) The protection of victims and witnesses and the preservation of evidence;

(k) The identification, tracing and freezing or seizure of proceeds, property and assets and instrumentalities of crimes for the purpose of eventual forfeiture, without prejudice to the rights of bona fide third parties; and

(*l*) Any other type of assistance which is not prohibited by the law of the requested State, with a view to facilitating the investigation and prosecution of crimes within the jurisdiction of the Court.

2. The Court shall have the authority to provide an assurance to a witness or an expert appearing before the Court that he or she will not

be prosecuted, detained or subjected to any restriction of personal freedom by the Court in respect of any act or omission that preceded the departure of that person from the requested State.

3. Where execution of a particular measure of assistance detailed in a request presented under paragraph 1, is prohibited in the requested State on the basis of an existing fundamental legal principle of general application, the requested State shall promptly consult with the Court to try to resolve the matter. In the consultations, consideration should be given to whether the assistance can be rendered in another manner or subject to conditions. If after consultations the matter cannot be resolved, the Court shall modify the request as necessary.

4. In accordance with Article 72, a State Party may deny a request for assistance, in whole or in part, only if the request concerns the production of any documents or disclosure of evidence which relates to its national security.

5. Before denying a request for assistance under paragraph 1 (1), the requested State shall consider whether the assistance can be provided subject to specified conditions, or whether the assistance can be provided at a later date or in an alternative manner, provided that if the Court or the Prosecutor accepts the assistance subject to conditions, the Court of the Prosecutor shall abide by them.

6. If a request for assistance is denied, the requested State Party shall promptly inform the Court or the Prosecutor of the reasons for such denial.

7. (a) The Court may request the temporary transfer of a person in custody for purposes of identification or for obtaining testimony or other assistance. The person may be transferred if the following conditions are fulfilled:

(i) The person freely gives his or her informed consent to the transfer; and

(ii) The requested State agrees to the transfer, subject to such conditions as that State and the Court may agree.

(b) The person being transferred shall remain in custody. When the purposes of the transfer have been fulfilled, the Court shall return the person without delay to the requested State.

8. (a) The Court shall ensure the confidentiality of documents and information, except as required for the investigation and proceedings described in the request.

(b) The requested State may, when necessary, transmit documents or information to the Prosecutor on a confidential basis. The Prosecutor may then use them solely for the purpose of generating new evidence;

(c) The requested State may, on its own motion or at the request of the Prosecutor, subsequently consent to the disclosure of such documents or information. They may then be used as evidence pursuant to the provisions of Parts 5 and 6 and in accordance with the Rules of Procedure and Evidence.

9. (a) (i) In the event that a State Party receives competing requests, other than for surrender or extradition, from the Court and from another State pursuant to an international obligation, the State Party shall endeavour, in consultation with the Court and the other State, to meet both requests, if necessary by postponing or attaching conditions to one or the other request.

(ii) Failing that, competing requests shall be resolved in accordance with the principles established in Article 90.

(b) Where, however, the request from the Court concerns information, property or persons which are subject to the control of a third State or an international organization by virtue of an international agreement, the requested States shall so inform the Court and the Court shall direct its request to the third State or international organization.

10. (a) The Court may, upon request, cooperate with and provide assistance to a State Party conducting an investigation into or trial in respect of conduct which constitutes a crime within the jurisdiction of the Court or which constitutes a serious crime under the national law of the requesting State.

(b) (i) The assistance provided under subparagraph (a) shall include, *inter alia*:

(1) The transmission of statements, documents or other types of evidence obtained in the course of an investigation or a trial conducted by the Court; and

(2) The questioning of any person detained by order of the Court;

(ii) In the case of assistance under subparagraph (b)(i)(1):

(1) If the documents or other types of evidence have been obtained with the assistance of a State, such transmission shall require the consent of that State;

(2) If the statements, documents or other types of evidence have been provided by a witness or expert, such transmission shall be subject to the provisions of Article 68.

(c) The Court may, under the conditions set out in this paragraph, grant a request for assistance under this paragraph from a State which is not a Party to the Statute.

Article 94. Postponement of execution of a request in respect of ongoing investigation or prosecution

1. If the immediate execution of a request would interfere with an ongoing investigation or prosecution of a case different from that to which the request relates, the requested State may postpone the execution of the request for a period of time agreed upon with the Court. However, the postponement shall be no longer than is necessary to complete the relevant investigation or prosecution in the requested State. Before making a decision to postpone, the requested State should

consider whether the assistance may be immediately provided subject to certain conditions.

2. If a decision to postpone is taken pursuant to paragraph 1, the Prosecutor may, however, seek measures to preserve evidence, pursuant to Article 93, paragraph 1(j).

Article 95. Postponement of execution of a request in respect of an admissibility challenge

Without prejudice to Article 53, paragraph 2, where there is an admissibility challenge under consideration by the Court pursuant to Articles 18 or 19, the requested State may postpone the execution of a request under this Part pending a determination by the Court, unless the Court has specifically ordered that the Prosecutor may pursue the collection of such evidence pursuant to Articles 18 or 19.

Article 96. Contents of request for other forms of assistance under Article 93

Upon the request for other forms of assistance referred to in Article 93 shall be made in writing. In urgent cases, a request may be made by any medium capable of delivering a written record, provided that the request shall be confirmed through the channel provided for in Article 87, paragraph 1 (a).

2. The request shall, as applicable, contain or be supported by the following:

(a) A concise statement of the purpose of the request and the assistance sought, including the legal basis and the grounds for the request;

(b) As much detailed information as possible about the location or identification of any person or place that must be found or identified in order for the assistance sought to be provided;

(c) A concise statement of the essential facts underlying the request;

(d) The reasons for and details of any procedure or requirement to be followed;

(e) Such information as may be required under the law of the requested State in order to execute the request; and

(f) Any other information relevant in order for the assistance sought to be provided.

3. Upon the request of the Court, a State Party shall consult with the Court, either generally or with respect to a specific matter, regarding any requirements under its national law that may apply under paragraph 2 (e). During the consultations, the State Party shall advise the Court of the specific requirements of its national law.

4. The provisions of this article shall, where applicable, also apply in respect of a request for assistance made to the Court.

Article 97. Consultations

Where a State Party receives a request under this Part in relation to which it identifies problems which may impede or prevent the execution of the request, that State shall consult with the Court without delay in order to resolve the matter. Such problems may include, *inter alia*:

(a) Insufficient information to execute the request;

(b) In the case of a request for surrender, the fact that despite best efforts, the person sought cannot be located or that the investigation conducted has determined that the person in the custodial State is clearly not the person named in the warrant; or

(c) The fact that execution of the request in its current form would require the requested State to breach a pre-existing treaty obligation undertaken with respect to another State.

Article 98. Cooperation with respect to waiver of immunity and consent to surrender

1. The Court may not proceed with a request for surrender or assistance which would require the requested State to act inconsistently with its obligations under international law with respect to the State or diplomatic immunity of a person or property of a third State, unless the Court can first obtain the cooperation of that third State for the waiver of the immunity.

2. The Court may not proceed with a request for surrender which would require the requested State to act inconsistently with its obligations under international agreements pursuant to which the consent of a sending State is required to surrender a person of that State to the Court, unless the Court can first obtain the cooperation of the sending State for the giving of consent for the surrender.

Article 99. Execution of requests under Articles 93 and 96

1. Requests for assistance shall be executed in accordance with the relevant procedure under the law of the requested State and, unless prohibited by such law, in the manner specified in the request, including following any procedure outlined therein or permitting persons specified in the request to be present at and assist in the execution process.

2. In the case of an urgent request, the documents or evidence produced in response shall, at the request of the Court, be sent urgently.

3. Replies from the requested State shall be transmitted in their original language and form.

4. Without prejudice to other articles in this Part, where it is necessary for the successful execution of a request which can be executed without any compulsory measures, including specifically the interview of or taking evidence from a person on a voluntary basis, including doing so without the presence of the authorities of the requested State Party if it is essential for the request to be executed, and the examination without modification of a public site or other public place, the Prosecutor may execute such request directly on the territory of a State as follows:

(a) When the State Party requested is a State on the territory of which the crime is alleged to have been committed, and there has been a determination of admissibility pursuant to Articles 18 or 19, the Prosecutor may directly execute such request following all possible consultations with the requested State Party;

(b) In other cases, the Prosecutor may execute such request following consultations with the requested State Party and subject to any reasonable conditions or concerns raised by that State Party. Where the requested State Party identifies problems with the execution of a request pursuant to this subparagraph it shall, without delay, consult with the Court to resolve the matter.

5. Provisions allowing a person heard or examined by the Court under Article 72 to invoke restrictions designed to prevent disclosure of confidential information connected with national defence or security shall also apply to the execution of requests for assistance under this article.

Article 100. Costs

1. The ordinary costs for execution of requests in the territory of the requested State shall be borne by that State, except for the following, which shall be borne by the Court:

(a) Costs associated with the travel and security of witnesses and experts or the transfer under Article 93 of persons in custody;

(b) Costs of translation, interpretation and transcription;

(c) Travel and subsistence costs of the judges, the Prosecutor, the Deputy Prosecutors, the Registrar, the Deputy Registrar and staff of any organ of the Court;

(d) Costs of any expert opinion or report requested by the Court;

(e) Costs associated with the transport of a person being surrendered to the Court by a custodial State; and

(f) Following consultations, any extraordinary costs that may result from the execution of a request.

2. The provisions of paragraph 1 shall, as appropriate, apply to requests from States Parties to the Court. In that case, the Court shall bear the ordinary costs of execution.

Article 101. Rule of speciality

1. A person surrendered to the Court under this Statute shall not be proceeded against, punished or detained for any conduct committed prior to surrender, other than the conduct or course of conduct which forms the basis of the crimes for which that person has been surrendered.

2. The Court may request a waiver of the requirements of paragraph 1 from the State which surrendered the person to the Court and, if necessary, the Court shall provide additional information in accor-

dance with Article 91. States Parties shall have the authority to provide a waiver to the Court and should endeavour to do so.

Article 102. Use of terms

For the purposes of this Statute:

(a) "surrender" means the delivering up of a person by a State to the Court, pursuant to this Statute.

(b) "extradition" means the delivering up of a person by one State to another as provided by treaty, convention or national legislation.

Part 10. Enforcement

Article 103. Role of States in enforcement of sentences of imprisonment

1. (a) A sentence of imprisonment shall be served in a State designated by the Court from a list of States which have indicated to the Court their willingness to accept sentenced persons.

(b) At the time of declaring its willingness to accept sentenced persons, a State may attach conditions to its acceptance as agreed by the Court and in accordance with this Part.

(c) A State designated in a particular case shall promptly inform the Court whether it accepts the Court's designation.

2. (a) The State of enforcement shall notify the Court of any circumstances, including the exercise of any conditions agreed under paragraph 1, which could materially affect the terms or extent of the imprisonment. The Court shall be given at least 45 days' notice of any such known or foreseeable circumstances. During this period, the State of enforcement shall take no action that might prejudice its obligations under Article 110.

(b) Where the Court cannot agree to the circumstances referred to in subparagraph (a), it shall notify the State of enforcement and proceed in accordance with Article 104, paragraph 1.

3. In exercising its discretion to make a designation under paragraph 1, the Court shall take into account the following:

(a) The principle that States Parties should share the responsibility for enforcing sentences of imprisonment, in accordance with principles of equitable distribution, as provided in the Rules of Procedure and Evidence;

(b) The application of widely accepted international treaty standards governing the treatment of prisoners;

(c) The views of the sentenced person; and

(d) The nationality of the sentenced person;

(e) Such other factors regarding the circumstances of the crime or the person sentenced, or the effective enforcement of the sentence, as may be appropriate in designating the State of enforcement.

4. If no State is designated under paragraph 1, the sentence of imprisonment shall be served in a prison facility made available by the host State, in accordance with the conditions set out in the headquarters agreement referred to in Article 3, paragraph 2. In such a case, the costs arising out of the enforcement of a sentence of imprisonment shall be borne by the Court.

Article 104. Change in designation of State of enforcement

1. The Court may, at any time, decide to transfer a sentenced person to a prison of another State.

2. A sentenced person may, at any time, apply to the Court to be transferred from the State of enforcement.

Article 105. Enforcement of the sentence

1. Subject to conditions which a State may have specified in accordance with Article 103, paragraph 1 (b), the sentence of imprisonment shall be binding on the States Parties, which shall in no case modify it.

2. The Court alone shall have the right to decide any application for appeal and revision. The State of enforcement shall not impede the making of any such application by a sentenced person.

Article 106. Supervision of enforcement of sentences and conditions of imprisonment

1. The enforcement of a sentence of imprisonment shall be subject to the supervision of the Court and shall be consistent with widely accepted international treaty standards governing treatment of prisoners.

2. The conditions of imprisonment shall be governed by the law of the State of enforcement and shall be consistent with widely accepted international treaty standards governing treatment of prisoners; in no case shall such conditions be more or less favourable than those available to prisoners convicted of similar offences in the State of enforcement.

3. Communications between a sentenced person and the Court shall be unimpeded and confidential.

Article 107. Transfer of the person upon completion of sentence

1. Following completion of the sentence, a person who is not a national of the State of enforcement may, in accordance with the law of the State of enforcement, be transferred to a State which is obliged to receive him or her, or to another State which agrees to receive him or her, taking into account any wishes of the person to be transferred to that State, unless the State of enforcement authorizes the person to remain in its territory.

2. If no State bears the costs arising out of transferring the person to another State pursuant to paragraph 1, such costs shall be borne by the Court.

3. Subject to the provisions of Article 108, the State of enforcement may also, in accordance with its national law, extradite or otherwise surrender the person to the State which has requested the extradition or surrender of the person for purposes of trial or enforcement of a sentence.

Article 108. Limitation on the prosecution or punishment of other offences

1. A sentenced person in the custody of the State of enforcement shall not be subject to prosecution or punishment or to extradition to a third State for any conduct engaged in prior to that person's delivery to the State of enforcement, unless such prosecution, punishment or extradition has been approved by the Court at the request of the State of enforcement.

2. The Court shall decide the matter after having heard the views of the sentenced person.

3. Paragraph 1 shall cease to apply if the sentenced person remains voluntarily for more than 30 days in the territory of the State of enforcement after having served the full sentence imposed by the Court, or returns to the territory of that State after having left it.

Article 109. Enforcement of fines and forfeiture measures

1. States Parties shall give effect to fines or forfeitures ordered by the Court under Part 7, without prejudice to the rights of bona fide third parties, and in accordance with the procedure of their national law.

2. If a State Party is unable to give effect to an order for forfeiture, it shall take measures to recover the value of the proceeds, property or assets ordered by the Court to be forfeited, without prejudice to the rights of bona fide third parties.

3. Property, or the proceeds of the sale of real property or, where appropriate, the sale of other property, which is obtained by a State Party as a result of its enforcement of a judgement of the Court shall be transferred to the Court.

Article 110. Review by the Court concerning reduction of sentence

1. The State of enforcement shall not release the person before expiry of the sentence pronounced by the Court.

2. The Court alone shall have the right to decide any reduction of sentence, and shall rule on the matter after having heard the person.

3. When the person has served two thirds of the sentence, or 25 years in the case of life imprisonment, the Court shall review the sentence to determine whether it should be reduced. Such a review shall not be conducted before that time.

4. In its review under paragraph 3, the Court may reduce the sentence if it finds that one or more of the following factors are present:

(a) The early and continuing willingness of the person to cooperate with the Court in its investigations and prosecutions;

(b) The voluntary assistance of the person in enabling the enforcement of the judgements and orders of the Court in other cases, and in particular providing assistance in locating assets subject to orders of fine, forfeiture or reparation which may be used for the benefit of victims; or

(c) Other factors establishing a clear and significant change of circumstances sufficient to justify the reduction of sentence, as provided in the Rules of Procedure and Evidence.

5. If the Court determines in its initial review under paragraph 3 that it is not appropriate to reduce the sentence, it shall thereafter review the question of reduction of sentence at such intervals and applying such criteria as provided for in the Rules of Procedure and Evidence.

Article 111. Escape

If a convicted person escapes from custody and flees the State of enforcement, that State may, after consultation with the Court, request the person's surrender from the State in which the person is located pursuant to existing bilateral or multilateral arrangements, or may request that the Court seek the person's surrender. It may direct that the person be delivered to the State in which he or she was serving the sentence or to another State designated by the Court.

Part 11. Assembly of States Parties

Article 112. Assembly of States Parties

1. An Assembly of States Parties to this Statute is hereby established. Each State Party shall have one representative in the Assembly who may be accompanied by alternates and advisers. Other States which have signed the Statute or the Final Act may be observers in the Assembly.

2. The Assembly shall:

(a) Consider and adopt, as appropriate, recommendations of the Preparatory Commission;

(b) Provide management oversight to the Presidency, the Prosecutor and the Registrar regarding the administration of the Court;

(c) Consider the reports and activities of the Bureau established under paragraph 3 and take appropriate action in regard thereto;

(d) Consider and decide the budget for the Court;

(e) Decide whether to alter, in accordance with Article 36, the number of judges;

(f) Consider pursuant to Article 87, paragraphs 5 and 7, any question relating to non-cooperation;

(g) Perform any other function consistent with this Statute or the Rules of Procedure and Evidence.

3. (a) The Assembly shall have a Bureau consisting of a President, two Vice–Presidents and 18 members elected by the Assembly for three-year terms.

(b) The Bureau shall have a representative character, taking into account, in particular, equitable geographical distribution and the adequate representation of the principal legal systems of the world.

(c) The Bureau shall meet as often as necessary, but at least once a year. It shall assist the Assembly in the discharge of its responsibilities.

4. The Assembly may establish such subsidiary bodies as may be necessary, including an independent oversight mechanism for inspection, evaluation and investigation of the Court, in order to enhance its efficiency and economy.

5. The President of the Court, the Prosecutor and the Registrar or their representatives may participate, as appropriate, in meetings of the Assembly and of the Bureau.

6. The Assembly shall meet at the seat of the Court or at the Headquarters of the United Nations once a year and, when circumstances so require, hold special sessions. Except as otherwise specified in this Statute, special sessions shall be convened by the Bureau on its own initiative or at the request of one third of the States Parties.

7. Each State Party shall have one vote. Every effort shall be made to reach decisions by consensus in the Assembly and in the Bureau. If consensus cannot be reached, except as otherwise provided in the Statute:

(a) Decisions on matters of substance must be approved by a two-thirds majority of those present and voting provided that an absolute majority of States Parties constitutes the quorum for voting;

(b) Decisions on matters of procedure shall be taken by a simple majority of States Parties present and voting.

8. A State Party which is in arrears in the payment of its financial contributions towards the costs of the Court shall have no vote in the Assembly and in the Bureau if the amount of its arrears equals or exceeds the amount of the contributions due from it for the preceding two full years. The Assembly may, nevertheless, permit such a State Party to vote in the Assembly and in the Bureau if it is satisfied that the failure to pay is due to conditions beyond the control of the State Party.

9. The Assembly shall adopt its own rules of procedure.

10. The official and working languages of the Assembly shall be those of the General Assembly of the United Nations.

Part 12. Financing

Article 113. Financial Regulations

Except as otherwise specifically provided, all financial matters related to the Court and the meetings of the Assembly of States Parties, including its Bureau and subsidiary bodies, shall be governed by this Statute and the Financial Regulations and Rules adopted by the Assembly of States Parties.

Article 114. Payment of expenses

Expenses of the Court and the Assembly of States Parties, including its Bureau and subsidiary bodies, shall be paid from the funds of the Court.

Article 115. Funds of the Court and of the Assembly of States Parties

The expenses of the Court and the Assembly of States Parties, including its Bureau and subsidiary bodies, as provided for in the budget decided by the Assembly of States Parties, shall be provided by the following sources:

(a) Assessed contributions made by States Parties;

(b) Funds provided by the United Nations, subject to the approval of the General Assembly, in particular in relation to the expenses incurred due to referrals by the Security Council.

Article 116. Voluntary contributions

Without prejudice to Article 115, the Court may receive and utilize, as additional funds, voluntary contributions from Governments, international organizations, individuals, corporations and other entities, in accordance with relevant criteria adopted by the Assembly of States Parties.

Article 117. Assessment of contributions

The contributions of States Parties shall be assessed in accordance with an agreed scale of assessment, based on the scale adopted by the United Nations for its regular budget and adjusted in accordance with the principles on which that scale is based.

Article 118. Annual audit

The records, books and accounts of the Court, including its annual financial statements, shall be audited annually by an independent auditor.

Part 13. Final Clauses

Article 119. Settlement of disputes

1. Any dispute concerning the judicial functions of the Court shall be settled by the decision of the Court.

2. Any other dispute between two or more States Parties relating to the interpretation or application of this Statute which is not settled through negotiations within three months of their commencement shall be referred to the Assembly of States Parties. The Assembly may itself seek to settle the dispute or make recommendations on further means of settlement of the dispute, including referral to the International Court of Justice in conformity with the Statute of that Court.

Article 120. Reservations

No reservations may be made to this Statute.

Article 121. Amendments

1. After the expiry of seven years from the entry into force of this Statute, any State Party may propose amendments thereto. The text of any proposed amendment shall be submitted to the Secretary–General of the United Nations, who shall promptly circulate it to all States Parties.

2. No sooner than three months from the date of notification, the next Assembly of States Parties shall, by a majority of those present and voting, decide whether to take up the proposal. The Assembly may deal with the proposal directly or convene a Review Conference if the issue involved so warrants.

3. The adoption of an amendment at a meeting of the Assembly of States Parties or at a Review Conference on which consensus cannot be reached shall require a two-thirds majority of States Parties.

4. Except as provided in paragraph 5, an amendment shall enter into force for all States Parties one year after instruments of ratification or acceptance have been deposited with the Secretary–General of the United Nations by seven-eighths of them.

5. Any amendment to Article 5 of this Statute shall enter into force for those States Parties which have accepted the amendment one year after the deposit of their instruments of ratification or acceptance. In respect of a State Party which has not accepted the amendment, the Court shall not exercise its jurisdiction regarding a crime covered by the amendment when committed by that State Party's nationals or on its territory.

6. If an amendment has been accepted by seven-eighths of States Parties in accordance with paragraph 4, any State Party which has not accepted the amendment may withdraw from the Statute with immediate effect, notwithstanding paragraph 1 of Article 127, but subject to paragraph 2 of Article 127, by giving notice no later than one year after the entry into force of such amendment.

7. The Secretary–General of the United Nations shall circulate to all States Parties any amendment adopted at a meeting of the Assembly of States Parties or at a Review Conference.

Article 122. Amendments to provisions of an institutional nature

1. Amendments to provisions of the Statute which are of an exclusively institutional nature, namely, Article 35, Article 36, paragraphs 8 and 9 Article 37, Article 38, Article 39, paragraphs 1 (first two sentences), 2 and 4, Article 42, paragraphs 4 to 9, Article 43, paragraphs 2 and 3, and Articles 44, 46, 47 and 49, may be proposed at any time, notwithstanding Article 121, paragraph 1, by any State Party. The text of any proposed amendment shall be submitted to the Secretary–General of the United Nations or such other person designated by the Assembly of States Parties who shall promptly circulate it to all States Parties and to others participating in the Assembly.

2. Amendments under this article on which consensus cannot be reached shall be adopted by the Assembly of States Parties or by a Review Conference, by a two-thirds majority of States Parties. Such amendments shall enter into force for all States Parties six months after their adoption by the Assembly or, as the case may be, by the Conference.

Article 123. Review of the Statute

1. Seven years after the entry into force of this Statute the Secretary–General of the United Nations shall convene a Review Conference to consider any amendments to this Statute. Such review may include, but is not limited to, the list of crimes contained in Article 5. The Conference shall be open to those participating in the Assembly of States Parties and on the same conditions.

2. At any time thereafter, at the request of a State Party and for the purposes set out in paragraph 1, the Secretary–General of the United Nations shall, upon approval by a majority of States Parties, convene a Review Conference.

3. The provisions of Article 121, paragraphs 3 to 7, shall apply to the adoption and entry into force of any amendment to the Statute considered at a Review Conference.

Article 124. Transitional Provision

Notwithstanding Article 12, paragraph 1, a State, on becoming a party to this Statute, may declare that, for a period of seven years after the entry into force of this Statute for the State concerned, it does not accept the jurisdiction of the Court with respect to the category of crimes referred to in Article 8 when a crime is alleged to have been committed by its nationals or on its territory. A declaration under this article may be withdrawn at any time. The provisions of this article shall be reviewed at the Review Conference convened in accordance with Article 123, paragraph 1.

Article 125. Signature, ratification, acceptance, approval or accession

1. This Statute shall be open for signature by all States in Rome, at the headquarters of the Food and Agriculture Organization of the United Nations, on 17 July 1998. Thereafter, it shall remain open for signature in Rome at the Ministry of Foreign Affairs of Italy until 17 October 1998. After that date, the Statute shall remain open for signature in New York, at United Nations Headquarters, until 31 December 2000.

2. This Statute is subject to ratification, acceptance or approval by signatory States. Instruments of ratification, acceptance or approval shall be deposited with the Secretary–General of the United Nations.

3. This Statute shall be open to accession by all States. Instruments of accession shall be deposited with the Secretary–General of the United Nations.

Article 126. Entry into force

1. This Statute shall enter into force on the first day of the month after the 60th day following the date of the deposit of the 60th instrument of ratification, acceptance, approval or accession with the Secretary–General of the United Nations.

2. For each State ratifying, accepting, approving or acceding to the Statute after the deposit of the 60th instrument of ratification, acceptance, approval or accession, the Statute shall enter into force on the first day of the month after the 60th day following the deposit by such State of its instrument of ratification, acceptance, approval or accession.

Article 127. Withdrawal

1. A State Party may, by written notification addressed to the Secretary–General of the United Nations, withdraw from this Statute. The withdrawal shall take effect one year after the date of receipt of the notification, unless the notification specifies a later date.

2. A State shall not be discharged, by reason of its withdrawal, from the obligations arising from this Statute while it was a Party to the Statute, including any financial obligations which may have accrued. Its withdrawal shall not affect any cooperation with the Court in connection with criminal investigations and proceedings in relation to which the withdrawing State had a duty to cooperate and which were commenced prior to the date on which the withdrawal became effective, nor shall it prejudice in any way the continued consideration of any matter which was already under consideration by the Court prior to the date on which the withdrawal became effective.

Article 128. Authentic texts

The original of this Statute, of which the Arabic, Chinese, English, French, Russian and Spanish texts are equally authentic, shall be deposited with the Secretary–General of the United Nations, who shall send certified copies thereof to all States.

IN WITNESS WHEREOF, the undersigned, being duly authorized thereto by their respective Governments, have signed this Statute.

DONE at Rome, this 17th day of July 1998.

Document 41
CONVENTION ON THE PREVENTION AND PUNISHMENT OF THE CRIME OF GENOCIDE

78 U.N.T.S. 277 (1948) (excerpt)

The Contracting Parties,

Having considered the declaration made by the General Assembly of the United Nations in its resolution 96(I) dated 11 December 1946 that genocide is a crime under international law, contrary to the spirit and aims of the United Nations and condemned by the civilized world;

Recognizing that at all periods of history genocide has inflicted great losses on humanity; and

Being convinced that, in order to liberate mankind from such an odious scourge, international co-operation is required;

Hereby agree as hereinafter provided.

Article I

The Contracting Parties confirm that genocide, whether committed in time of peace or in time of war, is a crime under international law which they undertake to prevent and to punish.

Article II

In the present Convention, genocide means any of the following acts committed with intent to destroy, in whole or in part, a national, ethnical, racial or religious group as such:

(a) Killing members of the group;

(b) Causing serious bodily or mental harm to members of the group;

(c) Deliberately inflicting on the group conditions of life calculated to bring about its physical destruction in whole or in part;

(d) Imposing measures intended to prevent births within the group;

(e) Forcibly transferring children of the group to another group.

Article III

The following acts shall be punishable:

(a) Genocide;

(b) Conspiracy to commit genocide;

(c) Direct and public incitement to commit genocide;

(d) Attempt to commit genocide;

(e) Complicity in genocide.

Article IV

Persons committing genocide or any of the other acts enumerated in Article III shall be punished, whether they are constitutionally responsible rulers, public officials or private individuals.

Article V

The Contracting Parties undertake to enact, in accordance with their respective Constitutions, the necessary legislation to give effect to the provisions of the present Convention and, in particular, to provide effective penalties for persons guilty of genocide or any of the other acts enumerated in Article III.

Article VI

Persons charged with genocide or any of the other acts enumerated in Article III shall be tried by a competent tribunal of the State in the territory of which the act was committed, or by such international penal tribunal as may have jurisdiction with respect to those Contracting Parties which shall have accepted its jurisdiction.

Article VII

Genocide and the other acts enumerated in Article III shall not be considered as political crimes for the purpose of extradition.

The Contracting Parties pledge themselves in such cases to grant extradition in accordance with their laws and treaties in force.

Article VIII

Any Contracting Party may call upon the competent organs of the United Nations to take such action under the Charter of the United Nations as they consider appropriate for the prevention and suppression of acts of genocide or any of the other acts enumerated in Article III.

Article IX

Disputes between the Contracting Parties relating to the interpretation, application or fulfilment of the present Convention, including those relating to the responsibility of a State for genocide or any of the other acts enumerated in Article II, shall be submitted to the International Court of Justice at the request of any of the parties to the dispute.

Document 42
INTERNATIONAL CONVENTION ON THE SUPPRESSION AND PUNISHMENT OF THE CRIME OF "APARTHEID"

Done in New York, Nov. 30, 1973; 1015 U.N.T.S. 243

Article I

(1) The States Parties to the present Convention declare that *apartheid* is a crime against humanity and that inhuman acts resulting from the policies and practices of *apartheid* and similar policies and practices of racial segregation and discrimination, as defined in Article II of the Convention, are crimes violating the principles of international law, in particular the purposes and principles of the Charter of the United Nations, and constituting a serious threat to international peace and security.

(2) States Parties to the present Convention declare criminal those organizations, institutions and individuals committing the crime of *apartheid.*

Article II

For the purpose of the present Convention, the term "the crime of *apartheid*" which shall include similar policies and practices of racial segregation and discrimination as practiced in southern Africa, shall apply to the following inhuman acts committed for the purpose of establishing and maintaining domination by one racial group of persons over any other racial group of persons and systematically oppressing them:

(a) Denial to a member or members of a racial group or groups of the right to life and liberty of person:

(i) By murder of members of a racial group or groups;

(ii) By the infliction upon the members of a racial group or groups of serious bodily or mental harm by the infringement of their freedom or dignity, or by subjecting them to torture or to cruel, inhuman or degrading treatment or punishment;

(iii) By arbitrary arrest and illegal imprisonment of the members of a racial group or groups;

(b) Deliberate imposition on a racial group or groups of living conditions calculated to cause its or their physical destruction in whole or in part;

(c) Any legislative measures and other measures calculated to prevent a racial group or groups from participation in the political, social, economic and cultural life of the country and the deliberate creation of conditions preventing the full development of such a group or groups, in particular by denying to members of a racial group or groups basic human rights and freedoms, including the right to work, the right to form recognized trade unions, the right to education, the right to leave and to return to their country, the right to freedom of opinion and expression, and the right to freedom of peaceful assembly and association;

(d) Any measures, including legislative measures, designed to divide the population along racial lines by the creation of separate reserves and ghettos for the members of a racial group or groups, the prohibition of mixed marriages among members of various racial groups, the expropriation of landed property belonging to a racial group or groups or to members thereof;

(e) Exploitation of the labour of the members of a racial group or groups, in particular by submitting them to forced labour;

(f) Persecution of organizations and persons, by depriving them of fundamental rights and freedoms, because they oppose *apartheid*.

Article III

International criminal responsibility shall apply, irrespective of the motive involved, to individuals, members of organizations and institutions and representatives of the State, whether residing in the territory of the State in which the acts are perpetrated or in some other State, whenever they:

(a) Commit, participate in, directly incite or conspire in the commission of the acts mentioned in Article II of the present Convention;

(b) Directly abet, encourage or co-operate in the commission of the crime of *apartheid*.

Article IV

The States Parties to the present Convention undertake:

(a) To adopt any legislative or other measure necessary to suppress as well as to prevent any encouragement of the crime of *apartheid* and similar segregationist policies or their manifestations and to punish persons guilty of that crime;

(b) To adopt legislative, judicial and administrative measures to prosecute, bring to trial and punish in accordance with their jurisdiction persons responsible for, or accused of, the acts defined in Article II of the present Convention, whether or not such persons reside in the territory of the State in which the acts are committed or are nationals of that State or of some other State or are stateless persons.

Article V

Persons charged with the acts enumerated in Article II of the present Convention may be tried by a competent tribunal of any State Party to the Convention which may acquire jurisdiction with respect to those State Parties which shall have accepted its jurisdiction.

Article VI

The States Parties to the present Convention undertake to accept and carry out in accordance with the Charter of the United Nations the decisions taken by the Security Council aimed at the prevention, suppression and punishment of the crime of *apartheid,* and to co-operate in the implementation of decisions adopted by other competent organs of the United Nations with a view to achieving the purposes of the Convention....

Article XI

(1) Acts enumerated in Article II of the present Convention shall not be considered political crimes for the purpose of extradition.

(2) The States Parties to the present Convention undertake in such cases to grant extradition with their legislation and with the treaties in force.

Document 43
INTERNATIONAL CONVENTION ON THE ELIMINATION OF ALL FORMS OF RACIAL DISCRIMINATION

660 U.N.T.S. 195 (opened for signature Mar. 7, 1966)

Part I

Article 1

1. In this Convention, the term "racial discrimination" shall mean any distinction, exclusion, restriction or preference based on race, colour, descent, or national or ethnic origin which has the purpose or effect of nullifying or impairing the recognition, enjoyment or exercise, on an equal footing, of human rights and fundamental freedoms in the political, economic, social, cultural or any other field of public life.

2. This Convention shall not apply to distinctions, exclusions, restrictions or preferences made by a State Party to this Convention between citizens and non-citizens.

3. Nothing in this Convention may be interpreted as affecting in any way the legal provisions of States Parties concerning nationality, citizenship or naturalization, provided that such provisions do not discriminate against any particular nationality.

4. Special measures taken for the sole purpose of securing adequate advancement of certain racial or ethnic groups or individuals requiring such protection as may be necessary in order to ensure such groups or individuals equal enjoyment or exercise of human rights and fundamental freedoms shall not be deemed racial discrimination, provided, however, that such measures do not, as a consequence, lead to the maintenance of separate rights for different racial groups and that they shall not be continued after the objectives for which they were taken have been achieved.

Article 2

1. States Parties condemn racial discrimination and undertake to pursue by all appropriate means and without delay a policy of eliminating racial discrimination in all its forms and promoting understanding among all races, and, to this end:

(a) Each State Party undertakes to engage in no act or practice of racial discrimination against persons, groups of persons or institutions and to ensure that all public authorities and public institutions, national and local, shall act in conformity with this obligation;

(b) Each State Party undertakes not to sponsor, defend or support racial discrimination by any persons or organizations;

(c) Each State Party shall take effective measures to review governmental, national and local policies, and to amend, rescind or nullify any laws and regulations which have the effect of creating or perpetuating racial discrimination wherever it exists;

(d) Each State Party shall prohibit and bring to an end, by all appropriate means, including legislation as required by circumstances, racial discrimination by any persons, group or organization;

(e) Each State Party undertakes to encourage, where appropriate, integrationist multi-racial organizations and movements and other means of eliminating barriers between races, and to discourage anything which tends to strengthen racial division.

2. States Parties shall, when the circumstances so warrant, take, in the social, economic, cultural and other fields, special and concrete measures to ensure the adequate development and protection of certain racial groups or individuals belonging to them, for the purpose of guaranteeing them the full and equal enjoyment of human rights and fundamental freedoms. These measures shall in no case entail as a consequence the maintenance or unequal or separate rights for different racial groups after the objectives for which they were taken have been achieved.

Article 3

States Parties particularly condemn racial segregation and apartheid and undertake to prevent, prohibit and eradicate all practices of this nature in territories under their jurisdiction.

Article 4

States Parties condemn all propaganda and all organizations which are based on ideas or theories of superiority of one race or group of persons of one colour or ethnic origin, or which attempt to justify or promote racial hatred and discrimination in any form, and undertake to adopt immediate and positive measures designed to eradicate all incitement to, or acts of, such discrimination and, to this end, with due regard to the principles embodied in the Universal Declaration of Human Rights and the rights expressly set forth in Article 5 of this Convention, *inter alia*:

(a) Shall declare an offence punishable by law all dissemination of ideas based on racial superiority or hatred, incitement to racial discrimination, as well as all acts of violence or incitement to such acts against any race or group of persons of another colour or ethnic origin, and also the provision of any assistance to racist activities, including the financing thereof;

(b) Shall declare illegal and prohibit organizations, and also organized and all other propaganda activities, which promote and incite racial discrimination, and shall recognize participation in such organizations or activities as an offence punishable by law;

(c) Shall not permit public authorities or public institutions, national or local, to promote or incite racial discrimination.

Article 5

In compliance with the fundamental obligations laid down in Article 2 of this Convention, States Parties undertake to prohibit and to eliminate racial discrimination in all its forms and to guarantee the right of everyone, without distinction as to race, colour, or national or ethnic origin, to equality before the law, notably in the enjoyment of the following rights:

(a) The right to equal treatment before the tribunals and all other organs administering justice;

(b) The right to security of person and protection by the State against violence or bodily harm, whether inflicted by government officials or by any individual, group or institution;

(c) Political rights, in particular the rights to participate in elections—to vote and to stand for election—on the basis of universal and equal suffrage, to take part in the Government as well as in the conduct of public affairs at any level and to have equal access to public service;

(d) Other civil rights, in particular:

(i) The right to freedom of movement and residence within the border of the State;

(ii) The right to leave any country, including one's own, and to return to one's country;

(iii) The right to nationality;

(iv) The right to marriage and choice of spouse;

(v) The right to own property alone as well as in association with others;

(vi) The right to inherit;

(vii) The right to freedom of thought, conscience and religion;

(viii) The right to freedom of opinion and expression;

(ix) The right to freedom of peaceful assembly and association;

(e) Economic, social and cultural rights, in particular:

(i) The rights to work, to free choice of employment, to just and favourable conditions of work, to protection against unemployment, to equal pay for equal work, to just and favourable remuneration;

(ii) The right to form and join trade unions;

(iii) The right to housing;

(iv) The right to public health, medical care, social security and social services;

(v) The right to education and training;

(vi) The right to equal participation in cultural activities;

(f) The right of access to any place or service intended for use by the general public, such as transport, hotels, restaurants, cafes, theatres and parks.

Article 6

States Parties shall assure to everyone within their jurisdiction effective protection and remedies, through the competent national tribunals and other State institutions, against any acts of racial discrimination which violate his human rights and fundamental freedoms contrary to this Convention, as well as the right to seek from such tribunals just and adequate reparation or satisfaction for any damage suffered as a result of such discrimination.

Article 7

States Parties undertake to adopt immediate and effective measures, particularly in the fields of teaching, education, culture and information, with a view to combating prejudices which lead to racial discrimination and to promoting understanding, tolerance and friendship among nations and racial or ethnical groups, as well as to propagating the purposes and principles of the Charter of the United Nations, the Universal Declaration of Human Rights, the United Nations Declaration on the Elimination of All Forms of Racial Discrimination, and this Convention.

PART II

Article 8

1. There shall be established a Committee on the Elimination of Racial Discrimination (hereinafter referred to as the Committee) consisting of eighteen experts of high moral standing and acknowledged impartiality elected by States Parties from among their nationals, who shall serve in their personal capacity, consideration being given to equitable geographical distribution and to the representation of the different forms of civilization as well as of the principal legal systems.

2. The members of the Committee shall be elected by secret ballot from a list of persons nominated by the States Parties. Each State Party may nominate one person from among its own nationals.

3. The initial election shall be held six months after the date of the entry into force of this Convention. At least three months before the date of each election the Secretary–General of the United Nations shall address a letter to the States Parties inviting them to submit their nominations within two months. The Secretary–General shall prepare a list in alphabetical order of all persons thus nominated, indicating the States Parties which have nominated them, and shall submit it to the States Parties.

4. Elections of the members of the Committee shall be held at a meeting of States Parties convened by the Secretary–General at United

Nations Headquarters. At that meeting, for which two-thirds of the States Parties shall constitute a quorum, the persons elected to the Committee shall be those nominees who obtain the largest number of votes and an absolute majority of the votes of the representatives of States Parties present and voting.

5. (a) The members of the Committee shall be elected for a term of four years. However, the terms of nine of the members elected at the first election shall expire at the end of two years; immediately after the first election the names of these nine members shall be chosen by lot by the Chairman of the Committee.

(b) For the filling of casual vacancies, the State Party whose expert has ceased to function as a member of the Committee shall appoint another expert from among its nationals, subject to the approval of the Committee.

6. States Parties shall be responsible for the expenses of the members of the Committee while they are in performance of Committee duties.

Article 9

1. States Parties undertake to submit to the Secretary–General of the United Nations, for consideration by the Committee, a report on the legislative, judicial, administrative or other measures which they have adopted and which give effect to the provisions of this Convention:

(a) within one year after the entry into force of the Convention for the State concerned; and

(b) thereafter every two years and whenever the Committee so requests. The Committee may request further information from the States Parties.

2. The Committee shall report annually, through the Secretary–General, to the General Assembly of the United Nations on its activities and may make suggestions and general recommendations based on the examination of the reports and information received from the States Parties. Such suggestions and general recommendations shall be reported to the General Assembly together with comments, if any, from States Parties.

Article 10

1. The Committee shall adopt its own rules of procedure.

2. The Committee shall elect its officers for a term of two years.

3. The secretariat of the Committee shall be provided by the Secretary–General of the United Nations.

4. The meetings of the Committee shall normally be held at United Nations Headquarters.

Article 11

1. If a State Party considers that another State Party is not giving effect to the provisions of this Convention, it may bring the matter to the

attention of the Committee. The Committee shall then transmit the communication to the State Party concerned. Within three months, the receiving State shall submit to the Committee written explanations or statements clarifying the matter and the remedy, if any, that may have been taken by that State.

2. If the matter is not adjusted to the satisfaction of both parties, either by bilateral negotiations or by any other procedure open to them, within six months after the receipt by the receiving State of the initial communication, either State shall have the right to refer the matter again to the Committee by notifying the Committee and also the other State.

3. The Committee shall deal with a matter referred to it in accordance with paragraph 2 of this article after it has ascertained that all available domestic remedies have been invoked and exhausted in the case, in conformity with the generally recognized principles of international law. This shall not be the rule where the application of the remedies is unreasonably prolonged.

4. In any matter referred to it, the Committee may call upon the States Parties concerned to supply any other relevant information.

5. When any matter arising out of this article is being considered by the Committee, the States Parties concerned shall be entitled to send a representative to take part in the proceedings of the Committee, without voting rights, while the matter is under consideration.

Article 12

1. (a) After the Committee has obtained and collated all the information it deems necessary, the Chairman shall appoint an ad hoc Conciliation Commission (hereinafter referred to as the Commission) comprising five persons who may or may not be members of the Committee. The members of the Commission shall be appointed with the unanimous consent of the parties to the dispute, and its good offices shall be made available to the States concerned with a view to an amicable solution of the matter on the basis or respect for this Convention.

(b) If the States Parties to the dispute fail to reach agreement within three months on all or part of the composition of the Commission, the members of the Commission not agreed upon by the States parties to the dispute shall be elected by secret ballot by a two-thirds majority vote of the Committee from among its own members.

2. The members of the Commission shall serve in their personal capacity. They shall not be nationals of the States parties to the dispute or of a State not Party to this Convention.

3. The Commission shall elect its own Chairman and adopt its own rules of procedure.

4. The meetings of the Commission shall normally be held at United Nations Headquarters or at any other convenient place as determined by the Commission.

5. The secretariat provided in accordance with Article 10, paragraph 3, of this Convention shall also service the Commission whenever a dispute among States Parties brings the Commission into being.

6. The States parties to the dispute shall share equally all the expenses of the members of the Commission in accordance with estimates to be provided by the Secretary–General of the United Nations.

7. The Secretary–General shall be empowered to pay the expenses of the members of the Commission, if necessary, before reimbursement by the States parties to the dispute in accordance with paragraph 6 of this article.

8. The information obtained and collated by the Committee shall be made available to the Commission, and the Commission may call upon the States concerned to supply any other relevant information.

Article 13

1. When the Commission has fully considered the matter, it shall prepare and submit to the Chairman of the Committee a report embodying its findings on all questions of fact relevant to the issue between the parties and containing such recommendations as it may think proper for the amicable solution of the dispute.

2. The Chairman of the Committee shall communicate the report of the Commission to each of the States Parties to the dispute. These States shall, within three months, inform the Chairman of the Committee whether or not they accept the recommendations contained in the report of the Commission.

3. After the period provided for in paragraph 2 of Chairman of the Committee shall communicate the report of the Commission and the declarations of the States Parties concerned to the other States Parties to this Convention.

Article 14

1. A State Party may at any time declare that it recognizes the competence of the Committee to receive and consider communications from individuals or groups of individuals within its jurisdiction claiming to be victims of a violation by that State Party of any of the rights set forth in this Convention. No communication shall be received by the Committee if it concerns a State Party which has not made such a declaration.

2. Any State Party which makes a declaration as provided for in paragraph 1 of this article may establish or indicate a body within its national legal order which shall be competent to receive and consider petitions from individuals and groups of individuals within its jurisdiction who claim to be victims of a violation of any of the rights set forth in this Convention and who have exhausted other available local remedies.

3. A declaration made in accordance with paragraph 1 of this article and the name of any body established or indicated in accordance with paragraph 2 of this article shall be deposited by the State Party

concerned with the Secretary–General of the United Nations, who shall transmit copies thereof to the other States Parties. A declaration may be withdrawn at any time by notification to the Secretary–General, but such a withdrawal shall not affect communications pending before the Committee.

4. A register of petitions shall be kept by the body established or indicated in accordance with paragraph 2 of this article, and certified copies of the register shall be filed annually through appropriate channels with the Secretary–General on the understanding that the contents shall not be publicly disclosed.

5. In the event of failure to obtain satisfaction from the body established or indicated in accordance with paragraph 2 of this article, the petitioner shall have the right to communicate the matter to the Committee within six months.

6. (a) The Committee shall confidentially bring any communication referred to it to the attention of the State Party alleged to be violating any provision of this Convention, but the identity of the individual or groups of individuals concerned shall not be revealed without his or their express consent. The Committee shall not receive anonymous communications.

(b) Within three months, the receiving State shall submit to the Committee written explanations or statements clarifying the matter and the remedy, if any, that may have been taken by that State.

7. (a) The Committee shall consider communications in the light of all information made available to it by the State Party concerned and by the petitioner. The Committee shall not consider any communication from a petitioner unless it has ascertained that the petitioner has exhausted all available domestic remedies. However, this shall not be the rule where the application of the remedies is unreasonably prolonged.

(b) The Committee shall forward its suggestions and recommendations, if any, to the State Party concerned and to the petitioner.

8. The Committee shall include in its annual report a summary of such communications and, where appropriate, a summary of the explanations and statements of the States Parties concerned and of its own suggestions and recommendations.

9. The Committee shall be competent to exercise the functions provided for in this article only when at least ten States Parties to this Convention are bound by declarations in accordance with paragraph 1 of this article. . . .

Article 20

1. The Secretary–General of the United Nations shall receive and circulate to all States which are or may become Parties to this Convention reservations made by States at the time of ratification or accession. Any State which objects to the reservation shall, within a period of

ninety days from the date of the said communication, notify the Secretary–General that it does not accept it.

2. A reservation incompatible with the object and purpose of this Convention shall not be permitted, nor shall a reservation the effect of which would inhibit the operation of any of the bodies established by this Convention be allowed. A reservation shall be considered incompatible or inhibitive if at least two-thirds of the States Parties to this Convention object to it.

3. Reservations may be withdrawn at any time by notification to this effect addressed to the Secretary–General. Such notification shall take effect on the date on which it is received....

Article 22

Any dispute between two or more States Parties with respect to the interpretation or application of this Convention, which is not settled by negotiation or by the procedures expressly provided for in this Convention, shall, at the request of any of the parties to the dispute, be referred to the International Court of Justice for decision, unless the disputants agree to another mode of settlement.

Document 44
CONVENTION ON THE ELIMINATION OF ALL FORMS OF DISCRIMINATION AGAINST WOMEN

1249 U.N.T.S. 13 (Dec. 18, 1979)

The States Parties to the present Convention,

Noting that the Charter of the United Nations reaffirms faith in fundamental human rights, in the dignity and worth of the human person and in the equal rights of men and women,

Noting that the Universal Declaration of Human Rights affirms the principle of the inadmissibility of discrimination and proclaims that all human beings are born free and equal in dignity and rights and that everyone is entitled to all the rights and freedoms set forth therein, without distinction of any kind including distinction based on sex,

Noting that States Parties to the International Covenant on Human Rights have the obligation to secure the equal rights or men and women to enjoy all economic, social, cultural, civil and political rights,

Considering the international conventions concluded under the auspices of the United Nations and the specialized agencies promoting equality of rights of men and women,

Noting also the resolutions, declarations and recommendations adopted by the United Nations and the specialized agencies promoting equality of rights of men and women, . . .

Concerned, however, that despite these various instruments extensive discrimination against women continues to exist,

Recalling that discrimination against women violates the principles of equality of rights and respect for human dignity, is an obstacle to the participation of women, on equal terms with men, in the political, social, economic and cultural life of their countries, hampers the growth of the prosperity of society and the family, and makes more difficult the full development of the potentialities of women in the service of their countries and of humanity,

Concerned that in situations of poverty women have the least access to food, health, education, training and opportunities for employment and other needs,

Convinced that the establishment of the new international economic order based on equity and justice will contribute significantly towards the promotion of equality between men and women,

Emphasizing that the eradication of *apartheid*, of all forms of racism, racial discrimination, colonialism, neo-colonialism, aggression, foreign occupation and domination and interference in the internal affairs of States is essential to the full enjoyment of the rights of men and women,

Convinced that the full and complete development of a country, the welfare of the world and the cause of peace require the maximum participation of women on equal terms with men in all fields,

Bearing in mind the great contribution of women to the welfare of the family and to the development of society, so far not fully recognized, the social significance of maternity and the role of both parents in the family and in the upbringing of children, and aware that the role of women in procreation should not be a basis for discrimination but that the upbringing of children requires a sharing of responsibility between men and women and society as a whole,

Aware that a change in the traditional role of men as well as the role of women in society and in the family is needed to achieve full equality between men and women,

Determined to implement the principles set forth in the Declaration on the Elimination of Discrimination against Women and, for that purpose, to adopt the measures required for the elimination of such discrimination in all its forms and manifestations,

Have agreed on the following:

PART I

Article 1

For the purposes of the present Convention, the term "discrimination against women" shall mean any distinction, exclusion or restriction made on the basis of sex which has the effect or purpose of impairing or nullifying the recognition, enjoyment or exercise by women, irrespective of their marital status, on a basis of equality of men and women, of human rights and fundamental freedoms in the political, economic, social, cultural, civil or any other field.

Article 2

States Parties condemn discrimination against women in all its forms, agree to pursue, by all appropriate means and without delay, a policy of eliminating discrimination against women and, to this end, undertake:

(a) To embody the principle of the equality of men and women in their national Constitutions or other appropriate legislation if not yet incorporated therein, and to ensure, through law and other appropriate means, the practical realization of this principle;

(b) To adopt appropriate legislative and other measures, including sanctions where appropriate, prohibiting all discrimination against women;

(c) To establish legal protection of the rights of women on an equal basis with men and to ensure through competent national tribunals and other public institutions the effective protection of women against any act of discrimination;

(d) To refrain from engaging in any act or practice of discrimination against women and to ensure that public authorities and institutions shall act in conformity with this obligation;

(e) To take all appropriate measures to eliminate discrimination against women by any person, organization or enterprise;

(f) To take all appropriate measures, including legislation, to modify or abolish existing laws, regulations, customs and practices which constitute discrimination against women;

(g) To repeal all national penal provisions which constitute discrimination against women.

Article 3

States Parties shall take in all fields, in particular in the political, social, economic and cultural fields, all appropriate measures, including legislation, to ensure the full development and advancement of women, for the purpose of guaranteeing them the exercise and enjoyment of human rights and fundamental freedoms on a basis of equality with men.

Article 4

1. Adoption by States Parties of temporary special measures aimed at accelerating *de facto* equality between men and women shall not be considered discrimination as defined in this Convention, but shall in no way entail, as a consequence, the maintenance of unequal or separate standards; these measures shall be discontinued when the objectives of equality of opportunity and treatment have been achieved.

2. Adoption by States Parties of special measures including those measures contained in the present Convention, aimed at protecting maternity, shall not be considered discriminatory.

Article 5

States Parties shall take all appropriate measures:

(a) To modify the social and cultural patterns of conduct of men and women, with a view to achieving the elimination of prejudices and customary and all other practices which are based on the idea of the inferiority or the superiority of either of the sexes or on stereotyped roles for men and women;

(b) To ensure that family education includes a proper understanding of maternity as a social function and the recognition of the common responsibility of men and women in the upbringing and development of their children, it being understood that the interest of the children is the primordial consideration in all cases.

Article 6

States Parties shall take all appropriate measures, including legislation, to suppress all forms of traffic in women and exploitation of prostitution of women.

PART II

Article 7

States Parties shall take all appropriate measures to eliminate discrimination against women in the political and public life of the country and, in particular, shall ensure, on equal terms with men, the right:

(a) To vote in all elections and public referenda and to be eligible for election to all publicly elected bodies;

(b) To participate in the formulation of government policy and the implementation thereof and to hold public office and perform all public functions at all levels of government;

(c) To participate in non-governmental organizations and associations concerned with the public and political life of the country.

Article 8

States Parties shall take all appropriate measures to ensure to women on equal terms with men and, without any discrimination, the opportunity to represent their Governments at the international level and to participate in the work of international organizations.

Article 9

1. States Parties shall grant women equal rights with men to acquire, change or retain their nationality. They shall ensure in particular that neither marriage to an alien nor change of nationality by the husband during marriage shall automatically change the nationality of the wife, render her stateless or force upon her the nationality of the husband.

2. States Parties shall grant women equal rights with men with respect to the nationality of their children.

PART III

Article 10

States Parties shall take all appropriate measures to eliminate discrimination against women in order to ensure to them equal rights with men in the field of education and in particular to ensure, on a basis of equality of men and women:

(a) The same conditions for career and vocational guidance, for access to studies and for the achievement of diplomas in educational establishments of all categories in rural as well as in urban areas; this equality shall be ensured in pre-school, general, technical, professional and higher technical education, as well as in all types of vocational training;

(b) Access to the same curricula, the same examinations, teaching staff with qualifications of the same standard and school premises and equipment of the same quality;

(c) The elimination of any stereotyped concept of the roles of men and women at all levels and in all forms of education by encouraging coeducation and other types of education which will help to achieve this aim and, in particular, by the revision of textbooks and school programmes and the adaptation of teaching methods;

(d) The same opportunities to benefit from scholarships and other study grants;

(e) The same opportunities for access to programmes of continuing education, including adult and functional literacy programmes, particularly those aimed at reducing, at the earliest possible time, any gap in education existing between men and women;

(f) The reduction of female student drop-out rates and the organization of programmes for girls and women who have left school prematurely;

(g) The same opportunities to participate actively in sports and physical education;

(h) Access to specific educational information to help to ensure the health and well-being of families, including information and advice on family planning.

Article 11

1. States Parties shall take all appropriate measures to eliminate discrimination against women in the field of employment in order to ensure, on a basis of equality of men and women, the same rights, in particular:

(a) The right to work as an inalienable right of all human beings;

(b) The right to the same employment opportunities, including the application of the same criteria for selection in matters of employment;

(c) The right to free choice of profession and employment, the right to promotion, job security and all benefits and conditions of service and the right to receive vocational training and retraining, including apprenticeships, advanced vocational training and recurrent training;

(d) The right to equal remuneration, including benefits, and to equal treatment in respect of work of equal value, as well as equality of treatment in the evaluation of the quality of work;

(e) The right to social security, particularly in cases of retirement, unemployment, sickness, invalidity and old age and other incapacity to work, as well as the right to paid leave;

(f) The right to protection of health and to safety in working conditions, including the safeguarding of the function of reproduction.

2. In order to prevent discrimination against women on the grounds of marriage or maternity and to ensure their effective right to work, States Parties shall take appropriate measures:

(a) To prohibit, subject to the imposition of sanctions, dismissal on the grounds of pregnancy or of maternity leave and discrimination in dismissals on the basis of marital status;

(b) To introduce maternity leave with pay or with comparable social benefits without loss of former employment, seniority or social allowances;

(c) To encourage the provision of the necessary supporting social services to enable parents to combine family obligations with work responsibilities and participation in public life, in particular through promoting the establishment and development of a network of child-care facilities;

(d) To provide special protection to women during pregnancy in types of work proved to be harmful to them.

3. Protective legislation relating to matters covered in this article shall be reviewed periodically in the light of scientific and technological knowledge and shall be revised, repealed or extended as necessary.

Article 12

1. States Parties shall take all appropriate measures to eliminate discrimination against women in the field of health care in order to ensure, on a basis of equality of men and women, access to health care services, including those related to family planning.

2. Notwithstanding the provisions of paragraph 1 above, States Parties shall ensure to women appropriate services in connection with pregnancy, confinement and the post-natal period, granting free services where necessary, as well as adequate nutrition during pregnancy and lactation.

Article 13

States Parties shall take all appropriate measures to eliminate discrimination against women in other areas of economic and social life in order to ensure, on a basis of equality of men and women the same rights, in particular:

(a) The right to family benefits;

(b) The right to bank loans, mortgages and other forms of financial credit;

(c) The right to participate in recreational activities, sports and in all aspects of cultural life.

Article 14

1. States Parties shall take into account the particular problems faced by rural women and the significant roles which they play in the economic survival of their families, including their work in the nonmonetized sectors of the economy, and shall take all appropriate measures to ensure the application of the provisions of this Convention to women in rural areas.

2. States Parties shall take all appropriate measures to eliminate discrimination against women in rural areas in order to ensure, on a basis of equality of men and women, that they participate in and benefit from rural development and, in particular, shall ensure to such women the right:

(a) To participate in the elaboration and implementation of development planning at all levels;

(b) To have access to adequate health care facilities, including information, counselling and services in family planning;

(c) To benefit directly from social security programmes;

(d) To obtain all types of training and education, formal and non-formal, including that relating to functional literacy, as well as the benefit of all community and extension services, *inter alia*, in order to increase their technical proficiency;

(e) To organize self-help groups and co-operatives in order to obtain equal access to economic opportunities through employment or self-employment;

(f) To participate in all community activities;

(g) To have access to agricultural credit and loans, marketing facilities, appropriate technology and equal treatment in land and agrarian reform as well as in land resettlement schemes;

(h) To enjoy adequate living conditions, particularly in relation to housing, sanitation, electricity and water supply, transport and communications.

PART IV

Article 15

1. States Parties shall accord to women equality with men before the law.

2. States Parties shall accord to women, in civil matters, a legal capacity identical to that of men and the same opportunities to exercise that capacity. They shall in particular give women equal rights to conclude contracts and to administer property and treat them equally in all stages of procedure in courts and tribunals.

3. States Parties agree that all contract and all other private instruments of any kind with a legal effect which is directed at restricting the legal capacity of women shall be deemed null and void.

4. States Parties shall accord to men and women the same rights with regard to the law relating to the movement of persons and the freedom to choose their residence and domicile.

Article 16

1. States Parties shall take all appropriate measures to eliminate discrimination against women in all matters relating to marriage and family relations and in particular shall ensure, on a basis of equality of men and women;

(a) The same right to enter into marriage;

(b) The same right freely to choose a spouse and to enter into marriage only with their free and full consent;

(c) The same rights and responsibilities during marriage and at its dissolution;

(d) The same rights and responsibilities as parents, irrespective of their marital status, in matters relating to their children. In all cases the interests of the children shall be paramount;

(e) The same rights to decide freely and responsibly on the number and spacing of their children and to have access to the information, education and means to enable them to exercise these rights;

(f) The same rights and responsibilities with regard to guardianship, wardship, trusteeship and adoption of children, or similar institutions where these concepts exist in national legislation. In all cases the interest of the children shall be paramount;

(g) The same personal rights as husband and wife, including the right to choose a family name, a profession and an occupation;

(h) The same rights for both spouses in respect of the ownership, acquisition, management, administration, enjoyment and disposition of property, whether free of charge or for a valuable consideration.

2. The betrothal and the marriage of a child shall have no legal effect and all necessary action, including legislation, shall be taken to specify a minimum age for marriage and to make the registration of marriages in an official registry compulsory.

PART V

Article 17

1. For the purpose of considering the progress made in the implementation of the present Convention, there shall be established a Committee on the Elimination of Discrimination against Women (hereinafter referred to as the Committee) consisting, at the time of entry into force of the Convention, of 18 and, after its ratification or accession by the thirty-fifth State Party, of 23 experts of high moral standing and competence in the field covered by the Convention. The experts shall be elected by States Parties from among their nationals and shall serve in their personal capacity, consideration being given to equitable geographi-

cal distribution and to the representation of the different forms of civilization as well as the principal legal systems.

2. The members of the Committee shall be elected by secret ballot from a list of persons nominated by States Parties. Each State Party may nominate one person from among its own nationals.

3. The initial election shall be held six months after the date of the entry into force of the present Convention. At least three months before the date of each election the Secretary–General of the United Nations shall address a letter to the States Parties inviting them to submit their nominations within two months. The Secretary–General shall prepare a list in alphabetical order of all persons thus nominated, indicating the States Parties which have nominated them, and shall submit it to the States Parties.

4. Elections of the members of the Committee shall be held at a meeting of States Parties convened by the Secretary–General at United Nations Headquarters. At that meeting, for which two thirds of the States Parties shall constitute a quorum, the persons elected to the Committee shall be those nominees who obtain the largest number of votes and an absolute majority of the votes of the representatives of States Parties present and voting.

5. The members of the Committee shall be elected for a term of four years. However, the terms of nine of the members elected at the first election shall expire at the end of two years; immediately after the first election the names of these nine members shall be chosen by lot by the Chairman of the Committee.

6. The election of the five additional members of the Committee shall be held in accordance with the provisions of paragraphs 2, 3 and 4 of the present article following the thirty-fifth ratification or accession. The terms of two of the additional members elected on this occasion shall expire at the end of two years, the names of these two members having been chosen by lot by the Chairman of the Committee.

7. For the filling of casual vacancies, the State Party whose expert has ceased to function as a member of the Committee shall appoint another expert from among its nationals, subject to the approval of the Committee.

8. The members of the Committee shall, with the approval of the General Assembly, receive emoluments from United Nations resources on such terms and conditions as the General Assembly may decide, having regard to the importance of the Committee's responsibilities.

9. The Secretary–General of the United Nations shall provide the necessary staff and facilities for the effective performance of the functions of the Committee under the present Convention.

Article 18

1. States Parties undertake to submit to the Secretary–General of the United Nations, for consideration by the Committee, a report on the legislative, judicial, administrative or other measures which they have

adopted to give effect to the provisions of the Convention and on the progress made in this respect:

(a) Within one year after the entry into force for the State concerned;

(b) Thereafter at least every four years and further whenever the Committee so requests.

2. Reports may indicate factors and difficulties affecting the degree of fulfillment of obligations under the present Convention.

Article 19

1. The Committee shall adopt its own rules of procedure.

2. The Committee shall elect its officers for a term of two years.

Article 20

1. The Committee shall normally meet for a period of not more than two weeks annually in order to consider the reports submitted in accordance with Article 18 of the present Convention.

2. The meetings of the Committee shall normally be held at United Nations Headquarters or at any other convenient place as determined by the Committee.

Article 21

1. The Committee shall, through the Economic and Social Council, report annually to the General Assembly on its activities and may make suggestions and general recommendations based on the examination of reports and information received from the States Parties. Such suggestions and general recommendations shall be included in the report of the Committee together with comments, if any, from States Parties.

2. The Secretary–General shall transmit the reports of the Committee to the Commission on the Status of Women for its information.

Article 22

Specialized agencies shall be entitled to be represented at the consideration of the implementation of such provisions of the present Convention as fall within the scope of their activities. The Committee may invite the specialized agencies to submit reports on the implementation of the Convention in areas falling within the scope of their activities.

PART VI

Article 23

Nothing in this Convention shall affect any provisions that are more conducive to the achievement of equality between men and women which may be contained:

(a) in the legislation of a State Party; or

(b) in any other international convention, treaty or agreement in force for that State.

Article 24

States Parties undertake to adopt all necessary measures at the national level aimed at achieving the full realization of the rights recognized in the present Convention....

Article 28

1. The Secretary–General of the United Nations shall receive and circulate to all States the text of reservations made by States at the time of ratification or accession.

2. A reservation incompatible with the object and purpose of the present Convention shall not be permitted.

3. Reservations may be withdrawn at any time by notification to this effect addressed to the Secretary–General of the United Nations who shall then inform all States thereof. Such notification shall take effect on the date on which it is received.

Article 29

1. Any dispute between two or more States Parties concerning the interpretation or application of the present Convention which is not settled by negotiation shall, at the request of one of them, be submitted to arbitration. If within six months from the date of the request for arbitration the parties are unable to agree on the organization of the arbitration, any one of those parties may refer the dispute to the International Court of Justice by request in conformity with the Statute of the Court.

2. Each State Party may at the time of signature or ratification of this Convention or accession thereto declare that it does not consider itself bound by paragraph 1 of this article. The other States Parties shall not be bound by paragraph 1 of this article with respect to any State Party which has made such a reservation.

3. Any State Party which has made a reservation in accordance with paragraph 2 of this article may at any time withdraw that reservation by notification to the Secretary–General of the United Nations.

Article 30

The present Convention, the Arabic, Chinese, English, French, Russian and Spanish texts of which are equally authentic, shall be deposited with the Secretary–General of the United Nations.

Document 45
CONVENTION ON THE RIGHTS OF THE CHILD

1577 U.N.T.S. 3

Preamble

The States Parties to the present Convention,

Considering that, in accordance with the principles proclaimed in the Charter of the United Nations, recognition of the inherent dignity and of the equal and inalienable rights of all members of the human family is the foundation of freedom, justice and peace in the world,

Bearing in mind that the peoples of the United Nations have, in the Charter, reaffirmed their faith in fundamental human rights and in the dignity and worth of the human person, and have determined to the promote social progress and better standards of life in larger freedom,

Recognizing that the United Nations has, in the Universal Declaration of Human Rights and in the International Covenants on Human Rights, proclaimed and agreed that everyone is entitled to the all the rights and freedoms set forth therein, without distinction of any kind, such as race, colour, sex, language, religion, political or other opinion, national or social origin, property, birth or other status,

Recalling that, in the Universal Declaration of Human Rights, the United Nations has proclaimed that childhood is entitled to special care and assistance,

Convinced that the family, as the fundamental group of society and the natural environment for the growth and well-being of all its members and particularly children, should be afforded the necessary protection and assistance so that it can fully assume its responsibilities within the community,

Recognizing that the child, for the full and harmonious development of his or her personality, should grow up in a family environment, in an atmosphere of happiness, love and understanding,

Considering that the child should be fully prepared to the live an individual life in society, and brought up in the spirit of the ideals proclaimed in the Charter of the United Nations, and in particular in the spirit of peace, dignity, tolerance, freedom, equality and solidarity,

Bearing in mind that the need to extend particular care to the child has been stated in the Geneva Declaration of the Rights of the Child of 1924 and in the Declaration of the Rights of the Child adopted by the General Assembly on 20 November 1959 and recognized in the Universal Declaration of Human Rights, in the International Covenant on Civil and Political Rights (in particular in Articles 23 and 24), in the International Covenant on Economic, Social and Cultural Rights (in particular in Article 10) and in the statutes and relevant instruments of specialized agencies and international organizations concerned with the welfare of children,

Bearing in mind that, as indicated in the Declaration of the Rights of the Child, "the child, by reason of his physical and mental immaturity, needs special safeguards and care, including appropriate legal protection, before as well as after birth,"

Recalling the provisions of the Declaration on Social and Legal Principles relating to the Protection and Welfare of Children, with Special Reference to Foster Placement and Adoption Nationally and Internationally; the United Nations Standard Minimum Rules for the Administration of Juvenile Justice (The Beijing Rules); and the Declaration on the Protection of Women and Children in Emergency and Armed Conflict,

Recognizing that, in all countries of the world, there are children living in exceptionally difficult conditions, and that such children need special consideration,

Taking due account of the importance of the traditions and cultural values of each people for the protection and harmonious development of the child,

Recognizing the importance of international co-operation for improving the living conditions of children in every country, in particular in the developing countries,

Have agreed as follows:

PART I

Article 1

For the purposes of the present Convention, a child means every human being below the age of eighteen years unless, under the law applicable to the child, majority is attained earlier.

Article 2

1. States Parties shall respect and ensure the rights set forth in the present Convention to each child within their jurisdiction without discrimination of any kind, irrespective of the child's or his or her parent's or legal guardian's race, colour, sex, language, religion, political or other opinion, national, ethnic or social origin, property, disability, birth or other status.

2. States Parties shall take all appropriate measures to ensure that the child is protected against all forms of discrimination or punishment on the basis of the status, activities, expressed opinions, or beliefs of the child's parents, legal guardians, or family members.

Article 3

1. In all actions concerning children, whether undertaken by public or private social welfare institutions, courts of law, administrative au-

thorities or legislative bodies, the best interests of the child shall be a primary consideration.

2. States Parties undertake to ensure the child such protection and care as is necessary for his or her well-being, taking into account the rights and duties of his or her parents, legal guardians, or other individuals legally responsible for him or her, and, to this end, shall take all appropriate legislative and administrative measures.

3. States Parties shall ensure that the institutions, services and facilities responsible for the care or protection of children shall conform with the standards established by competent authorities, particularly in the areas of safety, health, in the number and suitability of their staff, as well as competent supervision.

Article 4

States Parties shall undertake all appropriate legislative, administrative, and other measures for the implementation of the rights recognized in the present Convention. With regard to economic, social and cultural rights, States Parties shall undertake such measures to the maximum extent of their available resources and, where needed, within the framework of international co-operation.

Article 5

States Parties shall respect the responsibilities, rights and duties of parents or, where applicable, the members of the extended family or community as provided for by local custom, legal guardians or other persons legally responsible for the child, to provide, in a manner consistent with the evolving capacities of the child, appropriate direction and guidance in the exercise by the child of the rights recognized in the present Convention.

Article 6

1. States Parties recognize that every child has the inherent right to life.

2. States Parties shall ensure to the maximum extent possible the survival and development of the child.

Article 7

1. The child shall be registered immediately after birth and shall have the right from birth to a name, the right to acquire a nationality and, as far as possible, the right to know and be cared for by his or her parents.

2. States Parties shall ensure the implementation of these rights in accordance with their national law and their obligations under the relevant international instruments in this field, in particular where the child would otherwise be stateless.

Article 8

1. States Parties undertake to respect the right of the child to preserve his or her identity, including nationality, name and family relations as recognized by law without unlawful interference.

2. Where a child is illegally deprived of some or all of the elements of his or her identity, States Parties shall provide appropriate assistance and protection, with a view to speedily reestablishing his or her identity.

Article 9

1. States Parties shall ensure that a child shall not be separated from his or her parents against their will, except when competent authorities subject to judicial review determine, in accordance with applicable law and procedures, that such separation is necessary for the best interests of the child. Such determination may be necessary in a particular case such as one involving abuse or neglect of the child by the parents, or one where the parents are living separately and a decision must be made as to the child's place of residence.

2. In any proceedings pursuant to paragraph 1 of the present article, all interested parties shall be given an opportunity to participate in the proceedings and make their views known.

3. States Parties shall respect the right of the child who is separated from one or both parents to maintain personal relations and direct contact with both parents on a regular basis, except if it is contrary to the child's best interests.

4. Where such separation results from any action initiated by a State Party, such as the detention, imprisonment, exile, deportation or death (including death arising from any cause while the person is in the custody of the State) of one or both parents or of the child, that State Party shall, upon request, provide the parents, the child or, if appropriate, another member or the family with the essential information concerning the whereabouts of the absent member(s) of the family unless the provision of the information would be detrimental to the well-being of the child. States Parties shall further ensure that the submission of such a request shall of itself entail no adverse consequences for the person(s) concerned.

Article 10

1. In accordance with the obligation of States Parties under Article 9, paragraph 1, application by a child or his or her parents to enter or leave a State Party for the purpose of family reunification shall be dealt with by States Parties in a positive, humane and expeditious manner. States Parties shall further ensure that the submission of such a request shall entail no adverse consequences for the applicants and for the members of their family.

2. A child whose parents reside in different States shall have the right to maintain on a regular basis, save in exceptional circumstances, personal relations and direct contact with both parents. Towards that end and in accordance with the obligation of States Parties under Article 9, paragraph 1, States Parties shall respect the right of the child and his or her parents to leave any country, including their own, and to enter their own country. The right to leave any country shall be subject only to such restrictions as are prescribed by law and which are necessary to protect the national security, public order (*ordre public*), public health or

morals or the rights and freedoms of others and are consistent with the other rights recognized in the present Convention.

Article 11

1. States Parties shall take measures to combat the illicit transfer and non-return of children abroad.

2. To this end, States Parties shall promote the conclusion of bilateral or multilateral agreements or accession to existing agreements.

Article 12

1. States Parties shall assure to the child who is capable of forming his or her own views the right to express those views freely in all matters affecting the child, the views of the child being given due weight in accordance with the age and maturity of the child.

2. For this purpose, the child shall in particular be provided the opportunity to be heard in any judicial and administrative proceedings affecting the child, either directly, or through a representative or an appropriate body, in a manner consistent with the procedural rules of national law.

Article 13

1. The child shall have the right to freedom of expression; this right shall include freedom to seek, receive and impart information and ideas of all kinds, regardless of frontiers, either orally, in writing or in print, in the form of art, or through any other media of the child's choice.

2. The exercise of this right may be subject to certain restrictions, but these shall only be such as are provided by law and are necessary:

(a) For respect of the rights or reputations of others; or

(b) For the protection of national security or of public order (*ordre public*), or of public health or morals.

Article 14

1. States Parties shall respect the right of the child to freedom of thought, conscience and religion.

2. States Parties shall respect the rights and duties of the parents and, when applicable, legal guardians, to provide direction to the child in the exercise of his or her right in a manner consistent with the evolving capacities of the child.

3. Freedom to manifest one's religion or beliefs may be subject only to such limitations as are prescribed by law and are necessary to protect public safety, order, health or morals, or the fundamental rights and freedoms of others.

Article 15

1. States Parties recognize the rights of the child to freedom of association and to freedom of peaceful assembly.

2. No restrictions may be placed on the exercise of these rights other than those imposed in conformity with the law and which are necessary in a democratic society in the interests of national security or public safety, public order (*ordre public*), the protection of public health or morals or the protection of the rights and freedoms of others.

Article 16

1. No child shall be subjected to arbitrary or unlawful interference with his or her privacy, family, home or correspondence, nor to unlawful attacks on his or her honour and reputation.

2. The child has the right to the protection of the law against such interference or attacks.

Article 17

States Parties recognize the important function performed by the mass media and shall ensure that the child has access to information and material from a diversity of national and international sources, especially those aimed at the promotion of his or her social, spiritual and moral well-being and physical and mental health. To this end, States Parties shall:

(a) Encourage the mass media to disseminate information and material of social and cultural benefit to the child and in accordance with the spirit of Article 29;

(b) Encourage international co-operation in the production, exchange and dissemination of such information and material from a diversity of cultural, national and international sources;

(c) Encourage the production and dissemination of children's books;

(d) Encourage the mass media to have particular regard to the linguistic needs of the child who belongs to a minority group or who is indigenous;

(e) Encourage the development of appropriate guidelines for the protection of the child from information and material injurious to his or her well-being, bearing in mind the provisions of Articles 13 and 18.

Article 18

1. States Parties shall use their best efforts to ensure recognition of the principle that both parents have common responsibilities for the upbringing and development of the child. Parents or, as the case may be, legal guardians, have the primary responsibility for the upbringing and development of the child. The best interests of the child will be their basic concern.

2. For the purpose of guaranteeing and promoting the rights set forth in the present Convention, States Parties shall render appropriate assistance to parents and legal guardians in the performance of their child-rearing responsibilities and shall ensure the development of institutions, facilities and services for the care of children.

3. States Parties shall take all appropriate measures to ensure that children of working parents have the right to benefit from child-care services and facilities for which they are eligible.

Article 19

1. States Parties shall take all appropriate legislative, administrative, social and educational measures to protect the child from all forms of physical or mental violence, injury or abuse, neglect or negligent treatment, maltreatment or exploitation, including sexual abuse, while in the care of parent(s), legal guardian(s) or any other person who has the care of the child.

2. Such protective measures should, as appropriate, include effective procedures for the establishment of social programmes to provide necessary support for the child and for those who have the care of the child, as well as for other forms of prevention and for identification, reporting, referral, investigation, treatment and follow-up of instances of child maltreatment described heretofore, and, as appropriate, for judicial involvement.

Article 20

1. A child temporarily or permanently deprived of his or her family environment, or in whose own best interests cannot be allowed to remain in that environment, shall be entitled to special protection and assistance provided by the State.

2. States Parties shall in accordance with their national laws ensure alternative care for such a child.

3. Such care could include, *inter alia*, foster placement, *Kafala* of Islamic law, adoption, or if necessary placement in suitable institutions for the care of children. When considering solutions, due regard shall be paid to the desirability of continuity in a child's upbringing and to the child's ethnic, religious, cultural and linguistic background.

Article 21

States Parties that recognize and/or permit the system of adoption shall ensure that the best interests of the child shall be the paramount consideration and they shall:

(a) Ensure that the adoption of a child is authorized only by competent authorities who determine, in accordance with applicable law and procedures and on the basis of all pertinent and reliable information, that the adoption is permissible in view of the child's status concerning parents, relatives and legal guardians and that, if required, the persons concerned have given their informed consent to the adoption on the basis of such counselling as may be necessary;

(b) Recognize that inter-country adoption may be considered as an alternative means of child's care, if the child cannot be placed in a foster or an adoptive family or cannot in any suitable manner be cared for in the child's country of origin;

(c) Ensure that the child concerned by inter-country adoption enjoys safeguards and standards equivalent to those existing in the case of national adoption;

(d) Take all appropriate measures to ensure that, in inter-country adoption, the placement does not result in improper financial gain for those involved in it;

(e) Promote, where appropriate, the objectives of the present article by concluding bilateral or multilateral arrangements, and endeavour, within this framework, to ensure that the placement of the child in another country is carried out by competent authorities or organs.

Article 22

1. States Parties shall take appropriate measures to ensure that a child who is seeking refugee status or who is considered a refugee in accordance with applicable international and domestic law and procedures shall, whether unaccompanied or accompanied by his or her parents or by any other person, receive appropriate protection and humanitarian assistance in the enjoyment of applicable rights set forth in the present Convention and in other international human rights or humanitarian instruments to which the said States are Parties.

2. For this purpose, States Parties shall provide, as they consider appropriate, co-operation in any efforts by the United Nations and other competent intergovernmental organizations or non-governmental organizations co-operating with the United Nations to protect and assist such a child and to trace the parents or other members of the family of any refugee child in order to obtain information necessary for reunification with his or her family. In case where no parents or other members of the family can be found, the child shall be accorded the same protection as any other child permanently or temporarily deprived of his or her family environment for any reason, as set forth in the present Convention.

Article 23

1. States Parties recognize that a mentally or physically disabled child should enjoy a full and decent life, in conditions which ensure dignity, promote self-reliance and facilitate the child's active participation in the community.

2. States Parties recognize the right of the disabled child to special care and shall encourage and ensure the extension, subject to available resources, to the eligible child and those responsible for his or her care, of assistance for which application is made and which is appropriate to the child's condition and to the circumstances of the parents or others caring for the child.

3. Recognizing the special needs of a disabled child, assistance extended in accordance with paragraph 2 of the present article shall be provided free of charge, whenever possible, taking into account the financial resources of the parents or others caring for the child, and shall be designed to ensure that the disabled child has effective access to and receives education, training, health care services, rehabilitation services, preparation for employment and recreation opportunities in a manner

conducive to the child's achieving the fullest possible social integration and individual development, including his or her cultural and spiritual development.

4. States Parties shall promote, in the spirit of international co-operation, the exchange of appropriate information in the field of preventive health care and of medical, psychological and functional treatment of disabled children, including dissemination of and access to information concerning methods of rehabilitation, education and vocational services, with the aim of enabling States Parties to improve their capabilities and skills and to widen their experience in these areas. In this regard, particular account shall be taken of the needs of developing countries.

Article 24

1. States Parties recognize the right of the child to the enjoyment of the highest attainable standard of health and to facilities for the treatment of illness and rehabilitation of health. States Parties shall strive to ensure that no child is deprived of his or her right of access to such health care services.

2. States Parties shall pursue full implementation of this right and, in particular, shall take appropriate measures:

(a) To diminish infant and child mortality;

(b) To ensure the provision of necessary medical assistance and health care to all children with emphasis on the development of primary health care;

(c) To combat disease and malnutrition, including within the framework of primary health care, through, *inter alia*, the application of readily available technology and through the provision of adequate nutritious foods and clean drinking water, taking into consideration the dangers and risks of environmental pollution;

(d) To ensure appropriate pre-and post-natal health care for mothers;

(e) To ensure that all segments of society, in particular parents and children, are informed, have access to education and are supported in the use of basic knowledge of child health and nutrition, the advantages of breast-feeding, hygiene and environmental sanitation and the prevention of accidents;

(f) To develop preventive health care, guidance for parents, and family planning education and services.

3. States Parties shall take all effective and appropriate measures with a view to abolishing traditional practices prejudicial to the health of children.

4. States Parties undertake to promote and encourage international co-operation with a view to achieving progressively the full realization of the right recognized in the present article. In this regard, particular account shall be taken of the needs of developing countries.

Article 25

States Parties recognize the right of a child who has been placed by the competent authorities for the purposes of care, protection or treatment of his or her physical or mental health, to a periodic review of the treatment provided to the child and all other circumstances relevant to his or her placement.

Article 26

1. States Parties shall recognize for every child the right to benefit from social security, including social insurance, and shall take the necessary measures to achieve the full realization of this right in accordance with their national law.

2. The benefits should, where appropriate, be granted, taking into account the resources and the circumstances of the child and persons having responsibility for the maintenance of the child, as well as any other consideration relevant to an application for benefits made by or on behalf of the child.

Article 27

1. States Parties recognize the right of every child to a standard of living adequate for the child's physical, mental, spiritual, moral and social development.

2. The parent(s) or others responsible for the child have the primary responsibility to secure, within their abilities and financial capacities, the conditions of living necessary for the child's development.

3. States Parties, in accordance with national conditions and with their means, shall take appropriate measures to assist parents and others responsible for the child to implement this right and shall in case of need provide material assistance and support programmes, particularly with regard to nutrition, clothing and housing.

4. States Parties shall take all appropriate measures to secure the recovery of maintenance for the child from parents or other persons having financial responsibility for the child, both within the State Party and from abroad. In particular, where the person having financial responsibility for the child lives in a State different from that of the child, States Parties shall promote the accession to international agreements or the conclusion of such agreements, as well as the making of other appropriate arrangements.

Article 28

1. States Parties recognize the right of the child to education, and with a view to achieving this right progressively and on the basis of equal opportunity, they shall, in particular:

(a) Make primary education compulsory and available free to all;

(b) Encourage the development of different forms of secondary education, including general and vocational education, make them available and accessible to every child, and take appropriate measures such as the introduction of free education and offering financial assistance in case of need;

(c) Make higher education accessible to all on the basis of capacity by every appropriate means;

(d) Make educational and vocational information and guidance available and accessible to all children;

(e) Take measures to encourage regular attendance at schools and the reduction of drop-out rates.

2. States Parties shall take all appropriate measures to ensure that school discipline is administered in a manner consistent with the child's human dignity and in conformity with the present Convention.

3. States Parties shall promote and encourage international co-operation in matters relating to education, in particular with a view to contributing to the elimination of ignorance and illiteracy throughout the world and facilitating access to scientific and technical knowledge and modern teaching methods. In this regard, particular account shall be taken of the needs of developing countries.

Article 29

1. States Parties agree that the education of the child shall be directed to:

(a) The development of the child's personality, talents and mental and physical abilities to their fullest potential;

(b) The development of respect for human rights and fundamental freedoms, and for the principles enshrined in the Charter of the United Nations;

(c) The development of respect for the child's parents, his or her own cultural identity, language and values, for the national values of the country in which the child is living, the country from which he or she may originate, and for civilizations different from his or her own;

(d) The preparation of the child for responsible life in a free society, in the spirit of understanding, peace, tolerance, equality of sexes, and friendship among all peoples, ethnic, national and religious groups and persons of indigenous origin;

(e) The development of respect for the natural environment.

2. No part of the present article or Article 28 shall be construed so as to interfere with the liberty of individuals and bodies to establish and direct educational institutions, subject always to the observance of the principles set forth in paragraph 1 of the present article and to the requirements that the education given in such institutions shall conform to such minimum standards as may be laid down by the State.

Article 30

In those States in which ethnic, religious or linguistic minorities or persons of indigenous origin exist, a child belonging to such a minority or who is indigenous shall not be denied the right, in community with other members of his or her group, to enjoy his or her own culture, to profess and practice his or her own religion, or to use his or her own language.

Article 31

1. States Parties recognize the right of the child to rest and leisure, to engage in play and recreational activities appropriate to the age of the child and to participate freely in cultural life and the arts.

2. States Parties shall respect and promote the right of the child to participate fully in cultural and artistic life and shall encourage the provision of appropriate and equal opportunities for cultural, artistic, recreational and leisure activity.

Article 32

1. States Parties recognize the right of the child to be protected from economic exploitation and from performing any work that is likely to be hazardous or to interfere with the child's education, or to be harmful to the child's health or physical, mental, spiritual, moral or social development.

2. States Parties shall take legislative, administrative, social and educational measures to ensure the implementation of the present article. To this end, and having regard to the relevant provisions of other international instruments, States Parties shall in particular:

(a) Provide for a minimum ages or minimum ages for admission to employment;

(b) Provide for appropriate regulation of the hours and conditions of employment;

(c) Provide for appropriate penalties or other sanctions to ensure the effective enforcement of the present article.

Article 33

States Parties shall take all appropriate measures, including legislative, administrative, social and educational measures, to protect children from the illicit use of narcotic drugs and psychotropic substances as defined in the relevant international treaties, and to prevent the use of children in the illicit production and trafficking of such substances.

Article 34

States Parties undertake to protect the child from all forms of sexual exploitation and sexual abuse. For these purposes, States Parties shall in particular take all appropriate national, bilateral and multilateral measures to prevent:

(a) The inducement or coercion of a child to engage in any unlawful sexual activity;

(b) The exploitative use of children in prostitution or other unlawful sexual practices;

(c) The exploitative use of children in pornographic performances and materials.

Article 35

States Parties shall take all appropriate national, bilateral and multilateral measures to prevent the abduction of, the sale of or traffic in children for any purpose or in any form.

Article 36

States Parties shall protect the child against all other forms of exploitation prejudicial to any aspects of the child's welfare.

Article 37

States Parties shall ensure that:

(a) No child shall be subjected to torture or other cruel, inhuman or degrading treatment or punishment. Neither capital punishment nor life imprisonment without possibility of release shall be imposed for offences committed by persons below eighteen years of age;

(b) No child shall be deprived of his or her liberty unlawfully or arbitrarily. The arrest, detention or imprisonment of a child shall be in conformity with the law and shall be used only as a measure of last resort and for the shortest appropriate period of time;

(c) Every child deprived of liberty shall be treated with humanity and respect for the inherent dignity of the human person, and in a manner which takes into account the needs of persons of his or her age. In particular, every child deprived of liberty shall be separated from adults unless it is considered in the child's best interest not to do so and shall have the right to maintain contact with his or her family, through correspondence and visits, save in exceptional circumstances;

(d) Every child deprived of his or her liberty shall have the right to prompt access to legal and other appropriate assistance, as well as the right to challenge the legality of the deprivation of his or her liberty before a court or other competent, independent and impartial authority, and to a prompt decision on any such action.

Article 38

1. States Parties undertake to respect and to ensure respect for rules of international humanitarian law applicable to them in armed conflicts which are relevant to the child.

2. States Parties shall take all feasible measures to ensure that persons who have not attained the age of fifteen years do not take a direct part in hostilities.

3. States Parties shall refrain from recruiting any person who has not attained the age of fifteen years into their armed forces. In recruiting among those persons who have attained the age of fifteen years but who have not attained the age of eighteen years, States Parties shall endeavor to give priority to those who are oldest.

4. In accordance with their obligations under international humanitarian law to protect the civilian population in armed conflicts, States Parties shall take all feasible measures to ensure protection and care of children who are affected by an armed conflict.

Article 39

States Parties shall take all appropriate measures to promote physical and psychological recovery and social reintegration of a child victim of: any form of neglect, exploitation, or abuse; torture or any other form of cruel, inhuman or degrading treatment or punishment; or armed conflicts. Such recovery and reintegration shall take place in an environment which fosters the health, self-respect and dignity of the child.

Article 40

1. States Parties recognize the right of every child alleged as, accused of, or recognized as having infringed the penal law to be treated in a manner consistent with the promotion of the child's sense of dignity and worth, which reinforces the child's respect for the human rights and fundamental freedoms of others and which takes into account the child's age and the desirability of promoting the child's reintegration and the child's assuming a constructive role in society.

2. To this end, and having regard to the relevant provisions of international instruments, States Parties shall, in particular, ensure that:

(a) No child shall be alleged as, be accused of, or recognized as having infringed the penal law by reason of acts or omissions that were not prohibited by national or international law at the time they were committed;

(b) Every child alleged as or accused of having infringed the penal law has at least the following guarantees:

(i) To be presumed innocent until proven guilty according to law;

(ii) To be informed promptly and directly of the charges against him or her, and, if appropriate, through his or her parents or legal guardians, and to have legal or other appropriate assistance in the preparation and presentation of his or her defence;

(iii) To have the matter determined without delay by a competent, independent and impartial authority or judicial body in a fair hearing according to law, in the presence of legal or other appropriate assistance and, unless it is considered not to be in the best interest of the child, in particular, taking into account his or her age or situation, his or her parents or legal guardians;

(iv) Not to be compelled to give testimony or to confess guilt; to examine or have examined adverse witnesses and to obtain the participation and examination of witnesses on his or her behalf under conditions of equality;

(v) If considered to have infringed the penal law, to have this decision and any measures imposed in consequence thereof reviewed by a higher competent, independent and impartial authority or judicial body according to law;

(vi) To have the free assistance of an interpreter if the child cannot understand or speak the language used;

(vii) To have his or her privacy fully respected at all stages of the proceedings.

3. States Parties shall seek to promote the establishment of laws, procedures, authorities and institutions specifically applicable to children alleged as, accused of, or recognized as having infringed the penal law, and, in particular:

(a) The establishment of a minimum age below which children shall be presumed not to have the capacity to infringe the penal law;

(b) Whenever appropriate and desirable, measures for dealing with such children without resorting to judicial proceedings, providing that human rights and legal safeguards are fully respected.

4. A variety of dispositions, such as care, guidance and supervision orders; counselling; probation; foster care; education and vocational training programmes and other alternatives to institutional care shall be available to ensure that children are dealt with in a manner appropriate to their well-being and proportionate both to their circumstances and the offence.

Article 41

Nothing in the present Convention shall affect any provisions which are more conducive to the realization of the rights of the child and which may be contained in.

(a) The law of a State Party; or

(b) International law in force for that State.

PART II

Article 42

States Parties undertake to make the principles and provisions of the Convention widely known, by appropriate and active means, to adults and children alike.

Article 43

1. For the purpose of examining the progress made by States Parties in achieving the realization of the obligations undertaken in the present Convention, there shall be established a Committee on the Rights of the Child, which shall carry out the functions hereinafter provided.

2. The Committee shall consist of ten experts of high moral standing and recognized competence in the field covered by this Convention. The members of the Committee shall be elected by States Parties from among their nationals and shall serve in their personal capacity, consid-

eration being given to equitable geographical distribution, as well as to the principal legal systems.

3. The members of the Committee shall be elected by secret ballot from a list of persons nominated by States Parties. Each State Party may nominate one person from among its own nationals....

6. The members of the Committee shall be elected for a term of four years. They shall be eligible for re-election if renominated....

8. The Committee shall establish its own rules of procedure.

9. The Committee shall elect its officers for a period of two years....

11. The Secretary–General of the United Nations shall provide the necessary staff and facilities for the effective performance of the functions of the Committee under the present Convention....

Article 44

1. States Parties undertake to submit to the Committee, through the Secretary–General of the United Nations, reports on the measures they have adopted which give effect to the rights recognized herein and on the progress made on the enjoyment of those rights:

(a) Within two years of the entry into force of the Convention for the State Party concerned;

(b) Thereafter every five years.

2. Reports made under the present article shall indicate factors and difficulties, if any, affecting the degree of fulfillment of the obligations under the present Convention. Reports shall also contain sufficient information to provide the Committee with a comprehensive understanding of the implementation of the Convention in the country concerned.

3. A State Party which has submitted a comprehensive initial report to the Committee need not, in its subsequent reports submitted in accordance with paragraph 1 (b) of the present article, repeat basic information previously provided.

4. The Committee may request from States Parties further information relevant to the implementation of the Convention.

5. The Committee shall submit to the General Assembly, through the Economic and Social Council, every two years, reports on its activities.

6. States Parties shall make their reports widely available to the public in their own countries.

Article 45

1. In order to foster the effective implementation of the Convention and to encourage international co-operation in the field covered by the Convention:

(a) The specialized agencies, the United Nations Children's Fund, and other United Nations organs shall be entitled to be represented at the consideration of the implementation of such provisions of the present Convention as fall within the scope of their mandate. The Committee may invite the specialized agencies, the United Nations Children's Fund, and other competent bodies as it may consider appropriate to provide expert advice on the implementation of the Convention in areas falling within the scope of their respective mandates. The Committee may invite the specialized agencies, the United Nations Children's Fund, and other United Nations organs to submit reports on the implementation of the Convention in areas falling within the scope of their activities;

(b) The Committee shall transmit, as it may consider appropriate, to the specialized agencies, the United Nations Children's Fund, and other competent bodies, any reports from States Parties that contain a request, or indicate a need, for technical advice or assistance, along with the Committee's observations and suggestions, if any, on these requests or indications;

(c) The Committee may recommend to the General Assembly to request the Secretary–General to undertake on its behalf studies on specific issues relating to the rights of the child;

(d) The Committee may make suggestions and general recommendations based on information received pursuant to Articles 44 and 45 of the present Convention. Such suggestions and general recommendations shall be transmitted to any State Party concerned and reported to the General Assembly, together with comments, if any, from States Parties.

Document 46
CONVENTION ON THE RIGHTS OF PERSONS WITH DISABILITIES

U.N. G.A. Res. 61/106 (13 Dec. 2006)

The General Assembly,

Recalling its resolution 56/168 of 19 December 2001, by which it decided to establish an Ad Hoc Committee, open to the participation of all Member States and observers to the United Nations, to consider proposals for a comprehensive and integral international convention to promote and protect the rights and dignity of persons with disabilities, based on a holistic approach in the work done in the fields of social development, human rights and non-discrimination and taking into account the recommendations of the Commission on Human Rights and the Commission for Social Development,

Recalling also its previous relevant resolutions, the most recent of which was resolution 60/232 of 23 December 2005, as well as relevant resolutions of the Commission for Social Development and the Commission on Human Rights,

Welcoming the valuable contributions made by intergovernmental and non-governmental organizations and national human rights institutions to the work of the Ad Hoc Committee,

1. *Expresses its appreciation* to the Ad Hoc Committee for having concluded the elaboration of the draft Convention on the Rights of Persons with Disabilities and the draft Optional Protocol to the Convention;

2. *Adopts* the Convention on the Rights of Persons with Disabilities and the Optional Protocol to the Convention annexed to the present resolution, which shall be open for signature at United Nations Headquarters in New York as of 30 March 2007;

3. *Calls upon* States to consider signing and ratifying the Convention and the Optional Protocol as a matter of priority, and expresses the hope that they will enter into force at an early date;

4. *Requests* the Secretary–General to provide the staff and facilities necessary for the effective performance of the functions of the Conference of States Parties and the Committee under the Convention and the Optional Protocol after the entry into force of the Convention, as well as for the dissemination of information on the Convention and the Optional Protocol;

5. *Also requests* the Secretary–General to implement progressively standards and guidelines for the accessibility of facilities and services of the United Nations system, taking into account relevant provisions of the Convention, in particular when undertaking renovations;

6. *Requests* United Nations agencies and organizations, and invites intergovernmental and non-governmental organizations, to undertake efforts to disseminate information on the Convention and the Optional Protocol and to promote their understanding;

7. *Requests* the Secretary–General to submit to the General Assembly at its sixty-second session a report on the status of the Convention and the Optional Protocol and the implementation of the present resolution, under a sub-item entitled "Convention on the Rights of Persons with Disabilities".

Annex I

Convention on the Rights of Persons with Disabilities

Preamble

The States Parties to the present Convention,

(a) Recalling the principles proclaimed in the Charter of the United Nations which recognize the inherent dignity and worth and the equal and inalienable rights of all members of the human family as the foundation of freedom, justice and peace in the world,

(b) Recognizing that the United Nations, in the Universal Declaration of Human Rights and in the International Covenants on Human Rights, has proclaimed and agreed that everyone is entitled to all the rights and freedoms set forth therein, without distinction of any kind,

(c) Reaffirming the universality, indivisibility, interdependence and interrelatedness of all human rights and fundamental freedoms and the need for persons with disabilities to be guaranteed their full enjoyment without discrimination,

(d) Recalling the International Covenant on Economic, Social and Cultural Rights, the International Covenant on Civil and Political Rights, the International Convention on the Elimination of All Forms of Racial Discrimination, the Convention on the Elimination of All Forms of Discrimination against Women, the Convention against Torture and Other Cruel, Inhuman or Degrading Treatment or Punishment, the Convention on the Rights of the Child, and the International Convention on the Protection of the Rights of All Migrant Workers and Members of Their Families,

(e) Recognizing that disability is an evolving concept and that disability results from the interaction between persons with impairments and attitudinal and environmental barriers that hinders their full and effective participation in society on an equal basis with others,

(f) Recognizing the importance of the principles and policy guidelines contained in the World Programme of Action concerning Disabled Persons and in the Standard Rules on the Equalization of Opportunities for Persons with Disabilities in influencing the promotion, formulation and evaluation of the policies, plans, programmes and actions at the national, regional and international levels to further equalize opportunities for persons with disabilities,

(g) Emphasizing the importance of mainstreaming disability issues as an integral part of relevant strategies of sustainable development,

(h) Recognizing also that discrimination against any person on the basis of disability is a violation of the inherent dignity and worth of the human person,

(i) Recognizing further the diversity of persons with disabilities,

(j) Recognizing the need to promote and protect the human rights of all persons with disabilities, including those who require more intensive support,

(k) Concerned that, despite these various instruments and undertakings, persons with disabilities continue to face barriers in their participation as equal members of society and violations of their human rights in all parts of the world,

(l) Recognizing the importance of international cooperation for improving the living conditions of persons with disabilities in every country, particularly in developing countries,

(m) Recognizing the valued existing and potential contributions made by persons with disabilities to the overall well-being and diversity of their communities, and that the promotion of the full enjoyment by persons with disabilities of their human rights and fundamental freedoms and of full participation by persons with disabilities will result in their enhanced sense of belonging and in significant advances in the human, social and economic development of society and the eradication of poverty,

(n) Recognizing the importance for persons with disabilities of their individual autonomy and independence, including the freedom to make their own choices,

(o) Considering that persons with disabilities should have the opportunity to be actively involved in decision-making processes about policies and programmes, including those directly concerning them,

(p) Concerned about the difficult conditions faced by persons with disabilities who are subject to multiple or aggravated forms of discrimination on the basis of race, colour, sex, language, religion, political or other opinion, national, ethnic, indigenous or social origin, property, birth, age or other status,

(q) Recognizing that women and girls with disabilities are often at greater risk, both within and outside the home, of violence, injury or abuse, neglect or negligent treatment, maltreatment or exploitation,

(r) Recognizing that children with disabilities should have full enjoyment of all human rights and fundamental freedoms on an equal basis with other children, and recalling obligations to that end undertaken by States Parties to the Convention on the Rights of the Child,

(s) Emphasizing the need to incorporate a gender perspective in all efforts to promote the full enjoyment of human rights and fundamental freedoms by persons with disabilities,

(t) Highlighting the fact that the majority of persons with disabilities live in conditions of poverty, and in this regard recognizing the critical need to address the negative impact of poverty on persons with disabilities,

(u) Bearing in mind that conditions of peace and security based on full respect for the purposes and principles contained in the Charter of the United Nations and observance of applicable human rights instruments are indispensable for the full protection of persons with disabilities, in particular during armed conflicts and foreign occupation,

(v) Recognizing the importance of accessibility to the physical, social, economic and cultural environment, to health and education and to information and communication, in enabling persons with disabilities to fully enjoy all human rights and fundamental freedoms,

(w) Realizing that the individual, having duties to other individuals and to the community to which he or she belongs, is under a responsibility to strive for the promotion and observance of the rights recognized in the International Bill of Human Rights,

(x) Convinced that the family is the natural and fundamental group unit of society and is entitled to protection by society and the State, and that persons with disabilities and their family members should receive the necessary protection and assistance to enable families to contribute towards the full and equal enjoyment of the rights of persons with disabilities,

(y) Convinced that a comprehensive and integral international convention to promote and protect the rights and dignity of persons with disabilities will make a significant contribution to redressing the profound social disadvantage of persons with disabilities and promote their participation in the civil, political, economic, social and cultural spheres with equal opportunities, in both developing and developed countries,

Have agreed as follows:

Article 1

Purpose

The purpose of the present Convention is to promote, protect and ensure the full and equal enjoyment of all human rights and fundamental freedoms by all persons with disabilities, and to promote respect for their inherent dignity.

Persons with disabilities include those who have long-term physical, mental, intellectual or sensory impairments which in interaction with various barriers may hinder their full and effective participation in society on an equal basis with others.

Article 2

Definitions

For the purposes of the present Convention:

"Communication" includes languages, display of text, Braille, tactile communication, large print, accessible multimedia as well as written, audio, plain-language, human-reader and augmentative and alternative modes, means and formats of communication, including accessible information and communication technology;

"Language" includes spoken and signed languages and other forms of non-spoken languages;

"Discrimination on the basis of disability" means any distinction, exclusion or restriction on the basis of disability which has the purpose or effect of impairing or nullifying the recognition, enjoyment or exercise, on an equal basis with others, of all human rights and fundamental freedoms in the political, economic, social, cultural, civil or any other field. It includes all forms of discrimination, including denial of reasonable accommodation;

"Reasonable accommodation" means necessary and appropriate modification and adjustments not imposing a disproportionate or undue burden, where needed in a particular case, to ensure to persons with disabilities the enjoyment or exercise on an equal basis with others of all human rights and fundamental freedoms;

"Universal design" means the design of products, environments, programmes and services to be usable by all people, to the greatest extent possible, without the need for adaptation or specialized design. "Universal design" shall not exclude assistive devices for particular groups of persons with disabilities where this is needed.

Article 3

General principles

The principles of the present Convention shall be:

(a) Respect for inherent dignity, individual autonomy including the freedom to make one's own choices, and independence of persons;

(b) Non-discrimination;

(c) Full and effective participation and inclusion in society;

(d) Respect for difference and acceptance of persons with disabilities as part of human diversity and humanity;

(e) Equality of opportunity;

(f) Accessibility;

(g) Equality between men and women;

(h) Respect for the evolving capacities of children with disabilities and respect for the right of children with disabilities to preserve their identities.

Article 4

General obligations

1. States Parties undertake to ensure and promote the full realization of all human rights and fundamental freedoms for all persons with disabilities without discrimination of any kind on the basis of disability. To this end, States Parties undertake:

(a) To adopt all appropriate legislative, administrative and other measures for the implementation of the rights recognized in the present Convention;

(b) To take all appropriate measures, including legislation, to modify or abolish existing laws, regulations, customs and practices that constitute discrimination against persons with disabilities;

(c) To take into account the protection and promotion of the human rights of persons with disabilities in all policies and programmes;

(d) To refrain from engaging in any act or practice that is inconsistent with the present Convention and to ensure that public authorities and institutions act in conformity with the present Convention;

(e) To take all appropriate measures to eliminate discrimination on the basis of disability by any person, organization or private enterprise;

(f) To undertake or promote research and development of universally designed goods, services, equipment and facilities, as defined in article 2 of the present Convention, which should require the minimum possible adaptation and the least cost to meet the specific needs of a person with disabilities, to promote their availability and use, and to promote universal design in the development of standards and guidelines;

(g) To undertake or promote research and development of, and to promote the availability and use of new technologies, including information and communications technologies, mobility aids, devices and assistive technologies, suitable for persons with disabilities, giving priority to technologies at an affordable cost;

(h) To provide accessible information to persons with disabilities about mobility aids, devices and assistive technologies, including new technologies, as well as other forms of assistance, support services and facilities;

(i) To promote the training of professionals and staff working with persons with disabilities in the rights recognized in the present Convention so as to better provide the assistance and services guaranteed by those rights.

2. With regard to economic, social and cultural rights, each State Party undertakes to take measures to the maximum of its available resources and, where needed, within the framework of international cooperation, with a view to achieving progressively the full realization of these rights, without prejudice to those obligations contained in the present Convention that are immediately applicable according to international law.

3. In the development and implementation of legislation and policies to implement the present Convention, and in other decision-making processes concerning issues relating to persons with disabilities, States Parties shall closely consult with and actively involve persons with

disabilities, including children with disabilities, through their representative organizations.

4. Nothing in the present Convention shall affect any provisions which are more conducive to the realization of the rights of persons with disabilities and which may be contained in the law of a State Party or international law in force for that State. There shall be no restriction upon or derogation from any of the human rights and fundamental freedoms recognized or existing in any State Party to the present Convention pursuant to law, conventions, regulation or custom on the pretext that the present Convention does not recognize such rights or freedoms or that it recognizes them to a lesser extent.

5. The provisions of the present Convention shall extend to all parts of federal States without any limitations or exceptions.

Article 5

Equality and non-discrimination

1. States Parties recognize that all persons are equal before and under the law and are entitled without any discrimination to the equal protection and equal benefit of the law.

2. States Parties shall prohibit all discrimination on the basis of disability and guarantee to persons with disabilities equal and effective legal protection against discrimination on all grounds.

3. In order to promote equality and eliminate discrimination, States Parties shall take all appropriate steps to ensure that reasonable accommodation is provided.

4. Specific measures which are necessary to accelerate or achieve de facto equality of persons with disabilities shall not be considered discrimination under the terms of the present Convention.

Article 6

Women with disabilities

1. States Parties recognize that women and girls with disabilities are subject to multiple discrimination, and in this regard shall take measures to ensure the full and equal enjoyment by them of all human rights and fundamental freedoms.

2. States Parties shall take all appropriate measures to ensure the full development, advancement and empowerment of women, for the purpose of guaranteeing them the exercise and enjoyment of the human rights and fundamental freedoms set out in the present Convention.

Article 7

Children with disabilities

1. States Parties shall take all necessary measures to ensure the full enjoyment by children with disabilities of all human rights and fundamental freedoms on an equal basis with other children.

2. In all actions concerning children with disabilities, the best interests of the child shall be a primary consideration.

3. States Parties shall ensure that children with disabilities have the right to express their views freely on all matters affecting them, their views being given due weight in accordance with their age and maturity, on an equal basis with other children, and to be provided with disability and age-appropriate assistance to realize that right.

Article 8

Awareness-raising

1. States Parties undertake to adopt immediate, effective and appropriate measures:

(a) To raise awareness throughout society, including at the family level, regarding persons with disabilities, and to foster respect for the rights and dignity of persons with disabilities;

(b) To combat stereotypes, prejudices and harmful practices relating to persons with disabilities, including those based on sex and age, in all areas of life;

(c) To promote awareness of the capabilities and contributions of persons with disabilities.

2. Measures to this end include:

(a) Initiating and maintaining effective public awareness campaigns designed:

(i) To nurture receptiveness to the rights of persons with disabilities;

(ii) To promote positive perceptions and greater social awareness towards persons with disabilities;

(iii) To promote recognition of the skills, merits and abilities of persons with disabilities, and of their contributions to the workplace and the labour market;

(b) Fostering at all levels of the education system, including in all children from an early age, an attitude of respect for the rights of persons with disabilities;

(c) Encouraging all organs of the media to portray persons with disabilities in a manner consistent with the purpose of the present Convention;

(d) Promoting awareness-training programmes regarding persons with disabilities and the rights of persons with disabilities.

Article 9

Accessibility

1. To enable persons with disabilities to live independently and participate fully in all aspects of life, States Parties shall take appropriate measures to ensure to persons with disabilities access, on an equal basis with others, to the physical environment, to transportation, to information and communications, including information and communications technologies and systems, and to other facilities and services open or provided to the public, both in urban and in rural areas. These

measures, which shall include the identification and elimination of obstacles and barriers to accessibility, shall apply to, inter alia:

(a) Buildings, roads, transportation and other indoor and outdoor facilities, including schools, housing, medical facilities and workplaces;

(b) Information, communications and other services, including electronic services and emergency services.

2. States Parties shall also take appropriate measures:

(a) To develop, promulgate and monitor the implementation of minimum standards and guidelines for the accessibility of facilities and services open or provided to the public;

(b) To ensure that private entities that offer facilities and services which are open or provided to the public take into account all aspects of accessibility for persons with disabilities;

(c) To provide training for stakeholders on accessibility issues facing persons with disabilities;

(d) To provide in buildings and other facilities open to the public signage in Braille and in easy to read and understand forms;

(e) To provide forms of live assistance and intermediaries, including guides, readers and professional sign language interpreters, to facilitate accessibility to buildings and other facilities open to the public;

(f) To promote other appropriate forms of assistance and support to persons with disabilities to ensure their access to information;

(g) To promote access for persons with disabilities to new information and communications technologies and systems, including the Internet;

(h) To promote the design, development, production and distribution of accessible information and communications technologies and systems at an early stage, so that these technologies and systems become accessible at minimum cost.

Article 10

Right to life

States Parties reaffirm that every human being has the inherent right to life and shall take all necessary measures to ensure its effective enjoyment by persons with disabilities on an equal basis with others.

Article 11

Situations of risk and humanitarian emergencies

States Parties shall take, in accordance with their obligations under international law, including international humanitarian law and international human rights law, all necessary measures to ensure the protection and safety of persons with disabilities in situations of risk, including situations of armed conflict, humanitarian emergencies and the occurrence of natural disasters.

Article 12

Equal recognition before the law

1. States Parties reaffirm that persons with disabilities have the right to recognition everywhere as persons before the law.

2. States Parties shall recognize that persons with disabilities enjoy legal capacity on an equal basis with others in all aspects of life.

3. States Parties shall take appropriate measures to provide access by persons with disabilities to the support they may require in exercising their legal capacity.

4. States Parties shall ensure that all measures that relate to the exercise of legal capacity provide for appropriate and effective safeguards to prevent abuse in accordance with international human rights law. Such safeguards shall ensure that measures relating to the exercise of legal capacity respect the rights, will and preferences of the person, are free of conflict of interest and undue influence, are proportional and tailored to the person's circumstances, apply for the shortest time possible and are subject to regular review by a competent, independent and impartial authority or judicial body. The safeguards shall be proportional to the degree to which such measures affect the person's rights and interests.

5. Subject to the provisions of this article, States Parties shall take all appropriate and effective measures to ensure the equal right of persons with disabilities to own or inherit property, to control their own financial affairs and to have equal access to bank loans, mortgages and other forms of financial credit, and shall ensure that persons with disabilities are not arbitrarily deprived of their property.

Article 13

Access to justice

1. States Parties shall ensure effective access to justice for persons with disabilities on an equal basis with others, including through the provision of procedural and age-appropriate accommodations, in order to facilitate their effective role as direct and indirect participants, including as witnesses, in all legal proceedings, including at investigative and other preliminary stages.

2. In order to help to ensure effective access to justice for persons with disabilities, States Parties shall promote appropriate training for those working in the field of administration of justice, including police and prison staff.

Article 14

Liberty and security of person

1. States Parties shall ensure that persons with disabilities, on an equal basis with others:

(a) Enjoy the right to liberty and security of person;

(b) Are not deprived of their liberty unlawfully or arbitrarily, and that any deprivation of liberty is in conformity with the law, and that the existence of a disability shall in no case justify a deprivation of liberty.

2. States Parties shall ensure that if persons with disabilities are deprived of their liberty through any process, they are, on an equal basis with others, entitled to guarantees in accordance with international human rights law and shall be treated in compliance with the objectives and principles of the present Convention, including by provision of reasonable accommodation.

Article 15

Freedom from torture or cruel, inhuman or degrading treatment or punishment

1. No one shall be subjected to torture or to cruel, inhuman or degrading treatment or punishment. In particular, no one shall be subjected without his or her free consent to medical or scientific experimentation.

2. States Parties shall take all effective legislative, administrative, judicial or other measures to prevent persons with disabilities, on an equal basis with others, from being subjected to torture or cruel, inhuman or degrading treatment or punishment.

Article 16

Freedom from exploitation, violence and abuse

1. States Parties shall take all appropriate legislative, administrative, social, educational and other measures to protect persons with disabilities, both within and outside the home, from all forms of exploitation, violence and abuse, including their gender-based aspects.

2. States Parties shall also take all appropriate measures to prevent all forms of exploitation, violence and abuse by ensuring, inter alia, appropriate forms of gender- and age-sensitive assistance and support for persons with disabilities and their families and caregivers, including through the provision of information and education on how to avoid, recognize and report instances of exploitation, violence and abuse. States Parties shall ensure that protection services are age-, gender- and disability-sensitive.

3. In order to prevent the occurrence of all forms of exploitation, violence and abuse, States Parties shall ensure that all facilities and programmes designed to serve persons with disabilities are effectively monitored by independent authorities.

4. States Parties shall take all appropriate measures to promote the physical, cognitive and psychological recovery, rehabilitation and social reintegration of persons with disabilities who become victims of any form of exploitation, violence or abuse, including through the provision of protection services. Such recovery and reintegration shall take place in an environment that fosters the health, welfare, self-

respect, dignity and autonomy of the person and takes into account gender- and age-specific needs.

5. States Parties shall put in place effective legislation and policies, including women- and child-focused legislation and policies, to ensure that instances of exploitation, violence and abuse against persons with disabilities are identified, investigated and, where appropriate, prosecuted.

Article 17

Protecting the integrity of the person

Every person with disabilities has a right to respect for his or her physical and mental integrity on an equal basis with others.

Article 18

Liberty of movement and nationality

1. States Parties shall recognize the rights of persons with disabilities to liberty of movement, to freedom to choose their residence and to a nationality, on an equal basis with others, including by ensuring that persons with disabilities:

(a) Have the right to acquire and change a nationality and are not deprived of their nationality arbitrarily or on the basis of disability;

(b) Are not deprived, on the basis of disability, of their ability to obtain, possess and utilize documentation of their nationality or other documentation of identification, or to utilize relevant processes such as immigration proceedings, that may be needed to facilitate exercise of the right to liberty of movement;

(c) Are free to leave any country, including their own;

(d) Are not deprived, arbitrarily or on the basis of disability, of the right to enter their own country.

2. Children with disabilities shall be registered immediately after birth and shall have the right from birth to a name, the right to acquire a nationality and, as far as possible, the right to know and be cared for by their parents.

Article 19

Living independently and being included in the community

States Parties to the present Convention recognize the equal right of all persons with disabilities to live in the community, with choices equal to others, and shall take effective and appropriate measures to facilitate full enjoyment by persons with disabilities of this right and their full inclusion and participation in the community, including by ensuring that:

(a) Persons with disabilities have the opportunity to choose their place of residence and where and with whom they live on an equal basis with others and are not obliged to live in a particular living arrangement;

(b) Persons with disabilities have access to a range of in-home, residential and other community support services, including personal assistance necessary to support living and inclusion in the community, and to prevent isolation or segregation from the community;

(c) Community services and facilities for the general population are available on an equal basis to persons with disabilities and are responsive to their needs.

Article 20

Personal mobility

States Parties shall take effective measures to ensure personal mobility with the greatest possible independence for persons with disabilities, including by:

(a) Facilitating the personal mobility of persons with disabilities in the manner and at the time of their choice, and at affordable cost;

(b) Facilitating access by persons with disabilities to quality mobility aids, devices, assistive technologies and forms of live assistance and intermediaries, including by making them available at affordable cost;

(c) Providing training in mobility skills to persons with disabilities and to specialist staff working with persons with disabilities;

(d) Encouraging entities that produce mobility aids, devices and assistive technologies to take into account all aspects of mobility for persons with disabilities.

Article 21

Freedom of expression and opinion, and access to information

States Parties shall take all appropriate measures to ensure that persons with disabilities can exercise the right to freedom of expression and opinion, including the freedom to seek, receive and impart information and ideas on an equal basis with others and through all forms of communication of their choice, as defined in article 2 of the present Convention, including by:

(a) Providing information intended for the general public to persons with disabilities in accessible formats and technologies appropriate to different kinds of disabilities in a timely manner and without additional cost;

(b) Accepting and facilitating the use of sign languages, Braille, augmentative and alternative communication, and all other accessible means, modes and formats of communication of their choice by persons with disabilities in official interactions;

(c) Urging private entities that provide services to the general public, including through the Internet, to provide information and services in accessible and usable formats for persons with disabilities;

(d) Encouraging the mass media, including providers of information through the Internet, to make their services accessible to persons with disabilities;

(e) Recognizing and promoting the use of sign languages.

Article 22

Respect for privacy

1. No person with disabilities, regardless of place of residence or living arrangements, shall be subjected to arbitrary or unlawful interference with his or her privacy, family, home or correspondence or other types of communication or to unlawful attacks on his or her honour and reputation. Persons with disabilities have the right to the protection of the law against such interference or attacks.

2. States Parties shall protect the privacy of personal, health and rehabilitation information of persons with disabilities on an equal basis with others.

Article 23

Respect for home and the family

1. States Parties shall take effective and appropriate measures to eliminate discrimination against persons with disabilities in all matters relating to marriage, family, parenthood and relationships, on an equal basis with others, so as to ensure that:

(a) The right of all persons with disabilities who are of marriageable age to marry and to found a family on the basis of free and full consent of the intending spouses is recognized;

(b) The rights of persons with disabilities to decide freely and responsibly on the number and spacing of their children and to have access to age-appropriate information, reproductive and family planning education are recognized, and the means necessary to enable them to exercise these rights are provided;

(c) Persons with disabilities, including children, retain their fertility on an equal basis with others.

2. States Parties shall ensure the rights and responsibilities of persons with disabilities, with regard to guardianship, wardship, trusteeship, adoption of children or similar institutions, where these concepts exist in national legislation; in all cases the best interests of the child shall be paramount. States Parties shall render appropriate assistance to persons with disabilities in the performance of their childrearing responsibilities.

3. States Parties shall ensure that children with disabilities have equal rights with respect to family life. With a view to realizing these rights, and to prevent concealment, abandonment, neglect and segregation of children with disabilities, States Parties shall undertake to provide early and comprehensive information, services and support to children with disabilities and their families.

4. States Parties shall ensure that a child shall not be separated from his or her parents against their will, except when competent authorities subject to judicial review determine, in accordance with applicable law and procedures, that such separation is necessary for the

best interests of the child. In no case shall a child be separated from parents on the basis of a disability of either the child or one or both of the parents.

5. States Parties shall, where the immediate family is unable to care for a child with disabilities, undertake every effort to provide alternative care within the wider family, and failing that, within the community in a family setting.

Article 24

Education

1. States Parties recognize the right of persons with disabilities to education. With a view to realizing this right without discrimination and on the basis of equal opportunity, States Parties shall ensure an inclusive education system at all levels and lifelong learning directed to:

(a) The full development of human potential and sense of dignity and self-worth, and the strengthening of respect for human rights, fundamental freedoms and human diversity;

(b) The development by persons with disabilities of their personality, talents and creativity, as well as their mental and physical abilities, to their fullest potential;

(c) Enabling persons with disabilities to participate effectively in a free society.

2. In realizing this right, States Parties shall ensure that:

(a) Persons with disabilities are not excluded from the general education system on the basis of disability, and that children with disabilities are not excluded from free and compulsory primary education, or from secondary education, on the basis of disability;

(b) Persons with disabilities can access an inclusive, quality and free primary education and secondary education on an equal basis with others in the communities in which they live;

(c) Reasonable accommodation of the individual's requirements is provided;

(d) Persons with disabilities receive the support required, within the general education system, to facilitate their effective education;

(e) Effective individualized support measures are provided in environments that maximize academic and social development, consistent with the goal of full inclusion.

3. States Parties shall enable persons with disabilities to learn life and social development skills to facilitate their full and equal participation in education and as members of the community. To this end, States Parties shall take appropriate measures, including:

(a) Facilitating the learning of Braille, alternative script, augmentative and alternative modes, means and formats of communication and orientation and mobility skills, and facilitating peer support and mentoring;

(b) Facilitating the learning of sign language and the promotion of the linguistic identity of the deaf community;

(c) Ensuring that the education of persons, and in particular children, who are blind, deaf or deafblind, is delivered in the most appropriate languages and modes and means of communication for the individual, and in environments which maximize academic and social development.

4. In order to help ensure the realization of this right, States Parties shall take appropriate measures to employ teachers, including teachers with disabilities, who are qualified in sign language and/or Braille, and to train professionals and staff who work at all levels of education. Such training shall incorporate disability awareness and the use of appropriate augmentative and alternative modes, means and formats of communication, educational techniques and materials to support persons with disabilities.

5. States Parties shall ensure that persons with disabilities are able to access general tertiary education, vocational training, adult education and lifelong learning without discrimination and on an equal basis with others. To this end, States Parties shall ensure that reasonable accommodation is provided to persons with disabilities.

Article 25

Health

States Parties recognize that persons with disabilities have the right to the enjoyment of the highest attainable standard of health without discrimination on the basis of disability. States Parties shall take all appropriate measures to ensure access for persons with disabilities to health services that are gender-sensitive, including health-related rehabilitation. In particular, States Parties shall:

(a) Provide persons with disabilities with the same range, quality and standard of free or affordable health care and programmes as provided to other persons, including in the area of sexual and reproductive health and population-based public health programmes;

(b) Provide those health services needed by persons with disabilities specifically because of their disabilities, including early identification and intervention as appropriate, and services designed to minimize and prevent further disabilities, including among children and older persons;

(c) Provide these health services as close as possible to people's own communities, including in rural areas;

(d) Require health professionals to provide care of the same quality to persons with disabilities as to others, including on the basis of free and informed consent by, inter alia, raising awareness of the human rights, dignity, autonomy and needs of persons with disabilities through training and the promulgation of ethical standards for public and private health care;

(e) Prohibit discrimination against persons with disabilities in the provision of health insurance, and life insurance where such insurance is permitted by national law, which shall be provided in a fair and reasonable manner;

(f) Prevent discriminatory denial of health care or health services or food and fluids on the basis of disability.

Article 26

Habilitation and rehabilitation

1. States Parties shall take effective and appropriate measures, including through peer support, to enable persons with disabilities to attain and maintain maximum independence, full physical, mental, social and vocational ability, and full inclusion and participation in all aspects of life. To that end, States Parties shall organize, strengthen and extend comprehensive habilitation and rehabilitation services and programmes, particularly in the areas of health, employment, education and social services, in such a way that these services and programmes:

(a) Begin at the earliest possible stage, and are based on the multidisciplinary assessment of individual needs and strengths;

(b) Support participation and inclusion in the community and all aspects of society, are voluntary, and are available to persons with disabilities as close as possible to their own communities, including in rural areas.

2. States Parties shall promote the development of initial and continuing training for professionals and staff working in habilitation and rehabilitation services.

3. States Parties shall promote the availability, knowledge and use of assistive devices and technologies, designed for persons with disabilities, as they relate to habilitation and rehabilitation.

Article 27

Work and employment

1. States Parties recognize the right of persons with disabilities to work, on an equal basis with others; this includes the right to the opportunity to gain a living by work freely chosen or accepted in a labour market and work environment that is open, inclusive and accessible to persons with disabilities. States Parties shall safeguard and promote the realization of the right to work, including for those who acquire a disability during the course of employment, by taking appropriate steps, including through legislation, to, inter alia:

(a) Prohibit discrimination on the basis of disability with regard to all matters concerning all forms of employment, including conditions of recruitment, hiring and employment, continuance of employment, career advancement and safe and healthy working conditions;

(b) Protect the rights of persons with disabilities, on an equal basis with others, to just and favourable conditions of work, including equal opportunities and equal remuneration for work of equal value, safe and healthy working conditions, including protection from harassment, and the redress of grievances;

(c) Ensure that persons with disabilities are able to exercise their labour and trade union rights on an equal basis with others;

(d) Enable persons with disabilities to have effective access to general technical and vocational guidance programmes, placement services and vocational and continuing training;

(e) Promote employment opportunities and career advancement for persons with disabilities in the labour market, as well as assistance in finding, obtaining, maintaining and returning to employment;

(f) Promote opportunities for self-employment, entrepreneurship, the development of cooperatives and starting one's own business;

(g) Employ persons with disabilities in the public sector;

(h) Promote the employment of persons with disabilities in the private sector through appropriate policies and measures, which may include affirmative action programmes, incentives and other measures;

(i) Ensure that reasonable accommodation is provided to persons with disabilities in the workplace;

(j) Promote the acquisition by persons with disabilities of work experience in the open labour market;

(k) Promote vocational and professional rehabilitation, job retention and return-to-work programmes for persons with disabilities.

2. States Parties shall ensure that persons with disabilities are not held in slavery or in servitude, and are protected, on an equal basis with others, from forced or compulsory labour.

Article 28

Adequate standard of living and social protection

1. States Parties recognize the right of persons with disabilities to an adequate standard of living for themselves and their families, including adequate food, clothing and housing, and to the continuous improvement of living conditions, and shall take appropriate steps to safeguard and promote the realization of this right without discrimination on the basis of disability.

2. States Parties recognize the right of persons with disabilities to social protection and to the enjoyment of that right without discrimination on the basis of disability, and shall take appropriate steps to safeguard and promote the realization of this right, including measures:

(a) To ensure equal access by persons with disabilities to clean water services, and to ensure access to appropriate and affordable services, devices and other assistance for disability-related needs;

(b) To ensure access by persons with disabilities, in particular women and girls with disabilities and older persons with disabilities, to social protection programmes and poverty reduction programmes;

(c) To ensure access by persons with disabilities and their families living in situations of poverty to assistance from the State with disability-related expenses, including adequate training, counselling, financial assistance and respite care;

(d) To ensure access by persons with disabilities to public housing programmes;

(e) To ensure equal access by persons with disabilities to retirement benefits and programmes.

Article 29

Participation in political and public life

States Parties shall guarantee to persons with disabilities political rights and the opportunity to enjoy them on an equal basis with others, and shall undertake:

(a) To ensure that persons with disabilities can effectively and fully participate in political and public life on an equal basis with others, directly or through freely chosen representatives, including the right and opportunity for persons with disabilities to vote and be elected, inter alia, by:

(i) Ensuring that voting procedures, facilities and materials are appropriate, accessible and easy to understand and use;

(ii) Protecting the right of persons with disabilities to vote by secret ballot in elections and public referendums without intimidation, and to stand for elections, to effectively hold office and perform all public functions at all levels of government, facilitating the use of assistive and new technologies where appropriate;

(iii) Guaranteeing the free expression of the will of persons with disabilities as electors and to this end, where necessary, at their request, allowing assistance in voting by a person of their own choice;

(b) To promote actively an environment in which persons with disabilities can effectively and fully participate in the conduct of public affairs, without discrimination and on an equal basis with others, and encourage their participation in public affairs, including:

(i) Participation in non-governmental organizations and associations concerned with the public and political life of the country, and in the activities and administration of political parties;

(ii) Forming and joining organizations of persons with disabilities to represent persons with disabilities at international, national, regional and local levels.

Article 30

Participation in cultural life, recreation, leisure and sport

1. States Parties recognize the right of persons with disabilities to take part on an equal basis with others in cultural life, and shall take all appropriate measures to ensure that persons with disabilities:

(a) Enjoy access to cultural materials in accessible formats;

(b) Enjoy access to television programmes, films, theatre and other cultural activities, in accessible formats;

(c) Enjoy access to places for cultural performances or services, such as theatres, museums, cinemas, libraries and tourism services, and, as far as possible, enjoy access to monuments and sites of national cultural importance.

2. States Parties shall take appropriate measures to enable persons with disabilities to have the opportunity to develop and utilize their creative, artistic and intellectual potential, not only for their own benefit, but also for the enrichment of society.

3. States Parties shall take all appropriate steps, in accordance with international law, to ensure that laws protecting intellectual property rights do not constitute an unreasonable or discriminatory barrier to access by persons with disabilities to cultural materials.

4. Persons with disabilities shall be entitled, on an equal basis with others, to recognition and support of their specific cultural and linguistic identity, including sign languages and deaf culture.

5. With a view to enabling persons with disabilities to participate on an equal basis with others in recreational, leisure and sporting activities, States Parties shall take appropriate measures:

(a) To encourage and promote the participation, to the fullest extent possible, of persons with disabilities in mainstream sporting activities at all levels;

(b) To ensure that persons with disabilities have an opportunity to organize, develop and participate in disability-specific sporting and recreational activities and, to this end, encourage the provision, on an equal basis with others, of appropriate instruction, training and resources;

(c) To ensure that persons with disabilities have access to sporting, recreational and tourism venues;

(d) To ensure that children with disabilities have equal access with other children to participation in play, recreation and leisure and sporting activities, including those activities in the school system;

(e) To ensure that persons with disabilities have access to services from those involved in the organization of recreational, tourism, leisure and sporting activities.

Article 31

Statistics and data collection

1. States Parties undertake to collect appropriate information, including statistical and research data, to enable them to formulate and implement policies to give effect to the present Convention. The process of collecting and maintaining this information shall:

(a) Comply with legally established safeguards, including legislation on data protection, to ensure confidentiality and respect for the privacy of persons with disabilities;

(b) Comply with internationally accepted norms to protect human rights and fundamental freedoms and ethical principles in the collection and use of statistics.

2. The information collected in accordance with this article shall be disaggregated, as appropriate, and used to help assess the implementation of States Parties' obligations under the present Convention and to identify and address the barriers faced by persons with disabilities in exercising their rights.

3. States Parties shall assume responsibility for the dissemination of these statistics and ensure their accessibility to persons with disabilities and others.

Article 32

International cooperation

1. States Parties recognize the importance of international cooperation and its promotion, in support of national efforts for the realization of the purpose and objectives of the present Convention, and will undertake appropriate and effective measures in this regard, between and among States and, as appropriate, in partnership with relevant international and regional organizations and civil society, in particular organizations of persons with disabilities. Such measures could include, inter alia:

(a) Ensuring that international cooperation, including international development programmes, is inclusive of and accessible to persons with disabilities;

(b) Facilitating and supporting capacity-building, including through the exchange and sharing of information, experiences, training programmes and best practices;

(c) Facilitating cooperation in research and access to scientific and technical knowledge;

(d) Providing, as appropriate, technical and economic assistance, including by facilitating access to and sharing of accessible and assistive technologies, and through the transfer of technologies.

2. The provisions of this article are without prejudice to the obligations of each State Party to fulfil its obligations under the present Convention.

Article 33

National implementation and monitoring

1. States Parties, in accordance with their system of organization, shall designate one or more focal points within government for matters relating to the implementation of the present Convention, and shall give due consideration to the establishment or designation of a coordination

mechanism within government to facilitate related action in different sectors and at different levels.

2. States Parties shall, in accordance with their legal and administrative systems, maintain, strengthen, designate or establish within the State Party, a framework, including one or more independent mechanisms, as appropriate, to promote, protect and monitor implementation of the present Convention. When designating or establishing such a mechanism, States Parties shall take into account the principles relating to the status and functioning of national institutions for protection and promotion of human rights.

3. Civil society, in particular persons with disabilities and their representative organizations, shall be involved and participate fully in the monitoring process.

Article 34

Committee on the Rights of Persons with Disabilities

1. There shall be established a Committee on the Rights of Persons with Disabilities (hereafter referred to as "the Committee"), which shall carry out the functions hereinafter provided.

2. The Committee shall consist, at the time of entry into force of the present Convention, of twelve experts. After an additional sixty ratifications or accessions to the Convention, the membership of the Committee shall increase by six members, attaining a maximum number of eighteen members.

3. The members of the Committee shall serve in their personal capacity and shall be of high moral standing and recognized competence and experience in the field covered by the present Convention. When nominating their candidates, States Parties are invited to give due consideration to the provision set out in article 4, paragraph 3, of the present Convention.

4. The members of the Committee shall be elected by States Parties, consideration being given to equitable geographical distribution, representation of the different forms of civilization and of the principal legal systems, balanced gender representation and participation of experts with disabilities.

5. The members of the Committee shall be elected by secret ballot from a list of persons nominated by the States Parties from among their nationals at meetings of the Conference of States Parties. At those meetings, for which two thirds of States Parties shall constitute a quorum, the persons elected to the Committee shall be those who obtain the largest number of votes and an absolute majority of the votes of the representatives of States Parties present and voting.

6. The initial election shall be held no later than six months after the date of entry into force of the present Convention. At least four months before the date of each election, the Secretary-General of the United Nations shall address a letter to the States Parties inviting them to submit the nominations within two months. The Secretary-General shall subsequently prepare a list in alphabetical order of all persons thus

nominated, indicating the State Parties which have nominated them, and shall submit it to the States Parties to the present Convention.

7. The members of the Committee shall be elected for a term of four years. They shall be eligible for re-election once. However, the term of six of the members elected at the first election shall expire at the end of two years; immediately after the first election, the names of these six members shall be chosen by lot by the chairperson of the meeting referred to in paragraph 5 of this article.

8. The election of the six additional members of the Committee shall be held on the occasion of regular elections, in accordance with the relevant provisions of this article.

9. If a member of the Committee dies or resigns or declares that for any other cause she or he can no longer perform her or his duties, the State Party which nominated the member shall appoint another expert possessing the qualifications and meeting the requirements set out in the relevant provisions of this article, to serve for the remainder of the term.

10. The Committee shall establish its own rules of procedure.

11. The Secretary–General of the United Nations shall provide the necessary staff and facilities for the effective performance of the functions of the Committee under the present Convention, and shall convene its initial meeting.

12. With the approval of the General Assembly of the United Nations, the members of the Committee established under the present Convention shall receive emoluments from United Nations resources on such terms and conditions as the Assembly may decide, having regard to the importance of the Committee's responsibilities.

13. The members of the Committee shall be entitled to the facilities, privileges and immunities of experts on mission for the United Nations as laid down in the relevant sections of the Convention on the Privileges and Immunities of the United Nations.

Article 35

Reports by States Parties

1. Each State Party shall submit to the Committee, through the Secretary–General of the United Nations, a comprehensive report on measures taken to give effect to its obligations under the present Convention and on the progress made in that regard, within two years after the entry into force of the present Convention for the State Party concerned.

2. Thereafter, States Parties shall submit subsequent reports at least every four years and further whenever the Committee so requests.

3. The Committee shall decide any guidelines applicable to the content of the reports.

4. A State Party which has submitted a comprehensive initial report to the Committee need not, in its subsequent reports, repeat information previously provided. When preparing reports to the Commit-

tee, States Parties are invited to consider doing so in an open and transparent process and to give due consideration to the provision set out in article 4, paragraph 3, of the present Convention.

5. Reports may indicate factors and difficulties affecting the degree of fulfilment of obligations under the present Convention.

Article 36

Consideration of reports

1. Each report shall be considered by the Committee, which shall make such suggestions and general recommendations on the report as it may consider appropriate and shall forward these to the State Party concerned. The State Party may respond with any information it chooses to the Committee. The Committee may request further information from States Parties relevant to the implementation of the present Convention.

2. If a State Party is significantly overdue in the submission of a report, the Committee may notify the State Party concerned of the need to examine the implementation of the present Convention in that State Party, on the basis of reliable information available to the Committee, if the relevant report is not submitted within three months following the notification. The Committee shall invite the State Party concerned to participate in such examination. Should the State Party respond by submitting the relevant report, the provisions of paragraph 1 of this article will apply.

3. The Secretary–General of the United Nations shall make available the reports to all States Parties.

4. States Parties shall make their reports widely available to the public in their own countries and facilitate access to the suggestions and general recommendations relating to these reports.

5. The Committee shall transmit, as it may consider appropriate, to the specialized agencies, funds and programmes of the United Nations, and other competent bodies, reports from States Parties in order to address a request or indication of a need for technical advice or assistance contained therein, along with the Committee's observations and recommendations, if any, on these requests or indications.

Article 37

Cooperation between States Parties and the Committee

1. Each State Party shall cooperate with the Committee and assist its members in the fulfilment of their mandate.

2. In its relationship with States Parties, the Committee shall give due consideration to ways and means of enhancing national capacities for the implementation of the present Convention, including through international cooperation.

Article 38

Relationship of the Committee with other bodies

In order to foster the effective implementation of the present Convention and to encourage international cooperation in the field covered by the present Convention:

(a) The specialized agencies and other United Nations organs shall be entitled to be represented at the consideration of the implementation of such provisions of the present Convention as fall within the scope of their mandate. The Committee may invite the specialized agencies and other competent bodies as it may consider appropriate to provide expert advice on the implementation of the Convention in areas falling within the scope of their respective mandates. The Committee may invite specialized agencies and other United Nations organs to submit reports on the implementation of the Convention in areas falling within the scope of their activities;

(b) The Committee, as it discharges its mandate, shall consult, as appropriate, other relevant bodies instituted by international human rights treaties, with a view to ensuring the consistency of their respective reporting guidelines, suggestions and general recommendations, and avoiding duplication and overlap in the performance of their functions.

Article 39

Report of the Committee

The Committee shall report every two years to the General Assembly and to the Economic and Social Council on its activities, and may make suggestions and general recommendations based on the examination of reports and information received from the States Parties. Such suggestions and general recommendations shall be included in the report of the Committee together with comments, if any, from States Parties.

Article 40

Conference of States Parties

1. The States Parties shall meet regularly in a Conference of States Parties in order to consider any matter with regard to the implementation of the present Convention.

2. No later than six months after the entry into force of the present Convention, the Conference of States Parties shall be convened by the Secretary–General of the United Nations. The subsequent meetings shall be convened by the Secretary–General biennially or upon the decision of the Conference of States Parties.

Article 41

Depositary

The Secretary–General of the United Nations shall be the depositary of the present Convention.

Article 42

Signature

The present Convention shall be open for signature by all States and by regional integration organizations at United Nations Headquarters in New York as of 30 March 2007.

Article 43

Consent to be bound

The present Convention shall be subject to ratification by signatory States and to formal confirmation by signatory regional integration organizations. It shall be open for accession by any State or regional integration organization which has not signed the Convention.

Article 44

Regional integration organizations

1. "Regional integration organization" shall mean an organization constituted by sovereign States of a given region, to which its member States have transferred competence in respect of matters governed by the present Convention. Such organizations shall declare, in their instruments of formal confirmation or accession, the extent of their competence with respect to matters governed by the present Convention. Subsequently, they shall inform the depositary of any substantial modification in the extent of their competence.

2. References to "States Parties" in the present Convention shall apply to such organizations within the limits of their competence.

3. For the purposes of article 45, paragraph 1, and article 47, paragraphs 2 and 3, of the present Convention, any instrument deposited by a regional integration organization shall not be counted.

4. Regional integration organizations, in matters within their competence, may exercise their right to vote in the Conference of States Parties, with a number of votes equal to the number of their member States that are Parties to the present Convention. Such an organization shall not exercise its right to vote if any of its member States exercises its right, and vice versa.

Article 45

Entry into force

1. The present Convention shall enter into force on the thirtieth day after the deposit of the twentieth instrument of ratification or accession.

2. For each State or regional integration organization ratifying, formally confirming or acceding to the present Convention after the deposit of the twentieth such instrument, the Convention shall enter into force on the thirtieth day after the deposit of its own such instrument.

Article 46

Reservations

1. Reservations incompatible with the object and purpose of the present Convention shall not be permitted.

2. Reservations may be withdrawn at any time.

Article 47

Amendments

1. Any State Party may propose an amendment to the present Convention and submit it to the Secretary–General of the United Nations. The Secretary–General shall communicate any proposed amendments to States Parties, with a request to be notified whether they favour a conference of States Parties for the purpose of considering and deciding upon the proposals. In the event that, within four months from the date of such communication, at least one third of the States Parties favour such a conference, the Secretary–General shall convene the conference under the auspices of the United Nations. Any amendment adopted by a majority of two thirds of the States Parties present and voting shall be submitted by the Secretary–General to the General Assembly of the United Nations for approval and thereafter to all States Parties for acceptance.

2. An amendment adopted and approved in accordance with paragraph 1 of this article shall enter into force on the thirtieth day after the number of instruments of acceptance deposited reaches two thirds of the number of States Parties at the date of adoption of the amendment. Thereafter, the amendment shall enter into force for any State Party on the thirtieth day following the deposit of its own instrument of acceptance. An amendment shall be binding only on those States Parties which have accepted it.

3. If so decided by the Conference of States Parties by consensus, an amendment adopted and approved in accordance with paragraph 1 of this article which relates exclusively to articles 34, 38, 39 and 40 shall enter into force for all States Parties on the thirtieth day after the number of instruments of acceptance deposited reaches two thirds of the number of States Parties at the date of adoption of the amendment.

Article 48

Denunciation

A State Party may denounce the present Convention by written notification to the Secretary–General of the United Nations. The denunciation shall become effective one year after the date of receipt of the notification by the Secretary–General.

Article 49

Accessible format

The text of the present Convention shall be made available in accessible formats.

Article 50

Authentic texts

The Arabic, Chinese, English, French, Russian and Spanish texts of the present Convention shall be equally authentic.

IN WITNESS THEREOF the undersigned plenipotentiaries, being duly authorized thereto by their respective Governments, have signed the present Convention.

Annex II

Optional Protocol to the Convention on the Rights of Persons with Disabilities

The States Parties to the present Protocol have agreed as follows:

Article 1

1. State Party to the present Protocol ("State Party") recognizes the competence of the Committee on the Rights of Persons with Disabilities ("the Committee") to receive and consider communications from or on behalf of individuals or groups of individuals subject to its jurisdiction who claim to be victims of a violation by that State Party of the provisions of the Convention.

2. No communication shall be received by the Committee if it concerns a State Party to the Convention that is not a party to the present Protocol.

Article 2

The Committee shall consider a communication inadmissible when:

(a) The communication is anonymous;

(b) The communication constitutes an abuse of the right of submission of such communications or is incompatible with the provisions of the Convention;

(c) The same matter has already been examined by the Committee or has been or is being examined under another procedure of international investigation or settlement;

(d) All available domestic remedies have not been exhausted. This shall not be the rule where the application of the remedies is unreasonably prolonged or unlikely to bring effective relief;

(e) It is manifestly ill-founded or not sufficiently substantiated; or when

(f) The facts that are the subject of the communication occurred prior to the entry into force of the present Protocol for the State Party concerned unless those facts continued after that date.

Article 3

Subject to the provisions of article 2 of the present Protocol, the Committee shall bring any communications submitted to it confidentially to the attention of the State Party. Within six months, the receiving State shall submit to the Committee written explanations or statements clarifying the matter and the remedy, if any, that may have been taken by that State.

Article 4

1. At any time after the receipt of a communication and before a determination on the merits has been reached, the Committee may transmit to the State Party concerned for its urgent consideration a request that the State Party take such interim measures as may be necessary to avoid possible irreparable damage to the victim or victims of the alleged violation.

2. Where the Committee exercises its discretion under paragraph 1 of this article, this does not imply a determination on admissibility or on the merits of the communication.

Article 5

The Committee shall hold closed meetings when examining communications under the present Protocol. After examining a communication, the Committee shall forward its suggestions and recommendations, if any, to the State Party concerned and to the petitioner.

Article 6

1. If the Committee receives reliable information indicating grave or systematic violations by a State Party of rights set forth in the Convention, the Committee shall invite that State Party to cooperate in the examination of the information and to this end submit observations with regard to the information concerned.

2. Taking into account any observations that may have been submitted by the State Party concerned as well as any other reliable information available to it, the Committee may designate one or more of its members to conduct an inquiry and to report urgently to the Committee. Where warranted and with the consent of the State Party, the inquiry may include a visit to its territory.

3. After examining the findings of such an inquiry, the Committee shall transmit these findings to the State Party concerned together with any comments and recommendations.

4. The State Party concerned shall, within six months of receiving the findings, comments and recommendations transmitted by the Committee, submit its observations to the Committee.

5. Such an inquiry shall be conducted confidentially and the cooperation of the State Party shall be sought at all stages of the proceedings.

Article 7

1. The Committee may invite the State Party concerned to include in its report under article 35 of the Convention details of any measures taken in response to an inquiry conducted under article 6 of the present Protocol.

2. The Committee may, if necessary, after the end of the period of six months referred to in article 6, paragraph 4, invite the State Party concerned to inform it of the measures taken in response to such an inquiry.

Article 8

Each State Party may, at the time of signature or ratification of the present Protocol or accession thereto, declare that it does not recognize the competence of the Committee provided for in articles 6 and 7.

Article 9

The Secretary–General of the United Nations shall be the depositary of the present Protocol.

Article 10

The present Protocol shall be open for signature by signatory States and regional integration organizations of the Convention at United Nations Headquarters in New York as of 30 March 2007.

Article 11

The present Protocol shall be subject to ratification by signatory States of the present Protocol which have ratified or acceded to the Convention. It shall be subject to formal confirmation by signatory regional integration organizations of the present Protocol which have formally confirmed or acceded to the Convention. It shall be open for accession by any State or regional integration organization which has ratified, formally confirmed or acceded to the Convention and which has not signed the Protocol.

Article 12

1. "Regional integration organization" shall mean an organization constituted by sovereign States of a given region, to which its member States have transferred competence in respect of matters governed by the Convention and the present Protocol. Such organizations shall declare, in their instruments of formal confirmation or accession, the extent of their competence with respect to matters governed by the Convention and the present Protocol. Subsequently, they shall inform the depositary of any substantial modification in the extent of their competence.

2. References to "States Parties" in the present Protocol shall apply to such organizations within the limits of their competence.

3. For the purposes of article 13, paragraph 1, and article 15, paragraph 2, of the present Protocol, any instrument deposited by a regional integration organization shall not be counted.

4. Regional integration organizations, in matters within their competence, may exercise their right to vote in the meeting of States Parties, with a number of votes equal to the number of their member States that are Parties to the present Protocol. Such an organization shall not exercise its right to vote if any of its member States exercises its right, and vice versa.

Article 13

1. Subject to the entry into force of the Convention, the present Protocol shall enter into force on the thirtieth day after the deposit of the tenth instrument of ratification or accession.

2. For each State or regional integration organization ratifying, formally confirming or acceding to the present Protocol after the deposit of the tenth such instrument, the Protocol shall enter into force on the thirtieth day after the deposit of its own such instrument.

Article 14

1. Reservations incompatible with the object and purpose of the present Protocol shall not be permitted.

2. Reservations may be withdrawn at any time.

Article 15

1. Any State Party may propose an amendment to the present Protocol and submit it to the Secretary–General of the United Nations. The Secretary–General shall communicate any proposed amendments to States Parties, with a request to be notified whether they favour a meeting of States Parties for the purpose of considering and deciding upon the proposals. In the event that, within four months from the date of such communication, at least one third of the States Parties favour such a meeting, the Secretary–General shall convene the meeting under the auspices of the United Nations. Any amendment adopted by a majority of two thirds of the States Parties present and voting shall be submitted by the Secretary–General to the General Assembly of the United Nations for approval and thereafter to all States Parties for acceptance.

2. An amendment adopted and approved in accordance with paragraph 1 of this article shall enter into force on the thirtieth day after the number of instruments of acceptance deposited reaches two thirds of the number of States Parties at the date of adoption of the amendment. Thereafter, the amendment shall enter into force for any State Party on the thirtieth day following the deposit of its own instrument of acceptance. An amendment shall be binding only on those States Parties which have accepted it.

Article 16

A State Party may denounce the present Protocol by written notification to the Secretary–General of the United Nations. The denunciation shall become effective one year after the date of receipt of the notification by the Secretary–General.

Article 17

The text of the present Protocol shall be made available in accessible formats.

Article 18

The Arabic, Chinese, English, French, Russian and Spanish texts of the present Protocol shall be equally authentic.

IN WITNESS THEREOF the undersigned plenipotentiaries, being duly authorized thereto by their respective Governments, have signed the present Protocol.

. . .

Document 47
CONVENTION RELATING TO THE STATUS OF REFUGEES

189 U.N.T.S. 137 (1951) (excerpts)

Article 1. Definition of the term "refugee"

A. For the purposes of the present Convention, the term "refugee" shall apply to any person who: . . .

(2) As a result of events occurring before 1 January 1951 and owing to well-founded fear of being persecuted for reasons of race, religion, nationality, membership of a particular social group or political opinion, is outside the country of his nationality and is unable or, owing to such fear, is unwilling to avail himself of the protection of that country; or who, not having a nationality and being outside the country of his former habitual residence as a result of such events, is unable or, owing to such fear, is unwilling to return to it.

In the case of a person who has more than one nationality, the term "the country of his nationality" shall mean each of the countries of which he is a national and a person shall not be deemed to be lacking the protection of the country of his nationality if, without any valid reason based on well-founded fear, he has not availed himself of the protection of one of the countries of which he is a national. . . .

F. The provisions of this Convention shall not apply to any person with respect to whom there are serious reasons for considering that:

(a) he has committed a crime against peace, a war crime, or a crime against humanity, as defined in the international instruments drawn up to make provision in respect of such crimes;

(b) he has committed a serious non-political crime outside the country of refuge prior to his admission to that country as a refugee;

(c) he has been guilty of acts contrary to the purposes and principles of the United Nations. . . .

Article 2. General obligations

Every refugee has duties to the country in which he finds himself, which require in particular that he conform to its laws and regulations as well as to measures taken for the maintenance of public order.

Article 3. Non-discrimination

The Contracting States shall apply the provisions of this Convention to refugees without discrimination as to race, religion or country or origin. . . .

Article 9. Provisional Measures

Nothing is this Convention shall prevent a Contracting State, in time of war or other grave and exceptional circumstances, from taking provisionally measures which it considers to be essential to the national security in the case of a particular person, pending a determination by the Contracting State that the person is in fact a refugee and that the continuance of such measures is necessary in his case in the interests of national security....

Article 16. Access to courts

1. A refugee shall have free access to the courts of law on the territory of all Contracting States.

2. A refugee shall enjoy in the Contracting State in which he has his habitual residence the same treatment as a national in matters pertaining to access to the courts, including legal assistance and exemption from *cautio judicatum solvi*.

3. A refugee shall be accorded in the matters referred to in paragraph 2 in countries other than that in which he has his habitual residence the treatment granted to a national of the country of his habitual residence....

Article 31. Refugees unlawfully in the country of refuge

1. The Contracting States shall not impose penalties, on account of their illegal entry or presence, on refugees who, coming directly from a territory where their life or freedom was threatened in the sense of Article 1, enter or are present in their territory without authorization, provided they present themselves without delay to the authorities and show good cause for their illegal entry or presence.

2. The Contracting States shall not apply to the movements of such refugees restrictions other than those which are necessary and such restrictions shall only be applied until their status in the country is regularized or they obtain admission into another country. The Contracting States shall allow such refugees a reasonable period and all the necessary facilities to obtain admission into another country.

Article 32. Expulsion

1. The Contracting States shall not expel a refugee lawfully in their territory save on grounds of national security or public order.

2. The expulsion of such a refugee shall be only in pursuance of a decision reached in accordance with due process of law. Except where compelling reasons of national security otherwise require, the refugee shall be allowed to submit evidence to clear himself, and to appeal to and be represented for the purpose before competent authority or a person or persons specially designated by the competent authority.

3. The Contracting States shall allow such a refugee a reasonable period within which to seek legal admission into another country. The Contracting States reserve the right to apply during that period such internal measures as they may deem necessary.

Article 33. Prohibition of expulsion or return ("*refoulement*")

1. No Contracting State shall expel or return ("*refouler*") a refugee in any manner whatsoever to the frontiers of territories where his life or freedom would be threatened on account of his race, religion, nationality, membership of a particular social group or political opinion.

2. The benefit of the present provision may not, however, be claimed by a refugee whom there are reasonable grounds for regarding as a danger to the security of the country in which he is, or who, having been convicted by a final judgment of a particularly serious crime, constitutes a danger to the community of that country.

Article 34. Naturalization

The Contracting States shall as far as possible facilitate the assimilation and naturalization of refugees. They shall in particular make every effort to expedite naturalization proceedings and to reduce as far as possible the charges and costs of such proceedings. . . .

Document 48
PROTOCOL RELATING TO THE STATUS OF REFUGEES

606 U.N.T.S. 267 (1967) (excerpt)

Article I. General provision

1. The States Parties to the present Protocol undertake to apply Articles 2 to 34 inclusive of the Convention to refugees as hereinafter defined.

2. For the purpose of the present Protocol, the term "refugee" shall, except as regards the application of paragraph 3 of this article, means any person within the definition of Article 1 of the Convention as if the words "As a result of events occurring before 1 January 1951 and . . ." and the words ". . . as a result of such events", in Article 1 A (2) were omitted.

3. The present Protocol shall be applied by the States Parties hereto without any geographic limitation, save that existing declarations made by States already Parties to the Convention in accordance with Article 1 (B) (1) (a) of the Convention, shall, unless extended under Article 1 (B) (2) thereof, apply also under the present Protocol.

Document 49
INTERNATIONAL CONVENTION AGAINST THE TAKING OF HOSTAGES

1316 U.N.T.S. 205 (1979)

The States Parties to this Convention,

Having in mind the purposes and principles of the Charter of the United Nations concerning the maintenance of international peace and security and the promotion of friendly relations and co-operation among States,

Recognizing in particular that everyone has the right to life, liberty and security of person, as set out in the Universal Declaration of Human Rights and the International Covenant on Civil and Political Rights,

Reaffirming the principle of equal rights and self-determination of peoples as enshrined in the Charter of the United Nations and the Declaration on Principles of International Law concerning Friendly Relations and Co-operation among States in accordance with the Charter of the United Nations, as well as in other relevant resolutions of the General Assembly,

Considering that the taking of hostages is an offence of grave concern to the international community and that, in accordance with the provisions of this Convention, any person committing an act of hostage taking shall either be prosecuted or extradited,

Being convinced that it is urgently necessary to develop international co-operation between States in devising and adopting effective measures for the prevention, prosecution and punishment of all acts of taking of hostages as manifestations of international terrorism,

Have agreed as follows:

Article 1

1. Any person who seizes or detains and threatens to kill, to injure or to continue to detain another person (hereinafter referred to as the "hostage") in order to compel a third party, namely, a State, an international intergovernmental organization, a natural or juridical person, or a group of persons, to do or abstain from doing any act as an explicit or implicit condition for the release of the hostage commits the offence of taking of hostages ("hostage-taking") within the meaning of this Convention.

2. Any person who:

(a) attempts to commit an act of hostage-taking, or

(b) participates as an accomplice of anyone who commits or attempts to commit an act of hostage-taking likewise commits an offence for the purposes of this Convention.

Article 2

Each State Party shall make the offences set forth in Article 1 punishable by appropriate penalties which take into account the grave nature of those offences.

Article 3

1. The State Party in the territory of which the hostage is held by the offender shall take all measures it considers appropriate to ease the situation of the hostage, in particular, to secure his release and, after his release, to facilitate, when relevant, his departure.

2. If any object which the offender has obtained as a result of the taking of hostages comes into the custody of a State Party, that State Party shall return it as soon as possible to the hostage or the third party referred to in Article 1, as the case may be, or to the appropriate authorities thereof.

Article 4

States Parties shall co-operate in the prevention of the offences set forth in Article 1, particularly by:

(a) taking all practicable measures to prevent preparations in their respective territories for the commission of those offences within or outside their territories, including measures to prohibit in their territories illegal activities of persons, groups and organizations that encourage, instigate, organize or engage in the perpetration of acts of taking of hostages;

(b) exchanging information and co-ordinating the taking of administrative and other measures as appropriate to prevent the commission of those offences.

Article 5

1. Each State Party shall take such measures as may be necessary to establish its jurisdiction over any of the offences set forth in Article 1 which are committed:

(a) in its territory or on board a ship or aircraft registered in that State;

(b) by any of its nationals or, if that State considers it appropriate, by those stateless persons who have their habitual residence in its territory;

(c) in order to compel that State to do or abstain from doing any act; or

(d) with respect to a hostage who is a national of that State, if that State considers it appropriate.

2. Each State Party shall likewise take such measures as may be necessary to establish its jurisdiction over the offences set forth in Article 1 in cases where the alleged offender is present in its territory and it does not extradite him to any of the States mentioned in paragraph 1 of this article.

3. This Convention does not exclude any criminal jurisdiction exercised in accordance with internal law.

Article 6

1. Upon being satisfied that the circumstances so warrant, any State Party in the territory of which the alleged offender is present shall, in accordance with its laws, take him into custody or take other measures to ensure his presence for such time as is necessary to enable any criminal or extradition proceedings to be instituted. That State Party shall immediately make a preliminary inquiry into the facts.

2. The custody or other measures referred to in paragraph 1 of this article shall be notified without delay directly or through the Secretary–General of the United Nations to:

(a) the State where the offence was committed;

(b) the State against which compulsion has been directed or attempted;

(c) the State of which the natural or juridical person against whom compulsion has been directed or attempted is a national;

(d) the State of which the hostage is a national or in the territory of which he has his habitual residence;

(e) the State of which the alleged offender is a national or, if he is a stateless person, in the territory of which he has his habitual residence;

(f) the international intergovernmental organization against which compulsion has been directed or attempted;

(g) all other States concerned.

3. Any person regarding whom the measures referred to in paragraph 1 of this article are being taken shall be entitled:

(a) to communicate without delay with the nearest appropriate representative of the State of which he is a national or which is otherwise entitled to establish such communication or, if he is a stateless person, the State in the territory of which he has his habitual residence;

(b) to be visited by a representative of that State.

4. The rights referred to in paragraph 3 of this article shall be exercised in conformity with the laws and regulations of the State in the territory of which the alleged offender is present subject to the proviso, however, that the said laws and regulations must enable full effect to be given to the purposes for which the rights accorded under paragraph 3 of this article are intended.

5. The provisions of paragraphs 3 and 4 of this article shall be without prejudice to the right of any State Party having a claim to jurisdiction in accordance with paragraph 1(b) of Article 5 to invite the International Committee of the Red Cross to communicate with and visit the alleged offender.

6. The State which makes the preliminary inquiry contemplated in paragraph 1 of this article shall promptly report its findings to the States or organization referred to in paragraph 2 of this article and indicate whether it intends to exercise jurisdiction.

Article 7

The State Party where the alleged offender is prosecuted shall in accordance with its laws communicate the final outcome of the proceedings to the Secretary–General of the United Nations, who shall transmit the information to the other States concerned and the international intergovernmental organizations concerned.

Article 8

1. The State Party in the territory of which the alleged offender is found shall, if it does not extradite him, be obliged, without exception whatsoever and whether or not the offence was committed in its territory, to submit the case to its competent authorities for the purpose of prosecution, through proceedings in accordance with the laws of that State. Those authorities shall take their decision in the same manner as in the case of any ordinary offence of a grave nature under the law of that State.

2. Any person regarding whom proceedings are being carried out in connection with any of the offences set forth in Article 1 shall be guaranteed fair treatment at all stages of the proceedings, including enjoyment of all the rights and guarantees provided by the law of the State in the territory of which he is present.

Article 9

1. A request for the extradition of an alleged offender, pursuant to this Convention, shall not be granted if the requested State Party has substantial grounds for believing:

(a) that the request for extradition for an offence set forth in Article 1 has been made for the purpose of prosecuting or punishing a person on account of his race, religion, nationality, ethnic origin or political opinion; or

(b) that the person's position may be prejudiced:

(i) for any of the reasons mentioned in subparagraph (a) of this paragraph; or

(ii) for the reason that communication with him by the appropriate authorities of the State entitled to exercise rights of protection cannot be effected.

2. With respect to the offences as defined in this Convention the provisions of all extradition treaties and arrangements applicable be-

tween States Parties are modified as between States Parties to the extent that they are incompatible with this Convention.

Article 10

1. The offences set forth in Article 1 shall be deemed to be included as extraditable offences in any extradition treaty existing between States Parties. States Parties undertake to include such offences as extraditable offences in every extradition treaty to be concluded between them.

2. If a State Party which makes extradition conditional on the existence of a treaty receives a request for extradition from another State Party with which it has no extradition treaty, the requested State may at its option consider this Convention as the legal basis for extradition in respect of the offences set forth in Article 1. Extradition shall be subject to the other conditions provided by the law of the requested State.

3. States Parties which do not make extradition conditional on the existence of a treaty shall recognize the offences set forth in Article 1 as extraditable offences between themselves subject to the conditions provided by the law of the requested State.

4. The offences set forth in Article 1 shall be treated, for the purpose of extradition between States Parties, as if they had been committed not only in the place in which they occurred but also in the territories of the States required to establish their jurisdiction in accordance with paragraph 1 of Article 5.

Article 11

1. States Parties shall afford one another the greatest measure of assistance in connection with criminal proceedings brought in respect of the offences set forth in Article 1, including the supply of all evidence at their disposal necessary for the proceedings.

2. The provisions of paragraph 1 of this article shall not affect obligations concerning mutual judicial assistance embodied in any other treaty.

Article 12

In so far as the Geneva Conventions of 1949 for the protection of war victims or the Additional Protocols to those Conventions are applicable to a particular act of hostage-taking, and in so far as States Parties to this Convention are bound under those conventions to prosecute or hand over the hostage-taker, the present Convention shall not apply to an act of hostage-taking committed in the course of armed conflicts as defined in the Geneva Conventions of 1949 and the Protocols thereto, including armed conflicts mentioned in Article 1, paragraph 4, of Additional Protocol I of 1977, in which peoples are fighting against colonial domination and alien occupation and against racist regimes in the exercise of their right of self-determination, as enshrined in the Charter of the United Nations and the Declaration on Principles of International Law concerning Friendly Relations and Co-operation among States in accordance with the Charter of the United Nations.

Article 13

This Convention shall not apply where the offence is committed within a single State, the hostage and the alleged offender are nationals of that State and the alleged offender is found in the territory of that State.

Article 14

Nothing in this Convention shall be construed as justifying the violation of the territorial integrity or political independence of a State in contravention of the Charter of the United Nations.

Article 15

The provisions of this Convention shall not affect the application of the Treaties on Asylum, in force at the date of the adoption of this Convention, as between the States which are parties to those Treaties; but a State Party to this Convention may not invoke those Treaties with respect to another State Party to this Convention which is not a party to those treaties. . . .

Document 50
CONVENTION AGAINST TORTURE AND OTHER CRUEL, INHUMAN OR DEGRADING TREATMENT OR PUNISHMENT

1465 U.N.T.S. 85 (Dec. 10, 1984)

The States Parties to this Convention,

Considering that, in accordance with the principles proclaimed in the Charter of the United Nations, recognition of the equal and inalienable rights of all members of the human family is the foundation of freedom, justice and peace in the world,

Recognizing that those rights derive from the inherent dignity of the human person,

Considering the obligation of States under the Charter, in particular Article 55, to promote universal respect for, and observance of, human rights and fundamental freedoms,

Having regard to Article 5 of the Universal Declaration of Human Rights and Article 7 of the International Covenant on Civil and Political Rights, both of which provide that no one may be subjected to torture or to cruel, inhuman or degrading treatment or punishment,

Having regard also to the Declaration on the Protection of All Persons from Being Subjected to Torture and Other Cruel, Inhuman or Degrading Treatment or Punishment, adopted by the General Assembly on 9 December 1975 (resolution 3452 (XXX)),

Desiring to make more effective the struggle against torture and other cruel, inhuman or degrading treatment or punishment throughout the world,

Have agreed as follows:

PART I

Article 1

1. For the purposes of this Convention, torture means any act by which severe pain or suffering, whether physical or mental, is intentionally inflicted on a person for such purposes as obtaining from him or a third person information or a confession, punishing him for an act he or a third person has committed or is suspected of having committed, or intimidating or coercing him or a third person, or for any reason based on discrimination of any kind, when such pain or suffering is inflicted by or at the instigation of or with the consent or acquiescence of a public

official or other person acting in an official capacity. It does not include pain or suffering arising only from, inherent in or incidental to lawful sanctions.

2. This article is without prejudice to any international instrument or national legislation which does or may contain provisions of wider application.

Article 2

1. Each State Party shall take effective legislative, administrative, judicial or other measures to prevent acts of torture in any territory under its jurisdiction.

2. No exceptional circumstances whatsoever, whether a state of war or a threat of war, internal political instability or any other public emergency, may be invoked as a justification of torture.

3. An order from a superior officer or a public authority may not be invoked as a justification of torture.

Article 3

1. No State Party shall expel, return ("*refouler*") or extradite a person to another State where there are substantial grounds for believing that he would be in danger of being subjected to torture.

2. For the purpose of determining whether there are such grounds, the competent authorities shall take into account all relevant considerations including, where applicable, the existence in the State concerned of a consistent pattern of gross, flagrant or mass violations of human rights.

Article 4

1. Each State Party shall ensure that all acts of torture are offences under its criminal law. The same shall apply to an attempt to commit torture and to an act by any person which constitutes complicity or participation in torture.

2. Each State Party shall make these offences punishable by appropriate penalties which take into account their grave nature.

Article 5

1. Each State Party shall take such measures as may be necessary to establish its jurisdiction over the offences referred to in Article 4 in the following cases:

(a) When the offences are committed in any territory under its jurisdiction or on board a ship or aircraft registered in that State;

(b) When the alleged offender is a national of that State;

(c) When the victim is a national of that State if that State considers it appropriate.

2. Each State Party shall likewise take such measures as may be necessary to establish its jurisdiction over such offences in cases where the alleged offender is present in any territory under its jurisdiction and

it does not extradite him pursuant to Article 8 to any of the States mentioned in paragraph 1 of this article.

3. This Convention does not exclude any criminal jurisdiction exercised in accordance with internal law.

Article 6

1. Upon being satisfied, after an examination of information available to it, that the circumstances so warrant, any State Party in whose territory a person alleged to have committed any offence referred to in Article 4 is present, shall take him into custody or take other legal measures to ensure his presence. The custody and other legal measures shall be as provided in the law of that State but may be continued only for such time as is necessary to enable any criminal or extradition proceedings to be instituted.

2. Such State shall immediately make a preliminary inquiry into the facts.

3. Any person in custody pursuant to paragraph 1 of this article shall be assisted in communicating immediately with the nearest appropriate representative of the State of which he is a national, or, if he is a stateless person, to the representative of the State where he usually resides.

4. When a State, pursuant to this article, has taken a person into custody, it shall immediately notify the States referred to in Article 5, paragraph 1, of the fact that such person in is custody and of the circumstances which warrant his detention. The State which makes the preliminary inquiry contemplated in paragraph 2 of this article shall promptly report its findings to the said States and shall indicate whether it intends to exercise jurisdiction.

Article 7

1. The State Party in territory under whose jurisdiction a person alleged to have committed any offence referred to in Article 4 is found, shall in the cases contemplated in Article 5, if it does not extradite him, submit the case to its competent authorities for the purpose of prosecution.

2. These authorities shall take their decision in the same manner as in the case of any ordinary offence of a serious nature under the law of that State. In the cases referred to in Article 5, paragraph 2, the standards of evidence required for prosecution and conviction shall in no way be less stringent than those which apply in the cases referred to in Article 5, paragraph 1.

3. Any person regarding whom proceedings are brought in connection with any of the offenses referred to in Article 4 shall be guaranteed fair treatment at all stages of the proceedings.

Article 8

1. The offenses referred to in Article 4 shall be deemed to be included as extraditable offenses in any extradition treaty existing be-

tween States Parties. States Parties undertake to include such offenses as extraditable offenses in every extradition treaty to be concluded between them.

2. If a State Party which makes extradition conditional on the existence of a treaty receives a request for extradition from another State Party with which it has no extradition treaty, it may consider this Convention as the legal basis for extradition in respect of such offenses. Extradition shall be subject to the other conditions provided by the law of the requested State.

3. States Parties which do not make extradition conditional on the existence of a treaty shall recognize such offenses as extraditable offenses between themselves subject to the conditions provided by the law of the requested State.

4. Such offenses shall be treated, for the purpose of extradition between States Parties, as if they had been committed not only in the place in which they occurred but also in the territories of the States required to establish their jurisdiction in accordance with Article 5, paragraph 1.

Article 9

1. States Parties shall afford one another the greatest measure of assistance in connection with criminal proceedings brought in respect of any of the offenses referred to in Article 4, including the supply of all evidence at their disposal necessary for the proceedings.

2. States Parties shall carry out their obligations under paragraph 1 of this article in conformity with any treaties on mutual judicial assistance that may exist between them.

Article 10

1. Each State Party shall ensure that education and information regarding the prohibition against torture are fully included in the training of law enforcement personnel, civil or military, medical personnel, public officials and other persons who may be involved in the custody, interrogation or treatment of any individual subjected to any form of arrest, detention or imprisonment.

2. Each State Party shall include this prohibition in the rules or instructions issued in regard to the duties and functions of any such persons.

Article 11

Each State Party shall keep under systematic review interrogation rules, instructions, methods and practices as well as arrangements for the custody and treatment of persons subjected to any form of arrest, detention or imprisonment in any territory under its jurisdiction, with a view to preventing any cases of torture.

Article 12

Each State Party shall ensure that its competent authorities proceed to a prompt and impartial investigation, wherever there is reasonable ground to believe that an act of torture has been committed in any territory under its jurisdiction.

Article 13

Each State Party shall ensure that any individual who alleges he has been subjected to torture in any territory under its jurisdiction has the right to complain to and to have his case promptly and impartially examined by its competent authorities. Steps shall be taken to insure that the complainant and witnesses are protected against all ill-treatment or intimidation as a consequence of his complaint or any evidence given.

Article 14

1. Each State Party shall ensure in its legal system that the victim of an act of torture obtains redress and has an enforceable right to fair and adequate compensation including the means for as full rehabilitation as possible. In the event of the death of the victim as a result of an act of torture, his dependents shall be entitled to compensation.

2. Nothing in this article shall affect any right of the victim or other persons to compensation which may exist under national law.

Article 15

Each State Party shall ensure that any statement which is established to have been made as a result of torture shall not be involved as evidence in any proceedings, except against a person accused of torture as evidence that the statement was made.

Article 16

1. Each State Party shall undertake to prevent in any territory under its jurisdiction other acts of cruel, inhuman or degrading treatment or punishment which do not amount to torture as defined in Article 1, when such acts are committed by or at the instigation of or with the consent or acquiescence of a public official or other person acting in an official capacity. In particular, the obligations contained in Articles 10, 11, 12 and 13 shall apply with the substitution for references to torture of references to other forms of cruel, inhuman or degrading treatment or punishment.

2. The provisions of this Convention are without prejudice to the provisions of any other international instrument or national law which prohibit cruel, inhuman or degrading treatment or punishment or which relate to extradition or expulsion....

Document 51
INTER–AMERICAN CONVENTION ON THE FORCED DISAPPEARANCE OF PERSONS

Done in Belem do Para, Brazil, June 9, 1994

The Member States of the Organization of American States,

Disturbed by the persistence of the forced disappearance of persons;

Reaffirming that the true meaning of American solidarity and good neighborliness can be none other than that of consolidating in this Hemisphere, in the framework of democratic institutions, a system of individual freedom and social justice based on respect for essential human rights;

Considering that the forced disappearance of persons is an affront to the conscience of the Hemisphere and a grave and abominable offense against the inherent dignity of the human being, and one that contradicts the principles and purposes enshrined in the Charter of the Organization of American States;

Considering that the forced disappearance of persons violates numerous non-derogable and essential human rights enshrined in the American Convention on Human Rights, in the American Declaration of the Rights and Duties of Man, and in the Universal Declaration of Human Rights;

Recalling that the international protection of human rights is in the form of a convention reinforcing or complementing the protection provided by domestic law and is based upon the attributes of the human personality;

Reaffirming that the systematic practice of the forced disappearance of persons constitutes a crime against humanity;

Hoping that this Convention may help to prevent, punish, and eliminate the forced disappearance of persons in the Hemisphere and make a decisive contribution to the protection of human rights and the rule of law,

Resolve to adopt the following Inter–American Convention on the Forced Disappearance of Persons:

Article I

The States Parties to this Convention undertake:

(a) Not to practice, permit, or tolerate the forced disappearance of persons, even in states of emergency or suspension of individual guarantees;

(b) To punish within their jurisdictions those persons who commit or attempt to commit the crime of forced disappearance of persons and their accomplices and accessories;

(c) To cooperate with one another in helping to prevent, punish and eliminate the forced disappearance of persons;

(d) To take legislative, administrative, judicial, and any other measures necessary to comply with the commitments undertaken in this Convention.

Article II

For the purposes of this Convention, forced disappearance is considered to be the act of depriving a person or persons of his or their freedom, in whatever way, perpetrated by agents of the state or by persons or groups of persons acting with the authorization, support, or acquiescence of the state, followed by an absence of information or a refusal to acknowledge that deprivation of freedom or to give information on the whereabouts of that person, thereby impeding his or her recourse to the applicable legal remedies and procedural guarantees.

Article III

The States Parties undertake to adopt, in accordance with their constitutional procedures, the legislative measures that may be needed to define the forced disappearance of persons as an offense and to impose an appropriate punishment commensurate with its extreme gravity. This offense shall be deemed continuous or permanent as long as the fate or whereabouts of the victim has not been determined.

The States Parties may establish mitigating circumstances for persons who have participated in acts constituting forced disappearance when they help to cause the victim to reappear alive or provide information that sheds light on the forced disappearance of a person.

Article IV

The acts constituting the forced disappearance of persons shall be considered offenses in every State Party. Consequently, each State Party shall take measures to establish its jurisdiction over such cases in the following instances:

(a) When the forced disappearance of persons or any act constituting such offense was committed within its jurisdiction;

(b) When the accused is a national of that state;

(c) When the victim is a national of that state and that state sees fit to do so.

Every State Party shall, moreover, take the necessary measures to establish its jurisdiction over the crime described in this Convention when the alleged criminal is within its territory and it does not proceed to extradite him.

This Convention does not authorize any State Party to undertake, in the territory of another State Party, the exercise of jurisdiction or the performance of functions that are placed within the exclusive purview of the authorities of that other Party by its domestic law.

Article V

The forced disappearance of persons shall not be considered a political offense for purposes of extradition.

The forced disappearance of persons shall be deemed to be included among the extraditable offenses in every extradition treaty entered into between State Parties.

The States Parties undertake to include the offense of forced disappearance as one which is extraditable in every extradition treaty to be concluded between them in the future.

Every State Party that makes extradition conditional on the existence of a treaty and receives a request for extradition from another State Party with which it has no extradition treaty may consider this Convention as the necessary legal basis for extradition with respect to the offense of forced disappearance.

State Parties which do not make extradition conditional on the existence of a treaty shall recognize such offense as extraditable, subject to the conditions imposed by the law of the requested state.

Extradition shall be subject to the provisions set forth in the constitution and other laws of the requested state.

Article VI

When a State Party does not grant the extradition, the case shall be submitted to its competent authorities as if the offense had been committed within its jurisdiction, for the purposes of investigation and when appropriate, for criminal action, in accordance with its national law. Any decision adopted by these authorities shall be communicated to the state that has requested the extradition.

Article VII

Criminal prosecution for the forced disappearance of persons and the penalty judicially imposed on its perpetrator shall not be subject to statutes of limitations.

However, if there should be a norm of a fundamental character preventing application of the stipulation contained in the previous paragraph, the period of limitation shall be equal to that which applies to the gravest crime in the domestic laws of the corresponding State Party.

Article VIII

The defense of due obedience to superior orders or instructions that stipulate, authorize, or encourage forced disappearance shall not be admitted.

All persons who receive such orders have the right and duty not to obey them.

The States Parties shall ensure that the training of public law-enforcement personnel or officials includes the necessary education on the offense of forced disappearance of persons.

Article IX

Persons alleged to be responsible for the acts constituting the offense of forced disappearance of persons may be tried only in the competent jurisdictions of ordinary law in each state, to the exclusion of all other special jurisdictions, particularly military jurisdictions.

The acts constituting forced disappearance shall not be deemed to have been committed in the course of military duties.

Privileges, immunities, or special dispensations shall not be admitted in such trials, without prejudice to the provisions set forth in the Vienna Convention on Diplomatic Relations.

Article X

In no case may exceptional circumstances such as a state of war, the threat of war, internal political instability, or any other public emergency be invoked to justify the forced disappearance of persons. In such cases, the right to expeditious and effective judicial procedures and recourse shall be retained as a means of determining the whereabouts or state of health of a person who has been deprived of freedom, or of identifying the official who ordered or carried out such deprivation of freedom.

In pursuing such procedures or recourse, and in keeping with applicable domestic law, the competent judicial authorities shall have free and immediate access to all detention centers and to each of their units, and to all places where there is reason to believe the disappeared person might be found, including places that are subject to military jurisdiction.

Article XI

Every person deprived of liberty shall be held in an officially recognized place of detention and be brought before a competent judicial authority without delay, in accordance with applicable domestic law.

The States Parties shall establish and maintain official up-to-date registries of their detainees and, in accordance with their domestic law, shall make them available to relatives, judges, attorneys, any other person having a legitimate interest, and other authorities.

Article XII

The States Parties shall give each other mutual assistance in the search for, identification, location, and return of minors who have been removed to another state or detained therein as a consequence of the forced disappearance of their parents or guardians.

Article XIII

For the purposes of this Convention, the processing of petitions or communications presented to the Inter–American Commission on Human Rights alleging the forced disappearance of persons shall be subject to the procedures established in the American Convention on Human Rights and to the Statute and Regulations of the Inter–American Commission on Human Rights and to the Statute and Rules of Procedure of the Inter–American Court of Human Rights, including the provisions on precautionary measures.

Article XIV

Without prejudice to the provisions of the preceding article, when the Inter–American Commission on Human Rights receives a petition or communication regarding an alleged forced disappearance, its Executive Secretariat shall urgently and confidentially address the respective government and shall request that government to provide as soon as possible information as to the whereabouts of the allegedly disappeared person together with any other information it considers pertinent, and such request shall be without prejudice as to the admissibility of the petition.

Article XV

None of the provisions of this Convention shall be interpreted as limiting other bilateral or multilateral treaties or other agreements signed by the Parties.

This Convention shall not apply to the international armed conflicts governed by the 1949 Geneva Convention and its Protocol concerning protection of wounded, sick, and shipwrecked members of the armed forces; and prisoners of war and civilians in time of war.

Article XVI

This Convention is open for signature by the member states of the Organization of American States.

Article XVII

This Convention is subject to ratification. The instruments of ratification shall be deposited with the General Secretariat of the Organization of American States.

Article XVIII

This Convention shall be open to accession by any other state. The instruments of accession shall be deposited with the General Secretariat of the Organization of American States.

Article XIX

The states may make reservations with respect to this Convention when signing, ratifying or acceding to it, unless such reservations are incompatible with the object and purpose of the Convention and as long as they refer to one or more specific provisions.

Article XX

This Convention shall enter into force for the ratifying states on the thirtieth day from the date of deposit of the second instrument of ratification.

For each state ratifying or acceding to the Convention after the second instrument of ratification has been deposited, the Convention shall enter into force on the thirtieth day from the date on which that state deposited its instrument of ratification or accession.

Article XXI

This Convention shall remain in force indefinitely, but may be denounced by any State Party. The instrument of denunciation shall be deposited with the General Secretariat of the Organization of American States. The Convention shall cease to be in effect for the denouncing state and shall remain in force for the other State Parties one year from the date of deposit of the instrument of denunciation.

Article XXII

The original instrument of this Convention, the Spanish, English, Portuguese and French texts of which are equally authentic, shall be deposited with the General Secretariat of the Organization of American States, which shall forward certified copies thereof to the United Nations Secretariat, for registration and publication, in accordance with Article 102 of the Charter of the United Nations. The General Secretariat of the Organization of American States shall notify member states of the Organization and states acceding to the Convention of the signatures and deposit of instruments of ratification, accession or denunciation, as well as of any reservations that may be expressed.

In Witness Whereof the undersigned Plenipotentiaries, being duly authorized thereto by their respective governments, have signed this Convention, which shall be called the "Inter–American Convention on the Forced Disappearance of Persons."

Document 52
INTERNATIONAL CONVENTION FOR THE PROTECTION OF ALL PERSONS FROM ENFORCED DISAPPEARANCE

Adopted by U.N. G.A. Res. 61/177 (20 Dec. 2006)

Preamble

The States Parties to this Convention,

Considering the obligation of States under the Charter of the United Nations to promote universal respect for, and observance of, human rights and fundamental freedoms,

Having regard to the Universal Declaration of Human Rights,

Recalling the International Covenant on Economic, Social and Cultural Rights, the International Covenant on Civil and Political Rights and the other relevant international instruments in the fields of human rights, humanitarian law and international criminal law,

Also recalling the Declaration on the Protection of All Persons from Enforced Disappearance adopted by the General Assembly of the United Nations in its resolution 47/133 of 18 December 1992,

Aware of the extreme seriousness of enforced disappearance, which constitutes a crime and, in certain circumstances defined in international law, a crime against humanity,

Determined to prevent enforced disappearances and to combat impunity for the crime of enforced disappearance,

Considering the right of any person not to be subjected to enforced disappearance, the right of victims to justice and to reparation,

Affirming the right of any victim to know the truth about the circumstances of an enforced disappearance and the fate of the disappeared person, and the right to freedom to seek, receive and impart information to this end,

Have agreed on the following articles:

Part I

Article 1

1. No one shall be subjected to enforced disappearance.

2. No exceptional circumstances whatsoever, whether a state of war or a threat of war, internal political instability or any other public emergency, may be invoked as a justification for enforced disappearance.

Article 2

For the purposes of this Convention, "enforced disappearance" is considered to be the arrest, detention, abduction or any other form of deprivation of liberty by agents of the State or by persons or groups of persons acting with the authorization, support or acquiescence of the State, followed by a refusal to acknowledge the deprivation of liberty or by concealment of the fate or whereabouts of the disappeared person, which place such a person outside the protection of the law.

Article 3

Each State Party shall take appropriate measures to investigate acts defined in article 2 committed by persons or groups of persons acting without the authorization, support or acquiescence of the State and to bring those responsible to justice.

Article 4

Each State Party shall take the necessary measures to ensure that enforced disappearance constitutes an offence under its criminal law.

Article 5

The widespread or systematic practice of enforced disappearance constitutes a crime against humanity as defined in applicable international law and shall attract the consequences provided for under such applicable international law.

Article 6

1. Each State Party shall take the necessary measures to hold criminally responsible at least:

(a) Any person who commits, orders, solicits or induces the commission of, attempts to commit, is an accomplice to or participates in an enforced disappearance;

(b) A superior who:

(i) Knew, or consciously disregarded information which clearly indicated, that subordinates under his or her effective authority and control were committing or about to commit a crime of enforced disappearance;

(ii) Exercised effective responsibility for and control over activities which were concerned with the crime of enforced disappearance; and

(iii) Failed to take all necessary and reasonable measures within his or her power to prevent or repress the commission of an enforced disappearance or to submit the matter to the competent authorities for investigation and prosecution;

(c) Subparagraph (b) above is without prejudice to the higher standards of responsibility applicable under relevant international law to a military commander or to a person effectively acting as a military commander.

2. No order or instruction from any public authority, civilian, military or other, may be invoked to justify an offence of enforced disappearance.

Article 7

1. Each State Party shall make the offence of enforced disappearance punishable by appropriate penalties which take into account its extreme seriousness.

2. Each State Party may establish:

(a) Mitigating circumstances, in particular for persons who, having been implicated in the commission of an enforced disappearance, effectively contribute to bringing the disappeared person forward alive or make it possible to clarify cases of enforced disappearance or to identify the perpetrators of an enforced disappearance;

(b) Without prejudice to other criminal procedures, aggravating circumstances, in particular in the event of the death of the disappeared person or the commission of an enforced disappearance in respect of pregnant women, minors, persons with disabilities or other particularly vulnerable persons.

Article 8

Without prejudice to article 5,

1. A State Party which applies a statute of limitations in respect of enforced disappearance shall take the necessary measures to ensure that the term of limitation for criminal proceedings:

(a) Is of long duration and is proportionate to the extreme seriousness of this offence;

(b) Commences from the moment when the offence of enforced disappearance ceases, taking into account its continuous nature.

2. Each State Party shall guarantee the right of victims of enforced disappearance to an effective remedy during the term of limitation.

Article 9

1. Each State Party shall take the necessary measures to establish its competence to exercise jurisdiction over the offence of enforced disappearance:

(a) When the offence is committed in any territory under its jurisdiction or on board a ship or aircraft registered in that State;

(b) When the alleged offender is one of its nationals;

(c) When the disappeared person is one of its nationals and the State Party considers it appropriate.

2. Each State Party shall likewise take such measures as may be necessary to establish its competence to exercise jurisdiction over the offence of enforced disappearance when the alleged offender is present in any territory under its jurisdiction, unless it extradites or surrenders him or her to another State in accordance with its international obli-

gations or surrenders him or her to an international criminal tribunal whose jurisdiction it has recognized.

3. This Convention does not exclude any additional criminal jurisdiction exercised in accordance with national law.

Article 10

1. Upon being satisfied, after an examination of the information available to it, that the circumstances so warrant, any State Party in whose territory a person suspected of having committed an offence of enforced disappearance is present shall take him or her into custody or take such other legal measures as are necessary to ensure his or her presence. The custody and other legal measures shall be as provided for in the law of that State Party but may be maintained only for such time as is necessary to ensure the person's presence at criminal, surrender or extradition proceedings.

2. A State Party which has taken the measures referred to in paragraph 1 of this article shall immediately carry out a preliminary inquiry or investigations to establish the facts. It shall notify the States Parties referred to in article 9, paragraph 1, of the measures it has taken in pursuance of paragraph 1 of this article, including detention and the circumstances warranting detention, and of the findings of its preliminary inquiry or its investigations, indicating whether it intends to exercise its jurisdiction.

3. Any person in custody pursuant to paragraph 1 of this article may communicate immediately with the nearest appropriate representative of the State of which he or she is a national, or, if he or she is a stateless person, with the representative of the State where he or she usually resides.

Article 11

1. The State Party in the territory under whose jurisdiction a person alleged to have committed an offence of enforced disappearance is found shall, if it does not extradite that person or surrender him or her to another State in accordance with its international obligations or surrender him or her to an international criminal tribunal whose jurisdiction it has recognized, submit the case to its competent authorities for the purpose of prosecution.

2. These authorities shall take their decision in the same manner as in the case of any ordinary offence of a serious nature under the law of that State Party. In the cases referred to in article 9, paragraph 2, the standards of evidence required for prosecution and conviction shall in no way be less stringent than those which apply in the cases referred to in article 9, paragraph 1.

3. Any person against whom proceedings are brought in connection with an offence of enforced disappearance shall be guaranteed fair treatment at all stages of the proceedings. Any person tried for an offence of enforced disappearance shall benefit from a fair trial before a competent, independent and impartial court or tribunal established by law.

Article 12

1. Each State Party shall ensure that any individual who alleges that a person has been subjected to enforced disappearance has the right to report the facts to the competent authorities, which shall examine the allegation promptly and impartially and, where necessary, undertake without delay a thorough and impartial investigation. Appropriate steps shall be taken, where necessary, to ensure that the complainant, witnesses, relatives of the disappeared person and their defence counsel, as well as persons participating in the investigation, are protected against all ill-treatment or intimidation as a consequence of the complaint or any evidence given.

2. Where there are reasonable grounds for believing that a person has been subjected to enforced disappearance, the authorities referred to in paragraph 1 of this article shall undertake an investigation, even if there has been no formal complaint.

3. Each State Party shall ensure that the authorities referred to in paragraph 1 of this article:

(a) Have the necessary powers and resources to conduct the investigation effectively, including access to the documentation and other information relevant to their investigation;

(b) Have access, if necessary with the prior authorization of a judicial authority, which shall rule promptly on the matter, to any place of detention or any other place where there are reasonable grounds to believe that the disappeared person may be present.

4. Each State Party shall take the necessary measures to prevent and sanction acts that hinder the conduct of an investigation. It shall ensure in particular that persons suspected of having committed an offence of enforced disappearance are not in a position to influence the progress of an investigation by means of pressure or acts of intimidation or reprisal aimed at the complainant, witnesses, relatives of the disappeared person or their defence counsel, or at persons participating in the investigation.

Article 13

1. For the purposes of extradition between States Parties, the offence of enforced disappearance shall not be regarded as a political offence or as an offence connected with a political offence or as an offence inspired by political motives. Accordingly, a request for extradition based on such an offence may not be refused on these grounds alone.

2. The offence of enforced disappearance shall be deemed to be included as an extraditable offence in any extradition treaty existing between States Parties before the entry into force of this Convention.

3. States Parties undertake to include the offence of enforced disappearance as an extraditable offence in any extradition treaty subsequently to be concluded between them.

4. If a State Party which makes extradition conditional on the existence of a treaty receives a request for extradition from another State Party with which it has no extradition treaty, it may consider this Convention as the necessary legal basis for extradition in respect of the offence of enforced disappearance.

5. States Parties which do not make extradition conditional on the existence of a treaty shall recognize the offence of enforced disappearance as an extraditable offence between themselves.

6. Extradition shall, in all cases, be subject to the conditions provided for by the law of the requested State Party or by applicable extradition treaties, including, in particular, conditions relating to the minimum penalty requirement for extradition and the grounds upon which the requested State Party may refuse extradition or make it subject to certain conditions.

7. Nothing in this Convention shall be interpreted as imposing an obligation to extradite if the requested State Party has substantial grounds for believing that the request has been made for the purpose of prosecuting or punishing a person on account of that person's sex, race, religion, nationality, ethnic origin, political opinions or membership of a particular social group, or that compliance with the request would cause harm to that person for any one of these reasons.

Article 14

1. States Parties shall afford one another the greatest measure of mutual legal assistance in connection with criminal proceedings brought in respect of an offence of enforced disappearance, including the supply of all evidence at their disposal that is necessary for the proceedings.

2. Such mutual legal assistance shall be subject to the conditions provided for by the domestic law of the requested State Party or by applicable treaties on mutual legal assistance, including, in particular, the conditions in relation to the grounds upon which the requested State Party may refuse to grant mutual legal assistance or may make it subject to conditions.

Article 15

States Parties shall cooperate with each other and shall afford one another the greatest measure of mutual assistance with a view to assisting victims of enforced disappearance, and in searching for, locating and releasing disappeared persons and, in the event of death, in exhuming and identifying them and returning their remains.

Article 16

1. No State Party shall expel, return ("refouler"), surrender or extradite a person to another State where there are substantial grounds for believing that he or she would be in danger of being subjected to enforced disappearance.

2. For the purpose of determining whether there are such grounds, the competent authorities shall take into account all relevant consider-

ations, including, where applicable, the existence in the State concerned of a consistent pattern of gross, flagrant or mass violations of human rights or of serious violations of international humanitarian law.

Article 17

1. No one shall be held in secret detention.

2. Without prejudice to other international obligations of the State Party with regard to the deprivation of liberty, each State Party shall, in its legislation:

(a) Establish the conditions under which orders of deprivation of liberty may be given;

(b) Indicate those authorities authorized to order the deprivation of liberty;

(c) Guarantee that any person deprived of liberty shall be held solely in officially recognized and supervised places of deprivation of liberty;

(d) Guarantee that any person deprived of liberty shall be authorized to communicate with and be visited by his or her family, counsel or any other person of his or her choice, subject only to the conditions established by law, or, if he or she is a foreigner, to communicate with his or her consular authorities, in accordance with applicable international law;

(e) Guarantee access by the competent and legally authorized authorities and institutions to the places where persons are deprived of liberty, if necessary with prior authorization from a judicial authority;

(f) Guarantee that any person deprived of liberty or, in the case of a suspected enforced disappearance, since the person deprived of liberty is not able to exercise this right, any persons with a legitimate interest, such as relatives of the person deprived of liberty, their representatives or their counsel, shall, in all circumstances, be entitled to take proceedings before a court, in order that the court may decide without delay on the lawfulness of the deprivation of liberty and order the person's release if such deprivation of liberty is not lawful.

3. Each State Party shall assure the compilation and maintenance of one or more up-to-date official registers and/or records of persons deprived of liberty, which shall be made promptly available, upon request, to any judicial or other competent authority or institution authorized for that purpose by the law of the State Party concerned or any relevant international legal instrument to which the State concerned is a party. The information contained therein shall include, as a minimum:

(a) The identity of the person deprived of liberty;

(b) The date, time and place where the person was deprived of liberty and the identity of the authority that deprived the person of liberty;

(c) The authority that ordered the deprivation of liberty and the grounds for the deprivation of liberty;

(d) The authority responsible for supervising the deprivation of liberty;

(e) The place of deprivation of liberty, the date and time of admission to the place of deprivation of liberty and the authority responsible for the place of deprivation of liberty;

(f) Elements relating to the state of health of the person deprived of liberty;

(g) In the event of death during the deprivation of liberty, the circumstances and cause of death and the destination of the remains;

(h) The date and time of release or transfer to another place of detention, the destination and the authority responsible for the transfer.

Article 18

1. Subject to articles 19 and 20, each State Party shall guarantee to any person with a legitimate interest in this information, such as relatives of the person deprived of liberty, their representatives or their counsel, access to at least the following information:

(a) The authority that ordered the deprivation of liberty;

(b) The date, time and place where the person was deprived of liberty and admitted to the place of deprivation of liberty;

(c) The authority responsible for supervising the deprivation of liberty;

(d) The whereabouts of the person deprived of liberty, including, in the event of a transfer to another place of deprivation of liberty, the destination and the authority responsible for the transfer;

(e) The date, time and place of release;

(f) Elements relating to the state of health of the person deprived of liberty;

(g) In the event of death during the deprivation of liberty, the circumstances and cause of death and the destination of the remains.

2. Appropriate measures shall be taken, where necessary, to protect the persons referred to in paragraph 1 of this article, as well as persons participating in the investigation, from any ill-treatment, intimidation or sanction as a result of the search for information concerning a person deprived of liberty.

Article 19

1. Personal information, including medical and genetic data, which is collected and/or transmitted within the framework of the search for a disappeared person shall not be used or made available for purposes

other than the search for the disappeared person. This is without prejudice to the use of such information in criminal proceedings relating to an offence of enforced disappearance or the exercise of the right to obtain reparation.

2. The collection, processing, use and storage of personal information, including medical and genetic data, shall not infringe or have the effect of infringing the human rights, fundamental freedoms or human dignity of an individual.

Article 20

1. Only where a person is under the protection of the law and the deprivation of liberty is subject to judicial control may the right to information referred to in article 18 be restricted, on an exceptional basis, where strictly necessary and where provided for by law, and if the transmission of the information would adversely affect the privacy or safety of the person, hinder a criminal investigation, or for other equivalent reasons in accordance with the law, and in conformity with applicable international law and with the objectives of this Convention. In no case shall there be restrictions on the right to information referred to in article 18 that could constitute conduct defined in article 2 or be in violation of article 17, paragraph 1.

2. Without prejudice to consideration of the lawfulness of the deprivation of a person's liberty, States Parties shall guarantee to the persons referred to in article 18, paragraph 1, the right to a prompt and effective judicial remedy as a means of obtaining without delay the information referred to in article 18, paragraph 1. This right to a remedy may not be suspended or restricted in any circumstances.

Article 21

Each State Party shall take the necessary measures to ensure that persons deprived of liberty are released in a manner permitting reliable verification that they have actually been released. Each State Party shall also take the necessary measures to assure the physical integrity of such persons and their ability to exercise fully their rights at the time of release, without prejudice to any obligations to which such persons may be subject under national law.

Article 22

Without prejudice to article 6, each State Party shall take the necessary measures to prevent and impose sanctions for the following conduct:

(a) Delaying or obstructing the remedies referred to in article 17, paragraph 2 (f), and article 20, paragraph 2;

(b) Failure to record the deprivation of liberty of any person, or the recording of any information which the official responsible for the official register knew or should have known to be inaccurate;

(c) Refusal to provide information on the deprivation of liberty of a person, or the provision of inaccurate information, even though the legal requirements for providing such information have been met.

Article 23

1. Each State Party shall ensure that the training of law enforcement personnel, civil or military, medical personnel, public officials and other persons who may be involved in the custody or treatment of any person deprived of liberty includes the necessary education and information regarding the relevant provisions of this Convention, in order to:

(a) Prevent the involvement of such officials in enforced disappearances;

(b) Emphasize the importance of prevention and investigations in relation to enforced disappearances;

(c) Ensure that the urgent need to resolve cases of enforced disappearance is recognized.

2. Each State Party shall ensure that orders or instructions prescribing, authorizing or encouraging enforced disappearance are prohibited. Each State Party shall guarantee that a person who refuses to obey such an order will not be punished.

3. Each State Party shall take the necessary measures to ensure that the persons referred to in paragraph 1 of this article who have reason to believe that an enforced disappearance has occurred or is planned report the matter to their superiors and, where necessary, to the appropriate authorities or bodies vested with powers of review or remedy.

Article 24

1. For the purposes of this Convention, "victim" means the disappeared person and any individual who has suffered harm as the direct result of an enforced disappearance.

2. Each victim has the right to know the truth regarding the circumstances of the enforced disappearance, the progress and results of the investigation and the fate of the disappeared person. Each State Party shall take appropriate measures in this regard.

3. Each State Party shall take all appropriate measures to search for, locate and release disappeared persons and, in the event of death, to locate, respect and return their remains.

4. Each State Party shall ensure in its legal system that the victims of enforced disappearance have the right to obtain reparation and prompt, fair and adequate compensation.

5. The right to obtain reparation referred to in paragraph 4 of this article covers material and moral damages and, where appropriate, other forms of reparation such as:

(a) Restitution;

(b) Rehabilitation;

(c) Satisfaction, including restoration of dignity and reputation;

(d) Guarantees of non-repetition.

6. Without prejudice to the obligation to continue the investigation until the fate of the disappeared person has been clarified, each State Party shall take the appropriate steps with regard to the legal situation of disappeared persons whose fate has not been clarified and that of their relatives, in fields such as social welfare, financial matters, family law and property rights.

7. Each State Party shall guarantee the right to form and participate freely in organizations and associations concerned with attempting to establish the circumstances of enforced disappearances and the fate of disappeared persons, and to assist victims of enforced disappearance.

Article 25

1. Each State Party shall take the necessary measures to prevent and punish under its criminal law:

(a) The wrongful removal of children who are subjected to enforced disappearance, children whose father, mother or legal guardian is subjected to enforced disappearance or children born during the captivity of a mother subjected to enforced disappearance;

(b) The falsification, concealment or destruction of documents attesting to the true identity of the children referred to in subparagraph (a) above.

2. Each State Party shall take the necessary measures to search for and identify the children referred to in paragraph 1 (a) of this article and to return them to their families of origin, in accordance with legal procedures and applicable international agreements.

3. States Parties shall assist one another in searching for, identifying and locating the children referred to in paragraph 1 (a) of this article.

4. Given the need to protect the best interests of the children referred to in paragraph 1 (a) of this article and their right to preserve, or to have re-established, their identity, including their nationality, name and family relations as recognized by law, States Parties which recognize a system of adoption or other form of placement of children shall have legal procedures in place to review the adoption or placement procedure, and, where appropriate, to annul any adoption or placement of children that originated in an enforced disappearance.

5. In all cases, and in particular in all matters relating to this article, the best interests of the child shall be a primary consideration, and a child who is capable of forming his or her own views shall have the right to express those views freely, the views of the child being given due weight in accordance with the age and maturity of the child.

Part II

Article 26

1. A Committee on Enforced Disappearances (hereinafter referred to as "the Committee") shall be established to carry out the functions

provided for under this Convention. The Committee shall consist of ten experts of high moral character and recognized competence in the field of human rights, who shall serve in their personal capacity and be independent and impartial. The members of the Committee shall be elected by the States Parties according to equitable geographical distribution. Due account shall be taken of the usefulness of the participation in the work of the Committee of persons having relevant legal experience and of balanced gender representation.

2. The members of the Committee shall be elected by secret ballot from a list of persons nominated by States Parties from among their nationals, at biennial meetings of the States Parties convened by the Secretary–General of the United Nations for this purpose. At those meetings, for which two thirds of the States Parties shall constitute a quorum, the persons elected to the Committee shall be those who obtain the largest number of votes and an absolute majority of the votes of the representatives of States Parties present and voting.

3. The initial election shall be held no later than six months after the date of entry into force of this Convention. Four months before the date of each election, the Secretary–General of the United Nations shall address a letter to the States Parties inviting them to submit nominations within three months. The Secretary–General shall prepare a list in alphabetical order of all persons thus nominated, indicating the State Party which nominated each candidate, and shall submit this list to all States Parties.

4. The members of the Committee shall be elected for a term of four years. They shall be eligible for re-election once. However, the term of five of the members elected at the first election shall expire at the end of two years; immediately after the first election, the names of these five members shall be chosen by lot by the chairman of the meeting referred to in paragraph 2 of this article.

5. If a member of the Committee dies or resigns or for any other reason can no longer perform his or her Committee duties, the State Party which nominated him or her shall, in accordance with the criteria set out in paragraph 1 of this article, appoint another candidate from among its nationals to serve out his or her term, subject to the approval of the majority of the States Parties. Such approval shall be considered to have been obtained unless half or more of the States Parties respond negatively within six weeks of having been informed by the Secretary–General of the United Nations of the proposed appointment.

6. The Committee shall establish its own rules of procedure.

7. The Secretary–General of the United Nations shall provide the Committee with the necessary means, staff and facilities for the effective performance of its functions. The Secretary–General of the United Nations shall convene the initial meeting of the Committee.

8. The members of the Committee shall be entitled to the facilities, privileges and immunities of experts on mission for the United Nations, as laid down in the relevant sections of the Convention on the Privileges and Immunities of the United Nations.

9. Each State Party shall cooperate with the Committee and assist its members in the fulfilment of their mandate, to the extent of the Committee's functions that the State Party has accepted.

Article 27

A Conference of the States Parties will take place at the earliest four years and at the latest six years following the entry into force of this Convention to evaluate the functioning of the Committee and to decide, in accordance with the procedure described in article 44, paragraph 2, whether it is appropriate to transfer to another body–without excluding any possibility–the monitoring of this Convention, in accordance with the functions defined in articles 28 to 36.

Article 28

1. In the framework of the competencies granted by this Convention, the Committee shall cooperate with all relevant organs, offices and specialized agencies and funds of the United Nations, with the treaty bodies instituted by international instruments, with the special procedures of the United Nations and with the relevant regional intergovernmental organizations or bodies, as well as with all relevant State institutions, agencies or offices working towards the protection of all persons against enforced disappearances.

2. As it discharges its mandate, the Committee shall consult other treaty bodies instituted by relevant international human rights instruments, in particular the Human Rights Committee instituted by the International Covenant on Civil and Political Rights, with a view to ensuring the consistency of their respective observations and recommendations.

Article 29

1. Each State Party shall submit to the Committee, through the Secretary–General of the United Nations, a report on the measures taken to give effect to its obligations under this Convention, within two years after the entry into force of this Convention for the State Party concerned.

2. The Secretary–General of the United Nations shall make this report available to all States Parties.

3. Each report shall be considered by the Committee, which shall issue such comments, observations or recommendations as it may deem appropriate. The comments, observations or recommendations shall be communicated to the State Party concerned, which may respond to them, on its own initiative or at the request of the Committee.

4. The Committee may also request States Parties to provide additional information on the implementation of this Convention.

Article 30

1. A request that a disappeared person should be sought and found may be submitted to the Committee, as a matter of urgency, by relatives of the disappeared person or their legal representatives, their counsel or

any person authorized by them, as well as by any other person having a legitimate interest.

2. If the Committee considers that a request for urgent action submitted in pursuance of paragraph 1 of this article:

(a) Is not manifestly unfounded;

(b) Does not constitute an abuse of the right of submission of such requests;

(c) Has already been duly presented to the competent bodies of the State Party concerned, such as those authorized to undertake investigations, where such a possibility exists;

(d) Is not incompatible with the provisions of this Convention; and

(e) The same matter is not being examined under another procedure of international investigation or settlement of the same nature;

it shall request the State Party concerned to provide it with information on the situation of the persons sought, within a time limit set by the Committee.

3. In the light of the information provided by the State Party concerned in accordance with paragraph 2 of this article, the Committee may transmit recommendations to the State Party, including a request that the State Party should take all the necessary measures, including interim measures, to locate and protect the person concerned in accordance with this Convention and to inform the Committee, within a specified period of time, of measures taken, taking into account the urgency of the situation. The Committee shall inform the person submitting the urgent action request of its recommendations and of the information provided to it by the State as it becomes available.

4. The Committee shall continue its efforts to work with the State Party concerned for as long as the fate of the person sought remains unresolved. The person presenting the request shall be kept informed.

Article 31

1. A State Party may at the time of ratification of this Convention or at any time afterwards declare that it recognizes the competence of the Committee to receive and consider communications from or on behalf of individuals subject to its jurisdiction claiming to be victims of a violation by this State Party of provisions of this Convention. The Committee shall not admit any communication concerning a State Party which has not made such a declaration.

2. The Committee shall consider a communication inadmissible where:

(a) The communication is anonymous;

(b) The communication constitutes an abuse of the right of submission of such communications or is incompatible with the provisions of this Convention;

(c) The same matter is being examined under another procedure of international investigation or settlement of the same nature; or where

(d) All effective available domestic remedies have not been exhausted. This rule shall not apply where the application of the remedies is unreasonably prolonged.

3. If the Committee considers that the communication meets the requirements set out in paragraph 2 of this article, it shall transmit the communication to the State Party concerned, requesting it to provide observations and comments within a time limit set by the Committee.

4. At any time after the receipt of a communication and before a determination on the merits has been reached, the Committee may transmit to the State Party concerned for its urgent consideration a request that the State Party will take such interim measures as may be necessary to avoid possible irreparable damage to the victims of the alleged violation. Where the Committee exercises its discretion, this does not imply a determination on admissibility or on the merits of the communication.

5. The Committee shall hold closed meetings when examining communications under the present article. It shall inform the author of a communication of the responses provided by the State Party concerned. When the Committee decides to finalize the procedure, it shall communicate its views to the State Party and to the author of the communication.

Article 32

A State Party to this Convention may at any time declare that it recognizes the competence of the Committee to receive and consider communications in which a State Party claims that another State Party is not fulfilling its obligations under this Convention. The Committee shall not receive communications concerning a State Party which has not made such a declaration, nor communications from a State Party which has not made such a declaration.

Article 33

1. If the Committee receives reliable information indicating that a State Party is seriously violating the provisions of this Convention, it may, after consultation with the State Party concerned, request one or more of its members to undertake a visit and report back to it without delay.

2. The Committee shall notify the State Party concerned, in writing, of its intention to organize a visit, indicating the composition of the delegation and the purpose of the visit. The State Party shall answer the Committee within a reasonable time.

3. Upon a substantiated request by the State Party, the Committee may decide to postpone or cancel its visit.

4. If the State Party agrees to the visit, the Committee and the State Party concerned shall work together to define the modalities of the

visit and the State Party shall provide the Committee with all the facilities needed for the successful completion of the visit.

5. Following its visit, the Committee shall communicate to the State Party concerned its observations and recommendations.

Article 34

If the Committee receives information which appears to it to contain well-founded indications that enforced disappearance is being practiced on a widespread or systematic basis in the territory under the jurisdiction of a State Party, it may, after seeking from the State Party concerned all relevant information on the situation, urgently bring the matter to the attention of the General Assembly of the United Nations, through the Secretary–General of the United Nations.

Article 35

1. The Committee shall have competence solely in respect of enforced disappearances which commenced after the entry into force of this Convention.

2. If a State becomes a party to this Convention after its entry into force, the obligations of that State vis-à-vis the Committee shall relate only to enforced disappearances which commenced after the entry into force of this Convention for the State concerned.

Article 36

1. The Committee shall submit an annual report on its activities under this Convention to the States Parties and to the General Assembly of the United Nations.

2. Before an observation on a State Party is published in the annual report, the State Party concerned shall be informed in advance and shall be given reasonable time to answer. This State Party may request the publication of its comments or observations in the report.

Part III

Article 37

Nothing in this Convention shall affect any provisions which are more conducive to the protection of all persons from enforced disappearance and which may be contained in:

(a) The law of a State Party;

(b) International law in force for that State.

Article 38

1. This Convention is open for signature by all Member States of the United Nations.

2. This Convention is subject to ratification by all Member States of the United Nations. Instruments of ratification shall be deposited with the Secretary–General of the United Nations.

3. This Convention is open to accession by all Member States of the United Nations. Accession shall be effected by the deposit of an instrument of accession with the Secretary–General.

Article 39

1. This Convention shall enter into force on the thirtieth day after the date of deposit with the Secretary–General of the United Nations of the twentieth instrument of ratification or accession.

2. For each State ratifying or acceding to this Convention after the deposit of the twentieth instrument of ratification or accession, this Convention shall enter into force on the thirtieth day after the date of the deposit of that State's instrument of ratification or accession.

Article 40

The Secretary–General of the United Nations shall notify all States Members of the United Nations and all States which have signed or acceded to this Convention of the following:

(a) Signatures, ratifications and accessions under article 38;

(b) The date of entry into force of this Convention under article 39.

Article 41

The provisions of this Convention shall apply to all parts of federal States without any limitations or exceptions.

Article 42

1. Any dispute between two or more States Parties concerning the interpretation or application of this Convention which cannot be settled through negotiation or by the procedures expressly provided for in this Convention shall, at the request of one of them, be submitted to arbitration. If within six months from the date of the request for arbitration the Parties are unable to agree on the organization of the arbitration, any one of those Parties may refer the dispute to the International Court of Justice by request in conformity with the Statute of the Court.

2. A State may, at the time of signature or ratification of this Convention or accession thereto, declare that it does not consider itself bound by paragraph 1 of this article. The other States Parties shall not be bound by paragraph 1 of this article with respect to any State Party having made such a declaration.

3. Any State Party having made a declaration in accordance with the provisions of paragraph 2 of this article may at any time withdraw this declaration by notification to the Secretary–General of the United Nations.

Article 43

This Convention is without prejudice to the provisions of international humanitarian law, including the obligations of the High Contracting Parties to the four Geneva Conventions of 12 August 1949 and the two Additional Protocols thereto of 8 June 1977, or to the opportunity available to any State Party to authorize the International Committee of the Red Cross to visit places of detention in situations not covered by international humanitarian law.

Article 44

1. Any State Party to this Convention may propose an amendment and file it with the Secretary–General of the United Nations. The Secretary–General shall thereupon communicate the proposed amendment to the States Parties to this Convention with a request that they indicate whether they favour a conference of States Parties for the purpose of considering and voting upon the proposal. In the event that within four months from the date of such communication at least one third of the States Parties favour such a conference, the Secretary–General shall convene the conference under the auspices of the United Nations.

2. Any amendment adopted by a majority of two thirds of the States Parties present and voting at the conference shall be submitted by the Secretary–General of the United Nations to all the States Parties for acceptance.

3. An amendment adopted in accordance with paragraph 1 of this article shall enter into force when two thirds of the States Parties to this Convention have accepted it in accordance with their respective constitutional processes.

4. When amendments enter into force, they shall be binding on those States Parties which have accepted them, other States Parties still being bound by the provisions of this Convention and any earlier amendment which they have accepted.

Article 45

1. This Convention, of which the Arabic, Chinese, English, French, Russian and Spanish texts are equally authentic, shall be deposited with the Secretary–General of the United Nations.

2. The Secretary–General of the United Nations shall transmit certified copies of this Convention to all States referred to in article 38.

Document 53
U.N. G.A. RESOLUTION 46/51

U.N. Doc. A/46/654 (9 Dec. 1991)

The General Assembly, . . .

Recalling moreover the existing international conventions relating to various aspects of the problem of international terrorism, *inter alia,* the Convention on Offenses and Certain Other Acts Committed on Board Aircraft, signed at Tokyo on 14 September 1963, the Convention for the Suppression of Unlawful Seizure of Aircraft, signed at The Hague on 16 December 1970, the Convention for the Suppression of Unlawful Acts against the Safety of Civil Aviation, concluded at Montreal on 23 September 1971, the Convention on the Prevention and Punishment of Crimes against Internationally Protected Persons, including Diplomatic Agents, adopted in New York on 14 December 1973, the International Convention against the Taking of Hostages, adopted in New York on 17 December 1979, the Convention on the Physical Protection of Nuclear Material, adopted at Vienna on 3 March 1980, the Protocol for the Suppression of Unlawful Acts of Violence at Airports Serving International Civil Aviation, supplementary to the Convention for the Suppression of Unlawful Acts against the Safety of Civil Aviation, signed at Montreal on 24 February 1988, the Convention for the Suppression of Unlawful Acts against the Safety of Maritime Navigation, done at Rome on 10 March 1988, the Protocol for the Suppression of Unlawful Acts against the Safety of Fixed Platforms located on the Continental Shelf, done at Rome on 10 March 1988, and the Convention on the Marking of Plastic Explosives for the Purpose of Detection, done at Montreal on 1 March 1991,

Convinced that a policy of firmness and effective measures should be taken in accordance with international law in order that all acts, methods and practices of international terrorism may be brought to an end,

Taking note of Security Council resolution 638 (1989) of 31 July 1989 on the taking of hostages,

Deeply disturbed by the world-wide persistence of acts of international terrorism in all its forms, including those in which States are directly or indirectly involved, which endanger or take innocent lives, have a deleterious effect on international relations and may jeopardize the territorial integrity and security of States,

Calling attention to the growing connection between terrorist groups and drug traffickers,

Convinced of the importance of the observance by States of their obligations under the relevant international conventions to ensure that appropriate law enforcement measures are taken in connection with the offenses addressed in those conventions,

Convinced also of the importance of expanding and improving international cooperation among States, on a bilateral, regional and multilateral basis, which will contribute to the elimination of acts of international terrorism and their underlying causes and to the prevention and elimination of this criminal scourge,

Convinced further that international cooperation in combating and preventing terrorism will contribute to the strengthening of confidence among States, reduce tensions and create a better climate among them,

Mindful of the need to enhance the role of the United Nations and the relevant specialized agencies in combating international terrorism,

Mindful also of the necessity of maintaining and protecting the basic rights of, and guarantees for, the individual in accordance with the relevant international human rights instruments and generally accepted international standards,

Reaffirming the principle of self-determination of peoples as enshrined in the Charter of the United Nations,

Reaffirming also the inalienable right to self-determination and independence of all peoples under colonial and racist regimes and other forms of alien domination and foreign occupation, and upholding the legitimacy of their struggle, in particular the struggle of national liberation movements, in accordance with the purposes and principles of the Charter and the Declaration on Principles of International Law concerning Friendly Relations and Cooperation among States in accordance with the Charter of the United Nations,

Recognizing that the effectiveness of the struggle against terrorism could be enhanced by the establishment of a generally agreed definition of international terrorism,

Taking note of the report of the Secretary–General,

1. *Once again unequivocally condemns,* as criminal and unjustifiable, all acts, methods and practices of terrorism wherever and by whomever committed, including those which jeopardize the friendly relations among States and their security;

2. *Deeply deplores* the loss of human lives which results from such acts of terrorism, as well as the pernicious impact of these acts on relations and cooperation among States;

3. *Calls upon* all States to fulfil their obligations under international law to refrain from organizing, instigating, assisting or participating in terrorist acts in other States, or acquiescing in or encouraging activities within their territory directed towards the commission of such acts;

4. *Urges* all States to fulfil their obligations under international law and take effective and resolute measures for the speedy and final elimination of international terrorism and to that end, in particular:

(a) To prevent the preparation and operations in their respective territories, for commission within or outside their territories, of terrorist and subversive acts directed against other States and their citizens;

(b) To ensure the apprehension and prosecution or extradition of perpetrators of terrorist acts;

(c) To endeavor to conclude special agreements to that effect on a bilateral, regional and multilateral basis;

(d) To cooperate with one another in exchanging relevant information concerning the prevention and combating of terrorism;

(e) To take promptly all steps necessary to implement the existing international conventions on this subject to which they are parties, including the harmonization of their domestic legislation with those conventions;

5. *Appeals* to all States that have not yet done so to consider becoming party to the international conventions relating to various aspects of international terrorism referred to in the preamble to the present resolution;

6. *Urges* all States, unilaterally and in cooperation with other States, as well as relevant United Nations organs, to contribute to the progressive elimination of the causes underlying international terrorism and to pay special attention to all situations, including colonialism, racism and situations involving mass and flagrant violations of human rights and fundamental freedoms and those involving alien domination and foreign occupation, that may give rise to international terrorism and may endanger international peace and security;

7. *Firmly calls* for the immediate and safe release of all hostages and abducted persons, wherever and by whomever they are being held;

8. *Calls upon* all States to use their political influence in accordance with the Charter of the United Nations and the principles of international law to secure the safe release of all hostages and abducted persons and to prevent the commission of acts of hostage-taking and abduction;

9. *Expresses concern* at the growing and dangerous links between terrorist groups, drug traffickers and their paramilitary gangs, which have resorted to all types of violence, thus endangering the constitutional order of States and violating basic human rights;

10. *Welcomes* the efforts undertaken by the International Civil Aviation Organization aimed at promoting universal acceptance of, and strict compliance with, international air security conventions, and welcomes the recent adoption of the Convention on the Marking of Plastic Explosives for the Purpose of Detection;

11. *Requests* the other relevant specialized agencies and intergovernmental organizations, in particular the International Maritime Organization, the Universal Postal Union, the World Tourism Organization, the International Atomic Energy Agency and the United Nations Educational, Scientific and Cultural Organization, within their respec-

tive spheres of competence, to consider what further measures can usefully be taken to combat and eliminate terrorism;

12. *Requests* the Secretary–General to continue seeking the views of Member States on international terrorism in all its aspects and on ways and means of combating it, including the convening at an appropriate time, under the auspices of the United Nations, of an international conference to deal with international terrorism in the light of the proposal referred to in the penultimate preambular paragraph of General Assembly resolution 44/29 [calling for an international conference to define terrorism]; . . .

15. *Considers* that nothing in the present resolution could in any way prejudice the right to self-determination, freedom and independence, as derived from the Charter of the United Nations, of peoples forcibly deprived of that right referred to in the Declaration on Principles of International Law concerning Friendly Relations and Cooperation among States in accordance with the Charter of the United Nations, particularly peoples under colonial and racist regimes or other forms of alien domination, or the right of these peoples to struggle legitimately to this end and to seek and receive support in accordance with the principles of the Charter, the above-mentioned Declaration and the relevant General Assembly resolutions, including the present resolution.

Document 54
DECLARATION ON MEASURES TO ELIMINATE INTERNATIONAL TERRORISM

U.N. G.A. Res. 49/60 (9 Dec. 1994)

The General Assembly,

Recalling its resolution 46/51 of 9 December 1991 and its decision 48/411 of 9 December 1993,

Taking note of the report of the Secretary–General,

Having considered in depth the question of measures to eliminate international terrorism,

Convinced that the adoption of the declaration on measures to eliminate international terrorism should contribute to the enhancement of the struggle against international terrorism,

1. Approves the Declaration on Measures to Eliminate International Terrorism, the text of which is annexed to the present resolution;

2. Invites the Secretary–General to inform all States, the Security Council, the International Court of Justice and the relevant specialized agencies, organizations and organisms of the adoption of the Declaration;

3. Urges that every effort be made in order that the Declaration becomes generally known and is observed and implemented in full;

4. Urges States, in accordance with the provisions of the Declaration, to take all appropriate measures at the national and international levels to eliminate terrorism;. . . .

ANNEX

Declaration on Measures to Eliminate International Terrorism

The General Assembly,

Guided by the purposes and principles of the Charter of the United Nations,

Recalling the Declaration on Principles of International Law concerning Friendly Relations and Cooperation among States in accordance with the Charter of the United Nations, the Declaration on the Strengthening of International Security, the Definition of Aggression, the Declaration on the Enhancement of the Effectiveness of the Principle of Refraining from the Threat or Use of Force in International Relations, the Vienna Declaration and Programme of Action, adopted by the World Conference on Human Rights, the International Covenant on Economic,

Social and Cultural Rights and the International Covenant on Civil and Political Rights,

Deeply disturbed by the world-wide persistence of acts of international terrorism in all its forms and manifestations, including those in which States are directly or indirectly involved, which endanger or take innocent lives, have a deleterious effect on international relations and may jeopardize the security of States,

Deeply concerned by the increase, in many regions of the world, of acts of terrorism based on intolerance or extremism,

Concerned at the growing and dangerous links between terrorist groups and drug traffickers and their paramilitary gangs, which have resorted to all types of violence, thus endangering the constitutional order of States and violating basic human rights,

Convinced of the desirability for closer coordination and cooperation among States in combating crimes closely connected with terrorism, including drug trafficking, unlawful arms trade, money laundering and smuggling of nuclear and other potentially deadly materials, and bearing in mind the role that could be played by both the United Nations and regional organizations in this respect,

Firmly determined to eliminate international terrorism in all its forms and manifestations,

Convinced also that the suppression of acts of international terrorism, including those in which States are directly or indirectly involved, is an essential element for the maintenance of international peace and security,

Convinced further that those responsible for acts of international terrorism must be brought to justice,

Stressing the imperative need to further strengthen international cooperation between States in order to take and adopt practical and effective measures to prevent, combat and eliminate all forms of terrorism that affect the international community as a whole,

Conscious of the important role that might be played by the United Nations, the relevant specialized agencies and States in fostering widespread cooperation in preventing and combating international terrorism, inter alia, by increasing public awareness of the problem,

Recalling the existing international treaties relating to various aspects of the problem of international terrorism . . . ,

Welcoming the conclusion of regional agreements and mutually agreed declarations to combat and eliminate terrorism in all its forms and manifestations,

Convinced of the desirability of keeping under review the scope of existing international legal provisions to combat terrorism in all its forms and manifestations, with the aim of ensuring a comprehensive legal framework for the prevention and elimination of terrorism,

Solemnly declares the following:

I

1. The States Members of the United Nations solemnly reaffirm their unequivocal condemnation of all acts, methods and practices of terrorism, as criminal and unjustifiable, wherever and by whomever committed, including those which jeopardize the friendly relations among States and peoples and threaten the territorial integrity and security of States;

2. Acts, methods and practices of terrorism constitute a grave violation of the purposes and principles of the United Nations, which may pose a threat to international peace and security, jeopardize friendly relations among States, hinder international cooperation and aim at the destruction of human rights, fundamental freedoms and the democratic bases of society;

3. Criminal acts intended or calculated to provoke a state of terror in the general public, a group of persons or particular persons for political purposes are in any circumstance unjustifiable, whatever the considerations of a political, philosophical, ideological, racial, ethnic, religious or any other nature that may be invoked to justify them;

II

4. States, guided by the purposes and principles of the Charter of the United Nations and other relevant rules of international law, must refrain from organizing, instigating, assisting or participating in terrorist acts in territories of other States, or from acquiescing in or encouraging activities within their territories directed towards the commission of such acts;

5. States must also fulfil their obligations under the Charter of the United Nations and other provisions of international law with respect to combating international terrorism and are urged to take effective and resolute measures in accordance with the relevant provisions of international law and international standards of human rights for the speedy and final elimination of international terrorism, in particular:

(a) To refrain from organizing, instigating, facilitating, financing, encouraging or tolerating activities and to take appropriate practical measures to ensure that their respective territories are not used for terrorist installations or training camps, or for the preparation of organization of terrorist acts intended to be committed against other States or their citizens;

(b) To ensure the apprehension and prosecution or extradition of perpetrators of terrorist acts, in accordance with the relevant provisions of their national law;

(c) To endeavour to conclude special agreements to that effect on a bilateral, regional and multilateral basis, and to prepare, to that effect, model agreements on cooperation;

(d) To cooperate with one another in exchanging relevant information concerning the prevention and combating of terrorism;

(e) To take promptly all steps necessary to implement the existing international conventions on this subject to which they are parties, including the harmonization of their domestic legislation with those conventions;

(f) To take appropriate measures, before granting asylum, for the purpose of ensuring that the asylum seeker has not engaged in terrorist activities and, after granting asylum, for the purpose of ensuring that the refugee status is not used in a manner contrary to the provisions set out in subparagraph (a) above; . . .

III

9. The United Nations, the relevant specialized agencies and intergovernmental organizations and other relevant bodies must make every effort with a view to promoting measures to combat and eliminate acts of terrorism and to strengthening their role in this field; . . .

IV

11. All States are urged to promote and implement in good faith and effectively the provisions of the present Declaration in all its aspects;

12. Emphasis is placed on the need to pursue efforts aiming at eliminating definitively all acts of terrorism by the strengthening of international cooperation and progressive development of international law and its codification, as well as by enhancement of coordination between, and increase of the efficiency of, the United Nations and the relevant specialized agencies, organizations and bodies.

Document 55
PROTECTION OF HUMAN RIGHTS AND FUNDAMENTAL FREEDOMS WHILE COUNTERING TERRORISM

U.N. G.A. Res. 61/171 (19 Dec. 2006)

The General Assembly,

Reaffirming the purposes and principles of the Charter of the United Nations,

Reaffirming also the fundamental importance, including in response to terrorism and the fear of terrorism, of respecting all human rights and fundamental freedoms and the rule of law,

Recalling its resolutions 57/219 of 18 December 2002, 58/187 of 22 December 2003, 59/191 of 20 December 2004 and 60/158 of 16 December 2005, Commission on Human Rights resolutions 2003/68 of 25 April 2003, 2004/87 of 21 April 2004 and 2005/80 of 21 April 2005 and other relevant resolutions of the General Assembly and the Commission on Human Rights,

Reaffirming that States are under the obligation to protect all human rights and fundamental freedoms of all persons,

Reiterating the important contribution of measures taken at all levels against terrorism, consistent with international law, in particular international human rights law and refugee and humanitarian law, to the functioning of democratic institutions and the maintenance of peace and security and thereby to the full enjoyment of human rights, as well as the need to continue this fight, including through international cooperation and the strengthening of the role of the United Nations in this respect,

Deeply deploring the occurrence of violations of human rights and fundamental freedoms in the context of the fight against terrorism, as well as violations of international refugee law and international humanitarian law,

Recalling the establishment by the Commission on Human Rights, in its resolution 2005/80, of the mandate of the Special Rapporteur on the promotion and protection of human rights and fundamental freedoms while countering terrorism,

Recalling also its resolution 48/141 of 20 December 1993 and, inter alia, the responsibility of the United Nations High Commissioner for Human Rights to promote and protect the effective enjoyment of all human rights,

Welcoming the establishment of the Human Rights Council, which is responsible for promoting universal respect for the protection of all human rights and fundamental freedoms for all, without distinction of any kind and in a fair and equal manner,

Recognizing the importance of the United Nations Global Counter–Terrorism Strategy adopted by the General Assembly on 8 September 2006, and reaffirming its relevant clauses on the measures to ensure respect for human rights for all, international humanitarian law and the rule of law as the fundamental basis for the fight against terrorism,

Reaffirming that acts, methods and practices of terrorism in all its forms and manifestations are activities aimed at the destruction of human rights, fundamental freedoms and democracy, threatening the territorial integrity and security of States and destabilizing legitimately constituted Governments, and that the international community should take the necessary steps to enhance cooperation to prevent and combat terrorism,

Reaffirming its unequivocal condemnation of all acts, methods and practices of terrorism in all its forms and manifestations, wherever and by whomsoever committed, regardless of their motivation, as criminal and unjustifiable, and renewing its commitment to strengthen international cooperation to prevent and combat terrorism,

Reaffirming that terrorism cannot and should not be associated with any religion, nationality, civilization or ethnic group,

Recognizing that the respect for all human rights, the respect for democracy and the respect for the rule of law are interrelated and mutually reinforcing,

Noting the declarations, statements and recommendations of a number of human rights treaty monitoring bodies and special procedures on the question of the compatibility of counter-terrorism measures with human rights obligations,

Recalling Human Rights Council decision 1/102 of 30 June 2006,

1. *Reaffirms* that States must ensure that any measure taken to combat terrorism complies with their obligations under international law, in particular international human rights, refugee and humanitarian law;

2. *Deplores* the suffering caused by terrorism to the victims and their families, and expresses its profound solidarity with them;

3. *Reaffirms* the obligation of States, in accordance with article 4 of the International Covenant on Civil and Political Rights, to respect certain rights as non-derogable in any circumstances, recalls, in regard to all other Covenant rights, that any measures derogating from the provisions of the Covenant must be in accordance with that article in all cases, and underlines the exceptional and temporary nature of any such derogations;

4. *Calls upon* States to raise awareness about the importance of these obligations among national authorities involved in combating terrorism;

5. *Reaffirms* that counter-terrorism measures should be implemented in full consideration of minority rights and must not be discriminatory on the grounds of race, colour, sex, language, religion or social origin;

6. *Urges* States to fully respect non-refoulement obligations under international refugee and human rights law and, at the same time, to review, with full respect for these obligations and other legal safeguards, the validity of a refugee status decision in an individual case if credible and relevant evidence comes to light that indicates that the person in question has committed any criminal acts, including terrorist acts, falling under the exclusion clauses under international refugee law;

7. *Also urges* States, while countering terrorism, to ensure due process guarantees, consistent with all relevant provisions of the Universal Declaration of Human Rights, the International Covenant on Civil and Political Rights and the Geneva Conventions of 1949, in their respective fields of applicability;

8. *Opposes* any form of deprivation of liberty that amounts to placing a detained person outside the protection of the law, and urges States to respect the safeguards concerning the liberty, security and dignity of the person and to treat all prisoners in all places of detention in accordance with international law, including human rights law and international humanitarian law;

9. *Reaffirms* that it is imperative that all States work to uphold and protect the dignity of individuals and their fundamental freedoms, as well as democratic practices and the rule of law, while countering terrorism;

10. *Encourages* States, while countering terrorism, to take into account relevant United Nations resolutions and decisions on human rights, and encourages them to give due consideration to the recommendations of the special procedures and mechanisms and the relevant comments and views of United Nations human rights treaty bodies;

11. *Takes note with interest* of the report of the Secretary–General submitted pursuant to resolution 60/158;

12. *Welcomes* the ongoing dialogue established in the context of the fight against terrorism between the Security Council and its Counter–Terrorism Committee and the relevant bodies for the promotion and protection of human rights, and encourages the Security Council and its Counter–Terrorism Committee to strengthen the links and to continue to develop cooperation with relevant human rights bodies, in particular with the Office of the United Nations High Commissioner for Human Rights, the Special Rapporteur on the promotion and protection of human rights and fundamental freedoms while countering terrorism and other relevant special procedures and mechanisms of the Human Rights Council, giving due regard to the promotion and protection of human rights in the ongoing work pursuant to relevant Security Council resolutions relating to terrorism;

13. *Takes note with appreciation* of the report of the Special Rapporteur submitted pursuant to Commission on Human Rights resolution 2005/80;

14. *Acknowledges with appreciation* the cooperation between the Special Rapporteur and all relevant procedures and mechanisms of the Human Rights Council as well as the United Nations human rights treaty bodies, and urges them to continue their cooperation, in accordance with their mandates, and to coordinate their efforts, where appropriate, in order to promote a consistent approach on this subject;

15. *Requests* all Governments to cooperate fully with the Special Rapporteur in the performance of the tasks and duties mandated, including by reacting promptly to the urgent appeals of the Special Rapporteur and providing the information requested;

16. *Welcomes* the work done by the United Nations High Commissioner for Human Rights to implement the mandate given to her in resolution 60/158, and requests the High Commissioner to continue her efforts in this regard;

17. *Requests* the Secretary–General to submit a report on the implementation of the present resolution to the Human Rights Council and to the General Assembly at its sixty-second session;

18. *Decides* to consider at its sixty-second session the report of the Special Rapporteur on the promotion and protection of human rights and fundamental freedoms while countering terrorism.

Document 56
HUMAN RIGHTS AND TERRORISM

U.N. G.A. Res. 59/195 (20 Dec. 2004)

The General Assembly,

Guided by the Charter of the United Nations, the Universal Declaration of Human Rights, the Declaration on Principles of International Law concerning Friendly Relations and Cooperation among States in accordance with the Charter of the United Nations and the International Covenants on Human Rights, . . .

Recalling previous resolutions of the Commission on Human Rights on the issue of human rights and terrorism, as well as on hostage-taking,

Bearing in mind all other relevant General Assembly resolutions,

Bearing in mind also relevant Security Council resolutions,

Aware that, at the dawn of the twenty-first century, the world is witness to historic and far-reaching transformations, in the course of which forces of aggressive nationalism and religious and ethnic extremism continue to produce fresh challenges,

Alarmed that acts of terrorism in all its forms and manifestations aimed at the destruction of human rights have continued despite national and international efforts,

Convinced that terrorism in all its forms and manifestations, wherever and by whomever committed, can never be justified in any instance, including as a means to promote and protect human rights, . . .

Bearing in mind that the right to life is the basic human right, without which a human being can exercise no other right,

Bearing in mind also that terrorism creates an environment that destroys the right of people to live in freedom from fear,

Reiterating that all States have an obligation to promote and protect all human rights and fundamental freedoms and to ensure effective implementation of their obligations under international law,

Seriously concerned about the gross violations of human rights perpetuated by terrorist groups,

Expressing its deepest sympathy and condolences to all the victims of terrorism and their families,

Alarmed in particular at the possibility that terrorist groups may exploit new technologies to facilitate acts of terrorism, which may cause massive damage, including huge loss of life,

Emphasizing the need to intensify the fight against terrorism at the national level, to enhance effective international cooperation in combating terrorism in conformity with international law, including relevant

State obligations under international human rights and international humanitarian law, and to strengthen the role of the United Nations in this respect,

Emphasizing also that States shall deny safe haven to those who finance, plan, support or commit terrorist acts or provide safe haven,

Reaffirming that all measures to counter terrorism must be in strict conformity with international law, including international human rights standards and obligations,

Mindful of the need to protect the human rights of and guarantees for the individual in accordance with the relevant human rights principles and instruments, in particular the right to life,

Noting the growing consciousness within the international community of the negative effects of terrorism in all its forms and manifestations on the full enjoyment of human rights and fundamental freedoms and on the establishment of the rule of law and democratic freedoms enshrined in the Charter of the United Nations and the International Covenants on Human Rights,

Concerned by the tendencies to link terrorism and violence with religion, . . .

1. *Reiterates* its unequivocal condemnation of the acts, methods and practices of terrorism in all its forms and manifestations as activities aimed at the destruction of human rights, fundamental freedoms and democracy, threatening the territorial integrity and the security of States, destabilizing legitimately constituted Governments, undermining pluralistic civil society and having adverse consequences for the economic and social development of States;

2. *Strongly condemns* the violations of the right to life, liberty and security;

3. *Rejects* the identification of terrorism with any religion, nationality or culture;

4. *Profoundly deplores* the increasing number of innocent persons, including women, children and the elderly, killed, massacred and maimed by terrorists in indiscriminate and random acts of violence and terror, which cannot be justified in any circumstances;

5. *Expresses its solidarity* with the victims of terrorism;

6. *Reaffirms* the decision of the Heads of State and Government, as contained in the United Nations Millennium Declaration [res. 55/2], to take concerted action against international terrorism and to accede as soon as possible to all the relevant regional and international conventions;

7. *Urges* the international community to enhance cooperation at the regional and international levels in the fight against terrorism in all its forms and manifestations, in accordance with relevant international instruments, including those relating to human rights, with the aim of its eradication;

8. *Calls upon* States to take all necessary and effective measures, in accordance with relevant provisions of international law, including international human rights standards, to prevent, combat and eliminate terrorism in all its forms and manifestations, wherever and by whomever it is committed, and also calls upon States to strengthen, where appropriate, their legislation to combat terrorism in all its forms and manifestations;

9. *Urges* all States to deny safe haven to terrorists;

10. *Calls upon* States to take appropriate measures, in conformity with relevant provisions of national and international law, including human rights standards, before granting refugee status, for the purpose of ensuring that an asylum-seeker has not planned, facilitated or participated in the commission of terrorist acts, including assassinations, and to ensure, in conformity with international law, that refugee status is not abused by the perpetrators, organizers or facilitators of terrorist acts and that claims of political motivation are not recognized as grounds for refusing requests for the extradition of alleged terrorists; . . .

12. *Condemns* the incitement to ethnic hatred, violence and terrorism;

13. *Stresses* that every person, regardless of nationality, race, sex, religion or any other distinction, has a right to protection from terrorism and terrorist acts;

14. *Expresses concern* that the growing connection between terrorist groups and other criminal organizations engaged in the illegal traffic in arms and drugs at the national and international levels, as well as the consequent commission of serious crimes such as murder, extortion, kidnapping, assault, the taking of hostages and robbery, and requests the relevant United Nations bodies to continue to give special attention to this question;. . . .

Document 57
TORTURE AND OTHER CRUEL, INHUMAN OR DEGRADING TREATMENT OR PUNISHMENT

U.N. G.A. Res. 62/148 (18 Dec. 2007)

The General Assembly,

Reaffirming that no one shall be subjected to torture or to other cruel, inhuman or degrading treatment or punishment,

Recalling that freedom from torture and other cruel, inhuman or degrading treatment or punishment is a non-derogable right that must be protected under all circumstances, including in times of international or internal armed conflict or disturbance, and that the absolute prohibition of torture and other cruel, inhuman or degrading treatment or punishment is affirmed in relevant international instruments,

Recalling also that a number of international, regional and domestic courts, including the International Tribunal for the Prosecution of Persons Responsible for Serious Violations of International Humanitarian Law Committed in the Territory of the Former Yugoslavia since 1991, have recognized that the prohibition of torture is a peremptory norm of international law and have held that the prohibition of cruel, inhuman or degrading treatment or punishment is customary international law,

Recalling further the definition of torture contained in article 1 of the Convention against Torture and Other Cruel, Inhuman or Degrading Treatment or Punishment, without prejudice to any international instrument or national legislation which contains or may contain provisions of wider application,

Emphasizing the importance of properly interpreting and implementing the obligations of States with respect to torture and other cruel, inhuman or degrading treatment or punishment, and of abiding strictly by the definition of torture contained in article 1 of the Convention,

Noting that under the Geneva Conventions of 1949 torture and inhuman treatment are a grave breach and that under the statutes of the International Tribunal for the Former Yugoslavia and the International Criminal Tribunal for the Prosecution of Persons Responsible for Genocide and Other Serious Violations of International Humanitarian Law Committed in the Territory of Rwanda and Rwandan Citizens Responsible for Genocide and Other Such Violations Committed in the Territory of Neighbouring States between 1 January and 31 December 1994 and the Rome Statute of the International Criminal Court acts of torture can constitute crimes against humanity and, when committed in a situation of armed conflict, constitute war crimes,

Welcoming the establishment of national mechanisms for the prevention of torture pursuant to the obligations of States parties to the Optional Protocol to the Convention against Torture and Other Cruel, Inhuman or Degrading Treatment or Punishment, which entered into force on 22 June 2006,

Acknowledging the adoption of the International Convention for the Protection of All Persons from Enforced Disappearance in its resolution 61/177 of 20 December 2006, and recognizing that the entry into force of the Convention, expected before the sixty-third session of the General Assembly, will be a significant event,

Commending the persistent efforts of civil society organizations, including non-governmental organizations and the considerable network of centres for the rehabilitation of victims of torture, to combat torture and to alleviate the suffering of victims of torture,

Bearing in mind the special procedures review process being undertaken by the Human Rights Council, and its relevant resolutions,

1. *Condemns* all forms of torture and other cruel, inhuman or degrading treatment or punishment, including through intimidation, which are and shall remain prohibited at any time and in any place whatsoever and can thus never be justified, and calls upon all States to implement fully the absolute prohibition of torture and other cruel, inhuman or degrading treatment or punishment;

2. *Emphasizes* that States must take persistent, determined and effective measures to prevent and combat torture and other cruel, inhuman or degrading treatment or punishment, including their gender-based manifestations, and stresses that all acts of torture must be made offences under domestic criminal law;

3. *Also emphasizes* the importance of States ensuring proper follow-up to the recommendations and conclusions of the relevant treaty bodies and mechanisms, including the Committee against Torture, the Subcommittee on Prevention of Torture and Other Cruel, Inhuman or Degrading Treatment or Punishment and the Special Rapporteur of the Human Rights Council on torture and other cruel, inhuman or degrading treatment or punishment;

4. *Condemns* any action or attempt by States or public officials to legalize, authorize or acquiesce in torture and other cruel, inhuman or degrading treatment or punishment under any circumstances, including on grounds of national security or through judicial decisions;

5. *Stresses* that all allegations of torture or other cruel, inhuman or degrading treatment or punishment must be promptly and impartially examined by the competent national authority, and that those who encourage, order, tolerate or perpetrate acts of torture must be held responsible, brought to justice and severely punished, including the officials in charge of the place of detention where the prohibited act is found to have been committed;

6. *Takes note* in this respect of the Principles on the Effective Investigation and Documentation of Torture and Other Cruel, Inhuman or Degrading Treatment or Punishment (the Istanbul Principles) as a

useful tool in efforts to prevent and combat torture and of the updated set of principles for the protection of human rights through action to combat impunity;

7. *Calls upon* States parties to the Convention against Torture and Other Cruel, Inhuman or Degrading Treatment or Punishment to fulfil their obligation to submit for prosecution or extradite those alleged to have committed acts of torture;

8. *Encourages* all States to ensure that persons convicted of torture or other cruel, inhuman or degrading treatment or punishment have no subsequent involvement in the custody, interrogation or treatment of any person under arrest, detention, imprisonment or other deprivation of liberty;

9. *Emphasizes* that acts of torture in armed conflict are serious violations of international humanitarian law and in this regard constitute war crimes, that acts of torture can constitute crimes against humanity and that the perpetrators of all acts of torture must be prosecuted and punished;

10. *Strongly urges* States to ensure that any statement that is established to have been made as a result of torture shall not be invoked as evidence in any proceedings, except against a person accused of torture as evidence that the statement was made;

11. *Stresses* that States must not punish personnel who are involved in the custody, interrogation or treatment of any individual subjected to any form of arrest, detention or imprisonment or any other form of deprivation of liberty for not obeying orders to commit or conceal acts amounting to torture or other cruel, inhuman or degrading treatment or punishment;

12. *Urges* States not to expel, return ("refouler"), extradite or in any other way transfer a person to another State where there are substantial grounds for believing that the person would be in danger of being subjected to torture, and recognizes that diplomatic assurances, where used, do not release States from their obligations under international human rights, humanitarian and refugee law, in particular the principle of non-refoulement;

13. *Stresses* that national legal systems must ensure that victims of torture and other cruel, inhuman or degrading treatment or punishment obtain redress, are awarded fair and adequate compensation and receive appropriate social and medical rehabilitation, urges States to take effective measures to this end, and in this regard encourages the development of rehabilitation centres;

14. *Recalls* its resolution 43/173 of 9 December 1988 on the Body of Principles for the Protection of All Persons under Any Form of Detention or Imprisonment, and in this context stresses that ensuring that any individual arrested or detained is promptly brought before a judge or other independent judicial officer in person and permitting prompt and regular medical care and legal counsel as well as visits by family members and independent monitoring mechanisms are effective meas-

ures for the prevention of torture and other cruel, inhuman or degrading treatment or punishment;

15. *Reminds* all States that prolonged incommunicado detention or detention in secret places can facilitate the perpetration of torture and other cruel, inhuman or degrading treatment or punishment and can in itself constitute a form of such treatment, and urges all States to respect the safeguards concerning the liberty, security and dignity of the person;

16. *Calls upon* all States to take appropriate effective legislative, administrative, judicial and other measures to prevent and prohibit the production, trade, export and use of equipment that is specifically designed to inflict torture or other cruel, inhuman or degrading treatment or punishment;

17. *Urges* all States that have not yet done so to become parties to the Convention as a matter of priority;

18. *Invites* all States parties to the Convention that have not yet done so to make the declarations provided for in articles 21 and 22 of the Convention concerning inter-State and individual communications, to consider the possibility of withdrawing their reservations to article 20 of the Convention and to notify the Secretary–General of their acceptance of the amendments to articles 17 and 18 of the Convention with a view to enhancing the effectiveness of the Committee against Torture as soon as possible;

19. *Urges* States parties to comply strictly with their obligations under the Convention, including, in view of the high number of reports not submitted in time, their obligation to submit reports in accordance with article 19 of the Convention, and invites States parties to incorporate a gender perspective and information concerning children and juveniles and persons with disabilities when submitting reports to the Committee;

20. *Calls upon* States parties also to give early consideration to signing and ratifying the Optional Protocol to the Convention against Torture and Other Cruel, Inhuman or Degrading Treatment or Punishment, which provides further measures for use in the fight against and prevention of torture and other cruel, inhuman or degrading treatment or punishment;

21. *Welcomes* the work of the Committee and its report submitted in accordance with article 24 of the Convention, recommends that the Committee continue to include information on the follow-up by States to its recommendations, and supports the Committee in its intention to further improve the effectiveness of its working sessions;

22. *Calls upon* the United Nations High Commissioner for Human Rights, in conformity with her mandate established by the General Assembly in its resolution 48/141 of 20 December 1993, to continue to provide, at the request of States, advisory services for the prevention of torture and other cruel, inhuman or degrading treatment or punishment, including for the preparation of national reports to the Committee and for the establishment and operation of national preventive mecha-

nisms, as well as technical assistance for the development, production and distribution of teaching material for this purpose;

23. *Notes with appreciation* the interim report of the Special Rapporteur, and encourages the Special Rapporteur to continue to include in his recommendations proposals on the prevention and investigation of torture and other cruel, inhuman or degrading treatment or punishment, including its gender-based manifestations;

24. *Requests* the Special Rapporteur to continue to consider including in his report information on the follow-up by States to his recommendations, visits and communications, including progress made and problems encountered, and on other official contacts;

25. *Calls upon* all States to cooperate with and assist the Special Rapporteur in the performance of his task, to supply all necessary information requested by the Special Rapporteur, to fully and expeditiously respond to and follow up his urgent appeals, to give serious consideration to responding favourably to requests by the Special Rapporteur to visit their countries and to enter into a constructive dialogue with the Special Rapporteur on requested visits to their countries as well as with respect to the follow-up to his recommendations;

26. *Stresses* the need for the continued regular exchange of views among the Committee, the Subcommittee, the Special Rapporteur and other relevant United Nations mechanisms and bodies, as well as for the pursuance of cooperation with relevant United Nations programmes, notably the United Nations Crime Prevention and Criminal Justice Programme, with regional organizations and mechanisms, as appropriate, and civil society organizations, including non-governmental organizations, with a view to enhancing further their effectiveness and cooperation on issues relating to the prevention and eradication of torture, inter alia, by improving their coordination;

27. *Recognizes* the global need for international assistance to victims of torture, stresses the importance of the work of the Board of Trustees of the United Nations Voluntary Fund for Victims of Torture, appeals to all States and organizations to contribute annually to the Fund, preferably with a substantial increase in the level of contributions, and encourages contributions to the Special Fund established by the Optional Protocol to help finance the implementation of the recommendations made by the Subcommittee as well as education programmes of the national preventive mechanisms;

28. *Requests* the Secretary–General to continue to transmit to all States the appeals of the General Assembly for contributions to the Funds and to include the Funds on an annual basis among the programmes for which funds are pledged at the United Nations Pledging Conference for Development Activities;

29. *Also requests* the Secretary–General to submit to the Human Rights Council and to the General Assembly at its sixty-third session a report on the operations of the Funds;

30. *Further requests* the Secretary–General to ensure, within the overall budgetary framework of the United Nations, the provision of

adequate staff and facilities for the bodies and mechanisms involved in preventing and combating torture and assisting victims of torture or other cruel, inhuman or degrading treatment or punishment commensurate with the strong support expressed by Member States for preventing and combating torture and assisting victims of torture;

31. *Calls upon* all States, the Office of the United Nations High Commissioner for Human Rights and other United Nations bodies and agencies, as well as relevant intergovernmental and civil society organizations, including non-governmental organizations, to commemorate, on 26 June, the United Nations International Day in Support of Victims of Torture;

32. *Decides* to consider at its sixty-third session the reports of the Secretary–General, including the report on the United Nations Voluntary Fund for Victims of Torture and the Special Fund established by the Optional Protocol, the report of the Committee against Torture and the interim report of the Special Rapporteur on torture and other cruel, inhuman or degrading treatment or punishment.

Document 58
TOKYO CONVENTION ON OFFENCES AND CERTAIN OTHER ACTS COMMITTED ON BOARD AIRCRAFT

704 U.N.T.S. 219, 20 U.S.T. 2941, T.I.A.S. No. 6768 (1963)

The States Parties to this Convention

Have agreed as follows:

Chapter I—Scope of the Convention

Article 1

1. This Convention shall apply in respect of:

(a) offences against penal law;

(b) acts which, whether or not they are offences, may or do jeopardize the safety of the aircraft or of persons or property therein or which jeopardize good order and discipline on board.

2. Except as provided in Chapter III, this Convention shall apply in respect of offences committed or acts done by a person on board any aircraft registered in a Contracting State, while that aircraft is in flight or on the surface of the high seas or of any other area outside the territory of any State.

3. For the purposes of this Convention, an aircraft is considered to be in flight from the moment when power is applied for the purpose of take-off until the moment when the landing run ends.

4. This Convention shall not apply to aircraft used in military, customs or police services.

Article 2

Without prejudice to the provisions of Article 4 and except when the safety of the aircraft or of persons or property on board so requires, no provision of this Convention shall be interpreted as authorizing or requiring any action in respect of offences against penal laws of a political nature or those based on racial or religious discrimination.

Chapter II—Jurisdiction

Article 3

1. The State of registration of the aircraft is competent to exercise jurisdiction over offences and acts committed on board.

2. Each Contracting State shall take such measures as may be necessary to establish its jurisdiction as the State of registration over offences committed on board aircraft registered in such State.

3. This Convention does not exclude any criminal jurisdiction exercised in accordance with national law.

Article 4

A Contracting State which is not the State of registration may not interfere with an aircraft in flight in order to exercise its criminal jurisdiction over an offence committed on board except in the following cases:

(a) the offence has effect on the territory of such State;

(b) the offence has been committed by or against a national or permanent resident of such State;

(c) the offence is against the security of such State;

(d) the offence consists of a breach of any rules or regulations relating to the flight or manoeuvre of aircraft in force in such State;

(e) the exercise of jurisdiction is necessary to ensure the observance of any obligation of such State under a multilateral international agreement.

Chapter III—Powers of the aircraft commander

Article 5

1. The provisions of this Chapter shall not apply to offences and acts committed or about to be committed by a person on board an aircraft in flight in the airspace of the State of registration or over the high seas or any other area outside the territory of any State unless the last point of take-off or the next point of intended landing is situated in a State other than that of registration, or the aircraft subsequently flies in the airspace of a State other than that of registration with such person still on board.

2. Notwithstanding the provisions of Article 1, paragraph 3, an aircraft shall for the purposes of this Chapter, be considered to be in flight at any time from the moment when all its external doors are closed following embarkation until the moment when any such door is opened for disembarkation. In the case of a forced landing, the provisions of this Chapter shall continue to apply with respect to offences and acts committed on board until competent authorities of a State take over the responsibility for the aircraft and for the persons and property on board.

Article 6

1. The aircraft commander may, when he has reasonable grounds to believe that a person has committed, or is about to commit, on board the aircraft, an offence or act contemplated in Article 1, paragraph 1, impose upon such person reasonable measures including restraint which are necessary:

(a) to protect the safety of the air-craft, or of persons or property therein; or

(b) to maintain good order and discipline on board; or

(c) to enable him to deliver such person to competent authorities or to disembark him in accordance with the provisions of this Chapter.

2. The aircraft commander may require or authorize the assistance of other crew members and may request or authorize, but not require, the assistance of passengers to restrain any person whom he is entitled to restrain. Any crew member or passenger may also take reasonable preventive measures without such authorization when he has reasonable grounds to believe that such action is immediately necessary to protect the safety of the aircraft, or of persons or property therein.

Article 7

1. Measures of restraint imposed upon a person in accordance with Article 6 shall not be continued beyond any point at which the aircraft lands unless:

(a) such point is in the territory of a non-Contracting State and its authorities refuse to permit disembarkation of that person or those measures have been imposed in accordance with Article 6, paragraph 1 (c) in order to enable his delivery to competent authorities;

(b) the aircraft makes a forced landing and the aircraft commander is unable to deliver that person to competent authorities; or

(c) that person agrees to onward carriage under restraint.

2. The aircraft commander shall as soon as practicable, and if possible before landing in the territory of a State with a person on board who has been placed under restraint in accordance with the provisions of Article 6, notify the authorities of such State of the fact that a person on board is under restraint and of the reasons for such restraint.

Article 8

1. The aircraft commander may, in so far as it is necessary for the purpose of subparagraph (a) or (b) of paragraph 1 of Article 6, disembark in the territory of any State in which the aircraft lands any person who he has reasonable grounds to believe has committed, or is about to commit, on board the aircraft an act contemplated in Article 1, paragraph 1 (b).

2. The aircraft commander shall report to the authorities of the State in which he disembarks any person pursuant to this article, the fact of, and the reasons for, such disembarkation.

Article 9

1. The aircraft commander may deliver to the competent authorities of any Contracting State in the territory of which the aircraft lands any person who he has reasonable grounds to believe has committed on

board the aircraft an act which, in his opinion, is a serious offence according to the penal law of the State of registration of the aircraft.

2. The aircraft commander shall as soon as practicable and if possible before landing in the territory of a Contracting State with a person on board whom the aircraft commander intends to deliver in accordance with the preceding paragraph, notify the authorities of such State of his intention to deliver such person and the reasons therefor.

3. The aircraft commander shall furnish the authorities to whom any suspected offender is delivered in accordance with the provisions of this article with evidence and information which, under the law of the State of registration of the aircraft, are lawfully in his possession.

Article 10

For actions taken in accordance with this Convention, neither the aircraft commander, any other member of the crew, any passenger, the owner or operator of the aircraft, nor the person on whose behalf the flight was performed shall be held responsible in any proceeding on account of the treatment undergone by the person against whom the actions were taken.

Chapter IV—Unlawful Seizure of Aircraft

Article 11

1. When a person on board has unlawfully committed by force or threat thereof an act of interference, seizure, or other wrongful exercise of control of an aircraft in flight or when such an act is about to be committed, Contracting States shall take all appropriate measures to restore control of the aircraft to its lawful commander or to preserve his control of the aircraft.

2. In the cases contemplated in the preceding paragraph, the Contracting State in which the aircraft lands shall permit its passengers and crew to continue their journey as soon as practicable, and shall return the aircraft and its cargo to the persons lawfully entitled to possession.

Chapter V—Powers and Duties of States

Article 12

Any Contracting State shall allow the commander of an aircraft registered in another Contracting State to disembark any person pursuant to Article 8, paragraph 1.

Article 13

1. Any Contracting State shall take delivery of any person whom the aircraft commander delivers pursuant to Article 9, paragraph 1.

2. Upon being satisfied that the circumstances so warrant, any Contracting State shall take custody or other measures to ensure the presence of any person suspected of an act contemplated in Article 11, paragraph 1 and of any person of whom it has taken delivery. The custody and other measures shall be as provided in the law of that State

but may only be continued for such time as is reasonably necessary to enable any criminal or extradition proceedings to be instituted.

3. Any person in custody pursuant to the previous paragraph shall be assisted in communicating immediately with the nearest appropriate representative of the State of which he is a national.

4. Any Contracting State, to which a person is delivered pursuant to Article 9, paragraph 1, or in whose territory an aircraft lands following the commission of an act contemplated in Article 11, paragraph 1, shall immediately make a preliminary inquiry into the facts.

5. When a State, pursuant to this article, has taken a person into custody, it shall immediately notify the State of registration of the aircraft and the State of nationality of the detained person and, if it considers it advisable, any other interested State of the fact that such person is in custody and of the circumstances which warrant his detention. The State which makes the preliminary enquiry contemplated in paragraph 4 of this article shall promptly report its findings to the said States and shall indicate whether it intends to exercise jurisdiction.

Article 14

1. When any person has been disembarked in accordance with Article 8, paragraph 1, or delivered in accordance with Article 9, paragraph 1, or has disembarked after committing an act contemplated in Article 11, paragraph 1, and when such person cannot or does not desire to continue his journey and the State of landing refuses to admit him, that State may, if the person in question is not a national or permanent resident of that State, return him to the territory of the State of which he is a national or permanent resident or to the territory of the State in which he began his journey by air.

2. Neither disembarkation, nor delivery, nor the taking of custody or other measures contemplated in Article 13, paragraph 2, nor return of the person concerned, shall be considered as admission to the territory of the Contracting State concerned for the purpose of its law relating to entry or admission of persons and nothing in this Convention shall affect the law of a Contracting State relating to the expulsion of persons from its territory.

Article 15

1. Without prejudice to Article 14, any person who has been disembarked in accordance with Article 8, paragraph 1, or delivered in accordance with Article 9, paragraph 1, or has disembarked after committing an act contemplated in Article 11, paragraph 1, and who desires to continue his journey shall be at liberty as soon as practicable to proceed to any destination of his choice unless his presence is required by the law of the State of landing for the purpose of extradition or criminal proceedings.

2. Without prejudice to its law as to entry and admission to, and extradition and expulsion from its territory, a Contracting State in whose territory a person has been disembarked in accordance with Article 8, paragraph 1, or delivered in accordance with Article 9, para-

graph 1 or has disembarked and is suspected of having committed an act contemplated in Article 11, paragraph 1, shall accord to such person treatment which is no less favourable for his protection and security than that accorded to nationals of such Contracting State in like circumstances.

Chapter VI—Other Provisions

Article 16

1. Offences committed on aircraft registered in a Contracting State shall be treated, for the purpose of extradition, as if they had been committed not only in the place in which they have occurred but also in the territory of the State of registration of the aircraft.

2. Without prejudice to the provisions of the preceding paragraph, nothing in this Convention shall be deemed to create an obligation to grant extradition.

Article 17

In taking any measures for investigation or arrest or otherwise exercising jurisdiction in connection with any offence committed on board an aircraft the Contracting States shall pay due regard to the safety and other interests of air navigation and shall so act as to avoid unnecessary delay of the aircraft, passengers, crew or cargo.

Article 18

If Contracting States establish joint air transport operating organizations or international operating agencies, which operate aircraft not registered in any one State those States shall, according to the circumstances of the case, designate the State among them which, for the purposes of this Convention, shall be considered as the State of registration and shall give notice thereof to the International Civil Aviation Organization which shall communicate the notice to all States Parties to this Convention.

Chapter VII—Final Clauses

Article 19

Until the date on which this Convention comes into force in accordance with the provisions of Article 21, it shall remain open for signature on behalf of any State which at that date is a Member of the United Nations or of any of the Specialized Agencies.

Article 20

1. This Convention shall be subject to ratification by the signatory States in accordance with their constitutional procedures.

2. The instruments of ratification shall be deposited with the International Civil Aviation Organization.

Article 21

1. As soon as twelve of the signatory States have deposited their instruments of ratification of this Convention, it shall come into force

between them on the ninetieth day after the date of the deposit of the twelfth instrument of ratification. It shall come into force for each State ratifying thereafter on the ninetieth day after the deposit of its instrument of ratification.

2. As soon as this Convention comes into force, it shall be registered with the Secretary–General of the United Nations by the International Civil Aviation Organization.

Article 22

1. This Convention shall, after it has come into force, be open for accession by any State Member of the United Nations or of any of the Specialized Agencies.

2. The accession of a State shall be effected by the deposit of an instrument of accession with the International Civil Aviation Organization and shall take effect on the ninetieth day after the date of such deposit.

Article 23

1. Any Contracting State may denounce this Convention by notification addressed to the International Civil Aviation Organization.

2. Denunciation shall take effect six months after the date of receipt by the International Civil Aviation Organization of the notification of denunciation.

Article 24

1. Any dispute between two or more Contracting States concerning the interpretation or application of this Convention which cannot be settled through negotiation, shall, at the request of one of them, be submitted to arbitration. If within six months from the date of the request for arbitration the Parties are unable to agree on the organization of the arbitration, any one of those Parties may refer the dispute to the International Court of Justice by request in conformity with the Statute of the Court.

2. Each State may at the time of signature or ratification of this Convention or accession thereto, declare that it does not consider itself bound by the preceding paragraph. The other Contracting States shall not be bound by the preceding paragraph with respect to any Contracting State having made such a reservation.

3. Any Contracting State having made a reservation in accordance with the preceding paragraph may at any time withdraw this reservation by notification to the International Civil Aviation Organization.

Article 25

Except as provided in Article 24 no reservation may be made to this Convention.

Article 26

The International Civil Aviation Organization shall give notice to all States Members of the United Nations or of any of the Specialized Agencies:

(a) of any signature of this Convention and the date thereof;

(b) of the deposit of any instrument of ratification or accession and the date thereof;

(c) of the date on which this Convention comes into force in accordance with Article 21, paragraph 1;

(d) of the receipt of any notification of denunciation and the date thereof; and

(e) of the receipt of any declaration or notification made under Article 24 and the date thereof.

In Witness Whereof the undersigned Plenipotentiaries, having been duly authorized, have signed this Convention.

Done at Tokyo on the fourteenth day of September One Thousand Nine Hundred and Sixty-three in three authentic texts drawn up in the English, French and Spanish languages.

This Convention shall be deposited with the International Civil Aviation Organization with which, in accordance with Article 19, it shall remain open for signature and the said Organization shall send certified copies thereof to all States Members of the United Nations or of any Specialized Agency.

Document 59
MONTREAL CONVENTION FOR THE SUPPRESSION OF UNLAWFUL ACTS AGAINST THE SAFETY OF CIVIL AVIATION

974 U.N.T.S. 177, 24 U.S.T. 564, T.I.A.S. No. 7570 (1971)

Article 1

1. Any person commits an offence if he unlawfully and intentionally:

(a) performs an act of violence against a person on board an aircraft in flight if that act is likely to endanger the safety of that aircraft; or

(b) destroys an aircraft in service or causes damage to such aircraft which renders it incapable of flight or which is likely to endanger its safety in flight; or

(c) places or causes to be placed on an aircraft in service, by any means whatsoever, a device or substance which is likely to destroy that aircraft, or to cause damage to it which renders it incapable of flight, or to cause damage to it which is likely to endanger its safety in flight; or

(d) destroys or damages air navigation facilities or interferes with their operation, if any such act is likely to endanger the safety of aircraft in flight; or

(e) communicates information which he knows to be false, thereby endangering the safety of an aircraft in flight.

2. Any person also commits an offence if he:

(a) attempts to commit any of the offences mentioned in paragraph 1 of this article; or

(b) is an accomplice of a person who commits or attempts to commit any such offence.

Article 2

For the purposes of this Convention:

(a) an aircraft is considered to be in flight at any time from the moment when all its external doors are closed following embarkation until the moment when any such door is opened for disembarkation; in the case of a forced landing, the flight shall be deemed to continue until the competent authorities take over the responsibility for the aircraft and for the aircraft and for persons and property on board;

(b) an aircraft is considered to be in service from the beginning of the preflight preparation of the aircraft by ground personnel or by the crew for a specific flight until twenty-four hours after any landing; the period of service shall, in any event, extend for the entire period during which the aircraft is in flight as defined in paragraph (a) of this article.

Article 3

Each Contracting State undertakes to make the offences mentioned in Article 1 punishable by severe penalties.

Article 4

1. This Convention shall not apply to aircraft used in military, customs or police services.

2. In the cases contemplated in subparagraphs (a), (b), (c) and (e) of paragraph 1 of Article 1, this Convention shall apply, irrespective of whether the aircraft is engaged in an international or domestic flight, only if:

(a) the place of take-off or landing, actual or intended, of the aircraft is situated outside the territory of the State of registration of that aircraft; or

(b) the offence is committed in the territory of a State other than the State of registration of the aircraft.

3. Notwithstanding paragraph 2 of this article, in the cases contemplated in subparagraphs (a), (b), (c) and (e) of paragraph 1 of Article 1, this Convention shall also apply if the offender or the alleged offender is found in the territory of a State other than the State of registration of the aircraft.

4. With respect to the States mentioned in Article 9 and in the cases mentioned in subparagraphs (a), (b), (c) and (e) of paragraph 1 of Article 1, this Convention shall not apply if the places referred to in subparagraph (a) of paragraph 2 of this article are situated within the territory of the same State where that State is one of those referred to in Article 9, unless the offence is committed or the offender or alleged offender is found in the territory of a State other than that State.

5. In the cases contemplated in subparagraph (d) of paragraph 1 of Article 1, this Convention shall apply only if the air navigation facilities are used in international air navigation.

6. The provisions of paragraphs 2, 3, 4 and 5 of this article shall also apply in the cases contemplated in paragraph 2 of Article 1.

Article 5

1. Each Contracting State shall take such measures as may be necessary to establish its jurisdiction over the offences in the following cases:

(a) when the offence is committed in the territory of that State;

(b) when the offence is committed against or on board an aircraft registered in that State;

(c) when the aircraft on board which the offence is committed lands in its territory with the alleged offender still on board;

(d) when the offence is committed against or on board an aircraft leased without crew to a lessee who has his principal place of business or, if the lessee has no such place of business, his permanent residence, in that State.

2. Each Contracting State shall likewise take such measures as may be necessary to establish its jurisdiction over the offences mentioned in Article 1, paragraph 1 (a), (b) and (c), and in Article 1, paragraph 2, in so far as that paragraph relates to those offences, in the case where the alleged offender is present in its territory and it does not extradite him pursuant to Article 8 to any of the States mentioned in paragraph 1 of this article.

3. This Convention does not exclude any criminal jurisdiction exercised in accordance with national law.

Article 6

1. Upon being satisfied that the circumstances so warrant, any Contracting State in the territory of which the offender or the alleged offender is present, shall take him into custody or take other measures to ensure his presence. The custody and other measures shall be as provided in the law of that State but may only be continued for such time as is necessary to enable any criminal or extradition proceedings to be instituted.

2. Such State shall immediately make a preliminary enquiry into the facts.

3. Any person in custody pursuant to paragraph 1 of this article shall be assisted in communicating immediately with the nearest appropriate representative of the State of which he is a national.

4. When a State, pursuant to this article, has taken a person into custody, it shall immediately notify the States mentioned in Article 5, paragraph 1, the State of nationality of the detained person and, if it considers it advisable, any other interested States of the fact that such person is in custody and of the circumstances which warrant his detention. The State which makes the preliminary enquiry contemplated in paragraph 2 of this article shall promptly report its findings to the said States and shall indicate whether it intends to exercise jurisdiction.

Article 7

The Contracting State in the territory of which the alleged offender is found shall, if it does not extradite him, be obliged, without exception whatsoever and whether or not the offence was committed in its territory, to submit the case to its competent authorities for the purpose of prosecution. Those authorities shall take their decision in the same manner as in the case of any ordinary offence of a serious nature under the law of that State.

Article 8

1. The offences shall be deemed to be included as extraditable offences in any extradition treaty existing between Contracting States. Contracting States undertake to include the offences as extraditable offences in every extradition treaty to be concluded between them.

2. If a Contracting State which makes extradition conditional on the existence of a treaty receives a request for extradition from another Contracting State with which it has no extradition treaty, it may at its option consider this Convention as the legal basis for extradition in respect of the offences. Extradition shall be subject to the other conditions provided by the law of the requested State.

3. Contracting States which do not make extradition conditional on the existence of a treaty shall recognize the offences as extraditable offences between themselves subject to the conditions provided by the law of the requested State.

4. Each of the offences shall be treated, for the purpose of extradition between Contracting States, as if it had been committed not only in the place in which it occurred but also in the territories of the States required to establish their jurisdiction in accordance with Article 5, paragraph 1 (b), (c) and (d).

Article 11

1. Contracting States shall afford one another the greatest measure of assistance in connection with criminal proceedings brought in respect of the offences. The law of the State requested shall apply in all cases.

2. The Provisions of paragraph 1 of this article shall not affect obligations under any other treaty, bilateral or multilateral, which governs or will govern, in whole or in part, mutual assistance in criminal matters.

Article 14

1. Any dispute between two or more Contracting States concerning the interpretation or application of this Convention which cannot be settled through negotiation, shall, at the request of one of them, be submitted to arbitration. If within six months from the date of the request for arbitration the Parties are unable to agree on the organization of the arbitration, any of those Parties may refer the dispute to the International Court of Justice by request in conformity with the Statute of the Court.

2. Each State may at the time of signature or ratification of this Convention or accession thereto, declare that it does not consider itself bound by the preceding paragraph. The other Contracting States shall not be bound by the preceding paragraph with respect to any Contracting State having made such a reservation.

3. Any Contracting State having made a reservation in accordance with the preceding paragraph may at any time withdraw this reservation by notification to the Depository Governments.

Document 60
PROTOCOL FOR THE SUPPRESSION OF UNLAWFUL ACTS OF VIOLENCE AT AIRPORTS SERVING INTERNATIONAL CIVIL AVIATION, SUPPLEMENTARY TO THE CONVENTION FOR THE SUPPRESSION OF UNLAWFUL ACTS AGAINST THE SAFETY OF CIVIL AVIATION

International Civil Aviation Organization Doc. 9518 (signed at Montreal on 24 February 1988)

Article I

This Protocol supplements the Convention for the Suppression of Unlawful Acts against the Safety of Civil Aviation, done at Montreal on 23 September 1971 (hereinafter referred to as "the Convention"), and, as between the Parties to this Protocol, the Convention and the Protocol shall be read and interpreted together as one single instrument.

Article II

1. In Article 1 of the Convention, the following shall be added as new paragraph 1 *bis*:

"1 *bis*. Any person commits an offense if he unlawfully and intentionally using any device, substance or weapon:

(a) performs an act of violence against a person at an airport serving international civil aviation which causes or is likely to cause serious injury or death; or

(b) destroys or seriously damages the facilities of an airport serving international civil aviation or aircraft not in service located thereon or disrupts the services of the airport, if such an act endangers or is likely to endanger safety at that airport."

Article III

In Article 5 of the Convention, the following shall be added as paragraph 2 *bis*:

"2 *bis*. Each Contracting State shall likewise take such measures as may be necessary to establish its jurisdiction over the offenses mentioned in Article 1, paragraph 1 *bis*, and in Article 1, paragraph 2, in so far as that paragraph relates to these offenses, in the case where the alleged offender is present in its territory and it does not extradite him pursuant to Article 8 to the State mentioned in paragraph 1 (a) of this article."

Document 61
HAGUE CONVENTION ON THE SUPPRESSION OF UNLAWFUL SEIZURE OF AIRCRAFT (HIJACKING)

860 U.N.T.S. 105, 22 U.S.T. 1641, T.I.A.S. 7192 (1970)

Article 1

Any person who on board an aircraft in flight:

(a) unlawfully, by force or threat thereof, or by any other form of intimidation, seizes, or exercises control of, that aircraft, or attempts to perform any such act, or

(b) is an accomplice of a person who performs or attempts to perform any such act commits an offence (hereinafter referred to as "the offence")....

Article 3

1. For purposes of this Convention, an aircraft is considered to be in flight at any time from the moment when all its external doors are closed....

Article 4

1. Each Contracting State shall take such measures as may be necessary to establish its jurisdiction over the offence and any other act of violence against passengers of crew committed by the alleged offender in connection with the offence, in the following cases:

(a) when the offence is committed on board an aircraft registered in that State;

(b) when the aircraft on board which the offence is committed lands in its territory with the alleged offender still on board;

(c) when the offence is committed on board an aircraft leased without crew to a lessee who has his principal place of business or, if the lessee has no such place of business, his permanent residence, in that State.

2. Each Contracting State shall likewise take such measures as may be necessary to establish its jurisdiction over the offence in the case where the alleged offender is present in its territory and it does not extradite him pursuant to Article 8 to any of the States mentioned in paragraph 1 of this article.

3. This Convention does not exclude any criminal jurisdiction exercised in accordance with national law. ...

Document 62
CONVENTION ON THE PREVENTION AND PUNISHMENT OF CRIMES AGAINST INTERNATIONALLY PROTECTED PERSONS, INCLUDING DIPLOMATIC AGENTS

1035 U.N.T.S. 167, 28 U.S.T. 1975, T.I.A.S. No. 8532 (1973)

Article 1

For the purposes of this Convention:

1. "internationally protected person" means:

(a) a Head of State, including any member of a collegial body performing the functions of a Head of State under the constitution of the State concerned, a Head of Government or a Minister for Foreign Affairs, whenever any such person is in a foreign State, as well as members of his family who accompany him;

(b) any representative or official of a State or any official or other agent of an international organization of an intergovernmental character who, at the time when and in the place where a crime against him, his official premises, his private accommodation or his means of transport is committed, is entitled pursuant to international law to special protection from any attack on is person, freedom or dignity, as well as members of his family forming part of his household;

2. "alleged offender" means a person as to whom there is sufficient evidence to determine *prima facie* that he has committed or participated in one or more of the crimes set forth in Article 2.

Article 2

1. The intentional commission of:

(a) a murder, kidnapping or other attack upon the person or liberty of an internationally protected person;

(b) a violent attack upon the official premises, the private accommodation or the means of transport of an internationally protected person likely to endanger his person or liberty;

(c) a threat to commit any such attack;

(d) an attempt to commit any such attack; and

(e) an act constituting participation as an accomplice in any such attack shall be made by each State Party a crime under its internal law.

2. Each State Party shall make these crimes punishable by appropriate penalties which take into account their grave nature.

3. Paragraphs 1 and 2 of this article in no way derogate from the obligations of States Parties under international law to take all appropriate measure to prevent other attacks on the person, freedom or dignity of an internationally protect person.

Article 3

1. Each State Party shall take such measures as may be necessary to establish its jurisdiction over the crimes set forth in Article 2 in the following cases:

(a) when the crime is committed in the territory of that State or on board a ship or aircraft registered in that State;

(b) when the alleged offender is a national of that State;

(c) when the crime is committed against an internationally protected person as defined in Article 1 who enjoys his status as such by virtue of functions which he exercises on behalf of that State.

2. Each State Party shall likewise take such measures as may be necessary to establish its jurisdiction over these crimes in cases where the alleged offender is present in its territory and it does not extradite him pursuant to Article 8 to any of the States mentioned in paragraph 1 of this article.

3. This convention does not exclude any criminal jurisdiction exercised in accordance with internal law. . . .

Document 63
VIENNA CONVENTION ON DIPLOMATIC RELATIONS

500 U.N.T.S. 95, 23 U.S.T. 3227, T.I.A.S. No. 7502 (1961)

The States Parties to the present Convention,

Recalling that people of all nations from ancient times have recognized the status of diplomatic agents,

Having in mind the purposes and principles of the Charter of the United Nations concerning the sovereign equality of States, the maintenance of international peace and security, and the promotion of friendly relations among nations,

Believing that an international convention on diplomatic intercourse, privileges and immunities would contribute to the development of friendly relations among nations, irrespective of their differing constitutional and social systems,

Realizing that the purpose of such privileges and immunities is not to benefit individuals but to ensure the efficient performance of the functions of diplomatic missions as representing States,

Affirming that the rules of customary international law should continue to govern questions not expressly regulated by the provisions of the present Convention,

Have agreed as follows:

Article 1

For the purpose of the present Convention, the following expressions shall have the meanings hereunder assigned to them:

(a) the "head of the mission" is the person charged by the sending State with the duty of acting in that capacity;

(b) the "members of the mission" are the head of the mission and the members of the staff of the mission;

(c) the "members of the staff of the mission" are the members of the diplomatic staff, of the administrative and technical staff and of the service staff of the mission;

(d) the "members of the diplomatic staff" are the members of the staff of the mission having diplomatic rank;

(e) a "diplomatic agent" is the head of the mission or a member of the diplomatic staff of the mission;

(f) the "members of the administrative and technical staff" are the members of the staff of the mission employed in the administrative and technical service of the mission;

(g) the "members of the service staff" are the members of the staff of the mission in the domestic service of the mission;

(h) a "private servant" is a person who is in the domestic service of a member of the mission and who is not an employee of the sending State;

(i) the "premises of the mission" are the buildings or parts of buildings and the land ancillary thereto, irrespective of ownership, used for the purposes of the mission including the residence of the head of the mission.

Article 2

The establishment of diplomatic relations between States, and of permanent diplomatic missions, takes place by mutual consent.

Article 3

1. The functions of a diplomatic mission consist *inter alia* in:

(a) representing the sending State in the receiving State;

(b) protecting in the receiving State the interests of the sending State and of its nationals, within the limits permitted by international law;

(c) negotiating with the Government of the receiving State;

(d) ascertaining by all lawful means conditions and developments in the receiving State, and reporting thereon to the Government of the sending State;

(e) promoting friendly relations between the sending State and the receiving State, and developing their economic, cultural and scientific relations.

2. Nothing in the present Convention shall be construed as preventing the performance of consular functions by a diplomatic mission.

Article 4

1. The sending State must make certain that the *agrément* of the receiving State has been given for the person it proposes to accredit as head of the mission to that State.

2. The receiving State is not obliged to give reasons to the sending State for a refusal of *agrément*.

Article 5

1. The sending State may, after it has given due notification to the receiving States concerned, accredit a head of mission or assign any member of the diplomatic staff, as the case may be, to more than one State, unless there is express objection by any of the receiving States.

2. If the sending State accredits a head of mission to one or more other States it may establish a diplomatic mission headed by a *chargé d'affaires ad interim* in each State where the head of mission has not his permanent seat.

3. A head of mission or any member of the diplomatic staff of the mission may act as representative of the sending State to any international organization.

Article 6

Two or more States may accredit the same person as head of mission to another State, unless objection is offered by the receiving State.

Article 7

Subject to the provisions of Articles 5, 8, 9 and 11, the sending State may freely appoint the members of the staff of the mission. In the case of military, naval or air *attachés*, the receiving State may require their names to be submitted beforehand, for its approval.

Article 8

1. Members of the diplomatic staff of the mission should in principle be of the nationality of the sending State.

2. Members of the diplomatic staff of the mission may not he appointed from among persons having the nationality of the receiving State, except with the consent of that State which may be withdrawn at any time.

3. The receiving State may reserve the same right with regard to nationals of a third State who are not also nationals of the sending State.

Article 9

1. The receiving State may at any time and without having to explain its decision, notify the sending State that the head of the mission or any member of the diplomatic staff of the mission is *persona non grata* or that any other member of the staff of the mission is not acceptable. In any such case, the sending State shall, as appropriate, either recall the person concerned or terminate his functions with the mission. A person may be declared *non grata* or not acceptable before arriving in the territory of the receiving State.

2. If the sending State refuses or fails within a reasonable period to carry out its obligations under paragraph 1 of this article, the receiving State may refuse to recognize the person concerned as a member of the mission.

Article 10

1. The Ministry for Foreign Affairs of the receiving State, or such other ministry as may be agreed, shall be notified of:

(a) the appointment of members of the mission, their arrival and their final departure or the termination of their functions with the mission;

(b) the arrival and final departure of a person belonging to the family of a member of the mission and, where appropriate, the fact that a person becomes or ceases to be a member of the family of a member of the mission;

(c) the arrival and final departure of private servants in the employ of persons referred to in sub-paragraph (a) of this paragraph and, where appropriate, the fact that they are leaving the employ of such persons;

(d) the engagement and discharge of persons resident in the receiving State as members of the mission or private servants entitled to privileges and immunities.

2. Where possible, prior notification of arrival and final departure shall also be given.

Article 11

1. In the absence of specific agreement as to the size of the mission, the receiving State may require that the size of a mission be kept within limits considered by it to be reasonable and normal, having regard to circumstances and conditions in the receiving State and to the needs of the particular mission.

2. The receiving State may equally, within similar bounds and on a nondiscriminatory basis, refuse to accept officials of a particular category.

Article 12

The sending State may not, without the prior express consent of the receiving State, establish offices forming part of the mission in localities other than those in which the mission itself is established.

Article 13

1. The head of the mission is considered as having taken up his functions in the receiving State either when he has presented his credentials or when he has notified his arrival and a true copy of his credentials has been presented to the Ministry for Foreign Affairs of the receiving State, or such other ministry as may be agreed, in accordance with the practice prevailing in the receiving State which shall be applied in a uniform manner.

2. The order of presentation of credentials or of a true copy thereof will be determined by the date and time of the arrival of the head of the mission.

Article 14

1. Heads of mission are divided into three classes, namely:

(a) that of ambassadors or nuncios accredited to Heads of State, and other heads of mission of equal rank;

(b) that of envoys, ministers and internuncios accredited to Heads of State;

(c) that of *chargés d'affaires* accredited to Ministers of Foreign Affairs.

2. Except as concerns precedence and etiquette, there shall be no differentiation between heads of mission by reason of their class.

Article 15

The class to which the heads of their missions are to be assigned shall be agreed between States.

Article 16

1. Heads of mission shall take precedence in their respective classes in the order of the date and time of taking up their functions in accordance with Article 13.

2. Alterations in the credentials of a head of mission not involving any change of class shall not affect his precedence.

3. This article is without prejudice to any practice accepted by the receiving State regarding the precedence of the representative of the Holy See.

Article 17

The precedence of the members of the diplomatic staff of the mission shall be notified by the head of the mission to the Ministry for Foreign Affairs or such other ministry as may be agreed.

Article 18

The procedure to be observed in each State for the reception of heads of mission shall be uniform in respect of each class.

Article 19

1. If the post of head of the mission is vacant, or if the head of the mission is unable to perform his functions, a *chargé d'affaires ad interim* shall act provisionally as head of the mission. The name of the *chargé d'affaires ad interim* shall be notified, either by the head of the mission or, in case he is unable to do so, by the Ministry for Foreign Affairs of the sending State to the Ministry for Foreign Affairs of the receiving State or such other ministry as may be agreed.

2. In cases where no member of the diplomatic staff of the mission is present in the receiving State, a member of the administrative and technical staff may, with the consent of the receiving State, be designated by the sending State to be in charge of the current administrative affairs of the mission.

Article 20

The mission and its head shall have the right to use the flag and emblem of the sending State on the premises of the mission, including the residence of the head of the mission, and on his means of transport.

Article 21

1. The receiving State shall either facilitate the acquisition on its territory, in accordance with its laws, by the sending State of premises necessary for its mission or assist the latter in obtaining accommodation in some other way.

2. It shall also, where necessary, assist missions in obtaining suitable accommodation for their members.

Article 22

1. The premises of the mission shall be inviolable. The agents of the receiving State may not enter them, except with the consent of the head of the mission.

2. The receiving State is under a special duty to take all appropriate steps to protect the premises of the mission against any intrusion or damage and to prevent any disturbance of the peace of the mission or impairment of its dignity.

3. The premises of the mission, their furnishings and other property thereon and the means of transport of the mission shall be immune from search, requisition, attachment or execution.

Article 23

1. The sending State and the head of the mission shall be exempt from all national, regional or municipal dues and taxes in respect of the premises of the mission, whether owned or leased, other than such as represent payment for specific services rendered.

2. The exemption from taxation referred to in this article shall not apply to such dues and taxes payable under the law of the receiving State by persons contracting with the sending State or the head of the mission.

Article 24

The archives and documents of the mission shall be inviolable at any time and wherever they may be.

Article 25

The receiving State shall accord full facilities for the performance of the functions of the mission.

Article 26

Subject to its laws and regulations concerning zones entry into which is prohibited or regulated for reasons of national security, the receiving State shall ensure to all members of the mission freedom of movement and travel in its territory.

Article 27

1. The receiving State shall permit and protect free communication on the part of the mission for all official purposes. In communicating with the Government and the other missions and consulates of the

sending State, wherever situated, the mission may employ all appropriate means, including diplomatic couriers and messages in code or cipher. However, the mission may install and use a wireless transmitter only with the consent of the receiving State.

2. The official correspondence of the mission shall be inviolable. Official correspondence means all correspondence relating to the mission and its functions.

3. The diplomatic bag shall not be opened or detained.

4. The packages constituting the diplomatic bag must bear visible external marks of their character and may contain only diplomatic documents or articles intended for official use.

5. The diplomatic courier, who shall be provided with an official document indicating his status and the number of packages constituting the diplomatic bag, shall be protected by the receiving State in the performance of his functions. He shall enjoy personal inviolability and shall not be liable to any form of arrest or detention.

6. The sending State or the mission may designate diplomatic couriers ad hoc. In such cases the provisions of paragraph 5 of this Article shall also apply, except that the immunities therein mentioned shall cease to apply when such a courier has delivered to the consignee the diplomatic bag in his charge.

7. A diplomatic bag may be entrusted to the captain of a commercial aircraft scheduled to land at an authorized port of entry. He shall be provided with an official document indicating the number of packages constituting the bag but he shall not be considered to be a diplomatic courier. The mission may send one of its members to take possession of the diplomatic bag directly and freely from the captain of the aircraft.

Article 28

The fees and charges levied by the mission in the course of its official duties shall be exempt from all dues and taxes.

Article 29

The person of a diplomatic agent shall be inviolable. He shall not be liable to any form of arrest or detention. The receiving State shall treat him with due respect and shall take all appropriate steps to prevent any attack on his person, freedom or dignity.

Article 30

1. The private residence of a diplomatic agent shall enjoy the same inviolability and protection as the premises of the mission.

2. His papers, correspondence and, except as provided in paragraph 3 of Article 31, his property, shall likewise enjoy inviolability.

Article 31

1. A diplomatic agent shall enjoy immunity from the criminal jurisdiction of the receiving State. He shall also enjoy immunity from its civil and administrative jurisdiction, except in the case of:

(a) a real action relating to private immovable property situated in the territory of the receiving State, unless he holds it on behalf of the sending State for the purposes of the mission;

(b) an action relating to succession in which the diplomatic agent is involved as executor, administrator, heir or legatee as a private person and not on behalf of the sending State;

(c) an action relating to any professional or commercial activity exercised by the diplomatic agent in the receiving State outside his official functions.

2. A diplomatic agent is not obliged to give evidence as a witness.

3. No measures of execution may be taken in respect of a diplomatic agent except in the cases coming under sub-paragraphs (a), (b) and (c) of paragraph 1 of this article, and provided that the measures concerned can be taken without infringing the inviolability of his person or of his residence.

4. The immunity of a diplomatic agent from the jurisdiction of the receiving State does not exempt him from the jurisdiction of the sending State.

Article 32

1. The immunity from jurisdiction of diplomatic agents and of persons enjoying immunity under Article 37 may be waived by the sending State.

2. Waiver must always be express.

3. The initiation of proceedings by a diplomatic agent or by a person enjoying immunity from jurisdiction under Article 37 shall preclude him from invoking immunity from jurisdiction in respect of any counter-claim directly connected with the principal claim.

4. Waiver of immunity from jurisdiction in respect of civil or administrative proceedings shall not be held to imply waiver of immunity in respect of the execution of the judgment, for which a separate waiver shall be necessary.

Article 33

1. Subject to the provisions of paragraph 3 of this article, a diplomatic agent shall with respect to services rendered for the sending State be exempt from social security provisions which may be in force in the receiving State.

2. The exemption provided for in paragraph 1 of this article shall also apply to private servants who are in the sole employ of a diplomatic agent, on condition:

(a) that they are not nationals of or permanently resident in the receiving State; and

(b) that they are covered by the social security provisions which may be in force in the sending State or a third State.

3. A diplomatic agent who employs persons to whom the exemption provided for in paragraph 2 of this article does not apply shall observe the obligations which the social security provisions of the receiving State impose upon employers.

4. The exemption provided for in paragraphs 1 and 2 of this article shall not preclude voluntary participation in the social security system of the receiving State provided that such participation is permitted by that State.

5. The provisions of this article shall not affect bilateral or multilateral agreements concerning social security concluded previously and shall not prevent the conclusion of such agreements in the future.

Article 34

A diplomatic agent shall be exempt from all dues and taxes, personal or real, national, regional or municipal, except:

(a) indirect taxes of a kind which are normally incorporated in the price of goods or services;

(b) dues and taxes on private immovable property situated in the territory of the receiving State, unless he holds it on behalf of the sending State for the purposes of the mission;

(c) estate, succession or inheritance duties levied by the receiving State, subject to the provisions of paragraph 4 of Article 39;

(d) dues and taxes on private income having its source in the receiving State and capital taxes on investments made in commercial undertakings in the receiving State;

(e) charges levied for specific services rendered;

(f) registration, court or record fees, mortgage dues and stamp duty, with respect to immovable property, subject to the provisions of Article 23.

Article 35

The receiving State shall exempt diplomatic agents from all personal services, from all public service of any kind whatsoever, and from military obligations such as those connected with requisitioning, military contributions and billeting.

Article 36

1. The receiving State shall, in accordance with such laws and regulations as it may adopt, permit entry of and grant exemption from all customs duties, taxes, and related charges other than charges for storage, cartage and similar services, on:

(a) articles for the official use of the mission;

(b) articles for the personal use of a diplomatic agent or members of his family forming part of his household, including articles intended for his establishment.

2. The personal baggage of a diplomatic agent shall be exempt from inspection, unless there are serious grounds for presuming that it contains articles not covered by the exemptions mentioned in paragraph 1 of this article, or articles the import or export of which is prohibited by the law or controlled by the quarantine regulations of the receiving State. Such inspection shall be conducted only in the presence of the diplomatic agent or of his authorized representative.

Article 37

1. The members of the family of a diplomatic agent forming part of his household shall, if they are not nationals of the receiving State, enjoy the privileges and immunities specified in Articles 29 to 36.

2. Members of the administrative and technical staff of the mission, together with members of their families forming part of their respective households, shall, if they are not nationals of or permanently resident in the receiving State, enjoy the privileges and immunities specified in Articles 29 to 35, except that the immunity from civil and administrative jurisdiction of the receiving State specified in paragraph 1 of Article 31 shall not extend to acts performed outside the course of their duties. They shall also enjoy the privileges specified in Article 36, paragraph 1, in respect of articles imported at the time of first installation.

3. Members of the service staff of the mission who are not nationals of or permanently resident in the receiving State shall enjoy immunity in respect of acts performed in the course of their duties, exemption from dues and taxes on the emoluments they receive by reason of their employment and the exemption contained in Article 33.

4. Private servants of members of the mission shall, if they are not nationals of or permanently resident in the receiving State, be exempt from dues and taxes on the emoluments they receive by reason of their employment. In other respects, they may enjoy privileges and immunities only to the extent admitted by the receiving State. However, the receiving State must exercise its jurisdiction over those persons in such a manner as not to interfere unduly with the performance of the functions of the mission.

Article 38

1. Except insofar as additional privileges and immunities may be granted by the receiving State, a diplomatic agent who is a national of or permanently resident in that State shall enjoy only immunity from jurisdiction, and inviolability, in respect of official acts performed in the exercise of his functions.

2. Other members of the staff of the mission and private servants who are nationals of or permanently resident in the receiving State shall enjoy privileges and immunities only to the extent admitted by the receiving State. However, the receiving State must exercise its jurisdiction over those persons in such a manner as not to interfere unduly with the performance of the functions of the mission.

Article 39

1. Every person entitled to privileges and immunities shall enjoy them from the moment he enters the territory of the receiving State on proceeding to take up his post or, if already in its territory, from the moment when his appointment is notified to the Ministry for Foreign Affairs or such other ministry as may be agreed.

2. When the functions of a person enjoying privileges and immunities have come to an end, such privileges and immunities shall normally cease at the moment when he leaves the country, or on expiry of a reasonable period in which to do so, but shall subsist until that time, even in case of armed conflict. However, with respect to acts performed by such a person in the exercise of his functions as a member of the mission, immunity shall continue to subsist.

3. In case of the death of a member of the mission, the members of his family shall continue to enjoy the privileges and immunities to which they are entitled until the expiry of a reasonable period in which to leave the country.

4. In the event of the death of a member of the mission not a national of or permanently resident in the receiving State or a member of his family forming part of his household, the receiving State shall permit the withdrawal of the movable property of the deceased, with the exception of any property acquired in the country the export of which was prohibited at the time of his death. Estate, succession and inheritance duties shall not be levied on movable property the presence of which in the receiving State was due solely to the presence there of the deceased as a member of the mission or as a member of the family of a member of the mission.

Article 40

1. If a diplomatic agent passes through or is in the territory of a third State, which has granted him a passport visa if such visa was necessary, while proceeding to take up or to return to his post, or when returning to his own country, the third State shall accord him inviolability and such other immunities as may be required to ensure his transit or return. The same shall apply in the case of any members of his family enjoying privileges or immunities who are accompanying the diplomatic agent, or traveling separately to join him or to return to their country.

2. In circumstances similar to those specified in paragraph 1 of this article, third States shall not hinder the passage of members of the administrative and technical or service staff of a mission, and of members of their families, through their territories.

3. Third States shall accord to official correspondence and other official communications in transit, including messages in code or cipher, the same freedom and protection as is accorded by the receiving State. They shall accord to diplomatic couriers, who have been granted a passport visa if such visa was necessary, and diplomatic bags in transit the same inviolability and protection as the receiving State is bound to accord.

4. The obligations of third States under paragraphs 1, 2 and 3 of this article shall also apply to the persons mentioned respectively in those paragraphs, and to official communications and diplomatic bags, whose presence in the territory of the third State is due to *force majeure*.

Article 41

1. Without prejudice to their privileges and immunities, it is the duty of all persons enjoying such privileges and immunities to respect the laws and regulations of the receiving State. They also have a duty not to interfere in the internal affairs of that State.

2. All official business with the receiving State entrusted to the mission by the sending shall be conducted with or through the Ministry for Foreign Affairs of the receiving or such other ministry as may be agreed.

3. The premises of the mission must not be used in any manner incompatible with the functions of the mission as laid down in the present Convention or by other rules of general international law or by any special agreements in force between the sending and the receiving State.

Article 42

A diplomatic agent shall not in the receiving State practice for personal profit any professional or commercial activity.

Article 43

The function of a diplomatic agent comes to an end, *inter alia*:

(a) on notification by the sending State to the receiving State that the function of the diplomatic agent has come to an end;

(b) on notification by the receiving State to the sending State that, in accordance with paragraph 2 of Article 9, it refuses to recognize the diplomatic agent as a member of the mission.

Article 44

The receiving State must, even in case of armed conflict, grant facilities in order to enable persons enjoying privileges and immunities, other than nationals of the receiving State, and members of the families of such persons irrespective of their nationality, to leave at the earliest possible moment. It must, in particular, in case of need, place at their disposal the necessary means of transport for themselves and their property.

Article 45

If diplomatic relations are broken off between two States, or if a mission is permanently or temporarily recalled:

(a) the receiving State must, even in case of armed conflict, respect and protect the premises of the mission, together with its property and archives;

(b) the sending State may entrust the custody of the premises of the mission, together with its property and archives, to a third State acceptable to the receiving State;

(c) the sending State may entrust the protection of its interests and those of its nationals to a third State acceptable to the receiving State.

Article 46

A sending State may with the prior consent of a receiving State, and at the request of a third State not represented in the receiving State, undertake the temporary protection of the interests of the third State and of its nationals.

Article 47

1. In the application of the provisions of the present Convention, the receiving State shall not discriminate as between States.

2. However, discrimination shall not be regarded as taking place:

(a) where the receiving State applies any of the provisions of the present Convention restrictively because of a restrictive application of that provision to its mission in the sending State;

(b) where by custom or agreement States extend to each other more favourable treatment than is required by the provisions of the present Convention.

Article 48

The present Convention shall be open for signature by all States Members of the United Nations or of any of the specialized agencies or Parties to the Statute of the International Court of Justice, and by any other State invited by the General Assembly of the United Nations to become a Party to the Convention, as follows: until 31 October 1961 at the Federal Ministry for Foreign Affairs of Austria and subsequently, until 31 March 1962, at the United Nations Headquarters in New York.

Article 49

The present Convention is subject to ratification. The instruments of ratification shall be deposited with the Secretary–General of the United Nations.

Article 50

The present Convention shall remain open for accession by any State belonging to any of the four categories mentioned in Article 48. The instruments of accession shall be deposited with the Secretary–General of the United Nations.

Article 51

1. The present Convention shall enter into force on the thirtieth day following the date of deposit of the twenty-second instrument of ratification or accession with the Secretary–General of the United Nations.

2. For each State ratifying or acceding to the Convention after the deposit of the twenty-second instrument of ratification or accession, the Convention shall enter into force on the thirtieth day after deposit by such State of its instrument of ratification or accession.

Article 52

The Secretary–General of the United Nations shall inform all States belonging to any of the four categories mentioned in Article 48:

(a) of signatures to the present Convention and of the deposit of instruments of ratification or accession, in accordance with Articles 48, 49 and 50;

(b) of the date on which the present Convention will enter into force, in accordance with Article 51.

Article 53

The original of the present Convention, of which the Chinese, English, French, Russian and Spanish texts are equally authentic, shall be deposited with the Secretary General of the United Nations, who shall send certified copies thereof to all States belonging to any of the four categories mentioned in Article 48.

Document 64
VIENNA CONVENTION ON CONSULAR RELATIONS

596 U.N.T.S. 261 (1963) (extracts)

Article 5

Consular Functions

Consular functions consist in:

(a) protecting in the receiving State the interests of the sending State and of its nationals, both individuals and bodies corporate, within the limits permitted by international law;

(b) furthering the development of commercial, economic, cultural and scientific relations between the sending State and the receiving State and otherwise promoting friendly relations between them in accordance with the provisions of the present Convention;

(c) assisting by all lawful means conditions and developments in the commercial, economic, cultural and scientific life of the receiving State, reporting thereon to the Government of the sending State and giving information to persons interested;

(d) issuing passports and travel documents to nationals of the sending State, and visas or appropriate documents to persons wishing to travel to the sending State;

(e) helping and assisting nationals, both individuals and bodies corporate, of the sending State; . . .

(h) safeguarding, within the limits imposed by the laws and regulations of the receiving State, the interests of minors and other persons lacking full capacity who are nationals of the sending State, particularly where any guardianship or trusteeship is required with respect to such persons;

(i) subject to the practices and procedures obtaining in the receiving State, representing or arranging appropriate representation for nationals of the sending State before the tribunals and other authorities of the receiving State, for the purpose of obtaining, in accordance with the laws and regulations of the receiving State, provisional measures for the preservation of the rights and interests of these nationals, where, because of absence or any other reason, such nationals are unable at the proper time to assume the defense of their rights and interests;

(j) transmitting judicial and extra-judicial documents or executing letters rogatory or commissions to take evidence for the courts of the sending State in accordance with international agreements in force or, in the absence of such international agreements, in any other manner compatible with the laws and regulations of the receiving State;

(k) exercising rights of supervision and inspection provided for in the laws and regulations of the sending State in respect of vessels having the nationality of the sending State, and of aircraft registered in that State, and in respect of their crews;

(*l*) extending assistance to vessels and aircraft mentioned in sub-paragraph (k) of this article and to their crews, taking statements regarding the voyage of a vessel, examining and stamping the ship's papers, and, without prejudice to the powers of the authorities of the receiving State, conducting investigations into any incidents which occurred during the voyage, and settling disputes of any kind between the master, the officers and the seamen in so far as this may be authorized by the laws and regulations of the sending State;

(m) performing any other functions entrusted to a consular post by the sending State which are not prohibited by the laws and regulations of the receiving State or to which no objection is taken by the receiving State or which are referred to in the international agreements in force between the sending State and the receiving State.

Article 6

Exercise of Consular Functions Outside the Consular District

A consular officer may, in special circumstances, with the consent of the receiving State, exercise his functions outside his consular district.

Article 31

Inviolability of the Consular Premises

1. Consular premises shall be inviolable to the extent provided by this article.

2. The authorities of the receiving State shall not enter that part of the consular premises which is used exclusively for the purpose of the work of the consular post except with the consent of the head of the consular post or of his designee or of the head of the diplomatic mission of the sending State. The consent of the head of the consular post may, however, be assumed in case of fire or other disaster requiring prompt protective action.

3. Subject to the provisions of paragraph 2 of this article, the receiving State is under a special duty to take all appropriate steps to protect the consular premises against any intrusion or damage and to prevent any disturbance of the peace of the consular post or impairment of its dignity.

4. The consular premises, their furnishings, the property of the consular post and its means of transport shall be immune from any form of requisition for purposes of national defence or public utility. If expropriation is necessary for such purposes, all possible steps shall be taken to avoid impeding the performance of consular functions, and prompt, adequate and effective compensation shall be paid to the sending State.

Article 32

Exemption from Taxation of Consular Premises

1. Consular premises and the residence of the career head of the consular post of which the sending State or any person acting on its behalf is the owner or lessee shall be exempt from all national, regional or municipal dues and taxes whatsoever, other than such as represent payment for specific services rendered.

2. The exemption from taxation referred to in paragraph 1 of this article shall not apply to such dues and taxes if, under the law of the receiving State, they are payable to the person who contracted with the sending State or with the person acting on its behalf.

Article 33

Inviolability of the Consular Archives and Documents

The consular archives and documents shall be inviolable at all times and wherever they may be.

Article 36

Communication and Contact with Nationals of the Sending State

1. With a view to facilitating the exercise of consular functions relating to nationals of the sending State:

(a) consular officers shall be free to communicate with nationals of the sending State and to have access to them. Nationals of the sending State shall have the same freedom with respect to communication with and access to consular officers of the sending State;

(b) if he so requests, the competent authorities of the receiving State shall, without delay, inform the consular post of the sending State if, within its consular district, a national of that State is arrested or committed to prison or to custody pending trial or is detained in any other manner. Any communication addressed to the consular post by the person arrested, in prison, custody or detention shall also be forwarded by the said authorities without delay. The said authorities shall inform the person concerned without delay of his rights under this subparagraph;

(c) consular officers shall have the right to visit a national of the sending State who is in prison, custody or detention, to converse and correspond with him and to arrange for his legal representation. They shall also have the right to visit any national of the sending State who is in prison, custody or detention in their district in pursuance of a judgment. Nevertheless, consular officers shall refrain from taking action on behalf of a national who is in prison, custody or detention if he expressly opposes such action.

2. The rights referred to in paragraph 1 of this article shall be exercised in conformity with the laws and regulations of the receiving State, subject to the proviso, however, that the said laws and regulations must enable full effect to be given to the purposes for which the rights accorded under this article are intended.

Article 40

Protection of Consular Officers

The receiving State shall treat consular officers with due respect and shall take all appropriate steps to prevent any attack on their person, freedom or dignity.

Article 41

Personal Inviolability of Consular Officers

1. Consular officers shall not be liable to arrest or detention pending trial, except in the case of a grave crime and pursuant to a decision by the competent judicial authority.

2. Except in the case specified in paragraph 1 of this article, consular officers shall not be committed to prison or liable to any other form of restriction on their personal freedom save in execution of a judicial decision of final effect.

3. If criminal proceedings are instituted against a consular officer, he must appear before the competent authorities. Nevertheless, the proceedings shall be conducted with the respect due to him by reason of his official position and, except in the case specified in paragraph 1 of this article, in a manner which will hamper the exercise of consular functions as little as possible. When, in the circumstances mentioned in paragraph 1 of this article, it has become necessary to detain a consular officer, the proceedings against him shall be instituted with the minimum of delay.

Article 42

Notification of Arrest, Detention or Prosecution

In the event of the arrest or detention, pending trial, of a member of the consular staff, or of criminal proceedings being instituted against him, the receiving State shall promptly notify the head of the consular post. Should the latter be himself the object of any such measure, the receiving State shall notify the sending State through the diplomatic channel.

Article 43

Immunity from Jurisdiction

1. Consular officers and consular employees shall not be amenable to the jurisdiction of the judicial or administrative authorities of the receiving State in respect of acts performed in the exercise of consular functions.

2. The provisions of paragraph 1 of this article shall not, however, apply in respect of a civil action either:

(a) arising out of a contract concluded by a consular officer or a consular employee in which he did not contract expressly or impliedly as an agent of the sending State; or

(b) by a third party for damage arising from an accident in the receiving State caused by a vehicle, vessel or aircraft.

Article 44

Liability to Give Evidence

1. Members of a consular post may be called upon to attend as witnesses in the course of judicial or administrative proceedings. A consular employee or a member of the service staff shall not, except in cases mentioned in paragraph 3 of this article, decline to give evidence. If a consular officer should decline to do so, no coercive measure or penalty may be applied to him.

2. The authority requiring the evidence of a consular officer shall avoid interference with the performance of his functions. It may, when possible, take such evidence at his residence or at the consular post or accept a statement from him in writing.

3. Members of a consular post are under no obligation to give evidence concerning matters connected with the exercise of their functions or to produce official correspondence and documents relating thereto. They are also entitled to decline to give evidence as expert witnesses with regard to the law of the sending State.

Article 45

Waiver of Privileges and Immunities

1. The sending State may waive, with regard to a member of the consular post, any of the privileges and immunities provided for in articles 41, 43 and 44.

2. The waiver shall in all cases be express, except as provided for in paragraph 3 of this article, and shall be communicated to the receiving State in writing.

3. The initiation of proceedings by a consular officer or a consular employee in a matter where he might enjoy immunity from jurisdiction under Article 43 shall preclude him from invoking immunity from jurisdiction in respect of any counter-claim directly connected with the principal claim.

4. The waiver of immunity from jurisdiction for the purposes of civil or administrative proceedings shall not be deemed to imply waiver of immunity from the measures of execution resulting from the judicial decision; in respect of such measures, a separate waiver shall be necessary....

Article 49

Exemption from Taxation

1. Consular officers and consular employees and members of their families forming part of their households shall be exempt from all dues and taxes, personal or real, national, regional or municipal, except:

(a) indirect taxes of a kind which are normally incorporated in the price of goods or services;

(b) dues or taxes on private immovable property situated in the territory of the receiving State, subject to the provisions of Article 32;

(c) estate, succession or inheritance duties, and duties on transfers, levied by the receiving State, subject to the provisions of paragraph (b) of Article 51;

(d) dues and taxes on private income, including capital gains, having its source in the receiving State and capital taxes relating to investments made in commercial or financial undertakings in the receiving State;

(e) charges levied for specific services rendered;

(f) registration, court or record fees, mortgage dues and stamp duties, subject to the provisions of Article 32.

2. Members of the service staff shall be exempt from dues and taxes on the wages which they receive for their services. . . .

Article 55

Respect for the Laws and Regulations of the Receiving State

1. Without prejudice to their privileges and immunities, it is the duty of all persons enjoying such privileges and immunities to respect the laws and regulations of the receiving State. They also have a duty not to interfere in the internal affairs of that State.

2. The consular premises shall not be used in any manner incompatible with the exercise of consular functions.

3. The provisions of paragraph 2 of this article shall not exclude the possibility of offices or other institutions or agencies being installed in part of the building in which the consular premises are situated, provided that the premises assigned to them are separate from those used by the consular post. In that event, the said offices shall not, for the purposes of the present Convention, be considered to form part of the consular premises.

Article 56

Insurance Against Third Party Risks

Members of the consular post shall comply with any requirements imposed by the laws and regulations of the receiving State in respect of insurance against third party risks arising from the use of any vehicle, vessel or aircraft. . . .

Document 65
HAGUE CONVENTION ON THE SERVICE ABROAD OF JUDICIAL AND EXTRAJUDICIAL DOCUMENTS IN CIVIL OR COMMERCIAL MATTERS

658 U.N.T.S. 163, 20 U.S.T. 361 (1965)

The States signatory to the present Convention,

Desiring to create appropriate means to ensure that judicial and extrajudicial documents to be served abroad shall be brought to the notice of the addressee in sufficient time,

Desiring to improve the organization of mutual judicial assistance for that purpose by simplifying and expediting the procedure,

Have resolved to conclude a Convention to this effect and have agreed upon the following provisions:

Article 1

The present Convention shall apply to all cases, in civil or commercial matters, where there is occasion to transmit a judicial or extrajudicial document for service abroad.

This Convention shall not apply where the address of the person to be served with the document is not known.

Chapter I: Judicial Documents

Article 2

Each contracting State shall designate a Central Authority which will undertake to receive requests for service coming from other contracting States and to proceed in conformity with the provisions of Articles 3 to 6.

Each State shall organise the Central Authority in conformity with its own law.

Article 3

The authority or judicial officer competent under the law of the State in which the documents originate shall forward to the Central Authority of the State addressed a request conforming to the model annexed to the present Convention, without any requirement of legislation or other equivalent formality.

The document to be served or a copy thereof shall be annexed to the request. The request and the document shall both be furnished in duplicate.

Article 4

If the Central Authority considers that the request does not comply with the provisions of the present Convention it shall promptly inform the applicant and specify its objections to the request.

Article 5

The Central Authority of the State addressed shall itself serve the document or shall arrange to have it served by an appropriate agency, either–

(a) by a method proscribed by its internal law for the service of documents in domestic actions upon persons who are within its territory, or

(b) by a particular method requested by the applicant, unless such a method is incompatible with the law of the State addressed.

Subject to sub-paragraph (b) of the first paragraph of this article, the document may always be served by delivery to an addressee who accepts it voluntarily.

If the document is to be served under the first paragraph above, the Central Authority may require the document to be written in, or translated into, the official language or one of the official languages of the State addressed.

That part of the request, in the form attached to the present Convention, which contains a summary of the document to be served, shall be served with the document.

Article 6

The Central Authority of the State addressed or any authority which it may have designated for that purpose, shall complete a certificate in the form of the model annexed to the present Convention.

The certificate shall state that the document has been served and shall include the method, the place and the date of service and the person to whom the document was delivered. If the document has not been served, the certificate shall set out the reasons which have prevented service.

The applicant may require that a certificate not completed by a Central Authority or by a judicial authority shall be countersigned by one of these authorities.

The certificate shall be forwarded directly to the applicant.

Article 7

The standard terms in the method annexed to the present Convention shall in all cases be written either in French or in English. They may also be written in the official language, or in one of the official languages, of the State in which the documents originate.

The corresponding blanks shall be completed either in the language of the State addressed or in French or in English.

Article 8

Each contracting State shall be free to effect service of judicial documents upon persons abroad, without application of any compulsion, directly through its diplomatic or consular agents.

Any State may declare that it is opposed to such service within its territory, unless the document is the be served upon a national of the State in which the documents originate.

Article 9

Each contracting State shall be free, in addition, to use consular channels to forward documents, for the purpose of service, to those authorities of another contracting State which are designated by the latter for this purpose.

Each contracting State may, if exceptional circumstances so require, use diplomatic channels for the same purpose.

Article 10

Provided the State of destination does not object, the present Convention shall not interfere with–

(a) the freedom to send judicial documents, by postal channels, directly to persons abroad,

(b) the freedom of judicial officers, officials or other competent persons of the State of origin to effect service of judicial documents directly through the judicial officers, officials or other competent persons of the State of destination,

(c) the freedom of any person interested in a judicial proceeding to effect service of judicial documents directly through the judicial officers, officials or other competent persons of the State of destination.

Article 11

The present Convention shall not prevent two or more contracting States from agreeing to permit, for the purpose of service of judicial documents, channels of transmission other than those provided for in the preceding articles and, in particular, direct communication between their respective authorities.

Article 12

The service of judicial documents coming from a contracting State shall not give rise to any payment or reimbursement of taxes or costs for the services rendered by the State addressed.

The applicant shall pay or reimburse the costs occasioned by–

(a) the employment of a judicial officer or of a person competent under the law of the State of destination,

(b) the use of a particular method of service.

Article 13

Where a request for service complies with the terms of the present Convention, the State addressed may refuse to comply therewith only if it deems that compliance would infringe its sovereignty or security.

It may not refuse to comply solely on the ground that, under its internal law, it claims exclusive jurisdiction over the subject-matter of the action or that its internal law would not permit the action upon which the application is based.

The Central Authority shall, in case of refusal, promptly inform the applicant and state the reasons for the refusal.

Article 14

Difficulties which may arise in connection with the transmission of judicial documents for service shall be settled through diplomatic channels.

Article 15

Where a writ of summons or an equivalent document had to be transmitted abroad for the purpose of service, under the provisions of the present Convention, and the defendant has not appeared, judgment shall not be given until it is established that–

(a) the document was served by a method prescribed by the internal law of the State addressed for the service of documents in a domestic action upon persons who are within its territory, or

(b) the document was actually delivered to the defendant or to his residence by another method provided for by this Convention, and that in either of these cases the service or the delivery was effected in sufficient time to enable the defendant to defend.

Each contracting State shall be free to declare that the judge, notwithstanding the provisions of the first paragraph of this article, may give judgment even if no certificate of service or delivery has been received, if all the following conditions are fulfilled–

(a) the document was transmitted by one of the methods provided for in this Convention,

(b) a period of time of not less than six months, considered adequate by the judge in the particular case, has elapsed since the date of the transmission of the document,

(c) no certificate of any kind has been received, even though every reasonable effort has been made to obtain it through the competent authorities of the State addressed.

Notwithstanding the provisions of the preceding paragraphs the judge may order, in case of urgency, any provisional or protective measures.

Article 16

When a writ of summons or an equivalent document had to be transmitted abroad for the purpose of service, under the provisions of the present Convention, and a judgment has been entered against a defendant who has not appeared, the judge shall have the power to relieve the defendant from the effects of the expiration of the time for appeal from the judgment if the following conditions are fulfilled–

(a) the defendant, without any fault on his part, did not have knowledge of the document in sufficient tie to defend, or knowledge of the judgment in sufficient time to appeal, and

(b) the defendant has disclosed a prima facie defence to the action on the merits.

An application for relief may be filed only within a reasonable time after the defendant has knowledge of the judgment.

Each contracting State may declare that the application will not be entertained if it is filed after the expiration of a time to be stated in the declaration, but which shall in no case be less than one year following the date of the judgment.

This article shall not apply to judgments concerning status or capacity of persons.

Chapter II: Extrajudicial Documents

Article 17

Extrajudicial documents emanating from authorities and judicial officers of a contracting State may be transmitted for the purpose of service in another contracting State by the methods and under the provisions of the present Convention.

Article 18

Each contracting State may designate other authorities in addition to the Central Authority and shall determine the extent of their competence.

The applicant shall, however, in all cases, have the right to address a request directly to the Central Authority.

Federal States shall be free to designate more than one Central Authority.

Article 19

To the extent that the internal law of a contracting State permits methods of transmission, other than those provided for in the preceding article, or documents coming from abroad, for service within its territory, the present Convention shall not affect such provisions. . . .

Document 66
HAGUE CONVENTION ON THE TAKING OF EVIDENCE

847 U.N.T.S. 231, 23 U.S.T. 2555, T.I.A.S. No. 7444 (1970)

The States signatory to the present Convention,

Desiring to facilitate the transmission and execution or Letters of Request and to further the accommodation of the different methods which they use for this purpose,

Desiring to improve mutual judicial co-operation in civil or commercial matters,

Have resolved to conclude a Convention to this effect and have agreed upon the following provisions:

CHAPTER I. LETTERS OF REQUEST

Article 1

In civil or commercial matters a judicial authority of a Contracting State may, in accordance with the provisions of the law of that State, request the competent authority of another Contracting State, by means of a Letter of Request, to obtain evidence, or to perform some other judicial act.

A Letter shall not be used to obtain evidence which is not intended for use in judicial proceedings, commenced or contemplated.

The expression "other judicial act" does not cover the service of judicial documents or the issuance of any process by which judgments or orders are executed or enforced, or orders for provisional or protective measures.

Article 2

A Contracting State shall designate a Central Authority which will undertake to receive Letters of Request coming from a judicial authority of another Contracting State and to transmit them to the authority competent to execute them. Each State shall organize the Central Authority in accordance with its own law.

Letters shall be sent to the Central Authority of the State of execution without being transmitted through any other authority of that State.

Article 3

A Letter of Request shall specify:

(a) the authority requesting its execution and the authority requested to execute it, if known to the requesting authority;

(b) the names and addresses of the parties to the proceedings and their representatives, if any;

(c) the nature of the proceedings for which the evidence is required, giving all necessary information in regard thereto;

(d) the evidence to be obtained or other judicial act to be performed.

Where appropriate, the Letter shall specify, *inter alia*:

(e) the names and addresses of the persons to be examined;

(f) the questions to be put to the persons to be examined or a statement of the subject-matter about which they are to be examined;

(g) the documents or other property, real or personal, to be inspected;

(h) any requirement that the evidence is to be given on oath or affirmation, and any special form to be used;

(i) any special method or procedure to be followed under Article 9.

A Letter may also mention any information necessary for the application of Article 11. No legalization or other like formality may be required.

Article 4

A Letter of Request shall be in the language of the authority requested to execute it or be accompanied by a translation into that language.

Nevertheless, a Contracting State shall accept a Letter in either English or French, or a translation into one of these languages, unless it has made the reservation authorized by Article 33.

A Contracting State which has more than one official language and cannot, for reasons of internal law, accept Letters in one of these languages for the whole of its territory, shall, by declaration, specify the language in which the Letter or translation thereof shall be expressed for execution in the specified parts of its territory. In case of failure to comply with this declaration, without justifiable excuse, the costs of translation into the required language shall be borne by the State of origin.

A Contracting State may, by declaration, specify the language or languages other than those referred to in the preceding paragraphs, in which a Letter may be sent to its Central Authority.

Any translation accompanying a Letter shall be certified as correct, either by a diplomatic officer or consular agent or by a sworn translator or by any other person so authorized in either State.

Article 5

If the Central Authority considers that the request does not comply with the provisions of the present Convention, it shall promptly inform the authority of the State of origin which transmitted the Letter of Request, specifying the objections to the Letter.

Article 6

If the authority to whom a Letter of Request has been transmitted is not competent to execute it, the Letter shall be sent forthwith to the authority in the same State which is competent to execute it in accordance with the provisions of its own law.

Article 7

The requesting authority shall, if it so desires, be informed of the time when, and the place where, the proceedings will take place, in order that the parties concerned, and their representatives, if any, may be present. This information shall be sent directly to the parties or their representatives when the authority of the State of origin so requests.

Article 8

A Contracting State may declare that members of the judicial personnel of the requesting authority of another Contracting State may be present at the execution of a Letter of Request. Prior authorization by the competent authority designated by the declaring State may be required.

Article 9

The judicial authority which executes a Letter of Request shall apply its own law as to the methods and procedures to be followed.

However, it will follow a request of the requesting authority that a special method or procedure be followed, unless this is incompatible with the internal law of the State of execution or is impossible of performance by reason of its internal practice and procedure or by reason of practical difficulties.

A Letter of Request shall be executed expeditiously.

Article 10

In executing a Letter of Request the requested authority shall apply the appropriate measures of compulsion in the instances and to the same extent as are provided by its internal law for the execution of orders issued by the authorities of its own country or of requests made by parties in internal proceedings

Article 11

In the execution of a Letter of Request the person concerned may refuse to give evidence in so far as he has a privilege or duty to refuse to give the evidence:

(a) under the law of the State of execution; or

(b) under the law of the State of origin, and the privilege or duty has been specified in the Letter, or, at the instance of the requested authority, has been otherwise confirmed to that authority by the requesting authority.

A Contracting State may declare that, in addition, it will respect privileges and duties existing under the law of States other than the State of origin and the State of execution, to the extent specified in that declaration.

Article 12

The execution of a Letter of Request may be refused only to the extent that:

(a) in the State of execution the execution of the Letter does not fall within the functions of the judiciary; or

(b) the State addressed considers that its sovereignty or security would be prejudiced thereby.

Execution may not be refused solely on the ground that under its internal law the State of execution claims exclusive jurisdiction over the subject-matter of the action or that its internal law would not admit a right of action on it.

Article 13

The documents establishing the execution of the Letter of Request shall be sent by the requested authority to the requesting authority by the same channel which was used by the latter.

In every instance where the Letter is not executed in whole or in part, the requesting authority shall be informed immediately through the same channel and advised of the reasons.

Article 14

The execution of the Letter of Request shall not give rise to any reimbursement of taxes or costs of any nature.

Nevertheless, the State of execution has the right to require the State of origin to reimburse the fees paid to experts and interpreters and the costs occasioned by the use of a special procedure requested by the State of origin under Article 9, paragraph 2.

The requested authority whose law obliges the parties themselves to secure evidence, and which is not able itself to execute the Letter, may, after having obtained the consent of the requesting authority, appoint a suitable person to do so. When seeking this consent the requested authority shall indicate the approximate costs which would result from this procedure. If the requesting authority gives its consent it shall reimburse any costs incurred; without such consent the requesting authority shall not be liable for the costs.

CHAPTER II. TAKING OF EVIDENCE BY DIPLOMATIC OFFICERS, CONSULAR AGENTS AND COMMISSIONERS

Article 15

In a civil or commercial matter, a diplomatic officer or consular agent of a Contracting State may, in the territory of another Contracting

State and within the area where he exercises his functions, take the evidence without compulsion of nationals of a State which he represents in aid of proceedings commenced in the courts of a State which he represents.

A Contracting State may declare that evidence may be taken by a diplomatic officer or consular agent only if permission to that effect is given upon application made by him or on his behalf to the appropriate authority designated by the declaring State.

Article 16

A diplomatic officer or consular agent of a Contracting State may, in the territory of another Contracting State and within the area where he exercises his functions, also take the evidence, without compulsion, of nationals of the State in which he exercises his functions or of a third State, in aid of proceedings commenced in the courts of a State which he represents, if:

(a) a competent authority designated by the State in which he exercises his functions has given its permission either generally or in the particular case; and

(b) he complies with the conditions which the competent authority has specified in the permission.

A Contracting State may declare that evidence may be taken under this article without its prior permission.

Article 17

In a civil or commercial matter, a person duly appointed as a commissioner for the purpose may, without compulsion, take evidence in the territory of a Contracting State in aid of proceedings commenced in the courts of another Contracting State if:

(a) a competent authority designated by the State where the evidence is to be taken has given its permission either generally or in the particular case; and

(b) he complies with the conditions which the competent authority has specified in the permission.

A Contracting State may declare that evidence may be taken under this article without its prior permission.

Article 18

A Contracting State may declare that a diplomatic officer, consular agent or commissioner authorized to take evidence under Articles 15, 16 or 17, may apply to the competent authority designated by the declaring State for appropriate assistance to obtain the evidence by compulsion. The declaration may contain such conditions as the declaring State may see fit to impose.

If the authority grants the application it shall apply any measures of compulsion which are appropriate and are prescribed by its law for use in internal proceedings.

Article 19

The competent authority, in giving the permission referred to in Articles 15, 16 or 17, or in granting the application referred to in Article 18, may lay down such conditions as it deems fit, *inter alia,* as to the time and place of the taking of the evidence. Similarly it may require that it be given reasonable advance notice of the time, date and place of the taking of the evidence; in such a case a representative of the authority shall be entitled to be present at the taking of the evidence.

Article 20

In the taking of evidence under any article of this chapter persons concerned may be legally represented.

Article 21

Where a diplomatic officer, consular agent or commissioner is authorized under Articles 15, 16 or 17 to take evidence:

(a) he may take all kinds of evidence which are not incompatible with the law of the State where the evidence is taken or contrary to any permission granted pursuant to the above articles, and shall have power within such limits to administer an oath or take an affirmation;

(b) a request to a person to appear or to give evidence shall, unless the recipient is a national of the State where the action is pending, be drawn up in the language of the place where the evidence is taken or be accompanied by a translation into such language;

(c) the request shall inform the person that he may be legally represented and, in any State that has not filed a declaration under Article 18, shall also inform him that he is not compelled to appear or to give evidence;

(d) the evidence may be taken in the manner provided by the law applicable to the court in which the action is pending provided that such manner is not forbidden by the law of the State where the evidence is taken;

(e) a person requested to give evidence may invoke the privileges and duties to refuse to give the evidence contained in Article 11.

Article 22

The fact that an attempt to take evidence under the procedure laid down in this chapter has failed, owing to the refusal of a person to give evidence, shall not prevent an application being subsequently made to take the evidence in accordance with Chapter I.

CHAPTER III. GENERAL CLAUSES

Article 23

A Contracting State may at the time of signature, ratification or accession, declare that it will not execute Letters of Request issued for the purpose of obtaining pre-trial discovery of documents as known in Common Law countries.

Article 24

A Contracting State may designate other authorities in addition to the Central Authority and shall determine the extent of their competence. However, Letters of Request may in all cases be sent to the Central Authority.

Federal States shall be free to designate more than one Central Authority.

Article 25

A Contracting State which has more than one legal system may designate the authorities of one of such systems, which shall have exclusive competence to execute Letters of Request pursuant to this Convention.

Article 26

A Contracting State, if required to do so because of constitutional limitations, may request the reimbursement by the State of origin of fees and costs, in connection with the execution of Letters of Request, for the service of process necessary to compel the appearance of a person to give evidence, the costs of attendance of such persons, and the cost of any transcript of the evidence.

Where a State has made a request pursuant to the above paragraph, any other Contracting State may request from that State the reimbursement of similar fees and costs.

Article 27

The provisions of the present Convention shall not prevent a Contracting State from:

(a) declaring that Letters of Request may be transmitted to its judicial authorities through channels other than those provided for in Article 2;

(b) permitting, by internal law or practice, any act provided for in this Convention to be performed upon less restrictive conditions;

(c) permitting, by internal law or practice, methods of taking evidence other than those provided for in this Convention.

Article 28

The present Convention shall not prevent an agreement between any two or more Contracting States to derogate from:

(a) the provisions of Article 2 with respect to methods of transmitting Letters of Request;

(b) the provisions of Article 4 with respect to the languages which may be used;

(c) the provisions of Article 8 with respect to the presence of judicial personnel at the execution of Letters;

(d) the provisions of Article 11 with respect to the privileges and duties of witnesses to refuse to give evidence;

(e) the provisions of Article 13 with respect to the methods of returning executed Letters to the requesting authority;

(f) the provisions of Article 14 with respect to fees and costs;

(g) the provisions of Chapter II. . . .

Article 33

A State may, at the time of signature, ratification or accession exclude, in whole or in part. the application of the provisions of paragraph 2 of Article 4 and of Chapter II. No other reservation shall be permitted.

Each Contracting State may at any time withdraw a reservation it has made; the reservation shall cease to have effect on the sixtieth day after notification of the withdrawal.

When a State has made a reservation, any other State affected thereby may apply the same rule against the reserving State.

Article 34

A State may at any time withdraw or modify a declaration.

Article 35

A Contracting State shall, at the time of the deposit of its instrument of ratification or accession, or at a later date, inform the Ministry of Foreign Affairs of the Netherlands of the designation of authorities, pursuant to Articles 2, 8, 24 and 25.

A Contracting State shall likewise inform the Ministry, where appropriate, of the following:

(a) the designation of the authorities to whom notice must be given, whose permission may be required, and whose assistance may be invoked in the taking of evidence by diplomatic officers and consular agents, pursuant to Articles 15, 16 and 18 respectively;

(b) the designation of the authorities whose permission may be required in the taking of evidence by commissioners pursuant to Article 17 and of those who may grant the assistance provided for in Article 18;

(c) declarations pursuant to Articles 4, 8, 11, 15, 16, 17, 18, 23 and 27;

(d) any withdrawal or modification of the above designations and declarations;

(e) the withdrawal of any reservation.

Article 36

Any difficulties which may arise between Contracting States in connection with the operation of this Convention shall be settled through diplomatic channels. . . .

Document 67
FOREIGN SOVEREIGN IMMUNITIES ACT

28 U.S.C. §§ 1330, 1391, 1441(d), 1602–1611, *et seq.*

§ 1330. Actions Against Foreign States

(a) The district courts shall have original jurisdiction without regard to amount in controversy of any nonjury civil action against a foreign state as defined in section 1603 (a) of this title as to any claim for relief in personam with respect to which the foreign state is not entitled to immunity either under sections 1605–1607 of this title or under any applicable international agreement.

(b) Personal jurisdiction over a foreign state shall exist as to every claim for relief over which the district courts have jurisdiction under subsection (a) where service has been made under section 1608 of this title.

(c) For purposes of subsection (b), an appearance by a foreign state does not confer personal jurisdiction with respect to any claim for relief not arising out of any transaction or occurrence enumerated in section 1605–1607 of this title.

§ 1391. Venue Generally

... (f) A civil action against a foreign state as defined in subsection 1603 (a) of this title may be brought—

(1) in any judicial district in which a substantial part of the events or omissions giving rise to the claim occurred, or a substantial part of property that is the subject of the action is situated;

(3) in any judicial district in which the agency or instrumentality is licensed to do business or is doing business, if the action is brought against an agency or instrumentality of a foreign state as defined in section 1603 (b) of this title; or

(4) in the United States District Court for the District of Columbia if the action is brought against a foreign state or political subdivision thereof.

§ 1441. Actions Removable Generally

... (d) Any civil action brought in a State court against a foreign state as defined in section 1603 (a) of this title may be removed by the foreign state to the district court of the United States for the district and division embracing the place where such action is pending. Upon removal the action shall be tried by the court without jury. Where removal is based upon this subsection, the time limitations of section 1446 (b) of this chapter may be enlarged at any time for cause shown.

§ 1602. Findings and Declaration of Purpose

The Congress finds that the determination by the United States courts of the claims of foreign states to immunity from the jurisdiction of such courts would serve the interests of justice and would protect the rights of both foreign states and litigants in United States courts. Under international law, states are not immune from the jurisdiction of foreign courts insofar as their commercial activities are concerned, and their commercial property may be levied upon for the satisfaction of judgments rendered against them in connection with their commercial activities. Claims of foreign states to immunity should henceforth be decided by courts of the United States and of the States in conformity with the principles set forth in this chapter.

§ 1603. Definitions

For purposes of this chapter—

(a) A "foreign state," except as used in section 1608 of this title, includes a political subdivision of a foreign state or an agency or instrumentality of a foreign state as defined in subsection (b).

(b) An "agency or instrumentality of a foreign state" means any entity—

(1) which is a separate legal person, corporate or otherwise, and

(2) which is an organ of a foreign state or political subdivision thereof, or a majority of whose shares or other ownership interest is owned by a foreign state or political subdivision thereof, and

(3) which is neither a citizen of a State of the United States as defined in section 1332 (c) and (d) of this title, nor created under the laws of any third country.

(c) The "United States" includes all territory and waters, continental or insular, subject to the jurisdiction of the United States.

(d) A "commercial activity" means either a regular course of commercial conduct or a particular commercial transaction of act. The commercial character of an activity shall be determined by reference to the nature of the course of conduct or particular transaction or act, rather than by reference to its purpose.

(e) A "commercial activity carried on in the United States by a foreign state" means commercial activity carried on by such state and having substantial contact with the United States.

§ 1604. Immunity of a Foreign State from Jurisdiction

Subject to existing international agreements to which the United States is a party at the time of enactment of this Act a foreign state shall be immune from the jurisdiction of the courts of the United States and of the States except as provided in sections 1605 to 1607 of this chapter.

§ 1605. General Exceptions to the Jurisdictional Immunity of a Foreign State

(a) A foreign state shall not be immune from the jurisdiction of courts of the United States or of the States in any case—

(1) in which the foreign state has waived its immunity either explicitly or by implication, notwithstanding any withdrawal of the waiver which the foreign state may purport to effect except in accordance with the terms of the waiver;

(2) in which the action is based upon a commercial activity carried on in the United States by the foreign state; or upon an act performed in the United States in connection with a commercial activity of the foreign state elsewhere; or upon an act outside the territory of the United States in connection with a commercial activity of the foreign state elsewhere and that act causes a direct effect in the United States;

(3) in which rights in property taken in violation of international law are in issue and that property or any property exchanged for such property is present in the United States in connection with a commercial activity carried on in the United States by the foreign state; or that property or any property exchanged for such property is owned or operated by an agency or instrumentality of the foreign state and that agency or instrumentality is engaged in a commercial activity in the United States;

(4) in which rights in property in the United States acquired by succession or gift or rights in immovable property situated in the United States are in issue;

(5) not otherwise encompassed in paragraph (2) above, in which money damages are sought against a foreign state for personal injury or death, or damage to or loss of property, occurring in the United States and caused by the tortious act or omission of that foreign state or of any official or employee of that foreign state while acting within the scope of his office or employment; except this paragraph shall not apply to—

(A) any claim based upon the exercise or performance or the failure to exercise or perform a discretionary function regardless of whether the discretion be abused, or

(B) any claim arising out of malicious prosecution, abuse of process, libel, slander, misrepresentation, deceit, or interference with contract rights;

(6) in which the action is brought, either to enforce an agreement made by the foreign state with or for the benefit of a private party to submit to arbitration all or any differences which have arisen or which may arise between the parties with respect to a defined legal relationship, whether contractual or not, concerning a subject matter capable of settlement by arbitration under the laws of the United States, or to confirm an award made pursuant to such an agreement to arbitrate, if

(A) the arbitration takes place or is intended to take place in the United States,

(B) the agreement or award is or may be governed by a treaty or other international agreement in force for the United

States calling for the recognition and enforcement of arbitral awards,

(C) the underlying claim, save for the agreement to arbitrate, could have been brought in a United States court under this section or section 1607, or

(D) paragraph (1) of this subsection is otherwise applicable; or

(7) not otherwise covered by paragraph (2), in which money damages are sought against a foreign state for personal injury or death that was caused by an act of torture, extrajudicial killing, aircraft sabotage, hostage taking, or the provision of material support or resources (as defined in section 2339A of title 18) for such an act if such act or provision of material support is engaged in by an official, employee, or agent of such foreign state while acting within the scope of his or her office, employment, or agency, except that the court shall decline to hear a claim under this paragraph—

(A) if the foreign state was not designated as a state sponsor of terrorism under section 6(j) of the Export Administration Act of 1979 (50 U.S.C. App. 2405(j)) or section 620A of the Foreign Assistance Act of 1961 (22 U.S.C. 2371) at the time the act occurred, unless later so designated as a result of such act; and

(B) even if the foreign state is or was so designated, if–

(i) the act occurred in the foreign state against which the claim has been brought and the claimant has not afforded the foreign state a reasonable opportunity to arbitrate the claim in accordance with accepted international rules of arbitration; or

(ii) neither the claimant nor the victim was a national of the United States (as that term is defined in section 101 (a)(22) of the Immigration and Nationality Act [8 U.S.C. § 101(a)(22)]) when the act upon which the claim is based occurred.

(b) A foreign state shall not be immune from the jurisdiction of the courts of the United States in any case in which a suit in admiralty is brought to enforce a maritime lien against a vessel or cargo of the foreign state, which maritime lien is based upon a commercial activity of the foreign state: *Provided*, That—

(1) notice of the suit is given by delivery of a copy of the summons and of the complaint to the person, or his agent, having possession of the vessel or cargo against which the maritime lien is asserted; and if the vessel or cargo is arrested pursuant to process obtained on behalf of the party bringing the suit, the service of process of arrest shall be deemed to constitute valid delivery of such notice, but the party bringing the suit shall be liable for any damages sustained by the foreign state as a result of the arrest if the party bringing the suit had actual or constructive knowledge that the vessel or cargo of a foreign state was involved; and

(2) notice to the foreign state of the commencement of suit as provided in section 1608 of this title is initiated within ten days either of the delivery of notice as provided in paragraph (1) of this subsection or, in the case of a party who was unaware that the vessel or cargo of a foreign state was involved, of the date such party determined the existence of the foreign state's interest.

(c) Whenever notice is delivered under subsection (b)(1), the suit to enforce a maritime lien shall thereafter proceed and shall be heard and determined according to the principles of law and rules of practice of suits in rem whenever it appears that, had the vessel been privately owned and possessed, a suit in rem might have been maintained. A decree against the foreign state may include costs of the suit and, if the decree is for a money judgment, interest as ordered by the court, except that the court may not award judgment against the foreign state in an amount greater than the value of the vessel or cargo upon which the maritime lien arose. Such value shall be determined as of the time notice is served under subsection (b)(1). Decrees shall be subject to appeal and revision as provided in other cases of admiralty and maritime jurisdiction. Nothing shall preclude the plaintiff in any proper case from seeking relief in personam in the same action brought to enforce a maritime lien as provided in this section.

(d) A foreign state shall not be immune from the jurisdiction of the courts of the United States in any action brought to foreclose a preferred mortgage, as defined in the Ship Mortgage Act, 1920 (46 U.S.C. 911 and following [46 U.S.C. App. §§ 911 *et seq.*]). Such action shall be brought, heard, and determined in accordance with the provisions of that Act and in accordance with the principles of law and rules of practice of suits in rem, whenever it appears that had the vessel been privately owned and possessed a suit in rem might have been maintained.

(e) For purposes of paragraph (7) of subsection (a)—

(1) the terms "torture" and "extrajudicial killing" have the meaning given those terms in section 3 of the Torture Victim Protection Act of 1991;

(2) the term "hostage taking" has the meaning given that term in Article 1 of the International Convention Against the Taking of Hostages; and

(3) the term "aircraft sabotage" has the meaning given that term in Article 1 of the Convention for the Suppression of Unlawful Acts Against the Safety of Civil Aviation.

(f) No action shall be maintained under subsection (a)(7) unless the action is commenced not later than 10 years after the date on which the cause of action arose. All principles of equitable tolling, including the period during which the foreign state was immune from suit, shall apply in calculating this limitation period.

(g) Limitation on discovery.

(1) In general.

(A) Subject to paragraph (2), if an action is filed that would otherwise be barred by section 1604, but for subsection (a)(7), the court, upon request of the Attorney General, shall stay any request, demand, or order for discovery on the United States that the Attorney General certifies would significantly interfere with a criminal investigation or prosecution, or a national security operation, related to the incident that gave rise to the cause of action, until such time as the Attorney General advises the court that such request, demand, or order will no longer so interfere.

(B) A stay under this paragraph shall be in effect during the 12–month period beginning on the date on which the court issues the order to stay discovery. The court shall renew the order to stay discovery for additional 12–month periods upon motion by the United States if the Attorney General certifies that discovery would significantly interfere with a criminal investigation or prosecution, or a national security operation, related to the incident that gave rise to the cause of action.

(2) Sunset.

(A) Subject to subparagraph (B), no stay shall be granted or continued in effect under paragraph (1) after the date that is 10 years after the date on which the incident that gave rise to the cause of action occurred.

(B) After the period referred to in subparagraph (A), the court, upon request of the Attorney General, may stay any request, demand, or order for discovery on the United States that the court finds a substantial likelihood would–

(i) create a serious threat of death or serious bodily injury to any person;

(ii) adversely affect the ability of the United States to work in cooperation with foreign and international law enforcement agencies in investigating violations of United States law; or

(iii) obstruct the criminal case related to the incident that gave rise to cause of action or undermine the potential for a conviction in such case.

(3) Evaluation of evidence.—The court's evaluation of any request for a stay under this subsection filed by the Attorney General shall be conducted ex parte and in camera.

(4) Bar on motions to dismiss.—A stay of discovery under this subsection shall constitute a bar to the granting of motion to dismiss under rules 12(b)(6) and 56 of the Federal Rules of Civil Procedure.

(5) Construction.—Nothing in this subsection shall prevent the United States from seeking protective orders or asserting privileges ordinarily available to the United States.

§ 1606. Extent of Liability

As to any claim for relief with respect to which a foreign state is not entitled to immunity under section 1605 or 1607 of this chapter, the foreign state shall be liable in the same manner and to the same extent as a private individual under like circumstances; but a foreign state except for an agency or instrumentality thereof shall not be liable for punitive damages, except any action under section 1605 (a) (7) or 1610 (f); if, however, in any case wherein death was caused, the law of the place where the action or omission occurred provides, or has been construed to provide, for damages only punitive in nature, the foreign state shall be liable for actual or compensatory damages measured by the pecuniary injuries resulting from such death which were incurred by the persons for whose benefit the action was brought.

§ 1607. Counterclaims

In any action brought by a foreign state, or in which a foreign state intervenes, in a court of the United States or of a State, the foreign state shall not be accorded immunity with respect to any counterclaim—

(a) for which a foreign state would not be entitled to immunity under section 1605 of this chapter had such claim been brought in a separate action against the foreign state; or

(b) arising out of the transaction or occurrence that is the subject matter of the claim of the foreign state; or

(c) to the extent that the counterclaim does not seek relief exceeding in amount or differing in kind from that sought by the foreign state.

§ 1608. Service; Time to Answer; Default

(a) Service in the courts of the United States and of the States shall be made upon a foreign state or political subdivision of a foreign state:

(1) by delivery of a copy of the summons and complaint in accordance with any special agreement for service between the plaintiff and the foreign state or political subdivision; or

(2) if no special agreement exists, by delivery of a copy of the summons and complaint in accordance with an applicable international convention on service of judicial documents; or

(3) if service cannot be made under paragraphs (1) or (2), by sending a copy of the summons and complaint and a notice of suit, together with a translation of each into the official language of the foreign state, by any form of mail requiring a signed receipt, to be addressed and dispatched by the clerk of the court to the head of the ministry of foreign affairs of the foreign state concerned; or

(4) if service cannot be made within 30 days under paragraph (3), by sending two copies of the summons and complaint and a notice of suit, together with a translation of each into the official language of the foreign state, by any form of mail requiring a signed receipt, to be addressed and dispatched by the clerk of the court to the Secretary of State in Washington, District of Columbia, to the

attention of the Director of Special Consular Services—and the Secretary shall transmit one copy of the papers through diplomatic channels to the foreign state and shall send to the clerk of the court a certified copy of the diplomatic note indicating when the papers were transmitted.

As used in this subsection a "notice of suit" shall mean a notice addressed to a foreign state and in a form prescribed by the Secretary of State by regulation.

(b) Service in the courts of the United States and of the States shall be made upon an agency or instrumentality of a foreign state:

(1) by delivery of a copy of the summons and complaint in accordance with any special arrangement for service between the plaintiff and the agency or instrumentality; or

(2) if no special arrangement exists, by delivery of a copy of the summons and complaint either to an officer, a managing or general agent, or to any other agent authorized by appointment or by law to receive service of process in the United States; or in accordance with an applicable international convention on service of judicial documents; or

(3) if service cannot be made under paragraphs (1) or (2), and if reasonably calculated to give actual notice, by delivery of a copy of the summons and complaint, together with a translation of each into the official language of the foreign state–

(A) as directed by an authority of the foreign state or political subdivision in response to a letter rogatory or request or

(B) by any form of mail requiring a signed receipt, to be addressed and dispatched by the clerk of the court to the agency or instrumentality to be served, or

(C) as directed by order of the court consistent with the law of the place where service is to be made.

(c) Service shall be deemed to have been made—

(1) in the case of service under subsection (a)(4), as of the date of transmittal indicated in the certified copy of the diplomatic note; and

(2) in any other case under this section, as of the date of receipt indicated in the certification, signed and returned postal receipt, or other proof of service applicable to the method of service employed.

(d) In any action brought in a court of the United States or of a State, a foreign state, a political subdivision thereof, or an agency or instrumentality of a foreign state shall serve an answer or other responsive pleading to the complaint within sixty days after service has been made under this section.

(e) No judgment by default shall be entered by a court of the United States or of a State against a foreign state, a political subdivision thereof, or an agency or instrumentality of a foreign state, unless the claimant establishes his claim or right to relief by evidence satisfactory to the court. A copy of any such default judgment shall be sent to the foreign state or political subdivision in the manner prescribed for service in this section

§ 1609. Immunity from Attachment and Execution of Property of a Foreign State

Subject to existing international agreements to which the United States is a party at the time of enactment of this Act the property in the United States of a foreign state shall be immune from attachment, arrest and execution except as provided in sections 1610 and 1611 of this chapter.

§ 1610. Exceptions to the Immunity from Attachment or Execution

(a) The property in the United States of a foreign state, as defined in section 1603(a) of this chapter, used for a commercial activity in the United States, shall not be immune from attachment in aid of execution, or from execution, upon a judgment entered by a court of the United States or of a State after the effective date of this Act, if—

(1) the foreign state has waived its immunity from attachment in aid of execution or from execution either explicitly or by implication, notwithstanding any withdrawal of the waiver the foreign state may purport to effect except in accordance with the terms of the waiver, or

(2) the property is or was used for the commercial activity upon which the claim is based, or

(3) the execution relates to a judgment establishing rights in property which has been taken in violation of international law or which has been exchanged for property taken in violation of international law, or

(4) the execution relates to a judgment establishing rights in property—

(A) which is acquired by succession or gift, or

(B) which is immovable and situated in the United States: *Provided*, That such property is not used for purposes of maintaining a diplomatic or consular mission or the residence of the Chief of such mission, or

(5) the property consists of any contractual obligation or any proceeds from such a contractual obligation to indemnify or hold harmless the foreign state or its employees under a policy of automobile or other liability or casualty insurance covering the claim which merged into the judgment; or

(6) the judgment is based on an order confirming an arbitral award rendered against the foreign state, provided that attachment in aid of execution, or execution, would not be inconsistent with any provision in the arbitral agreement; or

(7) the judgment relates to a claim for which the foreign state is not immune under section 1605 (a)(7), regardless of whether the property is or was involved with the act upon which the claim is based.

(b) In addition to subsection (a), any property in the United States of an agency or instrumentality of a foreign state engaged in commercial activity in the United States shall not be immune from attachment in aid of execution, or from execution, upon a judgment entered by a court of the United States or of a State after the effective date of this Act, if—

(1) the agency or instrumentality has waived its immunity from attachment in aid of execution or from execution either explicitly or implicitly, notwithstanding any withdrawal of the waiver the agency or instrumentality may purport to effect except in accordance with the terms of the waiver, or

(2) the judgment relates to a claim for which the agency or instrumentality is not immune by virtue of section 1605(a)(2), (3), or (5), or (7), or 1605(b) of this chapter, regardless of whether the property is or was used for the activity upon which the claim is based.

(c) No attachment or execution referred to in subsections (a) and (b) of this section shall be permitted until the court has ordered such attachment and execution after having determined that a reasonable period of time has elapsed following the entry of judgment and the giving of any notice required under section 1608(e) of this chapter.

(d) The property of a foreign state, as defined in section 1603(a) of this chapter, used for a commercial activity in the United States, shall not be immune from attachment prior to the entry of judgment in any action brought in a court of the United States or of a State, or prior to the elapse of the period of time provided in subsection c of this section, if—

(1) the foreign state has explicitly waived its immunity from attachment prior to judgment, notwithstanding any withdrawal of the waiver the foreign state may purport to effect except in accordance with the terms of the waiver, and

(2) the purpose of the attachment is to secure satisfaction of a judgment that has been or may ultimately be entered against the foreign state, and not to obtain jurisdiction.

(e) The vessels of a foreign state shall not be immune from arrest in rem, interlocutory sale, and execution in actions brought to foreclose a preferred mortgage as provided in section 1605 (d).

(f) (1) (A) Notwithstanding any other provision of law, including but not limited to section 208 (f) of the Foreign Missions Act (22 U.S.C. 4308 (f)), and except as provided in subparagraph (B), any property with respect to which financial transactions are prohibited or regulated pursuant to section 5 (b) of the Trading with the Enemy Act (50 U.S.C. App. 5(b)), section 620(a) of the Foreign Assistance Act of 1961 (22 U.S.C. 2370 (a)), sections 202 and 203 of the International Emergency Economic Powers Act (50 U.S.C. 1701–1702), or any other proclamation, order, regulation, or license issued pursuant thereto, shall be subject to execution or attachment in aid of execution of any judgment relating to a claim for which a foreign state (including any agency or instrumentality or such state) claiming such property is not immune under section 1605(a) (7).

(B) Subparagraph (A) shall not apply if, at the time the property is expropriated or seized by the foreign state, the property has been held in title by a natural person or, if held in trust, has been held for the benefit of a natural person or persons.

(2) (A) At the request of any party in whose favor a judgment has been issued with respect to a claim for which the foreign state is not immune under section 1605(a) (7), the Secretary of the Treasury and the Secretary of State shall fully, promptly, and effectively assist any judgment creditor or any court that has issued any such judgment in identifying, locating, and executing against the property of that foreign state or any agency or instrumentality of such state.

(B) In providing such assistance, the Secretaries–

(i) may provide such information to the court under seal; and

(ii) shall provide such information in a manner sufficient to allow the court to direct the United States Marshall's office to promptly and effectively execute against that property.

§ 1611. Certain Types of Property Immune from Execution

(a) Notwithstanding the provisions of section 1610 of this chapter, the property of those organizations designated by the President as being entitled to enjoy the privileges, exemptions, and immunities provided by the International Organizations Immunities Act shall not be subject to attachment or any other judicial process impeding the disbursement of funds to, or on the order of, a foreign state as the result of an action brought in the courts of the United States or of the States.

(b) Notwithstanding the provisions of section 1610 of this chapter, the property of a foreign state shall be immune from attachment and from execution, if–

(1) the property is that of a foreign central bank or monetary authority held for its own account, unless such bank or authority, or its parent foreign government, has explicitly waived its immunity from attachment in aid of execution, or from execution, notwithstanding any withdrawal of the waiver which the bank, authority or government may purport to effect except in accordance with the terms of the waiver; or

(2) the property is, or is intended to be, used in connection with a military authority and

(A) is of a military character, or

(B) is under the control of a military authority or defense agency.

(c) Notwithstanding the provisions of section 1610 of this chapter, the property of a foreign state shall be immune from attachment and from execution in an action brought under section 302 of the Cuban Liberty and Democratic Solidarity (LIBERTAD) Act of 1996 to the extent that the property is a facility or installation used by an accredited diplomatic mission for official purposes.

Document 68
CIVIL LIABILITY FOR ACTS OF STATE SPONSORED TERRORISM

Pub. L. No. 104–208, Div. A, Title I, § 101(c) [Title V, § 589], Sept. 30, 1996, 110 Stat. 3009–172

(a) An official, employee, or agent of a foreign state designated as a state sponsor of terrorism designated under section 6 (j) of the Export Administration Act of 1979 [section 2405 (j) of the appendix to Title 50, War and National Defense] while acting within the scope of his or her office, employment, or agency shall be liable to a United States national or the national's legal representative for personal injury or death caused by acts of that official, employee, or agent for which the courts of the United States may maintain jurisdiction under section 1605(a)(7) of title 28, United States Code, for money damages which may include economic damages, solatium, pain, and suffering, and punitive damages if the acts were among those described in section 1605(a)(7).

(b) Provisions related to statute of limitations and limitations on discovery that would apply to an action brought under 28 U.S.C.1605 (f) and (g) shall also apply to actions brought under this section.

No action shall be maintained under this section if an official, employee, or agent of the United States, while acting within the scope of his or her office, employment, or agency would not be liable for such acts if carried out within the United States.

Document 69
UNITED NATIONS CONVENTION ON THE LAW OF THE SEA

1833 U.N.T.S. 3
Signed at Montego Bay, Jamaica, U.N. A/CONF. 62/122, 10 December 1982
Entered into force 16 November 1994

The States Parties to this Convention,

Prompted by the desire to settle, in a spirit of mutual understanding and co-operation, all issues relating to the law of the sea and aware of the historic significance of this Convention as an important contribution to the maintenance of peace, justice and progress for all peoples of the world,

Noting that developments since the United Nations Conferences on the Law of the Sea held at Geneva in 1958 and 1960 have accentuated the need for a new and generally acceptable Convention on the law of the sea,

Conscious that the problems of ocean space are closely interrelated and need to be considered as a whole,

Recognizing the desirability of establishing through this Convention, with due regard for the sovereignty of all States, a legal order for the seas and oceans which will facilitate international communication, and will promote the peaceful uses of the seas and oceans, the equitable and efficient utilization of their resources, the conservation of their living resources, and the study, protection and preservation of the marine environment,

Bearing in mind that the achievement of these goals will contribute to the realization of a just and equitable international economic order which takes into account the interests and needs of mankind as a whole and, in particular, the special interests and needs of developing countries, whether coastal or land-locked,

Desiring by this Convention to develop the principles embodied in resolution 2749 (XXV) of 17 December 1970 in which the General Assembly of the United Nations solemnly declared *inter alia* that the area of the sea-bed and ocean floor and the subsoil thereof, beyond the limits of national jurisdiction, as well as its resources, are the common heritage of mankind, the exploration and exploitation of which shall be carried out for the benefit of mankind as a whole, irrespective of the geographical location of States,

Believing that the codification and progressive development of the law of the sea achieved in this Convention will contribute to the strengthening of peace, security, co-operation and friendly relations among all nations in conformity with the principles of justice and equal rights and will promote the economic and social advancement of all peoples of the world, in accordance with the Purposes and Principles of the United Nations as set forth in the Charter,

Affirming that matters not regulated by this Convention continue to be governed by the rules and principles of general international law,

Have agreed as follows:

PART I. INTRODUCTION

Article 1

Use of Terms and Scope

1. For the purposes of this Convention:

(1) "Area" means the sea-bed and ocean floor and subsoil thereof beyond the limits of national jurisdiction;

(2) "Authority" means the International Sea–Bed Authority;

(3) "activities in the Area" means all activities of exploration for, and exploitation of, the resources of the Area;

(4) "pollution of the marine environment" means the introduction by man, directly or indirectly, of substances or energy into the marine environment, including estuaries, which results or is likely to result in such deleterious effects as harm to living resources and marine life, hazards to human health, hindrance to marine activities, including fishing and other legitimate uses of the sea, impairment of quality for use of sea water and reduction of amenities;

(5) (a) "dumping" means:

(i) any deliberate disposal of wastes or other matter from vessels, aircraft, platforms or other man-made structures at sea;

(ii) any deliberate disposal of vessels, aircraft, platforms or other man-made structures at sea

(b) "dumping" does not include:

(i) the disposal of wastes or other matter incidental to, or derived from the normal operations of vessels, aircraft, platforms or other man-made structures at sea and their equipment, other than wastes or other matter transported by or to vessels, aircraft, platforms or other man-made structures at sea, operating for the purpose of disposal of such matter or derived from the treatment of such wastes or other matter on such vessels, aircraft, platforms or structures;

(ii) placement of matter for a purpose other than the mere disposal thereof, provided that such placement is not contrary to the aims of this Convention.

2. (1) "States Parties" means States which have consented to be bound by this Convention and for which this Convention is in force.

(2) This Convention applies *mutatis mutandis* to the entities referred to in article 305, paragraph 1(b), (c), (d), (e) and (f), which become Parties to this Convention in accordance with the conditions

relevant to each, and to that extent "States Parties" refers to those entities.

PART II. TERRITORIAL SEA AND CONTIGUOUS ZONE

Section 1. General Provisions

Article 2

Legal Status of the Territorial Sea, of the Air Space Over the Territorial Sea and of its Bed and Subsoil

1. The sovereignty of a coastal State extends, beyond its land territory and internal waters and, in the case of an archipelagic State, its archipelagic waters, to an adjacent belt of sea, described as the territorial sea.

2. This sovereignty extends to the air space over the territorial sea as well as to its bed and subsoil.

3. The sovereignty over the territorial sea is exercised subject to this Convention and to other rules of international law.

Section 2. Limits of the Territorial Sea

Article 3

Breadth of the Territorial Sea

Every State has the right to establish the breadth of its territorial sea up to a limit not exceeding 12 nautical miles, measured from baselines determined in accordance with this Convention.

Article 4

Outer Limit of the Territorial Sea

The outer limit of the territorial sea is the line every point of which is at a distance from the nearest point of the baseline equal to the breadth of the territorial sea.

Article 5

Normal Baseline

Except where otherwise provided in this Convention, the normal baseline for measuring the breadth of the territorial sea is the low-water line along the coast as marked on large-scale charts officially recognized by the coastal State.

Article 6

Reefs

In the case of islands situated on atolls or of islands having fringing reefs, the baseline for measuring the breadth of the territorial sea is the seaward low-water line of the reef, as shown by the appropriate symbol on charts officially recognized by the coastal State.

Article 7

Straight Baselines

1. In localities where the coastline is deeply indented and cut into, or if there is a fringe of islands along the coast in its immediate vicinity,

the method of straight baselines joining appropriate points may be employed in drawing the baseline from which the breadth of the territorial sea is measured.

2. Where because of the presence of a delta and other natural conditions the coastline is highly unstable, the appropriate points may be selected along the furthest seaward extent of the low-water line and, notwithstanding subsequent regression of the low-water line, the straight baselines shall remain effective until changed by the coastal State in accordance with this Convention.

3. The drawing of straight baselines must not depart to any appreciable extent from the general direction of the coast, and the sea areas lying within the lines must be sufficiently closely linked to the land domain to be subject to the regime of internal waters.

4. Straight baselines shall not be drawn to and from low-tide elevations, unless lighthouses or similar installations which are permanently above sea level have been built on them or except in instances where the drawing of baselines to and from such elevations has received general international recognition.

5. Where the method of straight baselines is applicable under paragraph 1, account may be taken, in determining particular baselines, of economic interests peculiar to the region concerned, the reality and the importance of which are clearly evidenced by long usage.

6. The system of straight baselines may not be applied by a State in such a manner as to cut off the territorial sea of another State from the high seas or an exclusive economic zone.

Article 8

Internal Waters

1. Except as provided in Part IV, waters on the landward side of the baseline of the territorial sea form part of the internal waters of the State.

2. Where the establishment of a straight baseline in accordance with the method set forth in article 7 has the effect of enclosing as internal waters areas which had not previously been considered as such, a right of innocent passage as provided in this Convention shall exist in those waters.

Article 9

Mouths of Rivers

If a river flows directly into the sea, the baseline shall be a straight line across the mouth of the river between points on the low-water line of its banks.

Article 10

Bays

1. This article relates only to bays the coasts of which belong to a single State.

2. For the purposes of this Convention, a bay is a well-marked indentation whose penetration is in such proportion to the width of its mouth as to contain land-locked waters and constitute more than a mere curvature of the coast. An indentation shall not, however, be regarded as a bay unless its area is as large as, or larger than, that of the semi-circle whose diameter is a line drawn across the mouth of that indentation.

3. For the purpose of measurement, the area of an indentation is that lying between the low-water mark around the shore of the indentation and a line joining the low-water mark of its natural entrance points. Where, because of the presence of islands, an indentation has more than one mouth, the semicircle shall be drawn on a line as long as the sum total of the lengths of the lines across the different mouths. Islands within an indentation shall be included as if they were part of the water area of the indentation.

4. If the distance between the low-water marks of the natural entrance points of a bay does not exceed 24 nautical miles, a closing line may be drawn between these two low-water marks, and the waters enclosed thereby shall be considered as internal waters.

5. Where the distance between the low-water marks of the natural entrance points of a bay exceeds 24 nautical miles, a straight baseline of 24 nautical miles shall be drawn within the bay in such a manner as to enclose the maximum area of water that is possible with a line of that length.

6. The foregoing provisions do not apply to so-called "historic" bays, or in any case where the system of straight baselines provided for in article 7 is applied.

Article 11

Ports

For the purpose of delimiting the territorial sea, the outermost permanent harbour works which form an integral part of the harbour system are regarded as forming part of the coast. Off-shore installations and artificial islands shall not be considered as permanent harbour works.

Article 12

Roadsteads

Roadsteads which are normally used for the loading, unloading and anchoring of ships, and which would otherwise be situated wholly or partly outside the outer limit of the territorial sea, are included in the territorial sea.

Article 13

Low–Tide Elevations

1. A low-tide elevation is a naturally formed area of land which is surrounded by and above water at low tide but submerged at high tide.

Where a low-tide elevation is situated wholly or partly at a distance not exceeding the breadth of the territorial sea from the mainland or an island, the low-water line on that elevation may be used as the baseline for measuring the breadth of the territorial sea.

2. Where a low-tide elevation is wholly situated at a distance exceeding the breadth of the territorial sea from the mainland or an island, it has no territorial sea of its own.

Article 14

Combination of Methods for Determining Baselines

The coastal State may determine baselines in turn by any of the methods provided for in the foregoing articles to suit different conditions.

Article 15

Delimitation of the Territorial Sea Between States with Opposite or Adjacent Coasts

Where the coasts of two States are opposite or adjacent to each other, neither of the two States is entitled, failing agreement between them to the contrary, to extend its territorial sea beyond the median line every point of which is equidistant from the nearest points on the baselines from which the breadth of the territorial seas of each of the two States is measured. The above provision does not apply, however, where it is necessary by reason of historic title or other special circumstances to delimit the territorial seas of the two States in a way which is at variance therewith.

Article 16

Charts and Lists of Geographical Co–Ordinates

1. The baselines for measuring the breadth of the territorial sea determined in accordance with articles 7, 9 and 10, or the limits derived therefrom, and the lines of delimitation drawn in accordance with articles 12 and 15 shall be shown on charts of a scale or scales adequate for ascertaining their position. Alternatively, a list of geographical co-ordinates of points, specifying the geodetic datum, may be substituted.

2. The coastal State shall give due publicity to such charts or lists of geographical co-ordinates and shall deposit a copy of each such chart or list with the Secretary–General of the United Nations.

Section 3. Innocent Passage in the Territorial Sea

Subsection A. Rules Applicable to All Ships

Article 17

Right of Innocent Passage

Subject to this Convention, ships of all States, whether coastal or land-locked, enjoy the right of innocent passage through the territorial sea.

Article 18

Meaning of Passage

1. Passage means navigation through the territorial sea for the purpose of:

(a) traversing that sea without entering internal waters or calling at a roadstead or port facility outside internal waters; or

(b) proceeding to or from internal waters or a call at such roadstead or port facility.

2. Passage shall be continuous and expeditious. However, passage includes stopping and anchoring, but only in so far as the same are incidental to ordinary navigation or are rendered necessary by *force majeure* or distress or for the purpose of rendering assistance to persons, ships or aircraft in danger or distress.

Article 19

Meaning of Innocent Passage

1. Passage is innocent so long as it is not prejudicial to the peace, good order or security of the coastal State. Such passage shall take place in conformity with this Convention and with other rules of international law.

2. Passage of a foreign ship shall be considered to be prejudicial to the peace, good order or security of the coastal State if in the territorial sea it engages in any of the following activities:

(a) any threat or use of force against the sovereignty, territorial integrity or political independence of the coastal State, or in any other manner in violation of the principles of international law embodied in the Charter of the United Nations;

(b) any exercise or practice with weapons of any kind;

(c) any act aimed at collecting information to the prejudice of the defence or security of the coastal State;

(d) any act of propaganda aimed at affecting the defence or security of the coastal State;

(e) the launching, landing or taking on board of any aircraft;

(f) the launching, landing or taking on board of any military device;

(g) the loading or unloading of any commodity, currency or person contrary to the customs, fiscal, immigration or sanitary laws and regulations of the coastal State;

(h) any act of wilful and serious pollution contrary to this Convention;

(i) any fishing activities;

(j) the carrying out of research or survey activities;

(k) any act aimed at interfering with any systems of communication or any other facilities or installations of the coastal State;

(*l*) any other activity not having a direct bearing on passage.

Article 20

Submarines and Other Underwater Vehicles

In the territorial sea, submarines and other underwater vehicles are required to navigate on the surface and to show their flag.

Article 21

Laws and Regulations of the Coastal State
Relating to Innocent Passage

1. The coastal State may adopt laws and regulations, in conformity with the provisions of this Convention and other rules of international law, relating to innocent passage through the territorial sea, in respect of all or any of the following:

(a) the safety of navigation and the regulation of maritime traffic;

(b) the protection of navigational aids and facilities and other facilities or installations;

(c) the protection of cables and pipelines;

(d) the conservation of the living resources of the sea;

(e) the prevention of infringement of the fisheries laws and regulations of the coastal State;

(f) the preservation of the environment of the coastal State and the prevention, reduction and control of pollution thereof;

(g) marine scientific research and hydrographic surveys;

(h) the prevention of infringement of the customs, fiscal, immigration or sanitary laws and regulations of the coastal State.

2. Such laws and regulations shall not apply to the design, construction, manning or equipment of foreign ships unless they are giving effect to generally accepted international rules or standards.

3. The coastal State shall give due publicity to all such laws and regulations.

4. Foreign ships exercising the right of innocent passage through the territorial sea shall comply with all such laws and regulations and all generally accepted international regulations relating to the prevention of collisions at sea.

Article 22

Sea Lanes and Traffic Separation Schemes in the Territorial Sea

1. The coastal State may, where necessary having regard to the safety of navigation, require foreign ships exercising the right of innocent passage through its territorial sea to use such sea lanes and traffic separation schemes as it may designate or prescribe for the regulation of the passage of ships.

2. In particular, tankers, nuclear-powered ships and ships carrying nuclear or other inherently dangerous or noxious substances or materials may be required to confine their passage to such sea lanes.

3. In the designation of sea lanes and the prescription of traffic separation schemes under this article, the coastal State shall take into account:

(a) the recommendations of the competent international organization;

(b) any channels customarily used for international navigation;

(c) the special characteristics of particular ships and channels; and

(d) the density of traffic.

4. The coastal State shall clearly indicate such sea lanes and traffic separation schemes on charts to which due publicity shall be given.

Article 23

Foreign Nuclear–Powered Ships and Ships Carrying Nuclear or Other Inherently Dangerous or Noxious Substances

Foreign nuclear-powered ships and ships carrying nuclear or other inherently dangerous or noxious substances shall, when exercising the right of innocent passage through the territorial sea, carry documents and observe special precautionary measures established for such ships by international agreements.

Article 24

Duties of the Coastal State

1. The coastal State shall not hamper the innocent passage of foreign ships through the territorial sea except in accordance with this Convention. In particular, in the application of this Convention or of any laws or regulations adopted in conformity with this Convention, the coastal State shall not:

(a) impose requirements on foreign ships which have the practical effect of denying or impairing the right of innocent passage; or

(b) discriminate in form or in fact against the ships of any State or against ships carrying cargoes to, from or on behalf of any State.

2. The coastal State shall give appropriate publicity to any danger to navigation, of which it has knowledge, within its territorial sea.

Article 25

Rights of Protection of the Coastal State

1. The coastal State may take the necessary steps in its territorial sea to prevent passage which is not innocent.

2. In the case of ships proceeding to internal waters or a call at a port facility outside internal waters, the coastal State also has the right to take the necessary steps to prevent any breach of the conditions to

which admission of those ships to internal waters or such a call is subject.

3. The coastal State may, without discrimination in form or in fact among foreign ships, suspend temporarily in specified areas of its territorial sea the innocent passage of foreign ships if such suspension is essential for the protection of its security, including weapons exercises. Such suspension shall take effect only after having been duly published.

Article 26

Charges Which may be Levied Upon Foreign Ships

1. No charge may be levied upon foreign ships by reason only of their passage through the territorial sea.

2. Charges may be levied upon a foreign ship passing through the territorial sea as payment only for specific services rendered to the ship. These charges shall be levied without discrimination.

Subsection B. Rules Applicable to Merchant Ships and Government Ships Operated for Commercial Purposes

Article 27

Criminal Jurisdiction on Board a Foreign Ship

1. The criminal jurisdiction of the coastal State should not be exercised on board a foreign ship passing through the territorial sea to arrest any person or to conduct any investigation in connection with any crime committed on board the ship during its passage, save only in the following cases:

(a) if the consequences of the crime extend to the coastal State;

(b) if the crime is of a kind to disturb the peace of the country or the good order of the territorial sea;

(c) if the assistance of the local authorities has been requested by the master of the ship or by a diplomatic agent or consular officer of the flag State; or

(d) if such measures are necessary for the suppression of illicit traffic in narcotic drugs or psychotropic substances.

2. The above provisions do not affect the right of the coastal State to take any steps authorized by its laws for the purpose of an arrest or investigation on board a foreign ship passing through the territorial sea after leaving internal waters.

3. In the cases provided for in paragraphs 1 and 2, the coastal State shall, if the master so requests, notify a diplomatic agent or consular officer of the flag State before taking any steps, and shall facilitate contact between such agent or officer and the ship's crew. In cases of emergency this notification may be communicated while the measures are being taken.

4. In considering whether or in what manner an arrest should be made, the local authorities shall have due regard to the interests of navigation.

5. Except as provided in Part XII or with respect to violations of laws and regulations adopted in accordance with Part V, the coastal State may not take any steps on board a foreign ship passing through the territorial sea to arrest any person or to conduct any investigation in connection with any crime committed before the ship entered the territorial sea, if the ship, proceeding from a foreign port, is only passing through the territorial sea without entering internal waters.

Article 28

Civil Jurisdiction in Relation to Foreign Ships

1. The coastal State should not stop or divert a foreign ship passing through the territorial sea for the purpose of exercising civil jurisdiction in relation to a person on board the ship.

2. The coastal State may not levy execution against or arrest the ship for the purpose of any civil proceedings, save only in respect of obligations or liabilities assumed or incurred by the ship itself in the course or for the purpose of its voyage through the waters of the coastal State.

3. Paragraph 2 is without prejudice to the right of the coastal State, in accordance with its laws, to levy execution against or to arrest, for the purpose of any civil proceedings, a foreign ship lying in the territorial sea, or passing through the territorial sea after leaving internal waters.

Subsection C. Rules Applicable to Warships and Other Government Ships Operated for Non–Commercial Purposes

Article 29

Definition of Warships

For the purposes of this Convention, "warship" means a ship belonging to the armed forces of a State bearing the external marks distinguishing such ships of its nationality, under the command of an officer duly commissioned by the government of the State and whose name appears in the appropriate service list or its equivalent, and manned by a crew which is under regular armed forces discipline.

Article 30

Non–Compliance by Warships with the Laws and Regulations of the Coastal State

If any warship does not comply with the laws and regulations of the coastal State concerning passage through the territorial sea and disregards any request for compliance therewith which is made to it, the coastal State may require it to leave the territorial sea immediately.

Article 31

Responsibility of the Flag State for Damage Caused by a Warship or Other Government Ship Operated for Non–Commercial Purposes

The flag State shall bear international responsibility for any loss or damage to the coastal State resulting from the non-compliance by a warship or other government ship operated for non-commercial purposes with the laws and regulations of the coastal State concerning passage through the territorial sea or with the provisions of this Convention or other rules of international law.

Article 32

Immunities of Warships and Other Government Ships Operated for Non–Commercial Purposes

With such exceptions as are contained in subsection A and in articles 30 and 31, nothing in this Convention affects the immunities of warships and other government ships operated for non-commercial purposes.

Section 4. Contiguous Zone

Article 33

Contiguous Zone

1. In a zone contiguous to its territorial sea, described as the contiguous zone, the coastal State may exercise the control necessary to:

(a) prevent infringement of its customs, fiscal, immigration or sanitary laws and regulations within its territory or territorial sea;

(b) punish infringement of the above laws and regulations committed within its territory or territorial sea.

2. The contiguous zone may not extend beyond 24 nautical miles from the baselines from which the breadth of the territorial sea is measured.

PART III. STRAITS USED FOR INTERNATIONAL NAVIGATION

Section 1. General Provisions

Article 34

Legal Status of Waters Forming Straits Used for International Navigation

1. The regime of passage through straits used for international navigation established in this Part shall not in other respects affect the legal status of the waters forming such straits or the exercise by the States bordering the straits of their sovereignty or jurisdiction over such waters and their air space, bed and subsoil.

2. The sovereignty or jurisdiction of the States bordering the straits is exercised subject to this Part and to other rules of international law.

Article 35

Scope of this Part

Nothing in this Part affects:

(a) any areas of internal waters within a strait, except where the establishment of a straight baseline in accordance with the method set forth in article 7 has the effect of enclosing as internal waters areas which had not previously been considered as such;

(b) the legal status of the waters beyond the territorial seas of States bordering straits as exclusive economic zones or high seas; or

(c) the legal regime in straits in which passage is regulated in whole or in part by long-standing international conventions in force specifically relating to such straits.

Article 36

High Seas Routes or Routes Through Exclusive Economic Zones Through Straits Used for International Navigation

This Part does not apply to a strait used for international navigation if there exists through the strait a route through the high seas or through an exclusive economic zone of similar convenience with respect to navigational and hydrographical characteristics; in such routes, the other relevant Parts of this Convention, including the provisions regarding the freedoms of navigation and overflight, apply.

Section 2. Transit Passage

Article 37

Scope of this Section

This section applies to straits which are used for international navigation between one part of the high seas or an exclusive economic zone and another part of the high seas or an exclusive economic zone.

Article 38

Right of Transit Passage

1. In straits referred to in article 37, all ships and aircraft enjoy the right of transit passage, which shall not be impeded; except that, if the strait is formed by an island of a State bordering the strait and its mainland, transit passage shall not apply if there exists seaward of the island a route through the high seas or through an exclusive economic zone of similar convenience with respect to navigational and hydrographical characteristics.

2. Transit passage means the exercise in accordance with this Part of the freedom of navigation and overflight solely for the purpose of continuous and expeditious transit of the strait between one part of the high seas or an exclusive economic zone and another part of the high seas or an exclusive economic zone. However, the requirement of continuous and expeditious transit does not preclude passage through the strait for the purpose of entering, leaving or returning from a State bordering the strait, subject to the conditions of entry to that State.

3. Any activity which is not an exercise of the right of transit passage through a strait remains subject to the other applicable provisions of this Convention.

Article 39

Duties of Ships and Aircraft During Transit Passage

1. Ships and aircraft, while exercising the right of transit passage, shall:

(a) proceed without delay through or over the strait;

(b) refrain from any threat or use of force against the sovereignty, territorial integrity or political independence of States bordering the strait, or in any other manner in violation of the principles of international law embodied in the Charter of the United Nations;

(c) refrain from any activities other than those incident to their normal modes of continuous and expeditious transit unless rendered necessary by *force majeure* or by distress;

(d) comply with other relevant provisions of this Part.

2. Ships in transit passage shall:

(a) comply with generally accepted international regulations, procedures and practices for safety at sea, including the International Regulations for Preventing Collisions at Sea;

(b) comply with generally accepted international regulations, procedures and practices for the prevention, reduction and control of pollution from ships.

3. Aircraft in transit passage shall:

(a) observe the Rules of the Air established by the International Civil Aviation Organization as they apply to civil aircraft; state aircraft will normally comply with such safety measures and will at all times operate with due regard for the safety of navigation;

(b) at all times monitor the radio frequency assigned by the competent internationally designated air traffic control authority or the appropriate international distress radio frequency.

Article 40

Research and Survey Activities

During transit passage, foreign ships, including marine scientific research and hydrographic survey ships, may not carry out any research or survey activities without the prior authorization of the States bordering straits.

Article 41

Sea Lanes and Traffic Separation Schemes in Straits Used for International Navigation

1. In conformity with this Part, States bordering straits may designate sea lanes and prescribe traffic separation schemes for navigation in straits where necessary to promote the safe passage of ships.

2. Such States may, when circumstances require, and after giving due publicity thereto, substitute other sea lanes or traffic separation

schemes for any sea lanes or traffic separation schemes previously designated or prescribed by them.

3. Such sea lanes and traffic separation schemes shall conform to generally accepted international regulations.

4. Before designating or substituting sea lanes or prescribing or substituting traffic separation schemes, States bordering straits shall refer proposals to the competent international organization with a view to their adoption. The organization may adopt only such sea lanes and traffic separation schemes as may be agreed with the States bordering the straits, after which the States may designate, prescribe or substitute them.

5. In respect of a strait where sea lanes or traffic separation schemes through the waters of two or more States bordering the strait are being proposed, the States concerned shall co-operate in formulating proposals in consultation with the competent international organization.

6. States bordering straits shall clearly indicate all sea lanes and traffic separation schemes designated or prescribed by them on charts to which due publicity shall be given.

7. Ships in transit passage shall respect applicable sea lanes and traffic separation schemes established in accordance with this article.

Article 42

Laws and Regulations of States Bordering Straits Relating to Transit Passage

1. Subject to the provisions of this section, States bordering straits may adopt laws and regulations relating to transit passage through straits, in respect of all or any of the following:

(a) the safety of navigation and the regulation of maritime traffic, as provided in article 41;

(b) the prevention, reduction and control of pollution, by giving effect to applicable international regulations regarding the discharge of oil, oily wastes and other noxious substances in the strait;

(c) with respect to fishing vessels, the prevention of fishing, including the stowage of fishing gear;

(d) the loading or unloading of any commodity, currency or person in contravention of the customs, fiscal, immigration or sanitary laws and regulations of States bordering straits.

2. Such laws and regulations shall not discriminate in form or in fact among foreign ships or in their application have the practical effect of denying, hampering or impairing the right of transit passage as defined in this section.

3. States bordering straits shall give due publicity to all such laws and regulations.

4. Foreign ships exercising the right of transit passage shall comply with such laws and regulations.

5. The flag State of a ship or the State of registry of an aircraft entitled to sovereign immunity which acts in a manner contrary to such laws and regulations or other provisions of this Part shall bear international responsibility for any loss or damage which results to States bordering straits.

Article 43

Navigational and Safety Aids and Other Improvements and the Prevention, Reduction and Control of Pollution

User States and States bordering a strait should by agreement co-operate:

(a) in the establishment and maintenance in a strait of necessary navigational and safety aids or other improvements in aid of international navigation; and

(b) for the prevention, reduction and control of pollution from ships.

Article 44

Duties of States Bordering Straits

States bordering straits shall not hamper transit passage and shall give appropriate publicity to any danger to navigation or overflight within or over the strait of which they have knowledge. There shall be no suspension of transit passage.

Section 3. Innocent Passage

Article 45

Innocent Passage

1. The regime of innocent passage, in accordance with Part II, section 3 shall apply in straits used for international navigation:

(a) excluded from the application of the regime of transit passage under article 38 , paragraph 1; or

(b) between a part of the high seas or an exclusive economic zone and the territorial sea of a foreign State.

2. There shall be no suspension of innocent passage through such straits.

PART IV. ARCHIPELAGIC STATES

Article 46

Use of Terms

For the purposes of this Convention:

(a) "archipelagic State" means a State constituted wholly by one or more archipelagos and may include other islands;

(b) "archipelago" means a group of islands, including parts of islands, interconnecting waters and other natural features which are so closely interrelated that such islands, waters and other natural features form an intrinsic geographical, economic and political entity, or which historically have been regarded as such.

Article 47

Archipelagic Baselines

1. An archipelagic State may draw straight archipelagic baselines joining the outermost points of the outermost islands and drying reefs of the archipelago provided that within such baselines are included the main islands and an area in which the ratio of the area of the water to the area of the land, including atolls, is between 1 to 1 and 9 to 1.

2. The length of such baselines shall not exceed 100 nautical miles, except that up to 3 per cent of the total number of baselines enclosing any archipelago may exceed that length, up to a maximum length of 125 nautical miles.

3. The drawing of such baselines shall not depart to any appreciable extent from the general configuration of the archipelago.

4. Such baselines shall not be drawn to and from low-tide elevations, unless lighthouses or similar installations which are permanently above sea level have been built on them or where a low-tide elevation is situated wholly or partly at a distance not exceeding the breadth of the territorial sea from the nearest island.

5. The system of such baselines shall not be applied by an archipelagic State in such a manner as to cut off from the high seas or the exclusive economic zone the territorial sea of another State.

6. If a part of the archipelagic waters of an archipelagic State lies between two parts of an immediately adjacent neighbouring State, existing rights and all other legitimate interests which the latter State has traditionally exercised in such waters and all rights stipulated by agreement between those States shall continue and be respected.

7. For the purpose of computing the ratio of water to land under paragraph 1, land areas may include waters lying within the fringing reefs of islands and atolls, including that part of a steep-sided oceanic plateau which is enclosed or nearly enclosed by a chain of limestone islands and drying reefs lying on the perimeter of the plateau.

8. The baselines drawn in accordance with this article shall be shown on charts of a scale or scales adequate for ascertaining their position. Alternatively, lists of geographical co-ordinates of points, specifying the geodetic datum, may be substituted.

9. The archipelagic State shall give due publicity to such charts or lists of geographical co-ordinates and shall deposit a copy of each such chart or list with the Secretary–General of the United Nations.

Article 48

Measurement of the Breadth of the Territorial Sea, the Contiguous Zone, the Exclusive Economic Zone and the Continental Shelf

The breadth of the territorial sea, the contiguous zone, the exclusive economic zone and the continental shelf shall be measured from archipelagic baselines drawn in accordance with article 47.

Article 49

Legal Status of Archipelagic Waters, of the Air Space Over Archipelagic Waters and of Their Bed and Subsoil

1. The sovereignty of an archipelagic State extends to the waters enclosed by the archipelagic baselines drawn in accordance with article 47, described as archipelagic waters, regardless of their depth or distance from the coast.

2. This sovereignty extends to the air space over the archipelagic waters, as well as to their bed and subsoil, and the resources contained therein.

3. This sovereignty is exercised subject to this Part.

4. The regime of archipelagic sea lanes passage established in this Part shall not in other respects affect the status of the archipelagic waters, including the sea lanes, or the exercise by the archipelagic State of its sovereignty over such waters and their air space, bed and subsoil, and the resources contained therein.

Article 50

Delimitation of Internal Waters

Within its archipelagic waters, the archipelagic State may draw closing lines for the delimitation of internal waters, in accordance with articles 9, 10 and 11.

Article 51

Existing Agreements, Traditional Fishing Rights and Existing Submarine Cables

1. Without prejudice to Article 49, an archipelagic State shall respect existing agreements with other States and shall recognize traditional fishing rights and other legitimate activities of the immediately adjacent neighbouring States in certain areas falling within archipelagic waters. The terms and conditions for the exercise of such rights and activities, including the nature, the extent and the areas to which they apply, shall, at the request of any of the States concerned, be regulated by bilateral agreements between them. Such rights shall not be transferred to or shared with third States or their nationals.

2. An archipelagic State shall respect existing submarine cables laid by other States and passing through its waters without making a landfall. An archipelagic State shall permit the maintenance and replacement of such cables upon receiving due notice of their location and the intention to repair or replace them.

Article 52

Right of Innocent Passage

1. Subject to Article 53 and without prejudice to article 50, ships of all States enjoy the right of innocent passage through archipelagic waters, in accordance with Part II, section 3.

2. The archipelagic State may, without discrimination in form or in fact among foreign ships, suspend temporarily in specified areas of its archipelagic waters the innocent passage of foreign ships if such suspension is essential for the protection of its security. Such suspension shall take effect only after having been duly published.

Article 53

Right of Archipelagic Sea Lanes Passage

1. An archipelagic State may designate sea lanes and air routes thereabove, suitable for the continuous and expeditious passage of foreign ships and aircraft through or over its archipelagic waters and the adjacent territorial sea.

2. All ships and aircraft enjoy the right of archipelagic sea lanes passage in such sea lanes and air routes.

3. Archipelagic sea lanes passage means the exercise in accordance with this Convention of the rights of navigation and overflight in the normal mode solely for the purpose of continuous, expeditious and unobstructed transit between one part of the high seas or an exclusive economic zone and another part of the high seas or an exclusive economic zone.

4. Such sea lanes and air routes shall traverse the archipelagic waters and the adjacent territorial sea and shall include all normal passage routes used as routes for international navigation or overflight through or over archipelagic waters and, within such routes, so far as ships are concerned, all normal navigational channels, provided that duplication of routes of similar convenience between the same entry and exit points shall not be necessary.

5. Such sea lanes and air routes shall be defined by a series of continuous axis lines from the entry points of passage routes to the exit points. Ships and aircraft in archipelagic sea lanes passage shall not deviate more than 25 nautical miles to either side of such axis lines during passage, provided that such ships and aircraft shall not navigate closer to the coasts than 10 per cent of the distance between the nearest points on islands bordering the sea lane.

6. An archipelagic State which designates sea lanes under this article may also prescribe traffic separation schemes for the safe passage of ships through narrow channels in such sea lanes.

7. An archipelagic State may, when circumstances require, after giving due publicity thereto, substitute other sea lanes or traffic separation schemes for any sea lanes or traffic separation schemes previously designated or prescribed by it.

8. Such sea lanes and traffic separation schemes shall conform to generally accepted international regulations.

9. In designating or substituting sea lanes or prescribing or substituting traffic separation schemes, an archipelagic State shall refer proposals to the competent international organization with a view to their adoption. The organization may adopt only such sea lanes and traffic

separation schemes as may be agreed with the archipelagic State, after which the archipelagic State may designate, prescribe or substitute them.

10. The archipelagic State shall clearly indicate the axis of the sea lanes and the traffic separation schemes designated or prescribed by it on charts to which due publicity shall be given.

11. Ships in archipelagic sea lanes passage shall respect applicable sea lanes and traffic separation schemes established in accordance with this article.

12. If an archipelagic State does not designate sea lanes or air routes, the right of archipelagic sea lanes passage may be exercised through the routes normally used for internal navigation.

Article 54

Duties of Ships and Aircraft During Their Passage, Research and Survey Activities, Duties of the Archipelagic State and Laws and Regulations of the Archipelagic State Relating to Archipelagic Sea Lanes Passage

Articles 39, 40, 42 and 44 apply *mutatis mutandis* to archipelagic sea lanes passage.

PART V. EXCLUSIVE ECONOMIC ZONE

Article 55

Specific Legal Regime of the Exclusive Economic Zone

The exclusive economic zone is an area beyond and adjacent to the territorial sea, subject to the specific legal regime established in this Part, under which the rights and jurisdiction of the coastal State and the rights and freedoms of other States are governed by the relevant provisions of this Convention.

Article 56

Rights, Jurisdiction and Duties of the Coastal State in the Exclusive Economic Zone

1. In the exclusive economic zone, the coastal State has:

(a) sovereign rights for the purpose of exploring and exploiting, conserving and managing the natural resources, whether living or non-living, of the waters superjacent to the sea-bed and of the sea-bed and its subsoil, and with regard to other activities for the economic exploitation and exploration of the zone, such as the production of energy from the water, currents and winds;

(b) jurisdiction as provided for in the relevant provisions of this Convention with regard to:

(i) the establishment and use of artificial islands, installations and structures;

(ii) marine scientific research;

(iii) the protection and preservation of the marine environment;

(c) other rights and duties provided for in this Convention.

2. In exercising its rights and performing its duties under this Convention in the exclusive economic zone, the coastal State shall have due regard to the rights and duties of other States and shall act in a manner compatible with the provisions of this Convention.

3. The rights set out in this article with respect to the sea-bed and subsoil shall be exercised in accordance with Part VI.

Article 57

Breadth of the Exclusive Economic Zone

The exclusive economic zone shall not extend beyond 200 nautical miles from the baselines from which the breadth of the territorial sea is measured.

Article 58

Rights and Duties of Other States in the Exclusive Economic Zone

1. In the exclusive economic zone all States, whether coastal or land-locked, enjoy, subject to the relevant provisions of this Convention, the freedoms referred to in article 87 of navigation and overflight and of the laying of submarine cables and pipelines, and other internationally lawful uses of the sea related to these freedoms, such as those associated with the operation of ships, aircraft and submarine cables and pipelines, and compatible with the other provisions of this Convention.

2. Articles 88 to 115 and other pertinent rules of international law apply to the exclusive economic zone in so far as they are not incompatible with this Part.

3. In exercising their rights and performing their duties under this Convention in the exclusive economic zone, States shall have due regard to the rights and duties of the coastal State and shall comply with the laws and regulations adopted by the coastal State in accordance with the provisions of this Convention and other rules of international law in so far as they are not incompatible with this Part.

Article 59

Basis for the Resolution of Conflicts Regarding the Attribution of Rights and Jurisdiction in the Exclusive Economic Zone

In cases where this Convention does not attribute rights or jurisdiction to the coastal State or to other States within the exclusive economic zone, and a conflict arises between the interests of the coastal State and any other State or States, the conflict should be resolved on the basis of equity and in the light of all the relevant circumstances, taking into account the respective importance of the interests involved to the parties as well as to the international community as a whole.

Article 60

Artificial Islands, Installations and Structures in the Exclusive Economic Zone

1. In the exclusive economic zone, the coastal State shall have the exclusive right to construct and to authorize and regulate the construction, operation and use of:

(a) artificial islands;

(b) installations and structures for the purposes provided for in article 56 and other economic purposes;

(c) installations and structures which may interfere with the exercise of the rights of the coastal State in the zone.

2. The coastal State shall have exclusive jurisdiction over such artificial islands installations and structures, including jurisdiction with regard to customs, fiscal, health, safety and immigration laws and regulations.

3. Due notice must be given of the construction of such artificial islands, installations or structures, and permanent means for giving warning of their presence must be maintained. Any installations or structures which are abandoned or disused shall be removed to ensure safety of navigation, taking into account any generally accepted international standards established in this regard by the competent international organization. Such removal shall also have due regard to fishing, the protection of the marine environment and the rights and duties of other States. Appropriate publicity shall be given to the depth, position and dimensions of any installations or structures not entirely removed.

4. The coastal State may, where necessary, establish reasonable safety zones around such artificial islands, installations and structures in which it may take appropriate measures to ensure the safety both of navigation and of the artificial islands, installations and structures.

5. The breadth of the safety zones shall be determined by the coastal State, taking into account applicable international standards. Such zones shall be designed to ensure that they are reasonably related to the nature and function of the artificial islands, installations or structures, and shall not exceed a distance of 500 metres around them, measured from each point of their outer edge, except as authorized by generally accepted international standards or as recommended by the competent international organization. Due notice shall be given of the extent of safety zones.

6. All ships must respect these safety zones and shall comply with generally accepted international standards regarding navigation in the vicinity of artificial islands, installations, structures and safety zones.

7. Artificial islands, installations and structures and the safety zones around them may not be established where interference may be caused to the use of recognized sea lanes essential to international navigation.

8. Artificial islands, installations and structures do not possess the status of islands. They have no territorial sea of their own, and their

presence does not affect the delimitation of the territorial sea, the exclusive economic zone or the continental shelf.

Article 61

Conservation of the Living Resources

1. The coastal State shall determine the allowable catch of the living resources in its exclusive economic zone.

2. The coastal State, taking into account the best scientific evidence available to it, shall ensure through proper conservation and management measures that the maintenance of the living resources in the exclusive economic zone is not endangered by over-exploitation. As appropriate, the coastal State and competent international organizations, whether subregional, regional or global, shall co-operate to this end.

3. Such measures shall also be designed to maintain or restore populations of harvested species at levels which can produce the maximum sustainable yield, as qualified by relevant environmental and economic factors, including the economic needs of coastal fishing communities and the special requirements of developing States, and taking into account fishing patterns, the interdependence of stocks and any generally recommended international minimum standards, whether subregional, regional or global.

4. In taking such measures the coastal State shall take into consideration the effects on species associated with or dependent upon harvested species with a view to maintaining or restoring populations of such associated or dependent species above levels at which their reproduction may become seriously threatened.

5. Available scientific information, catch and fishing effort statistics, and other data relevant to the conservation of fish stocks shall be contributed and exchanged on a regular basis through competent international organizations, whether subregional, regional or global, where appropriate and with participation by all States concerned, including States whose nationals are allowed to fish in the exclusive economic zone.

Article 62

Utilization of the Living Resources

1. The coastal State shall promote the objective of optimum utilization of the living resources in the exclusive economic zone without prejudice to article 61.

2. The coastal State shall determine its capacity to harvest the living resources of the exclusive economic zone. Where the coastal State does not have the capacity to harvest the entire allowable catch, it shall, through agreements or other arrangements and pursuant to the terms, conditions, laws and regulations referred to in paragraph 4, give other States access to the surplus of the allowable catch, having particular regard to the provisions of articles 69 and 70, especially in relation to the developing States mentioned therein.

3. In giving access to other States to its exclusive economic zone under this article the coastal State shall take into account all relevant factors, including, *inter alia*, the significance of the living resources of the area to the economy of the coastal State concerned and its other national interests, the provisions of articles 69 and 70, the requirements of developing States in the subregion or region in harvesting part of the surplus and the need to minimize economic dislocation in States whose nationals have habitually fished in the zone or which have made substantial efforts in research and identification of stocks.

4. Nationals of other States fishing in the exclusive economic zone shall comply with the conservation measures and with the other terms and conditions established in the laws and regulations of the coastal State. These laws and regulations shall be consistent with this Convention and may relate, *inter alia*, to the following:

(a) licensing of fishermen, fishing vessels and equipment, including payment of fees and other forms of remuneration, which, in the case of developing coastal States, may consist of adequate compensation in the field of financing, equipment and technology relating to the fishing industry;

(b) determining the species which may be caught, and fixing quotas of catch, whether in relation to particular stocks or groups of stocks or catch per vessel over a period of time or to the catch by nationals of any State during a specified period;

(c) regulating seasons and areas of fishing, the types, sizes and amount of gear, and the types, sizes and number of fishing vessels that may be used;

(d) fixing the age and size of fish and other species that may be caught;

(e) specifying information required of fishing vessels, including catch and effort statistics and vessel position reports;

(f) requiring, under the authorization and control of the coastal State, the conduct of specified fisheries research programmes and regulating the conduct of such research, including the sampling of catches, disposition of samples and reporting of associated scientific data;

(g) the placing of observers or trainees on board such vessels by the coastal State;

(h) the landing of all or any part of the catch by such vessels in the ports of the coastal State;

(i) terms and conditions relating to joint ventures or other co-operative arrangements;

(j) requirements for the training of personnel and the transfer of fisheries technology, including enhancement of the coastal State's capability of undertaking fisheries research;

(k) enforcement procedures.

5. Coastal States shall give due notice of conservation and management laws and regulations.

Article 63

Stocks Occurring Within the Exclusive Economic Zones of Two or More Coastal States or Both Within the Exclusive Economic Zone and in an Area Beyond and Adjacent to It

1. Where the same stock or stocks of associated species occur within the exclusive economic zones of two or more coastal States, these States shall seek, either directly or through appropriate subregional or regional organizations, to agree upon the measures necessary to co-ordinate and ensure the conservation and development of such stocks without prejudice to the other provisions of this Part.

2. Where the same stock or stocks of associated species occur both within the exclusive economic zone and in an area beyond and adjacent to the zone, the coastal State and the States fishing for such stocks in the adjacent area shall seek, either directly or through appropriate subregional or regional organizations, to agree upon the measures necessary for the conservation of these stocks in the adjacent area.

Article 64

Highly Migratory Species

1. The coastal State and other States whose nationals fish in the region for the highly migratory species listed in Annex I shall co-operate directly or through appropriate international organizations with a view to ensuring conservation and promoting the objective of optimum utilization of such species throughout the region, both within and beyond the exclusive economic zone. In regions for which no appropriate international organization exists, the coastal State and other States whose nationals harvest these species in the region shall co-operate to establish such an organization and participate in its work.

2. The provisions of paragraph 1 apply in addition to the other provisions of this Part.

Article 65

Marine Mammals

Nothing in this Part restricts the right of a coastal State or the competence of an international organization, as appropriate, to prohibit, limit or regulate the exploitation of marine mammals more strictly than provided for in this Part. States shall co-operate with a view to the conservation of marine mammals and in the case of cetaceans shall in particular work through the appropriate international organizations for their conservation, management and study.

Article 66

Anadromous Stocks

1. States in whose rivers anadromous stocks originate shall have the primary interest in and responsibility for such stocks.

2. The State of origin of anadromous stocks shall ensure their conservation by the establishment of appropriate regulatory measures for fishing in all waters landward of the outer limits of its exclusive economic zone and for fishing provided for in paragraph 3(b). The State of origin may, after consultations with the other States referred to in paragraphs 3 and 4 fishing these stocks, establish total allowable catches for stocks originating in its rivers.

3. (a) Fisheries for anadromous stocks shall be conducted only in waters landward of the outer limits of exclusive economic zones, except in cases where this provision would result in economic dislocation for a State other than the State of origin. With respect to such fishing beyond the outer limits of the exclusive economic zone, States concerned shall maintain consultations with a view to achieving agreement on terms and conditions of such fishing giving due regard to the conservation requirements and the needs of the State of origin in respect of these stocks.

(b) The State of origin shall co-operate in minimizing economic dislocation in such other States fishing these stocks, taking into account the normal catch and the mode of operations of such States, and all the areas in which such fishing has occurred.

(c) States referred to in subparagraph (b), participating by agreement with the State of origin in measures to renew anadromous stocks, particularly by expenditures for that purpose, shall be given special consideration by the State of origin in the harvesting of stocks originating in its rivers.

(d) Enforcement of regulations regarding anadromous stocks beyond the exclusive economic zone shall be by agreement between the State of origin and the other States concerned.

4. In cases where anadromous stocks migrate into or through the waters landward of the outer limits of the exclusive economic zone of a State other than the State of origin, such State shall co-operate with the State of origin with regard to the conservation and management of such stocks.

5. The State of origin of anadromous stocks and other States fishing these stocks shall make arrangements for the implementation of the provisions of this article, where appropriate, through regional organizations.

Article 67

Catadromous Species

1. A coastal State in whose waters catadromous species spend the greater part of their life cycle shall have responsibility for the management of these species and shall ensure the ingress and egress of migrating fish.

2. Harvesting of catadromous species shall be conducted only in waters landward of the outer limits of exclusive economic zones. When conducted in exclusive economic zones, harvesting shall be subject to this article and the other provisions of this Convention concerning fishing in these zones.

3. In cases where catadromous fish migrate through the exclusive economic zone of another State, whether as juvenile or maturing fish, the management, including harvesting, of such fish shall be regulated by agreement between the State mentioned in paragraph 1 and the other State concerned. Such agreement shall ensure the rational management of the species and take into account the responsibilities of the State mentioned in paragraph 1 for the maintenance of these species.

Article 68

Sedentary Species

This Part does not apply to sedentary species as defined in article 77, paragraph 4.

Article 69

Right of Land–Locked States

1. Land-locked States shall have the right to participate, on an equitable basis, in the exploitation of an appropriate part of the surplus of the living resources of the exclusive economic zones of coastal States of the same subregion or region, taking into account the relevant economic and geographical circumstances of all the States concerned and in conformity with the provisions of this article and of articles 61 and 62.

2. The terms and modalities of such participation shall be established by the States concerned through bilateral, subregional or regional agreements taking into account, *inter alia*:

(a) the need to avoid effects detrimental to fishing communities or fishing industries of the coastal State;

(b) the extent to which the land-locked State, in accordance with the provisions of this article, is participating or is entitled to participate under existing bilateral, subregional or regional agreements in the exploitation of living resources of the exclusive economic zones of other coastal States;

(c) the extent to which other land-locked States and geographically disadvantaged States are participating in the exploitation of the living resources of the exclusive economic zone of the coastal State and the consequent need to avoid a particular burden for any single coastal State or a part of it;

(d) the nutritional needs of the populations of the respective States.

3. When the harvesting capacity of a coastal State approaches a point which would enable it to harvest the entire allowable catch of the living resources in its exclusive economic zone, the coastal State and other States concerned shall co-operate in the establishment of equitable arrangements on a bilateral, subregional or regional basis to allow for participation of developing land-locked States of the same subregion or region in the exploitation of the living resources of the exclusive economic zones of coastal States of the subregion or region, as may be appropriate in the circumstances and on terms satisfactory to all parties. In the

implementation of this provision the factors mentioned in paragraph 2 shall also be taken into account.

4. Developed land-locked States shall, under the provisions of this article, be entitled to participate in the exploitation of living resources only in the exclusive economic zones of developed coastal States of the same subregion or region having regard to the extent to which the coastal State, in giving access to other States to the living resources of its exclusive economic zone, has taken into account the need to minimize detrimental effects on fishing communities and economic dislocation in States whose nationals have habitually fished in the zone.

5. The above provisions are without prejudice to arrangements agreed upon in subregions or regions where the coastal States may grant to land-locked States of the same subregion or region equal or preferential rights for the exploitation of the living resources in the exclusive economic zones.

Article 70

Right of Geographically Disadvantaged States

1. Geographically disadvantaged States shall have the right to participate, on an equitable basis, in the exploitation of an appropriate part of the surplus of the living resources of the exclusive economic zones of coastal States of the same subregion or region, taking into account the relevant economic and geographical circumstances of all the States concerned and in conformity with the provisions of this article and of articles 61 and 62.

2. For the purposes of this Part, "geographically disadvantaged States" means coastal States, including States bordering enclosed or semi-enclosed seas, whose geographical situation makes them dependent upon the exploitation of the living resources of the exclusive economic zones of other States in the subregion or region for adequate supplies of fish for the nutritional purposes of their populations or parts thereof, and coastal States which can claim no exclusive economic zones of their own.

3. The terms and modalities of such participation shall be established by the States concerned through bilateral, subregional or regional agreements taking into account, *inter alia*:

(a) the need to avoid effects detrimental to fishing communities or fishing industries of the coastal State;

(b) the extent to which the geographically disadvantaged State, in accordance with the provisions of this article, is participating or is entitled to participate under existing bilateral, subregional or regional agreements in the exploitation of living resources of the exclusive economic zones of other coastal States;

(c) the extent to which other geographically disadvantaged States and landlocked States are participating in the exploitation of the living resources of the exclusive economic zone of the coastal State and the consequent need to avoid a particular burden for any single coastal State or a part of it;

(d) the nutritional needs of the populations of the respective States.

4. When the harvesting capacity of a coastal State approaches a point which would enable it to harvest the entire allowable catch of the living resources in its exclusive economic zone, the coastal State and other States concerned shall co-operate in the establishment of equitable arrangements on a bilateral, subregional or regional basis to allow for participation of developing geographically disadvantaged States of the same subregion or region in the exploitation of the living resources of the exclusive economic zones of coastal States of the subregion or region, as may be appropriate in the circumstances and on terms satisfactory to all parties. In the implementation of this provision the factors mentioned in paragraph 3 shall also be taken into account.

5. Developed geographically disadvantaged States shall, under the provisions of this article, be entitled to participate in the exploitation of living resources only in the exclusive economic zones of developed coastal States of the same subregion or region having regard to the extent to which the coastal State, in giving access to other States to the living resources of its exclusive economic zone, has taken into account the need to minimize detrimental effects on fishing communities and economic dislocation in States whose nationals have habitually fished in the zone.

6. The above provisions are without prejudice to arrangements agreed upon in subregions or regions where the coastal States may grant to geographically disadvantaged States of the same subregion or region equal or preferential rights for the exploitation of the living resources in the exclusive economic zones.

Article 71

Non–Applicability of Articles 69 and 70

The provisions of articles 69 and 70 do not apply in the case of a coastal State whose economy is overwhelmingly dependent on the exploitation of the living resources of its exclusive economic zone.

Article 72

Restrictions on Transfer of Rights

1. Rights provided under articles 69 and 70 to exploit living resources shall not be directly or indirectly transferred to third States or their nationals by lease or licence, by establishing joint ventures or in any other manner which has the effect of such transfer unless otherwise agreed by the States concerned.

2. The foregoing provision does not preclude the States concerned from obtaining technical or financial assistance from third States or international organizations in order to facilitate the exercise of the rights pursuant to articles 69 and 70, provided that it does not have the effect referred to in paragraph 1.

Article 73

Enforcement of Laws and Regulations of the Coastal State

1. The coastal State may, in the exercise of its sovereign rights to explore, exploit, conserve and manage the living resources in the exclu-

sive economic zone, take such measures, including boarding, inspection, arrest and judicial proceedings, as may be necessary to ensure compliance with the laws and regulations adopted by it in conformity with this Convention.

2. Arrested vessels and their crews shall be promptly released upon the posting of reasonable bond or other security.

3. Coastal State penalties for violations of fisheries laws and regulations in the exclusive economic zone may not include imprisonment, in the absence of agreements to the contrary by the States concerned, or any other form of corporal punishment.

4. In cases of arrest or detention of foreign vessels the coastal State shall promptly notify the flag State, through appropriate channels, of the action taken and of any penalties subsequently imposed.

Article 74

Delimitation of the Exclusive Economic Zone Between States With Opposite or Adjacent Coasts

1. The delimitation of the exclusive economic zone between States with opposite or adjacent coasts shall be effected by agreement on the basis of international law, as referred to in article 38 of the Statute of the International Court of Justice, in order to achieve an equitable solution.

2. If no agreement can be reached within a reasonable period of time, the States concerned shall resort to the procedures provided for in Part XV.

3. Pending agreement as provided for in paragraph 1, the States concerned, in a spirit of understanding and co-operation, shall make every effort to enter into provisional arrangements of a practical nature and, during this transitional period, not to jeopardize or hamper the reaching of the final agreement. Such arrangements shall be without prejudice to the final delimitation.

4. Where there is an agreement in force between the States concerned, questions relating to the delimitation of the exclusive economic zone shall be determined in accordance with the provisions of that agreement.

Article 75

Charts and Lists of Geographical Co–Ordinates

1. Subject to this Part, the outer limit lines of the exclusive economic zone and the lines of delimitation drawn in accordance with article 74 shall be shown on charts of a scale or scales adequate for ascertaining their position. Where appropriate, lists of geographical co-ordinates of points, specifying the geodetic datum, may be substituted for such outer limit lines or lines of delimitation.

2. The coastal State shall give due publicity to such charts or lists of geographical co-ordinates and shall deposit a copy of each such chart or list with the Secretary–General of the United Nations.

PART VI. CONTINENTAL SHELF

Article 76

Definition of the Continental Shelf

1. The continental shelf of a coastal State comprises the sea-bed and subsoil of the submarine areas that extend beyond its territorial sea throughout the natural prolongation of its land territory to the outer edge of the continental margin, or to a distance of 200 nautical miles from the baselines from which the breadth of the territorial sea is measured where the outer edge of the continental margin does not extend up to that distance.

2. The continental shelf of a coastal State shall not extend beyond the limits provided for in paragraphs 4 to 6.

3. The continental margin comprises the submerged prolongation of the land mass of the coastal State, and consists of the sea-bed and subsoil of the shelf the slope and the rise. It does not include the deep ocean floor with its oceanic ridges or the subsoil thereof.

4. (a) For the purposes of this Convention, the coastal State shall establish the outer edge of the continental margin wherever the margin extends beyond 200 nautical miles from the baselines from which the breadth of the territorial sea is measured, by either:

(i) a line delineated in accordance with paragraph 7 by reference to the outermost fixed points at each of which the thickness of sedimentary rocks is at least 1 per cent of the shortest distance from such point to the foot of the continental slope; or

(ii) a line delineated in accordance with paragraph 7 by reference to fixed points not more than 60 nautical miles from the foot of the continental slope.

(b) In the absence of evidence to the contrary, the foot of the continental slope shall be determined as the point of maximum change in the gradient at its base.

5. The fixed points comprising the line of the outer limits of the continental shelf on the sea-bed, drawn in accordance with paragraph 4(a)(i) and (ii), either shall not exceed 350 nautical miles from the baselines from which the breadth of the territorial sea is measured or shall not exceed 100 nautical miles from the 2,500 metre isobath, which is a line connecting the depth of 2,500 metres.

6. Notwithstanding the provisions of paragraph 5, on submarine ridges, the outer limit of the continental shelf shall not exceed 350 nautical miles from the baselines from which the breadth of the territorial sea is measured. This paragraph does not apply to submarine elevations that are natural components of the continental margin, such as its plateaux, rises, caps, banks and spurs.

7. The coastal State shall delineate the outer limits of its continental shelf, where that shelf extends beyond 200 nautical miles from the baselines from which the breadth of the territorial sea is measured, by

straight lines not exceeding 60 nautical miles in length, connecting fixed points, defined by coordinates of latitude and longitude.

8. Information on the limits of the continental shelf beyond 200 nautical miles from the baselines from which the breadth of the territorial sea is measured shall be submitted by the coastal State to the Commission on the Limits of the Continental Shelf set up under Annex II on the basis of equitable geographical representation. The Commission shall make recommendations to coastal States on matters related to the establishment of the outer limits of their continental shelf. The limits of the shelf established by a coastal State on the basis of these recommendations shall be final and binding.

9. The coastal State shall deposit with the Secretary–General of the United Nations charts and relevant information, including geodetic data, permanently describing the outer limits of its continental shelf. The Secretary–General shall give due publicity thereto.

10. The provisions of this article are without prejudice to the question of delimitation of the continental shelf between States with opposite or adjacent coasts.

Article 77

Rights of the Coastal State Over the Continental Shelf

1. The coastal State exercises over the continental shelf sovereign rights for the purpose of exploring it and exploiting its natural resources.

2. The rights referred to in paragraph 1 are exclusive in the sense that if the coastal State does not explore the continental shelf or exploit its natural resources, no one may undertake these activities without the express consent of the coastal State.

3. The rights of the coastal State over the continental shelf do not depend on occupation, effective or notional, or on any express proclamation.

4. The natural resources referred to in this Part consist of the mineral and other non-living resources of the sea-bed and subsoil together with living organisms belonging to sedentary species, that is to say, organisms which, at the harvestable stage, either are immobile on or under the sea-bed or are unable to move except in constant physical contact with the sea-bed or the subsoil.

Article 78

Legal Status of the Superjacent Waters and Air Space and the Rights and Freedoms of Other States

1. The rights of the coastal State over the continental shelf do not affect the legal status of the superjacent waters or of the air space above those waters.

2. The exercise of the rights of the coastal State over the continental shelf must not infringe or result in any unjustifiable interference with navigation and other rights and freedoms of other States as provided for in this Convention.

Article 79

Submarine Cables and Pipelines on the Continental Shelf

1. All States are entitled to lay submarine cables and pipelines on the continental shelf, in accordance with the provisions of this article.

2. Subject to its right to take reasonable measures for the exploration of the continental shelf, the exploitation of its natural resources and the prevention, reduction and control of pollution from pipelines, the coastal State may not impede the laying or maintenance of such cables or pipelines.

3. The delineation of the course for the laying of such pipelines on the continental shelf is subject to the consent of the coastal State.

4. Nothing in this Part affects the right of the coastal State to establish conditions for cables or pipelines entering its territory or territorial sea, or its jurisdiction over cables and pipelines constructed or used in connection with the exploration of its continental shelf or exploitation of its resources or the operations of artificial islands, installations and structures under its jurisdiction.

5. When laying submarine cables or pipelines, States shall have due regard to cables or pipelines already in position. In particular, possibilities of repairing existing cables or pipelines shall not be prejudiced.

Article 80

Artificial Islands, Installations and Structures on the Continental Shelf

Article 60 applies *mutatis mutandis* to artificial islands, installations and structures on the continental shelf.

Article 81

Drilling on the Continental Shelf

The coastal State shall have the exclusive right to authorize and regulate drilling on the continental shelf for all purposes.

Article 82

Payments and Contributions with Respect to the Exploitation of the Continental Shelf Beyond 200 Nautical Miles

1. The coastal State shall make payments or contributions in kind in respect of the exploitation of the non-living resources of the continental shelf beyond 200 nautical miles from the baselines from which the breadth of the territorial sea is measured.

2. The payments and contributions shall be made annually with respect to all production at a site after the first five years of production at that site. For the sixth year, the rate of payment or contribution shall be 1 per cent of the value or volume of production at the site. The rate shall increase by 1 per cent for each subsequent year until the twelfth year and shall remain at 7 per cent thereafter. Production does not include resources used in connection with exploitation.

3. A developing State which is a net importer of a mineral resource produced from its continental shelf is exempt from making such payments or contributions in respect of that mineral resource.

4. The payments or contributions shall be made through the Authority, which shall distribute them to States Parties to this Convention, on the basis of equitable sharing criteria, taking into account the interests and needs of developing States, particularly the least developed and the land-locked among them.

Article 83

Delimitation of the Continental Shelf Between States with Opposite or Adjacent Coasts

1. The delimitation of the continental shelf between States with opposite or adjacent coasts shall be effected by agreement on the basis of international law, as referred to in article 38 of the Statute of the International Court of Justice, in order to achieve an equitable solution.

2. If no agreement can be reached within a reasonable period of time, the States concerned shall resort to the procedures provided for in Part XV.

3. Pending agreement as provided for in paragraph 1, the States concerned, in a spirit of understanding and co-operation, shall make every effort to enter into provisional arrangements of a practical nature and, during this transitional period, not to jeopardize or hamper the reaching of the final agreement. Such arrangements shall be without prejudice to the final delimitation.

4. Where there is an agreement in force between the States concerned, questions relating to the delimitation of the continental shelf shall be determined in accordance with the provisions of that agreement.

Article 84

Charts and Lists of Geographical Co–Ordinates

1. Subject to this Part, the outer limit lines of the continental shelf and the lines of delimitation drawn in accordance with article 83 shall be shown on charts of a scale or scales adequate for ascertaining their position. Where appropriate, lists of geographical co-ordinates of points, specifying the geodetic datum, may be substituted for such outer limit lines or lines of delimitation.

2. The coastal State shall give due publicity to such charts or lists of graphical co-ordinates and shall deposit a copy of each such chart or list with the Secretary–General of the United Nations and, in the case of those showing the outer limit lines of the continental shelf, with the Secretary–General of the Authority.

Article 85

Tunnelling

This Part does not prejudice the right of the coastal State to exploit the subsoil by means of tunnelling, irrespective of the depth of water above the subsoil.

PART VII. HIGH SEAS

Section 1. General Provisions

Article 86

Application of the Provisions of this Part

The provisions of this Part apply to all parts of the sea that are not included in the exclusive economic zone, in the territorial sea or in the internal waters of a State, or in the archipelagic waters of an archipelagic State. This article does not entail any abridgement of the freedoms enjoyed by all States in the exclusive economic zone in accordance with article 58.

Article 87

Freedom of the High Seas

1. The high seas are open to all States, whether coastal or land-locked. Freedom of the high seas is exercised under the conditions laid down by this Convention and by other rules of international law. It comprises, *inter alia*, both for coastal and land-locked States:

(a) freedom of navigation;

(b) freedom of overflight;

(c) freedom to lay submarine cables and pipelines, subject to Part VI;

(d) freedom to construct artificial islands and other installations permitted under international law, subject to Part VI;

(e) freedom of fishing, subject to the conditions laid down in section 2;

(f) freedom of scientific research, subject to Parts VI and XIII.

2. These freedoms shall be exercised by all States with due regard for the interests of other States in their exercise of the freedom of the high seas, and also with due regard for the rights under this Convention with respect to activities in the Area.

Article 88

Reservation of the High Seas for Peaceful Purposes

The high seas shall be reserved for peaceful purposes.

Article 89

Invalidity of Claims of Sovereignty Over the High Seas

No State may validly purport to subject any part of the high seas to its sovereignty.

Article 90

Right of Navigation

Every State, whether coastal or land-locked, has the right to sail ships flying its flag on the high seas.

Article 91

Nationality of Ships

1. Every State shall fix the conditions for the grant of its nationality to ships, for the registration of ships in its territory, and for the right to fly its flag. Ships have the nationality of the State whose flag they are entitled to fly. There must exist a genuine link between the State and the ship.

2. Every State shall issue to ships to which it has granted the right to fly its flag documents to that effect.

Article 92

Status of Ships

1. Ships shall sail under the flag of one State only and, save in exceptional cases expressly provided for in international treaties or in this Convention, shall be subject to its exclusive jurisdiction on the high seas. A ship may not change its flag during a voyage or while in a port of call, save in the case of a real transfer of ownership or change of registry.

2. A ship which sails under the flags of two or more States, using them according to convenience, may not claim any of the nationalities in question with respect to any other State, and may be assimilated to a ship without nationality.

Article 93

Ships Flying the Flag of the United Nations, Its Specialized Agencies and the International Atomic Energy Agency

The preceding articles do not prejudice the question of ships employed on the official service of the United Nations, its specialized agencies or the International Atomic Energy Agency, flying the flag of the organization.

Article 94

Duties of the Flag State

1. Every State shall effectively exercise its jurisdiction and control in administrative, technical and social matters over ships flying its flag.

2. In particular every State shall:

(a) maintain a register of ships containing the names and particulars of ships flying its flag, except those which are excluded from generally accepted international regulations on account of their small size; and

(b) assume jurisdiction under its internal law over each ship flying its nag and its master, officers and crew in respect of administrative, technical and social matters concerning the ship.

3. Every State shall take such measures for ships flying its flag as are necessary to ensure safety at sea with regard, *inter alia*, to:

(a) the construction, equipment and seaworthiness of ships;

(b) the manning of ships, labour conditions and the training of crews, taking into account the applicable international instruments;

(c) the use of signals, the maintenance of communications and the prevention of collisions.

4. Such measures shall include those necessary to ensure:

(a) that each ship, before registration and thereafter at appropriate intervals, is surveyed by a qualified surveyor of ships, and has on board such charts, nautical publications and navigational equipment and instruments as are appropriate for the safe navigation of the ship;

(b) that each ship is in the charge of a master and officers who possess appropriate qualifications, in particular in seamanship, navigation, communications and marine engineering, and that the crew is appropriate in qualification and numbers for the type, size, machinery and equipment of the ship;

(c) that the master, officers and, to the extent appropriate, the crew are fully conversant with and required to observe the applicable international regulations concerning the safety of life at sea, the prevention of collisions, the prevention, reduction and control of marine pollution, and the maintenance of communications by radio.

5. In taking the measures called for in paragraphs 3 and 4 each State is required to conform to generally accepted international regulations, procedures and practices and to take any steps which may be necessary to secure their observance.

6. A State which has clear grounds to believe that proper jurisdiction and control with respect to a ship have not been exercised may report the facts to the flag State. Upon receiving such a report, the flag State shall investigate the matter and, if appropriate, take any action necessary to remedy the situation.

7. Each State shall cause an inquiry to be held by or before a suitably qualified person or persons into every marine casualty or incident of navigation on the high seas involving a ship flying its flag and causing loss of life or serious injury to nationals of another State or serious damage to ships or installations of another State or to the marine environment. The flag State and the other State shall co-operate in the conduct of any inquiry held by that other State into any such marine casualty or incident of navigation.

Article 95

Immunity of Warships on the High Seas

Warships on the high seas have complete immunity from the jurisdiction of any State other than the flag State.

Article 96

Immunity of Ships Used Only on Government Non–Commercial Service

Ships owned or operated by a State and used only on government non-commercial service shall, on the high seas, have complete immunity from the jurisdiction of any State other than the flag State.

Article 97

Penal Jurisdiction in Matters of Collision
or Any Other Incident of Navigation

1. In the event of a collision or any other incident of navigation concerning a ship on the high seas, involving the penal or disciplinary responsibility of the master or of any other person in the service of the ship, no penal or disciplinary proceedings may be instituted against such person except before the judicial or administrative authorities either of the flag State or of the State of which such person is a national.

2. In disciplinary matters, the State which has issued a master's certificate or a certificate of competence or licence shall alone be competent, after due legal process, to pronounce the withdrawal of such certificates, even if the holder is not a national of the State which issued them.

3. No arrest or detention of the ship, even as a measure of investigation, shall be ordered by any authorities other than those of the flag State.

Article 98

Duty to Render Assistance

1. Every State shall require the master of a ship flying its flag, in so far as he can do so without serious danger to the ship, the crew or the passengers:

(a) to render assistance to any person found at sea in danger of being lost;

(b) to proceed with all possible speed to the rescue of persons in distress, if informed of their need of assistance, in so far as such action may reasonably be expected of him;

(c) after a collision, to render assistance to the other ship, its crew and its passengers and, where possible, to inform the other ship of the name of his own ship, its port of registry and the nearest port at which it will call.

2. Every coastal State shall promote the establishment, operation and maintenance of an adequate and effective search and rescue service regarding safety on and over the sea and, where circumstances so require, by way of mutual regional arrangements co-operate with neighbouring States for this purpose.

Article 99

Prohibition of the Transport of Slaves

Every State shall take effective measures to prevent and punish the transport of slaves in ships authorized to fly its flag and to prevent the unlawful use of its flag for that purpose. Any slave taking refuge on board any ship, whatever its flag, shall *ipso facto* be free.

Article 100

Duty to Co–Operate in the Repression of Piracy

All States shall co-operate to the fullest possible extent in the repression of piracy on the high seas or in any other place outside the jurisdiction of any State.

Article 101

Definition of Piracy

Piracy consists of any of the following acts:

(a) any illegal acts of violence or detention, or any act of depredation, committed for private ends by the crew or the passengers of a private ship or a private aircraft, and directed:

(i) on the high seas, against another ship or aircraft, or against persons or property on board such ship or aircraft;

(ii) against a ship, aircraft, persons or property in a place outside the jurisdiction of any State;

(b) any act of voluntary participation in the operation of a ship or of an aircraft with knowledge of facts making it a pirate ship or aircraft;

(c) any act of inciting or of intentionally facilitating an act described in subparagraph (a) or (b).

Article 102

Piracy by a Warship, Government Ship or Government Aircraft Whose Crew Has Mutinied

The acts of piracy, as defined in Article 101, committed by a warship, government ship or government aircraft whose crew has mutinied and taken control of the ship or aircraft are assimilated to acts committed by a private ship or aircraft.

Article 103

Definition of a Pirate Ship or Aircraft

A ship or aircraft is considered a pirate ship or aircraft if it is intended by the persons in dominant control to be used for the purpose of committing one of the acts referred to in Article 101. The same applies if the ship or aircraft has been used to commit any such act, so long as it remains under the control of the persons guilty of that act.

Article 104

Retention or Loss of the Nationality of a Pirate Ship or Aircraft

A ship or aircraft may retain its nationality although it has become a pirate ship or aircraft. The retention or loss of nationality is determined by the law of the State from which such nationality was derived.

Article 105

Seizure of a Pirate Ship or Aircraft

On the high seas, or in any other place outside the jurisdiction of any State, every State may seize a pirate ship or aircraft, or a ship or aircraft taken by piracy and under the control of pirates, and arrest the persons and seize the property on board. The courts of the State which carried out the seizure may decide upon the penalties to be imposed, and may also determine the action to be taken with regard to the ships, aircraft or property, subject to the rights of third parties acting in good faith.

Article 106

Liability for Seizure Without Adequate Grounds

Where the seizure of a ship or aircraft on suspicion of piracy has been effected without adequate grounds, the State making the seizure shall be liable to the State the nationality of which is possessed by the ship or aircraft for any loss or damage caused by the seizure.

Article 107

Ships and Aircraft Which are Entitled to Seize on Account of Piracy

A seizure on account of piracy may be carried out only by warships or military aircraft, or other ships or aircraft clearly marked and identifiable as being on government service and authorized to that effect.

Article 108

Illicit Traffic in Narcotic Drugs or Psychotropic Substances

1. All States shall co-operate in the suppression of illicit traffic in narcotic drugs and psychotropic substances engaged in by ships on the high seas contrary to international conventions.

2. Any State which has reasonable grounds for believing that a ship flying its flag is engaged in illicit traffic in narcotic drugs or psychotropic substances may request the co-operation of other States to suppress such traffic.

Article 109

Unauthorized Broadcasting from the High Seas

1. All States shall co-operate in the suppression of unauthorized broadcasting from the high seas.

2. For the purposes of this Convention, "unauthorized broadcasting" means the transmission of sound radio or television broadcasts from a ship or installation on the high seas intended for reception by the general public contrary to international regulations, but excluding the transmission of distress calls.

3. Any person engaged in unauthorized broadcasting may be prosecuted before the court of:

(a) the flag State of the ship;

(b) the State of registry of the installation;

(c) the State of which the person is a national;

(d) any State where the transmissions can be received; or

(e) any State where authorized radio communication is suffering interference.

4. On the high seas, a State having jurisdiction in accordance with paragraph 3 may, in conformity with Article 110, arrest any person or ship engaged in unauthorized broadcasting and seize the broadcasting apparatus.

Article 110

Right of Visit

1. Except where acts of interference derive from powers conferred by treaty, a warship which encounters on the high seas a foreign ship, other than a ship entitled to complete immunity in accordance with articles 95 and 96, is not justified in boarding it unless there is reasonable ground for suspecting that:

(a) the ship is engaged in piracy;

(b) the ship is engaged in the slave trade;

(c) the ship is engaged in unauthorized broadcasting and the flag State of the warship has jurisdiction under article 109;

(d) the ship is without nationality; or

(e) though flying a foreign flag or refusing to show its flag, the ship is, in reality, of the same nationality as the warship.

2. In the cases provided for in paragraph 1, the warship may proceed to verify the ship's right to fly its flag. To this end, it may send a boat under the command of an officer to the suspected ship. If suspicion remains after the documents have been checked, it may proceed to a further examination on board the ship, which must be carried out with all possible consideration.

3. If the suspicions prove to be unfounded, and provided that the ship boarded has not committed any act justifying them, it shall be compensated for any loss or damage that may have been sustained.

4. These provisions apply *mutatis mutandis* to military aircraft.

5. These provisions also apply to any other duly authorized ships or aircraft clearly marked and identifiable as being on government service.

Article 111

Right of Hot Pursuit

1. The hot pursuit of a foreign ship may be undertaken when the competent authorities of the coastal State have good reason to believe that the ship has violated the laws and regulations of that State. Such pursuit must be commenced when the foreign ship or one of its boats is within the internal waters, the archipelagic waters, the territorial sea or the contiguous zone of the pursuing State, and may only be continued outside the territorial sea or the contiguous zone if the pursuit has not been interrupted. It is not necessary that, at the time when the foreign ship within the territorial sea or the contiguous zone receives the order

to stop, the ship giving the order should likewise be within the territorial sea or the contiguous zone. If the foreign ship is within a contiguous zone, as defined in Article 33, the pursuit may only be undertaken if there has been a violation of the rights for the protection of which the zone was established.

2. The right of hot pursuit shall apply *mutatis mutandis* to violations in the exclusive economic zone or on the continental shelf, including safety zones around continental shelf installations, of the laws and regulations of the coastal State applicable in accordance with this Convention to the exclusive economic zone or the continental shelf, including such safety zones.

3. The right of hot pursuit ceases as soon as the ship pursued enters the territorial sea of its own State or of a third State.

4. Hot pursuit is not deemed to have begun unless the pursuing ship has satisfied itself by such practicable means as may be available that the ship pursued or one of its boats or other craft working as a team and using the ship pursued as a mother ship is within the limits of the territorial sea, or, as the case may be, within the contiguous zone or the exclusive economic zone or above the continental shelf. The pursuit may only be commenced after a visual or auditory signal to stop has been given at a distance which enables it to be seen or heard by the foreign ship.

5. The right of hot pursuit may be exercised only by warships or military aircraft, or other ships or aircraft clearly marked and identifiable as being on government service and authorized to that effect.

6. Where hot pursuit is effected by an aircraft:

(a) the provisions of paragraphs 1 to 4 shall apply *mutatis mutandis*;

(b) the aircraft giving the order to stop must itself actively pursue the ship until a ship or another aircraft of the coastal State, summoned by the aircraft, arrives to take over the pursuit, unless the aircraft is itself able to arrest the ship. It does not suffice to justify an arrest outside the territorial sea that the ship was merely sighted by the aircraft as an offender or suspected offender, if it was not both ordered to stop and pursued by the aircraft itself or other aircraft or ships which continue the pursuit without interruption.

7. The release of a ship arrested within the jurisdiction of a State and escorted to a port of that State for the purposes of an inquiry before the competent authorities may not be claimed solely on the ground that the ship, in the course of its voyage, was escorted across a portion of the exclusive economic zone or the high seas, if the circumstances rendered this necessary.

8. Where a ship has been stopped or arrested outside the territorial sea in circumstances which do not justify the exercise of the right of hot pursuit, it shall be compensated for any loss or damage that may have been thereby sustained.

Article 112

Right to Lay Submarine Cables and Pipelines

1. All States are entitled to lay submarine cables and pipelines on the bed of the high seas beyond the continental shelf.

2. Article 79, paragraph 5, applies to such cables and pipelines.

Article 113

Breaking or Injury of a Submarine Cable or Pipeline

Every State shall adopt the laws and regulations necessary to provide that the breaking or injury by a ship flying its flag or by a person subject to its jurisdiction of a submarine cable beneath the high seas done wilfully or through culpable negligence, in such a manner as to be liable to interrupt or obstruct telegraphic or telephonic communications, and similarly the breaking or injury of a submarine pipeline or high-voltage power cable, shall be a punishable offence. This provision shall apply also to conduct calculated or likely to result in such breaking or injury. However, it shall not apply to any break or injury caused by persons who acted merely with the legitimate object of saving their lives or their ships, after having taken all necessary precautions to avoid such break or injury.

Article 114

Breaking or Injury by Owners of a Submarine Cable or Pipeline of Another Submarine Cable or Pipeline

Every State shall adopt the laws and regulations necessary to provide that, if persons subject to its jurisdiction who are the owners of a submarine cable or pipeline beneath the high seas, in laying or repairing that cable or pipeline, cause a break in or injury to another cable or pipeline, they shall bear the cost of the repairs.

Article 115

Indemnity for Loss Incurred in Avoiding Injury to a Submarine Cable or Pipeline

Every State shall adopt the laws and regulations necessary to ensure that the owners of ships who can prove that they have sacrificed an anchor, a net or any other fishing gear, in order to avoid injuring a submarine cable or pipeline, shall be indemnified by the owner of the cable or pipeline, provided that the owner of the ship has taken all reasonable precautionary measures beforehand.

Section 2. Conservation and Management of the Living Resources of the High Seas

Article 116

Right to Fish on the High Seas

All States have the right for their nationals to engage in fishing on the high seas subject to:

(a) their treaty obligations;

(b) the rights and duties as well as the interests of coastal States provided for, *inter alia*, in article 63, paragraph 2, and articles 64 to 67; and

(c) the provisions of this section.

Article 117

Duty of States to Adopt With Respect to Their Nationals Measures for the Conservation of the Living Resources of the High Seas

All States have the duty to take, or to co-operate with other States in taking, such measures for their respective nationals as may be necessary for the conservation of the living resources of the high seas.

Article 118

Co–Operation of States in the Conservation and Management of Living Resources

States shall co-operate with each other in the conservation and management of living resources in the areas of the high seas. States whose nationals exploit identical living resources, or different living resources in the same area, shall enter into negotiations with a view to taking the measures necessary for the conservation of the living resources concerned. They shall, as appropriate, cooperate to establish subregional or regional fisheries organizations to this end.

Article 119

Conservation of the Living Resources of the High Seas

1. In determining the allowable catch and establishing other conservation measures for the living resources in the high seas, States shall:

(a) take measures which are designed, on the best scientific evidence available to the States concerned, to maintain or restore populations of harvested species at levels which can produce the maximum sustainable yield, as qualified by relevant environmental and economic factors, including the special requirements of developing States, and taking into account fishing patterns, the interdependence of stocks and any generally recommended international minimum standards, whether subregional, regional or global;

(b) take into consideration the effects on species associated with or dependent upon harvested species with a view to maintaining or restoring populations of such associated or dependent species above levels at which their reproduction may become seriously threatened.

2. Available scientific information, catch and fishing effort statistics, and other data relevant to the conservation of fish stocks shall be contributed and exchanged on a regular basis through competent international organizations, whether subregional, regional or global, where appropriate and with participation by all States concerned.

3. States concerned shall ensure that conservation measures and their implementation do not discriminate in form or in fact against the fishermen of any State.

Article 120

Marine Mammals

Article 65 also applies to the conservation and management of marine mammals in the high seas.

PART VIII. REGIME OF ISLANDS

Article 121

Regime of Islands

1. An island is a naturally formed area of land, surrounded by water, which is above water at high tide.

2. Except as provided for in paragraph 3, the territorial sea, the contiguous zone, the exclusive economic zone and the continental shelf of an island are determined in accordance with the provisions of this Convention applicable to other land territory.

3. Rocks which cannot sustain human habitation or economic life of their own shall have no exclusive economic zone or continental shelf.

PART IX. ENCLOSED OR SEMI–ENCLOSED SEAS

Article 122

Definition

For the purposes of this Convention, "enclosed or semi-enclosed sea" means a gulf, basin or sea surrounded by two or more States and connected to another sea or the ocean by a narrow outlet or consisting entirely or primarily of the territorial seas and exclusive economic zones of two or more coastal States.

Article 123

Co–Operation of States Bordering Enclosed or Semi–Enclosed Seas

States bordering an enclosed or semi-enclosed sea should co-operate with each other in the exercise of their rights and in the performance of their duties under this Convention. To this end they shall endeavour, directly or through an appropriate regional organization:

(a) to co-ordinate the management, conservation, exploration and exploitation of the living resources of the sea;

(b) to co-ordinate the implementation of their rights and duties with respect to the protection and preservation of the marine environment;

(c) to co-ordinate their scientific research policies and undertake where appropriate joint programmes of scientific research in the area;

(d) to invite, as appropriate, other interested States or international organizations to co-operate with them in furtherance of the provisions of this article.

PART X. RIGHT OF ACCESS OF LAND–LOCKED STATES TO AND FROM THE SEA AND FREEDOM OF TRANSIT

Article 124

Use of Terms

1. For the purposes of this Convention:

(a) "land-locked State" means a State which has no sea-coast;

(b) "transit State" means a State, with or without a sea-coast, situated between a land-locked State and the sea, through whose territory traffic in transit passes;

(c) "traffic in transit" means transit of persons, baggage, goods and means of transport across the territory of one or more transit States, when the passage across such territory, with or without trans-shipment, warehousing, breaking bulk or change in the mode of transport, is only a portion of a complete journey which begins or terminates within the territory of the land-locked State;

(d) "means of transport" means:

(i) railway rolling stock, sea, lake and river craft and road vehicles;

(ii) where local conditions so require, porters and pack animals.

2. Land-locked States and transit States may, by agreement between them, include as means of transport pipelines and gas lines and means of transport other than those included in paragraph 1.

Article 125

Right of Access to and from the Sea and Freedom of Transit

1. Land-locked States shall have the right of access to and from the sea for the purpose of exercising the rights provided for in this Convention including those relating to the freedom of the high seas and the common heritage of mankind. To this end, land-locked States shall enjoy freedom of transit through the territory of transit States by all means of transport.

2. The terms and modalities for exercising freedom of transit shall be agreed between the land-locked States and transit States concerned through bilateral, subregional or regional agreements.

3. Transit States, in the exercise of their full sovereignty over their territory, shall have the right to take all measures necessary to ensure that the rights and facilities provided for in this Part for land-locked States shall in no way infringe their legitimate interests.

Article 126

Exclusion of Application of the Most–Favoured–Nation Clause

The provisions of this Convention, as well as special agreements relating to the exercise of the right of access to and from the sea, establishing rights and facilities on account of the special geographical position of land-locked States are excluded from the application of the most-favoured-nation clause.

Article 127

Customs Duties, Taxes and Other Charges

1. Traffic in transit shall not be subject to any customs duties, taxes or other charges except charges levied for specific services rendered in connection with such traffic.

2. Means of transport in transit and other facilities provided for and used by land-locked States shall not be subject to taxes or charges higher than those levied for the use of means of transport of the transit State.

Article 128

Free Zones and Other Customs Facilities

For the convenience of traffic in transit, free zones or other customs facilities may be provided at the ports of entry and exit in the transit States, by agreement between those States and the land-locked States.

Article 129

Co–Operation in the Construction and Improvement of Means of Transport

Where there are no means of transport in transit States to give effect to the freedom of transit or where the existing means, including the port installations and equipment, are inadequate in any respect, the transit States and land-locked States concerned may co-operate in constructing or improving them.

Article 130

Measures to Avoid or Eliminate Delays or Other Difficulties of a Technical Nature in Traffic in Transit

1. Transit States shall take all appropriate measures to avoid delays or other difficulties of a technical nature in traffic in transit.

2. Should such delays or difficulties occur, the competent authorities of the transit States and land-locked States concerned shall co-operate towards their expeditious elimination.

Article 131

Equal Treatment in Maritime Ports

Ships flying the flag of land-locked States shall enjoy treatment equal to that accorded to other foreign ships in maritime ports.

Article 132

Grant of Greater Transit Facilities

This Convention does not entail in any way the withdrawal of transit facilities which are greater than those provided for in this

Convention and which are agreed between States Parties to this Convention or granted by a State Party. This Convention also does not preclude such grant of greater facilities in the future.

PART XI. THE AREA

Section 1. General Provisions

Article 133

Use of Terms

For the purposes of this Part:

(a) "resources" means all solid, liquid or gaseous mineral resources in situ in the Area at or beneath the sea-bed, including polymetallic nodules;

(b) resources, when recovered from the Area, are referred to as "minerals".

Article 134

Scope of this Part

1. This Part applies to the Area.

2. Activities in the Area shall be governed by the provisions of this Part.

3. The requirements concerning deposit of, and publicity to be given to, the charts or lists of geographical co-ordinates showing the limits referred to in article 1, paragraph 1 (1), are set forth in Part VI.

4. Nothing in this article affects the establishment of the outer limits of the continental shelf in accordance with Part VI or the validity of agreements relating to delimitation between States with opposite or adjacent coasts.

Article 135

Legal status of the Superjacent Waters and Air Space

Neither this Part nor any rights granted or exercised pursuant thereto shall affect the legal status of the waters superjacent to the Area or that of the air space above those waters.

Section 2. Principles Governing the Area

Article 136

Common Heritage of Mankind

The Area and its resources are the common heritage of mankind.

Article 137

Legal Status of the Area and its Resources

1. No State shall claim or exercise sovereignty or sovereign rights over any part of the Area or its resources, nor shall any State or natural or juridical person appropriate any part thereof. No such claim or

exercise of sovereignty or sovereign rights nor such appropriation shall be recognized.

2. All rights in the resources of the Area are vested in mankind as a whole on whose behalf the Authority shall act. These resources are not subject to alienation. The minerals recovered from the Area, however, may only be alienated in accordance with this Part and the rules, regulations and procedures of the Authority.

3. No State or natural or juridical person shall claim, acquire or exercise rights with respect to the minerals recovered from the Area except in accordance with this Part. Otherwise, no such claim, acquisition or exercise of such rights shall be recognized.

Article 138

General Conduct of States in Relation to the Area

The general conduct of States in relation to the Area shall be in accordance with the provisions of this Part, the principles embodied in the Charter of the United Nations and other rules of international law in the interests of maintaining peace and security and promoting international co-operation and mutual understanding.

Article 139

Responsibility to Ensure Compliance and Liability for Damage

1. States Parties shall have the responsibility to ensure that activities in the Area, whether carried out by States Parties, or state enterprises or natural or juridical persons which possess the nationality of States Parties or are effectively controlled by them or their nationals, shall be carried out in conformity with this Part. The same responsibility applies to international organizations for activities in the Area carried out by such organizations.

2. Without prejudice to the rules of international law and Annex III, article 22, damage caused by the failure of a State Party or international organization to carry out its responsibilities under this Part shall entail liability, States Parties or international organizations acting together shall bear joint and several liability. A State Party shall not however be liable for damage caused by any failure to comply with this Part by a person whom it has sponsored under article 153, paragraph 2(b), if the State Party has taken all necessary and appropriate measures to secure effective compliance under article 153, paragraph 4, and Annex III, article 4, paragraph 4.

3. States Parties that are members of international organizations shall take appropriate measures to ensure the implementation of this article with respect to such organizations.

Article 140

Benefit of Mankind

1. Activities in the Area shall, as specifically provided for in this Part, be carried out for the benefit of mankind as a whole, irrespective of the geographical location of States, whether coastal or land-locked, and

taking into particular consideration the interests and needs of developing States and of peoples who have not attained full independence or other self-governing status recognized by the United Nations in accordance with General Assembly resolution 1514 (XV) and other relevant General Assembly resolutions.

2. The Authority shall provide for the equitable sharing of financial and other economic benefits derived from activities in the Area through any appropriate mechanism on a non-discriminatory basis, in accordance with article 160, paragraph 2 (f) (i).

Article 141

Use of the Area Exclusively for Peaceful Purposes

The Area shall be open to use exclusively for peaceful purposes by all States, whether coastal or land-locked, without discrimination and without prejudice to the other provisions of this Part.

Article 142

Rights and Legitimate Interests of Coastal States

1. Activities in the Area, with respect to resource deposits in the Area which lie across limits of national jurisdiction, shall be conducted with due regard to the rights and legitimate interests of any coastal State across whose jurisdiction such deposits lie.

2. Consultations, including a system of prior notification, shall be maintained with the State concerned, with a view to avoiding infringement of such rights and interests. In cases where activities in the Area may result in the exploitation of resources lying within national jurisdiction, the prior consent of the coastal State concerned shall be required.

3. Neither this Part nor any rights granted or exercised pursuant thereto shall affect the rights of coastal States to take such measures consistent with the relevant provisions of Part XII as may be necessary to prevent, mitigate or eliminate grave and imminent danger to their coastline, or related interests from pollution or threat thereof or from other hazardous occurrences resulting from or caused by any activities in the Area.

Article 143

Marine Scientific Research

1. Marine scientific research in the Area shall be carried out exclusively for peaceful purposes and for the benefit of mankind as a whole in accordance with Part XIII.

2. The Authority may carry out marine scientific research concerning the Area and its resources, and may enter into contracts for that purpose. The Authority shall promote and encourage the conduct of marine scientific research in the Area, and shall co-ordinate and disseminate the results of such research and analysis when available.

3. States Parties may carry out marine scientific research in the Area. States Parties shall promote international co-operation in marine scientific research in the Area by:

(a) participating in international programmes and encouraging co-operation in marine scientific research by personnel of different countries and of the Authority;

(b) ensuring that programmes are developed through the Authority or other international organizations as appropriate for the benefit of developing States and technologically less developed States with a view to:

(i) strengthening their research capabilities;

(ii) training their personnel and the personnel of the Authority in the techniques and applications of research;

(iii) fostering the employment of their qualified personnel in research in the Area;

(c) effectively disseminating the results of research and analysis when available, through the Authority or other international channels when appropriate.

Article 144

Transfer of Technology

1. The Authority shall take measures in accordance with this Convention:

(a) to acquire technology and scientific knowledge relating to activities in the Area; and

(b) to promote and encourage the transfer to developing States of such technology and scientific knowledge so that all States Parties benefit therefrom.

2. To this end the Authority and States Parties shall cooperate in promoting the transfer of technology and scientific knowledge relating to activities in the Area so that the Enterprise and all States Parties may benefit therefrom. In particular they shall initiate and promote:

(a) programmes for the transfer of technology to the Enterprise and to developing States with regard to activities in the Area, including, *inter alia*, facilitating the access of the Enterprise and of developing States to the relevant technology, under fair and reasonable terms and conditions;

(b) measures directed towards the advancement of the technology of the Enterprise and the domestic technology of developing States, particularly by providing opportunities to personnel from the Enterprise and from developing States for training in marine science and technology and for their full participation in activities in the Area.

Article 145

Protection of the Marine Environment

Necessary measures shall be taken in accordance with this Convention with respect to activities in the Area to ensure effective protection for the marine environment from harmful effects which may arise from such activities. To this end the Authority shall adopt appropriate rules, regulations and procedures for *inter alia*:

(a) the prevention, reduction and control of pollution and other hazards to the marine environment, including the coastline, and of interference with the ecological balance of the marine environment, particular attention being paid to the need for protection from harmful effects of such activities as drilling, dredging, excavation, disposal of waste, construction and operation or maintenance of installations, pipelines and other devices related to such activities;

(b) the protection and conservation of the natural resources of the Area and the prevention of damage to the flora and fauna of the marine environment.

Article 146

Protection of Human Life

With respect to activities in the Area, necessary measures shall be taken to ensure effective protection of human life. To this end the Authority shall adopt appropriate rules, regulations and procedures to supplement existing international law as embodied in relevant treaties.

Article 147

Accommodation of Activities in the Area and in the Marine Environment

1. Activities in the Area shall be carried out with reasonable regard for other activities in the marine environment.

2. Installations used for carrying out activities in the Area shall be subject to the following conditions:

(a) such installations shall be erected, emplaced and removed solely in accordance with this Part and subject to the rules, regulations and procedures of the Authority. Due notice must be given of the erection, emplacement and removal of such installations, and permanent means for giving warning of their presence must be maintained;

(b) such installations may not be established where interference may be caused to the use of recognized sea lanes essential to international navigation or in areas of intense fishing activity;

(c) safety zones shall be established around such installations with appropriate markings to ensure the safety of both navigation and the installations. The configuration and location of such safety zones shall not be such as to form a belt impeding the lawful access of shipping to particular maritime zones or navigation along international sea lanes;

(d) such installations shall be used exclusively for peaceful purposes;

(e) such installations do not possess the status of islands. They have no territorial sea of their own, and their presence does not affect the delimitation of the territorial sea, the exclusive economic zone or the continental shelf.

3. Other activities in the marine environment shall be conducted with reasonable regard for activities in the Area.

Article 148

Participation of Developing States in Activities in the Area

The effective participation of developing States in activities in the Area shall be promoted as specifically provided for in this Part, having due regard to their special interests and needs, and in particular to the special need of the landlocked and geographically disadvantaged among them to overcome obstacles arising from their disadvantaged location, including remoteness from the Area and difficulty of access to and from it.

Article 149

Archaeological and Historical Objects

All objects of an archaeological and historical nature found in the Area shall be preserved or disposed of for the benefit of mankind as a whole, particular regard being paid to the preferential rights of the State or country of origin, or the State of cultural origin, or the State of historical and archaeological origin.

Section 3. Development of Resources of the Area

Article 150

Policies Relating to Activities in the Area

Activities in the Area shall, as specifically provided for in this Part, be carried out in such a manner as to foster healthy development of the world economy and balanced growth of international trade, and to promote international co-operation for the over-all development of all countries, especially developing States, and with a view to ensuring:

(a) the development of the resources of the Area;

(b) orderly, safe and rational management of the resources of the Area, including the efficient conduct of activities in the Area and, in accordance with sound principles of conservation, the avoidance of unnecessary waste;

(c) the expansion of opportunities for participation in such activities consistent in particular with articles 144 and 148;

(d) participation in revenues by the Authority and the transfer of technology to the Enterprise and developing States as provided for in this Convention;

(e) increased availability of the minerals derived from the Area as needed in conjunction with minerals derived from other sources, to ensure supplies to consumers of such minerals;

(f) the promotion of just and stable prices remunerative to producers and fair to consumers for minerals derived both from the

Area and from other sources, and the promotion of long-term equilibrium between supply and demand;

(g) the enhancement of opportunities for all States Parties, irrespective of their social and economic systems or geographical location, to participate in the development of the resources of the Area and the prevention of monopolization of activities in the Area;

(h) the protection of developing countries from adverse effects on their economies or on their export earnings resulting from a reduction in the price of an affected mineral, or in the volume of exports of that mineral, to the extent that such reduction is caused by activities in the Area, as provided in article 151;

(i) the development of the common heritage for the benefit of mankind as a whole; and

(j) conditions of access to markets for the imports of minerals produced from the resources of the Area and for imports of commodities produced from such minerals shall not be more favourable than the most favourable applied to imports from other sources.

Article 151

Production Policies

1. (a) Without prejudice to the objectives set forth in article 150 and for the purpose of implementing subparagraph (h) of that article, the Authority, acting through existing forums or such new arrangements or agreements as may be appropriate, in which all interested parties, including both producers and consumers, participate, shall take measures necessary to promote the growth, efficiency and stability of markets for those commodities produced from the minerals derived from the Area, at prices remunerative to producers and fair to consumers. All States Parties shall co-operate to this end.

(b) The Authority shall have the right to participate in any commodity conference dealing with those commodities and in which all interested parties including both producers and consumers participate. The Authority shall have the right to become a party to any arrangement or agreement resulting from such conferences. Participation of the Authority in any organs established under those arrangements or agreements shall be in respect of production in the Area and in accordance with the relevant rules of those organs.

(c) The Authority shall carry out its obligations under the arrangements or agreements referred to in this paragraph in a manner which assures a uniform and non-discriminatory implementation in respect of all production in the Area of the minerals concerned. In doing so, the Authority shall act in a manner consistent with the terms of existing contracts and approved plans of work of the Enterprise.

2. (a) During the interim period specified in paragraph 3, commercial production shall not be undertaken pursuant to an approved plan of work until the operator has applied for and has been issued a production authorization by the Authority. Such production authori-

zations may not be applied for or issued more than five years prior to the planned commencement of commercial production under the plan of work unless, having regard to the nature and timing of project development, the rules, regulations and procedures of the Authority prescribe another period.

(b) In the application for the production authorization, the operator shall specify the annual quantity of nickel expected to be recovered under the approved plan of work. The application shall include a schedule of expenditures to be made by the operator after he has received the authorization which are reasonably calculated to allow him to begin commercial production on the date planned.

(c) For the purposes of subparagraphs (a) and (b), the Authority shall establish appropriate performance requirements in accordance with Annex III, article 17.

(d) The Authority shall issue a production authorization for the level of production applied for unless the sum of that level and the levels already authorized exceeds the nickel production ceiling, as calculated pursuant to paragraph 4 in the year of issuance of the authorization, during any year of planned production falling within the interim period.

(e) When issued, the production authorization and approved application shall become a part of the approved plan of work.

(f) If the operator's application for a production authorization is denied pursuant to subparagraph (d), the operator may apply again to the Authority at any time.

3. The interim period shall begin five years prior to 1 January of the year in which the earliest commercial production is planned to commence under an approved plan of work. If the earliest commercial production is delayed beyond the year originally planned, the beginning of the interim period and the production ceiling originally calculated shall be adjusted accordingly. The interim period shall last 25 years or until the end of the Review Conference referred to in article 155 or until the day when such new arrangements or agreements as are referred to in paragraph 1 enter into force, whichever is earliest. The Authority shall resume the power provided in this article for the remainder of the interim period if the said arrangements or agreements should lapse or become ineffective for any reason whatsoever.

4. (a) The production ceiling for any year of the interim period shall be the sum of:

(i) the difference between the trend line values for nickel consumption as calculated pursuant to subparagraph (b), for the year immediately prior to the year of the earliest commercial production and the year immediately prior to the commencement of the interim period; and

(ii) sixty per cent of the difference between the trend line values for nickel consumption, as calculated pursuant to subparagraph (b), for the year for which the production authorization is being applied for and the year immediately prior to the year of the earliest commercial production.

(b) For the purposes of subparagraph (a):

(i) trend line values used for computing the nickel production ceiling shall be those annual nickel consumption values on a trend line computed during the year in which a production authorization is issued. The trend line shall be derived from a linear regression of the logarithms of actual nickel consumption for the most recent 15–year period for which such data are available, time being the independent variable. This trend line shall be referred to as the original trend line;

(ii) if the annual rate of increase of the original trend line is less than 3 per cent, then the trend line used to determine the quantities referred to in subparagraph (a) shall instead be one passing through the original trend line at the value for the first year of the relevant 15–year period, and increasing at 3 per cent annually; provided however that the production ceiling established for any year of the interim period may not in any case exceed the difference between the original trend line value for that year and the original trend line value for the year immediately prior to the commencement of the interim period.

5. The Authority shall reserve to the Enterprise for its initial production a quantity of 38,000 metric tonnes of nickel from the available production ceiling calculated pursuant to paragraph 4.

6. (a) An operator may in any year produce less than or up to 8 per cent more than the level of annual production of minerals from polymetallic nodules specified in his production authorization, provided that the over-all amount of production shall not exceed that specified in the authorization. Any excess over 8 per cent and up to 20 per cent in any year, or any excess in the first and subsequent years following two consecutive years in which excesses occur, shall be negotiated with the Authority, which may require the operator to obtain a supplementary production authorization to cover additional production.

(b) Applications for such supplementary production authorizations shall be considered by the Authority only after all pending applications by operators who have not yet received production authorizations have been acted upon and due account has been taken of other likely applicants. The Authority shall be guided by the principle of not exceeding the total production allowed under the production ceiling in any year of the interim period. It shall not authorize the production under any plan of work of a quantity in excess of 46,500 metric tonnes of nickel per year.

7. The levels of production of other metals such as copper, cobalt and manganese extracted from the polymetallic nodules that are recovered pursuant to a production authorization should not be higher than those which would have been produced had the operator produced the maximum level of nickel from those nodules pursuant to this article. The Authority shall establish rules, regulations and procedures pursuant to Annex III, article 17, to implement this paragraph.

8. Rights and obligations relating to unfair economic practices under relevant multilateral trade agreements shall apply to the explora-

tion for and exploitation of minerals from the Area. In the settlement of disputes arising under this provision, States Parties which are Parties to such multilateral trade agreements shall have recourse to the dispute settlement procedures of such agreements.

9. The Authority shall have the power to limit the level of production of minerals from the Area, other than minerals from polymetallic nodules, under such conditions and applying such methods as may be appropriate by adopting regulations in accordance with article 161, paragraph 8.

10. Upon the recommendation of the Council on the basis of advice from the Economic Planning Commission, the Assembly shall establish a system of compensation or take other measures of economic adjustment assistance including co-operation with specialized agencies and other international organizations to assist developing countries which suffer serious adverse effects on their export earnings or economies resulting from a reduction in the price of an affected mineral or in the volume of exports of that mineral, to the extent that such reduction is caused by activities in the Area. The Authority on request shall initiate studies on the problems of those States which are likely to be most seriously affected with a view to minimizing their difficulties and assisting them in their economic adjustment.

Article 152

Exercise of Powers and Functions by the Authority

1. The Authority shall avoid discrimination in the exercise of its powers and functions, including the granting of opportunities for activities in the Area.

2. Nevertheless, special consideration for developing States, including particular consideration for the land-locked and geographically disadvantaged among them, specifically provided for in this Part shall be permitted.

Article 153

System of Exploration and Exploitation

1. Activities in the Area shall be organized, carried out and controlled by the Authority on behalf of mankind as a whole in accordance with this article as well as other relevant provisions of this Part and the relevant Annexes, and the rules, regulations and procedures of the Authority.

2. Activities in the Area shall be carried out as prescribed in paragraph 3:

(a) by the Enterprise, and

(b) in association with the Authority by States Parties, or state enterprises or natural or juridical persons which possess the nationality of States Parties or are effectively controlled by them or their nationals, when sponsored by such States, or any group of the foregoing which meets the requirements provided in this Part and in Annex III.

3. Activities in the Area shall be carried out in accordance with a formal written plan of work drawn up in accordance with Annex III and approved by the Council after review by the Legal and Technical Commission. In the case of activities in the Area carried out as authorized by the Authority by the entities specified in paragraph 2(b), the plan of work shall, in accordance with Annex III, article 3, be in the form of a contract. Such contracts may provide for joint arrangements in accordance with Annex III, article 11.

4. The Authority shall exercise such control over activities in the Area as is necessary for the purpose of securing compliance with the relevant provisions of this Part and the Annexes relating thereto, and the rules, regulations and procedures of the Authority, and the plans of work approved in accordance with paragraph 3. States Parties shall assist the Authority by taking all measures necessary to ensure such compliance in accordance with article 139.

5. The Authority shall have the right to take at any time any measures provided for under this Part to ensure compliance with its provisions and the exercise of the functions of control and regulation assigned to it thereunder or under any contract. The Authority shall have the right to inspect all installations in the Area used in connection with activities in the Area.

6. A contract under paragraph 3 shall provide for security of tenure. Accordingly, the contract shall not be revised, suspended or terminated except in accordance with Annex III, articles 18 and 19.

Article 154

Periodic Review

Every five years from the entry into force of this Convention, the Assembly shall undertake a general and systematic review of the manner in which the international regime of the Area established in this Convention has operated in practice. In the light of this review the Assembly may take, or recommend that other organs take, measures in accordance with the provisions and procedures of this Part and the Annexes relating thereto which will lead to the improvement of the operation of the regime.

Article 155

The Review Conference

1. Fifteen years from 1 January of the year in which the earliest commercial production commences under an approved plan of work, the Assembly shall convene a conference for the review of those provisions of this Part and the relevant Annexes which govern the system of exploration and exploitation of the resources of the Area. The Review Conference shall consider in detail, in the light of the experience acquired during that period:

(a) whether the provisions of this Part which govern the system of exploration and exploitation of the resources of the Area have achieved their aims in all respects, including whether they have benefited mankind as a whole;

(b) whether, during the 15–year period, reserved areas have been exploited in an effective and balanced manner in comparison with non-reserved areas;

(c) whether the development and use of the Area and its resources have been undertaken in such a manner as to foster healthy development of the world economy and balanced growth of international trade;

(d) whether monopolization of activities in the Area has been prevented;

(e) whether the policies set forth in articles 150 and 151 have been fulfilled; and

(f) whether the system has resulted in the equitable sharing of benefits derived from activities in the Area, taking into particular consideration the interests and needs of the developing States.

2. The Review Conference shall ensure the maintenance of the principle of the common heritage of mankind, the international regime designed to ensure equitable exploitation of the resources of the Area for the benefit of all countries, especially the developing States, and an Authority to organize, conduct and control activities in the Area. It shall also ensure the maintenance of the principles laid down in this Part with regard to the exclusion of claims or exercise of sovereignty over any part of the Area, the rights of States and their general conduct in relation to the Area, and their participation in activities in the Area in conformity with this Convention, the prevention of monopolization of activities in the Area, the use of the Area exclusively for peaceful purposes, economic aspects of activities in the Area, marine scientific research, transfer of technology, protection of the marine environment, protection of human life, rights of coastal States, the legal status of the waters superjacent to the Area and that of the air space above those waters and accommodation between activities in the Area and other activities in the marine environment.

3. The decision-making procedure applicable at the Review Conference shall be the same as that applicable at the Third United Nations Conference on the Law of the Sea. The Conference shall make every effort to reach agreement on any amendments by way of consensus and there should be no voting on such matters until all efforts at achieving consensus have been exhausted.

4. If, five years after its commencement, the Review Conference has not reached agreement on the system of exploration and exploitation of the resources of the Area, it may decide during the ensuing 12 months, by a three-fourths majority of the States Parties, to adopt and submit to the States Parties for ratification or accession such amendments changing or modifying the system as it determines necessary and appropriate. Such amendments shall enter into force for all States

Parties 12 months after the deposit of instruments of ratification or accession by three fourths of the States Parties.

5. Amendments adopted by the Review Conference pursuant to this article shall not affect rights acquired under existing contracts.

Section 4. The Authority

Subsection A. General Provisions

Article 156

Establishment of the Authority

1. There is hereby established the International Sea–Bed Authority, which shall function in accordance with this Part.

2. All States Parties are *ipso facto* members of the Authority.

3. Observers at the Third United Nations Conference on the Law of the Sea who have signed the Final Act and who are not referred to in article 305, paragraph 1 (c), (d), (e) or (f), shall have the right to participate in the Authority as observers, in accordance with its rules, regulations and procedures.

4. The seat of the Authority shall be in Jamaica.

5. The Authority may establish such regional centres or offices as it deems necessary for the exercise of its functions.

Article 157

Nature and Fundamental Principles of the Authority

1. The Authority is the organization through which States Parties shall, in accordance with this Part, organize and control activities in the Area, particularly with a view to administering the resources of the Area.

2. The powers and functions of the Authority shall be those expressly conferred upon it by this Convention. The Authority shall have such incidental powers, consistent with this Convention, as are implicit in and necessary for the exercise of those powers and functions with respect to activities in the Area.

3. The Authority is based on the principle of the sovereign equality of all its members.

4. All members of the Authority shall fulfil in good faith the obligations assumed by them in accordance with this Part in order to ensure to all of them the rights and benefits resulting from membership.

Article 158

Organs of the Authority

1. There are hereby established, as the principal organs of the Authority, an Assembly, a Council and a Secretariat.

2. There is hereby established the Enterprise, the organ through which the Authority shall carry out the functions referred to in article 170, paragraph 1.

3. Such subsidiary organs as may be found necessary may be established in accordance with this Part.

4. Each principal organ of the Authority and the Enterprise shall be responsible for exercising those powers and functions which are conferred upon it. In exercising such powers and functions each organ shall avoid taking any action which may derogate from or impede the exercise of specific powers and functions conferred upon another organ.

Subsection B. The Assembly

Article 159

Composition, Procedure and Voting

1. The Assembly shall consist of all the members of the Authority. Each member shall have one representative in the Assembly, who may be accompanied by alternates and advisers.

2. The Assembly shall meet in regular annual sessions and in such special sessions as may be decided by the Assembly, or convened by the Secretary–General at the request of the Council or of a majority of the members of the Authority.

3. Sessions shall take place at the seat of the Authority unless otherwise decided by the Assembly.

4. The Assembly shall adopt its rules of procedure. At the beginning of each regular session, it shall elect its President and such other officers as may be required. They shall hold office until a new President and other officers are elected at the next regular session.

5. A majority of the members of the Assembly shall constitute a quorum.

6. Each member of the Assembly shall have one vote.

7. Decisions on questions of procedure, including decisions to convene special sessions of the Assembly, shall be taken by a majority of the members present and voting.

8. Decisions on questions of substance shall be taken by a two-thirds majority of the members present and voting, provided that such majority includes a majority of the members participating in the session. When the issue arises as to whether a question is one of substance or not, that question shall be treated as one of substance unless otherwise decided by the Assembly by the majority required for decisions on questions of substance.

9. When a question of substance comes up for voting for the first time, the President may, and shall, if requested by at least one fifth of the members of the Assembly, defer the issue of taking a vote on that question for a period not exceeding five calendar days. This rule may be applied only once to any question, and shall not be applied so as to defer the question beyond the end of the session.

10. Upon a written request addressed to the President and sponsored by at least one fourth of the members of the Authority for an advisory opinion on the conformity with this Convention of a proposal

before the Assembly on any matter, the Assembly shall request the Sea-Bed Disputes Chamber of the International Tribunal for the Law of the Sea to give an advisory opinion thereon and shall defer voting on that proposal pending receipt of the advisory opinion by the Chamber. If the advisory opinion is not received before the final week of the session in which it is requested, the Assembly shall decide when it will meet to vote upon the deferred proposal.

Article 160

Powers and Functions

1. The Assembly, as the sole organ of the Authority consisting of all the members, shall be considered the supreme organ of the Authority to which the other principal organs shall be accountable as specifically provided for in this Convention. The Assembly shall have the power to establish general policies in conformity with the relevant provisions of this Convention on any question or matter within the competence of the Authority.

2. In addition, the powers and functions of the Assembly shall be:

(a) to elect the members of the Council in accordance with article 161;

(b) to elect the Secretary-General from among the candidates proposed by the Council;

(c) to elect, upon the recommendation of the Council, the members of the Governing Board of the Enterprise and the Director-General of the Enterprise;

(d) to establish such subsidiary organs as it finds necessary for the exercise of its functions in accordance with this Part. In the composition of these subsidiary organs due account shall be taken of the principle of equitable geographical distribution and of special interests and the need for members qualified and competent in the relevant technical questions dealt with by such organs;

(e) to assess the contributions of members to the administrative budget of the Authority in accordance with an agreed scale of assessment based upon the scale used for the regular budget of the United Nations until the Authority shall have sufficient income from other sources to meet its administrative expenses;

(f) (i) to consider and approve, upon the recommendation of the Council the rules, regulations and procedures on the equitable sharing of financial and other economic benefits derived from activities in the Area and the payments and contributions made pursuant to article 82, taking into particular consideration the interests and needs of developing States and peoples who have not attained full independence or other self-governing status. If the Assembly does not approve the recommendations of the Council, the Assembly shall return them to the Council for reconsideration in the light of the views expressed by the Assembly;

(ii) to consider and approve the rules, regulations and procedures of the Authority, and any amendments thereto, provisionally adopted by the Council pursuant to article 162, paragraph 2 (*o*)(ii). These rules, regulations and procedures shall relate to prospecting, exploration and exploitation in the Area, the financial management and internal administration of the Authority, and, upon the recommendation of the Governing Board of the Enterprise, to the transfer of funds from the Enterprise to the Authority;

(g) to decide upon the equitable sharing of financial and other economic benefits derived from activities in the Area, consistent with this Convention and the rules, regulations and procedures of the Authority;

(h) to consider and approve the proposed annual budget of the Authority submitted by the Council;

(i) to examine periodic reports from the Council and from the Enterprise and special reports requested from the Council or any other organ of the Authority;

(j) to initiate studies and make recommendations for the purpose of promoting international co-operation concerning activities in the Area and encouraging the progressive development of international law relating thereto and its codification;

(k) to consider problems of a general nature in connection with activities in the Area arising in particular for developing States, as well as those problems for States in connection with activities in the Area that are due to their geographical location, particularly for land-locked and geographically disadvantaged States;

(*l*) to establish, upon the recommendation of the Council, on the basis of advice from the Economic Planning Commission, a system of compensation or other measures of economic adjustment assistance as provided in article 151, paragraph 10;

(m) to suspend the exercise of rights and privileges of membership pursuant to article 185;

(n) to discuss any question or matter within the competence of the Authority and to decide as to which organ of the Authority shall deal with any such question or matter not specifically entrusted to a particular organ, consistent with the distribution of powers and functions among the organs of the Authority.

Subsection C. The Council

Article 161

Composition, Procedure and Voting

1. The Council shall consist of 36 members of the Authority elected by the Assembly in the following order:

(a) four members from among those States Parties which, during the last five years for which statistics are available, have either consumed more than 2 per cent of total world consumption or have had net imports of more than 2 per cent of total world imports of the commodities produced from the categories of minerals to be derived from the Area, and in any case one State from the Eastern European (Socialist) region, as well as the largest consumer;

(b) four members from among the eight States Parties which have the largest investments in preparation for and in the conduct of activities in the Area, either directly or through their nationals, including at least one State from the Eastern European (Socialist) region;

(c) four members from among States Parties which on the basis of production in areas under their jurisdiction are major net exporters of the categories of minerals to be derived from the Area, including at least two developing States whose exports of such minerals have a substantial bearing upon their economies;

(d) six members from among developing States Parties, representing special interests. The special interests to be represented shall include those of States with large populations, States which are land-locked or geographically disadvantaged, States which are major importers of the categories of minerals to be derived from the Area, States which are potential producers of such minerals, and least developed States;

(e) eighteen members elected according to the principle of ensuring an equitable geographical distribution of seats in the Council as a whole, provided that each geographical region shall have at least one member elected under this subparagraph. For this purpose, the geographical regions shall be Africa, Asia, Eastern European (Socialist), Latin America and Western European and Others.

2. In electing the members of the Council in accordance with paragraph 1, the Assembly shall ensure that:

(a) land-locked and geographically disadvantaged States are represented to a degree which is reasonably proportionate to their representation in the Assembly;

(b) coastal States, especially developing States, which do not qualify under paragraph 1 (a), (b), (c) or (d) are represented to a degree which is reasonably proportionate to their representation in the Assembly;

(c) each group of States Parties to be represented on the Council is represented by those members, if any, which are nominated by that group.

3. Elections shall take place at regular sessions of the Assembly. Each member of the Council shall be elected for four years. At the first election, however, the term of one half of the members of each group referred to in paragraph 1 shall be two years.

4. Members of the Council shall be eligible for re-election, but due regard should be paid to the desirability of rotation of membership.

5. The Council shall function at the seat of the Authority, and shall meet as often as the business of the Authority may require, but not less than three times a year.

6. A majority of the members of the Council shall constitute a quorum.

7. Each member of the Council shall have one vote.

8. (a) Decisions on questions of procedure shall be taken by a majority of the members present and voting.

(b) Decisions on questions of substance arising under the following provisions shall be taken by a two-thirds majority of the members present and voting, provided that such majority includes a majority of the members of the Council: article 162, paragraph 2, subparagraphs (f); (g); (h); (i); (n); (p); (v); article 191.

(c) Decisions on questions of substance arising under the following provisions shall be taken by a three-fourths majority of the members present and voting, provided that such majority includes a majority of the members of the Council: article 162, paragraph 1; article 162, paragraph 2, subparagraphs (a); (b); (c); (d); (e); (*l*); (q); (r); (s); (t); (u) in cases of non-compliance by a contractor or a sponsor; (w) provided that orders issued thereunder may be binding for not more than 30 days unless confirmed by a decision taken in accordance with subparagraph (d); article 162, paragraph 2, subparagraphs (x); (y); (z); article 163, paragraph 2; article 174, paragraph 3; Annex IV, article 11.

(d) Decisions on questions of substance arising under the following provisions shall be taken by consensus: article 162, paragraph 2(m) and (*o*); adoption of amendments to Part XI.

(e) For the purposes of subparagraphs (d), (f) and (g), "consensus" means the absence of any formal objection. Within 14 days of the submission of a proposal to the Council, the President of the Council shall determine whether there would be a formal objection to the adoption of the proposal. If the President determines that there would be such an objection, the President shall establish and convene, within three days following such determination, a conciliation committee consisting of not more than nine members of the Council, with the President as chairman, for the purpose of reconciling the differences and producing a proposal which can be adopted by consensus. The committee shall work expeditiously and report to the Council within 14 days following its establishment. If the committee is unable to recommend a proposal which can be adopted by consensus, it shall set out in its report the grounds on which the proposal is being opposed.

(f) Decisions on questions not listed above which the Council is authorized to take by the rules, regulations and procedures of the Authority or otherwise shall be taken pursuant to the subparagraphs of this paragraph specified in the rules, regulations and procedures or, if not specified therein, then pursuant to the subparagraph determined by the Council if possible in advance, by consensus.

(g) When the issue arises as to whether a question is within subparagraph (a), (b), (c) or (d), the question shall be treated as being within the subparagraph requiring the higher or highest majority or consensus as the case may be, unless otherwise decided by the Council by the said majority or by consensus.

9. The Council shall establish a procedure whereby a member of the Authority not represented on the Council may send a representative to attend a meeting of the Council when a request is made by such member, or a matter particularly affecting it is under consideration. Such a representative shall be entitled to participate in the deliberations but not to vote.

Article 162

Powers and Functions

1. The Council is the executive organ of the Authority. The Council shall have the power to establish, in conformity with this Convention and the general policies established by the Assembly, the specific policies to be pursued by the Authority on any question or matter within the competence of the Authority.

2. In addition, the Council shall:

(a) supervise and co-ordinate the implementation of the provisions of this Part on all questions and matters within the competence of the Authority and invite the attention of the Assembly to cases of non-compliance;

(b) propose to the Assembly a list of candidates for the election of the Secretary–General;

(c) recommend to the Assembly candidates for the election of the members of the Governing Board of the Enterprise and the Director–General of the Enterprise;

(d) establish, as appropriate, and with due regard to economy and efficiency, such subsidiary organs as it finds necessary for the exercise of its functions in accordance with this Part. In the composition of subsidiary organs, emphasis shall be placed on the need for members qualified and competent in relevant technical matters dealt with by those organs provided that due account shall be taken of the principle of equitable geographical distribution and of special interests;

(e) adopt its rules of procedure including the method of selecting its president;

(f) enter into agreements with the United Nations or other international organizations on behalf of the Authority and within its competence, subject to approval by the Assembly;

(g) consider the reports of the Enterprise and transmit them to the Assembly with its recommendations;

(h) present to the Assembly annual reports and such special reports as the Assembly may request;

(i) issue directives to the Enterprise in accordance with article 170;

(j) approve plans of work in accordance with Annex III, article 6. The Council shall act upon each plan of work within 60 days of its submission by the Legal and Technical Commission at a session of the Council in accordance with the following procedures:

(i) if the Commission recommends the approval of a plan of work, it shall be deemed to have been approved by the Council if no member of the Council submits in writing to the President within 14 days a specific objection alleging non-compliance with the requirements of Annex III, article 6. If there is an objection, the conciliation procedure set forth in article 161, paragraph 8(e), shall apply. If, at the end of the conciliation procedure, the objection is still maintained, the plan of work shall be deemed to have been approved by the Council unless the Council disapproves it by consensus among its members excluding any State or States making the application or sponsoring the applicant;

(ii) if the Commission recommends the disapproval of a plan of work or does not make a recommendation, the Council may approve the plan of work by a three-fourths majority of the members present and voting, provided that such majority includes a majority of the members participating in the session;

(k) approve plans of work submitted by the Enterprise in accordance with Annex IV, article 12, applying, *mutatis mutandis*, the procedures set forth in subparagraph (j);

(*l*) exercise control over activities in the Area in accordance with article 153, paragraph 4, and the rules, regulations and procedures of the Authority;

(m) take, upon the recommendation of the Economic Planning Commission, necessary and appropriate measures in accordance with article 150, subparagraph (h), to provide protection from the adverse economic effects specified therein;

(n) make recommendations to the Assembly, on the basis of advice from the Economic Planning Commission, for a system of compensation or other measures of economic adjustment assistance as provided in article 151, paragraph 10;

(*o*) (i) recommend to the Assembly rules, regulations and procedures on the equitable sharing of financial and other economic benefits derived from activities in the Area and the payments and contributions made pursuant to article 82, taking into particular consideration the interests and needs of the developing States and peoples who have not attained full independence or other self-governing status;

(ii) adopt and apply provisionally, pending approval by the Assembly, the rules, regulations and procedures of the Authority, and any amendments thereto, taking into account the recommendations of the Legal and Technical Commission or other subordinate organ concerned. These rules, regulations and procedures shall relate to prospecting, exploration and exploitation in the Area and the financial management and internal administration of the Authority. Priority shall be given to the adoption of rules, regulations and procedures for the exploration for and exploitation of polymetallic nodules. Rules, regulations and procedures for the exploration for and exploitation of any resource other than polymetallic nodules shall be adopted within three years from the date of a request to the Authority by any of its members to adopt such rules, regulations and procedures in respect of such resource. All rules, regulations and procedures shall remain in effect on a provisional basis until approved by the Assembly or until amended by the Council in the light of any views expressed by the Assembly;

(p) review the collection of all payments to be made by or to the Authority in connection with operations pursuant to this Part;

(q) make the selection from among applicants for production authorizations pursuant to Annex III, article 7, where such selection is required by that provision;

(r) submit the proposed annual budget of the Authority to the Assembly for its approval;

(s) make recommendations to the Assembly concerning policies on any question or matter within the competence of the Authority;

(t) make recommendations to the Assembly concerning suspension of the exercise of the rights and privileges of membership pursuant to article 185;

(u) institute proceedings on behalf of the Authority before the Sea-Bed Disputes Chamber in cases of non-compliance;

(v) notify the Assembly upon a decision by the Sea-Bed Disputes Chamber in proceedings instituted under subparagraph (u), and make any recommendations which it may find appropriate with respect to measures to be taken;

(w) issue emergency orders, which may include orders for the suspension or adjustment of operations, to prevent serious harm to the marine environment arising out of activities in the Area;

(x) disapprove areas for exploitation by contractors or the Enterprise in cases where substantial evidence indicates the risk of serious harm to the marine environment;

(y) establish a subsidiary organ for the elaboration of draft financial rules, regulations and procedures relating to:

(i) financial management in accordance with articles 171 to 175; and

(ii) financial arrangements in accordance with Annex III, article 13 and article 17, paragraph 1 (c);

(z) establish appropriate mechanisms for directing and supervising a staff of inspectors who shall inspect activities in the Area to determine whether this Part, the rules, regulations and procedures of the Authority, and the terms and conditions of any contract with the Authority are being complied with.

Article 163

Organs of the Council

1. There are hereby established the following organs of the Council:

(a) an Economic Planning Commission;

(b) a Legal and Technical Commission.

2. Each Commission shall be composed of 15 members, elected by the Council from among the candidates nominated by the States Parties. However, if necessary, the Council may decide to increase the size of either Commission having due regard to economy and efficiency.

3. Members of a Commission shall have appropriate qualifications in the area of competence of that Commission. States Parties shall nominate candidates of the highest standards of competence and integrity with qualifications in relevant fields so as to ensure the effective exercise of the functions of the Commissions.

4. In the election of members of the Commissions, due account shall be taken of the need for equitable geographical distribution and the representation of special interests.

5. No State Party may nominate more than one candidate for the same Commission. No person shall be elected to serve on more than one Commission.

6. Members of the Commissions shall hold office for a term of five years. They shall be eligible for re-election for a further term.

7. In the event of the death, incapacity or resignation of a member of a Commission prior to the expiration of the term of office, the Council shall elect for the remainder of the term, a member from the same geographical region or area of interest.

8. Members of Commissions shall have no financial interest in any activity relating to exploration and exploitation in the Area. Subject to their responsibilities to the Commissions upon which they serve, they shall not disclose, even after the termination of their functions, any industrial secret, proprietary data which are transferred to the Authority in accordance with Annex III, article 14, or any other confidential information coming to their knowledge by reason of their duties for the Authority.

9. Each Commission shall exercise its functions in accordance with such guidelines and directives as the Council may adopt.

10. Each Commission shall formulate and submit to the Council for approval such rules and regulations as may be necessary for the efficient conduct of the Commission's functions.

11. The decision-making procedures of the Commissions shall be established by the rules, regulations and procedures of the Authority. Recommendations to the Council shall, where necessary, be accompanied by a summary on the divergencies of opinion in the Commission.

12. Each Commission shall normally function at the seat of the Authority and shall meet as often as is required for the efficient exercise of its functions.

13. In the exercise of its functions, each Commission may, where appropriate, consult another commission, any competent organ of the United Nations or of its specialized agencies or any international organizations with competence in the subject-matter of such consultation.

Article 164

The Economic Planning Commission

1. Members of the Economic Planning Commission shall have appropriate qualifications such as those relevant to mining, management of mineral resource activities, international trade or international economics. The Council shall endeavour to ensure that the membership of the Commission reflects all appropriate qualifications. The Commission shall include at least two members from developing States whose exports of the categories of minerals to be derived from the Area have a substantial bearing upon their economies.

2. The Commission shall:

(a) propose, upon the request of the Council, measures to implement decisions relating to activities in the Area taken in accordance with this Convention;

(b) review the trends of and the factors affecting supply, demand and prices of materials which may be derived from the Area, bearing in mind the interests of both importing and exporting countries, and in particular of the developing States among them;

(c) examine any situation likely to lead to the adverse effects referred to in article 150, subparagraph (h), brought to its attention by the State Party or States Parties concerned, and make appropriate recommendations to the Council;

(d) propose to the Council for submission to the Assembly, as provided in article 151, paragraph 10, a system of compensation or other measures of economic adjustment assistance for developing States which suffer adverse effects caused by activities in the Area. The Commission shall make the recommendations to the Council that are necessary for the application of the system or other measures adopted by the Assembly in specific cases.

Article 165

The Legal and Technical Commission

1. Members of the Legal and Technical Commission shall have appropriate qualifications such as those relevant to exploration for and exploitation and processing of mineral resources, oceanology, protection

of the marine environment, or economic or legal matters relating to ocean mining and related fields of expertise. The Council shall endeavour to ensure that the membership of the Commission reflects all appropriate qualifications.

2. The Commission shall:

(a) make recommendations with regard to the exercise of the Authority's functions upon the request of the Council;

(b) review formal written plans of work for activities in the Area in accordance with article 153, paragraph 3, and submit appropriate recommendations to the Council. The Commission shall base its recommendations solely on the grounds stated in Annex III and shall report fully thereon to the Council;

(c) supervise, upon the request of the Council, activities in the Area, where appropriate, in consultation and collaboration with any entity carrying out such activities or State or States concerned and report to the Council;

(d) prepare assessments of the environmental implications of activities in the Area;

(e) make recommendations to the Council on the protection of the marine environment, taking into account the views of recognized experts in that field;

(f) formulate and submit to the Council the rules regulations and procedures referred to in article 162, paragraph 2(*o*) taking into account all relevant factors including assessments of the environmental implications of activities in the Area;

(g) keep such rules, regulations and procedures under review and recommend to the Council from time to time such amendments thereto as it may deem necessary or desirable;

(h) make recommendations to the Council regarding the establishment of a monitoring programme to observe, measure evaluate and analyse by recognized scientific methods, on a regular basis, the risks or effects of pollution of the marine environment resulting from activities in the Area, ensure that existing regulations are adequate and are complied with and co-ordinate the implementation of the monitoring programme approved by the Council;

(i) recommend to the Council that proceedings be instituted on behalf of the Authority before the Sea-Bed Disputes Chamber, in accordance with this Part and the relevant Annexes taking into account particularly article 187;

(j) make recommendations to the Council with respect to measures to be taken, upon a decision by the Sea-Bed Disputes Chamber in proceedings instituted in accordance with subparagraph (i);

(k) make recommendations to the Council to issue emergency orders, which may include orders for the suspension or adjustment of operations, to prevent serious harm to the marine environment arising out of activities in the Area. Such recommendations shall be taken up by the Council on a priority basis;

(*l*) make recommendations to the Council to disapprove areas for exploitation by contractors or the Enterprise in cases where substantial evidence indicates the risk of serious harm to the marine environment;

(m) make recommendations to the Council regarding the direction and supervision of a staff of inspectors who shall inspect activities in the Area to determine whether the provisions of this Part, the rules, regulations and procedures of the Authority and the terms and conditions of any contract with the Authority are being complied with;

(n) calculate the production ceiling and issue production authorizations on behalf of the Authority pursuant to article 151, paragraphs 2 to 7, following any necessary selection among applicants for production authorizations by the Council in accordance with Annex III, article 7.

3. The members of the Commission shall, upon request by any State Party or other party concerned, be accompanied by a representative of such State or other party concerned when carrying out their function of supervision and inspection.

Subsection D. The Secretariat

Article 166

The Secretariat

1. The Secretariat of the Authority shall comprise a Secretary–General and such staff as the Authority may require.

2. The Secretary–General shall be elected for four years by the Assembly from among the candidates proposed by the Council and may be re-elected.

3. The Secretary–General shall be the chief administrative officer of the Authority, and shall act in that capacity in all meetings of the Assembly, of the Council and of any subsidiary organ, and shall perform such other administrative functions as are entrusted to the Secretary–General by these organs.

4. The Secretary–General shall make an annual report to the Assembly on the work of the Authority.

Article 167

The Staff of the Authority

1. The staff of the Authority shall consist of such qualified scientific and technical and other personnel as may be required to fulfil the administrative functions of the Authority.

2. The paramount consideration in the recruitment and employment of the staff and in the determination of their conditions of service shall be the necessity of securing the highest standards of efficiency, competence and integrity. Subject to this consideration, due regard shall be paid to the importance of recruiting the staff on as wide a geographical basis as possible.

3. The staff shall be appointed by the Secretary–General. The terms and conditions on which they shall be appointed, remunerated and dismissed shall be in accordance with the rules, regulations and procedures of the Authority.

Article 168

International Character of the Secretariat

1. In the performance of their duties the Secretary–General and the staff shall not seek or receive instructions from any government or from any other source external to the Authority. They shall refrain from any action which might reflect on their position as international officials responsible only to the Authority. Each State Party undertakes to respect the exclusively international character of the responsibilities of the Secretary–General and the staff and not to seek to influence them in the discharge of their responsibilities. Any violation of responsibilities by a staff member shall be submitted to the appropriate administrative tribunal as provided in the rules, regulations and procedures of the Authority.

2. The Secretary–General and the staff shall have no financial interest in any activity relating to exploration and exploitation in the Area. Subject to their responsibilities to the Authority, they shall not disclose, even after the termination of their functions, any industrial secret, proprietary data which are transferred to the Authority in accordance with Annex III, article 14, or any other confidential information coming to their knowledge by reason of their employment with the Authority.

3. Violations of the obligations of a staff member of the Authority set forth in paragraph 2 shall, on the request of a State Party affected by such violation, or a natural or juridical person, sponsored by a State Party as provided in article 153, paragraph 2(b), and affected by such violation, be submitted by the Authority against the staff member concerned to a tribunal designated by the rules, regulations and procedures of the Authority. The Party affected shall have the right to take part in the proceedings. If the tribunal so recommends, the Secretary–General shall dismiss the staff member concerned.

4. The rules, regulations and procedures of the Authority shall contain such provisions as are necessary to implement this article.

Article 169

Consultation and Co–Operation with International and Non–Governmental Organizations

1. The Secretary–General shall, on matters within the competence of the Authority, make suitable arrangements, with the approval of the Council, for consultation and co-operation with international and non-governmental organizations recognized by the Economic and Social Council of the United Nations.

2. Any organization with which the Secretary–General has entered into an arrangement under paragraph 1 may designate representatives

to attend meetings of the organs of the Authority as observers in accordance with the rules of procedure of these organs. Procedures shall be established for obtaining the views of such organizations in appropriate cases.

3. The Secretary–General may distribute to States Parties written reports submitted by the non-governmental organizations referred to in paragraph 1 on subjects in which they have special competence and which are related to the work of the Authority.

Subsection E. The Enterprise

Article 170

The Enterprise

1. The Enterprise shall be the organ of the Authority which shall carry out activities in the Area directly, pursuant to article 153, paragraph 2(a), as well as the transporting, processing and marketing of minerals recovered from the Area.

2. The Enterprise shall, within the framework of the international legal personality of the Authority, have such legal capacity as is provided for in the Statute set forth in Annex IV. The Enterprise shall act in accordance with this Convention and the rules, regulations and procedures of the Authority, as well as the general policies established by the Assembly, and shall be subject to the directives and control of the Council.

3. The Enterprise shall have its principal place of business at the seat of the Authority.

4. The Enterprise shall, in accordance with article 173, paragraph 2, and Annex IV, article 11, be provided with such funds as it may require to carry out its functions, and shall receive technology as provided in article 144 and other relevant provisions of this Convention.

Subsection F. Financial Arrangements of the Authority

Article 171

Funds of the Authority

The funds of the Authority shall include:

(a) assessed contributions made by members of the Authority in accordance with article 160, paragraph 2(e);

(b) funds received by the Authority pursuant to Annex III, article 13, in connection with activities in the Area;

(c) funds transferred from the Enterprise in accordance with Annex IV, article 10;

(d) funds borrowed pursuant to article 174;

(e) voluntary contributions made by members or other entities; and (f) payments to a compensation fund, in accordance with article 151, paragraph 10, whose sources are to be recommended by the Economic Planning Commission.

Article 172

Annual Budget of the Authority

The Secretary–General shall draft the proposed annual budget of the Authority and submit it to the Council. The Council shall consider the proposed annual budget and submit it to the Assembly, together with any recommendations thereon. The Assembly shall consider and approve the proposed annual budget in accordance with article 160, paragraph 2(h).

Article 173

Expenses of the Authority

1. The contributions referred to in article 171, subparagraph (a), shall be paid into a special account to meet the administrative expenses of the Authority until the Authority has sufficient funds from other sources to meet those expenses.

2. The administrative expenses of the Authority shall be a first call upon the funds of the Authority. Except for the assessed contributions referred to in article 171, subparagraph (a), the funds which remain after payment of administrative expenses may, *inter alia*:

(a) be shared in accordance with article 140 and article 160, paragraph 2(g);

(b) be used to provide the Enterprise with funds in accordance with article 170, paragraph 4;

(c) be used to compensate developing States in accordance with article 151, paragraph 10, and article 160, paragraph 2(1).

Article 174

Borrowing Power of the Authority

1. The Authority shall have the power to borrow funds.

2. The Assembly shall prescribe the limits on the borrowing power of the Authority in the financial regulations adopted pursuant to article 160, paragraph 2(f).

3. The Council shall exercise the borrowing power of the Authority.

4. States Parties shall not be liable for the debts of the Authority.

Article 175

Annual Audit

The records, books and accounts of the Authority, including its annual financial statements, shall be audited annually by an independent auditor appointed by the Assembly.

Subsection G. Legal Status, Privileges and Immunities

Article 176

Legal Status

The Authority shall have international legal personality and such legal capacity as may be necessary for the exercise of its functions and the fulfilment of its purposes.

Article 177

Privileges and Immunities

To enable the Authority to exercise its functions, it shall enjoy in the territory of each State Party the privileges and immunities set forth in this subsection. The privileges and immunities relating to the Enterprise shall be those set forth in Annex IV, article 13.

Article 178

Immunity from Legal Process

The Authority, its property and assets, shall enjoy immunity from legal process except to the extent that the Authority expressly waives this immunity in a particular case.

Article 179

Immunity from Search and Any Form of Seizure

The property and assets of the Authority, wherever located and by whomever held, shall be immune from search, requisition, confiscation, expropriation or any other form of seizure by executive or legislative action.

Article 180

Exemption from Restrictions, Regulations, Controls and Moratoria

The property and assets of the Authority shall be exempt from restrictions, regulations, controls and moratoria of any nature....

Section 5. Settlement of Disputes and Advisory Opinions

Article 186

Sea–Bed Disputes Chamber of the International Tribunal for the Law of the Sea

The establishment of the Sea–Bed Disputes Chamber and the manner which it shall exercise its jurisdiction shall be governed by the provisions of this section, of Part XV and of Annex VI.

Article 187

Jurisdiction of the Sea–Bed Disputes Chamber

The Sea–Bed Disputes Chamber shall have jurisdiction under this Part and the Annexes relating thereto in disputes with respect to activities in the Area falling within the following categories:

(a) disputes between States Parties concerning the interpretation or application of this Part and the Annexes relating thereto;

(b) disputes between a State Party and the Authority concerning:

(i) acts or omissions of the Authority or of a State Party alleged to be in violation of this Part or the Annexes relating thereto or of rules, regulations and procedures of the Authority adopted in accordance therewith; or

(ii) acts of the Authority alleged to be in excess of jurisdiction or a misuse of power;

(c) disputes between parties to a contract, being States Parties, the Authority or the Enterprise, state enterprises and natural or juridical persons referred to in article 153, paragraph 2 (b), concerning:

(i) the interpretation or application of a relevant contract or a plan of work; or

(ii) acts or omissions of a party to the contract relating to activities in the Area and directed to the other party or directly affecting its legitimate interests;

(d) disputes between the Authority and a prospective contractor who has been sponsored by a State as provided in article 153, paragraph 2 (b), and has duly fulfilled the conditions referred to in article 13, paragraph 2, concerning the refusal of a contract or a legal issue arising in the negotiation of the contract;

(e) disputes between the Authority and a State Party, a state enterprise or a natural or juridical person sponsored by a State Party as provided for in article 153, paragraph 2(b), where it is alleged that the Authority has incurred liability as provided in Annex III, article 22;

(f) any other disputes for which the jurisdiction of the Chamber is specifically provided in this Convention.

Article 188

Submission of Disputes to a Special Chamber of the International Tribunal for the Law of the Sea or an Ad Hoc Chamber of the Sea–Bed Disputes Chamber or to Binding Commercial Arbitration

1. Disputes between States Parties referred to in article 187, subparagraph (a), may be submitted:

(a) at the request of the parties to the dispute, to a special chamber of the International Tribunal for the Law of the Sea to be formed in accordance with Annex VI, articles 15 and 17; or

(b) at the request of any party to the dispute, to an ad hoc chamber of the Sea–Bed Disputes Chamber to be formed in accordance with Annex VI, article 36.

2. (a) Disputes concerning the interpretation or application of a contract referred to in article 187, subparagraph (c) (i), shall be submitted, at the request of any party to the dispute, to binding commercial arbitration, unless the parties otherwise agree. A commercial arbitral tribunal to which the dispute is submitted shall have no jurisdiction to decide any question of interpretation of this Convention. When the dispute also involves a question of the interpretation of Part XI and the Annexes relating thereto, with respect to activities in the Area, that question shall be referred to the Sea–Bed Disputes Chamber for a ruling.

(b) If, at the commencement of or in the course of such arbitration, the arbitral tribunal determines, either at the request of any party to the dispute or *proprio motu*, that its decision depends upon a ruling of the Sea–Bed Disputes Chamber, the arbitral tribunal shall refer such question to the Sea–Bed Disputes Chamber for such ruling. The arbitral tribunal shall then proceed to render its award in conformity with the ruling of the Sea–Bed Disputes Chamber.

(c) In the absence of a provision in the contract on the arbitration procedure to be applied in the dispute, the arbitration shall be conducted in accordance with the UNCITRAL Arbitration Rules or such other arbitration rules as may be prescribed in the rules, regulations and procedures of the Authority, unless the parties to the dispute otherwise agree.

Article 189

Limitation on Jurisdiction with Regard to Decisions of the Authority

The Sea–Bed Disputes Chamber shall have no jurisdiction with regard to the exercise by the Authority of its discretionary powers in accordance with this Part; in no case shall it substitute its discretion for that of the Authority. Without prejudice to article 191, in exercising its jurisdiction pursuant to article 187, the Sea–Bed Disputes Chamber shall not pronounce itself on the question of whether any rules, regulations and procedures of the Authority are in conformity with this Convention, nor declare invalid any such rules, regulations and procedures. Its jurisdiction in this regard shall be confined to deciding claims that the application of any rules, regulations and procedures of the Authority in individual cases would be in conflict with the contractual obligations of the parties to the dispute or their obligations under this Convention, claims concerning excess of jurisdiction or misuse of power, and to claims for damages to be paid or other remedy to be given to the party concerned for the failure of the other party to comply with its contractual obligations or its obligations under this Convention.

Article 190

Participation and Appearance of Sponsoring States Parties in Proceedings

1. If a natural or juridical person is a party to a dispute referred to in article 187, the sponsoring State shall be given notice thereof and shall have the right to participate in the proceedings by submitting written or oral statements.

2. If an action is brought against a State Party by a natural or juridical person sponsored by another State Party in a dispute referred to in article 187, subparagraph (c), the respondent State may request the State sponsoring that person to appear in the proceedings on behalf of that person. Failing such appearance, the respondent State may arrange to be represented by a juridical person of its nationality.

Article 191

Advisory Opinions

The Sea–Bed Disputes Chamber shall give advisory opinions at the request of the Assembly or the Council on legal questions arising within the scope of their activities. Such opinions shall be given as a matter of urgency.

PART XII. PROTECTION AND PRESERVATION OF THE MARINE ENVIRONMENT

Section 1. General Provisions

Article 192

General Obligation

States have the obligation to protect and preserve the marine environment.

Article 193

Sovereign Right of States to Exploit Their Natural Resources

States have the sovereign right to exploit their natural resources pursuant to their environmental policies and in accordance with their duty to protect and preserve the marine environment.

Article 194

Measures to Prevent, Reduce and Control Pollution of the Marine Environment

1. States shall take, individually or jointly as appropriate, all measures consistent with this Convention that are necessary to prevent, reduce and control pollution of the marine environment from any source, using for this purpose the best practicable means at their disposal and in accordance with their capabilities, and they shall endeavour to harmonize their policies in this connection.

2. States shall take all measures necessary to ensure that activities under their jurisdiction or control are so conducted as not to cause damage by pollution to other States and their environment, and that pollution arising from incidents or activities under their jurisdiction or control does not spread beyond the areas where they exercise sovereign rights in accordance with this Convention.

3. The measures taken pursuant to this Part shall deal with all sources of pollution of the marine environment. These measures shall include, *inter alia*, those designed to minimize to the fullest possible extent:

(a) the release of toxic, harmful or noxious substances, especially those which are persistent, from land-based sources, from or through the atmosphere or by dumping;

(b) pollution from vessels, in particular measures for preventing accidents and dealing with emergencies, ensuring the safety of operations at sea, preventing intentional and unintentional discharges, and regulating the design, construction, equipment, operation and manning of vessels;

(c) pollution from installations and devices used in exploration or exploitation of the natural resources of the sea-bed and subsoil, in particular measures for preventing accidents and dealing with emergencies, ensuring the safety of operations at sea, and regulating the design, construction, equipment, operation and manning of such installations or devices;

(d) pollution from other installations and devices operating in the marine environment, in particular measures for preventing accidents and dealing with emergencies, ensuring the safety of operations at sea, and regulating the design, construction, equipment, operation and manning of such installations or devices.

4. In taking measures to prevent, reduce or control pollution of the marine environment, States shall refrain from unjustifiable interference with activities carried out by other States in the exercise of their rights and in pursuance of their duties in conformity with this Convention.

5. The measures taken in accordance with this Part shall include those necessary to protect and preserve rare or fragile ecosystems as well as the habitat of depleted, threatened or endangered species and other forms of marine life.

Article 195

Duty Not to Transfer Damage or Hazards or Transform One Type of Pollution into Another

In taking measures to prevent, reduce and control pollution of the marine environment, States shall act so as not to transfer, directly or indirectly, damage or hazards from one area to another or transform one type of pollution into another.

Article 196

Use of Technologies or Introduction of Alien or New Species

1. States shall take all measures necessary to prevent, reduce and control pollution of the marine environment resulting from the use of technologies under their jurisdiction or control, or the intentional or accidental introduction of species, alien or new, to a particular part of the marine environment, which may cause significant and harmful changes thereto.

2. This article does not affect the application of this Convention regarding the prevention, reduction and control of pollution of the marine environment.

Section 2. Global and Regional Co–Operation

Article 197

Co–Operation on a Global or Regional Basis

States shall co-operate on a global basis and, as appropriate, on a regional basis, directly or through competent international organizations, in formulating and elaborating international rules, standards and recommended practices and procedures consistent with this Convention, for the protection and preservation of the marine environment, taking into account characteristic regional features.

Article 198

Notification of Imminent or Actual Damage

When a State becomes aware of cases in which the marine environment is in imminent danger of being damaged or has been damaged by pollution, it shall immediately notify other States it deems likely to be affected by such damage, as well as the competent international organizations.

Article 199

Contingency Plans Against Pollution

In the cases referred to in article 198, States in the area affected, in accordance with their capabilities, and the competent international organizations shall co-operate, to the extent possible, in eliminating the effects of pollution and preventing or minimizing the damage. To this end, States shall jointly develop and promote contingency plans for responding to pollution incidents in the marine environment.

Article 200

Studies, Research Programmes and Exchange of Information and Data

States shall co-operate, directly or through competent international organizations, for the purpose of promoting studies, undertaking programmes of scientific research and encouraging the exchange of information and data acquired about pollution of the marine environment. They shall endeavour to participate actively in regional and global programmes to acquire knowledge for the assessment of the nature and extent of pollution, exposure to it, and its pathways, risks and remedies.

Article 201

Scientific Criteria for Regulations

In the light of the information and data acquired pursuant to article 200, States shall co-operate, directly or through competent international organizations, in establishing appropriate scientific criteria for the formulation and elaboration of rules, standards and recommended practices and procedures for the prevention, reduction and control of pollution of the marine environment.

Section 3. Technical Assistance

Article 202

Scientific and Technical Assistance to Developing States

States shall, directly or through competent international organizations:

(a) promote programmes of scientific, educational, technical and other assistance to developing States for the protection and preservation of the marine environment and the prevention, reduction and control of marine pollution. Such assistance shall include, *inter alia*:

(i) training of their scientific and technical personnel;

(ii) facilitating their participation in relevant international programmes;

(iii) supplying them with necessary equipment and facilities;

(iv) enhancing their capacity to manufacture such equipment;

(v) advice on and developing facilities for research, monitoring, educational and other programmes;

(b) provide appropriate assistance, especially to developing States, for the minimization of the effects of major incidents which may cause serious pollution of the marine environment;

(c) provide appropriate assistance, especially to developing States, concerning the preparation of environmental assessments.

Article 203

Preferential Treatment for Developing States

Developing States shall, for the purposes of prevention, reduction and control of pollution of the marine environment or minimization of its effects, be granted preference by international organizations in:

(a) the allocation of appropriate funds and technical assistance; and

(b) the utilization of their specialized services.

Section 4. Monitoring and Environmental Assessment

Article 204

Monitoring of the Risks or Effects of Pollution

1. States shall, consistent with the rights of other States, endeavour, as far as practicable, directly or through the competent international organizations, to observe, measure, evaluate and analyse, by recognized scientific methods, the risks or effects of pollution of the marine environment.

2. In particular, States shall keep under surveillance the effects of any activities which they permit or in which they engage in order to determine whether these activities are likely to pollute the marine environment.

Article 205

Publication of Reports

States shall publish reports of the results obtained pursuant to article 204 or provide such reports at appropriate intervals to the competent international organizations, which should make them available to all States.

Article 206

Assessment of Potential Effects of Activities

When States have reasonable grounds for believing that planned activities under their jurisdiction or control may cause substantial pollution of or significant and harmful changes to the marine environment, they shall, as far as practicable, assess the potential effects of such activities on the marine environment and shall communicate reports of the results of such assessments in the manner provided in article 205.

Section 5. International Rules and National Legislation to Prevent, Reduce and Control Pollution of the Marine Environment

Article 207

Pollution from Land–Based Sources

1. States shall adopt laws and regulations to prevent, reduce and control pollution of the marine environment from land-based sources, including rivers, estuaries, pipelines and outfall structures, taking into account internationally agreed rules, standards and recommended practices and procedures.

2. States shall take other measures as may be necessary to prevent, reduce and control such pollution.

3. States shall endeavour to harmonize their policies in this connection at the appropriate regional level.

4. States, acting especially through competent international organizations or diplomatic conference, shall endeavour to establish global and regional rules, standards and recommended practices and procedures to prevent, reduce and control pollution of the marine environment from land-based sources, taking into account characteristic regional features, the economic capacity of developing States and their need for economic development. Such rules, standards and recommended practices and procedures shall be reexamined from time to time as necessary.

5. Laws, regulations, measures, rules, standards and recommended practices and procedures referred to in paragraphs 1, 2 and 4 shall include those designed to minimize, to the fullest extent possible, the release of toxic, harmful or noxious substances, especially those which are persistent, into the marine environment.

Article 208

Pollution from Sea–Bed Activities Subject to National Jurisdiction

1. Coastal States shall adopt laws and regulations to prevent, reduce and control pollution of the marine environment arising from or in connection with seabed activities subject to their jurisdiction and from artificial islands, installations and structures under their jurisdiction, pursuant to articles 60 and 80.

2. States shall take other measures as may be necessary to prevent, reduce and control such pollution.

3. Such laws, regulations and measures shall be no less effective than international rules, standards and recommended practices and procedures.

4. States shall endeavour to harmonize their policies in this connection at the appropriate regional level.

5. States, acting especially through competent international organizations or diplomatic conference, shall establish global and regional rules, standards and recommended practices and procedures to prevent, reduce and control pollution of the marine environment referred to in paragraph 1. Such rules, standards and recommended practices and procedures shall be re-examined from time to time as necessary.

Article 209

Pollution from Activities in the Area

1. International rules, regulations and procedures shall be established in accordance with Part XI to prevent, reduce and control pollution of the marine environment from activities in the Area. Such rules, regulations and procedures shall be re-examined from time to time as necessary.

2. Subject to the relevant provisions of this section, States shall adopt laws and regulations to prevent, reduce and control pollution of the marine environment from activities in the Area undertaken by vessels, installations, structures and other devices flying their flag or of their registry or operating under their authority, as the case may be. The requirements of such laws and regulations shall be no less effective than the international rules, regulations and procedures referred to in paragraph 1.

Article 210

Pollution by Dumping

1. States shall adopt laws and regulations to prevent, reduce and control pollution of the marine environment by dumping.

2. States shall take other measures as may be necessary to prevent, reduce and control such pollution.

3. Such laws, regulations and measures shall ensure that dumping is not carried out without the permission of the competent authorities of States.

4. States, acting especially through competent international organizations or diplomatic conference, shall endeavour to establish global and regional rules, standards and recommended practices and procedures to prevent, reduce and control such pollution. Such rules, standards and recommended practices and procedures shall be re-examined from time to time as necessary.

5. Dumping within the territorial sea and the exclusive economic zone or onto the continental shelf shall not be carried out without the express prior approval of the coastal State, which has the right to permit, regulate and control such dumping after due consideration of the matter with other States which by reason of their geographical situation may be adversely affected thereby.

6. National laws, regulations and measures shall be no less effective in preventing, reducing and controlling such pollution than the global rules and standards.

Article 211

Pollution from Vessels

1. States, acting through the competent international organization or general diplomatic conference, shall establish international rules and standards to prevent, reduce and control pollution of the marine environment from vessels and promote the adoption, in the same manner, wherever appropriate, of routing systems designed to minimize the threat of accidents which might cause pollution of the marine environment, including the coastline, and pollution damage to the related interests of coastal States. Such rules and standards shall, in the same manner, be re-examined from time to time as necessary.

2. States shall adopt laws and regulations for the prevention, reduction and control of pollution of the marine environment from vessels flying their flag or of their registry. Such laws and regulations shall at least have the same effect as that of generally accepted international rules and standards established through the competent international organization or general diplomatic conference.

3. States which establish particular requirements for the prevention, reduction and control of pollution of the marine environment as a condition for the entry of foreign vessels into their ports or internal waters or for a call at their off-shore terminals shall give due publicity to such requirements and shall communicate them to the competent international organization. Whenever such requirements are established in identical form by two or more coastal States in an endeavour to harmonize policy, the communication shall indicate which States are participating in such co-operative arrangements. Every State shall require the master of a vessel flying its flag or of its registry, when navigating within the territorial sea of a State participating in such co-operative arrangements, to furnish, upon the request of that State, information as to whether it is proceeding to a State of the same region participating in such co-operative arrangements and, if so, to indicate whether it complies with the port entry requirements of that State. This article is without prejudice to the continued exercise by a vessel of its right of innocent passage or to the application of article 25, paragraph 2.

4. Coastal States may, in the exercise of their sovereignty within their territorial sea, adopt laws and regulations for the prevention, reduction and control of marine pollution from foreign vessels, including vessels exercising the right of innocent passage. Such laws and regulations shall, in accordance with Part 11, section 3, not hamper innocent passage of foreign vessels.

5. Coastal States, for the purpose of enforcement as provided for in section 6, may in respect of their exclusive economic zones adopt laws and regulations for the prevention, reduction and control of pollution from vessels conforming to and giving effect to generally accepted international rules and standards established through the competent international organization or general diplomatic conference.

6. (a) Where the international rules and standards referred to in paragraph 1 are inadequate to meet special circumstances and

coastal States have reasonable grounds for believing that a particular, clearly defined area of their respective exclusive economic zones is an area where the adoption of special mandatory measures for the prevention of pollution from vessels is required for recognized technical reasons in relation to its oceanographical and ecological conditions, as well as its utilization or the protection of its resources and the particular character of its traffic, the coastal States, after appropriate consultations through the competent international organization with any other States concerned, may, for that area, direct a communication to that organization, submitting scientific and technical evidence in support and information on necessary reception facilities. Within 12 months after receiving such a communication, the organization shall determine whether the conditions in that area correspond to the requirements set out above. If the organization so determines, the coastal States may, for that area, adopt laws and regulations for the prevention, reduction and control of pollution from vessels implementing such international rules and standards or navigational practices as are made applicable, through the organization, for special areas. These laws and regulations shall not become applicable to foreign vessels until 15 months after the submission of the communication to the organization.

(b) The coastal States shall publish the limits of any such particular, clearly defined area.

(c) If the coastal States intend to adopt additional laws and regulations for the same area for the prevention, reduction and control of pollution from vessels, they shall, when submitting the aforesaid communication, at the same time notify the organization thereof. Such additional laws and regulations may relate to discharges or navigational practices but shall not require foreign vessels to observe design, construction, manning or equipment standards other than generally accepted international rules and standards; they shall become applicable to foreign vessels 15 months after the submission of the communication to the organization, provided that the organization agrees within 12 months after the submission of the communication.

7. The international rules and standards referred to in this article should include *inter alia* those relating to prompt notification to coastal States, whose coastline or related interests may be affected by incidents, including maritime casualties, which involve discharges or probability of discharges.

Article 212

Pollution from or through the Atmosphere

1. States shall adopt laws and regulations to prevent, reduce and control pollution of the marine environment from or through the atmosphere, applicable to the air space under their sovereignty and to vessels flying their flag or vessels or aircraft of their registry, taking into account internationally agreed rules, standards and recommended practices and procedures and the safety of air navigation.

2. States shall take other measures as may be necessary to prevent, reduce and control such pollution.

3. States, acting especially through competent international organizations or diplomatic conference, shall endeavour to establish global and regional rules, standards and recommended practices and procedures to prevent, reduce and control such pollution.

Section 6. Enforcement

Article 213

Enforcement with Respect to Pollution from Land–Based Sources

States shall enforce their laws and regulations adopted in accordance with article 207 and shall adopt laws and regulations and take other measures necessary to implement applicable international rules and standards established through competent international organizations or diplomatic conference to prevent, reduce and control pollution of the marine environment from land-based sources.

Article 214

Enforcement with Respect to Pollution from Sea–Bed Activities

States shall enforce their laws and regulations adopted in accordance with article 208 and shall adopt laws and regulations and take other measures necessary to implement applicable international rules and standards established through competent international organizations or diplomatic conference to prevent, reduce and control pollution of the marine environment arising from or in connection with sea-bed activities subject to their jurisdiction and from artificial islands, installations and structures under their jurisdiction, pursuant to articles 60 and 80.

Article 215

Enforcement with Respect to Pollution from Activities in the Area

Enforcement of international rules, regulations and procedures established in accordance with Part XI to prevent, reduce and control pollution of the marine environment from activities in the Area shall be governed by that Part.

Article 216

Enforcement with Respect to Pollution by Dumping

1. Laws and regulations adopted in accordance with this Convention and applicable international rules and standards established through competent international organizations or diplomatic conference for the prevention, reduction and control of pollution of the marine environment by dumping shall be enforced:

(a) by the coastal State with regard to dumping within its territorial sea or its exclusive economic zone or onto its continental shelf;

(b) by the flag State with regard to vessels flying its flag or vessels or aircraft of its registry;

(c) by any State with regard to acts of loading of wastes or other matter occurring within its territory or at its off-shore terminals.

2. No State shall be obliged by virtue of this article to institute proceedings when another State has already instituted proceedings in accordance with this article.

Article 217

Enforcement by Flag States

1. States shall ensure compliance by vessels flying their flag or of their registry with applicable international rules and standards, established through the competent international organization or general diplomatic conference, and with their laws and regulations adopted in accordance with this Convention for the prevention, reduction and control of pollution of the marine environment from vessels and shall accordingly adopt laws and regulations and take other measures necessary for their implementation. Flag States shall provide for the effective enforcement of such rules, standards, laws and regulations, irrespective of where a violation occurs.

2. States shall, in particular, take appropriate measures in order to ensure that vessels flying their flag or of their registry are prohibited from sailing, until they can proceed to sea in compliance with the requirements of the international rules and standards referred to in paragraph 1, including requirements in respect of design, construction, equipment and manning of vessels.

3. States shall ensure that vessels flying their flag or of their registry carry on board certificates required by and issued pursuant to international rules and standards referred to in paragraph 1. States shall ensure that vessels flying their flag are periodically inspected in order to verify that such certificates are in conformity with the actual condition of the vessels. These certificates shall be accepted by other States as evidence of the condition of the vessels and shall be regarded as having the same force as certificates issued by them, unless there are clear grounds for believing that the condition of the vessel does not correspond substantially with the particulars of the certificates.

4. If a vessel commits a violation of rules and standards established through the competent international organization or general diplomatic conference, the flag State, without prejudice to articles 218, 220 and 228, shall provide for immediate investigation and where appropriate institute proceedings in respect of the alleged violation irrespective of where the violation occurred or where the pollution caused by such violation has occurred or has been spotted.

5. Flag States conducting an investigation of the violation may request the assistance of any other State whose co-operation could be useful in clarifying the circumstances of the case. States shall endeavour to meet appropriate requests of flag States.

6. States shall, at the written request of any State, investigate any violation alleged to have been committed by vessels flying their flag. If satisfied that sufficient evidence is available to enable proceedings to be brought in respect of the alleged violation, flag States shall without delay institute such proceedings in accordance with their laws.

7. Flag States shall promptly inform the requesting State and the competent international organization of the action taken and its outcome. Such information shall be available to all States.

8. Penalties provided for by the laws and regulations of States for vessels flying their flag shall be adequate in severity to discourage violations wherever they occur.

Article 218

Enforcement by Port States

1. When a vessel is voluntarily within a port or at an off-shore terminal of a State, that State may undertake investigations and, where the evidence so warrants, institute proceedings in respect of any discharge from that vessel outside the internal waters, territorial sea or exclusive economic zone of that State in violation of applicable international rules and standards established through the competent international organization or general diplomatic conference.

2. No proceedings pursuant to paragraph 1 shall be instituted in respect of a discharge violation in the internal waters, territorial sea or exclusive economic zone of another State unless requested by that State, the flag State, or a State damaged or threatened by the discharge violation, or unless the violation has caused or is likely to cause pollution in the internal waters, territorial sea or exclusive economic zone of the State instituting the proceedings.

3. When a vessel is voluntarily within a port or at an off-shore terminal of a State, that State shall, as far as practicable, comply with requests from any State for investigation of a discharge violation referred to in paragraph 1, believed to have occurred in, caused, or threatened damage to the internal waters, territorial sea or exclusive economic zone of the requesting State. It shall likewise, as far as practicable, comply with requests from the flag State for investigation of such a violation, irrespective of where the violation occurred.

4. The records of the investigation carried out by a port State pursuant to this article shall be transmitted upon request to the flag State or to the coastal State. Any proceedings instituted by the port State on the basis of such an investigation may, subject to section 7, be suspended at the request of the coastal State when the violation has occurred within its internal waters, territorial sea or exclusive economic zone. The evidence and records of the case, together with any bond or other financial security posted with the authorities of the port State, shall in that event be transmitted to the coastal State. Such transmittal shall preclude the continuation of proceedings in the port State.

Article 219

Measures Relating to Seaworthiness of Vessels to Avoid Pollution

Subject to section 7, States which, upon request or on their own initiative, have ascertained that a vessel within one of their ports or at one of their offshore terminals is in violation of applicable international rules and standards relating to seaworthiness of vessels and thereby threatens damage to the marine environment shall, as far as practicable, take administrative measures to prevent the vessel from sailing. Such States may permit the vessel to proceed only to the nearest appropriate repair yard and, upon removal of the causes of the violation, shall permit the vessel to continue immediately.

Article 220

Enforcement by Coastal States

1. When a vessel is voluntarily within a port or at an off-shore terminal of a State, that State may, subject to section 7, institute proceedings in respect of any violation of its laws and regulations adopted in accordance with this Convention or applicable international rules and standards for the prevention, reduction and control of pollution from vessels when the violation has occurred within the territorial sea or the exclusive economic zone of that State.

2. Where there are clear grounds for believing that a vessel navigating in the territorial sea of a State has, during its passage therein, violated laws and regulations of that State adopted in accordance with this Convention or applicable international rules and standards for the prevention, reduction and control of pollution from vessels, that State, without prejudice to the application of the relevant provisions of Part II, section 3, may undertake physical inspection of the vessel relating to the violation and may, where the evidence so warrants institute proceedings, including detention of the vessel, in accordance with its laws, subject to the provisions of section 7.

3. Where there are clear grounds for believing that a vessel navigating in the exclusive economic zone or the territorial sea of a State has, in the exclusive economic zone, committed a violation of applicable international rules and standards for the prevention, reduction and control of pollution from vessels or laws and regulations of that State conforming and giving effect to such rules and standards, that State may require the vessel to give information regarding its identity and port of registry, its last and its next port of call and other relevant information required to establish whether a violation has occurred.

4. States shall adopt laws and regulations and take other measures so that vessels flying their flag comply with requests for information pursuant to paragraph 3.

5. Where there are clear grounds for believing that a vessel navigating in the exclusive economic zone or the territorial sea of a State has, in the exclusive economic zone, committed a violation referred to in paragraph 3 resulting in a substantial discharge causing or threatening significant pollution of the marine environment, that State may under-

take physical inspection of the vessel for matters relating to the violation if the vessel has refused to give information or if the information supplied by the vessel is manifestly at variance with the evident factual situation and if the circumstances of the case justify such inspection.

6. Where there is clear objective evidence that a vessel navigating in the exclusive economic zone or the territorial sea of a State has, in the exclusive economic zone, committed a violation referred to in paragraph 3 resulting in a discharge causing major damage or threat of major damage to the coastline or related interests of the coastal State, or to any resources of its territorial sea or exclusive economic zone, that State may, subject to section 7, provided that the evidence so warrants, institute proceedings, including detention of the vessel, in accordance with its laws.

7. Notwithstanding the provisions of paragraph 6, whenever appropriate procedures have been established, either through the competent international organization or as otherwise agreed, whereby compliance with requirements for bonding or other appropriate financial security has been assured, the coastal State if bound by such procedures shall allow the vessel to proceed.

8. The provisions of paragraphs 3, 4, 5, 6 and 7 also apply in respect of national laws and regulations adopted pursuant to article 211, paragraph 6.

Article 221

Measures to Avoid Pollution Arising from Maritime Casualties

1. Nothing in this Part shall prejudice the right of States, pursuant to international law, both customary and conventional, to take and enforce measures beyond the territorial sea proportionate to the actual or threatened damage to protect their coastline or related interests, including fishing, from pollution or threat of pollution following upon a maritime casualty or acts relating to such a casualty, which may reasonably be expected to result in major harmful consequences.

2. For the purposes of this article, "maritime casualty" means a collision of vessels, stranding or other incident of navigation, or other occurrence on board a vessel or external to it resulting in material damage or imminent threat of material damage to a vessel or cargo.

Article 222

Enforcement with Respect to Pollution from or through the Atmosphere

States shall enforce, within the air space under their sovereignty or with regard to vessels flying their flag or vessels or aircraft of their registry, their laws and regulations adopted in accordance with article 212, paragraph 1, and with other provisions of this Convention and shall adopt laws and regulations and take other measures necessary to implement applicable international rules and standards established through competent international organizations or diplomatic conference to prevent, reduce and control pollution of the marine environment from or through the atmosphere, in conformity with all relevant international rules and standards concerning the safety of air navigation.

Section 7. Safeguards

Article 223

Measures to Facilitate Proceedings

In proceedings instituted pursuant to this Part, States shall take measures to facilitate the hearing of witnesses and the admission of evidence submitted by authorities of another State, or by the competent international organization, and shall facilitate the attendance at such proceedings of official representatives of the competent international organization, the flag State and any State affected by pollution arising out of any violation. The official representatives attending such proceedings shall have such rights and duties as may be provided under national laws and regulations or international law.

Article 224

Exercise of Powers of Enforcement

The powers of enforcement against foreign vessels under this Part may only be exercised by officials or by warships, military aircraft, or other ships or aircraft clearly marked and identifiable as being on government service and authorized to that effect.

Article 225

Duty to Avoid Adverse Consequences in the Exercise of the Powers of Enforcement

In the exercise under this Convention of their powers of enforcement against foreign vessels, States shall not endanger the safety of navigation or otherwise create any hazard to a vessel, or bring it to an unsafe port or anchorage, or expose the marine environment to an unreasonable risk.

Article 226

Investigation of Foreign Vessels

1. (a) States shall not delay a foreign vessel longer than is essential for purposes of the investigations provided for in articles 216, 218 and 220. Any physical inspection of a foreign vessel shall be limited to an examination of such certificates, records or other documents as the vessel is required to carry by generally accepted international rules and standards or of any similar documents which it is carrying; further physical inspection of the vessel may be undertaken only after such an examination and only when:

(i) there are clear grounds for believing that the condition of the vessel or its equipment does not correspond substantially with the particulars of those documents;

(ii) the contents of such documents are not sufficient to confirm or verify a suspected violation; or

(iii) the vessel is not carrying valid certificates and records.

(b) If the investigation indicates a violation of applicable laws and regulations or international rules and standards for the protection and preservation of the marine environment, release shall be made promptly subject to reasonable procedures such as bonding or other appropriate financial security.

(c) Without prejudice to applicable international rules and standards relating to the seaworthiness of vessels, the release of a vessel may, whenever it would present an unreasonable threat of damage to the marine environment, be refused or made conditional upon proceeding to the nearest appropriate repair yard. Where release has been refused or made conditional, the flag State of the vessel must be promptly notified, and may seek release of the vessel in accordance with Part XV.

2. States shall co-operate to develop procedures for the avoidance of unnecessary physical inspection of vessels at sea.

Article 227

Non–Discrimination with Respect to Foreign Vessels

In exercising their rights and performing their duties under this Part, States shall not discriminate in form or in fact against vessels of any other State.

Article 228

Suspension and Restrictions on Institution of Proceedings

1. Proceedings to impose penalties in respect of any violation of applicable laws and regulations or international rules and standards relating to the prevention, reduction and control of pollution from vessels committed by a foreign vessel beyond the territorial sea of the State instituting proceedings shall be suspended upon the taking of proceedings to impose penalties in respect of corresponding charges by the flag State within six months of the date on which proceedings were first instituted, unless those proceedings relate to a case of major damage to the coastal State or the flag State in question has repeatedly disregarded its obligation to enforce effectively the applicable international rules and standards in respect of violations committed by its vessels. The flag State shall in due course make available to the State previously instituting proceedings a full dossier of the case and the records of the proceedings, whenever the flag State has requested the suspension of proceedings in accordance with this article. When proceedings instituted by the flag State have been brought to a conclusion, the suspended proceedings shall be terminated. Upon payment of costs incurred in respect of such proceedings, any bond posted or other financial security provided in connection with the suspended proceedings shall be released by the coastal State.

2. Proceedings to impose penalties on foreign vessels shall not be instituted after the expiry of three years from the date on which the violation was committed, and shall not be taken by any State in the event of proceedings having been instituted by another State subject to the provisions set out in paragraph 1.

3. The provisions of this article are without prejudice to the right of the flag State to take any measures, including proceedings to impose penalties, according to its laws irrespective of prior proceedings by another State.

Article 229

Institution of Civil Proceedings

Nothing in this Convention affects the institution of civil proceedings in respect of any claim for loss or damage resulting from pollution of the marine environment.

Article 230

Monetary Penalties and the Observance of Recognized Rights of the Accused

1. Monetary penalties only may be imposed with respect to violations of national laws and regulations or applicable international rules and standards for the prevention, reduction and control of pollution of the marine environment, committed by foreign vessels beyond the territorial sea.

2. Monetary penalties only may be imposed with respect to violations of national laws and regulations or applicable international rules and standards for the prevention, reduction and control of pollution of the marine environment, committed by foreign vessels in the territorial sea, except in the case of a wilful and serious act of pollution in the territorial sea.

3. In the conduct of proceedings in respect of such violations committed by a foreign vessel which may result in the imposition of penalties, recognized rights of the accused shall be observed.

Article 231

Notification to the Flag State and Other States Concerned

States shall promptly notify the flag State and any other State concerned of any measures taken pursuant to section 6 against foreign vessels, and shall submit to the flag State all official reports concerning such measures. However, with respect to violations committed in the territorial sea, the foregoing obligations of the coastal State apply only to such measures as are taken in proceedings. The diplomatic agents or consular officers and where possible the maritime authority of the flag State, shall be immediately informed of any such measures taken pursuant to section 6 against foreign vessels.

Article 232

Liability of States Arising from Enforcement Measures

States shall be liable for damage or loss attributable to them arising from measures taken pursuant to section 6 when such measures are unlawful or exceed those reasonably required in the light of available information. States shall provide for recourse in their courts for actions in respect of such damage or loss.

Article 233

Safeguards with Respect to Straits Used for International Navigation

Nothing in sections 5, 6 and 7 affects the legal regime of straits used for international navigation. However, if a foreign ship other than those referred to in section 10 has committed a violation of the laws and regulations referred to in article 42, paragraph 1 (a) and (b),causing or threatening major damage to the marine environment of the straits, the States bordering the straits may take appropriate enforcement measures and if so shall respect *mutatis mutandis* the provisions of this section.

Section 8. Ice–Covered Areas

Article 234

Ice–Covered Areas

Coastal States have the right to adopt and enforce non-discriminatory laws and regulations for the prevention, reduction and control of marine pollution from vessels in ice-covered areas within the limits of the exclusive economic zone, where particularly severe climatic conditions and the presence of ice covering such areas for most of the year create obstructions or exceptional hazards to navigation, and pollution of the marine environment could cause major harm to or irreversible disturbance of the ecological balance. Such laws and regulations shall have due regard to navigation and the protection and preservation of the marine environment based on the best available scientific evidence.

Section 9. Responsibility and Liability

Article 235

Responsibility and Liability

1. States are responsible for the fulfilment of their international obligations concerning the protection and preservation of the marine environment. They shall be liable in accordance with international law.

2. States shall ensure that recourse is available in accordance with their legal systems for prompt and adequate compensation or other relief in respect of damage caused by pollution of the marine environment by natural or juridical persons under their jurisdiction.

3. With the objective of assuring prompt and adequate compensation in respect of all damage caused by pollution of the marine environment, States shall co-operate in the implementation of existing international law and the further development of international law relating to

responsibility and liability for the assessment of and compensation for damage and the settlement of related disputes, as well as, where appropriate, development of criteria and procedures for payment of adequate compensation, such as compulsory insurance or compensation funds.

Section 10. Sovereign Immunity

Article 236

Sovereign Immunity

The provisions of this Convention regarding the protection and preservation of the marine environment do not apply to any warship, naval auxiliary, other vessels or aircraft owned or operated by a State and used, for the time being, only on government non-commercial service. However, each State shall ensure, by the adoption of appropriate measures not impairing operations or operational capabilities of such vessels or aircraft owned or operated by it, that such vessels or aircraft act in a manner consistent, so far as is reasonable and practicable, with this Convention.

Section 11. Obligations Under Other Conventions on the Protection and Preservation of the Marine Environment

Article 237

Obligations Under Other Conventions on the Protection and Preservation of the Marine Environment

1. The provisions of this Part are without prejudice to the specific obligations assumed by States under special conventions and agreements concluded previously which relate to the protection and preservation of the marine environment and to agreements which may be concluded in furtherance of the general principles set forth in this Convention.

2. Specific obligations assumed by States under special conventions, with respect to the protection and preservation of the marine environment, should be carried out in a manner consistent with the general principles and objectives of this Convention.

PART XIII. MARINE SCIENTIFIC RESEARCH

Section 1. General Provisions

Article 238

Right to Conduct Marine Scientific Research

All States, irrespective of their geographical location, and competent international organizations have the right to conduct marine scientific research subject to the rights and duties of other States as provided for in this Convention.

Article 239

Promotion of Marine Scientific Research

States and competent international organizations shall promote and facilitate the development and conduct of marine scientific research in accordance with this Convention.

Article 240

General Principles for the Conduct of Marine Scientific Research

In the conduct of marine scientific research the following principles shall apply:

(a) marine scientific research shall be conducted exclusively for peaceful purposes;

(b) marine scientific research shall be conducted with appropriate scientific methods and means compatible with this Convention;

(c) marine scientific research shall not unjustifiably interfere with other legitimate uses of the sea compatible with this Convention and shall be duly respected in the course of such uses;

(d) marine scientific research shall be conducted in compliance with all relevant regulations adopted in conformity with this Convention including those for the protection and preservation of the marine environment.

Article 241

Non–Recognition of Marine Scientific Research Activities as the Legal Basis for Claims

Marine scientific research activities shall not constitute the legal basis for any claim to any part of the marine environment or its resources.

Section 2. International Co–Operation

Article 242

Promotion of International Co–Operation

1. States and competent international organizations shall, in accordance with the principle of respect for sovereignty and jurisdiction and on the basis of mutual benefit, promote international co-operation in marine scientific research for peaceful purposes.

2. In this context, without prejudice to the rights and duties of States under this Convention, a State, in the application of this Part, shall provide, as appropriate, other States with a reasonable opportunity to obtain from it, or with its co-operation, information necessary to prevent and control damage to the health and safety of persons and to the marine environment.

Article 243

Creation of Favourable Conditions

States and competent international organizations shall co-operate, through the conclusion of bilateral and multilateral agreements, to create favourable conditions for the conduct of marine scientific research in the marine environment and to integrate the efforts of scientists in studying the essence of phenomena and processes occurring in the marine environment and the interrelations between them.

Article 244

Publication and Dissemination of Information and Knowledge

1. States and competent international organizations shall, in accordance with this Convention, make available by publication and dissemination through appropriate channels information on proposed major programmes and their objectives as well as knowledge resulting from marine scientific research.

2. For this purpose, States, both individually and in co-operation with other States and with competent international organizations, shall actively promote the flow of scientific data and information and the transfer of knowledge resulting from marine scientific research, especially to developing States, as well as the strengthening of the autonomous marine scientific research capabilities of developing States through, *inter alia*, programmes to provide adequate education and training of their technical and scientific personnel.

Section 3. Conduct and Promotion of Marine Scientific Research

Article 245

Marine Scientific Research in the Territorial Sea

Coastal States, in the exercise of their sovereignty, have the exclusive right to regulate, authorize and conduct marine scientific research in their territorial sea. Marine scientific research therein shall be conducted only with the express consent of and under the conditions set forth by the coastal State.

Article 246

Marine Scientific Research in the Exclusive Economic Zone and on the Continental Shelf

1. Coastal States, in the exercise of their jurisdiction, have the right to regulate, authorize and conduct marine scientific research in their exclusive economic zone and on their continental shelf in accordance with the relevant provisions of this Convention.

2. Marine scientific research in the exclusive economic zone and on the continental shelf shall be conducted with the consent of the coastal State.

3. Coastal States shall, in normal circumstances, grant their consent for marine scientific research projects by other States or competent international organizations in their exclusive economic zone or on their

continental shelf to be carried out in accordance with this Convention exclusively for peaceful purposes and in order to increase scientific knowledge of the marine environment for the benefit of all mankind. To this end, coastal States shall establish rules and procedures ensuring that such consent will not be delayed or denied unreasonably.

4. For the purposes of applying paragraph 3, normal circumstances may exist in spite of the absence of diplomatic relations between the coastal State and the researching State.

5. Coastal States may however in their discretion withhold their consent to the conduct of a marine scientific research project of another State or competent international organization in the exclusive economic zone or on the continental shelf of the coastal State if that project:

(a) is of direct significance for the exploration and exploitation of natural resources, whether living or non-living;

(b) involves drilling into the continental shelf, the use of explosives or the introduction of harmful substances into the marine environment;

(c) involves the construction, operation or use of artificial islands, installations and structures referred to in articles 60 and 80;

(d) contains information communicated pursuant to article 248 regarding the nature and objectives of the project which is inaccurate or if the researching State or competent international organization has outstanding obligations to the coastal State from a prior research project.

6. Notwithstanding the provisions of paragraph 5, coastal States may not exercise their discretion to withhold consent under subparagraph (a) of that paragraph in respect of marine scientific research projects to be undertaken in accordance with the provisions of this Part on the continental shelf, beyond 200 nautical miles from the baselines from which the breadth of the territorial sea is measured, outside those specific areas which coastal States may at any time publicly designate as areas in which exploitation or detailed exploratory operations focused on those areas are occurring or will occur within a reasonable period of time. Coastal States shall give reasonable notice of the designation of such areas, as well as any modifications thereto, but shall not be obliged to give details of the operations therein.

7. The provisions of paragraph 6 are without prejudice to the rights of coastal States over the continental shelf as established in article 77.

8. Marine scientific research activities referred to in this article shall not unjustifiably interfere with activities undertaken by coastal States in the exercise of their sovereign rights and jurisdiction provided for in this Convention.

Article 247

Marine Scientific Research Projects Undertaken by or under the Auspices of International Organizations

A coastal State which is a member of or has a bilateral agreement with an international organization, and in whose exclusive economic zone or on whose continental shelf that organization wants to carry out a marine scientific research project, directly or under its auspices, shall be deemed to have authorized the project to be carried out in conformity with the agreed specifications if that State approved the detailed project when the decision was made by the organization for the undertaking of the project, or is willing to participate in it, and has not expressed any objection within four months of notification of the project by the organization to the coastal State.

Article 248

Duty to Provide Information to the Coastal State

States and competent international organizations which intend to undertake marine scientific research in the exclusive economic zone or on the continental shelf of a coastal State shall, not less than six months in advance of the expected starting date of the marine scientific research project, provide that State with a full description of:

(a) the nature and objectives of the project;

(b) the method and means to be used, including name, tonnage, type and class of vessels and a description of scientific equipment;

(c) the precise geographical areas in which the project is to be conducted;

(d) the expected date of first appearance and final departure of the research vessels, or deployment of the equipment and its removal, as appropriate;

(e) the name of the sponsoring institution, its director, and the person in charge of the project; and (f) the extent to which it is considered that the coastal State should be able to participate or to be represented in the project.

Article 249

Duty to Comply with Certain Conditions

1. States and competent international organizations when undertaking marine scientific research in the exclusive economic zone or on the continental shelf of a coastal State shall comply with the following conditions:

(a) ensure the right of the coastal State, if it so desires, to participate or be represented in the marine scientific research project, especially on board research vessels and other craft or scientific research installations, when practicable, without payment of any remuneration to the scientists of the coastal State and without obligation to contribute towards the costs of the project;

(b) provide the coastal State, at its request, with preliminary reports, as soon as practicable, and with the final results and conclusions after the completion of the research;

(c) undertake to provide access for the coastal State, at its request, to all data and samples derived from the marine scientific research project and likewise to furnish it with data which may be copied and samples which may be divided without detriment to their scientific value;

(d) if requested, provide the coastal State with an assessment of such data, samples and research results or provide assistance in their assessment or interpretation;

(e) ensure, subject to paragraph 2, that the research results are made internationally available through appropriate national or international channels, as soon as practicable;

(f) inform the coastal State immediately of any major change in the research programme;

(g) unless otherwise agreed, remove the scientific research installations or equipment once the research is completed.

2. This article is without prejudice to the conditions established by the laws and regulations of the coastal State for the exercise of its discretion to grant or withhold consent pursuant to article 246, paragraph 5, including requiring prior agreement for making internationally available the research results of a project of direct significance for the exploration and exploitation of natural resources.

Article 250

Communications Concerning Marine Scientific Research Projects

Communications concerning the marine scientific research projects shall be made through appropriate official channels, unless otherwise agreed.

Article 251

General Criteria and Guidelines

States shall seek to promote through competent international organizations the establishment of general criteria and guidelines to assist States in ascertaining the nature and implications of marine scientific research.

Article 252

Implied Consent

States or competent international organizations may proceed with a marine scientific research project six months after the date upon which the information required pursuant to article 248 was provided to the coastal State unless within four months of the receipt of the communication containing such information the coastal State has informed the State or organization conducting the research that:

(a) it has withheld its consent under the provisions of article 246; or

(b) the information given by that State or competent international organization regarding the nature or objectives of the project does not conform to the manifestly evident facts; or

(c) it requires supplementary information relevant to conditions and the information provided for under articles 248 and 249; or

(d) outstanding obligations exist with respect to a previous marine scientific research project carried out by that State or organization, with regard to conditions established in article 249.

Article 253

Suspension or Cessation of Marine Scientific Research Activities

1. A coastal State shall have the right to require the suspension of any marine scientific research activities in progress within its exclusive economic zone or on its continental shelf if:

(a) the research activities are not being conducted in accordance with the information communicated as provided under article 248 upon which the consent of the coastal State was based; or

(b) the State or competent international organization conducting the research activities fails to comply with the provisions of article 249 concerning the rights of the coastal State with respect to the marine scientific research project.

2. A coastal State shall have the right to require the cessation of any marine scientific research activities in case of any non-compliance with the provisions of article 248 which amounts to a major change in the research project or the research activities.

3. A coastal State may also require cessation of marine scientific research activities if any of the situations contemplated in paragraph 1 are not rectified within a reasonable period of time.

4. Following notification by the coastal State of its decision to order suspension or cessation, States or competent international organizations authorized to conduct marine scientific research activities shall terminate the research activities that are the subject of such a notification.

5. An order of suspension under paragraph 1 shall be lifted by the coastal State and the marine scientific research activities allowed to continue once the researching State or competent international organization has complied with the conditions required under articles 248 and 249.

Article 254

Rights of Neighbouring Land–Locked and Geographically Disadvantaged States

1. States and competent international organizations which have submitted to a coastal State a project to undertake marine scientific research referred to in article 246, paragraph 3, shall give notice to the neighbouring land-locked and geographically disadvantaged States of the proposed research project, and shall notify the coastal State thereof.

2. After the consent has been given for the proposed marine scientific research project by the coastal State concerned, in accordance with article 246 and other relevant provisions of this Convention, States and competent international organizations undertaking such a project shall provide to the neighbouring land-locked and geographically disad-

vantaged States, at their request and when appropriate, relevant information as specified in article 248 and article 249, paragraph 1 (f).

3. The neighbouring land-locked and geographically disadvantaged States referred to above shall, at their request, be given the opportunity to participate, whenever feasible, in the proposed marine scientific research project through qualified experts appointed by them and not objected to by the coastal State, in accordance with the conditions agreed for the project, in conformity with the provisions of this Convention, between the coastal State concerned and the State or competent international organizations conducting the marine scientific research.

4. States and competent international organizations referred to in paragraph 1 shall provide to the above-mentioned land-locked and geographically disadvantaged States, at their request, the information and assistance specified in article 249, paragraph 1 (d), subject to the provisions of article 249, paragraph 2.

Article 255

Measures to Facilitate Marine Scientific Research and Assist Research Vessels

States shall endeavour to adopt reasonable rules, regulations and procedures to promote and facilitate marine scientific research conducted in accordance with this Convention beyond their territorial sea and, as appropriate, to facilitate, subject to the provisions of their laws and regulations, access to their harbours and promote assistance for marine scientific research vessels which comply with the relevant provisions of this Part.

Article 256

Marine Scientific Research in the Area

All States, irrespective of their geographical location, and competent international organizations have the right, in conformity with the provisions of Part XI, to conduct marine scientific research in the Area.

Article 257

Marine Scientific Research in the Water Column Beyond the Exclusive Economic Zone

All States, irrespective of their geographical location, and competent international organizations have the right, in conformity with this Convention, to conduct marine scientific research in the water column beyond the limits of the exclusive economic zone.

Section 4. Scientific Research Installations or Equipment in the Marine Environment

Article 258

Deployment and Use

The deployment and use of any type of scientific research installations or equipment in any area of the marine environment shall be subject to the same conditions as are prescribed in this Convention for the conduct of marine scientific research in any such area.

Article 259

Legal Status

The installations or equipment referred to in this section do not possess the status of islands. They have no territorial sea of their own, and their presence does not affect the delimitation of the territorial sea, the exclusive economic zone or the continental shelf.

Article 260

Safety Zones

Safety zones of a reasonable breadth not exceeding a distance of 500 metres may be created around scientific research installations in accordance with the relevant provisions of this Convention. All States shall ensure that such safety zones are respected by their vessels.

Article 261

Non–Interference with Shipping Routes

The deployment and use of any type of scientific research installations or equipment shall not constitute an obstacle to established international shipping routes.

Article 262

Identification Markings and Warning Signals

Installations or equipment referred to in this section shall bear identification markings indicating the State of registry or the international organization to which they belong and shall have adequate internationally agreed warning signals to ensure safety at sea and the safety of air navigation, taking into account rules and standards established by competent international organizations.

Section 5. Responsibility and Liability

Article 263

Responsibility and Liability

1. States and competent international organizations shall be responsible for ensuring that marine scientific research, whether undertaken by them or on their behalf, is conducted in accordance with this Convention.

2. States and competent international organizations shall be responsible and liable for the measures they take in contravention of this Convention in respect of marine scientific research conducted by other States, their natural or juridical persons or by competent international organizations, and shall provide compensation for damage resulting from such measures.

3. States and competent international organizations shall be responsible and liable pursuant to article 235 for damage caused by

pollution of the marine environment arising out of marine scientific research undertaken by them or on their behalf.

Section 6. Settlement of Disputes and Interim Measures

Article 264

Settlement of Disputes

Disputes concerning the interpretation or application of the provisions of this Convention with regard to marine scientific research shall be settled in accordance with Part XV, sections 2 and 3.

Article 265

Interim Measures

Pending settlement of a dispute in accordance with Part XV, sections 2 and 3, the State or competent international organization authorized to conduct a marine scientific research project shall not allow research activities to commence or continue without the express consent of the coastal State concerned.

PART XIV. DEVELOPMENT AND TRANSFER OF MARINE TECHNOLOGY

Section 1. General Provisions

Article 266

Promotion of the Development and Transfer of Marine Technology

1. States, directly or through competent international organizations, shall cooperate in accordance with their capabilities to promote actively the development and transfer of marine science and marine technology on fair and reasonable terms and conditions.

2. States shall promote the development of the marine scientific and technological capacity of States which may need and request technical assistance in this field, particularly developing States, including land-locked and geographically disadvantaged States, with regard to the exploration, exploitation, conservation and management of marine resources, the protection and preservation of the marine environment, marine scientific research and other activities in the marine environment compatible with this Convention, with a view to accelerating the social and economic development of the developing States.

3. States shall endeavour to foster favourable economic and legal conditions for the transfer of marine technology for the benefit of all parties concerned on an equitable basis.

Article 267

Protection of Legitimate Interests

States, in promoting co-operation pursuant to article 266, shall have due regard for all legitimate interests including, *inter alia*, the rights and duties of holders, suppliers and recipients of marine technology.

Article 268

Basic Objectives

States, directly or through competent international organizations, shall promote:

(a) the acquisition, evaluation and dissemination of marine technological knowledge and facilitate access to such information and data;

(b) the development of appropriate marine technology;

(c) the development of the necessary technological infrastructure to facilitate the transfer of marine technology;

(d) the development of human resources through training and education of nationals of developing States and countries and especially the nationals of the least developed among them;

(e) international co-operation at all levels, particularly at the regional, subregional and bilateral levels.

Article 269

Measures to Achieve the Basic Objectives

In order to achieve the objectives referred to in article 268, States, directly or through competent international organizations, shall endeavour, *inter alia*, to:

(a) establish programmes of technical co-operation for the effective transfer of all kinds of marine technology to States which may need and request technical assistance in this field, particularly the developing land-locked and geographically disadvantaged States, as well as other developing States which have not been able either to establish or develop their own technological capacity in marine science and in the exploration and exploitation of marine resources or to develop the infrastructure of such technology;

(b) promote favourable conditions for the conclusion of agreements, contracts and other similar arrangements, under equitable and reasonable conditions;

(c) hold conferences, seminars and symposia on scientific and technological subjects, in particular on policies and methods for the transfer of marine technology;

(d) promote the exchange of scientists and of technological and other experts;

(e) undertake projects and promote joint ventures and other forms of bilateral and multilateral co-operation.

Section 2. International Co–Operation

Article 270

Ways and Means of International Co–Operation

International co-operation for the development and transfer of marine technology shall be carried out, where feasible and appropriate, through existing bilateral, regional or multilateral programmes, and also through expanded and new programmes in order to facilitate marine scientific research, the transfer of marine technology, particularly in new fields, and appropriate international funding for ocean research and development.

Article 271

Guidelines, Criteria and Standards

States, directly or through competent international organizations, shall promote the establishment of generally accepted guidelines, criteria and standards for the transfer of marine technology on a bilateral basis or within the framework of international organizations and other fora, taking into account, in particular, the interests and needs of developing States.

Article 272

Co–Ordination of International Programmes

In the field of transfer of marine technology, States shall endeavour to ensure that competent international organizations co-ordinate their activities, including any regional or global programmes, taking into account the interests and needs of developing States, particularly land-locked and geographically disadvantaged States.

Article 273

Co–Operation with International Organizations and the Authority

States shall co-operate actively with competent international organizations and the Authority to encourage and facilitate the transfer to developing States, their nationals and the Enterprise of skills and marine technology with regard to activities in the Area.

Article 274

Objectives of the Authority

Subject to all legitimate interests including, *inter alia*, the rights and duties of holders, suppliers and recipients of technology, the Authority, with regard to activities in the Area, shall ensure that:

(a) on the basis of the principle of equitable geographical distribution, nationals of developing States, whether coastal, land-locked or geographically disadvantaged, shall be taken on for the purposes of training as members of the managerial, research and technical staff constituted for its undertakings;

(b) the technical documentation on the relevant equipment, machinery, devices and processes is made available to all States, in particular developing States which may need and request technical assistance in this field;

(c) adequate provision is made by the Authority to facilitate the acquisition of technical assistance in the field of marine technology by States which may need and request it, in particular developing

States, and the acquisition by their nationals of the necessary skills and know-how, including professional training;

(d) States which may need and request technical assistance in this field, in particular developing States, are assisted in the acquisition of necessary equipment, processes, plant and other technical know-how through any financial arrangements provided for in this Convention.

Section 3. National and Regional Marine Scientific and Technological Centres

Article 275

Establishment of National Centres

1. States, directly or through competent international organizations and the Authority, shall promote the establishment, particularly in developing coastal States, of national marine scientific and technological research centres and the strengthening of existing national centres, in order to stimulate and advance the conduct of marine scientific research by developing coastal States and to enhance their national capabilities to utilize and preserve their marine resources for their economic benefit.

2. States, through competent international organizations and the Authority, shall give adequate support to facilitate the establishment and strengthening of such national centres so as to provide for advanced training facilities and necessary equipment, skills and know-how as well as technical experts to such States which may need and request such assistance.

Article 276

Establishment of Regional Centres

1. States, in co-ordination with the competent international organizations, the Authority and national marine scientific and technological research institutions, shall promote the establishment of regional marine scientific and technological research centres, particularly in developing States, in order to stimulate and advance the conduct of marine scientific research by developing States and foster the transfer of marine technology.

2. All States of a region shall co-operate with the regional centres therein to ensure the more effective achievement of their objectives.

Article 277

Functions of Regional Centres

The functions of such regional centres shall include, *inter alia*:

(a) training and educational programmes at all levels on various aspects of marine scientific and technological research, particularly marine biology, including conservation and management of living resources, oceanography, hydrography, engineering, geological exploration of the sea-bed, mining and desalination technologies;

(b) management studies;

(c) study programmes related to the protection and preservation of the marine environment and the prevention, reduction and control of pollution;

(d) organization of regional conferences, seminars and symposia;

(e) acquisition and processing of marine scientific and technological data and information;

(f) prompt dissemination of results of marine scientific and technological research in readily available publications;

(g) publicizing national policies with regard to the transfer of marine technology and systematic comparative study of those policies;

(h) compilation and systematization of information on the marketing of technology and on contracts and other arrangements concerning patents;

(i) technical co-operation with other States of the region.

Section 4. Co–Operation Among International Organizations

Article 278

Co–Operation Among International Organizations

The competent international organizations referred to in this Part and in Part XIII shall take all appropriate measures to ensure, either directly or in close cooperation among themselves, the effective discharge of their functions and responsibilities under this Part.

PART XV. SETTLEMENT OF DISPUTES

Section 1. General Provisions

Article 279

Obligation to Settle Disputes by Peaceful Means

States Parties shall settle any dispute between them concerning the interpretation or application of this Convention by peaceful means in accordance with Article 2, paragraph 3, of the Charter of the United Nations and, to this end, shall seek a solution by the means indicated in Article 33, paragraph 1, of the Charter.

Article 280

Settlement of Disputes by Any Peaceful Means Chosen by the Parties

Nothing in this Part impairs the right of any States Parties to agree at any time to settle a dispute between them concerning the interpretation or application of this Convention by any peaceful means of their own choice.

Article 281

Procedure Where No Settlement Has Been Reached by the Parties

1. If the States Parties which are parties to a dispute concerning the interpretation or application of this Convention have agreed to seek settlement of the dispute by a peaceful means of their own choice, the

procedures provided for in this Part apply only where no settlement has been reached by recourse to such means and the agreement between the parties does not exclude any further procedure.

2. If the parties have also agreed on a time-limit, paragraph 1 applies only upon the expiration of that time-limit.

Article 282

Obligations Under General, Regional or Bilateral Agreements

If the States Parties which are parties to a dispute concerning the interpretation or application of this Convention have agreed, through a general, regional or bilateral agreement or otherwise, that such dispute shall, at the request of any party to the dispute, be submitted to a procedure that entails a binding decision, that procedure shall apply in lieu of the procedures provided for in this Part, unless the parties to the dispute otherwise agree.

Article 283

Obligation to Exchange Views

1. When a dispute arises between States Parties concerning the interpretation or application of this Convention, the parties to the dispute shall proceed expeditiously to an exchange of views regarding its settlement by negotiation or other peaceful means.

2. The parties shall also proceed expeditiously to an exchange of views where a procedure for the settlement of such a dispute has been terminated without a settlement or where a settlement has been reached and the circumstances require consultation regarding the manner of implementing the settlement.

Article 284

Conciliation

1. A State Party which is a party to a dispute concerning the interpretation or application of this Convention may invite the other party or parties to submit the dispute to conciliation in accordance with the procedure under Annex V, section 1, or another conciliation procedure.

2. If the invitation is accepted and if the parties agree upon the conciliation procedure to be applied, any party may submit the dispute to that procedure.

3. If the invitation is not accepted or the parties do not agree upon the procedure, the conciliation proceedings shall be deemed to be terminated.

4. Unless the parties otherwise agree, when a dispute has been submitted to conciliation, the proceedings may be terminated only in accordance with the agreed conciliation procedure.

Article 285

Application of this Section to Disputes Submitted Pursuant to Part XI

This section applies to any dispute which pursuant to Part XI, section 5, is to be settled in accordance with procedures provided for in this Part. If an entity other than a State Party is a party to such a dispute, this section applies *mutatis mutandis*.

Section 2. Compulsory Procedures Entailing Binding Decisions

Article 286

Application of Procedures Under this Section

Subject to section 3, any dispute concerning the interpretation or application of this Convention shall, where no settlement has been reached by recourse to section 1, be submitted at the request of any party to the dispute to the court or tribunal having jurisdiction under this section.

Article 287

Choice of Procedure

1. When signing, ratifying or acceding to this Convention or at any time thereafter, a State shall be free to choose, by means of a written declaration, one or more of the following means for the settlement of disputes concerning the interpretation or application of this Convention:

(a) the International Tribunal for the Law of the Sea established in accordance with Annex VI;

(b) the International Court of Justice;

(c) an arbitral tribunal constituted in accordance with Annex VII;

(d) a special arbitral tribunal constituted in accordance with Annex VIII for one or more of the categories of disputes specified therein.

2. A declaration made under paragraph 1 shall not affect or be affected by the obligation of a State Party to accept the jurisdiction of the Sea–Bed Disputes Chamber of the International Tribunal for the Law of the Sea to the extent and in the manner provided for in Part XI, section 5.

3. A State Party, which is a party to a dispute not covered by a declaration in force, shall be deemed to have accepted arbitration in accordance with Annex VII.

4. If the parties to a dispute have accepted the same procedure for the settlement of the dispute, it may be submitted only to that procedure, unless the parties otherwise agree.

5. If the parties to a dispute have not accepted the same procedure for the settlement of the dispute, it may be submitted only to arbitration in accordance with Annex VII, unless the parties otherwise agree.

6. A declaration made under paragraph 1 shall remain in force until three months after notice of revocation has been deposited with the Secretary–General of the United Nations.

7. A new declaration, a notice of revocation or the expiry of a declaration does not in any way affect proceedings pending before a court or tribunal having jurisdiction under this article, unless the parties otherwise agree.

8. Declarations and notices referred to in this article shall be deposited with the Secretary–General of the United Nations, who shall transmit copies thereof to the States Parties.

Article 288

Jurisdiction

1. A court or tribunal referred to in article 287 shall have jurisdiction over any dispute concerning the interpretation or application of this Convention which is submitted to it in accordance with this Part.

2. A court or tribunal referred to in article 287 shall also have jurisdiction over any dispute concerning the interpretation or application of an international agreement related to the purposes of this Convention, which is submitted to it in accordance with the agreement.

3. The Sea–Bed Disputes Chamber of the International Tribunal for the Law of the Sea established in accordance with Annex VI, and any other chamber or arbitral tribunal referred to in Part XI, section 5, shall have jurisdiction in any matter which is submitted to it in accordance therewith.

4. In the event of a dispute as to whether a court or tribunal has jurisdiction, the matter shall be settled by decision of that court or tribunal.

Article 289

Experts

In any dispute involving scientific or technical matters, a court or tribunal exercising jurisdiction under this section may, at the request of a party or *proprio motu*, select in consultation with the parties no fewer than two scientific or technical experts chosen preferably from the relevant list prepared in accordance with Annex VIII, article 2, to sit with the court or tribunal but without the right to vote.

Article 290

Provisional Measures

1. If a dispute has been duly submitted to a court or tribunal which considers that *prima facie* it has jurisdiction under this Part or Part XI, section 5, the court or tribunal may prescribe any provisional measures which it considers appropriate under the circumstances to preserve the respective rights of the parties to the dispute or to prevent serious harm to the marine environment, pending the final decision.

2. Provisional measures may be modified or revoked as soon as the circumstances justifying them have changed or ceased to exist.

3. Provisional measures may be prescribed, modified or revoked under this article only at the request of a party to the dispute and after the parties have been given an opportunity to be heard.

4. The court or tribunal shall forthwith give notice to the parties to the dispute, and to such other States Parties as it considers appropriate, of the prescription, modification or revocation of provisional measures.

5. Pending the constitution of an arbitral tribunal to which a dispute is being submitted under this section, any court or tribunal agreed upon by the parties or, failing such agreement within two weeks from the date of the request for provisional measures, the International Tribunal for the Law of the Sea or, with respect to activities in the Area, the Sea–Bed Disputes Chamber, may prescribe, modify or revoke provisional measures in accordance with this article if it considers that *prima facie* the tribunal which is to be constituted would have jurisdiction and that the urgency of the situation so requires. Once constituted, the tribunal to which the dispute has been submitted may modify, revoke or affirm those provisional measures, acting in conformity with paragraphs 1 to 4.

6. The parties to the dispute shall comply promptly with any provisional measures prescribed under this article.

Article 291

Access

1. All the dispute settlement procedures specified in this Part shall be open to States Parties.

2. The dispute settlement procedures specified in this Part shall be open to entities other than States Parties only as specifically provided for in this Convention.

Article 292

Prompt Release of Vessels and Crews

1. Where the authorities of a State Party have detained a vessel flying the flag of another State Party and it is alleged that the detaining State has not complied with the provisions of this Convention for the prompt release of the vessel or its crew upon the posting of a reasonable bond or other financial security, the question of release from detention may be submitted to any court or tribunal agreed upon by the parties or, failing such agreement within 10 days from the time of detention, to a court or tribunal accepted by the detaining State under article 287 or to the International Tribunal for the Law of the Sea, unless the parties otherwise agree.

2. The application for release may be made only by or on behalf of the flag State of the vessel.

3. The court or tribunal shall deal without delay with the application for release and shall deal only with the question of release, without

prejudice to the merits of any case before the appropriate domestic forum against the vessel, its owner or its crew. The authorities of the detaining State remain competent to release the vessel or its crew at any time.

4. Upon the posting of the bond or other financial security determined by the court or tribunal, the authorities of the detaining State shall comply promptly with the decision of the court or tribunal concerning the release of the vessel or its crew.

Article 293

Applicable Law

1. A court or tribunal having jurisdiction under this section shall apply this Convention and other rules of international law not incompatible with this Convention.

2. Paragraph 1 does not prejudice the power of the court or tribunal having jurisdiction under this section to decide a case *ex aequo et bono*, if the parties so agree.

Article 294

Preliminary Proceedings

1. A court or tribunal provided for in article 287 to which an application is made in respect of a dispute referred to in article 297 shall determine at the request of a party, or may determine *proprio motu*, whether the claim constitutes an abuse of legal process or whether *prima facie* it is well founded. If the court or tribunal determines that the claim constitutes an abuse of legal process or is *prima facie* unfounded, it shall take no further action in the case.

2. Upon receipt of the application, the court or tribunal shall immediately notify the other party or parties of the application, and shall fix a reasonable time-limit within which they may request it to make a determination in accordance with paragraph 1.

3. Nothing in this article affects the right of any party to a dispute to make preliminary objections in accordance with the applicable rules of procedure.

Article 295

Exhaustion of Local Remedies

Any dispute between States Parties concerning the interpretation or application of this Convention may be submitted to the procedures provided for in this section only after local remedies have been exhausted where this is required by international law.

Article 296

Finality and Binding Force of Decisions

1. Any decision rendered by a court or tribunal having jurisdiction under this section shall be final and shall be complied with by all the parties to the dispute.

2. Any such decision shall have no binding force except between the parties and in respect of that particular dispute.

Section 3. Limitations and Exceptions to Applicability of Section 2

Article 297

Limitations on Applicability of Section 2

1. Disputes concerning the interpretation or application of this Convention with regard to the exercise by a coastal State of its sovereign rights or jurisdiction provided for in this Convention shall be subject to the procedures provided for in section 2 in the following cases:

(a) when it is alleged that a coastal State has acted in contravention of the provisions of this Convention in regard to the freedoms and rights of navigation, overflight or the laying of submarine cables and pipelines, or in regard to other internationally lawful uses of the sea specified in article 58;

(b) when it is alleged that a State in exercising the aforementioned freedoms, rights or uses has acted in contravention of this Convention or of laws or regulations adopted by the coastal State in conformity with this Convention and other rules of international law not incompatible with this Convention; or

(c) when it is alleged that a coastal State has acted in contravention of specified international rules and standards for the protection and preservation of the marine environment which are applicable to the coastal State and which have been established by this Convention or through a competent international organization or diplomatic conference in accordance with this Convention.

2. (a) Disputes concerning the interpretation or application of the provisions of this Convention with regard to marine scientific research shall be settled in accordance with section 2, except that the coastal State shall not be obliged to accept the submission to such settlement of any dispute arising out of:

(i) the exercise by the coastal State of a right or discretion in accordance with article 246, or

(ii) a decision by the coastal State to order suspension or cessation of a research project in accordance with article 253.

(b) A dispute arising from an allegation by the researching State that with respect to a specific project the coastal State is not exercising its rights under articles 246 and 253 in a manner compatible with this Convention shall be submitted, at the request of either party, to conciliation under Annex V, section 2, provided that the conciliation commission shall not call in question the exercise by the coastal State of its discretion to designate specific areas as referred to in article 246, paragraph 6, or of its discretion to withhold consent in accordance with article 246, paragraph 5.

3. (a) Disputes concerning the interpretation or application of the provisions of this Convention with regard to fisheries shall be settled in accordance with section 2, except that the coastal State shall not

be obliged to accept the submission to such settlement of any dispute relating to its sovereign rights with respect to the living resources in the exclusive economic zone or their exercise, including its discretionary powers for determining the allowable catch, its harvesting capacity, the allocation of surpluses to other States and the terms and conditions established in its conservation and management laws and regulations.

(b) Where no settlement has been reached by recourse to section 1 of this Part, a dispute shall be submitted to conciliation under Annex V, section 2, at the request of any party to the dispute, when it is alleged that:

(i) a coastal State has manifestly failed to comply with its obligations to ensure through proper conservation and management measures that the maintenance of the living resources in the exclusive economic zone is not seriously endangered;

(ii) a coastal State has arbitrarily refused to determine, at the request of another State, the allowable catch and its capacity to harvest living resources with respect to stocks which that other State is interested in fishing, or

(iii) a coastal State has arbitrarily refused to allocate to any State, under articles 62, 69 and 70 and under the terms and conditions established by the coastal State consistent with this Convention, the whole or part of the surplus it has declared to exist.

(c) In no case shall the conciliation commission substitute its discretion for that of the coastal State.

(d) The report of the conciliation commission shall be communicated to the appropriate international organizations.

(e) In negotiating agreements pursuant to articles 69 and 70, States Parties, unless they otherwise agree, shall include a clause on measures which they shall take in order to minimize the possibility of a disagreement concerning the interpretation or application of the agreement, and on how they should proceed if a disagreement nevertheless arises.

Article 298

Optional Exceptions to Applicability of Section 2

1. When signing, ratifying or acceding to this Convention or at any time thereafter, a State may, without prejudice to the obligations arising under section 1, declare in writing that it does not accept any one or more of the procedures provided for in section 2 with respect to one or more of the following categories of disputes:

(a) (i) disputes concerning the interpretation or application of articles 15, 74 and 83 relating to sea boundary delimitations, or those involving historic bays or titles, provided that a State having made such a declaration shall, when such a dispute arises subsequent to the entry into force of this Convention and where no agreement within a reasonable period of time is reached in negotiations between the parties, at the request of any party to the dispute, accept submission of the matter to conciliation under Annex V, section 2; and provided further that any dispute that necessarily involves the concurrent consideration of any unsettled dispute concerning sovereignty or other rights over continental or insular land territory shall be excluded from such submission;

(ii) after the conciliation commission has presented its report, which shall state the reasons on which it is based, the parties shall negotiate an agreement on the basis of that report; if these negotiations do not result in an agreement, the parties shall, by mutual consent, submit the question to one of the procedures provided for in section 2, unless the parties otherwise agree;

(iii) this subparagraph does not apply to any sea boundary dispute finally settled by an arrangement between the parties, or to any such dispute which is to be settled in accordance with a bilateral or multilateral agreement binding upon those parties;

(b) disputes concerning military activities, including military activities by government vessels and aircraft engaged in non-commercial service, and disputes concerning law enforcement activities in regard to the exercise of sovereign rights or jurisdiction excluded from the jurisdiction of a court or tribunal under article 297, paragraph 2 or 3;

(c) disputes in respect of which the Security Council of the United Nations is exercising the functions assigned to it by the Charter of the United Nations, unless the Security Council decides to remove the matter from its agenda or calls upon the parties to settle it by the means provided for in this Convention.

2. A State Party which has made a declaration under paragraph 1 may at any time withdraw it, or agree to submit a dispute excluded by such declaration to any procedure specified in this Convention.

3. A State Party which has made a declaration under paragraph 1 shall not be entitled to submit any dispute falling within the excepted category of disputes to any procedure in this Convention as against another State Party, without the consent of that party.

4. If one of the States Parties has made a declaration under paragraph 1 (a), any other State Party may submit any dispute falling within an excepted category against the declarant party to the procedure specified in such declaration.

5. A new declaration, or the withdrawal of a declaration, does not in any way affect proceedings pending before a court or tribunal in accordance with this article, unless the parties otherwise agree.

6. Declarations and notices of withdrawal of declarations under this article shall be deposited with the Secretary–General of the United Nations, who shall transmit copies thereof to the States Parties.

Article 299

Right of the Parties to Agree Upon a Procedure

1. A dispute excluded under article 297 or excepted by a declaration made under article 298 from the dispute settlement procedures provided for in section 2 may be submitted to such procedures only by agreement of the parties to the dispute.

2. Nothing in this section impairs the right of the parties to the dispute to agree to some other procedure for the settlement of such dispute or to reach an amicable settlement.

PART XVI. GENERAL PROVISIONS

Article 300

Good Faith and Abuse of Rights

States Parties shall fulfil in good faith the obligations assumed under this Convention and shall exercise the rights, jurisdiction and freedoms recognized in this Convention in a manner which would not constitute an abuse of right.

Article 301

Peaceful Uses of the Seas

In exercising their rights and performing their duties under this Convention, States Parties shall refrain from any threat or use of force against the territorial integrity or political independence of any State, or in any other manner inconsistent with the principles of international law embodied in the Charter of the United Nations.

Article 302

Disclosure of Information

Without prejudice to the right of a State Party to resort to the procedures for the settlement of disputes provided for in this Convention, nothing in this Convention shall be deemed to require a State Party, in the fulfilment of its obligations under this Convention, to supply information the disclosure of which is contrary to the essential interests of its security.

Article 303

Archaeological and Historical Objects Found at Sea

1. States have the duty to protect objects of an archaeological and historical nature found at sea and shall co-operate for this purpose.

2. In order to control traffic in such objects, the coastal State may, in applying article 33, presume that their removal from the sea-bed in the zone referred to in that article without its approval would result in an infringement within its territory or territorial sea of the laws and regulations referred to in that article.

3. Nothing in this article affects the rights of identifiable owners, the law of salvage or other rules of admiralty, or laws and practices with respect to cultural exchanges.

4. This article is without prejudice to other international agreements and rules of international law regarding the protection of objects of an archaeological and historical nature.

Article 304

Responsibility and Liability for Damage

The provisions of this Convention regarding responsibility and liability for damage are without prejudice to the application of existing rules and the development of further rules regarding responsibility and liability under international law.

PART XVII. FINAL PROVISIONS

Article 305

Signature

1. This Convention shall be open for signature by:

(a) all States;

(b) Namibia, represented by the United Nations Council for Namibia;

(c) all self-governing associated States which have chosen that status in an act of self-determination supervised and approved by the United Nations in accordance with General Assembly resolution 1514 (XV) and which have competence over the matters governed by this Convention, including the competence to enter into treaties in respect of those matters;

(d) all self-governing associated States which, in accordance with their respective instruments of association, have competence over the matters governed by this Convention, including the competence to enter into treaties in respect of those matters;

(e) all territories which enjoy full internal self-government, recognized as such by the United Nations, but have not attained full independence in accordance with General Assembly resolution 1514 (XV) and which have competence over the matters governed by this Convention, including the competence to enter into treaties in respect of those matters;

(f) international organizations, in accordance with Annex IX.

2. This Convention shall remain open for signature until 9 December 1984 at the Ministry of Foreign Affairs of Jamaica and also, from 1 July 1983 until 9 December 1984, at United Nations Headquarters in New York.

Article 306

Ratification and Formal Confirmation

This Convention is subject to ratification by States and the other entities referred to in article 305, paragraph 1 (b), (c), (d) and (e), and to formal confirmation, in accordance with Annex IX, by the entities referred to in article 305, paragraph 1 (f). The instruments of ratification and of formal confirmation shall be deposited with the Secretary-General of the United Nations.

Article 307

Accession

This Convention shall remain open for accession by States and the other entities referred to in article 305. Accession by the entities referred to in article 305, paragraph 1 (f), shall be in accordance with Annex IX. The instruments of accession shall be deposited with the Secretary-General of the United Nations.

Article 308

Entry Into Force

1. This Convention shall enter into force 12 months after the date of deposit of the sixtieth instrument of ratification or accession.

2. For each State ratifying or acceding to this Convention after the deposit of the sixtieth instrument of ratification or accession, the Convention shall enter into force on the thirtieth day following the deposit of its instrument of ratification or accession, subject to paragraph 1.

3. The Assembly of the Authority shall meet on the date of entry into force of this Convention and shall elect the Council of the Authority. The first Council shall be constituted in a manner consistent with the purpose of article 161 if the provisions of that article cannot be strictly applied.

4. The rules, regulations and procedures drafted by the Preparatory Commission shall apply provisionally pending their formal adoption by the Authority in accordance with Part XI.

5. The Authority and its organs shall act in accordance with resolution II of the Third United Nations Conference on the Law of the Sea relating to preparatory investment and with decisions of the Preparatory Commission taken pursuant to that resolution.

Article 309

Reservations and Exceptions

No reservations or exceptions may be made to this Convention unless expressly permitted by other articles of this Convention.

Article 310

Declarations and Statements

Article 309 does not preclude a State, when signing, ratifying or acceding to this Convention, from making declarations or statements, however phrased or named, with a view, *inter alia*, to the harmonization of its laws and regulations with the provisions of this Convention, provided that such declarations or statements do not purport to exclude or to modify the legal effect of the provisions of this Convention in their application to that State.

Article 311

Relation to Other Conventions and International Agreements

1. This Convention shall prevail, as between States Parties, over the Geneva Conventions on the Law of the Sea of 29 April 1958.

2. This Convention shall not alter the rights and obligations of States Parties which arise from other agreements compatible with this Convention and which do not affect the enjoyment by other States Parties of their rights or the performance of their obligations under this Convention.

3. Two or more States Parties may conclude agreements modifying or suspending the operation of provisions of this Convention, applicable solely to the relations between them, provided that such agreements do not relate to a provision derogation from which is incompatible with the effective execution of the object and purpose of this Convention, and provided further that such agreements shall not affect the application of the basic principles embodied herein, and that the provisions of such agreements do not affect the enjoyment by other States Parties of their rights or the performance of their obligations under this Convention.

4. States Parties intending to conclude an agreement referred to in paragraph 3 shall notify the other States Parties through the depositary of this Convention of their intention to conclude the agreement and of the modification or suspension for which it provides.

5. This article does not affect international agreements expressly permitted or preserved by other articles of this Convention.

6. States Parties agree that there shall be no amendments to the basic principle relating to the common heritage of mankind set forth in article 136 and that they shall not be party to any agreement in derogation thereof.

Article 312

Amendment

1. After the expiry of a period of 10 years from the date of entry into force of this Convention, a State Party may, by written communication addressed to the Secretary–General of the United Nations, propose specific amendments to this Convention, other than those relating to activities in the Area, and request the convening of a conference to consider such proposed amendments. The Secretary–General shall circulate such communication to all States Parties. If, within 12 months from the date of the circulation of the communication, not less than one half of the States Parties reply favourably to the request, the Secretary–General shall convene the conference.

2. The decision-making procedure applicable at the amendment conference shall be the same as that applicable at the Third United Nations Conference on the Law of the Sea unless otherwise decided by

the conference. The conference should make every effort to reach agreement on any amendments by way of consensus and there should be no voting on them until all efforts at consensus have been exhausted.

Article 313

Amendment by Simplified Procedure

1. A State Party may, by written communication addressed to the Secretary-General of the United Nations, propose an amendment to this Convention, other than an amendment relating to activities in the Area, to be adopted by the simplified procedure set forth in this article without convening a conference. The Secretary-General shall circulate the communication to all States Parties.

2. If, within a period of 12 months from the date of the circulation of the communication, a State Party objects to the proposed amendment or to the proposal for its adoption by the simplified procedure, the amendment shall be considered rejected. The Secretary-General shall immediately notify all States Parties accordingly.

3. If, 12 months from the date of the circulation of the communication, no State Party has objected to the proposed amendment or to the proposal for its adoption by the simplified procedure, the proposed amendment shall be considered adopted. The Secretary-General shall notify all States Parties that the proposed amendment has been adopted.

Article 314

Amendments to the Provisions of this Convention Relating Exclusively to Activities in the Area

1. A State Party may, by written communication addressed to the Secretary-General of the Authority, propose an amendment to the provisions of this Convention relating exclusively to activities in the Area, including Annex VI, section 4. The Secretary-General shall circulate such communication to all States Parties. The proposed amendment shall be subject to approval by the Assembly following its approval by the Council. Representatives of States Parties in those organs shall have full powers to consider and approve the proposed amendment. The proposed amendment as approved by the Council and the Assembly shall be considered adopted.

2. Before approving any amendment under paragraph 1, the Council and the Assembly shall ensure that it does not prejudice the system of exploration for and exploitation of the resources of the Area, pending the Review Conference in accordance with article 155.

Article 315

Signature, Ratification of, Accession to and Authentic Texts of Amendments

1. Once adopted, amendments to this Convention shall be open for signature by States Parties for 12 months from the date of adoption, at United Nations Headquarters in New York, unless otherwise provided in the amendment itself.

2. Articles 306, 307 and 320 apply to all amendments to this Convention.

Article 316

Entry Into Force of Amendments

1. Amendments to this Convention, other than those referred to in paragraph 5, shall enter into force for the States Parties ratifying or acceding to them on the thirtieth day following the deposit of instruments of ratification or accession by two thirds of the States Parties or by 60 States Parties, whichever is greater. Such amendments shall not affect the enjoyment by other States Parties of their rights or the performance of their obligations under this Convention.

2. An amendment may provide that a larger number of ratifications or accessions shall be required for its entry into force than are required by this article.

3. For each State Party ratifying or acceding to an amendment referred to in paragraph 1 after the deposit of the required number of instruments of ratification or accession, the amendment shall enter into force on the thirtieth day following the deposit of its instrument of ratification or accession.

4. A State which becomes a Party to this Convention after the entry into force of an amendment in accordance with paragraph 1 shall, failing an expression of a different intention by that State:

(a) be considered as a Party to this Convention as so amended; and

(b) be considered as a Party to the unamended Convention in relation to any State Party not bound by the amendment.

5. Any amendment relating exclusively to activities in the Area and any amendment to Annex VI shall enter into force for all States Parties one year following the deposit of instruments of ratification or accession by three fourths of the States Parties.

6. A State which becomes a Party to this Convention after the entry into force of amendments in accordance with paragraph 5 shall be considered as a Party to this Convention as so amended.

Article 317

Denunciation

1. A State Party may, by written notification addressed to the Secretary–General of the United Nations, denounce this Convention and may indicate its reasons. Failure to indicate reasons shall not affect the validity of the denunciation. The denunciation shall take effect one year after the date of receipt of the notification, unless the notification specifies a later date.

2. A State shall not be discharged by reason of the denunciation from the financial and contractual obligations which accrued while it was a Party to this Convention, nor shall the denunciation affect any right,

obligation or legal situation of that State created through the execution of this Convention prior to its termination for that State.

3. The denunciation shall not in any way affect the duty of any State Party to fulfil any obligation embodied in this Convention to which it would be subject under international law independently of this Convention.

Article 318

Status of Annexes

The Annexes form an integral part of this Convention and, unless expressly provided otherwise, a reference to this Convention or to one of its Parts includes a reference to the Annexes relating thereto.

Article 319

Depositary

1. The Secretary–General of the United Nations shall be the depositary of this Convention and amendments thereto.

2. In addition to his functions as depositary, the Secretary–General shall:

(a) report to all States Parties, the Authority and competent international organizations on issues of a general nature that have arisen with respect to this Convention;

(b) notify the Authority of ratifications and formal confirmations of and accessions to this Convention and amendments thereto, as well as of denunciations of this Convention;

(c) notify States Parties of agreements in accordance with article 311, paragraph 4;

(d) circulate amendments adopted in accordance with this Convention to States Parties for ratification or accession;

(e) convene necessary meetings of States Parties in accordance with this Convention.

3. (a) The Secretary–General shall also transmit to the observers referred to in article 156:

(i) reports referred to in paragraph 2 (a);

(ii) notifications referred to in paragraph 2 (b) and (c); and

(iii) texts of amendments referred to in paragraph 2 (d), for their information.

(b) The Secretary–General shall also invite those observers to participate as observers at meetings of States Parties referred to in paragraph 2(e).

Article 320

Authentic Texts

The original of this Convention, of which the Arabic, Chinese, English, French, Russian and Spanish texts are equally authentic, shall, subject to article 305, paragraph 2, be deposited with the Secretary-General of the United Nations. . . .

Annex I. Highly Migratory Species

1. Albacore tuna: *Thunnus alalunga.*

2. Bluefin tuna: *Thunnus thynnus.*

3. Bigeye tuna: *Thunnus obesus.*

4. Skipjack tuna: *Katsuwonus pelamis.*

5. Yellowfin tuna: *Thunnus albacares.*

6. Blackfin tuna: *Thunnus atlanticus.*

7. Little tuna: *Euthynnus alletteratus; Euthynnus affinis.*

8. Southern bluefin tuna: *Thunnus maccoyii.*

9. Frigate mackerel: *Auxis thazard; Auxis rochei.*

10. Pomfrets: Family *Bramidae.*

11. Marlins: *Tetrapturus angustirostris; Tetrapturus belone; Tetrapturus pnuegeri; Tetrapturus albidus; Tetrapturus audax; Tetrapturus georgei; Makaira mazara; Makaira indica; Makaira nigricans.*

12. Sail-fishes: *Istiophorus platypterus; Istiophorus albicans.*

13. Swordfish: *Xiphias gladius.*

14. Sauries: *Scomberesox saurus; Cololabis saira; Cololabis adocetus; Scomberesox saurus scombroides.*

15. Dolphin: *Coryphaena hippurus; Coryphaena equiselis.*

16. Oceanic sharks: *Hexanchus griseus; Cetorhinus maximus;* Family *Alopiidae; Rhincodon typus;* Family *Carcharhinidae;* Family *Sphyrnidae*; Family *Isurida.*

17. Cetaceans: Family *Physeteridae,* Family *Balaenopteridae;* Family *Balaenidae;* Family *Eschrichtiidae;* Family *Monodontidae;* Family *Ziphiidae;* Family *Delphinidae.*

Annex II. Commission on the Limits of the Continental Shelf

Article 1

In accordance with the provisions of Article 76, a Commission on the Limits of the Continental Shelf beyond 200 nautical miles shall be established in conformity with the following articles.

Article 2

1. The Commission shall consist of 21 members who shall be experts in the field of geology, geophysics or hydrography, elected by States Parties to this Convention from among their nationals, having due regard to the need to ensure equitable geographical representation, who shall serve in their personal capacities.

2. The initial election shall be held as soon as possible but in any case within 18 months after the date of entry into force of this Convention. At least three months before the date of each election, the Secre-

tary–General of the United Nations shall address a letter to the States Parties, inviting the submission of nominations, after appropriate regional consultations, within three months. The Secretary–General shall prepare a list in alphabetical order of all persons thus nominated and shall submit it to all the States Parties.

3. Elections of the members of the Commission shall be held at a meeting of States Parties convened by the Secretary–General at United Nations Headquarters. At that meeting, for which two thirds of the States Parties shall constitute a quorum, the persons elected to the Commission shall be those nominees who obtain a two-thirds majority of the votes of the representatives of States Parties present and voting. Not less than three members shall be elected from each geographical region.

4. The members of the Commission shall be elected for a term of five years. They shall be eligible for re-election.

5. The State Party which submitted the nomination of a member of the Commission shall defray the expenses of that member while in performance of Commission duties. The coastal State concerned shall defray the expenses incurred in respect of the advice referred to in Article 3, paragraph 1 (b), of this Annex. The secretariat of the Commission shall be provided by the Secretary–General of the United Nations.

Article 3

1. The functions of the Commission shall be:

(a) to consider the data and other material submitted by coastal States concerning the outer limits of the continental shelf in areas where those limits extend beyond 200 nautical miles, and to make recommendations in accordance with Article 76 and the Statement of Understanding adopted on 29 August 1980 by the Third United Nations Conference on the Law of the Sea;

(b) to provide scientific and technical advice, if requested by the coastal State concerned during the preparation of the data referred to in subparagraph (a).

2. The Commission may co-operate, to the extent considered necessary and useful, with the Intergovernmental Oceanographic Commission of UNESCO, the International Hydrographic Organization and other competent international organizations with a view to exchanging scientific and technical information which might be of assistance in discharging the Commission's responsibilities.

Article 4

Where a coastal State intends to establish, in accordance with Article 76, the outer limits of its continental shelf beyond 200 nautical miles, it shall submit particulars of such limits to the Commission along with supporting scientific and technical data as soon as possible but in any case within 10 years of the entry into force of this Convention for that State. The coastal State shall at the same time give the names of any Commission members who have provided it with scientific and technical advice.

Article 5

Unless the Commission decides otherwise, the Commission shall function by way of sub-commissions composed of seven members, appointed in a balanced manner taking into account the specific elements of each submission by a coastal State. Nationals of the coastal State making the submission who are members of the Commission and any Commission member who has assisted a coastal State by providing scientific and technical advice with respect to the delineation shall not be a member of the sub-commission dealing with that submission but has the right to participate as a member in the proceedings of the Commission concerning the said submission. The coastal State which has made a submission to the Commission may send its representatives to participate in the relevant proceedings without the right to vote.

Article 6

1. The sub-commission shall submit its recommendations to the Commission.

2. Approval by the Commission of the recommendations of the subcommission shall be by a majority of two thirds of Commission members present and voting.

3. The recommendations of the Commission shall be submitted in writing to the coastal State which made the submission and to the Secretary–General of the United Nations.

Article 7

Coastal States shall establish the outer limits of the continental shelf in conformity with the provisions of Article 76, paragraph 8, and in accordance with the appropriate national procedures.

Article 8

In the case of disagreement by the coastal State with the recommendations of the Commission, the coastal State shall, within a reasonable time, make a revised or new submission to the Commission.

Article 9

The actions of the Commission shall not prejudice matters relating to delimitation of boundaries between States with opposite or adjacent coasts. . . .

Annex VI. Statute of the International Tribunal for the Law of the Sea

Article 1. General Provisions

1. The International Tribunal for the Law of the Sea is constituted and shall function in accordance with the provisions of this Convention and this Statute.

2. The seat of the Tribunal shall be in the Free and Hanseatic City of Hamburg in the Federal Republic of Germany.

3. The Tribunal may sit and exercise its functions elsewhere whenever it considers this desirable.

4. A reference of a dispute to the Tribunal shall be governed by the provisions of Parts XI and XV.

Section 1. Organization of the Tribunal

Article 2. Composition

1. The Tribunal shall be composed of a body of 21 independent members, elected from among persons enjoying the highest reputation for fairness and integrity and of recognized competence in the field of the law of the sea.

2. In the Tribunal as a whole the representation of the principal legal systems of the world and equitable geographical distribution shall be assured.

Article 3. Membership

1. No two members of the Tribunal may be nationals of the same State. A person who for the purposes of membership in the Tribunal could be regarded as a national of more than one State shall be deemed to be a national of the one in which he ordinarily exercises civil and political rights.

2. There shall be no fewer than three members from each geographical group as established by the General Assembly of the United Nations.

Article 4. Nominations and Elections

1. Each State Party may nominate not more than two persons having the qualifications prescribed in article 2 of this Annex. The members of the Tribunal shall be elected from the list of persons thus nominated.

2. At least three months before the date of the election, the Secretary–General of the United Nations in the case of the first election and the Registrar of the Tribunal in the case of subsequent elections shall address a written invitation to the States Parties to submit their nominations for members of the Tribunal within two months. He shall prepare a list in alphabetical order of all the persons thus nominated, with an indication of the States Parties which have nominated them, and shall submit it to the States Parties before the seventh day of the last month before the date of each election.

3. The first election shall be held within six months of the date of entry into force of this Convention.

4. The members of the Tribunal shall be elected by secret ballot. Elections shall be held at a meeting of the States Parties convened by the Secretary–General of the United Nations in the case of the first election and by a procedure agreed to by the States Parties in the case of subsequent elections. Two thirds of the States Parties shall constitute a quorum at that meeting. The persons elected to the Tribunal shall be those nominees who obtain the largest number of votes and a two-thirds

majority of the States Parties present and voting, provided that such majority includes a majority of the States Parties.

Article 5. Term of Office

1. The members of the Tribunal shall be elected for nine years and may be re-elected; provided, however, that of the members elected at the first election, the terms of seven members shall expire at the end of three years and the terms of seven more members shall expire at the end of six years.

2. The members of the Tribunal whose terms are to expire at the end of the above-mentioned initial periods of three and six years shall be chosen by lot to be drawn by the Secretary–General of the United Nations immediately after the first election.

3. The members of the Tribunal shall continue to discharge their duties until their places have been filled. Though replaced, they shall finish any proceedings which they may have begun before the date of their replacement.

4. In the case of the resignation of a member of the Tribunal, the letter of resignation shall be addressed to the President of the Tribunal. The place becomes vacant on the receipt of that letter.

Article 6. Vacancies

1. Vacancies shall be filled by the same method as that laid down for the first election, subject to the following provision: the Registrar shall, within one month of the occurrence of the vacancy, proceed to issue the invitations provided for in article 4 of this Annex, and the date of the election shall be fixed by the President of the Tribunal after consultation with the States Parties.

2. A member of the Tribunal elected to replace a member whose term of office has not expired shall hold office for the remainder of his predecessor's term.

Article 7. Incompatible Activities

1. No member of the Tribunal may exercise any political or administrative function, or associate actively with or be financially interested in any of the operations of any enterprise concerned with the exploration for or exploitation of the resources of the sea or the sea-bed or other commercial use of the sea or the sea-bed.

2. No member of the Tribunal may act as agent, counsel or advocate in any case.

3. Any doubt on these points shall be resolved by decision of the majority of the other members of the Tribunal present.

Article 8. Conditions Relating to Participation of Members in a Particular Case

1. No member of the Tribunal may participate in the decision of any case in which he has previously taken part as agent, counsel or

advocate for one of the parties, or as a member of a national or international court or tribunal, or in any other capacity.

2. If, for some special reason, a member of the Tribunal considers that he should not take part in the decision of a particular case, he shall so inform the President of the Tribunal.

3. If the President considers that for some special reason one of the members of the Tribunal should not sit in a particular case, he shall give him notice accordingly.

4. Any doubt on these points shall be resolved by decision of the majority of the other members of the Tribunal present.

Article 9. Consequence of Ceasing to Fulfil Required Conditions

If, in the unanimous opinion of the other members of the Tribunal, a member has ceased to fulfil the required conditions, the President of the Tribunal shall declare the seat vacant.

Article 10. Privileges and Immunities

The members of the Tribunal, when engaged on the business of the Tribunal, shall enjoy diplomatic privileges and immunities.

Article 11. Solemn Declaration by Members

Every member of the Tribunal shall, before taking up his duties, make a solemn declaration in open session that he will exercise his powers impartially and conscientiously.

Article 12. President, Vice–President and Registrar

1. The Tribunal shall elect its President and Vice–President for three years; they may be re-elected.

2. The Tribunal shall appoint its Registrar and may provide for the appointment of such other officers as may be necessary.

3. The President and the Registrar shall reside at the seat of the Tribunal.

Article 13. Quorum

1. All available members of the Tribunal shall sit; a quorum of 11 elected members shall be required to constitute the Tribunal.

2. Subject to article 17 of this Annex, the Tribunal shall determine which members are available to constitute the Tribunal for the consideration of a particular dispute, having regard to the effective functioning of the chambers as provided for in articles 14 and 15 of this Annex.

3. All disputes and applications submitted to the Tribunal shall be heard and determined by the Tribunal, unless article 14 of this Annex applies, or the parties request that it shall be dealt with in accordance with article 15 of this Annex.

Article 14. Sea–Bed Disputes Chamber

A Sea–Bed Disputes Chamber shall be established in accordance with the provisions of section 4 of this Annex. Its jurisdiction, powers and functions shall be as provided for in Part XI, section 5.

Article 15. Special Chambers

1. The Tribunal may form such chambers, composed of three or more of its elected members, as it considers necessary for dealing with particular categories of disputes.

2. The Tribunal shall form a chamber for dealing with a particular dispute submitted to it if the parties so request. The composition of such a chamber shall be determined by the Tribunal with the approval of the parties.

3. With a view to the speedy dispatch of business, the Tribunal shall form annually a chamber composed of five of its elected members which may hear and determine disputes by summary procedure. Two alternative members shall be selected for the purpose of replacing members who are unable to participate in a particular proceeding.

4. Disputes shall be heard and determined by the chambers provided for in this article if the parties so request.

5. A judgment given by any of the chambers provided for in this article and in article 14 of this Annex shall be considered as rendered by the Tribunal.

Article 16. Rules of the Tribunal

The Tribunal shall frame rules for carrying out its functions. In particular it shall lay down rules of procedure.

Article 17. Nationality of Members

1. Members of the Tribunal of the nationality of any of the parties to a dispute shall retain their right to participate as members of the Tribunal.

2. If the Tribunal, when hearing a dispute, includes upon the bench a member of the nationality of one of the parties, any other party may choose a person to participate as a member of the Tribunal.

3. If the Tribunal, when hearing a dispute, does not include upon the bench a member of the nationality of the parties, each of those parties may choose a person to participate as a member of the Tribunal.

4. This article applies to the chambers referred to in articles 14 and 15 of this Annex. In such cases, the President, in consultation with the parties, shall request specified members of the Tribunal forming the chamber, as many as necessary, to give place to the members of the Tribunal of the nationality of the parties concerned, and, failing such, or if they are unable to be present, to the members specially chosen by the parties.

5. Should there be several parties in the same interest, they shall, for the purpose of the preceding provisions, be considered as one party

only. Any doubt on this point shall be settled by the decision of the Tribunal.

6. Members chosen in accordance with paragraphs 2, 3 and 4 shall fulfil the conditions required by articles 2, 8 and 11 of this Annex. They shall participate in the decision on terms of complete equality with their colleagues.

Article 18. Remuneration of Members

1. Each elected member of the Tribunal shall receive an annual allowance and, for each day on which he exercises his functions, a special allowance, provided that in any year the total sum payable to any member as special allowance shall not exceed the amount of the annual allowance.

2. The President shall receive a special annual allowance.

3. The Vice–President shall receive a special allowance for each day on which he acts as President.

4. The members chosen under article 17 of this Annex, other than elected members of the Tribunal, shall receive compensation for each day on which they exercise their functions.

5. The salaries, allowances and compensation shall be determined from time to time at meetings of the States Parties, taking into account the work load of the Tribunal. They may not be decreased during the term of office.

6. The salary of the Registrar shall be determined at meetings of the States Parties, on the proposal of the Tribunal.

7. Regulations adopted at meetings of the States Parties shall determine the conditions under which retirement pensions may be given to members of the Tribunal and to the Registrar, and the conditions under which members of the Tribunal and Registrar shall have their traveling expenses refunded.

8. The salaries, allowances, and compensation shall be free of all taxation.

Article 19. Expenses of the Tribunal

1. The expenses of the Tribunal shall be borne by the States Parties and by the Authority on such terms and in such a manner as shall be decided at meetings of the States Parties.

2. When an entity other than a State Party or the Authority is a party to a case submitted to it, the Tribunal shall fix the amount which that party is to contribute towards the expenses of the Tribunal.

Section 2. Competence

Article 20. Access to the Tribunal

1. The Tribunal shall be open to States Parties.

2. The Tribunal shall be open to entities other than States Parties in any case expressly provided for in Part XI or in any case submitted

pursuant to any other agreement conferring jurisdiction on the Tribunal which is accepted by all the parties to that case.

Article 21. Jurisdiction

The jurisdiction of the Tribunal comprises all disputes and all applications submitted to it in accordance with this Convention and all matters specifically provided for in any other agreement which confers jurisdiction on the Tribunal.

Article 22. Reference of Disputes Subject to Other Agreements

If all the parties to a treaty or convention already in force and concerning the subject-matter covered by this Convention so agree, any disputes concerning the interpretation or application of such treaty or convention may, in accordance with such agreement, be submitted to the Tribunal.

Article 23. Applicable Law

The Tribunal shall decide all disputes and applications in accordance with article 293.

Section 3. Procedure

Article 24. Institution of Proceedings

1. Disputes are submitted to the Tribunal, as the case may be, either by notification of a special agreement or by written application, addressed to the Registrar. In either case, the subject of the dispute and the parties shall be indicated.

2. The Registrar shall forthwith notify the special agreement or the application to all concerned.

3. The Registrar shall also notify all States Parties.

Article 25. Provisional Measures

1. In accordance with article 290, the Tribunal and its Sea–Bed Disputes Chamber shall have the power to prescribe provisional measures.

2. If the Tribunal is not in session or a sufficient number of members is not available to constitute a quorum, the provisional measures shall be prescribed by the chamber of summary procedure formed under article 15, paragraph 3, of this Annex. Notwithstanding article 15, paragraph 4, of this Annex, such provisional measures may be adopted at the request of any party to the dispute. They shall be subject to review and revision by the Tribunal.

Article 26. Hearing

1. The hearing shall be under the control of the President or, if he is unable to preside, of the Vice–President. If neither is able to preside, the senior judge present of the Tribunal shall preside.

2. The hearing shall be public, unless the Tribunal decides otherwise or unless the parties demand that the public be not admitted.

Article 27. Conduct of Case

The Tribunal shall make orders for the conduct of the case, decide the form and time in which each party must conclude its arguments, and make all arrangements connected with the taking of evidence.

Article 28. Default

When one of the parties does not appear before the Tribunal or fails to defend its case, the other party may request the Tribunal to continue the proceedings and make its decision. Absence of a party or failure of a party to defend its case shall not constitute a bar to the proceedings. Before making its decision, the Tribunal must satisfy itself not only that it has jurisdiction over the dispute, but also that the claim is well founded in fact and law.

Article 29. Majority for Decision

1. All questions shall be decided by a majority of the members of the Tribunal who are present.

2. In the event of an equality of votes, the President or the member of the Tribunal who acts in his place shall have a casting vote.

Article 30. Judgment

1. The judgment shall state the reasons on which it is based.

2. It shall contain the names of the members of the Tribunal who have taken part in the decision.

3. If the judgment does not represent in whole or in part the unanimous opinion of the members of the Tribunal, any member shall be entitled to deliver a separate opinion.

4. The judgment shall be signed by the President and by the Registrar. It shall be read in open court, due notice having been given to the parties to the dispute.

Article 31. Request to Intervene

1. Should a State Party consider that it has an interest of a legal nature which may be affected by the decision in any dispute, it may submit a request to the Tribunal to be permitted to intervene.

2. It shall be for the Tribunal to decide upon this request.

3. If a request to intervene is granted, the decision of the Tribunal in respect of the dispute shall be binding upon the intervening State Party in so far as it relates to matters in respect of which that State Party intervened.

Article 32. Right to Intervene in Cases of Interpretation or Application

1. Whenever the interpretation or application of this Convention is in question, the Registrar shall notify all States Parties forthwith.

2. Whenever pursuant to article 21 or 22 of this Annex the interpretation or application of an international agreement is in question, the Registrar shall notify all the parties to the agreement.

3. Every party referred to in paragraphs 1 and 2 has the right to intervene in the proceedings; if it uses this right, the interpretation given by the judgment will be equally binding upon it.

Article 33. Finality and Binding Force of Decisions

1. The decision of the Tribunal is final and shall be complied with by all the parties to the dispute.

2. The decision shall have no binding force except between the parties in respect of that particular dispute.

3. In the event of dispute as to the meaning or scope of the decision, the Tribunal shall construe it upon the request of any party.

Article 34. Costs

Unless otherwise decided by the Tribunal, each party shall bear its own costs.

Section 4. Sea–Bed Disputes Chamber

Article 35. Composition

1. The Sea–Bed Disputes Chamber referred to in article 14 of this Annex shall be composed of 11 members, selected by a majority of the elected members of the Tribunal from among them.

2. In the selection of the members of the Chamber, the representation of the principal legal systems of the world and equitable geographical distribution shall be assured. The Assembly of the Authority may adopt recommendations of a general nature relating to such representation and distribution.

3. The members of the Chamber shall be selected every three years and may be selected for a second term.

4. The Chamber shall elect its President from among its members, who shall serve for the term for which the Chamber has been selected.

5. If any proceedings are still pending at the end of any three-year period for which the Chamber has been selected, the Chamber shall complete the proceedings in its original composition.

6. If a vacancy occurs in the Chamber, the Tribunal shall select a successor from among its elected members, who shall hold office for the remainder of his predecessor's term.

7. A quorum of seven of the members selected by the Tribunal shall be required to constitute the Chamber.

Article 36. Ad Hoc Chambers

1. The Sea–Bed Disputes Chamber shall form an ad hoc chamber, composed of three of its members, for dealing with a particular dispute submitted to it in accordance with article 188, paragraph 1 (b). The composition of such a chamber shall be determined by the Sea–Bed Disputes Chamber with the approval of the parties.

2. If the parties do not agree on the composition of an ad hoc chamber, each party to the dispute shall appoint one member, and the

third member shall be appointed by them in agreement. If they disagree, or if any party fails to make an appointment, the President of the Sea-Bed Disputes Chamber shall promptly make the appointment or appointments from among its members, after consultation with the parties.

3. Members of the ad hoc chamber must not be in the service of, or nationals of, any of the parties to the dispute.

Article 37. Access

The Chamber shall be open to the States Parties, the Authority and the other entities referred to in Part XI, section 5.

Article 38. Applicable Law

In addition to the provisions of article 293, the Chamber shall apply:

(a) the rules, regulations and procedures of the Authority adopted in accordance with this Convention; and

(b) the terms of contracts concerning activities in the Area in matters relating to those contracts.

Article 39. Enforcement of Decisions of the Chamber

The decisions of the Chamber shall be enforceable in the territories of the States Parties in the same manner as judgments or orders of the highest court of the State Party in whose territory the enforcement is sought.

Article 40. Applicability of Other Sections of this Annex

1. The other sections of this Annex which are not incompatible with this section apply to the Chamber.

2. In the exercise of its functions relating to advisory opinions, the Chamber shall be guided by the provisions of this Annex relating to procedure before the Tribunal to the extent to which it recognizes them to be applicable.

Section 5. Amendments

Article 41. Amendments

1. Amendments to this Annex, other than amendments to section 4, may be adopted only in accordance with article 313 or by consensus at a conference convened in accordance with this Convention.

2. Amendments to section 4 may be adopted only in accordance with article 314.

3. The Tribunal may propose such amendments to this Statute as it may consider necessary, by written communications to the States Parties for their consideration in conformity with paragraphs 1 and 2.

Annex VII. Arbitration

Article 1. Institution of Proceedings

Subject to the provisions of Part XV, any party to a dispute may submit the dispute to the arbitral procedure provided for in this Annex by written notification addressed to the other party or parties to the dispute. The notification shall be accompanied by a statement of the claim and the grounds on which it is based.

Article 2. List of Arbitrators

1. A list of arbitrators shall be drawn up and maintained by the Secretary–General of the United Nations. Every State Party shall be entitled to nominate four arbitrators, each of whom shall be a person experienced in maritime affairs and enjoying the highest reputation for fairness, competence and integrity. The names of the persons so nominated shall constitute the list.

2. If at any time the arbitrators nominated by a State Party in the list so constituted shall be fewer than four, that State Party shall be entitled to make further nominations as necessary.

3. The name of an arbitrator shall remain on the list until withdrawn by the State Party which made the nomination, provided that such arbitrator shall continue to serve on any arbitral tribunal to which that arbitrator has been appointed until the completion of the proceedings before that arbitral tribunal.

Article 3. Constitution of Arbitral Tribunal

For the purpose of proceedings under this Annex, the arbitral tribunal shall, unless the parties otherwise agree, be constituted as follows:

(a) Subject to subparagraph (g), the arbitral tribunal shall consist of five members.

(b) The party instituting the proceedings shall appoint one member to be chosen preferably from the list referred to in article 2 of this Annex, who may be its national. The appointment shall be included in the notification referred to in article 1 of this Annex.

(c) The other party to the dispute shall, within 30 days of receipt of the notification referred to in article 1 of this Annex, appoint one member to be chosen preferably from the list, who may be its national. If the appointment is not made within that period, the party instituting the proceedings may, within two weeks of the expiration of that period, request that the appointment be made in accordance with subparagraph (e).

(d) The other three members shall be appointed by agreement between the parties. They shall be chosen preferably from the list and shall be nationals of third States unless the parties otherwise agree. The parties to the dispute shall appoint the President of the arbitral tribunal from among those three members. If, within 60 days of receipt of the notification referred to in article 1 of this Annex, the parties are unable to reach agreement on the appointment of one or more of the members of the tribunal to be appointed by agreement, or on the appointment of the President, the remaining appointment or appointments shall be made in accordance with subparagraph (e), at the request of a party to the dispute. Such request shall be made within two weeks of the expiration of the aforementioned 60–day period.

(e) Unless the parties agree that any appointment under subparagraphs (c) and (d) be made by a person or a third State chosen by the parties, the President of the International Tribunal for the Law of the Sea shall make the necessary appointments. If the President is unable to act under this subparagraph or is a national of one of the parties to the dispute, the appointment shall be made by the next senior member of the International Tribunal for the Law of the Sea who is available and is not a national of one of the parties. The appointments referred to in this subparagraph shall be made from the list referred to in article 2 of this Annex within a period of 30 days of the receipt of the request and in consultation with the parties. The members so appointed shall be of different nationalities and may not be in the service of, ordinarily resident in the territory of, or nationals of, any of the parties to the dispute.

(f) Any vacancy shall be filled in the manner prescribed for the initial appointment.

(g) Parties in the same interest shall appoint one member of the tribunal jointly by agreement. Where there are several parties having separate interests or where there is disagreement as to whether they are of the same interest, each of them shall appoint one member of the tribunal. The number of members of the tribunal appointed separately by the parties shall always be smaller by one than the number of members of the tribunal to be appointed jointly by the parties.

(h) In disputes involving more than two parties, the provisions of subparagraphs (a) to (f) shall apply to the maximum extent possible.

Article 4. Functions of Arbitral Tribunal

An arbitral tribunal constituted under article 3 of this Annex shall function in accordance with this Annex and the other provisions of this Convention.

Article 5. Procedure

Unless the parties to the dispute otherwise agree, the arbitral tribunal shall determine its own procedure, assuring to each party a full opportunity to be heard and to present its case.

Article 6. Duties of Parties to a Dispute

The parties to the dispute shall facilitate the work of the arbitral tribunal and, in particular, in accordance with their law and using all means at their disposal, shall:

(a) provide it with all relevant documents, facilities and information; and

(b) enable it when necessary to call witnesses or experts and receive their evidence and to visit the localities to which the case relates.

Article 7. Expenses

Unless the arbitral tribunal decides otherwise because of the particular circumstances of the case, the expenses of the tribunal, including the remuneration of its members, shall be borne by the parties to the dispute in equal shares.

Article 8. Required Majority for Decisions

Decisions of the arbitral tribunal shall be taken by a majority vote of its members. The absence or abstention of less than half of the members shall not constitute a bar to the tribunal reaching a decision. In the event of an equality of votes, the President shall have a casting vote.

Article 9. Default of Appearance

If one of the parties to the dispute does not appear before the arbitral tribunal or fails to defend its case, the other party may request the tribunal to continue the proceedings and to make its award. Absence of a party or failure of a party to defend its case shall not constitute a bar to the proceedings. Before making its award, the arbitral tribunal must satisfy itself not only that it has jurisdiction over the dispute but also that the claim is well founded in fact and law.

Article 10. Award

The award of the arbitral tribunal shall be confined to the subject-matter of the dispute and state the reasons on which it is based. It shall contain the names of the members who have participated and the date of the award.

Any member of the tribunal may attach a separate or dissenting opinion to the award.

Article 11. Finality of Award

The award shall be final and without appeal, unless the parties to the dispute have agreed in advance to an appellate procedure. It shall be complied with by the parties to the dispute.

Article 12. Interpretation or Implementation of Award

1. Any controversy which may arise between the parties to the dispute as regards the interpretation or manner of implementation of the award may be submitted by either party for decision to the arbitral tribunal which made the award. For this purpose, any vacancy in the tribunal shall be filled in the manner provided for in the original appointments of the members of the tribunal.

2. Any such controversy may be submitted to another court or tribunal under article 287 by agreement of all the parties to the dispute.

Article 13. Application to Entities other than States Parties

The provisions of this Annex shall apply *mutatis mutandis* to any dispute involving entities other than States Parties.

Annex VIII. Special Arbitration

Article 1. Institution of Proceedings

Subject to Part XV, any party to a dispute concerning the interpretation or application of the articles of this Convention relating to (1) fisheries, (2) protection and preservation of the marine environment, (3) marine scientific research, or (4) navigation, including pollution from vessels and by dumping may submit the dispute to the special arbitral procedure provided for in this Annex by written notification addressed to the other party or parties to the dispute. The notification shall be accompanied by a statement of the claim and the grounds on which it is based.

Article 2. Lists of Experts

1. A list of experts shall be established and maintained in respect of each of the fields of (1) fisheries, (2) protection and preservation of the marine environment, (3) marine scientific research, and (4) navigation, including pollution from vessels and by dumping.

2. The lists of experts shall be drawn up and maintained, in the field of fisheries by the Food and Agriculture Organization of the United Nations, in the field of protection and preservation of the marine environment by the United Nations Environment Programme, in the field of marine scientific research by the Inter–Governmental Oceanographic Commission, in the field of navigation, including pollution from vessels and by dumping, by the International Maritime Organization, or in each case by the appropriate subsidiary body concerned to which such organization, programme or commission has delegated this function.

3. Every State Party shall be entitled to nominate two experts in each field whose competence in the legal, scientific or technical aspects of such field is established and generally recognized and who enjoy the highest reputation for fairness and integrity. The names of the persons so nominated in each field shall constitute the appropriate list.

4. If at any time the experts nominated by a State Party in the list so constituted shall be fewer than two, that State Party shall be entitled to make further nominations as necessary.

5. The name of an expert shall remain on the list until withdrawn by the State Party which made the nomination, provided that such expert shall continue to serve on any special arbitral tribunal to which that expert has been appointed until the completion of the proceedings before that special arbitral tribunal.

Article 3. Constitution of Special Arbitral Tribunal

For the purpose of proceedings under this Annex, the special arbitral tribunal shall, unless the parties otherwise agree, be constituted as follows:

(a) Subject to subparagraph (g), the special arbitral tribunal shall consist of five members.

(b) The party instituting the proceedings shall appoint two members to be chosen preferably from the appropriate list or lists referred to in article 2 of this Annex relating to the matters in dispute, one of whom may be its national. The appointments shall be included in the notification referred to in article 1 of this Annex.

(c) The other party to the dispute shall, within 30 days of receipt of the notification referred to in article 1 of this Annex, appoint two members to be chosen preferably from the appropriate list or lists relating to the matters in dispute, one of whom may be its national. If the appointments are not made within that period, the party instituting the proceedings may, within two weeks of the expiration of that period, request that the appointments be made in accordance with subparagraph (e).

(d) The parties to the dispute shall by agreement appoint the President of the special arbitral tribunal, chosen preferably from the appropriate list, who shall be a national of a third State, unless the parties otherwise agree. If, within 30 days of receipt of the notification referred to in article 1 of this Annex, the parties are unable to reach agreement on the appointment of the President, the appointment shall be made in accordance with subparagraph (e), at the request of a party to the dispute. Such request shall be made within two weeks of the expiration of the aforementioned 30–day period.

(e) Unless the parties agree that the appointment be made by a person or a third State chosen by the parties, the Secretary–General of the United Nations shall make the necessary appointments within 30 days of receipt of a request under subparagraphs (c) and (d). The appointments referred to in this subparagraph shall be made from the appropriate list or lists of experts referred to in article 2 of this Annex and in consultation with the parties to the dispute and the appropriate international organization. The members so appointed shall be of different nationalities and may not be in the service of, ordinarily resident in the territory of, or nationals of, any of the parties to the dispute.

(f) Any vacancy shall be filled in the manner prescribed for the initial appointment.

(g) Parties in the same interest shall appoint two members of the tribunal jointly by agreement. Where there are several parties having separate interests or where there is disagreement as to whether they are of the same interest, each of them shall appoint one member of the tribunal.

(h) In disputes involving more than two parties, the provisions of subparagraphs (a) to (f) shall apply to the maximum extent possible.

Article 4. General Provisions

Annex VII, articles 4 to 13, apply *mutatis mutandis* to the special arbitration proceedings in accordance with this Annex.

Article 5. Fact Finding

1. The parties to a dispute concerning the interpretation or application of the provisions of this Convention relating to (1) fisheries, (2) protection and preservation of the marine environment, (3) marine scientific research, or (4) navigation, including pollution from vessels and by dumping, may at any time agree to request a special arbitral tribunal constituted in accordance with article 3 of this Annex to carry out an inquiry and establish the facts giving rise to the dispute.

2. Unless the parties otherwise agree, the findings of fact of the special arbitral tribunal acting in accordance with paragraph 1, shall be considered as conclusive as between the parties.

3. If all the parties to the dispute so request, the special arbitral tribunal may formulate recommendations which, without having the force of a decision, shall only constitute the basis for a review by the parties of the questions giving rise to the dispute.

4. Subject to paragraph 2, the special arbitral tribunal shall act in accordance with the provisions of this Annex, unless the parties otherwise agree.

Document 70
AGREEMENT RELATING TO THE IMPLEMENTATION OF PART XI OF THE UNITED NATIONS CONVENTION ON THE LAW OF THE SEA OF 10 DECEMBER 1982

U.N. G.A. Res. 48/263 (28 July 1994)

The General Assembly, ...

Welcoming the report of the Secretary–General on the outcome of his informal consultations, including the draft of an agreement relating to the implementation of Part XI, . . .

1. *Expresses its appreciation* to the Secretary–General for his report on the informal consultations;

2. *Reaffirms* the unified character of the United Nations Convention on the Law of the Sea of 10 December 1982;

3. *Adopts* the Agreement relating to the implementation of Part XI of the United Nations Convention on the Law of the Sea of 10 December 1982 (hereinafter referred to as the "Agreement"), the text of which is annexed to the present resolution;

4. *Affirms* that the Agreement shall be interpreted and applied together with Part XI as a single instrument;

5. *Considers* that future ratifications or formal confirmations of or accessions to the Convention shall represent also consent to be bound by the Agreement and that no State or entity may establish its consent to be bound by the Agreement unless it has previously established or establishes at the same time its consent to be bound by the Convention; . . . .

Annex

Agreement Relating to the Implementation of Part XI of the United Nations Convention on the Law of the Sea of 10 December 1982

The States Parties to this Agreement,

Recognizing the important contribution of the United Nations Convention on the Law of the Sea of 10 December 1982 (hereinafter referred to as "the Convention") to the maintenance of peace, justice and progress for all peoples of the world,

Reaffirming that the seabed and ocean floor and subsoil thereof, beyond the limits of national jurisdiction (hereinafter referred to as "the Area"), as well as the resources of the Area, are the common heritage of mankind,

Mindful of the importance of the Convention for the protection and preservation of the marine environment and of the growing concern for the global environment,

Having considered the report of the Secretary–General of the United Nations on the results of the informal consultations among States held from 1990 to 1994 on outstanding issues relating to Part XI and related provisions of the Convention (hereinafter referred to as "Part XI"),

Noting the political and economic changes, including market-oriented approaches, affecting the implementation of Part XI,

Wishing to facilitate universal participation in the Convention,

Considering that an agreement relating to the implementation of Part XI would best meet that objective,

Have agreed as follows:

Article 1. Implementation of Part XI

1. The States Parties to this Agreement undertake to implement Part XI in accordance with this Agreement.

2. The Annex forms an integral part of this Agreement.

Article 2. Relationship between this Agreement and Part XI

1. The provisions of this Agreement and Part XI shall be interpreted and applied together as a single instrument. In the event of any inconsistency between this Agreement and Part XI, the provisions of this Agreement shall prevail.

2. Articles 309 to 319 of the Convention shall apply to this Agreement as they apply to the Convention.

Article 3. Signature

This Agreement shall remain open for signature at United Nations Headquarters by the States and entities referred to in article 305, paragraph 1 (a), (c), (d), (e) and (f), of the Convention for 12 months from the date of its adoption.

Article 4. Consent to be Bound

1. After the adoption of this Agreement, any instrument of ratification or formal confirmation of or accession to the Convention shall also represent consent to be bound by this Agreement.

2. No State or entity may establish its consent to be bound by this Agreement unless it has previously established or establishes at the same time its consent to be bound by the Convention.

3. A State or entity referred to in article 3 may express its consent to be bound by this Agreement by:

(a) Signature not subject to ratification, formal confirmation or the procedure set out in article 5;

(b) Signature subject to ratification or formal confirmation, followed by ratification or formal confirmation;

(c) Signature subject to the procedure set out in article 5; or

(d) Accession.

Article 5. Simplified Procedure

1. A State or entity which has deposited before the date of the adoption of this Agreement an instrument of ratification or formal confirmation of or accession to the Convention and which has signed this Agreement in accordance with article 4, paragraph 3 (c), shall be considered to have established its consent to be bound by this Agreement 12 months after the date of its adoption, unless that State or entity notifies the depositary in writing before that date that it is not availing itself of the simplified procedure set out in this article.

2. In the event of such notification, consent to be bound by this Agreement shall be established in accordance with article 4, paragraph 3 (b).

Article 6. Entry into Force

1. This Agreement shall enter into force 30 days after the date on which 40 States have established their consent to be bound in accordance with articles 4 and 5, provided that such States include at least seven of the States referred to in paragraph 1 (a) of resolution II of the Third United Nations Conference on the Law of the Sea (hereinafter referred to as "resolution II") and that at least five of those States are developed States.

2. For each State or entity establishing its consent to be bound by this Agreement after the requirements set out in paragraph 1 have been fulfilled, this Agreement shall enter into force on the thirtieth day following the date of establishment of its consent to be bound.

Article 7. Provisional Application

1. If on 16 November 1994 this Agreement has not entered into force, it shall be applied provisionally pending its entry into force by:

(a) States which have consented to its adoption in the General Assembly of the United Nations, except any such State which before 16 November 1994 notifies the depositary in writing either that it will not so apply this Agreement or that it will consent to such application only upon subsequent signature or notification in writing;

(b) States and entities which sign this Agreement, except any such State or entity which notifies the depositary in writing at the time of signature that it will not so apply this Agreement;

(c) States and entities which consent to its provisional application by so notifying the depository in writing;

(d) States which accede to this Agreement.

2. All such States and entities shall apply this Agreement provisionally in accordance with their national or internal laws and regulations, with effect from 16 November 1994 or the date of signature, notification of consent or accession, if later.

3. Provisional application shall terminate upon the date of entry into force of this Agreement. In any event, provisional application shall terminate on 16 November 1998 if at that date the requirement in article 6, paragraph 1, of consent to be bound by this Agreement by at least seven of the States (of which at least five must be developed States) referred to in paragraph 1 (a) of resolution II has not been fulfilled.

Article 8. States Parties

1. For the purposes of this Agreement, "States Parties" means States which have consented to be bound by this Agreement and for which this Agreement is in force.

2. This Agreement applies *mutatis mutandis* to the entities referred to in article 305, paragraph 1 (c), (d), (e) and (f), of the Convention which become Parties to this Agreement in accordance with the conditions relevant to each, and to that extent "States Parties" refers to those entities. . . .

Annex

Section 1. Costs to States Parties and Institutional Arrangements

1. The International Seabed Authority (hereinafter referred to as "the Authority") is the organization through which States Parties to the Convention shall, in accordance with the regime for the Area established in Part XI and this Agreement, organize and control activities in the Area, particularly with a view to administering the resources of the Area. The powers and functions of the Authority shall be those expressly conferred upon it by the Convention. The Authority shall have such incidental powers, consistent with the Convention, as are implicit in, and necessary for, the exercise of those powers and functions with respect to activities in the Area.

2. In order to minimize costs to States Parties, all organs and subsidiary bodies to be established under the Convention and this Agreement shall be cost-effective. This principle shall also apply to the frequency, duration and scheduling of meetings.

3. The setting up and the functioning of the organs and subsidiary bodies of the Authority shall be based on an evolutionary approach, taking into account the functional needs of the organs and subsidiary bodies concerned in order that they may discharge effectively their respective responsibilities at various stages of the development of activities in the Area.

4. The early functions of the Authority upon entry into force of the Convention shall be carried out by the Assembly, the Council, the Secretariat, the Legal and Technical Commission and the Finance Committee. The functions of the Economic Planning Commission shall be

performed by the Legal and Technical Commission until such time as the Council decides otherwise or until the approval of the first plan of work for exploitation.

5. Between the entry into force of the Convention and the approval of the first plan of work for exploitation, the Authority shall concentrate on:

(a) Processing of applications for approval of plans of work for exploration in accordance with Part XI and this Agreement;

(b) Implementation of decisions of the Preparatory Commission for the International Seabed Authority and for the International Tribunal for the Law of the Sea (hereinafter referred to as "the Preparatory Commission") relating to the registered pioneer investors and their certifying States, including their rights and obligations, in accordance with article 308, paragraph 5, of the Convention and resolution II, paragraph 13;. . . .

(f) Adoption of rules, regulations and procedures necessary for the conduct of activities in the Area as they progress. Notwithstanding the provisions of Annex III, article 17, paragraph 2 (b) and (c), of the Convention, such rules, regulations and procedures shall take into account the terms of this Agreement, the prolonged delay in commercial deep seabed mining and the likely pace of activities in the Area;. . . .

6. (a) An application for approval of a plan of work for exploration shall be considered by the Council following the receipt of a recommendation on the application from the Legal and Technical Commission. The processing of an application for approval of a plan of work for exploration shall be in accordance with the provisions of the Convention, including Annex III thereof, and this Agreement, and subject to the following:

(i) A plan of work for exploration submitted on behalf of a State or entity, or any component of such entity, referred to in resolution II, paragraph 1 (a) (ii) or (iii), other than a registered pioneer investor, which had already undertaken substantial activities in the Area prior to the entry into force of the Convention, or its successor in interest, shall be considered to have met the financial and technical qualifications necessary for approval of a plan of work if the sponsoring State or States certify that the applicant has expended an amount equivalent to at least US $30 million in research and exploration activities and has expended no less than 10 per cent of that amount in the location, survey and evaluation of the area referred to in the plan of work. If the plan of work otherwise satisfies the requirements of the Convention and any rules, regulations and procedures adopted pursuant thereto, it shall be approved by the Council in the form of a contract. The provisions of section 3, paragraph 11, of this Annex shall be interpreted and applied accordingly;

(ii) Notwithstanding the provisions of resolution II, paragraph 8 (a), a registered pioneer investor may request approval of a plan of work for exploration within 36 months of the entry into force of the Convention. The plan of work for exploration shall consist of documents, reports and other data submitted to the Preparatory Commission both before and after registration and shall be accompanied by a certificate of compliance, consisting of a factual report describing the status of fulfilment of obligations under the pioneer investor regime, issued by the Preparatory Commission in accordance with resolution II, paragraph 11 (a). Such a plan of work shall be considered to be approved. Such an approved plan of work shall be in the form of a contract concluded between the Authority and the registered pioneer investor in accordance with Part XI and this Agreement. The fee of US $250,000 paid pursuant to resolution II paragraph 7 (a), shall be deemed to be the fee relating to the exploration phase pursuant to section 8, paragraph 3, of this Annex. Section 3, paragraph 11, of this Annex shall be interpreted and applied accordingly;

(iii) In accordance with the principle of non-discrimination, a contract with a State or entity or any component of such entity referred to in subparagraph (a)(i) shall include arrangements which shall be similar to and no less favourable than those agreed with any registered pioneer investor referred to in subparagraph (a)(ii).... (b) The approval of a plan of work for exploration shall be in accordance with article 153, paragraph 3, of the Convention....

8. An application for approval of a plan of work for exploration, subject to paragraph 6 (a)(i) or (ii), shall be processed in accordance with the procedures set out in section 3, paragraph 11, of this Annex.

9. A plan of work for exploration shall be approved for a period of 15 years. Upon the expiration of a plan of work for exploration, the contractor shall apply for a plan of work for exploitation unless the contractor has already done so or has obtained an extension for the plan of work for exploration. Contractors may apply for such extensions for periods of not more than five years each. Such extensions shall be approved if the contractor has made efforts in good faith to comply with the requirements of the plan of work but for reasons beyond the contractor's control has been unable to complete the necessary preparatory work for proceeding to the exploitation stage or if the prevailing economic circumstances do not justify proceeding to the exploitation stage.

10. Designation of a reserved area for the Authority in accordance with Annex III, article 8, of the Convention shall take place in connection with approval of an application for a plan of work for exploration or approval of an application for a plan of work for exploration and exploitation.

11. Notwithstanding the provisions of paragraph 9, an approved plan of work for exploration which is sponsored by at least one State

provisionally applying this Agreement shall terminate if such a State ceases to apply this Agreement provisionally and has not become a member on a provisional basis in accordance with paragraph 12 or has not become a State Party.

12. Upon the entry into force of this Agreement, States and entities referred to in article 3 of this Agreement which have been applying it provisionally in accordance with article 7 and for which it is not in force may continue to be members of the Authority on a provisional basis pending its entry into force for such States and entities, in accordance with the following subparagraphs: . . .

(b) If this Agreement enters into force after 15 November 1996, such States and entities may request the Council to grant continued membership in the Authority on a provisional basis for a period or periods not extending beyond 16 November 1998. The Council shall grant such membership with effect from the date of the request if it is satisfied that the State or entity has been making efforts in good faith to become a party to the Agreement and the Convention;. . . .

(d) Notwithstanding the provisions of paragraph 9, an approved plan of work in the form of a contract for exploration which was sponsored pursuant to subparagraph (c)(ii) by a State which was a member on a provisional basis shall terminate if such membership ceases and the State or entity has not become a State Party;

(e) If such a member has failed to make its assessed contributions or otherwise failed to comply with its obligations in accordance with this paragraph, its membership on a provisional basis shall be terminated.

13. The reference in Annex III, article 10, of the Convention to performance which has not been satisfactory shall be interpreted to mean that the contractor has failed to comply with the requirements of an approved plan of work in spite of a written warning or warnings from the Authority to the contractor to comply therewith.

14. The Authority shall have its own budget. Until the end of the year following the year during which this Agreement enters into force, the administrative expenses of the Authority shall be met through the budget of the United Nations. Thereafter, the administrative expenses of the Authority shall be met by assessed contributions of its members, including any members on a provisional basis, in accordance with articles 171, subparagraph (a), and 173 of the Convention and this Agreement, until the Authority has sufficient funds from other sources to meet those expenses. The Authority shall not exercise the power referred to in article 74, paragraph 1, of the Convention to borrow funds to finance its administrative budget.

15. The Authority shall elaborate and adopt, in accordance with article 162, paragraph 2 (*o*)(ii), of the Convention, rules, regulations and procedures based on the principles contained in sections 2, 5, 6, 7 and 8 of this Annex, as well as any additional rules, regulations and procedures necessary to facilitate the approval of plans of work for exploration or exploitation, in accordance with the following subparagraphs. . . .

17. The relevant provisions of Part XI, section 4, of the Convention shall be interpreted and applied in accordance with this Agreement.

Section 2. The Enterprise

1. The Secretariat of the Authority shall perform the functions of the Enterprise until it begins to operate independently of the Secretariat. The Secretary–General of the Authority shall appoint from within the staff of the Authority an interim Director–General to oversee the performance of these functions by the Secretariat. . . .

2. The Enterprise shall conduct its initial deep seabed mining operations through joint ventures. Upon the approval of a plan of work for exploitation for an entity other than the Enterprise, or upon receipt by the Council of an application for a joint-venture operation with the Enterprise, the Council shall take up the issue of the functioning of the Enterprise independently of the Secretariat of the Authority. If joint-venture operations with the Enterprise accord with sound commercial principles, the Council shall issue a directive pursuant to article 170, paragraph 2, of the Convention providing for such independent functioning.

3. The obligation of States Parties to fund one mine site of the Enterprise as provided for in Annex IV, article 11, paragraph 3, of the Convention shall not apply and States Parties shall be under no obligation to finance any of the operations in any mine site of the Enterprise or under its joint-venture arrangements.

4. The obligations applicable to contractors shall apply to the Enterprise. Notwithstanding the provisions of article 153, paragraph 3, and Annex III, article 3, paragraph 5, of the Convention, a plan of work for the Enterprise upon its approval shall be in the form of a contract concluded between the Authority and the Enterprise.

5. A contractor which has contributed a particular area to the Authority as a reserved area has the right of first refusal to enter into a joint-venture arrangement with the Enterprise for exploration and exploitation of that area. If the Enterprise does not submit an application for a plan of work for activities in respect of such a reserved area within 15 years of the commencement of its functions independent of the Secretariat of the Authority or within 15 years of the date on which that area is reserved for the Authority, whichever is the later, the contractor which contributed the area shall be entitled to apply for a plan of work for that area provided it offers in good faith to include the Enterprise as a joint-venture partner.

6. Article 170, paragraph 4, Annex IV and other provisions of the Convention relating to the Enterprise shall be interpreted and applied in accordance with this section.

Section 3. Decision–Making

1. The general policies of the Authority shall be established by the Assembly in collaboration with the Council.

2. As a general rule, decision-making in the organs of the Authority should be by consensus.

3. If all efforts to reach a decision by consensus have been exhausted, decisions by voting in the Assembly on questions of procedure shall be taken by a majority of members present and voting, and decisions on questions of substance shall be taken by a two-thirds majority of members present and voting, as provided for in article 159, paragraph 8, of the Convention.

4. Decisions of the Assembly on any matter for which the Council also has competence or on any administrative, budgetary or financial matter shall be based on the recommendations of the Council. If the Assembly does not accept the recommendation of the Council on any matter, it shall return the matter to the Council for further consideration. The Council shall reconsider the matter in the light of the views expressed by the Assembly.

5. If all efforts to reach a decision by consensus have been exhausted, decisions by voting in the Council on questions of procedure shall be taken by a majority of members present and voting, and decisions on questions of substance, except where the Convention provides for decisions by consensus in the Council, shall be taken by a two-thirds majority of members present and voting, provided that such decisions are not opposed by a majority in any one of the chambers referred to in paragraph 9. In taking decisions the Council shall seek to promote the interests of all the members of the Authority.

6. The Council may defer the taking of a decision in order to facilitate further negotiation whenever it appears that all efforts at achieving consensus on a question have not been exhausted.

7. Decisions by the Assembly or the Council having financial or budgetary implications shall be based on the recommendations of the Finance Committee.

8. The provisions of article 161, paragraph 8 (b) and (c), of the Convention shall not apply.

9. (a) Each group of States elected under paragraph 15 (a) to (c) shall be treated as a chamber for the purposes of voting in the Council. The developing States elected under paragraph 15 (d) and (e) shall be treated as a single chamber for the purposes of voting in the Council.

(b) Before electing the members of the Council, the Assembly shall establish lists of countries fulfilling the criteria for membership in the groups of States in paragraph 15 (a) to (d). If a State fulfils the criteria for membership in more than one group, it may only be proposed by one group for election to the Council and it shall represent only that group in voting in the Council.

10. Each group of States in paragraph 15 (a) to (d) shall be represented in the Council by those members nominated by that group. Each group shall nominate only as many candidates as the number of seats required to be filled by that group. When the number of potential candidates in each of the groups referred to in paragraph 15 (a) to (e)

exceeds the number of seats available in each of those respective groups, as a general rule, the principle of rotation shall apply. States members of each of those groups shall determine how this principle shall apply in those groups.

11. (a) The Council shall approve a recommendation by the Legal and Technical Commission for approval of a plan of work unless by a two-thirds majority of its members present and voting, including a majority of members present and voting in each of the chambers of the Council, the Council decides to disapprove a plan of work. If the Council does not make a decision on a recommendation for approval of a plan of work within a prescribed period, the recommendation shall be deemed to have been approved by the Council at the end of that period. The prescribed period shall normally be 60 days unless the Council decides to provide for a longer period. If the Commission recommends the disapproval of a plan of work or does not make a recommendation, the Council may nevertheless approve the plan of work in accordance with its rules of procedure for decision-making on questions of substance.

(b) The provisions of article 162, paragraph 2 (j), of the Convention shall not apply.

12. Where a dispute arises relating to the disapproval of a plan of work, such dispute shall be submitted to the dispute settlement procedures set out in the Convention.

13. Decisions by voting in the Legal and Technical Commission shall be by a majority of members present and voting.

14. Part XI, section 4, subsections B and C, of the Convention shall be interpreted and applied in accordance with this section.

15. The Council shall consist of 36 members of the Authority elected by the Assembly in the following order:

(a) Four members from among those States Parties which, during the last five years for which statistics are available, have either consumed more than 2 per cent in value terms of total world consumption or have had net imports of more than 2 per cent in value terms of total world imports of the commodities produced from the categories of minerals to be derived from the Area, provided that the four members shall include one State from the Eastern European region having the largest economy in that region in terms of gross domestic product and the State, on the date of entry into force of the Convention, having the largest economy in terms of gross domestic product, if such States wish to be represented in this group;

(b) Four members from among the eight States Parties which have made the largest investments in preparation for and in the conduct of activities in the Area, either directly or through their nationals;

(c) Four members from among States Parties which, on the basis of production in areas under their jurisdiction, are major net exporters of the categories of minerals to be derived from the Area, including at least two developing States whose exports of such minerals have a substantial bearing upon their economies;

(d) Six members from among developing States Parties, representing special interests. The special interests to be represented shall include those of States with large populations, States which are land-locked or geographically disadvantaged, island States, States which are major importers of the categories of minerals to be derived from the Area, States which are potential producers of such minerals and least developed States;

(e) Eighteen members elected according to the principle of ensuring an equitable geographical distribution of seats in the Council as a whole, provided that each geographical region shall have at least one member elected under this subparagraph. For this purpose, the geographical regions shall be Africa, Asia, Eastern Europe, Latin America and the Caribbean and Western Europe and Others.

16. The provisions of article 161, paragraph 1, of the Convention shall not apply.

Section 4. Review Conference

The provisions relating to the Review Conference in article 155, paragraphs 1, 3 and 4, of the Convention shall not apply. Notwithstanding the provisions of article 314, paragraph 2, of the Convention, the Assembly, on the recommendation of the Council, may undertake at any time a review of the matters referred to in article 155, paragraph 1, of the Convention. Amendments relating to this Agreement and Part XI shall be subject to the procedures contained in articles 314, 315 and 316 of the Convention, provided that the principles, regime and other terms referred to in article 155, paragraph 2, of the Convention shall be maintained and the rights referred to in paragraph 5 of that article shall not be affected.

Section 5. Transfer of Technology

1. In addition to the provisions of article 144 of the Convention, transfer of technology for the purposes of Part XI shall be governed by the following principles:

(a) The Enterprise, and developing States wishing to obtain deep seabed mining technology, shall seek to obtain such technology on fair and reasonable commercial terms and conditions on the open market, or through joint-venture arrangements;

(b) If the Enterprise or developing States are unable to obtain deep seabed mining technology, the Authority may request all or any of the contractors and their respective sponsoring State or States to cooperate with it in facilitating the acquisition of deep seabed mining technology by the Enterprise or its joint venture, or by a developing State or States seeking to acquire such technology on fair and reasonable commercial terms and conditions, consistent with the effective protection of intellectual property rights. States Parties undertake to cooperate fully and effectively with the Authority for this purpose and to ensure that contractors sponsored by them also cooperate fully with the Authority;....

2. The provisions of Annex III, article 5, of the Convention shall not apply.

Section 6. Production Policy

1. The production policy of the Authority shall be based on the following principles:

(a) Development of the resources of the Area shall take place in accordance with sound commercial principles;

(b) The provisions of the General Agreement on Tariffs and Trade, its relevant codes and successor or superseding agreements shall apply with respect to activities in the Area;

(c) In particular, there shall be no subsidization of activities in the Area except as may be permitted under the agreements referred to in subparagraph (b). Subsidization for the purpose of these principles shall be defined in terms of the agreements referred to in subparagraph (b);

(d) There shall be no discrimination between minerals derived from the Area and from other sources. There shall be no preferential access to markets for such minerals or for imports of commodities produced from such minerals, in particular:

(i) By the use of tariff or non-tariff barriers; and

(ii) Given by States Parties to such minerals or commodities produced by their state enterprises or by natural or juridical persons which possess their nationality or are controlled by them or their nationals;

(e) The plan of work for exploitation approved by the Authority in respect of each mining area shall indicate an anticipated production schedule which shall include the estimated maximum amounts of minerals that would be produced per year under the plan of work;

(f) The following shall apply to the settlement of disputes concerning the provisions of the agreements referred to in subparagraph (b):

(i) Where the States Parties concerned are parties to such agreements, they shall have recourse to the dispute settlement procedures of those agreements;

(ii) Where one or more of the States Parties concerned are not parties to such agreements, they shall have recourse to the dispute settlement procedures set out in the Convention;

(g) In circumstances where a determination is made under the agreements referred to in subparagraph (b) that a State Party has engaged in subsidization which is prohibited or has resulted in adverse effects on the interests of another State Party and appropriate steps have not been taken by the relevant State Party or States

Parties, a State Party may request the Council to take appropriate measures.

2. The principles contained in paragraph 1 shall not affect the rights and obligations under any provision of the agreements referred to in paragraph 1 (b), as well as the relevant free trade and customs union agreements, in relations between States Parties which are parties to such agreements.

3. The acceptance by a contractor of subsidies other than those which may be permitted under the agreements referred to in paragraph 1 (b) shall constitute a violation of the fundamental terms of the contract forming a plan of work for the carrying out of activities in the Area.

4. Any State Party which has reason to believe that there has been a breach of the requirements of paragraphs 1 (b) to (d) or 3 may initiate dispute settlement procedures in conformity with paragraph 1 (f) or (g). . . .

7. The provisions of article 151, paragraphs 1 to 7 and 9, article 162, paragraph 2 (q), article 165, paragraph 2 (n), and Annex III, article 6, paragraph 5, and article 7, of the Convention shall not apply.

Section 7. Economic Assistance

1. The policy of the Authority of assisting developing countries which suffer serious adverse effects on their export earnings or economies resulting from a reduction in the price of an affected mineral or in the volume of exports of that mineral, to the extent that such reduction is caused by activities in the Area, shall be based on the following principles:

(a) The Authority shall establish an economic assistance fund from a portion of the funds of the Authority which exceeds those necessary to cover the administrative expenses of the Authority. The amount set aside for this purpose shall be determined by the Council from time to time, upon the recommendation of the Finance Committee. Only funds from payments received from contractors, including the Enterprise, and voluntary contributions shall be used for the establishment of the economic assistance fund;

(b) Developing land-based producer States whose economies have been determined to be seriously affected by the production of minerals from the deep seabed shall be assisted from the economic assistance fund of the Authority;

(c) The Authority shall provide assistance from the fund to affected developing land-based producer States, where appropriate, in cooperation with existing global or regional development institutions which have the infrastructure and expertise to carry out such assistance programmes;

(d) The extent and period of such assistance shall be determined on a case-by-case basis. In doing so, due consideration shall be given to the nature and magnitude of the problems encountered by affected developing land-based producer States.

2. Article 151, paragraph 10, of the Convention shall be implemented by means of measures of economic assistance referred to in paragraph 1. Article 160, paragraph 2 (*l*), article 162, paragraph 2 (n), article 164, paragraph 2 (d), article 171, subparagraph (f), and article 173, paragraph 2 (c), of the Convention shall be interpreted accordingly.

Section 8. Financial Terms of Contracts

1. The following principles shall provide the basis for establishing rules, regulations and procedures for financial terms of contracts:

(a) The system of payments to the Authority shall be fair both to the contractor and to the Authority and shall provide adequate means of determining compliance by the contractor with such system;

(b) The rates of payments under the system shall be within the range of those prevailing in respect of land-based mining of the same or similar minerals in order to avoid giving deep seabed miners an artificial competitive advantage or imposing on them a competitive disadvantage;

(c) The system should not be complicated and should not impose major administrative costs on the Authority or on a contractor. Consideration should be given to the adoption of a royalty system or a combination of a royalty and profit-sharing system. If alternative systems are decided upon, the contractor has the right to choose the system applicable to its contract. Any subsequent change in choice between alternative systems, however, shall be made by agreement between the Authority and the contractor;

(d) An annual fixed fee shall be payable from the date of commencement of commercial production. This fee may be credited against other payments due under the system adopted in accordance with subparagraph (c). The amount of the fee shall be established by the Council;

(e) The system of payments may be revised periodically in the light of changing circumstances. Any changes shall be applied in a non-discriminatory manner. Such changes may apply to existing contracts only at the election of the contractor. Any subsequent change in choice between alternative systems shall be made by agreement between the Authority and the contractor;

(f) Disputes concerning the interpretation or application of the rules and regulations based on these principles shall be subject to the dispute settlement procedures set out in the Convention.

2. The provisions of Annex III, article 13, paragraphs 3 to 10, of the Convention shall not apply.

3. With regard to the implementation of Annex III, article 13, paragraph 2, of the Convention, the fee for processing applications for approval of a plan of work limited to one phase, either the exploration phase or the exploitation phase, shall be US $250,000.

Section 9. The Finance Committee

1. There is hereby established a Finance Committee. The Committee shall be composed of 15 members with appropriate qualifications

relevant to financial matters. States Parties shall nominate candidates of the highest standards of competence and integrity.

2. No two members of the Finance Committee shall be nationals of the same State Party.

3. Members of the Finance Committee shall be elected by the Assembly and due account shall be taken of the need for equitable geographical distribution and the representation of special interests. Each group of States referred to in section 3, paragraph 15 (a), (b), (c) and (d), of this Annex shall be represented on the Committee by at least one member. Until the Authority has sufficient funds other than assessed contributions to meet its administrative expenses, the membership of the Committee shall include representatives of the five largest financial contributors to the administrative budget of the Authority. Thereafter, the election of one member from each group shall be on the basis of nomination by the members of the respective group, without prejudice to the possibility of further members being elected from each group.

4. Members of the Finance Committee shall hold office for a term of five years. They shall be eligible for re-election for a further term. . . .

7. Decisions by the Assembly and the Council on the following issues shall take into account recommendations of the Finance Committee:

(a) Draft financial rules, regulations and procedures of the organs of the Authority and the financial management and internal financial administration of the Authority;

(b) Assessment of contributions of members to the administrative budget of the Authority in accordance with article 160, paragraph 2 (e), of the Convention;

(c) All relevant financial matters, including the proposed annual budget prepared by the Secretary–General of the Authority in accordance with article 172 of the Convention and the financial aspects of the implementation of the programmes of work of the Secretariat;

(d) The administrative budget;

(e) Financial obligations of States Parties arising from the implementation of this Agreement and Part XI as well as the administrative and budgetary implications of proposals and recommendations involving expenditure from the funds of the Authority;

(f) Rules, regulations and procedures on the equitable sharing of financial and other economic benefits derived from activities in the Area and the decisions to be made thereon.

8. Decisions in the Finance Committee on questions of procedure shall be taken by a majority of members present and voting. Decisions on questions of substance shall be taken by consensus.

9. The requirement of article 162, paragraph 2 (y), of the Convention to establish a subsidiary organ to deal with financial matters shall be deemed to have been fulfilled by the establishment of the Finance Committee in accordance with this section.

Document 71
TREATY BETWEEN THE GOVERNMENT OF THE UNITED STATES OF AMERICA AND THE GOVERNMENT OF CANADA ON MUTUAL LEGAL ASSISTANCE IN CRIMINAL MATTERS

1990 Can. T. S. No. 19

The Government of the United States of America and the Government of Canada,

Desiring to improve the effectiveness of both countries in the investigation, prosecution and suppression of crime through cooperation and mutual assistance in law enforcement matters,

Have agreed as follows:

Article I

Definitions

For the purposes of this Treaty:

"Central Authority" means—

(a) for Canada, the Minister of Justice or officials designated by him;

"Competent Authority" means any law enforcement authority with responsibility for matter related to the investigation or prosecution of offenses;

"Offence" means—

(a) for Canada, an offense created by a law of Parliament that may be prosecuted upon indictment, or an offence created by the Legislature of a Province specified in the Annex;

(b) for the United States, an offence for which the statutory penalty is a term of imprisonment of one year or more, or an offence specified in the Annex;

"Public Interest" means any substantial interest related to a national security or other essential public policy;

"Request" means a request made under this Treaty.

Article II

Scope of Application

1. The Parties shall provide, in accordance with the provisions of this Treaty, mutual legal assistance in all matters relating to the investigation, prosecution and suppression of offences.

2. Assistance shall include:

(a) examining objects and sites;

(b) exchanging information and objects;

(c) locating or identifying persons;

(d) serving documents;

(e) taking the evidence of persons;

(f) providing documents and records;

(g) transferring persons in custody;

(h) executing requests for searches and seizures.

3. Assistance shall be provided without regard to whether the conduct under investigation or prosecution in the Requesting State constitutes an offence or may be prosecuted by the Requested State.

4. This Treaty is intended solely for mutual legal assistance between Parties. The provisions of this Treaty shall not give rise to a right on the part of a private party to obtain, suppress or exclude any evidence or impede the execution of a request.

Article III

Other Assistance

1. The Parties, including their competent authorities, may provide assistance pursuant to other agreements, arrangements or practices.

2. The Central Authorities may agree, in exceptional circumstances, to provide assistance pursuant to this Treaty in respect of illegal acts that do not constitute an offence within the definition of offence in Article I.

Article IV

Obligation To Request Assistance

1. A Party seeking to obtain documents, records or other articles known to be located in the territory of the other Party shall request assistance pursuant to Article III(1).

2. Where denial of a request or delay in its execution may jeopardize successful completion of an investigation or prosecution, the Parties shall promptly consult, at the instance of either Party, to consider alternative means of assistance.

3. Unless the Parties otherwise agree, the consultations shall be considered terminated 30 days after they have been requested, and the Parties' obligations under this Article shall then be deemed to have been fulfilled.

Article V

Limitations on Compliance

1. The Requested State may deny assistance to the extent that—

(a) the request is not made in conformity with the provisions of this Treaty; or

(b) execution of the request is contrary to its public interest, as determined by its Central Authority.

2. The Requested State may postpone assistance if execution of the request would interfere with an ongoing investigation or prosecution in the Requested State.

3. Before denying or postponing assistance pursuant to this Article, the Requested State, through its Central Authority—

(a) shall promptly inform the Requesting State of the reason for considering denial or postponement; and

(b) shall consult with the Requesting State to determine whether assistance may be given subject to such terms and conditions as the Requested State deems necessary.

4. If the Requesting State accepts assistance subject to the terms conditions referred to in paragraph 3(b), it shall comply with said terms and conditions.

Article VI

Requests

1. Requests shall be made by the Central Authority of the Requesting State directly to the Central Authority of the Requested State.

2. Requests shall be made in writing where compulsory process is required in the Requested State or where otherwise required by the Requested State. In urgent circumstances, such requests may be made orally, but shall be confirmed in writing forthwith.

3. A request shall contain such information as the Requested State requires to execute the request, including—

(a) the name of the competent authority conducting the investigation or proceeding to which the request relates;

(b) the subject matter and nature of the investigation or proceeding to which the request relates;

(c) a description of the evidence, information or other assistance sought;

(d) the purpose for which the evidence, information or other assistance is sought, and at any time limitations relevant thereto; and

(e) requirements for confidentiality.

4. The Courts of the Requesting State shall be authorized to order lawful disclosure of such information as is necessary to enable the Requested State to execute the request.

5. The Requested State shall use its best efforts to keep confidential a request and its contents except when otherwise authorized by the Requesting State.

Article VII

Execution of Requests

1. The Central Authority of the Requested State shall promptly execute the request or, when appropriate, transmit it to the competent authorities, who shall make best efforts to execute the request. The Courts of the Requested State shall have jurisdiction to issue subpoenas, search warrants or other orders necessary to execute the request.

2. A request shall be executed in accordance with the law of the Requested State and, to the extent not prohibited by law of the Requested State, in accordance with the directions stated in the request.

Article VIII

Costs

1. The Requested State shall assume all ordinary expenses of executing a request within its boundaries, except—

(a) fees of experts;

(b) expenses of translation and transcription; and

(c) travel and incidental expenses of persons traveling to the Requested State to attend the execution of a request.

2. The Requesting State shall assume all ordinary expenses required to present evidence from the Requested State in the requesting State, including—

(a) travel and incidental expenses of witnesses traveling to the Requesting State, including those of accompanying officials; and

(b) fees of experts.

3. If during the execution of the request it becomes apparent that expenses of an extraordinary nature are required to fulfill the request, the Parties shall consult to determine the terms and conditions under which the execution of the request may continue.

4. The Parties shall agree, pursuant to Article XVIII, on practical measures as appropriate for the reporting and payment of costs in conformity with this article.

Article IX

Limitations of Use

1. The Central Authority of the Requested State may require, after consultation with the Central Authority of the Requesting State, that information or evidence furnished be kept confidential or be disclosed or used only subject to terms and conditions it may specify.

2. The Requesting State shall not disclose or use information or evidence furnished for purposes other than those stated in the request

without the prior consent of the Central Authority of the Requested State.

3. Information or evidence made public in the Requesting State in accordance with paragraph 2 may be used for any purpose.

Article X

Location or Identity of Persons

The competent authorities of the Requested State shall make best efforts to ascertain the location and identity of persons specified in the request.

Article XI

Service of Documents

1. The Requested State shall serve any document transmitted to it for the purpose of service.

2. The Requesting State shall transmit a request for the service of a document pertaining to a response or appearance in the Requesting State within a reasonable time before the scheduled response or appearance.

3. A request for the service of a document pertaining to an appearance in the Requesting State shall include such notice as the Central Authority of the Requesting State is reasonably able to provide of outstanding warrants or other judicial orders in criminal matters against the person to be served.

4. The Requested State shall return a proof of service in the manner required by the Requesting State or in any manner agreed upon pursuant to Article XVIII.

Article XII

Taking of Evidence in the Requested State

1. A person requested to testify and produce documents, records or other articles in the Requested State may be compelled by subpoena or order to appear and testify and produce such documents, records and other articles, in accordance with the requirements of the law of the Requested State.

2. Every person whose attendance is required for the purpose of giving testimony under this article is entitled to such fees and allowances as may be provided for by the law of the Requested State.

Article XIII

Government Documents and Records

1. The Requested State shall provide copies of publicly available documents and records of government departments and agencies.

2. The Requested State may provide copies of any document, record or information in the possession of a government department or agency, but not publicly available, to the same extent and under the

same conditions as would be available to its own law enforcement and judicial authorities.

Article XIV

Certification and Authentication

1. Copies of documents and records provided under Article XII or Article XIII shall be certified or authenticated in the manner required by the Requesting State or in any manner agreed upon pursuant to Article XVIII.

2. No document or record otherwise admissible in evidence in the Requesting State, certified or authenticated under paragraph 2, shall require further certification or authentication.

Article XV

Transfer of Persons in Custody

1. A person in custody in the Requested State whose presence is requested in the Requesting State for the purposes of this Treaty shall be transferred from the Requested State to the Requesting State for that purpose, provided the person in custody consents and the Requested State has no reasonable basis to deny the request.

2. The Requesting State shall have the authority and duty to keep the person in custody at all times and return the person to the custody of the Requested State immediately after the execution of the request.

Article XVI

Search and Seizure

1. A request for search and seizure shall be executed in accordance with the requirements of the law of the Requested State.

2. The competent authority that has executed a request for search and seizure shall provide such certifications as may be required by the Requesting State concerning, but not limited to, the circumstances of the seizure, identity of the item seized and integrity of its condition, and continuity of possession thereof.

3. Such certifications may be admissible in evidence in a judicial proceeding in the Requesting State as proof of the truth of the matters certified therein, in accordance with the law of the Requesting State.

4. No item seized shall be provided to the Requesting State until that State has agreed to such terms and conditions as may be required by the Requested State to protect third party interests in the item to be transferred.

Article XVII

Proceeds of Crime

1. The Central Authority of either Party shall notify the Central Authority of the other Party of proceeds of crime believed to be located in the territory of the other party.

2. The Parties shall assist each other to the extent permitted by their respective laws in proceedings related to the forfeiture of the proceeds of crime, restitution to the victims of crime, and the collection of fines imposed as a sentence in a criminal prosecution.

Article XVIII

Improvement of Assistance

1. The Parties agree to consult as appropriate to develop other specific agreements or arrangements, formal or informal, on mutual legal assistance.

2. The Parties may agree on such practical measures as may be necessary to facilitate the implementation of this Treaty.

Article XIX

Ratification and Entry Into Force

1. This Treaty shall be ratified, and the instruments of ratification shall be exchanged at Washington, D.C., as soon as possible.

2. This Treaty shall enter into force upon the exchange of instruments of ratification.

Article XX

Termination

Either Party may terminate this Treaty by giving written notice to the other Party at any time. Termination shall become effective six months after receipt of such notice.

Annex

The definition of offence includes offenses created by the Legislature of Province of Canada or offenses under the law of the United States in the following categories:

(1) securities;

(2) wildlife protection;

(3) environmental protection; and

(4) consumer protection.

Document 72
CONVENTION ON INTERNATIONAL CIVIL AVIATION [THE CHICAGO CONVENTION]

15 U.N.T.S. 295, T.I.A.S. No. 1591 (1944)

Whereas the future development of international civil aviation can greatly help to create and preserve friendship and understanding among the nations and peoples of the world, yet its abuse can become a threat to the general security; and

Whereas it is desirable to avoid friction and to promote that cooperation between nations and peoples upon which the peace of the world depends;

Therefore the undersigned governments having agreed on certain principles and arrangements in order that international civil aviation may be developed in a safe and orderly manner and that international air transport services may be established on the basis of equality of opportunity and operated soundly and economically;

Have accordingly concluded this Convention to that end.

PART I. AIR NAVIGATION

CHAPTER I. GENERAL PRINCIPLES AND APPLICATION OF THE CONVENTION

Article 1. Sovereignty

The contracting States recognize that every State has complete and exclusive sovereignty over the airspace above its territory.

Article 2. Territory

For the purposes of this Convention the territory of a State shall be deemed to be the land areas and territorial waters adjacent thereto under the sovereignty, suzerainty, protection or mandate of such State.

Article 3. Civil and State Aircraft

(a) This Convention shall be applicable only to civil aircraft, and shall not be applicable to state aircraft.

(b) Aircraft used in military, customs and police services shall be deemed to be state aircraft.

(c) No state aircraft of a contracting State shall fly over the territory of another State or land thereon without authorization by special agreement or otherwise, and in accordance with the terms thereof.

(d) The contracting States undertake, when issuing regulations for their state aircraft, that they will have due regard for the safety of navigation of civil aircraft.

Article 4. Misuse of Civil Aviation

Each contracting State agrees not to use civil aviation inconsistent with the aims of this Convention for any purpose.

CHAPTER II. FLIGHT OVER TERRITORY OF CONTRACTING STATES

Article 5. Right of Non–Scheduled Flight

Each contracting State agrees that all aircraft of the other contracting States, being aircraft not engaged in scheduled international air services shall have the right, subject to the observance of the terms of this Convention, to make flights into or in transit non-stop across its territory and to make stops for non-traffic purposes without the necessity of obtaining prior permission, and subject to the right of the State flown over to require landing. Each contracting State nevertheless reserves the right, for reasons of safety of flight, to require aircraft desiring to proceed over regions which are inaccessible or without adequate air navigation facilities to follow prescribed routes, or to obtain special permission for such flights.

Such aircraft, if engaged in the carriage of passengers, cargo, or mail for remuneration or hire on other than scheduled international air services, shall also, subject to the provisions of Article 7, have the privilege of taking on or discharging passengers, cargo, or mail, subject to the right of any State where such embarkation or discharge takes place to impose such regulations, conditions or limitations as it may consider desirable.

Article 6. Scheduled Air Services

No scheduled international air service may be operated over or into the territory of a contracting State, except with the special permission or other authorization of that State, and in accordance with the terms of such permission or authorization.

Article 7. Cabotage

Each contracting State shall have the right to refuse permission to the aircraft of other contracting States to take on in its territory passengers, mail and cargo carried for remuneration or hire and destined for another point within its territory. Each contracting State undertakes not to enter into any arrangements which specifically grant any such privilege on an exclusive basis to any other State or an airline of any other State, and not to obtain any such exclusive privilege from any other State.

Article 8. Pilotless Aircraft

No aircraft capable of being flown without a pilot shall be flown without a pilot over the territory of a contracting State without special authorization by that State and in accordance with the terms of such authorization. Each contracting State undertakes to insure that the flight of such aircraft without a pilot in regions open to civil aircraft shall be so controlled as to obviate danger to civil aircraft.

Article 9. Prohibited Areas

(a) Each contracting State may, for reasons of military necessity or public safety, restrict or prohibit uniformly the aircraft of other States from flying over certain areas of its territory, provided that no distinction in this respect is made between the aircraft of the State whose territory is involved, engaged in international scheduled airline services, and the aircraft of the other contracting States likewise engaged. Such prohibited areas shall be of reasonable extent and location so as not to interfere unnecessarily with air navigation. Descriptions of such prohibited areas in the territory of a contracting State, as well as any subsequent alterations therein, shall be communicated as soon as possible to the other contracting States and to the International Civil Aviation Organization.

(b) Each contracting State reserves also the right, in exceptional circumstances or during a period of emergency, or in the interest of public safety, and with immediate effect, temporarily to restrict or prohibit flying over the whole or any part of its territory, on condition that such restriction or prohibition shall be applicable without distinction of nationality to aircraft of all other States.

(c) Each contracting State, under such regulations as it may prescribe, may require any aircraft entering the areas contemplated in subparagraphs (a) or (h) above to effect a landing as soon as practicable thereafter at some designated airport within its territory.

Article 10. Landing at Customs Airport

Except in a case where, under the terms of this Convention or a special authorization, aircraft are permitted to cross the territory of a contracting State without landing, every aircraft which enters the territory of a contracting State shall, if the regulations of that State so require, land at an airport designated by that State for the purpose of customs and other examination. On departure from the territory of a contracting State, such aircraft shall depart from a similarly designated customs airport. Particulars of all designated customs airports shall be published by the State and transmitted to the International Civil Aviation Organization established under Part II of this Convention for communication to all other contracting States.

Article 11. Applicability of Air Regulations

Subject to the provisions of this Convention, the laws and regulations of a contracting State relating to the admission to or departure from its territory of aircraft engaged in international air navigation, or to the operation and navigation of such aircraft while within its territory, shall be applied to the aircraft of all contracting States without distinction as to nationality, and shall be complied with by such aircraft upon entering or departing from or while within the territory of that State.

Article 12. Rules of the Air

Each contracting State undertakes to adopt measures to insure that every aircraft flying over or maneuvering within its territory and that every aircraft carrying its nationality mark, wherever such aircraft may be, shall comply with the rules and regulations relating to the flight and maneuver of aircraft there in force. Each contracting State undertakes to keep its own regulations in these respects uniform, to the greatest possible extent, with those established from time to time under this Convention. Over the high seas, the rules in force shall be those established under this Convention. Each contracting State undertakes to insure the prosecution of all persons violating the regulations applicable.

Article 13. Entry and Clearance Regulations

The laws and regulations of a contracting State as to the admission to or departure from its territory of passengers, crew or cargo of aircraft, such as regulations relating to entry, clearance, immigration, passports, customs, and quarantine shall be complied with by or on behalf of such passengers, crew or cargo upon entrance into or departure from, or while within the territory of that State.

Article 14. Prevention of Spread of Disease

Each contracting State agrees to take effective measures to prevent the spread by means of air navigation of cholera, typhus (epidemic), smallpox, yellow fever, plague, and such other communicable diseases as the contracting States shall from time to time decide to designate, and to that end contracting States will keep in close consultation with the agencies concerned with international regulations relating to sanitary measures applicable to aircraft. Such consultation shall be without prejudice to the application of any existing international convention on this subject to which the contracting States may be parties.

Article 15. Airport and Similar Charges

Every airport in a contracting State which is open to public use of its national aircraft shall likewise, subject to the provisions of Article 68, be open under uniform conditions to the aircraft of all the other contracting States. The like uniform conditions shall apply to the use, by aircraft of every contracting State, of all air navigation facilities, including radio and meteorological services, which may be provided for public use for the safety and expedition of air navigation.

Any charges that may be imposed or permitted to be imposed by a contracting State for the use of such airports and air navigation facilities by the aircraft of any other contracting State shall not be higher,

(a) As to aircraft not engaged in scheduled international air services, than those that would be paid by its national aircraft of the same class engaged in similar operations, and

(b) As to aircraft engaged in scheduled international air services, than those that would be paid by its national aircraft engaged in similar international air services.

All such charges shall be published and communicated to the International Civil Aviation Organization: provided that, upon representation by an interested contracting State, the charges imposed for the use of airports and other facilities shall be subject to review by the Council, which shall report and make recommendations thereon for the consideration of the State or States concerned. No fees, dues or other charges shall be imposed by any contracting State in respect solely of the right of transit over or entry into or exit from its territory of any aircraft of a contracting State or persons or property thereon.

Article 16. Search of Aircraft

The appropriate authorities of each of the contracting States shall have the right, without unreasonable delay, to search aircraft of the other contracting States on landing or departure, and to inspect the certificates and other documents prescribed by this Convention.

CHAPTER III. NATIONALITY OF AIRCRAFT

Article 17. Nationality of Aircraft

Aircraft have the nationality of the State in which they are registered.

Article 18. Dual Registration

An aircraft cannot be validly registered in more than one State, but its registration may be changed from one State to another.

Article 19. National Laws Governing Registration

The registration or transfer of registration of aircraft in any contracting State shall be made in accordance with its laws and regulations.

Article 20. Display of Marks

Every aircraft engaged in international air navigation shall bear its appropriate nationality and registration marks....

Article 28. Air Navigation Facilities and Standard Systems

Each contracting State undertakes, so far as it may find practicable, to:

(a) Provide, in its territory, airports, radio services, meteorological services and other air navigation facilities to facilitate international air navigation in accordance with the standards and practices recommended or established from time to time, pursuant to this Convention;

(b) Adopt and put into operation the appropriate standard systems of communications procedure, codes, markings, signals, lighting and other operational practices and rules which may be recommended or established from time to time, pursuant to this Convention;

(c) Collaborate in international measures to secure the publication of aeronautical maps and charts in accordance with standards which may be recommended or established from time to time, pursuant to this Convention. . . .

CHAPTER VI. INTERNATIONAL STANDARDS AND RECOMMENDED PRACTICES

Article 37. Adoption of International Standards and Procedures

Each contracting State undertakes to collaborate in securing the highest practicable degree of uniformity in regulations, standards, procedures, and organization in relation to aircraft, personnel, airways and auxiliary services in all matters in which such uniformity will facilitate and improve air navigation.

To this end the International Civil Aviation Organization shall adopt and amend from time to time, as may be necessary, international standards and recommended practices and procedures dealing with:

(a) Communications systems and air navigation aids, including ground marking;

(b) Characteristics of airports and landing areas;

(c) Rules of the air and air traffic control practices;

(d) Licensing of operating and mechanical personnel;

(e) Airworthiness of aircraft;

(f) Registration and identification of aircraft;

(g) Collection and exchange of meteorological information;

(h) Log books;

(i) Aeronautical maps and charts;

(j) Customs and immigration procedures;

(k) Aircraft in distress and investigation of accidents;

and such other matters concerned with the safety, regularity, and efficiency of air navigation as may from time to time appear appropriate. . . .

PART II. THE INTERNATIONAL CIVIL AVIATION ORGANIZATION

CHAPTER VII. THE ORGANIZATION

Article 43. Name and Composition

An organization to be named the International Civil Aviation Organization is formed by the Convention. It is made up of an Assembly, a Council, and such other bodies as may be necessary.

Article 44. Objectives

The aims and objectives of the Organization are to develop the principles and techniques of international air navigation and to foster the planning and development of international air transport so as to:

(a) Insure the safe and orderly growth of international civil aviation throughout the world;

(b) Encourage the arts of aircraft design and operation for peaceful purposes;

(c) Encourage the development of airways, airports, and air navigation facilities for international civil aviation;

(d) Meet the needs of the peoples of the world for safe, regular, efficient and economical air transport;

(e) Prevent economic waste caused by unreasonable competition;

(f) Insure that the rights of contracting States are fully respected and that every contracting State has a fair opportunity to operate international airlines;

(g) Avoid discrimination between contracting States;

(h) Promote safety of flight in international air navigation;

(i) Promote generally the development of all aspects of international civil aeronautics.

Article 54. Mandatory Functions of Council

The Council shall:

(a) Submit annual reports to the Assembly;

(b) Carry out the directions of the Assembly and discharge the duties and obligations which are laid on it by this Convention;

(c) Determine its organization and rules of procedure;

(d) Appoint and define the duties of an Air Transport Committee, which shall be chosen from among the representatives of the members of the Council, and which shall be responsible to it;

(e) Establish an Air Navigation Commission, in accordance with the provisions of Chapter X;

(f) Administer the finances of the Organization in accordance with the provisions of Chapters XII and XV;

(g) Determine the emoluments of the President of the Council;

(h) Appoint a chief executive officer who shall be called the Secretary General, and make provision for the appointment of such other personnel as may be necessary in accordance with the provisions of Chapter XI;

(i) Request, collect, examine and publish information relating to the advancement of air navigation and the operation of international air services, including information about the costs of operation and particulars of subsidies paid to airlines from public funds;

(j) Report to contracting States any infraction of this Convention, as well as any failure to carry out recommendations or determinations of the Council;

(k) Report to the Assembly any infraction of this Convention where a contracting State has failed to take appropriate action within a reasonable time after notice of the infraction;

(*l*) Adopt, in accordance with the provisions of Chapter VI of this Convention, international standards and recommended practices; for convenience, designate them as Annexes to this Convention; and notify all contracting States of the action taken;

(m) Consider recommendations of the Air Navigation Commission for amendment of the Annexes and take action in accordance with the provisions of Chapter XX;

(n) Consider any matter relating to the Convention which any contracting State refers to it.

Article 55. Permissive Functions of Council

The Council may:

(a) Where appropriate and as experience may show to be desirable, create subordinate air transport commissions on a regional or other basis and define groups of states or airlines with or through which it may deal to facilitate the carrying out of the aims of this Convention;

(b) Delegate to the Air Navigation Commission duties additional to those set forth in the Convention and revoke or modify such delegations of authority at any time;

(c) Conduct research into all aspects of air transport and air navigation which are of international importance, communicate the results of the research to the contracting States, and facilitate the exchange of information between contracting States on air transport and air navigation matters;

(d) Study any matters affecting the organization and operation of international air transport, including the international ownership and operation of international air services on trunk routes, and submit to the Assembly plans in relation thereto;

(e) Investigate, at the request of any contracting Party, any situation which may appear to present avoidable obstacles to the development of international air navigation; and, after such investigation, issue such reports as may appear to it desirable....

CHAPTER XIX. WAR

Article 89. War and Emergency Conditions

In case of war, the provisions of this Convention shall not affect the freedom of action of any of the contracting States affected, whether as belligerents or as neutrals. The same principle shall apply in the case of any contracting State which declares a state of national emergency and notifies the fact to the Council.

Document 73
CONVENTION FOR THE UNIFICATION OF CERTAIN RULES RELATING TO INTERNATIONAL TRANSPORTATION BY AIR [THE WARSAW CONVENTION]

137 L.N.T.S. 11, T.S. No. 876, 49 Stat. 3000 (1929)

Article 1

(1) This convention shall apply to all international transportation of persons, baggage, or goods performed by aircraft for hire. It shall apply equally to gratuitous transportation by aircraft performed by an air transportation enterprise.

(2) For the purposes of this convention the expression "international transportation" shall mean any transportation in which, according to the contract made by the parties, the place of departure and the place of destination, whether or not there be a break in the transportation or a transshipment, are situated either within the territories of two High Contracting Parties, or within the territory of a single High Contracting Party, if there is an agreed stopping place within a territory subject to the sovereignty, suzerainty, mandate or authority of another power, even though that power is not a party to this convention. Transportation without such agreed stopping place between territories subject to the sovereignty, suzerainty, mandate, or authority of the same High Contracting Party shall not be deemed to be international for the purposes of this convention.

(3) Transportation to be performed by several successive air carriers shall be deemed, for the purposes of this convention, to be one undivided transportation, if it has been regarded by the parties as a single operation, whether it has been agreed upon under the form of a single contract or of a series of contracts....

Article 2

(1) This convention shall apply to transportation performed by the state or by legal entities constituted under public law provided it falls within the conditions laid down in Article 1.

(2) This convention shall not apply to transportation performed under the terms of any international postal convention.

Article 3

(1) For the transportation of passengers the carriers must deliver a passenger ticket which shall contain the following particulars:

(a) The place and date of issue;

(b) The place of departure and of destination;

(c) The agreed stopping places, provided that the carrier may reserve the right to alter the stopping places in case of necessity, and that if he exercises that right, the alteration shall not have the effect of depriving the transportation of its international character;

(d) The name and address of the carrier or carriers;

(e) A statement that the transportation is subject to the rules relating to liability established by this convention.

(2) The absence, irregularity, or loss of the passenger ticket shall not affect the existence or the validity of the contract of transportation, which shall none the less be subject to the rules of this convention. Nevertheless, if the carrier accepts a passenger without a passenger ticket having been delivered he shall not be entitled to avail himself of those provisions of this convention which exclude or limit his liability....

Article 17

The carrier shall be liable for damage sustained in the event of the death or wounding of a passenger or any other bodily injury suffered by a passenger, if the accident which caused the damage so sustained took place on board the aircraft or in the course of any of the operations of embarking or disembarking.

Article 18

(1) The carrier shall be liable for damage sustained in the event of the destruction or loss of, or damage to, any checked baggage or any goods, if the occurrence which caused the damage so sustained took place during the transportation by air.

(2) The transportation by air within the meaning of the preceding paragraph shall comprise the period during which the baggage or goods are in charge of the carrier, whether in an airport or on board an aircraft, or, in the case of a landing outside an airport, in any place whatsoever....

Article 19

The carrier shall be liable for damage occasioned by delay in the transportation by air of passengers, baggage, or goods.

Article 20

(1) The carrier shall not be liable if he proves that he and his agents have taken all necessary measures to avoid the damage or that it was impossible for him or them to take such measures....

Article 21

If the carrier proves that the damage was caused by or contributed to by the negligence of the injured person the court may, in accordance with the provisions of its own law, exonerate the carrier wholly or partly from his liability.

Article 22

(1) In the transportation of passengers the liability of the carrier for each passenger shall be limited to the sum of 125,000 francs. ... Nevertheless, by special contract, the carrier and the passenger may agree to a higher limit of liability....

Article 23

Any provision tending to relieve the carrier of liability or to fix a lower limit than that which is laid down in this convention shall be null and void....

Article 24

(1) In the cases covered by Articles 18 and 19 any action for damages, however founded, can only be brought subject to the conditions and limits set out in this convention.

(2) In the cases covered by Article 17 the provisions of the preceding paragraph shall also apply, without prejudice to the questions as to who are the persons who have the right to bring suit and what are their respective rights.

Article 25

(1) The carrier shall not be entitled to avail himself of the provisions of this convention which exclude or limit his liability, if the damage is caused by his wilful misconduct or by such default on his part as, in accordance with the law of the court to which the case is submitted, is considered to be equivalent to wilful misconduct.

(2) Similarly the carrier shall not be entitled to avail himself of the said provisions, if the damage is caused under the same circumstances by any agent of the carrier acting within the scope of his employment.

Article 28

(1) An action for damages must be brought, at the option of the plaintiff, in the territory of one of the High Contracting Parties, either before the court of the domicile of the carrier or of his principal place of business, or where he has a place of business through which the contract has been made, or before the court at the place of destination.

(2) Questions of procedure shall be governed by the law of the court to which the case is submitted.

Article 29

(1) The right to damages shall be extinguished if an action is not brought within 2 years, reckoned from the date of arrival at the destination, or from the date on which the aircraft ought to have arrived, or from the date on which the transportation stopped.

(2) The method of calculating the period of limitations shall be determined by the law of the court to which the case is submitted....

Article 32

Any clause contained in the contract and all special agreements entered into before the damage occurred by which the parties purport to infringe the rules laid down by this convention, whether by deciding the law to be applied, or by altering the rules as to jurisdiction, shall be null and void. Nevertheless for the transportation of goods arbitration clauses shall be allowed, subject to this convention, if the arbitration is to take place within one of the jurisdictions referred to in the first paragraph of Article 28. . . .

Document 74
TREATY ON PRINCIPLES GOVERNING THE ACTIVITIES OF STATES IN THE EXPLORATION AND USE OF OUTER SPACE, INCLUDING THE MOON AND OTHER CELESTIAL BODIES [THE OUTER SPACE TREATY]

610 U.N.T.S. 205, 18 U.S.T. 2410, T.I.A.S. No. 6347 (1967)

Article I

The exploration and use of outer space, including the moon and other celestial bodies, shall be carried out for the benefit and in the interests of all countries, irrespective of their degree of economic or scientific development, and shall be the province of all mankind.

Outer space, including the moon and other celestial bodies, shall be free for exploration and use by all States without discrimination of any kind, on a basis of equality and in accordance with international law, and there shall be free access to all areas of celestial bodies.

There shall be freedom of scientific investigation in outer space, including the moon and other celestial bodies, and States shall facilitate and encourage international co-operation in such investigation.

Article II

Outer space, including the moon and other celestial bodies, is not subject to national appropriation by claim of sovereignty, by means of use or occupation, or by any other means.

Article III

States Parties to the Treaty shall carry on activities in the exploration and use of outer space, including the moon and other celestial bodies, in accordance with international law, including the Charter of the United Nations, in the interest of maintaining international peace and security and promoting international co-operation and understanding.

Article IV

States Parties to the Treaty undertake not to place in orbit around the Earth any objects carrying nuclear weapons or any other kinds of weapons of mass destruction, install such weapons on celestial bodies, or station such weapons in outer space in any other manner.

The moon and other celestial bodies shall be used by all States Parties to the Treaty exclusively for peaceful purposes. The establishment of military bases, installations and fortifications, the testing of any type of weapons and the conduct of military maneuvers on celestial bodies shall be forbidden. The use of military personnel for scientific research or for any other peaceful purposes shall not be prohibited. The use of any equipment or facility necessary for peaceful exploration of the moon and other celestial bodies shall also not be prohibited.

Article V

States Parties to the Treaty shall regard astronauts as envoys of mankind in outer space and shall render to them all possible assistance in the event of accident, distress, or emergency landing on the territory of another State Party or on the high seas. When astronauts make such a landing, they shall be safely and promptly returned to the State of registry of their space vehicle.

In carrying on activities in outer space and on celestial bodies, the astronauts of one State Party shall render all possible assistance to the astronauts of other States Parties.

States Parties to the Treaty shall immediately inform the other States Parties to the Treaty or the Secretary–General of the United Nations of any phenomena they discover in outer space, including the moon and other celestial bodies, which could constitute a danger to the life or health of astronauts.

Article VI

States Parties to the Treaty shall bear international responsibility for national activities in outer space, including the moon and other celestial bodies, whether such activities are carried on by governmental agencies or by non-governmental entities, and for assuring that national activities are carried out in conformity with the provisions set forth in the present Treaty. The activities of non-governmental entities in outer space, including the moon and other celestial bodies, shall require authorization and continuing supervision by the appropriate State Party to the Treaty. When activities are carried on in outer space, including the moon and other celestial bodies, by an international organization, responsibility for compliance with this Treaty shall be borne both by the international organization and by the States Parties to the Treaty participating in such organization.

Article VII

Each State Party to the Treaty that launches or procures the launching of an object into outer space, including the moon and other celestial bodies, and each State Party from whose territory or facility an object is launched, is internationally liable for damage to another State Party to the Treaty or to its natural or juridical persons by such object or its component parts on the Earth, in air space or in outer space, including the moon and other celestial bodies.

Article VIII

A State Party to the Treaty on whose registry an object launched into outer space is carried shall retain jurisdiction and control over such object, and over any personnel thereof, while in outer space or on a celestial body. Ownership of objects launched into outer space, including objects landed or constructed on a celestial body, and of their component parts, is not affected by their presence in outer space or on a celestial body or by their return to the Earth. Such objects or component parts found beyond the limits of the State Party to the Treaty on whose registry they are carried shall be returned to that State Party, which shall, upon request, furnish identifying data prior to their return.

Article IX

In the exploration and use of outer space, including the moon and other celestial bodies, States Parties to the Treaty shall be guided by the principle of co-operation and mutual assistance and shall conduct all their activities in outer space, including the moon and other celestial bodies, with due regard to the corresponding interests of all other States Parties to the Treaty. States Parties to the Treaty shall pursue studies of outer space, including the moon and other celestial bodies, and conduct exploration of them so as to avoid their harmful contamination and also adverse changes in the environment of the Earth resulting from the introduction of extraterrestrial matter and, where necessary, shall adopt appropriate measures for this purpose. If a State Party to the Treaty has reason to believe that an activity or experiment planned by it or its nationals in outer space, including the moon and other celestial bodies, would cause potentially harmful interference with activities of other States Parties in the peaceful exploration and use of outer space, including the moon and other celestial bodies, it shall undertake appropriate international consultations before proceeding with any such activity or experiment. A State Party to the Treaty which has reason to believe that an activity or experiment planned by another State Party in outer space, including the moon and other celestial bodies, would cause potentially harmful interference with activities in the peaceful exploration and use of outer space, including the moon and other celestial bodies, may request consultation concerning the activity or experiment.

Article X

In order to promote international co-operation in the exploration and use of outer space, including the moon and other celestial bodies, in conformity with the purposes of this Treaty, the States Parties to the Treaty shall consider on a basis of equality any requests by other States Parties to the Treaty to be afforded an opportunity to observe the flight of space objects launched by those States.

The nature of such an opportunity for observation and the conditions under which it could be afforded shall be determined by agreement between the States concerned.

Article XI

In order to promote international co-operation in the peaceful exploration and use of outer space, States Parties to the Treaty conducting activities in outer space, including the moon and other celestial of bodies, agree to inform the Secretary–General of the United Nations as well as the public and the international scientific community, to the greatest extent feasible and practicable, of the nature, conduct, locations and results of such activities. On receiving the said information, the Secretary–General the United Nations should be prepared to disseminate it immediately and effectively.

Article XII

All stations, installations, equipment and space vehicles on the moon and other celestial bodies shall be open to representatives of other States Parties to the Treaty on a basis of reciprocity. Such representatives shall give reasonable advance notice of a projected visit, in order that appropriate consultations may be held and that maximum precautions may be taken to assure safety and to avoid interference with normal operations in the facility to be visited.

Article XIII

The provisions of this Treaty shall apply to the activities of States Parties to the Treaty in the exploration and use of outer space, including the moon and other celestial bodies, whether such activities are carried on by a single State Party to the Treaty or jointly with other States, including cases where they are carried on within the framework of international intergovernmental organizations.

Any practical questions arising in connection with activities carried on by international inter-governmental organizations in the exploration and use of outer space, including the moon and other celestial bodies, shall be resolved by the States Parties to the Treaty either with the appropriate international organization or with one or more States members of that international organization, which are Parties to this Treaty. . . .

Article XV

Any State Party to the Treaty may propose amendments to this Treaty. Amendments shall enter into force for each State Party to the Treaty accepting the amendments upon their acceptance by a majority of the States Parties to the Treaty and thereafter for each remaining State Party to the Treaty on the date of acceptance by it.

Article XVI

Any State Party to the Treaty may give notice of its withdrawal from the Treaty one year after its entry into force by written notification to the Depositary Governments. Such withdrawal shall take effect one year from the date of receipt of this notification. . . .

Document 75
CONVENTION ON INTERNATIONAL LIABILITY FOR DAMAGE CAUSED BY SPACE OBJECTS

961 U.N.T.S. 187, 24 U.S.T. 2389, T.I.A.S. No. 7762 (1972)

The States Parties to this Convention,

Recognizing the common interest of all mankind in furthering the exploration and use of outer space for peaceful purposes,

Recalling the Treaty on Principles Governing the Activities of States in the Exploration and Use of Outer Space, including the Moon and Other Celestial Bodies,

Taking into consideration that, notwithstanding the precautionary measures to be taken by States and international intergovernmental organizations involved in the launching of space objects, damage may on occasion be caused by such objects,

Recognizing the need to elaborate effective international rules and procedures concerning liability for damage caused by space objects and to ensure, in particular, the prompt payment under the terms of this Convention of a full and equitable measure of compensation to victims of such damage,

Believing that the establishment of such rules and procedures would contribute to the strengthening of international cooperation in the field of the exploration and use of outer space for peaceful purposes,

Have agreed on the following:

Article I

For the purposes of this Convention:

(a) The term "damage" means loss of life, personal injury or other impairment of health; or loss of or damage to property of States or of persons, natural or juridical, or property of international intergovernmental organizations;

(b) The term "launching" includes attempted launching;

(c) The term "launching State" means:

(i) The State which launches or procures the launching of a space object;

(ii) A State from whose territory or facility a space object is launched;

(d) The term "space object" includes component parts of a space object as well as its launch vehicle and parts thereof.

Article II

A launching State shall be absolutely liable to pay compensation for damage caused by its space object on the surface of the earth or to aircraft in flight.

Article III

In the event of damage being caused elsewhere than on the surface of the earth to a space object of one launching State or to persons or property on board such a space object by a space object of another launching State, the latter shall be liable only if the damage is due to its fault or the fault of persons for whom it is responsible.

Article IV

1. In the event of damage being caused elsewhere than on the surface of the earth to a space object of one launching State or to persons or property on board such a space object by a space object of another launching State, and of damage thereby being caused to a third State or to its natural or juridical persons, the first two States shall be jointly and severally liable to the third State, to the extent indicated by the following:

(a) If the damage has been caused to the third State on the surface of the earth or to aircraft in flight, their liability to the third State shall be absolute;

(b) If the damage has been caused to a space object of the third State or to persons or property on board that space object elsewhere than on the surface of the earth, their liability to the third State shall be based on the fault of either of the first two States or on the fault of persons for whom either is responsible.

2. In all cases of joint and several liability referred to in paragraph 1 of this article, the burden of compensation for the damage shall be apportioned between the first two States in accordance with the extent to which they were at fault; if the extent of the fault of each of these States cannot be established, the burden of compensation shall be apportioned equally between them. Such apportionment shall be without prejudice to the right of the third State to seek the entire compensation due under this Convention from any or all of the launching States which are jointly and severally liable.

Article V

1. Whenever two or more States jointly launch a space object, they shall be jointly and severally liable for any damage caused.

2. A launching State which has paid compensation for damage shall have the right to present a claim for indemnification to other participants in the joint launching. The participants in a joint launching may conclude agreements regarding the apportioning among themselves of the financial obligation in respect of which they are jointly and

severally liable. Such agreements shall be without prejudice to the right of a State sustaining damage to seek the entire compensation due under this Convention from any or all of the launching States which are jointly and severally liable.

3. A State from whose territory or facility a space object is launched shall be regarded as a participant in a joint launching.

Article VI

1. Subject to the provisions of paragraph 2 of this article, exoneration from absolute liability shall be granted to the extent that a launching State establishes that the damage has resulted either wholly or partially from gross negligence or from an act or omission done with intent to cause damage on the part of a claimant State or of natural or juridical persons it represents.

2. No exoneration whatever shall be granted in cases where the damage has resulted from activities conducted by a launching State which are not in conformity with international law including, in particular, the Charter of the United Nations and the Treaty on Principles Governing the Activities of States in the Exploration and Use of Outer Space, including the Moon and Other Celestial Bodies.

Article VII

The provisions of this Convention shall not apply to damage caused by a space object of a launching State to:

(a) Nationals of that launching State;

(b) Foreign nationals during such time as they are participating in the operation of that space object from the time of its launching or at any stage thereafter until its descent, or during such time as they are in the immediate vicinity of a planned launching or recovery area as the result of an invitation by that launching State.

Article VIII

1. A State which suffers damage, or whose natural or juridical persons suffer damage, may present to a launching State a claim for compensation for such damage.

2. If the State of nationality has not presented a claim, another State may, in respect of damage sustained in its territory by any natural or juridical person, present a claim to a launching State.

3. If neither the State of nationality nor the State in whose territory the damage was sustained has presented a claim or notified its intention of presenting a claim, another State may, in respect of damage sustained by its permanent residents, present a claim to a launching State.

Article IX

A claim for compensation for damage shall be presented to a launching State through diplomatic channels. If a State does not maintain diplomatic relations with the launching State concerned, it may request another State to present its claim to that launching State or otherwise represent its interests under this Convention. It may also present its claim through the Secretary-General of the United Nations, provided the claimant State and the launching State are both Members of the United Nations.

Article X

1. A claim for compensation for damage may be presented to a launching State not later than one year following the date of the occurrence of the damage or the identification of the launching State which is liable.

2. If, however, a State does not know of the occurrence of the damage or has not been able to identify the launching State which is liable, it may present a claim within one year following the date on which it learned of the aforementioned facts; however, this period shall in no event exceed one year following the date on which the State could reasonably be expected to have learned of the facts through the exercise of due diligence.

3. The time-limits specified in paragraphs 1 and 2 of this article shall apply even if the full extent of the damage may not be known. In this event, however, the claimant State shall be entitled to revise the claim and submit additional documentation after the expiration of such time-limits until one year after the full extent of the damage is known.

Article XI

1. Presentation of a claim to a launching State for compensation for damage under this Convention shall not require the prior exhaustion of any local remedies which may be available to a claimant State or to natural or juridical persons it represents.

2. Nothing in this Convention shall prevent a State, or natural or juridical persons it might represent, from pursuing a claim in the courts or administrative tribunals or agencies of a launching State. A State shall not, however, be entitled to present a claim under this Convention in respect of the same damage for which a claim is being pursued in the courts or administrative tribunals or agencies of a launching State or under another international agreement which is binding on the States concerned.

Article XII

The compensation which the launching State shall be liable to pay for damage under this Convention shall be determined in accordance with international law and the principles of justice and equity, in order to provide such reparation in respect of the damage as will restore the person, natural or juridical, State or international organization on whose behalf the claim is presented to the condition which would have existed if the damage had not occurred.

Article XIII

Unless the claimant State and the State from which compensation is due under this Convention agree on another form of compensation, the compensation shall be paid in the currency of the claimant State or, if that State so requests, in the currency of the State from which compensation is due.

Article XIV

If no settlement of a claim is arrived at through diplomatic negotiations as provided for in Article IX, within one year from the date on which the claimant State notifies the launching State that it has submitted the documentation of its claim, the parties concerned shall establish a Claims Commission at the request of either party.

Article XV

1. The Claims Commission shall be composed of three members: one appointed by the claimant State, one appointed by the launching State and the third member, the Chairman, to be chosen by both parties jointly. Each party shall make its appointment within two months of the request for the establishment of the Claims Commission.

2. If no agreement is reached on the choice of the Chairman within four months of the request for the establishment of the Commission, either party may request the Secretary–General of the United Nations to appoint the Chairman within a further period of two months.

Article XVI

1. If one of the parties does not make its appointment within the stipulated period, the Chairman shall, at the request of the other party, constitute a single-member Claims Commission.

2. Any vacancy which may arise in the Commission for whatever reason shall be filled by the same procedure adopted for the original appointment.

3. The Commission shall determine its own procedure.

4. The Commission shall determine the place or places where it shall sit and all other administrative matters.

5. Except in the case of decisions and awards by a single-member Commission, all decisions and awards of the Commission shall be by majority vote.

Article XVII

No increase in the membership of the Claims Commission shall take place by reason of two or more claimant States or launching States being joined in any one proceeding before the Commission. The claimant States so joined shall collectively appoint one member of the Commission in the same manner and subject to the same conditions as would be the case for a single claimant State. When two or more launching States are so joined, they shall collectively appoint one member of the Commission in the same way. If the claimant States or the launching States do not make the appointment within the stipulated period, the Chairman shall constitute a single-member Commission.

Article XVIII

The Claims Commission shall decide the merits of the claim for compensation and determine the amount of compensation payable, if any.

Article XIX

1. The Claims Commission shall act in accordance with the provisions of Article XII.

2. The decision of the Commission shall be final and binding if the parties have so agreed; otherwise the Commission shall render a final and recommendatory award, which the parties shall consider in good faith. The Commission shall state the reasons for its decision or award.

3. The Commission shall give its decision or award as promptly as possible and no later than one year from the date of its establishment, unless an extension of this period is found necessary by the Commission.

4. The Commission shall make its decision or award public. It shall deliver a certified copy of its decision or award to each of the parties and to the Secretary–General of the United Nations.

Article XX

The expenses in regard to the Claims Commission shall be borne equally by the parties, unless otherwise decided by the Commission.

Article XXI

If the damage caused by a space object presents a large-scale danger to human life or seriously interferes with the living conditions of the population or the functioning of vital centres, the States Parties, and in particular the launching State, shall examine the possibility of rendering appropriate and rapid assistance to the State which has suffered the damage, when it so requests. However, nothing in this article shall affect the rights or obligations of the States Parties under this Convention.

Article XXII

1. In this Convention, with the exception of Articles XXIV to XXVII, references to States shall be deemed to apply to any international intergovernmental organization which conducts space activities if the organization declares its acceptance of the rights and obligations provided for in this Convention and if a majority of the States members of the organization are States Parties to this Convention and to the Treaty on Principles Governing the Activities of States in the Exploration and Use of Outer Space, including the Moon and Other Celestial Bodies.

2. States members of any such organization which are States Parties to this Convention shall take all appropriate steps to ensure that the organization makes a declaration in accordance with the preceding paragraph.

3. If an international intergovernmental organization is liable for damage by virtue of the provisions of this Convention, that organization

and those of its members which are States Parties to this Convention shall be jointly and severally liable; provided, however, that:

(a) Any claim for compensation in respect of such damage shall be first presented to the organization;

(b) Only where the organization has not paid, within a period of six months, any sum agreed or determined to be due as compensation for such damage, may the claimant State invoke the liability of the members which are States Parties to this Convention for the payment of that sum.

4. Any claim, pursuant to the provisions of this Convention, for compensation in respect of damage caused to an organization which has made a declaration in accordance with paragraph 1 of this article shall be presented by a State member of the organization which is a State Party to this Convention.

Article XXIII

1. The provisions of this Convention shall not affect other international agreements in force in so far as relations between the States Parties to such agreements are concerned.

2. No provision of this Convention shall prevent States from concluding international agreements reaffirming, supplementing or extending its provisions. . . .

†